Follow My Footprints

•

THE BRANDEIS SERIES

IN AMERICAN JEWISH HISTORY,

CULTURE, AND LIFE

Jonathan D. Sarna, Editor

Leon A. Jick, 1992
The Americanization of the Synagogue, *1820–1870*

Sylvia Barack Fishman, 1992
Follow My Footprints: Changing Images of Women in American Jewish Fiction

Follow My Footprints

Changing Images of Women in American Jewish Fiction

EDITED AND WITH INTRODUCTORY ESSAY AND NOTES BY

Sylvia Barack Fishman

BRANDEIS UNIVERSITY PRESS

PUBLISHED BY UNIVERSITY PRESS OF NEW ENGLAND

Hanover and London

BRANDEIS UNIVERSITY PRESS
Published by University Press of New England, Hanover, NH 03755

Printed in the United States of America 5 4 3 2 1
CIP data appear at the end of the book

This book is dedicated to

my parents

RABBI NATHAN ABRAHAM *and* LILLIAN ASTRACHAN BARACK

and to

the loving memory of my grandparents

RAV JOSEPH DOV-BER *and* ESTHER GUREVITCH ASTRACHAN

REB PERETZ *and* ETA KOTCHKA BARACK,

who brought their living faith to a new land

and implanted it in the hearts of their children

Everything will remember
That I was here.
The ships will be the color
Of my clothing,
The birds will use my voice for singing,
The fisherman on the rock
Will ponder my poem,
The river
Will follow my footprints.

—Rajzel Zychlinska

Contents

THE EVOLUTION OF LITERARY TYPES: THE "JEWISH MOTHER" AND THE "JEWISH AMERICAN PRINCESS"

REAL WOMEN: JEWISH MOTHERS AND DAUGHTERS EXPLORE NEW PATHS

CONTEMPORARY SOLDIER WOMEN IN A CHANGING WORLD

Preface

This anthology focuses on women in Jewish fiction and presents a vivid panorama of Jewish life in the United States over the past one hundred years. *Follow My Footprints* begins with the roots of much American Jewish experience, on muddy paths of Russian shtetls and in the teeming tenements and intellectual ferment of prewar Warsaw; it moves to the poverty and painful cultural dislocation of immigrant communities, rises to the affluence and assimilation of American Jewish life at midcentury, and concludes with the feminist exploration and reempowerment of women in the 1970s and 1980s. The authors include some of the most critically celebrated writers of twentieth-century Yiddish and American Jewish literature—indeed of world literature—as well as popular authors whose novels shaped American Jewish opinion and younger authors who represent important new trends in American Jewish fiction. Their fiction graphically and poignantly conveys the profound transformation of American Jewish life in our times.

My awareness of the need for this reader arose from experience in teaching the courses Women in Jewish Culture and American Jewish Literature to undergraduate and graduate students at Brown and Brandeis universities and to adults in university continuing education programs and a variety of other settings. Like others teaching such courses, I have been impressed by the enthusiastic reception, intellectual excitement, and increased understanding evoked by literary subject matter—and frustrated by the difficulty of locating literary and critical materials in a cohesive and easily accessible format. Early and more recent fiction goes in and out of print and is often available only in prohibitively expensive hardcover books. The ideal course—beginning with Yiddish writers in translation and concluding with the most recent fiction by American Jewish women—has previously often been, in practice, truncated at both ends by logistical impossibilities.

It is my pleasure to present in this anthology a collection of short stories and excerpts from novels that have, in my experience, proved most effective in capturing and conveying the sweep of the historical, social, economic, and cultural trends that have shaped modern Jewish life in general and the experiences of Jewish women in particular. These fictional portrayals of women illuminate not only changes in the lives of American Jewish women but also transformations of the American Jewish family and the continuing conflict between traditional Jewish values and the American secular/Christian environment.

The images of women included in this anthology's readings have been created by twenty-one men and women. For readers who question the inclusion of male authors in a book about women, I emphasize that this collection is designed to function not as a showcase for authors of either gender but as a literary social history. I have found that readers respond to the stories and novels excerpted here not only by analyzing the literature but also by examining their own perceptions of the roles of Jewish women and the nature of Jewish identity. Many are motivated to pursue further reading and research in specific related areas. The "Suggestions for Further Reading" that concludes this anthology is designed to provide such readers with tools to begin their own focused and detailed critical explorations.

During the final stages of preparing this volume, the manuscript was made available to my current college students. Their responses to the material have been extremely useful, and it is to them and to the classes who preceded them, students who read avidly, who were enthralled, moved, provoked, outraged, won over, troubled, and stirred to wonder by the selections included here, that my first expressions of gratitude freely go. My students have been my companions on a voyage of discovery, as my teachers were at an earlier time, and I consider myself fortunate indeed to have shared with both teachers and students the pleasures of reading and learning together.

Second, I am happily indebted to my colleagues at Brandeis University. The Maurice and Marilyn Cohen Center for Modern Jewish Studies generously aided in the publications costs for this anthology. In addition, gratitude is due, as always, my friends and co-workers at the Cohen Center, Gary A. Tobin, Marshall Sklare, Lawrence Sternberg, Mordechai Rimor, Gabriel Berger, and Sylvia Riese, for creating an environment in which joys and frustrations as well as ideas are shared. The Center also provided me with student assistants Raquel Kosovske and Francine Green, whose intellectual interests coincided wonderfully with many subjects explored in this book. Each performed an assortment of tasks with intelligence, diligence, and devotion; Raquel not only worked with me for over a year, struggling with the vagaries of the computer and other technological "helpers," but also brought important issues to my attention. I warmly wish them every success in their own professional and personal lives.

Special thanks go to Jehuda Reinharz, director of the Tauber Institute for the Study of European Jewry, whose energy, perceptiveness, and wise guidance have been crucial to the publication of this anthology. Moreover, I am delighted to acknowledge the helpful suggestions of my readers and editors, including Jeanne West at the University Press of New England, who believed in this project and whose quiet assurance fortified my own; Sylvia Fuks Fried, of the Tauber Institute, who generously lent her intensive editorial skills and her extensive familiarity with Yiddish and American Jewish literature to repeated careful readings of the manuscript; Marc Brettler, of Brandeis University's Near Eastern and Judaic Studies Department, who read the sections on biblical and rabbinic literature and made important suggestions; Lawrence Sternberg, who read the sections on immigration and American Jewish life; and my husband, Philip Fishman, who remains my most irrepressible critic and my fiercest advocate and enabler. My colleagues in Brandeis University's Women's Studies Program, especially Joyce Antler and Shulamit Reinharz, former and present directors of the program, have been valuable advisors and loyal allies. The suggestions of my colleagues have worked to improve the quality of this book; I, of course, take responsibility for the final product.

Waltham, Massachusetts S. B. F.
December 1991

cal helper. [illegible] the important issues to my attention. I warmly [illegible] professional and personal lives.

Special thanks go to [illegible], director of the [illegible] Institute for the Study of [illegible] and wise guidance [illegible] the production of this anthology. [illegible] suggestions [illegible] readers and [illegible] rounded [illegible] own. [illegible] of the [illegible] her inter- [illegible] and Ameri- can Jewish literature [illegible] Depart- [illegible] and made important suggestions [illegible] the sections on [illegible] [illegible] could [illegible] responsibility for the final product.

[illegible]

Follow My Footprints

•

The Faces of Women: An Introductory Essay

Our Literature, Ourselves

Literature shapes and reflects popular conceptions of the nature and capacities of women, and the self-images of many contemporary American girls and women are influenced not only by changing political, social, and economic conditions but also by a lifetime of contact with literary portrayals of female characters. Such portrayals exist on many brow levels and are derived from diverse religious, cultural, folkloric, and mythic traditions. Many have been nurtured by images from ancient heritages, such as classical Greek and Latin myth and drama, and by narrative characters and allegorical women in the Old and New Testaments.

In the open environment of modern American society the mix of literary heritages describing female nature is rich indeed, including widely divergent pictures. Some have become so familiar that their very names evoke an emotional ambiance: the earnest and spunky problem-solving heroines of books for young girls; the orphan told she "should have been a boy" who surmounts the limitations of her environment through her intense imagination (*Anne of Green Gables*); empowered and powerless Shakespearean characters such as Lady Macbeth, Portia, Juliet, and Desdemona; the independent heroines of novels by Jane Austen, the Brontë sisters, and George Eliot; the pure-hearted martyr doomed and betrayed by honorable and dishonorable men alike (*Tess of the D'Urbervilles*); the bitchy, manipulative survivor (Scarlett O'Hara in *Gone with the Wind*); the fickle, shallow love-object with money in her laughter (Daisy in *The Great Gatsby*); the grasping, greedy wives of Philip Wylie and the overbearing mothers of Philip Roth. In the late 1960s and 1970s, feminism opened the doors for new themes, and readers encountered the courageous experiments in integrity of Doris Lessing's protagonists, embattled modern women struggling with *Small Changes* and attempting to break out of *The Women's Room*, and the sexual adventures of women trying to conquer their *Fear of Flying*. In addition, in recent years, American women have had the opportunity to "meet" an even broader cast of female images in the fiction of African-American, Native American, third world, and Oriental authors in a growing number of novels such as *The Song of Solomon*, *The Color Purple*, *The Beet Queen*, *Memoirs of a Woman Warrior*, *The Joy Luck Club*, *The Floating World*, and *Jasmine*.

This discussion singles out and focuses on the significant positive and negative models provided by Jewish literature. Within the pantheon of world and American literature, Jewish literature, ranging from ancient to modern works, has provided a rich and various source of female imagery and characterization. One of the most striking cultural biases that emerges in an exploration of changing portrayals of women in Jewish literature is that images of opinionated, active, strong women have been close to ubiquitous from biblical through modern times. Despite their obvious differences, biblical figures such as Rebecca, Deborah, and the proverbial Woman of Valor and twentieth-century literary creations such as Marjorie Morgenstern Morningstar and Sophie Portnoy have certain qualities in common: each is a forceful Jewish woman who tries to control her life and the events around her. Intelligent, articulate, and aggressive, the strong women of Jewish literature do not passively accept what fate has to offer; instead, they try to shape destiny—and often their friends and families—to more closely resemble their vision of a rectified reality. In the words of Sholem Asch, describing his heroine Rachel-Leah, they behave like "soldiers" called upon "to do battle with life."

Modifications in the expected role and status of Jewish women have been integrally intertwined with more comprehensive cultural changes in areas such as education, occupation, patterns of family formation, and religious observance. American Jews have been the paradigm of an immigrant/ethnic group responding to and being transformed by the opportunities provided by the American dream. Thus, by studying changing depictions of women in American Jewish fiction, one learns not only about developments in the lives of women but also a great deal about the social history of American Jews. One also can discover in American Jewish fictional depictions of women a microcosm of changing values in American society as a whole.

The readings begin with depictions of the Eastern European milieu in the works of writers whose background experiences were typical of a large proportion of Jews before they emigrated to the United States; the primary focus of the volume is on American Jewish writers over the past century, whose fiction illuminates profound and often surprising shifts in attitudes toward women in general as well as toward Jewish women in particular.

The Eastern European writers and many American Jewish writers were exposed to—and sometimes steeped in—Jewish literary and cultural traditions that reach back through two thousand years of Diaspora existence to the Bible itself. To understand fully the transformation of the role of Jewish women as it is reflected in and influenced by Jewish literature, it is useful to survey briefly some key portrayals of ancient Israelite women—and rabbinic response to those women—in early Jewish literature. For although Jewish literature has often focused on vigorous women rather than passive women, the strong woman has evoked ambivalent responses throughout Jewish history.

Antecedents: A Glimpse into Biblical and Rabbinic Portrayals of Women

The strong woman is one constant type in Jewish literature from the Bible onward, but her interpretation and critical reception varies strikingly. The creators of the Hebrew Bible often seem to approve of female enterprise, resourcefulness, and articulateness—provided that those qualities were used to further divine plans and spiritual or nationalistic goals and not merely the personal ambitions of the women involved.[1] It should be noted that the standards of divine providence and group survival, rather than personal success, were used to evaluate male characters as well. Moreover, the tendency of biblical female characters to defy human patriarchal authority often serves to establish divine authority more effectively and to further what are presented by the text as divine providential imperatives. Thus, the Hebrew Bible depicts, among others, women who defy or supersede male authority, such as Rebecca, Tamar, Jocebed, and Miriam; women who find their own way to God's ear and heart, such as Ruth and Hannah; and the occasional women who lead their people politically, such as Deborah and Huldah.[2]

The Hebrew Bible describes in detail the independent judgment and cleverness of women like Rebecca and the leadership and courage of women like Deborah because Rebecca, on a family level, and Deborah, on a national level, use their intelligence and strength to help guarantee the survival of the Israelite people. Rebecca deceives her husband Isaac to make sure that the spiritual birthright, which innately belongs to Jacob, is linked to the material birthright that will support him and his descendants. Tamar uses her sexuality to take her rightful place in the lineage of the tribal dynasty, compelling the autocratic Judah to see and admit his error; later Jewish tradition "rewards" her behavior by positing that out of the union of Judah and Tamar comes the royal line of David and, eventually, the Messiah.[3]

Miriam and her mother, Jocebed, who served as midwives according to the Midrash, battle both the brutality of an infanticidal pharaoh and the depressed passivity of Jewish husbands, who were afraid to produce more children; through their efforts, not only Moses, the leader, but indeed an entire generation of Israelites who fled Egypt into the desert were born and sheltered.[4] Hannah rejects her husband's insistence that his love should compensate her for their infertility; she prays to God on her own behalf most effectively. In later times, Hannah's heartfelt prayer, with lips moving but no sound issuing, became the preferred mode of Jewish worship. Additionally, Hannah keeps the bargain she made with God and yields up her son Samuel at a tender age to a holy life among the priests so that he may eventually assume his role as national leader.[5] Ruth leaves her comfortable home and links her destiny with that of the Jewish people and the Jewish God, not because of love for any man but because of some intangible superiority she finds in another woman, her mother-in-law, Naomi.[6] Deborah judges her people and supervises the military activities of her general, Barak.[7]

The "interpretive communities"[8] of rabbis who read and studied the Bible and who together participated over the centuries in creating the opus of Talmudic and post-Talmudic commentaries, however, convey mixed feelings about many resourceful, aggressive biblical women. Although disagreements and widely divergent viewpoints most assuredly exist—indeed are among the most striking characteristics of rabbinic dialogue—certain themes and tendencies often recur. One such tendency is to suppress the public prominence of biblical women and to discourage any impulse to view independent women as role models.[9]

Rabbinical sources, for example, sometimes recast the images of female leaders in the Bible, such as Deborah, within their commentaries: she was given the unflattering name of Deborah ("bee"), says the Talmudic Tractate *Megilah* (14a–b), because she was arrogant, calling for Barak rather than going to see him, as was appropriate for a woman, and later praising herself by saying, "I arose, a mother in Israel" (Judges 5:7). Similarly, the prophetess Huldah is given the name "weasel" because she "displayed haughtiness and disrespect toward men."[10] Deborah's striking song also evoked differing responses. Although the Talmudic Tractate *Pesachim* (66b) minimized the significance of the song by claiming that the spirit of holy prophecy departed from her while she composed it, the *Zohar* (Lev. 19b)[11] says that Deborah and Hannah were unique women because their songs in praise of God were superior to those of men. The prophetess Miriam, also the author of a song, is rewritten by the Midrash[12] into a more consistent, more family oriented—and less powerful, public, ambitious—character, according to Devora Steinmetz:

Miriam is named as the actor in only two biblical episodes, the Song at the Sea and the gossip. In both, Miriam appears in the Bible to be claiming, implicitly or explicitly, her share of Moses' leadership. In Exodus, she leads the women in a song parallel to the song in which Moses leads the men. And in Numbers she questions Moses' right to exclusive leadership since she, too, is a prophetess. Both of these stories are rewritten by the Midrash: in the context of her song, the Midrash recalls Miriam's prophecy about the yet unborn redeemer of Israel, and into her complaint against Moses, the Midrash reads Miriam's concern about the continuity of that redeemer's leadership. The Midrash, then, has a more sympathetic view of Miriam, but also a more passive notion of her participation in the leadership of the nation. . . . Miriam, it seems, is cast by the rabbis in the mold of the biblical matriarchs. Like them, and unlike the biblical Miriam who sings with the women and complains about Moses, the midrashic Miriam claims no share of leadership for herself, but strives to insure that there be a male heir to carry on leadership of the developing nation.[13]

Even the seemingly irreproachable Hannah in the Book of 1 Samuel is reinterpreted by the rabbinic literature so that her personality is less impressive and her role in the story is less significant. Rabbinical interpreters were disturbed both by Hannah's strength and prominence and by her husband's obvious devotion to her happiness, to the exclusion of her familial responsibilities. In midrashic texts, Hannah's personality is reshaped so that she appears less intelligent and self-disciplined and seems instead to be driven by her biological destiny, complaining that her breasts have been unused. At the same time, her husband's role in the story is beefed up, and his qualities are praised by the midrashic text (Brachot 31b). According to Nechama Aschkenasy, "the midrashim revolving around Hannah prove without doubt that the sages attempted to bring the biblical story into conformity with prevalent sexist attitudes."[14]

Interestingly, just as rabbis disagreed on the significance of the attitudes and behaviors of women in the Bible, the interpretive communities of contemporary feminist readers disagree as well. One major point of contention is the significance of the preoccupation with procreation seen in the story of Hannah, which is so characteristic of women in the Hebrew Bible. Some feminist readers see in the repeated stories of frustrated motherhood realistic portraits of women with limited options; these readers argue that no matter how brilliant or talented the woman, she had no psychological, social, or economic niche in biblical societies unless she became a mother—indeed, that having male progeny was more important than having a living husband. Others see such portraits of women as male wish fulfillment; they argue that the women of the Hebrew Bible may not necessarily have wanted children but that the patriarchal authors of the Bible needed to present women as being obsessed with motherhood.[15] Taking the former viewpoint, Susan Niditch observes, "If her husband dies, the woman must rely on her children for support. In terms of long-range security in the social structure, it is more important for a woman to become her children's mother than her husband's wife."[16]

Given these circumstances, it is all the more extraordinary that in the biblical text Hannah's husband, recognizing the extreme importance of male children in their social scheme, attempts to console her with what Aschkenasy characterizes as "an egalitarian, nonpatriarchal" statement, "when he says 'Am I not better to thee than ten sons?' (v. 8)." Aschkenasy notes that although they live in "a male-centered economy, where sons were important as a means of strengthening the extended family and a woman's function was, of necessity, that of procreating," Hannah's husband liberally "views himself as the loving partner whose duty it is to make his wife happy. He does not define his relationship with his wife in terms of her familial or sexual duties, but in terms of his contribution to her contentment."[17]

Another evocative example of rabbinic reinterpretation of enterprising female characters in the Bible is provided by the commentary on Dinah. In the biblical text (Genesis 34), Dinah goes out into the field and is raped by a non-Israelite from a nearby tribe, who subsequently falls in love with her and wants to marry her. Dinah's "honor" is salvaged by her brothers in a scheme that is so manipulative and brutal that their father Jacob disassociates himself from it. Regardless of the wisdom or folly of their behavior, it is clear that Dinah's feelings and preferences were never solicited or considered. Rabbinical commentators, as reported in *Midrash Rabbah* (80:1–12, *Vayishlakh*)[18] use this troubling story as the occasion for homiletics condemning female independence, enterprise, and sexuality. "And Dinah went out," says the Midrash, continuing, "Dinah, the daughter of Leah." Just as the matriarch Leah brazenly went out to the fields to acquire the aphrodisiac mandrakes from her sister Rachel in a vain attempt to win their husband Jacob's love, so Dinah brazenly went out to the field for unknown purposes—instead of staying home where she belonged. Resh Lakish[19] notes, "a woman is not immoral until her daughter is immoral"; Leah went out to meet Jacob "adorned like a harlot," and so, by implication, did Dinah go out. In vulgar modern parlance, Dinah "got what she deserved," according to rabbinical commentary. Thus, female enterprise is linked to lasciviousness and ends in tragedy.

Rabbinic unease with women whom they perceived as overstepping their bounds, however, should be taken in the context of the relatively inferior position of women in surrounding cultures and also in the context of the overridingly respectful and protective attitude toward women within Jewish law. As Judith Romney Wegner suggests, "the sages of the Mishnah" came to the ultimate conclusion that in Jewish law "women share with men a common humanity." She notes that the "social and religious agendas of feminists in the three monotheistic traditions diverge more than they converge":

In the last analysis the otherness of women resides most obviously and undeniably in their sexual differentiation from men and in the function this serves. . . . women may in that respect, but only in that respect, be viewed as Other; in all other contexts of private law, the system must—as indeed, it does—treat them very much like men. It is only in the public domain that the sages manage to avoid this result. This they do by the simple expedient of excluding women from the separate-but-equal world of cultural creation forged by men to express, not the otherness of women but the otherness of men.[20]

Despite the gender-related subordination of women in Jewish law, the emphasis on female procreative and domestic roles, and the discomfort of rabbinic literature with prominent or aggressive women, rabbinic law and literature does not suggest that women lack souls or spiritual qualities. On the contrary, according to Jewish law, a grown woman is spiritually and religiously responsible directly to God (and *not*, as in Milton's *Paradise Lost*, "he for God only, she for God in him"). Indeed, a woman's primary responsibility is not to marry and procreate but to live the most morally and spiritually elevated life possible, a point that is emphasized in the *Akedat Yitzhak*[21] as the author explains Jacob's anger at Rachel when she pleads with him, "Give me children or I die." Nechama Leibowitz comments on the rabbinic text:

Jacob's anger is here explained as being directed at Rachel's forgetting the true and chief purpose of her existence which, according to the *Akedat Yitzhak* is no different from her partner's, the man's. "Like him you may understand and advance in the intellectual and moral field as did the matriarchs and many righteous women and prophetesses, as the literal meaning of Proverbs 31 about the woman of worth indicates." She in her yearnings for a child saw her whole world circumscribed by the second purpose of woman's existence—according to the *Akedat Yitzhak* the *secondary* purpose!—to become a mother. Without it her life was not worth living, 'Or else I die.' This was treasonable repudiation of her function, a flight from her destiny and purpose, shirking the duties imposed on her, not in virtue of her being a woman, but in virtue of her being a human being.[22]

Several explanations have been suggested for rabbinic unease with independent or prominent Jewish women, which actually became more pronounced over the centuries and is still a factor in contemporary Orthodox thought.[23] The most benign suggestion is that domestic women became indispensable to the survival of Judaism. Within the hostile external environments of most Diaspora cultures, the home became crucial for the transmission and continuation of Jewish culture; female devotion to the family and the Jewish household was necessary to help guarantee the survival of the Jewish people.[24] Moreover, the hostility of the environment was not always defined by oppression; on the contrary, as modern attitudes emerged, the emphasis on women as domestic paragons was strongly underscored by the assimilatory opportunities offered by emancipation, as Paula Hyman discusses.[25] Partially because women were critical in the home as enablers, leadership qualities that might encourage women to leave the home and take more active public roles seemed threatening.

A second explanation is that rabbinical commentators throughout history may have been influenced by the misogynist attitudes present in surrounding cultures; thus, Hellenistic, Christian, and Moslem attitudes toward women would all have had some impact on Jewish perceptions of women as well. According to scholars such as Rachel Biale, for example, the rabbinic law (Halakhah[26]) has not excluded women from public religious life nearly as much as did the folk cultures that surrounded it. It was folk culture, not postbiblical Jewish law, for example, that perpetuated the notion of menstrual contamination and made menstruating women feel unwelcome in synagogues in certain European Jewish communities. Contrary to popular opinion, Biale suggests, "the law may have preceded common practice in what to the contemporary eye are liberal, compassionate attitudes toward women.[27]

A third explanation, one frequently articulated by Jewish feminists, is that Jewish religious texts, with some notable exceptions, have been androcentric since their inception in the Bible, and later rabbinical explanations are simply exacerbating an already existing condition. Most feminist scholars of Judaism would be inclined to agree with Judith Plaskow's view that "*Halakhah* is formulated by men in a patriarchal culture" and that "feminism questions any definition of 'normative' Judaism that excludes women's experience." Within this most overarching feminist critique of historical Judaism, men—but not women—are the true audience addressed by God and by Moses, who warn the Israelites to "go not near a woman" as they prepare to receive the Ten Commandments—although, according to Jewish tradition, all Jews and their descendants were standing at Sinai. Women, according to this train of interpretation, were accessories to the spiritual lives of men and were almost always relegated to the role of the ineluctable "other."[28]

Sexuality and the Role of Women

While women in many Jewish societies were expected to be strong and competent in the home, the home-based business, and sometimes the community marketplace, they were excluded from several highly meaningful roles in Jewish life. For most of Jewish history, the role of women within Judaism was shaped by halakhah. Although this body of law prescribed behavior for Jewish women, women were not involved in the formal discussion or decision-making processes—they were passive recipients of a nonrepresentative system.[29] Most significantly, for much of Jewish history women were denied access to the intellectual life of the community, which centered around the study of sacred texts, primarily the Talmud. Second, they were denied a public role in Jewish worship. The practical results of these exclusions were that women were removed from some of the major sites of fellowship: the daily prayers in the synagogue and the group study that was ideally considered to be a lifelong activity for Jewish males.[30]

These exclusions were based on certain assumptions in Jewish rabbinic law about the nature of women. Although depictions of women differed from rabbi to rabbi—and some were far more flattering to women than others—certain commonalities prevailed. The rabbis assumed that, as a practical matter, the vast majority of women would be absorbed in domestic responsibilities for most of their adult lives. They also assumed that men as a group were easily inflamed into sexual thoughts and that a woman's uncovered hair, her arms or legs, even her voice could, perhaps unwittingly, distract a man from sacred tasks such as prayer or study. One of the rationales for the exclusion of women from public worship was that women's physical attractions were perceived as a sexual snare for men. Sexuality was carefully prevented from intruding into the worlds of study and prayer by preventing women from intruding into those worlds.

Although women were certainly not absent from the synagogue, as they were from the study hall, their presence was not required. Although Maimonides rules that women should pray daily, the presence of women is irrelevant to communal prayer. Men are required by Jewish law to pray three specific times daily, and they are encouraged to pray in groups of at least ten men, a minyan[31] (prayer quorum). Women are not obligated to pray at a specific time, just as they are not obligated to perform many time-specific laws, because their familial duties take priority. In many traditional Jewish societies, women did attend services on Sabbaths and holidays; but when they joined men in prayer, they were required to do so behind a partition, the *mekhitzah*,[32] to prevent their disrupting male concentration on the prayers.

However, this does *not* mean that study and prayer were considered to be "sacred" while sexuality was considered to be "profane." On the contrary, sexuality itself was perceived as a good and sacred aspect of life within the marital framework and at the proper time and place. An erotic life that satisfied both husband and wife was seen by the rabbis as an important component of *shalom bayit*, the serene and orderly household that was perceived as the basic building block of Jewish society. (Deliberate celibacy was considered to be an aberration, and both unmarried men and women were regarded with pity or suspicion in Jewish societies.) Both within the Hebrew Bible and within rabbinic law, sexuality was viewed as a key element of human nature, a drive that had the capacity to enhance or to destroy life, to be put to positive and constructive or to dangerous uses.

Female eroticism, sensuality, and nurturing qualities were viewed by the authors of such biblical books as Proverbs and the Song of Songs as part of the arsenal used by the good and wise woman to attract a man and to keep him on the productive and moral path of life. In Proverbs, for example, the wife Wisdom figure is deliberately described in terms quite similar to that of the adulteress Folly figure: both women are pictured as attractive beings offering the "young man" who is the ostensible object of his father/poet's advice the seductions of sexual pleasure and banquets of food. The young man must develop his discrimination so that he knows which woman to pick, and his father admonishes him to love his wife fully so that he is not tempted by the illicit and dangerous invitations of the adulteress: "Let thy fountain be blessed: and rejoice with the wife of thy youth. Let her be as the loving hind and the pleasant roe; let her breasts satisfy thee at all times; and be thou always ravished with her love." In the framework of Proverbs, the moral choice for a woman is to be a faithful wife rather than an adventuress-adulteress who offers her potential lover "bread eaten in secret" when her husband is out of town; the moral choice for the man is to marry and to eschew the false promises of the adventuress, whose "mouth is smoother than oil; but her end is bitter as wormwood, sharp as a two-edged sword" (Proverbs 5: 18–19).

This positive attitude toward eroticism within marriage was retained within much of later Hebrew literature as well. Medieval Hebrew wedding poems, for example, drew heavily on "the prelapsarian love of Adam and Eve in the Garden of Eden and the love of the bride and groom in the Song of Songs," according to Tova Rosen, in love lyrics such as the following:

> The time for love making has come!
> Go down, why do you tarry
> To pasture in her garden?
>
> She keeps her fresh pomegranates out of sight,
> But you, do not fear when she brings them out. . . .[33]

Female sexuality was viewed as a powerful force for either good or evil. Once a woman married, her sexuality was consecrated to her husband. Married women were sexually off-limits for any men except their husbands, and according to biblical law the punishment for extramarital intercourse involving a married woman was death for both the man and the woman. The child of an extramarital affair was a *mamzer*, a bastard, and was forbidden to marry into the legitimate Jewish community for ten generations. The product of a premarital affair, however, was *not* a bastard, according to Jewish law, and had the same legal status, including marriage, as any other Jewish child. However, the social sanctions against premarital sexuality for Jewish girls were very strong in every traditional Jewish community.

Jewish law recognized women's sexual rights within marriage. First, a married woman had the right to sexual fulfillment. The rabbis assumed that women desire sexual activity just as men do but that women may be shy about initiating sexuality; they also assumed that men who had certain lifestyles, such as those who traveled or the scholarly types, might occasionally be so distracted that they neglected the emotional well-being of their wives. For this reason, rabbinic law stipulated the minimum frequency with which husbands should offer their wives sexual activity. Second, within Jewish law every woman had the right to refuse sexual advances that did not please her. Jewish law recognized the reality of marital rape and forbade it. The author of *Iggeret Ha-Kodesh*,[34] for example, advises husbands:

> you ought to engage her first in matters which please her heart and mind and cheer her. . . . And you should say such things some of which will urge her to passion and intercourse, to affection, desire and lovemaking. . . . And you shall not possess her against her will nor force her because in that kind of a union there is no divine presence [Shekhinah[35]] because your intentions are opposite to hers and her wish does not agree with yours. And do not quarrel with her nor beat her for the sake of having intercourse. The rabbis say in Tractate Yoma: "As a lion smashes and eats and has no shame, so a boor beats and possesses and has no shame." Rather you should attract her with charming words and seductions. . . . And do not possess her while she is asleep because the two intentions are not one and her wish does not agree with yours. [*Iggeret Ha-Kodesh*, Chapter 6, "The Fifth Way—Concerning the Quality of Intercourse"][36]

Nevertheless, because women's sexuality presented a "problem" for men when they were engaged in study or prayer, women were barred from two activities that not only were central to the intellectual and public religious life of the society but provided access to communal power and prestige as well. Moreover, women were portrayed by some Talmudic texts as being unsuited for rigorous study. Many rabbis concede that the "exceptional" or "unusual" woman might have the capacity and the interest to engage in rigorous study of Jewish texts, but later rabbinic opinion tended to assume that women as a group are not appropriate candidates for such study.[37] One Talmudic text, for example, asserts that "women are light headed" (Kiddushin 80 b). The most extreme attitudes are perhaps expressed by Rabbi Eliezer Ben Hyrcanus, who argues that "he who teaches his daughter [the oral law] it is as if he taught her licentiousness" (Sotah 20a) and that it is "better that the Torah be burned than that it be studied by women" (Yerushalmi Sotah 3:4). Partially as a result of these attitudes, rigorous study of

Jewish texts by women did not become widespread in traditional Jewish societies until the twentieth century,[38] and in many Orthodox schools even today girls are not provided with access to or the tools for Talmud study.

Indeed, within rabbinic tradition, Beruriah, a woman who dared to overstep her bounds and steep herself in the study of learned texts, is treated with disturbing harshness. The wife of the celebrated Rabbi Meir and daughter of Rabbi Hanina ben Teradion, Beruriah was said to have studied three hundred laws from three hundred teachers in one day (*Pesachim* 62b)—a hyperbole that testifies to Beruriah's quickness and retention of mind. In a variety of anecdotes, she was described not only as brilliant and insightful but as a paragon of pious belief in God's wisdom as well (see, for example, Brachot 10a, Eruvim 53b, and Midrash Proverbs 30:10). However, as Sondra Henry and Emily Taitz summarize, Beruriah came to a sordidly bitter end:

> . . . in order to prove to her that the prejudices against women were not unfounded, and in order to test her, Rabbi Meir secretly arranged for her seduction by one of his pupils. When Beruriah felt herself tempted by the advances of the pupil, she killed herself in realization of her weakness. . . . Rabbi Meir is said to have fled, brokenhearted, to Babylonia after her death (Avodah Zarah 18b). Rashi,[39] the famous 11th century Biblical commentator, elaborated on this story, giving it more credence as a result. One may well wonder what purpose the denigration of Beruriah served for those who chose to repeat this story and believe it.[40]

Contributing to the image of women as creatures delimited by their sexuality were the laws of marital purity, *taharat hamishpakhah*. Based on the biblical taboo against cohabiting with a menstruating woman, an elaborate complex of laws grew up, not only prohibiting sexual relations between husband and wife for a minimum of twelve days a month (an assumed five-day menstrual period and an addition seven "white" days following) but discouraging as well any physical contact whatsoever during that time. Elaborate precautions were suggested by some writers to prevent any inadvertent breach of the laws by a forgetful spouse. Some rabbis advised women not to dress attractively during their *niddut*, unavailable time, but this concept was overturned by Rabbi Akiva, who was concerned that such behavior would undermine the quality of the overall marital relationship: "The early authorities said that she may not pretty herself with makeup nor put on colorful clothes, until Rabbi Akiva came and taught: If you hold this view you will soon make her unattractive to her husband and eventually he will divorce her" (Shabbat 64b).

Within the context of the way Jewish law approaches all appetites, this preoccupation with detail is not unusual: traditional Jewish law provides systems of discipline for all human appetites, and to modern sensibilities these laws can easily appear arcane. For example, within the dietary laws of kashrut the biblical taboo against seething a kid in its mother's milk is understood by the rabbis as a prohibition against mixing milk and meat foods, ultimately resulting in the keeping of separate dishes for milk and meat. However, human beings internalize feelings about sexuality in a way quite foreign to their feelings about food. Therefore, although it is quite true that the laws of *kashrut* are at least as complex as the laws of *taharat hamishpakhah*, their psychological impact may have been quite different.

As writers such as I. L. Peretz, Sholem Asch, I. B. Singer, Tova Reich, E. M. Broner, Kim Chernin, Cynthia Ozick, and Rebecca Goldstein, among others, illustrate in their fiction, rabbinic laws surrounding female sexuality sometimes had profound psychological effects on the way both men and women viewed women. Rabbinic law had the effect of creating an extremely stable society, a society that in many ways protected and respected women and that celebrated certain aspects of sexuality[41] but, also in many ways, stereotyped the image of women, especially in regard to perceptions of women's intellectual and leadership capacities. Moreover, the fiction of many Yiddish and American Jewish writers illustrates the fact that women who for any reason were marginal to traditional Jewish society—because of marital status, intellectual or artistic talents, or nonmarital sexual interests—were punished by society through pariah status and other means.

Within the shorthand of daily life, in which few women learned the intricacies of Jewish law and the nuances of Talmudic descriptions of female nature, the image of the woman was sometimes telescoped and distorted. Thus, female sexuality, which some rabbis saw as "dangerous" in that it might distract men from sacred tasks, was sometimes (albeit mistakenly, from the standpoint of Jewish law) seen as being simply dangerous. In traditional Jewish communities there were some men who leaned toward asceticism and who attempted to minimize the impact of sexuality on their environments even further than stipulated by Jewish law. Some Jewish communities, in addition, were much affected by notions of menstrual contamination drawn from the superstitions of surrounding cultures. For women wedded to men who feared female sexuality or living in communities in which such fears were rife, it was little comfort that in other households or other communities different attitudes prevailed. Similarly, whereas women initially were released from many time-based commandments because it was assumed that their maternal responsibilities would take priority, the popular image of women sometimes indicated that women were incapable of such activities or that such activities would be unseemly for women. Thus, women's subordinate and limited position in Jewish life was tied into their sexuality and into what was sometimes perceived as their prevailingly sexual natures.

The Woman of Valor

Despite historical fluctuations in the reputation of the assertive Jewish woman, however, the Woman of Valor described in Proverbs 31 continued to be considered the epitome of ideal womanhood. Universal praise is accorded by traditional Jewish sources to the strength and assertiveness of this prototypical Jewish ideal woman. She is forceful, splendidly meeting the inner needs of her household and earning income outside her home through real estate and other ventures. Confident and competent, she is neither selfish nor narrow; she labors for social reform by caring for the needy. After describing her active life, the author notes that her husband and children are honored in the community. Because her aggressive behavior is exercised only on behalf of her family and the needy and because she does not personally seek out public honor, for centuries she was seen as the role model for the Jewish wife. Indeed, in Ashkenazi[42] households for the past several hundred years the proverbial description of the Woman of Valor has been sung every Friday night as a form of homage to the actual woman of the household, who, after a week of work that often included breadwinning in the form of some sort of marketplace activity, in addition to domestic chores, had prepared the Sabbath loaves and lit the Sabbath candles.

The woman of valor was not only an ancient cultural and literary ideal but persisted as a familiar personality type in Central and Eastern Europe. Some such talented women were lucky enough to thrive in middle-class surroundings, and others used their considerable skills to struggle with ever-present poverty. The multifaceted, much-talented woman of valor was perhaps most famously epitomized by Glueckel of Hameln (1646–1724), an aggressive businesswoman and mother of thirteen who also wrote her memoirs in Yiddish, supplying historians with one of the best pictures of the social, economic, and cultural life of Central European Jews during that time.[43] More recently, women who functioned both as Jewish matriarchs and as businesswomen have been described in the memoirs of Bella Chagall, who recalls her middle-class mother in *Burning Lights*,[44] and by Chaim Grade, who elegizes his impoverished mother in *My Mother's Sabbath Days*.[45] Many American Jews can recall European or immigrant grandmothers and aunts who worked as storekeepers or seamstresses, presided over orderly and hospitable homes, and often dominated family life as well.

However, the cruel impoverishment experienced by many Jews during lengthy periods of Jewish history often fell especially hard on the shoulders of women, giving glowing descriptions of the woman of valor a bitterly ironic significance, as witnessed by Hayim Nachman Bialik, the great genius of the Hebrew literary renaissance, in his famous poem, "My Song."

As the following excerpt illustrates, Bialik shows how each sphere in which the woman of valor excelled provided one more burden to women like his widowed mother in their daily struggle for survival:

She went to market, blood and marrow spent,
returned at evening crushed to her last breath,
each cursed penny gained vexatiously
made moist with her heart's blood and soaked in gall.
At home at last, a harassed, driven beast
she did not put her candle out till dawn
but plied her needle, mending shirts and socks,
and dumbly sighing out her aching heart.

. . . At break of day, at cock-crow she arose,
in silence moved about her household chores.
In bed, in my dark room, by feeble light
I watched her bend her frail form to the dough,
her thin hands kneading, kneading stubbornly,
the stool rocking beneath the baking trough.
Each pressure of the hand, each pinch, each rub
drove through the wall the whisper of a sigh:
"Lord of the world, support and strengthen me.
What strength have I? What is a woman's life?"
My heart knew well what tears fell in the dough;
and when she gave her children warm new bread,
bread of her baking, bread of her pain, her woe,
I swallowed sighs that seeped into my bones.[46]

Unlike the children of the biblical Woman of Valor, who rose up to call their mother happy, Bialik must give voice to the "dumb sighs," the unarticulated misery of a woman who could not, like the biblical wife, "clothe her children in scarlet"—except for the scarlet stain of her own heart's blood.

The Eastern European Milieu: Toward a Feminist Sensibility

By and large, literary images of women in the Eastern European milieu come from fiction written by men, especially the Yiddish short story writers and novelists; the literary expressions of female Yiddish writers focused largely on poetry, and very few of them published fiction.[47] The writers with whom the readings in this anthology begin were acutely aware of the strengths and the weaknesses of the position of women in traditional Jewish life. The intricacies of traditional Jewish law and culture were not esoteric to them; rather, they were an intrinsic element in the intellectual equipment with which they interpreted experience. Indeed, one of the characteristics common to the fiction of these Yiddish writers was that they were intimately familiar with and yet critical of traditional Jewish culture.

Although the writing of Yiddish authors from I. L. Peretz to Chaim Grade spans a century, from the 1880s to the 1980s, these writers shared certain background elements. Despite the fact that the outside world underwent enormous transformations from the first to the last of these writers, the growing years of each were shaped by the traditional religious culture of Jewish societies and by the religious texts of the yeshiva;[48] their adolescence and young adult years were energized by Westernized intellectual ferment. The Haskalah,[49] the Jewish Enlightenment, had a profound effect on the early Yiddish writers; for the later writers, a variety of modern social and political movements that followed in the wake of the Haskalah were influential as well. Steeped in both the intricacies of traditional Judaism and the intellectual freedoms of secular Western humanism, nationalism, and socialism, the fiction of these Yiddish writers, sometimes elegiac, sometimes intensely critical, reflects their relationship with the culture that spawned them.

Each of the Yiddish writers, some of whom were the precursors of and some the contemporaries of American Jewish writers who wrote fiction in English, places his fiction in a variety of settings, including, among others, the intensely Jewish environment of the shtetl[50] or the densely Jewish urban area. When I. L. Peretz, Sholem Aleichem, Sholem Asch, I. B. Singer, and Chaim Grade place their fiction in traditional Jewish communities, they put their characters into a socioeconomic climate that is at vast odds with those of contemporary America. Suffering from severe economic hardships and starvation, restrictive state policies, and periodic, officially incited pogroms, the everyday lives of Jewish women in such settings were arduous indeed. In these environments, women often did not focus on their subordination by men; they were more directly aware of their mutual subordination by the hostile societies that surrounded them. As Aschkenasy comments, "Oppression from within Hebraic tradition represented a small part of the woman's predicament. Throughout Jewish history, the woman participated with the man in the image of the persecuted, and shared with him the status of the pariah and the unwanted stranger among people who only reluctantly allowed him to dwell in their midst."[51] Unfortunately, such persecution persisted, taking different forms, until well into the middle of the twentieth century.

Nevertheless, the burdens of poverty and persecution fell especially heavily on the shoulders of Jewish women. Moreover, some of them were additionally emotionally debilitated by the misogynistic attitudes voiced by the people around them. Yiddish writers depict in vivid and empathetic detail both strong, resourceful Jewish women who shape their own destinies and also weaker Jewish women, who are victimized by poverty and repressive cultural norms. Peretz, Sholem Aleichem, and Asch especially have portrayed the pathos and desperation of the lives of powerless women. Asch's "weekday mother" in *Salvation*, for example, is a weak but loving woman whose gentle spirit and frail health fail in an environment that convinces her of her own worthlessness in the eyes of God and men. Sholem Aleichem's Shayna Sheindel in *The Adventures of Menachem Mendel*, albeit portrayed in darkly humorous eptistolary narratives, is a lonely, wretched creature, driven to shrewishness by her incompetent husband, who abandons her and her children.

Perhaps the most damning indictment of cultural mysogyny is found in I. L. Peretz's collection of stories, *In This World and the Next*, the earliest of the works here anthologized. Peretz depicts a religious ethos distorted from its original direction and purpose and laying waste to the inner lives of countless women. He portrays agonized young women who marry rich old men in order to save their families from malnutrition and disease, and pathological middle-aged women who have adopted the psychology of the male oppressor so thoroughly that they reject their own female sexuality and cripple their daughters' emotional lives as well. In "A Marred Holiday" (pages 64–71 in this anthology), a mother living with a newlywed couple brutally warns her daughter that if she does not scrupulously avoid sexual contact with her husband during religiously prohibited days she will suffer both in this world and the world to come. The overbearing mother squelches all sensuality and spontaneity in her daughter by convincing her that a woman is "a pitiful creature, no more than a turkey hen, the Lord forgive us. But when it comes to pregnancy, to childbirth—why then her life actually hangs by a hair. That's when the Days of Atonement come upon her. And what do we poor things have for the salvation of our souls . . . right off women in childbirth and little children start dying off."[52]

In other Peretz stories, some women are so filled with despair that life no longer seems worth living.[53] As Ruth Wisse notes, "Peretz was particularly eloquent in his defense of the Jewish woman who was expected to carry the financial burden of the family she was raising so that she could then sit as her scholarly husband's 'footstool' in heaven. . . . [Peretz showed] at what terrible cost to women the unworldliness and holiness of Jewish manhood was often attained."[54] "A Woman's Wrath" (pages 71–75 in this anthology) traces the shifting emotions of a woman overwhelmed by expectations she cannot meet. Watching her husband study, the newest baby sleeping at her side, a prematurely aged mother is at first filled with joy and satisfaction as she listens to her husband's Talmudic chanting. However, she soon remembers that Passover is coming and that "the candlesticks and her earrings are in pawn, that the trunk is empty and the brass lamp has been sold," that in fact "the baby is ailing and there isn't a drop of milk in the house." Distraught, she lashes out verbally at her oblivious husband, at first frightening him into speechlessness and pallor. However, in a masterful scene, her husband realizes by degrees that his wife is overcome by emotion, that she has in fact no control over herself. He soon regains control of the situation by verbally brutalizing her with a cruel distortion of traditional Jewish values—which the wife, because of her vastly inferior Jewish education, is unable to recognize as a distortion:

> "Hell! Everlasting flames! You'll be hung by your tongue—you'll receive all the four punishments of the supreme tribunal!"
>
> She is silent; her face is as white as chalk. He feels that he is not acting right, that he ought not to torture her thus, that this is dishonest, but by now he is no longer able to hold himself in check. All the rancor that had been lurking in his soul is now poured forth without restraint.

Convinced that she is cut off from the joys of both this world and the world to come, the anguished, emaciated woman frantically tries to hang herself. But at the last moment a black humor gleams from the story; as the mother stands on the table with a rope around her neck, she sees her baby about to fall out of his cradle. A mother to the end, she has been socialized to think of others even in her moment of darkest despair. She takes care of all, and even the youngest child has power over her life and her destiny. Furious, she climbs down and silences him with her withered breast. "There, you glutton," she gasps at the little man. "There, sip away—torture me."[55]

Within the short stories, memoirs, and novels of many Yiddish writers, two attitudes emerge that might well be classified as sympathetic to feminist concerns: first, a deep understanding of the day-to-day trials and obstacles experienced by women, such as those seen in the Peretz stories anthologized here; and second, a conviction that women's natures are as multifaceted as those of men—that women, like men, are subject to rational and sensual impulses, the demands of what may be termed mind and body.

In some stories, these sympathetic attitudes emerge through the glorification of the strong, idealistic Jewish woman, who often had to cope with the impact of modernity in the guise of socialism, nationalism, and Zionism, as well as with the demands of traditional Jewish life. These women are often portrayed by Yiddish writers as soldier women in a changing world. Among the women who possess an impressive level of dignity and power, some are Orthodox Jewesses, such as Mother Vella in Chaim Grade's *My Mother's Sabbath Days* (pages 117–139 in this anthology), who heroically maintains her integrity and preserves traditional Jewish mores while retaining loving communication with rebellious children. Vella is presented not only through the young Grade's eyes but also through the eyes of a young, irreligious Zionist and his father, an ultra-Orthodox rabbi. Both the tradition-bound and the rebellious men respect and admire her, finding great dignity and strength beneath her modest demeanor.

Many of the strong women in Yiddish fiction, however, have already moved away from traditional Jewish religious life. They are idealistic participants in the brave new world of *isms* that swept through Jewish communities. Sholem Aleichem's Masha in his 1907 novel, *In the Storm*, is a charismatic, dynamic young Socialist who electrifies her comrades into action. Compared to her, the male heroes seem shadowy and insubstantial. Tamara, in the same novel, is the beautiful daughter of a hypocritically "religious" and stultifyingly bourgeois environment, who redeems her soul in the crucible of idealistic ferment.

Indeed, of all the Yiddish writers anthologized here, Sholem Aleichem is in some ways the most "liberated" as regards the images of the women he depicts. In the "Tevye the Dairyman" series (see "Hodel," pages 77–89 in this anthology), for example, Tevye accepts and celebrates the fact that several of his daughters are intellectuals, they "gobble books like dumplings," and he hires a tutor for them despite his very modest means. Sholem Aleichem endows Tevye with profound respect, not only for his daughters' intellectual qualities but even more for the moral and spiritual qualities of Hodel, the most idealistic and ideologically motivated of his daughters. When one of his younger daughters is on the verge of marrying for money—ostensibly Tevye's goal all along—Tevye is appalled. He wants to know why she can't be more like Hodel, working to change the world and marrying a kindred intellectual spirit for love alone. With his characteristic genius, Sholem Aleichem makes Tevye almost unaware that he holds these views; Tevye frequently struts about asserting that women are simple or overemotional. However, the reader is meant to see through Tevye's chauvinistic poses, as he stridently declares, "Tevye does not cry like an old woman" and turns aside to wipe the tears from his eyes.

Turn-of-the-century Jewish society still retained some of the cultural values of premodern times. Jewish women in late-nineteenth- and early-twentieth-century Eastern Europe lived primarily in urban settings, and yet their demanding lives had something in common with that of farm women, pioneer women, and other women living in societies in which the labor of both men and women is mortally necessary. As emphasized by Barbara Ehrenreich and Deidre English, women in premodern societies, which they typify as Old Order, performed roles that both men and women perceived as important, full, and productive despite their subordinate status. Although "the patriarchy of the Old Order was reinforced at every level of social organization and belief" and although women in such societies saw the authority of their husbands as deriving ultimately from God "to a degree that is almost unimaginable from our vantage point within industrial society, the Old Order is *gynocentric*: the skills and work of women are indispensable." Women's skills in such societies are wide-ranging and respected, often including planting, sewing, spinning, cooking and preserving, raising children, and nursing and healing illnesses. As Ehrenreich and English suggest, a woman "could hardly think of herself as a 'misfit' in a world which depended so heavily on her skills and her work."[56]

The women and the environments described by many modern Yiddish writers in some ways resemble the "Old Order" analyzed by Ehrenreich and English, even after socialism, nationalism, and Zionism had irrevocably transformed the thinking and behavior of many Jews. Sholem Asch, for example, makes a specific point of the fact that his heroine Rachel-Leah Hurvitz, in *Three Cities* (pages 91–115 in this anthology), retains the same thought processes and attitude toward herself as did her pious grandmother and mother, although she lives among the emancipated Jews of Warsaw. In his description of a day in the life of the middle-aged Rachel-Leah, the activities he details include grinding morning coffee with a mill she holds between her legs, boiling the coffee and preparing breakfast for her family and a roomful of her husband's ravenous adolescent students, packing lunches, finding lodging and jobs for new students, caring for sick and/or impoverished neighborhood people, preparing and serving dinner to family and students, and again boiling vats of water to scrub the pots, pans, and floors after dinner. Asch hastens to assure the reader that Rachel-Leah thrives on this regimen. He emphasizes especially her vigorous self-esteem:

> Yet it would be a mistake to assume that all the worries, her own and other people's with which Frau Hurvitz contended had furrowed her face or aged her prematurely. The contrary seemed to be the case; the more she had to do the higher rose her energy, strength and spirit. The inexhaustible reserve of nervous force that was stored in her—presumably an inheritance from generations of peasant ancestors—made her young-looking, elastic in her movements and as fresh in her appearance as a country girl. When she went downstairs the whole house knew her step, for it was unmistakable; the stairs quivered under her tread and yet she always flew whether going up or down. Although she was over forty she looked like a woman of thirty. Sorrow and care had not bowed her proud figure. Full-bosomed and ripe, she advanced like a soldier in an army of mothers, knowing her duty and her own value.[57]

Although Asch draws on the biblical description of the idealized woman of valor in his portrayal of Rachel-Leah, he depicts in his novel a multifaceted believable character as well. In keeping with the general model of "Old Order" women, Rachel-Leah accepts the notion of male intellectual superiority; as she scrubs pots and pans, she happily reflects to herself that "women were intended to help men in the struggle" toward heaven, or spiritual worlds, or socialist equality, depending on the man. However, Asch also depicts this same Rachel-Leah leading large groups of men and women in dangerous public demonstrations for justice and confronting armed authorities with fiery and unself-conscious courage.

Moreover, perhaps contrary to stereotype, Rachel-Leah has a very positive sense of her own physical self; she cherishes her femininity. Asch depicts Rachel-Leah's rich, sensual inner life, as each evening she bolts the door and bathes, "standing naked in a great tub" and pouring "water from a ladle over her supple athletic body." Here she becomes like the Shulamite in the Song of Solomon, as "the dreams of her youth rose up again; green dells of her childhood, cool streams in which she had bathed as a girl, secret glades in fragrant spring woods; all lived again in her memory as she poured the lukewarm rain-water over her head." Rachel-Leah's private time Asch calls the "Sabbath hour" of each weekday. Astonishingly, in describing Rachel-Leah at her bath, Asch alludes not only to the bridegroom in the Song of Solomon but also to a prayer in the Rosh Hashanah liturgy in which God is compared to a shepherd reviewing his flocks: "As a shepherd passes in review his well-tended flocks, Rachel-Leah now reviewed her days and her dreams." Rachel-Leah is, in her serene and private physicality, alone, self-sufficient, thinking her own thoughts, as one divine.[58]

When Rachel-Leah's thoughts drift, at the end of this episode, to an anguished reflection on the imprisonment of her beloved son somewhere in Russia, she is lost in memories of a simpler, more serene time, when he was an infant and she nursed him, nurturing him and keeping him safe. Now she is unable to keep him safe, and she weeps out of anxiety for his future and out of nostalgia for a time gone by. Surprised in the midst of her reverie by Merkin, a protagonist sexually attracted to women who remind him of his long-dead mother, Rachel-Leah manages to extricate herself honorably without damaging Merkin's fragile ego; her behavior is by implication favorably contrasted with that of the glamorous, sophisticated, assimilated Olga Michaelovna in the first third of Asch's trilogy, who, when similarly courted by Merkin, is so flattered by the attentions of a younger man that she capitulates and sleeps with him even though he is her daughter's fiancé.

On one level, Asch here displays an unusual understanding of certain organic connections in the psychological and sensual realms. On another level, Asch is consciously evoking the traditional Jewish mythic image of "mother Rachel," who weeps for the safety of her exiled children. It is characteristic of Asch to juxtapose traditional Jewish images and concepts with the startling psychological insights that fascinated him.

Significantly, authors such as Peretz, Sholem Aleichem, and Grade, as well as Asch, never rejected the Jewish character of their Jewish heroines. If anything, they glorified their Jewish characteristics. The epitome of feminine beauty in their Yiddish fiction is the "Sabbath mother," the fully adult Jewish matron pausing from her hectic round of responsibilities, well-scrubbed and radiant, resplendent in her Sabbath garb. Nor is the "Sabbath mother," as she is portrayed by these Yiddish writers, the sexless madonna typical of some strands in Christian culture; Asch and Peretz both pay approving attention to the inherently sensual nature of their heroines, and Sholem Aleichem's Tevye the Dairyman brags that when his daughters "fall in love, they fall in with their whole hearts." However, the sensuality of these Jewish heroines is generally expressed among courting couples or within the chaste bonds of matrimony. Although unfettered sexuality certainly exists in Yiddish novels and stories, it is often presented as suffused with internal and external danger.

I. B. Singer can hardly be categorized as a feminist—his attitude toward women in many novels and stories is notoriously reductive—but he does display insight into and empathy for persons who are marginal to organized Jewish society, such as women who sought sexual outlets in unconventional settings, or intellectual women, who were certainly marginal to preemancipation Jewish society. Singer has produced numerous pieces of fiction, such as "Taibele and Her Demon," "The Spinoza of Market Street," and "The Unseen," that portray with great sympathy, charm, and warmth the difficult and devious ways in which marginal women and men follow their hormones and their hearts.

Singer's short story "Yentl the Yeshiva Boy" (pages 141–60 in this anthology) effectively depicts the very complicated emotions and behavior of a young woman whose intellectual passion is so profound that she undergoes the charade of being a young male yeshiva student, Anshel. She finds the study of Talmud immensely fulfilling. However, Yentl is tormented by the androgynous exterior she has assumed. She realizes that religious prescriptions for gender-related dress and behavior have a rationale, that they promote a unified—if limited—perception of reality; dressed as a man, Yentl discovers that her male persona is confusing even to her: "In her dream she had been at the same time a man and a woman, wearing both a woman's bodice and a man's fringed garment. . . . Only now did Yentl grasp the meaning of the Torah's prohibition against wearing the clothes of the other sex. By doing so one deceived not only others but also oneself. Even the soul was perplexed, finding itself incarnate in a strange body."[59]

Singer explores Yentl's potential capacity not only for androgyny but also for bisexuality: although she is powerfully drawn to and emotionally aroused by a young man, Avigdor, she marries his beloved, Hadass; Singer alludes to erotic fulfillment between the masquerading Anshel-Yentl and the naive, deceived Hadass.[60] Ultimately, Yentl is willing to live a shadow life, sacrificing long-lasting human relationships and personal happiness in order to travel from city to city and study the Talmud. When she leaves, both Hadass and Avigdor yearn after her and name their firstborn child for her. Yentl, despite her heroic attempt to take control over her own life, walks out of Singer's story in a very precarious position indeed.

Modernity presented Jewish women with alternative life-styles, and many broke free of traditional Jewish sexual and social constrictions. However, such women often felt torn between the Jewish traditions in which they were raised and the opportunities and challenges of more open societies. A number of women were accomplished Yiddish poets,[61] and their poems express the tension many women felt between their frustration with and their loyalty to the women who preceded them. Such warring emotions, for example, are vividly explored in Kadia Molodowsky's poignant series of poems entitled "Women Songs," which begin with a vignette of the confrontation between the poet and her female ancestors:

> The faces of women long dead, of our family,
> come back in the night, come in dreams to me saying:
> We have kept our blood pure through long generations,
> we brought it to you like a sacred wine
> from the kosher cellars of our hearts.
> And one of them whispers:
> I remained deserted, when my two rosy apples
> still hung on the tree
> and I gritted away the long nights of waking between my white teeth.
>
> I will go to meet the grandmothers, saying:
> Your sighs were the whips that lashed me
> and drove my young life to the threshold
> to escape from your kosher beds.
> But wherever the street grows dark you pursue me—
> wherever a shadow falls.
>
> Your whimperings race like the autumn wind past me
> and your words are the silken cord
> still binding my thoughts.
> My life is a page ripped out of a holy book
> and part of the first line is missing.[62]

Like many emancipated Jewish intellectuals and Yiddish writers in the late-nineteenth and early-twentieth centuries, Molodowsky speaks of rejecting traditional Jewish religious behavior, but she feels bound by treasured emotional ties, the blood of her grandmothers a "silken cord," to the lives of the Jewish women of the past. She stands both inside and outside Jewish tradition, as critic Kathryn Hellerstein demonstrates, "in a position of unique ambivalence."[63] Still for her, as she writes in another poem, "The singing of the wind / is the singing of the Sabbath. / And my heart's song /

is an eternal Sabbath."[64] Or as Malka Heifetz Tussman, whose poetry often celebrates the variegated voices of Jewish women, writes slyly, the emancipated Jewish woman's impurity may be more of a problem for an assumedly Orthodox God than for the woman herself: "I say to the Almighty: / Ever homeless Wanderer, / I would, / if but my heart were pure, / invite / you in to spend the night."[65]

Dislocation and Survival in Immigrant America

When European Jewish women and their families emigrated to America, the contexts of Jewish life were radically altered. Although many immigrants came to the New World hoping for comfort and opportunity, they found confusion, poverty, and exploitation instead. Society was often turned upside down, as formerly middle-class, well-educated families found themselves plunged into abject poverty, while formerly impoverished and ignorant emigrés became entrepreneurial successes. Most jobs demanded a six- or seven-day work week, and religious traditions were quickly or reluctantly abandoned by immigrants who faced starvation if they did not meet the requirements of their employers.

Life for immigrant women was especially difficult. Few families were able to survive on the earnings of the husband alone, and both girls and married women worked long hours. Women who came at the beginning of the mass emigration period (1880–1924) often worked as seamstresses at home or peddled food or worked in a small family store. Many took in boarders, further increasing the congestion of their tenement domiciles and decreasing any hope of privacy. Later immigrants provided the major work force in the mushrooming garment industry, with girls typically working in the factories and married women doing piecework at home. In his memoirs, Alfred Kazin describes the pivotal role of the mother, which was typical of many immigrant households:

> The kitchen gave a special character to our lives: my mother's character. All my memories of that kitchen are dominated by the nearness of my mother sitting all day long at her sewing machine, by the clacking of the treadle against the linoleum floor, by the patient twist of her right shoulder as she automatically pushed at the wheel with one hand or lifted the foot to free the needle where it had gotten stuck in a thick piece of material. The kitchen was her life. Year by year, as I began to take in her fantastic capacity for labor and her anxious zeal, I realized it was ourselves she kept stitched together.[66]

Ironically, laws enacted to do away with home sweatshops actually imposed greater privations on the family, for poor women were forced to leave very young children so that they could work in the factory, rather than working at the kitchen table and caring for young children at home. A vignette from Samuel Ornitz's novel *The Bride of the Sabbath* describes the mother of a nursing infant called back to work. An older child carries his baby sister and a pot with his mother's dinner up five flights to the factory loft. His mother nurses the baby while she eats, and when the baby is satisfied, so is she. She turns back immediately to her work, without the time to look back at her children as they leave.

Jewish immigrants found themselves in an environment where few of the traditional values seemed to apply. Contemporaneous nonfiction pieces such as the memoirs of women like Mary Antin and E. G. Stern (alias Leah Morton), as well as the descriptive essays of observers such as Hutchins Hapgood, William Dean Howells, Henry James, Lincoln Steffens, and Jacob Riis, provide us with pictures of a society in the midst of violent transitions, with enormous cultural gaps often opening up between one generation and the next.[67] American-born or -raised Jewish daughters and sons often longed fiercely to blend in with the American landscape and were mortified by the European accents and habits of their parents. American Jewish writers during the period of mass immigrations described a world in which female strength and aggressiveness was still needed but was already beginning to be derided. In immigrant settings characterized by poverty and danger, to be an enabler was a calling requiring intelligence, skill, and shrewdness as well as great reserves of physical and emotional strength; however, in this caldron of dislocation and adaptation, both societal and literary attitudes toward the competent, forceful soldier woman—in particular the Jewish soldier woman—began to change.

Many immigrant women felt confused and almost powerless in this strange new society. Their clothes, their language, and their attitudes toward life did not seem to fit their new homes.[68] Those who did not find employment outside the home often learned English slowly and found their way around their new cities more slowly still. Late-nineteenth- and early-twentieth-century American Jewish writers often described the plight of such immigrant American Jewish women with great sympathy and sensitivity. Abraham Cahan's Gitl in "Yekl" (upon which the movie *Hester Street* is based) is an innocent creature who loses her vulgar husband to the assimilated charms of another woman but eventually finds a better man (pages 164–74 in this anthology).

Cahan's Flora, in "The Imported Bridegroom," on the other hand, is a bright, ambitious, and manipulative girl who schemes to achieve her goals. The sophisticated, elegant daughter of a wealthy and seemingly Americanized Jew, Flora has a very clear sense of what she wants from life; however, like most women of her time, she must accomplish her goals vicariously, by manipulating the men in her life. Although manipulation is not a much-admired behavior in postfeminist America, for American Jewish women who aspired to marriage and a traditional life-style at the turn of the century, there were basically two choices: to act upon others or to be acted upon by others. Existence, therefore, often became a power struggle between husband and wife and between parents and their children. The third option—to pursue an independent and often single course in life—was too intimidating for women like Flora to contemplate. Flora yearns to marry an uptown doctor, and it seems for a time that she will be able to trick her father and her fiancé into fulfilling her dreams. In the end, however, she is defeated by circumstances and the equally strong wills of the men, and she may have lost them both.

One of the most lyrical descriptions of a disoriented and yet heroic Jewish mother is found in Henry Roth's *Call It Sleep*, a novel that movingly exposes the way in which dysfunctional families sometimes survive through the sacrificial efforts of women (pages 195–211 in this anthology). Genya, the protagonist's mother, speaks an eloquent, expressive Yiddish but can barely string an English sentence together. When she wanders outside a few-block radius of her home, she gets lost and is terrified. And yet, in Roth's novel, the seemingly passive, cautious Genya is shown to be a woman with great reserves of strength and hidden sensuality. Singlehandedly, she provides an oasis of sanity and love for her sensitive, terrified son and her psychotic husband and quietly saves her family.

Genya's character is primarily revealed through the reactions of the men who desire her: her vulnerable, adoring son; her tormented, dependent husband; and Luter, the lecherous lodger. Although Genya has little use for authoritarian religious structures and homiletics or for rigid pieties, she maintains traditional Jewish customs on Sabbaths and holidays, and her identity is enriched by the imagery of the Sabbath mother in the eyes of her son. Additional facets of Genya's personality are revealed when her flaming-haired, vulgar, irrepressible sister Bertha arrives on the scene. Bertha, impulsive, openly defiant, a domineering Jewish female who would be instantly recognizable to audiences of the Yiddish theater as well as to later Jewish satirists such as Woody Allen and Philip Roth, serves as a foil for Genya. With Bertha, Genya's careful, protective reserve is dropped, and the reader learns much about Genya's tragic past and motivations. Henry Roth's portrayal of Genya, like the complex heroines of some Yiddish writers, serves as a potent reminder that the literary imagination can indeed transcend gender.

While Genya is clearly a heroine to her needy son, even in immigrant society, Jewish mothers already suffered from the belittling gaze of their

American children. For some second-generation Americans, the raw energy and aggressive behavior of their mothers was suspect—it was un-American. The best chronicler of the rejection of immigrant mothers is Anzia Yezierska, herself a child of the tenements. She writes with equal skill of the agony of the mothers and the agony of the children as they faced each other across a seemingly impassable chasm.

One of Yezierska's most searing works, ironically called "The Fat of the Land," tells the story of Hannah Breineh, who manages to raise many children despite dire poverty (pages 176–93 in this anthology). When family finances improve, as her children grow older, they move uptown to the prestigious "allrightnik's row"—that is, Riverside Drive. But Hannah Breineh is wretched on Riverside Drive, despite the luxury, because she has no freedom to shop, to cook, to conduct her life as she pleases. Her children provide for her physically but do little to hide their scorn for her foreign and uncouth manner. Hannah Breineh's daughter Fanny, especially, is openly appalled and humiliated by her mother. For many daughters in immigrant Jewish literature, the major issue was becoming American. They wanted to be well-educated, soft-spoken, elegantly dressed, refined American ladies. These daughters saw their European Jewish mothers as the antithesis of all of these things. Their mothers did not dress like American women; they spoke too loudly and often with accents; they looked at the world through different eyes. Many of the daughters felt ashamed of their mothers. Moreover, they felt their mothers were ruining their chances for getting ahead. As Fanny tells her brothers, a girl is "always judged by her mother."

Similarly, Rachel Ravinsky, the protagonist of "Children of Loneliness," another Anzia Yezierska story, feels that her parents are dragging her backward "by the hair into the darkness of past ages." Thinking about the gentile man she has grown to love at college, Rachel wonders how she can "possibly introduce such a born and bred American to her low, ignorant, dirty parents." Mrs. Ravinsky, caught between her husband's rigidly righteous convictions and her daughter's scathing rejection, shrivels and grows "old with a sense of her own futility."

For Hannah Breineh and Mrs. Ravinsky, as for many impoverished immigrant mothers, the difficult acquisition and preparation of food became the focus of daily activity.[69] For many mothers, that nurturing activity remained the one link that connected them to their increasingly sophisticated and scornful Americanized offspring. When their children, like Rachel Ravinsky, rejected even their food, such mothers were wounded to their souls: "Ain't even my cooking good no more either. . . . God from the world, for what do I need yet any more my life? Nothing I do for my child is no use no more. . . . How I was hurrying to run by the butcher before everybody else, so as to pick out the grandest, fattest piece of brust. . . . And I put my hand away from my heart and put a whole fresh egg into the *lotkes*, and I stuffed the stove full of coal like a millionaire so as to get the *lotkes* fried so nice and brown; and now you give a kick on everything I done." Yaakov Ravinsky laughs bitterly at his wife's continuing love for their daughter. He tells her, with cruel yet accurate brutality, that Rachel "makes herself so refined, she can't stand it when we use the knife or fork the wrong way; but her heart is that of a brutal Cossack, and she spills her own father's and mother's blood like water."[70]

Michael Gold's fictionalized autobiography of life on the lower East Side describes Jewish women who drifted into lives as prostitutes and madams, as well as a vivid, energetic mother who speaks her mind on dishonesty and injustice in the best tradition of the Woman of Valor and has very definite ideas on the ingestion of proper foodstuffs:

> She woke at five, cooked our breakfast at home, then had to walk a mile to her job. She came home at five-thirty, and made supper, cleaned the house, was busy on her feet until bedtime. It hurt my father's masculine pride to see his wife working for wages. But my mother liked it all; she was proud of earning money, and she liked her fights in the restaurant. . . . The manager there was a fat blond Swede with a *Kaeserliche* mustache, and the manners of a Mussolini. All the workers feared this bull-necked tyrant, except my mother. She told him "what was what." When the meat was rotten, when the drains were clogged and smelly, or the dishwashers overworked, she told him so. She scolded him as if he were her child, and he listened meekly.
>
> "Your food is *Dreck*, it is fit only for pigs," she told the manager bluntly. And once she begged me to promise never to eat hamburger steak in a restaurant when I grew up. "Swear it to me, Mikey!" she said. "Never, never eat hamburger." "I swear it, momma." "Poison!" she went on passionately. "They don't care if they poison people, as long as there's money in it."[71]

Almost four decades later, Philip Roth would describe Sophie Portnoy making a similar demand of little Alexander in *Portnoy's Complaint*, but rather than seeing such a mother's behavior through bemused and basically admiring eyes, as Gold does, Philip Roth would see her fiery admonitions as a symptom of crippling and controlling behavior.

Interestingly, few writers in the first two decades of the twentieth century chose to focus their short stories and novels on the successful activism of Jewish women. In 1909–1910 about two-thirds of the women employed in the garment industry were Jewish; within that industry, Jewish women—described with admiration as *vunderbare farbrente meydlekh* (wonderful, fervent girls)—provided the primary leadership and support for the emerging unions, partially because many had brought socialist values with them from Eastern Europe and Russia. Newspaper reporters and other observers of the scene described the ferocity and eloquence of the Jewish girls who led the strike of twenty thousand shirtwaist workers on November 22, 1909, for example, as Howe summarizes:

> As the evening dragged along, and speaker followed speaker, there suddenly raced up to the platform, from the depths of the hall, a frail teen-age girl named Clara Lemlich. . . . She burst into a flow of passionate Yiddish which would remain engraved in thousands of memories: "I am a working girl, one of those striking against intolerable conditions. I am tired of listening to speakers who talk in generalities. What we are here for is to decide whether or not to strike. I offer a resolution that a general strike be declared—now." . . . Thousands of hands went up: "If I turn traitor to the cause I now pledge, may this hand wither from the arm I raise."[72]

Immigrant and second-generation fiction by Cahan, Yezierska, and many others does capture, however, the tremendous importance of education in transforming the lives of American Jewish women—and in exacerbating the chasm between mothers and daughters. A study of working women in evening schools in New York City in 1910 and 1911 showed that 40 percent of the women were foreign-born Jews; 25 percent of Hunter College graduates in 1916 were Jewish women of Eastern European origin.[73] Those who were successful were able to go on to get jobs as secretaries, bookkeepers, or salesclerks in the finer stores; these jobs were seen as highly desirable, and indeed they represented a very different life from twelve-hour days in factories. Many educated second-generation Jewish women became schoolteachers and social workers in numbers far disproportionate to their place in the immigrant population; early on, teaching and social work came to be considered "Jewish professions."

Later, American Jewish authors who wrote out of the Depression did depict the social activism of women, but much of the proletarian fiction of such writers as Tess Slesinger and Leane Zugsmith has little focus on the Jewish identity of characters or Jewish subject matter. Similarly, Jo Sinclair's (Ruth Seid) early proletarian fiction, such as "Tony and the WPA" (1938),[74] has little direct connection to her Jewish roots as the daughter of immigrants; not until the publication of *The Wasteland*[75] in 1946 did Sinclair incorporate Jewish themes into her fiction for general audiences.[76]

The price of acculturation was very high, and for many Jewish women it amounted to a jettisoning of crucial areas of their inner life. The areas of loss depended on the woman. For some, traditional religious behavior was sacrificed as un-American. For others, Jewish religious ritual had long since been abandoned in the struggle for socialist equality. Some, especially those living in urban centers, were able to continue with their socialistic endeavors on American shores, and these women were extremely influential in creating and supporting union movements in the United States. For those women who were isolated from such centers of socialist struggle, however, the revolutionary fervor that was the core of their lives before emigration found no outlet in America. Women who lost the opportunity to live out their dreams found themselves bereaved, with no vocabulary to articulate their loss and grief.

Tillie Olsen writes frequently both of women who have lost their sense of direction and of strong women involved in socialist activities, but only in *Tell Me a Riddle* (pages 213–44 in this anthology) does the Jewish identity of her characters become obvious or salient. In *Tell Me a Riddle*, Eva, a brilliant, eloquent young Russian revolutionary, comes to this country, marries, and has seven children. Her husband, according to the American custom, is the one who is usually out of the house—at work, at meetings, at clubs—while she remains at home with the children. She is an affectionate, creative mother who takes the wash basin outside to do her laundry on a beautiful day and shows her little ones how to blow soap bubbles with the hollow stalks of wild onion in the yard.

But Eva has no time to read, no time to listen to music, no time to discuss politics with friends. As an older woman, she is very bitter, hating her husband for the way he allowed their family life to divest her of her intellectual and spiritual birthright. She withdraws emotionally from her husband and children and even her grandchildren, yearning for time before she dies to move to the rhythms of her own heart. On her deathbed, she sings snatches of songs she remembers from the revolution. One of them longs for a time when each individual will be valued for him or herself, "every life a song."

The Evolution of Literary Types: The Jewish Mother and the Jewish American Princess

It was to be a long time before American Jewish women, within and outside of novels, would be free to explore their own inner natures. Instead, the midtwentieth-century American literary scene proliferated with books that ridiculed or discouraged the ambitions of Jewish women for intellect, vocation, or self-esteem. The soldier woman qualities that were so admirable to the Yiddish writers were infuriating to midtwentieth-century American Jewish novelists. The world had changed dramatically for American Jews, and different female qualities seemed necessary and admirable in this changed world. Most American Jewish women during and after World War II lived in pleasant neighborhoods, not in grimy tenements. They had 2.8 children, not 8 or 10 children. They washed their clothes in laundromats or in their own washing machines, instead of boiling vats of water on the stove. But they were as smart and as aggressive and as articulate as ever; like Asch's Rachel-Leah, they dramatized their lives and were on the lookout for ever-present dangers that might threaten them and their families. But because the very real dangers of Jewish life in Europe had disappeared from the American Jewish environment, their level of anxiety seemed inappropriate. In lieu of outside employment and in the absence of external challenges such as war or poverty, many American women became caught up in a cycle of consumerism that was easily satirized and mocked. In the hands of American Jewish novelists, both the consumerism and the satire were given a Jewish flavor.

The attitude of Jewish authors toward Jewish women was in many ways symptomatic of their attitude toward middle-class Jewish America. Some of the most widely read midtwentieth-century American Jewish writers were second-generation American men whose lives had been permeated both with consciousness of their Jewishness and with an acute awareness of the differences between Jewish mores and values and those of the United States in its most conformist mode. Jewish women seemed to personify the foreignness of Jewish culture. Apple-pie America might be represented by a blond, sweet woman with a kind of childlike prettiness, a woman who always supported her man and seldom contradicted him; conversely, America might be embodied in the glorious, uninhibited sexuality and putative stupidity of the ubiquitous "blond bombshell" or "sex kitten."

As Philip Roth characterized the assimilative hunger of second-generation American Jewish men, "O America! America! it may have been gold in the streets to my grandparents, it may have been a chicken in every pot to my father and mother, but to me, a child whose earliest movie memories are of Ann Rutherford and Alice Faye, America is a *shikse* nestling under your arm whispering love love love love love!"[77] And if America at its most attractive was the sunny smile and smooth yellow hair of a non-Jewish woman, then Jewish women were both un-American and undesirable.

The problematic, distinctive nature of American Jewish women was presented in two basic stock characters: the "Jewish mother" and the "Jewish American princess." Some European Yiddish writers had already created the figure of the overbearing Jewish matron, but their actual targets were the ineffectual husbands who created the necessity for their wives' forcefulness. In America, however, the rationale for criticism shifted. The forceful Jewish woman was compared unfavorably with more restrained gentile women. In Jewish literature the aggressive, verbal, clever Jewish woman was often caricatured as pushy and unattractive compared to the refined, polite, domestic, docile, and ornamental image of the "real" American non-Jewish woman.

Interestingly, Jewish daughters came under fire first, and satirical stereotypes of unmarried Jewish women remained prevalent throughout the 1970s and 1980s. Indeed, when undergraduates in a spring 1991 class on

"Women in Jewish Culture" were asked if they ever thought of the Jewish woman in terms of the stereotypical Jewish American princess the most forthright and fulsome descriptions came from Jewish females. Significantly, some students were resistant to the idea that the JAP image was fundamentally either misogynist or antisemitic, despite ample documentation. As one student put it, "I come from the Five Towns [Long Island], and where I come from calling someone a JAP is a compliment. Being a JAP means that you've made it. Being a JAP means you have money and prestige, and you know how to use both. A JAP knows and wears what is stylish—she knows exactly where to buy it and how to put things together. And a JAP knows how to get other people to do things for her. Isn't that power? What's more American than power? Being a JAP is being a powerful woman."[78]

This unironic and remarkably naive description of the so-called Jewish American princess is a fundamentally accurate depiction of the sociological beginnings of this stereotype. The yearning to be American, to fit in, was translated in many upwardly mobile families into providing both sons and daughters with every advantage that would enable them to appear and behave as real Americans. For both boys and girls this meant acquiring secular education far beyond the norm for their non-Jewish cohort; for boys it meant being helped with a start in business or professional life as well. But for women, who in the American consumer culture that surrounded them were steered toward being attractive and being effective and conspicuous consumers, a different kind of "higher education" was necessary.

American Jewish writers satirically describe the young woman whose parents were grooming her to fit into upper-middle-class American norms, as they saw them. Although some Jewish writers satirize Jewish men as well, depicting a variety of vulgar, aggressive, materialistic Jewish males, their discomfort with Jewish family life is more often channeled into a preoccupation with Jewish women. Ironically, the negative literary stereotypes of materialistic, manipulative Jewish women that were promulgated by American Jewish writers were only the most recent in a long line of antisemitic literary stereotypes of materialistic Jews in the annals of English literature. As Francine Klagsbrun notes, "All the old stereotypes of Jews come into play in the term JAP. In this day, polite Christian society would not openly make anti-Jewish slurs. But JAP is okay. JAP is a kind of code word. It's a way of symbolically winking, poking with an elbow, and saying, 'well, you know how Jews are—so materialistic and pushy.' What is interesting is that this code word can be used in connection with women—the Jewish American Princess—and nobody protests its intrinsic antisemitism."[79] Eventually, this stereotype was articulated in a genre of humor called JAP jokes. Such jokes, which are often vicious in nature, continue to circulate, although they have now been exposed for their intrinsically antisemitic and misogynist content; JAP humor often suggests that Jewish women are sexually manipulative or unresponsive, that they are obsessively materialistic and exploit their husbands financially, and even that they should be physically exterminated.[80]

A gap often developed between the way Jewish women felt about their families from the inside of the experience and the way they looked from the outside. That gap is brilliantly captured by Herman Wouk in his depiction of one of the best-known Jewish princesses, Marjorie Morningstar (pages 248–55 in this anthology). As Wouk's protagonist, Marjorie Morgenstern, walks down the aisle on her wedding day, she looks into the face of the man she almost married, her beloved nemesis, the playboy playwright Noel Airman. At that moment, Marjorie sees her wedding through Noel's eyes as if she were looking through a ghastly green filter, and she knows that through the filter of his perceptions her spectacular and long-awaited wedding is nothing more than "a blaze of silly Shirley glory." To view her family and the man she really loves and wants to marry through her own affectionate eyes, she must brush away the green filter of Noel's jaundiced attitudes.

It is Airman who first fully describes the princess stereotype to the young and inexperienced Marjorie early in the novel, under the generic name of "Shirley." The youthful appearances, lighthearted personalities, and ostensible career aspirations of unmarried Jewish women are all a sham, Airman insists, because they really are after what women have always wanted "and always will—big diamond engagement ring, house in a good neighborhood, furniture, children, well-made clothes, furs." Although they insist that they despise "domestic dullness," says Airman, in the end they marry "dentists, doctors, woolen manufacturers, lawyers" and settle in for a lifetime of shopping and bourgeois social events. Marjorie correctly condemns Airman's caricature of the Shirley and spiritedly tells him he is "a damned intellectual snob . . . and a bit of an antisemite."[81]

The character of Marjorie actually has more depth than is sometimes appreciated, as does her pragmatic, dryly witty mother. Both mother and daughter would prefer to maintain control over their surroundings and other human beings, but only because they wish to accomplish certain practical ends, not simply for the acquisition of power itself. In this, each resembles the character of Cahan's Flora in "The Imported Bridegroom" (1898).[82] Vital, brave, complicated, and charming—as well as unfailingly manipulative—Marjorie struggles valiantly with a culture that sends her mixed messages about the nature of femininity, sexuality, and the purpose of life. Marjorie takes genuine chances, sleeping with Airman and falling in love with Eden, a secretive, drug-addicted, anti-Nazi hero. However, although she clearly grows and matures through these experiences, Wouk punishes her for the chances she takes. When Marjorie finally meets and agrees to marry a solidly responsible Jewish professional, both he and she are grief-stricken and distraught that Marjorie is no longer a virgin. Marjorie confesses her affair—"every word like vomit in her mouth"—and both of them regard her sexual experience as "a physical deformity, like a crippled arm."

Wouk indicates that Marjorie has done the correct thing, that she has followed her inescapable and life-affirming destiny, when she ultimately discards inappropriate dreams of glory and chooses the traditional religion and values she has grown up with, a stable man she has grown to love, "and children, and a warm happy home." Narrator Wally Wronken comments at the conclusion of the novel that Marjorie now sounds just like her mother, a woman he has always liked. Contemporary readers may well find troubling Marjorie's abrupt abandonment of her career dreams, as well as her obsession with physical virginity, but there is no doubt that Marjorie's feelings accurately reflect normative attitudes among American Jews in the 1950s.

In contrast to searching yet practical Marjorie, Brenda Patimkin, heiress to the Patimkin plumbing fortune in Philip Roth's *Goodbye, Columbus*, loves power for its own sake and fights fairly or unfairly as the need arises to maintain the competitive upper hand over every significant person in her life (pages 258–85 in this anthology). Neal, Roth's poor but intellectual protagonist from urban Jewish Newark, reflects that Brenda, who has had her nose "fixed" so that it will look less Jewish, tries to "fix" her relationships with people as well. She competes with her mother, her father, her little sister, and Neal. Through the pages of Roth's novella, the reader sees both Brenda and her younger sister being shaped by their parents into self-centered and power-hungry women. Because they are both bright and energetic, they absorb these lessons well.

Moreover, Brenda does not feel that she must be a productive person. Her parents have sent her mixed messages about what life requires of her, the primary message being that she is required only to please herself and to be a loyal daughter.[83] Sporadically, however, her mother, perhaps remembering her own, more deprived adolescence, castigates Brenda for her parasitic behavior. In one memorable fight with her mother, Brenda angrily rejects the notion that she ought to contribute in any way to the household community:

> "When's the last time you lifted a finger to help around here?"
> "I'm not a slave. . . . I'm a daughter."
> "You ought to learn what a day's work means."
> "Why?" Brenda said. "Why?"

"Because you're lazy," Mrs. Patimkin answered, "and you think the world owes you a living."

"Whoever said that?"

"You ought to earn some money and buy your own clothes."

"Why? Good God, Mother, Daddy could live off the stocks alone, for God's sake. What are you complaining about?"

"When's the last time you washed the dishes?"

"Jesus Christ!" Brenda flared, "Carlota washes the dishes!"[84]

The Jewish mother was the next target of the satirical efforts of Jewish men. In a epoch when psychiatrists advised women that the only road to feminine fulfillment and happiness was acceptance of a submissive and supportive role, Jewish male writers often portrayed Jewish women in a grotesque mirror image of the proverbial Woman of Valor. These fictional Jewish women had their own ideas and tried to conquer their husbands and sons; they used food, hygiene, and guilt as weapons of domination.

Fear of maternal domination was far from an exclusively Jewish preoccupation in midtwentieth-century America. Indeed, Philip Wylie's *Generation of Vipers* (1942) scathingly accused "dear old Mom" of tying all of male America to her apron strings through heavy-handed emotional manipulation.[85] Erik Erikson in 1950 wholeheartedly accepted the notion of "Momism," the phenomenon of the pathologically dominating mother who infantalizes and emasculates both husbands and sons.[86] Although fear and loathing of the domineering mother began as a culture-wide systemic misogynistic impulse, it soon became highly associated with the Jewish mother in particular. The Jewish mother, like the Jewish American princess, became a staple of American Jewish fiction. And, like the princess, the cartoon figure of the omniscient, omnipotent Jewish mother has enjoyed an amazingly long shelf life in the popular imagination, no doubt due partially to the talents of Jewish writers and filmmakers.

Jewish mothers were repeatedly caricatured as the apotheosis of the crippling "smothering mother," absurdly exaggerating whatever dangers she might find on the midtwentieth-century American landscape. The Jewish mother as terrorist is a peculiarly American hybrid, very assimilated and yet very Jewish. Herbert Gold's mother in *Family*, for example, is worried because her divorced son is thin, "skin and bones," so she prepares a breakfast of strangely brown scrambled eggs. When he vomits over the polished marble hallways at a job interview, his mother is puzzled: with traditional Jewish maternal solicitude—but with highly nontraditional methods—she had put quantities of religiously prohibited bacon grease in the eggs to fatten him up.

The hysterical mother par excellence is surely Roth's Sophie Portnoy in *Portnoy's Complaint* (pages 285–95 in this anthology). Sophie Ginsky Portnoy is so obsessed with her son Alex that she tries to control every aspect of his life, especially those connected to the alimentary canal. When Alex is at the table or when Alex is in the bathroom, Sophie Portnoy wants to know exact details on the nature of his meal or his defecation. She feels that through knowing and controlling every aspect of his life she can protect him from as yet unknown dangers: "'He eats French fries,' she says, and sinks into a kitchen chair to Weep Her Heart Out once and for all. 'He goes after school with Melvin Weiner and stuffs himself with French-fried potatoes. Jack, you tell him, I'm only his mother. Tell him what the end is going to be. Alex,' she says passionately, looking to where I am edging out of the room, '*tateleh*, it begins with diarrhea, but do you know how it ends? With a sensitive stomach like yours, do you know how it finally ends? *Wearing a plastic bag to do your business in!*'"

Not only is Sophie Portnoy's overprotectiveness satirized, but her intelligence, strength, and articulateness is denigrated as well. She is, the novel tells us, an intelligent woman with poetic sensibilities. She encourages Alex in his schoolwork and listens to him attentively for hours, praising him as though he were "the Pope." She is, as well, a generous woman who, like Asch's Rachel-Leah, moves about the kitchen with energy and joy and is tirelessly concerned about others, a principled woman who, like Grade's Mother Vella, expects high religious performance from her children. However, Roth pillories Sophie Portnoy for many of the same female qualities that Asch, Grade, and earlier Jewish writers admired.[87] Few Jewish writers looked beyond the surface of women's lives. The woman of valor had fallen upon hard times.

Real Women: Jewish Mothers and Daughters Explore New Paths

If the typical woman in Old Order societies gained some measure of self-esteem because she knew, like Rachel-Leah, "her duty and her own value," women in the changing society of midtwentieth-century America were often unhappy partially because of confusion about their proper role. Many, no longer content to follow in their mothers' footprints, had not yet defined what they wished to be instead. For some, the exploration of new paths was further complicated by anguished feelings of resentment and guilt toward the mothers they loved and hated and, at least psychologically and often physically as well, were leaving behind. They feared to be too close to their mothers because they did not wish to become like them, but they felt that in abandoning their mothers' life-styles they were adding to the burdens that had already oppressed and diminished the older women.[88]

Explorations of mother–daughter relationships, already an intriguing element in earlier American Jewish fiction, emerged as a major motif in mid- and late-twentieth-century novels and short stories. Indeed, although Jewish fiction shared in a culture-wide, growing American interest in the mother–daughter dyad, the Jewish presentation of the relationship had some special characteristics. Marianne Hirsch demonstrates that "the mother/daughter plot" has been a powerfully evocative motif in literature; she asks important questions that are germane to this discussion, such as "What is unique about the attachment between mothers and daughters? Do cultural, ethnic, and class differences, and differences in sexual preference shape the details of their interaction? And where are the voices of the mothers, where are their experiences with maternal pleasure and frustration, joy and anger? . . . What explains the fact that in fiction and theory we find only rarely the most common aspects of mother–daughter interaction, anger for example?"[89]

For women who derive from distinctive ethnic groups, especially those with strong hierarchical traditions, such as traditional Jewish, Chinese, and Japanese societies, the stakes in the conflict between mothers and daughters are complicated even beyond their general psychological import. Partially because of the high cultural stakes of the struggle between American Jewish parents and their offspring, in American Jewish literature anger is a freely expressed emotion. Starting with mother–daughter relationships in the literature of Yezierska and Olsen and moving forward to works by Piercy, Gornick, Goldstein, Broner, Chernin, and Roiphe, among others, one repeatedly finds mothers and daughters confronting each other; one might easily say that anger is the signature emotion of the genre. Moreover, Jewish authors seem somewhat more likely than average to present the world as viewed through the eyes of a mother, and the mother's perspective is vividly represented in the fiction and memoirs of Peretz, Asch, Yezierska, Olsen, Chernin, and Roiphe.

The prevalence of anger and of maternal viewpoints in Jewish-authored mother–daughter stories arises partially because such motifs are powerfully symbolic of the ambivalence of American Jewish women in a transitional world. Many women find themselves caught, like Yezierska's immigrant heroines, between feelings of loyalty to their traditional Jewish mothers and attraction to their gentile lovers; that conflict is a vivid and graphic symbol of the pull of the past and the lure of the new. The painful predicament of women caught between American and Jewish values was perhaps most pronounced for those families in which poverty exacerbated the division between generations. Several outstanding pieces of fiction explore the confusion of urban women who try to straddle two worlds, without even the financial backing to assure them that they can fully enter American culture if they are willing to leave the Jewish world.

Bernard Malamud's works deal with the conflict between the humanistic values of prophetic Judaism—which he characterizes as "the Jewish heart"—and the amoral materialism that lies at the heart of capitalistic American society. However, most often women are accessories to the action in Malamud's fiction, rather than central or fully developed characters. One of the significant exceptions is the character of Helen Bober in Malamud's 1959 novel, *The Assistant* (pages 300–10 in this anthology). Helen, daughter of a kindhearted, impoverished grocer, Morris Bober, is a young woman of unusual integrity, moral fiber, and intellectual and spiritual potential. However, she is trapped by her socioeconomic position and fears she will never be able to escape her "miserable Bober fate." When a love affair develops between Helen and Frank Alpine, an Italian drifter with a criminal record who becomes her father's grocery assistant, Helen is torn by ambivalent feelings. Is she betraying her parents and her people by loving a non-Jew? Is she betraying her ambitions for higher education and the intellectual life by allying herself with an uneducated man?

To Helen's mother, however, the relationship between Frank and Helen is an unequivocal "tragedy." Helen's mother, Ida, confronts Morris—much as Sholem Aleichem's Golda confronts Tevye and accuses of him of bringing Pertschik into the house so that he may court Hodel—and accuses the grocer of bringing Alpine into the house for Helen. Malamud creates an affecting portrait of mother and daughter, revealing their characters both from within, through their own thought processes, and from without, in the way they are perceived by others. The ties that bind Helen and Ida together and the distances of experience and expectation that separate them from each other testify eloquently to the moral ambiguity that accompanies and complicates mother-daughter relationships in the best American Jewish literature.

Very often in American Jewish literature the intelligent, ambitious daughter feels that she has more in common with her father than with her mother; it is the father who is the kindred spirit. This alliance between father and daughter can leave the mother feeling displaced and alienated from her daughter's love when the daughter moves beyond the need for simple nurture. Thus, in E. M. Broner's novel, *Her Mothers*, Beatrix, the protagonist, for years makes her mother feel as though she is unworthy of Beatrix's friendship and regard. Beatrix's mother is acutely aware of the way her daughter snubs her, as she complains: "You had your father sign your report card; when you told about your day, about your night, you looked at your father; when you spoke of foreign affairs, money affairs, travel affairs you looked at your father." Because Beatrix is a mother as well as a daughter, she learns through her own experience how great a gift is the reconciliation of a daughter's embrace.[90]

One of the most effective portraits of a confused young woman who feels drawn to her father and guiltily estranged from her mother is found in Seymour Epstein's 1964 novel, *Leah* (pages 312–31 in this anthology). Many readers have expressed astonishment that *Leah* is authored by a man; the book's delicate, nuanced presentation of the protagonist's psychology illustrates yet again the gender-transcending power of the literary imagination. Leah is a sensitive, thoughtful woman whose empathetic personality draws many men to her. However, none of these men seems to meet her emotional needs, partially because she finds her father's dramatic personality and ostentatious joie de vivre so compelling that all other men suffer by comparison. Leah's father gives her advice about men that is somewhat similar to the advice Marsha Zelenko gives to Marjorie Morningstar: he encourages Leah to live life to the limit, to reach for beauty, truth, and imaginative excellence, rather than for materialistic security. This is especially difficult for a woman like Leah, who works because she must—for a paycheck rather than in fulfillment of inner-directed career goals, a woman who repeatedly meets seemingly ordinary men.

Leah's relationship with her father is intensified by his desertion of her mother, ostensibly because of her mother's lack of emotional responsiveness, her "granite" nature, her paucity of imagination. Leah, like many of the daughters of abandoned mothers described in American Jewish literature, blames her mother for her father's dereliction. She has shared her father's view of her mother for most of her life. However, when an emotional crisis in her own life makes her vulnerable enough to open up to her mother, Leah discovers that her mother exhibits warmth, responsiveness, and inner resources that she had never known or appreciated. She could not have been more amazed, she says, had "pink doves flown out of my mother's mouth."

For the first time in her memory, Leah consciously and positively identifies with her mother; this new identification increases her own sense of direction and self-esteem, making it possible for her to accept a suitor who has genuinely understood and cared for her for many years. For Leah, identification with her mother is liberating. It also makes it possible for her to confront her father with his own hypocrisy, as he grasps for the materialistic security he has always derided. The words with which Leah's outburst erupts are instructive: "I have a mother!" Leah cries out to her father on a windy street corner. She is capable at last of making her own life.

Divided parental allegiances are additionally complicated when the daughters, like Epstein's Leah or Grace Paley's Faith Darwin Asbury, have more in common intellectually with their fathers than with their mothers. Faith, the frequent heroine of Paley's superb short stories in *Enormous Changes at the Last Minute* and *Later the Same Day*, is a searching, idealistic Jewish woman with two sons, whose parents have decided to take early retirement in the Children of Judea Retirement Home. Paley presents an accurate but extraordinarily gentle and balanced picture of the infantilizing mother and her impatient daughter. In "Faith in the Afternoon" Mrs. Darwin greets the news that Faith's husband Ricardo has abandoned Faith by chiding, "Oh, well, Faithy, you know you have a terrible temper." In "Dreamers in a Dead Language" (pages 333–47 in this anthology), Mrs. Darwin holds Faith's hand and recalls the time when Faith was a baby who sucked applesauce off her fingers. Seemingly unable to comprehend that Faith is a grown, independent woman, she urges Faith to wash her hands more carefully.

Despite the fact that Mrs. Darwin treats Faith like a little girl who has forgotten to wash, she is a sympathetically drawn figure. Faith tolerates her mother's ministrations with reasonable aplomb. What Faith can't tolerate is a revelation her father makes to her later, that he would like to divorce his wife but he can't—because he never married her. When they were young, they were socialist idealists who didn't believe in marriage, he says. Faith bursts out angrily: "Oh, *you* were idealists. . . . Well, Pa, you know I have three lovers right this minute. I don't know which one I'll choose to finally marry. . . . I'm just like you, an idealist. The whole world is getting more idealistic all the time. It's so idealistic. People want only the best, only perfection."[91]

Faith is angry because her father is acting like Ricardo, the gentile husband who left her to pursue other women. Her father speaks as though he will leave her mother a lonely, deserted woman like herself. "So," she shouts at her father, "You and Ricardo ought to get a nice East Side pad with a separate entrance so you can entertain separate girls." Although they are very different in terms of self-knowledge and intellectual capacity, Faith and her mother are both secularized, compassionate, caring women who retain much of the Jewish cultural ethos of concern for others. It seems they may end by having a very similar fate.

This tendency of history to repeat itself in the lives of women is at the heart of much mother-daughter conflict as reported in American Jewish fiction. A common pattern—indeed, a pattern that recalls some of the immigrant fiction as well—depicts a daughter whose entire life is lived in reaction to her mother. Obsessed by the conviction that she does not want to repeat her mother's mistakes, the daughter never truly achieves independence from the past. Frequently, behind the destructive mother–daughter relationship in these contemporary works of American Jewish fiction there is a man whose expectations and demands pit women against each other.

A world of such women is evoked in Vivian Gornick's memoir, *Fierce Attachments* (pages 348–64 in this anthology), which focuses on thwarted women who turn inward, blighting the lives of subsequent generations of women. The Bronx apartment of the protagonist's youth is a rich and colorful world of women, in which her mother is powerful—and yet bitterly aware that she is removed from the patriarchal power structure of the world of work. The Bronx women send mixed messages about the world of men and work to the protagonist as she grows up: men are longed for, hated, admired, and disdained. Concomitantly, the women's ghetto in the apartment building is both safe and threatening, sometimes shimmering with lesbian overtones, sometimes as claustrophobic as the grave. It partakes of the characteristics of a literary community of women as described by Nina Auerbach, in that it is a kind of matriarchal society that both empowers women yet blocks the progress of young women toward independence and maturity in an outside world that is, finally, both patriarchal and heterosexual.[92] Each of Gornick's women struggles to establish a workable relationship with the men in her life, often unsuccessfully. Seeing their personal potential stunted by male demands, priorities, and expectations, some women react with anger, some with denial, and some with apathy and despair.

Gornick's protagonist is obsessed by her mother and by the past partially because her mother withdrew from appropriate nurturing during a pathologically extended period of grieving for her dead husband. As an adolescent, Gornick's protagonist becomes convinced that she can keep her mother alive and functioning only through the sheer strength of her presence and her will. Mothers can withdraw from their daughters for other reasons, as Daphne Merkin illustrates in her novel *Enchantment*. In Merkin's novel, Hannah Lehman grows up in an affluent German-Jewish Orthodox home on New York's Upper West Side. In contrast with the more familiar stereotype of the "smothering" Jewish mother, Hannah feels that her mother ignores her. Both infatuated with her mother—enchanted—and alienated from her, Hannah finds that all of her subsequent relationships are disturbed. Her mother's emotional withdrawal controls Hannah's life just as surely as another mother's direct manipulation.[93]

Daughters in many pieces of recent American Jewish fiction observe their mothers being neglected or abandoned, and their first impulses are to blame the mother for "provoking" mistreatment and to distance themselves from the mother's fate by showing how "different" they are from their mothers. In *Leah* and in "Dreamers in a Dead Language," one way in which daughters distance themselves from their mothers is to identify strongly with their fathers, until life circumstances thrust gender bonds upon them. In much American Jewish fiction, another effective way in which the Jewish daughter distances herself from the Jewish mother is to marry or become sexually involved with a partner overtly quite different from the man who married—and then neglected or abandoned—mother; the most "different" type of man is frequently non-Jewish.

Anne Roiphe, in *Lovingkindness* (pages 366–81 in this anthology), makes these emotional currents between mother and daughter explicit. *Lovingkindness* expands the reactive mother-daughter pattern to three generations: the grandmother, a wealthy, heavily made-up, card-playing, dependent, and conventionally Jewish woman whose husband cheats on her; the mother, Annie, an independent, intellectual, assimilated woman who marries a non-Jew to escape the same fate her mother suffered; and the disturbed granddaughter, Andrea, an emotionally fragile girl who goes from a punk life-style to extreme religiosity in Yeshiva Rachel, a girl's school that educates and indoctrinates "born-again" Jews in Jerusalem, to escape her own mother's values system and behavior.

Roiphe's protagonist remembers her mother weeping day after day over her husband's philandering and neglect; Annie is sure it is her mother's fault: "I believed that if she tried harder she could make him kind and gentle, considerate and loving, that rosebushes could grow in our living room and that birds could fly free in our dining room. I believed that if she worked at it he would stop leaving lipstick-stained shirts on his armchair and come home for dinner and put his arms around her and whisper in her ear and they could put on a record and dance together."[94]

Partially in order to protect herself from the emptiness of her mother's life, Annie seeks out a totally different kind of relationship. Annie determines that she will marry a spectacularly gentile man. Like Philip Roth's Jewish men who rejected Jewish women because they hope to buy American identity in the bed of a gentile, Annie too tries to buy acculturation in the arms of a true American:

> I was wanting something exotic, something American, something that spoke of picket fences, white clapboard houses, Fourth of July parades in which children sold lemonade as the Lions and Elks wearing fezzes walked past to the sound of the trumpet and the Veterans of Foreign Wars waved to their families as they marched in uniforms that stretched across stomachs greatly sucked in for the occasion. I wanted to bed with a man who had drunk in the Declaration of Independence with his mother's milk, who knew the purple mountain's majesty because he had inherited the vision from the kind of man who had made stone boulders into even fences. I wanted a man who was not a tourist in towns where the white steeples stung the sky. . . . I wanted a man who couldn't tell a Yiddish joke.

Annie's choice turns out to be a poor one, and she finds herself increasingly neglected by and then widowed by (perhaps semi-intentionally) her drunken, poetic, gentile husband. Mother-daughter history repeats itself as Annie watches her daughter, named Andrea to evoke the Aegean Isles, reject her values and life-style as definitively as she had rejected her own mother's. Annie reflects long on the nature of mother love as it is depicted in Greek myth and drama and as it plays itself out in contemporary life. Although Annie is appalled by Andrea's coup de grace in becoming a born-again Jew, after traveling to Jerusalem, Annie's negative attitude toward Judaism softens. Annie—and Roiphe—bear witness to the beauty and depth of a woman's restricted life in an ultra-Orthodox Jewish community. We have come full circle from the writings of Anzia Yezierska. Yezierska describes the daughter's longing to escape from the foreignness and restrictions of the Jewish past. Annie's daughter wants to return to them.

Stricken with ambivalence and doubt, Anne Roiphe's heroine wonders if women's liberation is after all a mere evolutional aberration, which will be erased by the growing forces of fundamentalism. She wonders if women in the future will be relegated, as her daughter has chosen to be relegated, to the quiet byways of the domestic realm. In her questions about the past and future of the personal lives of women and the entanglement of those lives both in Jewish values and in the lives of their mother and daughters, Roiphe's Annie is emblematic of an entire generation of women struggling to find their own path in a transitional society.

Contemporary Soldier Women in a Changing World

American Jewish women struggled not only with their own mothers and daughters but with a plethora of challenges in the shifting landscape of America in the 1970s and 1980s. The whole world was seemingly open to them: they could pursue education as far as their intellectual capacities and ambitions could take them; they could enter any vocational field; they could follow their sexual inclinations into numerous or monogamous, lesbian or heterosexual liaisons; they could have seven children while pursuing a career in gastroenterology or postpone or avoid having children altogether. In terms of their relationship with Judaism, they could attain rabbinical ordination or they could completely estrange themselves from Jewish life. The choices were at times bewildering.

American Jewish literature has faithfully recorded the battles undertaken by Jewish women in this extraordinary time of change. The impact of external forces on the women portrayed in Jewish fiction has shifted perceptibly from decade to decade. Thus, despite the appearance of enormous external change early in the emergence of the contemporary feminist movement, Jewish female protagonists in the early 1970s were often depicted as being victimized by society, being deluded and denuded, being left with what were in actuality "Small Changes,"[95] as Marge Piercy insists in her diligent chronicle of the stormy, experimental cultural environment of the late 1960s and early 1970s. Piercy portrays Miriam, a bright, talented, lively Jewish female professional who has affairs simultaneously with two gentile men, neither of whom accords her the respect she deserves and whose friendship with each other sometimes seems more real than their relationship with Miriam. Later she marries a seemingly stable Jewish man, but when she wants to augment motherhood with a very modest career, he is ready to leave his "pushy" "orange and purple" Jewish wife for a docile "pastel" non-Jewish subordinate.

Piercy's observation about society's punitive attitude toward vibrant Jewish women jibes with poet Adrienne Rich's essay about being half-Jewish, "Split at the Root." She recalls that the route to success for Jewish women until very recently consisted in their being able to suppress their Jewishness:

> With enough excellence, you could presumably make it stop mattering that you were Jewish; you could become the *only* Jew in the gentile world, a Jew so "civilized," so far from "common," so attractively combining southern gentility with European cultural values that no one would ever confuse you with the raw, "pushy" Jews of New York. . . . We—my sister, mother, and I—were constantly urged to speak quietly in public, to dress without ostentation, to repress all vividness or spontaneity, to assimilate with a world which might see us as too flamboyant. I suppose that my mother, pure gentile though she was, could be seen as acting "common" or "Jewish" if she laughed too loudly or spoke aggressively.[96]

One thinks also of Hortense Calisher's memories of growing up Jewish in the South, dealing with a mother who, despite her activity in the Temple Sisterhood, "didn't want to be Jewish," who "sneered at the name of a high school friend I had brought home, whose head of blond fuzz she had termed 'kike hair.' . . . when I went uncombed or unkempt I was accused of having the same." And yet the young Hortense understands also that she is a vehicle for familial continuity, for "when we elders die, you will be our keepers."[97]

By the late 1970s and 1980s, women in American Jewish fiction were most often not only doing active battle with their surroundings but achieving significant triumphs as well, in the fiction of some male as well as female authors. Pushiness—that is, assertive behavior and clearly and forcefully articulated opinions—made a comeback. The soldier woman was back in style, rescued by the general women's liberation movements and by Jewish feminist writing. Interestingly, women have become frequent protagonists of American Jewish short stories and novels during these two decades, not only because far greater numbers of Jewish female authors have recently published books than in earlier historical periods but also because the extent of change in the lives of contemporary Jewish women has been dramatic and full of conflict, offering a broad spectrum of themes to writers of fiction. Thus, a focus on female protagonists and significant supporting characters is found not only in the works of female authors and new figures on the American Jewish literary scene in the 1970s and 1980s but also in the recent works of some established male literary figures, who previously did not seem much interested in women except as accessories to men's lives.

Indeed, it might fairly be stated that feminist exploration is one of the most significant new movements in American Jewish literature, as it is in American Jewish life. This literary exploration has achieved a rather startling prominence in all varieties of literature, running the entire gamut from difficult, critically acclaimed fiction to glossy, melodramatic, shallow romantic novels. As a general observation, the female protagonists in popular Jewish romances are almost always breathtakingly beautiful, and no matter how agonizing their experiences, they almost always achieve the predictable romantic and material successes that are a sine qua non of the genre. Although this anthology does not draw from that category, it is significant to note that, unlike such novels in the past, today's beautiful protagonists (1) are often identifiably, proudly Jewish, and (2) achieve their goals not through the ministrations of a handsome and mysterious gentleman but through their own intelligent, energetic efforts. The image of the woman in contemporary American Jewish literature has been rehabilitated and transformed even at the most basic, grass-roots level.

Jewish women now appear as protagonists in fiction whose scope extends far beyond "the Oedipal swamp" (to borrow a phrase from Philip Roth). Among major themes that have emerged in recent American Jewish fiction focusing on women, some of the most important include the role of the Holocaust in the identity of survivors, their children, and the broader Jewish community; Israel as a focal point of American Jewish identity and as a setting for the exploration of Jewish identity; a variety of religious and cultural subgroups within Jewish life, such as Sephardi Jewish communities, ultra-Orthodox communities, and feminist groups; sexual subgroups, such as Jewish lesbians and homosexuals; and the tension between intellectual and sensual, personal and professional, Jewish and humanistic agendas in the lives of contemporary American Jewish women. Moreover, feminist themes are often linked with Israel, the Holocaust, and Jewish subgroups and societies in recent American Jewish fiction.

Some feminist literature has been experimental in theme, style, or content. A good example of the creative freedom that marks some self-consciously feminist American Jewish literature can be found in E. M. Broner's *A Weave of Women*,[98] which describes a dozen women and three girls who dream of and plan for a feminist vision of utopia in Israel. They create their own Israeli/Jewish/feminist liturgy, together with its own ceremonial literature and myth. Broner's experimental style blends Hebrew, Yiddish, and biblical motifs within narrative, drama, and poetic forms.

Her fiction is an example of what might be termed mythic exploration of feminist issues. Another example of this type of fiction is Kim Chernin's *The Flame Bearers*,[99] which depicts a sect of Jewish women devoted to a female aspect of godhead called Chochma, the Bride. Other works by the prolific Chernin include feminist-oriented and Jewishly intense essays, such as those found in *Reinventing Eve*,[100] and memoirs such as *In My Mother's House*.[101] In one memorable episode in *Reinventing Eve*, Chernin experiences a spiritual epiphany with a unique Jewish "goddess" in an Israeli village, together with little girls and an aged woman, as the others pray in the synagogue on the High Holidays.

More commonly, however, feminist issues within Jewish and American culture have been explored in familiar American Jewish settings. The female protagonists of recent American Jewish fiction have had to struggle with a multiplicity of identities: they are Jewish, they are Americans, they are daughters and wives and lovers and mothers, they are moderns, they are heirs to an ancient tradition. Equally important, American Jewish women are not depicted as balancing these competing demands exclusively according to their own internal preferences; influences from sweeping historical events to the significant others in women's lives often distort the decision-making process.

The effect of history on the lives of individual women is movingly addressed in Gloria Goldreich's *Four Days* (pages 386–401 in this anthology). While the novel focuses on the moral decision of Ina, a middle-aged daughter of Holocaust survivors, over whether to abort an unplanned pregnancy, an interrelated subplot examines the character of Ina's mother, Shirley Cherne. When Shirley, as a young mother, is incarcerated in a concentration camp with her little daughter, she is passionately maternal, a thin, tenderly loving, indomitable wraith of a woman who manages against all odds to keep her little girl hidden and safe. Once in America, however, Shirley metamorphoses into a plump, hard-edged, pragmatic, and phlegmatic businesswoman who has little time or energy for that same daughter. Ina puzzles over the nature of femininity and maternity and the true identity of her Holocaust mother.[102]

The complex interaction between mothers who are Holocaust survivors and their daughters has been the subject of some of the most compelling recent literature. Rebecca Goldstein's story "The Legacy of Raizel Kaidish," for example, portrays a mother who engineers her daughter's personality through the strongest kind of emotional manipulation; she tries to create of her daughter a selfless, dispassionately altruistic saint, all in an effort to expiate her own profound moral failure within the hell of the concentration camps. Only on her deathbed does she acknowledge that she has been wrong to sacrifice her daughter's autonomy.[103] Cynthia Ozick, in *The*

Shawl, portrays a very different kind of mother, Rosa Lublin, who, like Goldreich's Shirley Cherne, struggles to hide, protect, and nurture her small daughter. But Lublin's daughter is betrayed, discovered, and killed. Rosa, like Demeter unwilling to abandon Persephone to the gods of death and darkness, wills her daughter Magda into life and existence within her own imagination. She imagines every detail of her daughter's physical and emotional existence, her talents, her attitudes, her feelings. Within Rosa's mind, her dead daughter is vital, beautiful, and fierce, "a tigress."[104]

The Holocaust also looms in the background of Saul Bellow's 1989 novella, *The Bellarosa Connection*. Narrated by an elderly Jewish man, the brilliant and wealthy founder of the Mnemosyne Institute in Philadelphia, the narrative ostensibly describes the relationship between two Jewish men, Holocaust survivor Harry Fonstein and the Broadway producer Billy Rose, who saves Fonstein and many other Jews from the Nazis; in reality, however, the book is animated and dominated by the figure of Sorella Fonstein, Harry's wife. Sorella Fonstein seems at first glance like a character created in order to poke fun: the narrator recalls that when he first met her, "Sorella's obesity, her beehive coif, the preposterous pince-nez—a 'lady' put-on—made me wonder: What is it with such people? Are they female impersonators, drag queens?"[105]

Significantly, the Jewish women portrayed in most of Bellow's previous novels are often misfits who display grotesque behaviors or appearances. The three main female figures in Bellow's *Mr. Sammler's Planet* (1969), for example, are each devoted to the protagonist but are regarded by him as grossly inferior in their physical, moral, and intellectual capacities. Sammler's daughter Shula is genuinely mad, a pathetic, bewigged creature who scavenges Broadway trash baskets and goes about creating havoc in her own and other people's lives. Sammler thinks that Shula's emotional instability is somehow linked to her thin hair, a quirky symbol of her twisted femininity.[106] Sammler also thinks that the widow, Margotte, who tries to take care of him is "sweet but on the theoretical side very tedious, and when she settled down to an earnest theme, one was lost . . . because mornings could disappear while Margotte in her goodness speculated." Perhaps most egregiously, Angela Gruner, the sexually hyperactive daughter of Sammler's generous cousin, emits a plethora of sexual odors, speaks constantly of her numerous affairs, and evokes from her otherwise kindhearted father such epithets as " 'Bitch' when his daughter approached with all her flesh in motion—thighs, hips, bosom displayed with a certain fake innocence. . . . Under his breath, Gruner said 'Cow!' or 'Sloppy cunt!' "[107]

In contrast, Sorella Fonstein, while certainly as physically grotesque as any of Bellow's previous female characters, is described with admiration, sympathy, and approval, an admiration all the more astonishing given her doorway-filling, chair-straining size; she is, as the protagonist comments succinctly, "off the continuum." Bellow characterizes Sorella as a new and totally original type of soldier woman, a woman of immense honesty and courage as well as immense bulk and a woman who triumphs morally over the powerful, womanizing Billy Rose and over the soul-killing materialism of the "Shirley" stereotype.[108]

For decades, Bellow has effectively explored the dialectic of appetite and repulsion that female sexuality evokes in some men. Although fascinating as a psychological phenomenon, the love–hate relationship that men have with women's bodies has been the basis of profound discrimination against women at many times and in many cultures. This discrimination has attracted the attention of Jewish women writing today, who often include in their fiction male characters who project their own psychological ambivalence onto female physical characteristics and virtually convert normal female physiology into a type of pathology.

One of the most devastatingly witty and accurate satires on the male projectionist fallacy is found in Cynthia Ozick's *The Cannibal Galaxy*, which portrays Hester Lilt, a world-renowned philosopher who enters her daughter in the Jewish day school of principal Joseph Brill. Lilt suffers socially because of her dual nature—at times she is isolated or even ostracized by a society that continues to insist, "either mind or body." Initially, Lilt impresses Joseph Brill as another order of being from most women, especially from other mothers, because she is rational, honest, and direct. Brill thinks that most mothers are like frenzied creatures on a hormonal flood but that Hester—the intellectual female—is necessarily different:

> It was strange to think she had a child. Profoundly, illimitably, he knew the mothers; she was not like any of them. The unselfconscious inexorable secretion ran in all of them. From morning to night they were hurtled forward by the explosions of internal rivers, with their roar of force and pressure. The mothers were rafts on their own instinctual flood . . . that was why they lived and how: to make a roiling moat around their offspring . . . they were in the pinch of nature's vise. . . . And their offspring too would one day be the same: aggressive, arrogant, pervicacious."

Having decided that most mothers are all body, all instinctive frenzy to protect their offspring, but that Hester is different and all mind, Brill blurts out to her that her daughter is an inferior creature and is not worth the love of her intellectual mother. He is shocked by the white fury with which Lilt answers him. Brill decides that "she was like the others: nature's trick, it comes in with the milk of the teat."

Nature's trick, of course, is that both men and women have dual natures, a duality that has been expressed via many literary formulas down through the centuries. Both men and women are pulled between the demands of intellect and rationality, on the one hand, and the demands of emotion,

contemporary American Jewish literature still exhibit squeamishness about their female nature.

Rebecca Goldstein's *The Mind-Body Problem* (pages 419–38 in this anthology) wittily captures many facets of the discomfort American Jewish women can still feel about themselves. That discomfort ranges from a lack of self-esteem, in which a woman is made to feel deficient because she is both attractive and intelligent, to a real revulsion against female physiology. In Goldstein's book, one woman comes to see her mind as the enemy that threatens her chances for a happy marriage. Another woman articulates the pathological attitudes toward the female body that both Bellow and Ozick put into the mouths of men; here, women have absorbed destructive male attitudes so thoroughly that they see their bodies as the enemy.[114]

Goldstein surveys the many prejudices that confront the brilliant, multifaceted woman. Her female protagonist, Renee Feuer, is a beautiful young woman who goes to Princeton to get a Ph.D. in philosophy and studies philosophical approaches to the dichotomy between the intellect (the mind) and the senses (the body). Her professors do not take her seriously—she is too beautiful—until she gains legitimacy by marrying a world-famous mathematical genius. The genius wants Renee to abandon her career and make herself his organizer and enabler. Renee's best friend, Ava, an attractive classmate from Barnard who has now become an intentionally ugly academic, reinforces the idea that femininity and intellectualism are mutually exclusive, that "feminine is dumb," and that a woman who hopes to be taken seriously as a scientist must "stamp out all traces of girlishness."

Ava's insistence that she cannot see herself both as a woman and as an intellectual is true not only of women in the sciences but often of women in the arts as well. Hortense Calisher argues that many female writers and painters have absorbed the judgments of their male colleagues. They are terrified that if they are perceived as female artists their art will be somehow trivialized or diminished: "She knows her own capacity for the universal, and will not have it contaminated with the particular—if the particularity is feminine. Looking abroad, it can be seen what happens to women who do ride their femininity in the literary races: Doris Lessing, tied to psychiatry, suffragettism, and the vaginal reflex." It is their flight *away* from overt femaleness, however, that actually does reduce the power of some female writers, Calisher suggests. Only by speaking out with their own voices can the full power of their artistic vision be realized.[115]

For many years, some female writers suppressed aspects of their experience in order to assimilate into the dominantly patriarchal literary environment. Similarly, Jewish writers for many years catered to the predominantly non-Jewish literary establishment either by ignoring Jewish subject matter or by treating Jewish characters as a species of precocious "others," existential heroes or court jesters, whose value consisted in their standing both inside and outside Christian or secular societies and commenting on them. Few American Jewish writers prior to 1965 explored what being Jewish meant for the Jews themselves.[116] Just as female writers today are reclaiming their own womanly voices, Jewish writers are regaining their Jewish voices. Jewish female writers, doubly marginal, for many years disguising two primary aspects of their identity, are at last writing out of their full vision. Writers such as Cynthia Ozick, Rebecca Goldstein, and others draw on the full, complex, often contradictory and conflicting particularisms of their female Jewish American experience and vision.

Contemporary American Jewish writers often focus specifically on women's struggles to be treated as multifaceted individuals. Their works illustrate the fact that the battle is far from over. As surely as is I. B. Singer's Yentl the yeshiva boy, Rebecca Goldstein's Ava is convinced that she must dress, act, and think like a man in order to be considered, by others and by herself, a bona fide intellectual. She must reject her female nature, mind *and* body, to participate in the discipline she loves, albeit it is physics rather than the Talmud that she studies, and it is drab, androgynous clothing rather than a *taalith* that she dons. As keenly as did Jewish heroines of past decades, Renee Feuer rejects the rigid pieties of her mother's life, but she longs for the melodies and flavors, the spiritual and communal richness of traditional Jewish culture. Depictions of Jewish women have become broader, deeper, and more believable than they had been in recent decades, but the problems Jewish female protagonists face bear more than a passing resemblance to the problems of Jewish women in the past.

A new and yet curiously traditional protagonist has emerged in contemporary American Jewish fiction: the strong, intelligent woman who struggles with conflicts arising from within and from without. The scope of female protagonists in American Jewish fiction is more diverse than it has been for decades, reflecting changing economic and societal conditions for American women. Despite radical changes in the social realities and in the literary depictions of women in recent American Jewish literature, however, the ancestry of the contemporary soldier woman remains a venerable one, enriched immeasurably by historical and literary precedents.

Notes

1. Athalya Brenner, in *The Israelite Woman: Social Role and Literary Type in Biblical Narrative* (Great Britain: JSOT Press, 1985) devotes a scholarly monograph to classifying the many different models of women in the Bible. She comments succinctly on the character of those women who are the focus of this essay: "Her plot is bound to succeed because she acts not for personal pleasure or profit, but for a sacred aim" (p. 82); they "are motivated neither by

pleasure-seeking nor by financial or social ambitions"; because their motives are in line with an accepted values system, "the authors who record their tales are on their side" (p. 108). See also Carol Meyers, *Discovering Eve: Ancient Israelite Women in Context* (New York and Oxford: Oxford University Press, 1988).

2. There are four prophetesses in the Hebrew Bible: Miriam, Deborah, Huldah, and Noadiah. For discussion of their characters and contributions, see S. D. Goitein, "Women as Creators of Biblical Genres," *Prooftexts* 8, no. 1 (January 1988), pp. 1–33; and Brenner, *The Israelite Woman*, pp. 57–66.

3. Mieke Bal, *Lethal Love: Feminist Literary Readings of Biblical Love Stories* (Bloomington and Indianapolis: Indiana University Press, 1987), provides very interesting insights into the Tamar story. She emphasizes Tamar's role as a "focalizer," who "sees what Judah does not see. In 14, she sees the injustice done to her. In 16–17, she sees that Judah is not to be trusted. Judah, in turn, sees a whore instead of a relative. In 25, she forces him to see the truth." Bal underscores the fact that Judah, before Tamar confronted him, was "ready to misuse his power and condemn to death the woman guilty of his own act" (pp. 100–103).

4. Phyllis Trible, "Depatriarchalizing in Biblical Interpretation," in *The Jewish Woman: New Perspectives*, ed. Elizabeth Koltun (New York: Schocken Books, 1976), pp. 217–40; and Alicia Ostriker, "Liberated Theology," *Tikkun* 6, no. 2 (March/April 1991), pp. 43–45, both comment on the way in which a group of women working together defeat patriarchal authority in this episode. Trible notes that "women nurture the revolution. The Hebrew midwives disobey Pharoh [sic]. His own daughter thwarts him, and her maidens assist. This Egyptian princess schemes with female slaves, mother and daughter, to adopt a Hebrew child. . . . As the first to defy the oppressor, women alone take the initiative which leads to deliverance (Exod. 1:15–2:20). If Pharoh had realized the power of these women, he might have reversed his decree" (p. 221). Ostriker refers to the "striking conspiracy of women (midwives, Moses' mother, his sister, and Pharoh's daughter) united across class and ethnic lines to break a Pharoh's law" (p. 44).

5. Nechama Aschkenasy, in *Eve's Journey: Feminine Images in Hebraic Literary Tradition* (Philadelphia: University of Pennsylvania Press, 1986), argues that "it soon becomes clear to the careful reader that, though the larger context of this narrative does not require it, the narrator has painstakingly etched a character of great strength and forcefulness and that . . . it is the single-minded and determined woman, not her famous offspring, who is meant to sustain the reader's interest and sympathy. . . . Hannah is dignified, determined, and extremely eloquent, and her vision transcends the immediate and the domestic" (pp. 12–13).

6. Bal, in *Lethal Love*, usefully points out that upon their return to Israel, "Ruth is badly off: she is a woman, a widow, a foreigner, and childless. Her tribe lives in hostility with the Jews (Num. 25). Naomi is not a foreigner, but she is a childless widow, and too old to change that situation. . . . Ruth's and Naomi's problems are economic." Boaz, outwardly so established and secure, the "perfect citizen," shares a related problem: he too is aging and childless. Bal suggests a complex and carefully worked out interpretation of the sexual themes of the book, noting that the elders bless the union of Boaz and Ruth with a reference to the earlier story of Judah and Tamar (Gen. 38) and that Ruth's approach to the sleeping Boaz in the threshing house in the dead of night is easily seen as a sexual encouragement of their eventual marriage (pp. 68–88).

7. See the following biblical passages: Rebecca, Genesis 24:15–67; Tamar, Genesis 38; Ruth, the Book of Ruth; Deborah, the Book of Judges; Hannah, I Samuel 1:2–2:21.

8. This term is drawn from Stanley E. Fish, *Is There a Text in This Class?* (Cambridge, Mass.: Harvard University Press, 1980).

9. See Linda Kuzmack, "Aggadic Approaches to Biblical Women," in *The Jewish Woman: New Perspectives*, ed. Elizabeth Koltun (New York: Schocken Books, 1976), pp. 248–56.

10. Aschkenasy, *Eve's Journey*, p. 14.

11. The *Zohar*, compiled in the thirteenth and fourteenth centuries, is the central work in the literature of the Kabbalah, a movement of Jewish mysticism.

12. The Midrash is a particular genre of rabbinic literature that combines homily, biblical analysis and exegesis, legends, and occasionally legal principles. These pieces provide a run-

ning commentary on specific books of the Bible, often linking them to other passages in the Bible, but thematically are only loosely clustered around the original texts.

13. Devora Steinmetz, "A Portrait of Miriam in Rabbinic Midrash," *Prooftexts* 8 (1988), pp. 35–65, 57–58.

14. Aschkenasy, *Eve's Journey*, p. 13.

15. Aschkenasy, in discussing the rabbinic diminution of Hannah, states that the procreative yearning of such biblical women as Sarah, Rachel, Tamar, and Hannah is not superimposed on female characters by patriarchal male authors, a common assumption among some critics. Mieke Bal, for example, insists that Tamar's "action does not provide her with the husband that was her goal. But it does provide Judah with the offspring he was longing for. As in many biblical tales, the woman is used for her indispensable share in the course of history, as the sidestep that restores broken chronology" (*Lethal Love*, p. 102); similarly, Esther Fuchs argues that biblical motherhood is a "patriarchal mechanism" and not the "personal tendency of women" because God intervenes only to facilitate the impregnation of married women ("The Literary Characterization of Mothers and Sexual Politics in the Hebrew Bible," *Semia* 46 (1989), pp. 151–66, 160). In contrast with this more commonly held view among feminist readers of the Hebrew Bible, Aschkenasy (*Eve's Journey*) argues that biblical women themselves longed for offspring at least as intensely as did men—indeed, that these offspring provided women with a purpose and place in the daily world, while to men the same offspring represented a link with the future. Instead, the position of women in ancient societies was such that even—or perhaps especially—strong and talented women experienced a desperate longing for male progeny: "Only by having a child, by educating him and shaping his life could such a woman find release for all her hidden talents." Thus, "Hannah's diversified talents seem to be incongruous with her monolithic pursuit of motherhood, and indicate the paucity of opportunities that existed in ancient times for expression of creativity" (p. 12).

16. Susan Niditch, "The Wronged Woman Righted: An Analysis of Genesis 38," *Harvard Theological Review* 72 (1979), pp. 143–49.

17. Aschkenasy, *Eve's Journey*, pp. 12–13.

18. The translation used here is found in H. Friedman and Maurice Simon, trans., *The Midrash Rabba: Genesis* (London, Jerusalem, and New York: Soncino Press, 1977).

19. Resh Lakish, Simeon ben Lakish, who lived during the third century B.C.E., became one of the leading Torah sages in the Tiberias academy, which was headed by Rabbi Yohanan.

20. Wegner, *Chattel or Person? The Status of Women in the Mishnah* (New York and Oxford: Oxford University Press, 1988), "The Mishnaic Woman and Feminist Theory," pp. 183, 197.

21. *Akedat Yitzhak* is a philosophic commentary to the Five Books of Moses, composed by Isaac Arama (1420–1494), a Spanish Talmudist.

22. Nechama Leibowitz, *Studies in Bereshit (Genesis) in the Context of Ancient and Modern Jewish Commentary*, trans. Aryeh Newman (Jerusalem: World Zionist Organization Department for Torah Education and Culture, 1972), pp. 334–35.

23. See Wegner, *Chattel or Person?*; Yvonne Haddad and Willison Findly, eds., *Women, Religion, and Social Change* (Albany, N.Y.: SUNY Press, 1985); Rachel Biale, *Women and Jewish Law: An Exploration of Women's Issues in Halakhic Sources* (New York: Schocken Books, 1984); Bernadette Brooten, *Women Leaders in the Ancient Synagogue* (Chico, Calif.: Scholars Press, 1982); Ze'ev Falk, *Jewish Matrimonial Law in the Middle Ages* (Oxford: Oxford University Press, 1966); Judith Hauptman, "Images of Women in the Talmud," in *Religion and Sexism*, ed. Rosemary Reuther (New York: Simon and Schuster, 1974), pp. 184–212; Susannah Heschel, ed., *On Being a Jewish Feminist* (New York: Schocken Books, 1983).

24. See, for example, Aschkenasy, *Eve's Journey*, p. 15.

25. Paula Hyman, "The Modern Jewish Family: Image and Reality," in *The Jewish Family: Myth and Reality*, ed. Steven M. Cohen and Paula E. Hyman (New York and London: Holmes and Meier, 1986), pp. 179–93.

26. The halakhah, its name derived from the Hebrew word to go or to walk, is the body of Jewish law as formulated over the centuries by rabbinic scholars; these laws prescribe in great detail the preferred behavior of the Jew in regard to every aspect of life.

27. Rachel Biale, *Women and Jewish Law*, p. 7.

28. For Judaism as a historically androcentric religion, see Judith Plaskow, "Standing Again at Sinai: Jewish Memory from a Feminist Perspective," *Tikkun* 1, no. 2; *Standing Again at Sinai: Judaism from a Feminist Perspective* (New York: Harper &.Row, 1990).

29. For further discussion of the changing role of contemporary Jewish women, see Sylvia Barack Fishman, "The Impact of Feminism on American Jewish Life" in *The American Jewish Year Book, 1989*, ed. David Singer and Ruth Seldin (New York and Philadelphia: American Jewish Committee and the Jewish Publication Society, 1989), pp. 3–62.

30. Blu Greenberg, *On Women and Judaism: A View from Tradition* (Philadelphia: Jewish Publication Society, 1981), pp. 62–63, summarizes the laws and concepts that most determined a Jewish woman's role thus:

> Talmudic law spelled out every facet of the law as it applied to the woman. She was exempt from those positive commandments that must be performed at specific times, such as wearing the *tzitzit* and the *tefillin*, reciting the *Shema*, and the three complete daily services (Kiddushin 29a; Eruvin 96b; Berakhot 20a-b, Menahot 43a). She was exempt also from certain commandments that were not time specific (Eruvin 96b). In various communal or group events, she could be a participant-observer but had no equal status in performance of ritual. This held true for the *mitzvah* of *sukkah*, the celebration of *simhat bet ha-sho'evah*, the redemption of the firstborn, inclusion in the *minyan* for grace after meals, and reading the Torah at the communal prayer service (Sukkah 2:18, 53a; Kiddushin 34a; Megillah 47b, 23a).

31. A minyan is a quorum of ten Jewish men necessary for certain group prayers to be read.

32. A *mekhitzah* is a partition separating men from women in Orthodox synagogues. This separation can be effected through an actual partition or by placing the women's section in a balcony or adjoining room.

33. Tova Rosen, "On Tongues Being Bound and Let Loose: Women in Medieval Hebrew Literature," *Prooftexts* 8 (1988), pp. 67–87; quotation, p. 77.

34. The *Iggeret Ha-Kodesh*, literally the "holy epistle," is an anonymous thirteenth-century Kabbalistic work that broke ground as the first work to openly apply Jewish mystical teachings to everyday behavior. It deals extensively with sexual relations between husband and wife.

35. The Shekhinah is one of several Hebrew names referring to the Divine presence; it is usually taken to embody the feminine aspects of Godhead.

36. For a fascinating and thorough discussion of sexuality within marriage according to Jewish law, see Biale, *Women and Jewish Law*, pp. 121–46.

37. Saul Berman, "The Status of Women in Halakhic Judaism," in *The Jewish Woman: New Perspectives*, ed. Elizabeth Koltun (New York: Schocken Books, 1976), pp. 114–28, details trends promoting, opposing, and presenting compromise positions in regard to women studying:

> . . . during the Tannaitic period there were three distinct positions. . . . While the Mishnah reflects the extreme positions of Ben Azzai arguing for obligation and Rabbi Eliezer propounding that it is prohibited . . . the Tosefta suggests an intermediate position in which women are not obligated to study Torah but would not be prohibited from doing so. Amoraic discussion already reflects only this intermediate stance. . . . However, this position fades during the period of the Rishonim, to be replaced with variants of the more extreme position of Rabbi Eliezer. Among the Aharonim, two divergent approaches [are found]. . . . One such line constructs its case for permission to teach women both Written and Oral Torah on a purely functional base. Thus the Hafetz Hayyim and others have argued that the fact that Jewish women are beneficiaries of a secular education makes it mandatory for us to assure their knowledge of Scripture and rabbinic thought. . . . Rabbi Joseph Karo suggests that women are obligated to study those laws which pertain to them. But it is Schneur Zalman of Liadi who formulates a broad principle by which women are obligated to study all laws of the Torah, both Biblical and rabbinic, except those concerning mitzvot which they are not obligated to perform. (pp. 118–20)

38. The slow, cumulative growth of Jewish education for women is linked to the process of emancipation and acculturation to Western society. In Germany, where the Jewish com-

munity was profoundly affected by the ideals of the Haskalah (Jewish Enlightenment), both the burgeoning Reform movement and the enlightened neo-Orthodox movement of Samson Raphael Hirsch sponsored formal Jewish education for girls. In Eastern Europe, where the Jewish community proved more resistent to Westernization, such schooling came somewhat later. After World War I, some secular Jewish schools, both Yiddishist and Hebraist, provided formal education for girls. Most important, Sara Schnirer, the Polish daughter of a Belzer Hassid, established in 1917 the Bais Yaakov movement, which revolutionized Jewish education for girls in the Orthodox world. Today, intensive Jewish education of girls is widely accepted by all Orthodox elements as an absolute necessity.

39. Rashi, an acronym of the name Rabbi Solomon ben Isaac, lived from 1040 to 1105 in Troyes, France. He is the most influential and widely studied rabbinic commentator on the Bible and Talmud.

40. Sondra Henry and Emily Taitz, *Written Out of History* (New York: Biblio Press, 1988), pp. 54–58.

41. For three modern, positive commentaries on the spiritual import of women's immersion in the waters of the ritual bath, see Rachel Adler, "Tumah and Taharah—Mikveh," in *The Jewish Catalog*, comp. and ed. Richard Siegel, Michael Strassfeld, and Sharon Strassfeld (Philadelphia: Jewish Publication Society, 1973); Barbara Rosman Penzer and Amy Zweiback-Levenson, "Spiritual Cleansing: A Mikvah Ritual for Brides," *Reconstructionist*, September 1986, pp. 25–29; Blu Greenberg, "In Defense of the Daughters of Israel," *On Women and Judaism*, pp. 105–24.

42. The term *Ashkenazi* refers to Jewish persons of Eastern, Central, or Northern European descent, in distinction from Sephardi Jews, who descend from Spanish or Mediterranean areas.

43. *The Life of Glueckel of Hameln, Written by Herself* (New York: Thomas Yoseloff, 1962).

44. Bella Chagall, *Burning Lights* (New York: Schocken Books, 1946).

45. Chaim Grade, *My Mother's Sabbath Days* (New York: Alfred A. Knopf, 1986, originally published in Yiddish as *Der Mames Shabosim*, 1955).

46. Hayim Nachman Bialik, "My Song," trans. Ruth Nevo, *Voices within the Ark: The Modern Jewish Poets*, ed. Howard Schwartz and Anthony Rudolf (New York: Avon Books, 1980), pp. 57–59. The editors provide the following short biography of Bialik:

> Hayim Nachman Bialik was born in 1873 to a poor family in the Ukraine. He received the traditional Jewish training in Talmud. After establishing himself in literary and publishing circles in Odessa, Bialik translated classics of European literature into Hebrew, edited the Aggada and the Hebrew poets of Spain, established the Dvir publishing house, and became the leading poet of the Hebrew national renaissance. Before settling in Palestine in 1924, he wrote in both Hebrew and Yiddish. He died in 1934. (p. 51)

47. Some exceptions were Kadia Molodowsky, who wrote dramatic vignettes and one novel as well as poetry (see note 62), and Isaac Bashevis Singer's sister, Esther Singer Kreitmen, whose storytelling talents and intellectualism seemed so bizarre in the shtetl that they were a source of misery to herself and others, according to British novelist Clive Sinclair. See Clive Sinclair, "Esther Singer Kreitmen: The Trammeled Talent of Isaac Bashevis Singer's Neglected Sister," *Lilith*, Spring 1991, pp. 8–9.

48. The yeshiva is a school of higher learning for the study of classical Jewish texts, especially for the study of Talmudic literature. Although persons enrolled in the yeshiva can study for rabbinic ordination, these schools are not attended exclusively by those who wish to enter the rabbinate.

49. The Haskalah, the Jewish Enlightenment, began in Germany in the 19th century and later spread into Eastern European Jewish communities.

50. Shtetls were predominantly Jewish areas located outside of major metropolitan areas; however, they were urban and not rural or buccolic in atmosphere.

51. Aschkenasy, *Eve's Journey*, p. 231.

52. I. L. Peretz, "A Marred Holiday," in *In This World and the Next: Selected Writings*, trans. Moshe Spiegel (New York: Thomas Yoseloff, 1958), pp. 186–194; quotation, p. 190.

53. For an overview of Peretz's sympathetic treatment of women, see Ruth Adler, *Women*

of the Shtetl—Through the Eyes of Y. L. Peretz (Cranbury, N.J.: Associated University Presses, 1980).

54. Ruth Wisse, ed., *The I. L. Peretz Reader* (New York: Schocken Books, 1990), p. xx.

55. Ibid., pp. 239–43.

56. Barbara Ehrenreich and Deidre English, *For Her Own Good: 150 Years of the Expert's Advice to Women* (New York: Doubleday, Anchor Books, 1979), pp. 8–9.

57. Sholem Asch, *Three Cities* (New York: G. P. Putnam's Sons, 1933; New York: Carrol & Graf, 1983), pp. 313–14.

58. Ibid., pp. 320–21.

59. I. B. Singer, "Yentl the Yeshiva Boy," *The Collected Stories of Isaac Bashevis Singer* (New York: Farrar Strauss and Giroux, 1982), pp. 149–169; quotation, p. 155.

60. Evelyn Torten Beck, "Teaching about Jewish Lesbians in Literature: From *Zeitl and Rickel* to *The Tree of Begats*," in *Lesbian Studies: Present and Future*, ed. Margaret Cruikshank (Old Westbury, N.Y.: Feminist Press, 1982), pp. 81–87.

61. In addition to the poets quoted in this essay, see Anna Margolin (1887–1952), Celia Dropkin (1888–1956), Dvorah Fogel (1902–1942), Rosa Gutman-Jasny (born 1903), and Rachel Korn (1898–1982).

62. Kadia Molodowsky, "Women Songs, I," trans. Adrienne Rich, in *A Treasury of Yiddish Poetry*, ed. Irving Howe and Eliezer Greenberg (New York, Chicago, and San Francisco: Holt, Rinehart and Winston, 1969), p. 284. Molodowsky was born in Lithuania in 1894, and, like many Jewish intellectuals, she lived and wrote in Warsaw for many years. An activist in the Yiddish movement, she taught in Yiddish schools and wrote verse and poetic tales for both adults and children. After her emigration to New York in 1935, she wrote several volumes of poetry, a book of children's literature, a drama, and a novel, *At the Gate* (1967), before her death in 1975.

63. Kathryn Hellerstein, "Songs of Herself: A Lineage of Women Yiddish Poets," *Studies in American Jewish Literature* 9, no. 2 (Fall 1990), pp. 138–150, explicates Molodowsky's 1927 sequence of poems, "Women Songs," and shows how Molodowsky uses the image of blood to evoke the ambivalent attitude toward female sexuality within traditional Judaism:

> On one figurative level, this is the blood of the heart, of a womanhood made pure and virtuous; and, in fact, the blood itself is likened to the virtue inherent in a ritually correct way of living. However, because women's blood inevitably suggests the blood of the menses and childbirth, too, the poem brings to mind the 'impurity' of women which they can correct only through the halakhic rituals of purification. The overcharged nature of the blood figure is only complicated by the word tsnies. . . . In Yiddish, this Hebraic word has a range of meanings—virtue, modesty, chastity—that are applied almost exclusively in reference to women, specifically to sexual purity. The pure blood of *tsnies*, or modest virtue, then becomes—when conveyed through women—the impure blood of procreation and sexual prohibition. (pp. 143–45)

64. Kadia Molodowsky, "Song of the Sabbath," trans. Jean Valentine, *A Treasury of Yiddish Poetry*, ed. Irving Howe and Eliezer Greenberg (New York, Chicago and San Francisco: Holt, Rinehart and Winston, 1969), pp. 285–286.

65. Malka Heifetz Tussman, "I Say," trans. Marcia Falk, in *Voices within the Ark: The Modern Jewish Poets*, ed. Howard Schwartz and Anthony Rudolf (New York: Avon Books, 1980), p. 360. Tussman, born in the Ukraine in 1896, emigrated to the United States in 1912. She has written several volumes of poetry and translated Dylan Thomas, Akhmatova, and Tagore into Yiddish.

66. Cited in Irving Howe with Kenneth Libo, *World of Our Fathers: The Journey of East European Jews to America and the Life They Found and Made* (New York: Simon and Schuster, 1976), p. 172.

67. See Mary Antin, *From Plotzk to Boston* (1899; reprint, New York: Marcus Wiener, 1986) and *The Promised Land* (1912; reprint, Boston: Houghton Mifflin, 1969); Leah Morton, *I Am a Woman—and a Jew* (1926; reprint, New York: Marcus Wiener, 1986); Hutchens Hapgood, *The Spirit of the Ghetto: Studies of the Jewish Quarter of New York* (1902; reprint, New York: Funk & Wagnalls, 1965); Milton Hindus, *The Old East Side: An Anthology* (Phila-

delphia: The Jewish Publication Society of America, 1969). See also Pamela S. Nadell, "The Journey to America by Steam: The Jews of Eastern Europe in Transition," *American Jewish History* 71 (December 1981), pp. 269–84.

68. See Sydney Stahl Weinberg, *The World of Our Mothers* (Chapel Hill: University of North Carolina Press, 1988).

69. See Howe, *World of Our Fathers*, pp. 174–75.

70. Anzia Yezierska, "Children of Loneliness," *The Open Cage*, pp. 145–63.

71. Michael Gold, *Jews without Money* (1930; reprint, New York: Carrol & Graf, 1985), pp. 246–47.

72. Howe, *World of Our Fathers*, pp. 297–300; see also Charlotte Baum, Paula Hyman, and Sonia Michel, *The Jewish Woman in America* (New York: New American Library, 1978).

73. Paula Hyman, "Gender and the Immigrant Jewish Experience in the United States," *Jewish Women in Historical Perspective*, pp. 222–42, p. 232.

74. Jo Sinclair, "Tony and the WPA," *The New Masses*, Sept. 6, 1938, pp. 19–20.

75. Jo Sinclair, *The Wasteland* (1946; reprint, Philadelphia, New York, Jerusalem: The Jewish Publication Society, 1987); in her introduction to the JPS volume, Vivian Gornick comments that this novel was before its time in linking the problems of marginality experienced by Jews, blacks, and homosexuals; she notes that Sinclair "made the ghetto in which her inner-city Jews live a reflection of the ghetto within themselves."

76. See Alan Wald, *The New York Intellectuals: The Rise and Decline of the Anti-Stalinist Left from the 1930s to the 1980s* (Chapel Hill: University of North Carolina Press, 1987), pp. 64–74.

77. Philip Roth, *Portnoy's Complaint* (New York: Fawcett Crest, 1967), pp. 164–65.

78. Classroom conversation around Philip Roth's *Goodbye, Columbus*, Judaic Studies 6B, Brown University, April 2, 1991, student J. R., female, Jewish, sophomore.

79. Francine Klagsbrun, "JAP: The new antisemitic code word," *Lilith* 17 (Fall 1987), p. 11. See also "Jewish Women Campaign Against 'Princess' Jokes," *The New York Times*, Sept. 7, 1987.

80. College campuses report repeated incidences of the harassment of Jewish women, sometimes with crowds of men shreiking, "JAP, JAP, JAP" at a passing Jewish woman. In perhaps the most bizarre instance of the social acceptability of the JAP image, an Arizona husband actually escaped imprisonment for the murder of his wife by the success of the defense lawyer's claim that his wife was a "Jewish American princess" and therefore impossible to live with. Ruth Knafo Setton, author of "Street of the Whores" in this anthology, has surveyed the malice of the JAP image and the real havoc it has created in people's lives in "Jewish American Princess: The Lethal Stereotype," *Matrix* (December 1989), p. 9. See also Elaine DeRosa, "Crime and Punishment: Author of Book on Steinberg Murder Explores Injustice of Justice System," *Greater Phoenix Jewish News*, July 29, 1988, pp. 10–12; Sherry Chayat, "JAP-Baiting on the College Scene"; Judith Allen Rubenstein, "The Graffiti Wars"; Susan Schnur, "When Is a JAP Not a Yuppie: Blazes of Truth," *Lilith* 17 (1987), pp. 6–7, 8–9, 10–11, respectively; Gary Spenser, "JAP-Baiting on a College Campus: An Example of Gender and Ethnic Stereotyping" (July 1987; available from the Syracuse University Department of Sociology; includes lengthy bibliography); "Image of the Jewish Woman: Myth and Reality" (a guide for discussion of stereotypes of Jewish women, available from the Program Affairs Department of B'nai B'rith Women, Washington, D.C.); Selma R. Siegel, "The Jewish Mother and the Jewish American Princess," *Jewish Currents*, February 1987, pp. 23–28.

81. Herman Wouk, *Marjorie Morningstar* (New York: Doubleday, 1955; New York: Simon & Schuster, Pocket Books, 1973), pp. 228–30.

82. In terms of character, none of these women has the least in common with Ibsen's Hedda Gabbler, however, whose pathological quest for power denies the selfhood of others and ultimately embraces death rather than life.

83. See Janet Handler Burstein, "Lost Children in Contemporary American Jewish Literature," *Studies in American Jewish Literature* 9, no. 1 (Spring 1990), pp. 9–19.

84. Philip Roth, *Goodbye, Columbus* (Boston: Houghton Mifflin, 1959; New York: Bantam Books, 1976), p. 46.

85. Philip Wylie, *Generation of Vipers* (New York: Holt, Rinehart and Winston, 1955), p. 198.

86. Erik Erikson, *Childhood and Society* (New York: W. W. Norton, 1950).

87. For discussions of Roth's women, see Barry Gross, "Sophie Portnoy and 'The Opossum's Death': American Sexism and Jewish Anti-Gentilism," *Studies in American Jewish Literature* 3 (1983), pp. 166–79, who correctly states, "Portnoy's complaint against his mother is, in effect, a complaint against being Jewish. . . . she is a moral force, exemplar and propagator of values, values of responsibility and duty" (pp. 167–68).

88. Adrienne Rich, *Of Women Born: Motherhood as Experience and Institution* (New York: Norton, 1976), puts it most succinctly: "Easier by far to hate and reject a mother outright than to see beyond her to the forces acting upon her. . . . there may also be a deep underlying pull toward her . . . the fear not of one's mother or of motherhood but of becoming one's mother" (p. 235). For a masterful presentation of this phenomenon as a psychological factor in the development of eating disorders, see Kim Chernin, *The Hungry Self: Women, Eating, and Identity* (New York: Harper and Row, 1986).

89. Marianne Hirsch, *The Mother/Daughter Plot: Narrative, Psychoanalysis, Feminism* (Bloomington and Indianapolis: Indiana University Press, 1989), p. 23.

90. E. M. Broner, *Her Mothers* (Bloomington: Indiana University Press, 1985), pp. 116, 142.

91. Grace Paley, "Dreamer in a Dead Language," in *Later the Same Day* (New York: Farrar, Strauss and Giroux, 1985), pp. 11–36; quotation, pp. 30–31.

92. Nina Auerbach, *Communities of Women: An Idea in Fiction* (Cambridge, Mass.: Harvard University Press, 1978).

93. Daphne Merkin, *Enchantment* (San Diego and New York: Harcourt Brace Jovanovich, 1986).

94. Anne Roiphe, *Lovingkindness* (New York: Warner Books, by permission of Summit Books, A Division of Simon & Schuster, Inc., 1987), p. 56.

95. Marge Piercy, *Small Changes* (New York: Fawcett Crest, by permission of Doubleday and Company, Inc., 1974).

96. Adrienne Rich, "Split at the Root," *Blood, Bread and Poetry: Selected prose 1979–1985* (London: Virago Press, by permission of W. W. Norton and Company, 1987, pp. 110–11.

97. Hortense Calisher, *Kissing Cousins: A Memory* (New York: Weidenfeld & Nicolson, 1988).

98. E. M. Broner, *A Weave of Women* (New York: Holt, Rinehart, & Winston, 1978).

99. Kim Chernin, *The Flame Bearers* (New York: Random House, 1986).

100. Kim Chernin, *Reinventing Eve: Modern Woman in Search of Herself* (New York: Times Books, 1987).

101. Kim Chernin, *In My Mother's House* (New Haven, Conn.: Ticknor & Fields, 1983).

102. Gloria Goldreich, *Four Days* (New York: Harcourt Brace Jovanovich, 1980).

103. Rebecca Goldstein, "The Legacy of Raizel Kaidish," *New Traditions* 2 (Spring 1985); reprinted in Joyce Antler, ed., *America and I* (Boston: Beacon Press, 1989).

104. Cynthia Ozick, *The Shawl* (New York: Alfred A. Knopf, 1989).

105. Saul Bellow, *The Bellarosa Connection* (New York: Viking Penguin, 1989), p. 19.

106. Saul Bellow, *Mr. Sammler's Planet* (Greenwich, Conn.: Fawcett Publications, by permission of The Viking Press, Inc., 1971, p. 24.

107. Ibid., pp. 17, 74.

108. Ibid., pp. 32–33, 41.

109. Perhaps one of the best known formulations of this gender-divided universe is found in G. B. Shaw's *Man and Superman*.

110. Cynthia Ozick, "Puttermesser and Xanthippe," in *Levitation: Five Fictions* (New York: E. P. Dutton, 1983).

111. Evelyn Torten Beck, ed., *Nice Jewish Girls: A Lesbian Anthology* (Trumansburg, N.Y.: Crossing Press, 1984); Alice Bloch, *The Law of Return* (Watertown, N.Y.: Persephone Press, 1983); Melanie Kaye-Kantrowitz, *My Jewish Face and Other Stories* (San Francisco: Spinsters Books, 1990); Edith Konecky, *A Place at the Table* (New York: Ballantine, 1990); Lesléa New-

man, *A Letter to Harvey Milk* (Ithaca, N.Y.: Firebrand Books, 1988) and *Secrets* (Norwich, Vt.: New Victoria Publishers, 1990); Cynthia Rich, *Desert Years: Undreaming the American Dream* (San Francisco: Spinsters Books, 1989); Sarah Schulman, *The Sophie Horowitz Story* (Tallahassee, Fla.: Naiad Press, 1984); and Irena Zahava, ed., *Speaking for Ourselves: Short Stories by Jewish Lesbians* (Freedom, Calif.: Crossing Press, 1990).

112. Gloria Kirchheimer, "Food of Love," in *The Tribe of Dina: A Jewish Woman's Anthology* ed. Melanie Kaye-Kantrowitz and Irena Klepfisz (Boston: Beacon Press, 1989).

113. This is of course not a phenomenon exclusive to Jewish women, although it does take on a particular coloration in Jewish culture. For a good discussion of sexual self-hatred in the recent fiction of American female authors, see Ann Barr Snitow, "The Front Line: Notes on Sex in Novels by Women, 1969–1979," *Signs: Journal of Women in Culture and Society* 5, no. 4 (1980), pp. 702–18.

114. Rebecca Goldstein, *The Mind-Body Problem* (New York: Dell, 1983).

115. Hortense Calisher, "No Important Woman Writer," in *Women's Liberation and Literature*, ed. Elaine Showalter (New York: Harcourt Brace Jovanovich, 1971), pp. 223–30.

116. For a full exploration of the new particularistic, "liturgical" Jewish fiction, see Sylvia Barack Fishman, "American Jewish Fiction Turns Inward," in *American Jewish Year Book, 1991* ed. David Singer and Ruth Seldin (Philadelphia and New York: Jewish Publication Society, 1991), pp. 34–66.

The Eastern European Milieu

Toward a Feminist Sensibility

I. L. Peretz

Born in Zamosc, Poland in 1851 or 1852, Yitzak Leybush Peretz was a prodigy who began his Talmud studies at age six. Although Peretz was raised in an Orthodox environment and was thoroughly well versed in Jewish texts, he taught himself French and German in order to read secular works. He experimented writing in Polish, Yiddish, and Hebrew, but it was in Yiddish that his voice emerged most powerfully. His Yiddish poem "Monish," published in 1887 in *Die Yiddishe Bibliothek*, established him as a literary craftsman. It was in the Yiddish short story, however, that Peretz truly excelled. Peretz's short stories combine lyrical pathos, uncanny insight, and dramatic force. They appear deceptively simple, but they are actually quite sophisticated and complex, blending elements of biblical and rabbinic Hebrew language and metaphor, with stylistic techniques from authors such as Chekhov, Gorky, Ibsen, and Heine.

Peretz's fiction often displays socialist values. He speaks for the oppressed, and few were more oppressed in his milieu than impoverished women. In some stories, Peretz portrays the Jewish woman as a powerless pawn, victimized by the selfishness of a male-dominated social and religious system. Interestingly, such stories are seldom anthologized in English. The American reading public is far more likely to be familiar with (and to misread) Peretz stories that obliquely criticize some elements of European Jewish life while appearing to be charmingly simple folktales. In two stories from the collection *In This World and the Next*, reprinted here, Peretz clearly condemns a cultural system that distorts religious prescriptions and convinces women that they are worthless. He paints a scathing picture of men who pursue a life of study and scholarship at the physical and emotional expense of their overworked wives and daughters; he shows as well that women sometimes internalize these distorted attitudes and treat each other with shocking callousness.

Although he spent a number of years living and writing in New York,

Peretz returned to Europe and died in Warsaw in 1915, deeply disheartened by the sight of the suffering inflicted on the Jews during World War I.

•

"A Marred Holiday"

The eve of Sabbath. Near the threshold is a little pile of rubbish, waiting to be swept out. The noodles, boiled and drained, are in their bowl—all that remains to be done is to pour a spoonful of chicken soup over them to prevent their sticking together. The table is set with vodka for the kiddush, and with two white loaves covered by a small damask napkin.

Zorech, the young master of the house, has already washed up. He is squeezing the water out of his ritual sidelocks between the thumb and index finger of each hand. Miriam, the young housewife, is standing near him and cleaning his Sabbath kaftan.

"Oh, you . . . careless fellow!" she says, smiling. "It's only a year and a half after the wedding, and yet, see what the kaftan looks like! See—there's a spot of candle-grease on the lapel!" She scrapes the spot off with a fingernail and then runs a brush over that segment of cloth.

"That's enough!" Zorech pleads with her. "Your hands will get tired from that. You've already exhausted your strength; drop it!"

"No great matter! I'd rather have my hands ache a little than have them saying in the synagogue that your wife is so lazy and careless that she won't even clean your Sabbath clothes."

She notices another tiny spot, bends over the garment and goes on with her cleaning. Her small pale face has flushed, her eyes are glittering, and she is breathing hard. But she has gained her end: Zorech kisses her head.

"What do you like about it so much? The way I have tied my headkerchief?" Then she adds softly: "You ought to be ashamed before my mother, at least."

Her kerchief (which covers her whole head), and the stern vigilance of her mother, who has now turned her back to the two, making believe she is looking for her prayerbook in the closet—these are the two things which haunt and crush Miriam.

Before her wedding Miriam had had two long, thick braids; all the girls had envied her flaxen-fair silky hair. When she had gone down the street people had said to themselves "There goes Temptation itself!" Zorech, when he had become her fiance, used to be aquiver with joy whenever he had touched her head. But did he continue to make that gesture often?

They had been betrothed half a year, and had seen each other only a few times. One evening, on the holiday of Rejoicing over the Torah, they had managed to slip out before the ceremony of the procession with the Holy Scrolls, and on one other occasion they had met during Passover, while strolling beyond the town limits. That was the time after they had been caught redhanded! What rumors sprang up after that, and what gossip! The rabbi, having summoned the parents, informed them that though he hadn't the least doubt of the innocence of the young people, *his* advice would be, just the same, to schedule the wedding right away now.

Long Serel, Miriam's mother, actually hadn't had time to get all the featherbeds and pillows ready; Zorech's father, who made his living by making ropes, had not yet collected all the dowry; but the wedding was held then just the same. And, before the wedding ceremony, Miriam's silky, flaxen-fair tresses had been shorn! Miriam had wept bitterly while this was being done. At the same time, Zorech had been sitting amid a crowd of young people, but as he told the story afterward, he had sensed the moment when the scissors had touched her hair. It was just as if something sharp had slashed across his heart. At the wedding supper both of them had looked as if they had lost God knows what.

Oh, that headkerchief of hers!

Her hair would have grown to its former length, except that the religious laws made it compulsory for a married woman to keep it cropped. Zorech, it's true, maintained that there were certain towns where Jewish women wore the ritual wigs prescribed for married women and at the same time kept their natural hair, but then everybody knew that Zorech was a bit of a freethinker.

"If God would help me, and I should win a lottery," he used to say (to get rich at his trade would really be too great a miracle), "I'd leave my mother-in-law a couple of thousand, while Miriam and I myself would move to a big city to live!"

But Miriam would not hear a word of all this. She would implore Zorech not to say such things, kissing and hugging him to make him keep still.

In the first place, in whose care were they to leave her mother? True, her mother would actually have money then, but she was no longer young. What if she should fall ill, God forbid? There wouldn't be anybody to give her a sip of water, even then. Secondly, Miriam herself was afraid of committing a sin. True enough, such towns did exist, Zorech knew what he was talking about. But God knows what sort of towns they were! After all, there had been such places as Sodom and Gomorrah, spoken of in the Old Testament; there had been still others, where the ways of the inhabitants were still worse! Iron bedsteads which strangers had to be made to fit (Miriam must have had Procrustes in mind), children smeared with honey so the ants would eat them. "And who knows, perhaps the Lord will look down, hold counsel with the angels and then, no later than tomorrow, will decide to run the Sodoms and Gomorrahs of today off the face of the earth?"

Miriam knew, however, that God, may His name be blessed, was forbearing. He must surely be patiently waiting now to see if the people would repent.

"Well, now," Zorech had told her, "does that mean that one must renounce life altogether?"

"No, Zorech," she had answered. "Only I don't want to do such things. If you are told you mustn't do something, it means you mustn't."

She had to endure still more from her mother. Long Serel loved her daughter with greater capacity than any ten mothers could. She would never say a harsh word to Miriam, but ever since that time when Miriam had been caught actually walking alone with her fiance, on the outskirts of the town, her mother was constantly suspecting her of something and was safeguarding her.

"Your soul," she would say to Miriam, "is pure, but your heart is yielding, whereas to withstand the Tempter one must have a will of iron. A human being must fight like a lion, for the Tempter is more dangerous than a serpent."

And she had taken to admonishing her kindhearted but weakwilled daughter, this pure yet unstable soul, in order to teach her how to resist the demon Tempter. But after each such lesson Miriam felt out of sorts: her chest ached; she was suffocated by nightmares. No sooner did Zorech leave the house than Miriam's mother would launch into her admonitions. Serel herself was a well-informed person; she could read the jargon fluently and had gone through the whole Pentateuch with its sundry commentaries as well as through several other holy books. Hell was something she knew all about—she was as familiar with it as with her own house. She knew just where the sinners were boiled in pitch, where they were seared with the Black Fire, and where the devils roasted them on spits, like so many spring chickens. She knew all the interior arrangements of the other worlds—for what sins they hanged you up by your tongue, for which you were cast into the void between heaven and earth, where the eagles and the ravens plucked out pieces of your sinful flesh. She knew the transgressions for which you had to go scurrying through forests where the wild beasts nipped at your heels; she knew too, for what transgressions your skin would be flayed and you would be enveloped in thorns, on top of which you'd have to dip up water with a pitcher that had no bottom. The only salvation lay in the fulness of God's mercy—all He asked was repentance.

Miriam would listen to all this with a face as white as chalk, her heart pounding and her lips trembling.

She was filled with fear; she knew that sin was lying in wait for mortals everywhere. Things were still worse during those certain days of the month when woman is beset by evil spirits, when the effluvia of hell dance about her . . . when she must not even look into a mirror, lest it become spotted with tarnish. Woman's breath as filled with impurities then, and her clothes were strewn with he devils and monsters of hell. How afraid of Zorech Miriam was at such times!

But the mother's fears began even before the coming of this period each month. She would ask her daughter almost every minute:

"Little daughter, perhaps it is already time? Are you concealing the matter—do you want to ruin your young life by such a heavy sin? Look, maybe it has happened already? Perhaps you weren't observant enough before?"

"Mamma dear," Miriam asked her once, "why does Zorech regard this matter so lightly? He actually laughs when I toss him the keys!"*

"That's not right, child; it's a great sin," the mother had assured her. "But that's how men are by nature. Come, do they know? And what has man to fear? He'll skim through a chapter of the Mishna, and at once six pages of his sins are cancelled. And when are they ever called to account, these men? Once a year, on the Day of Atonement! But woman—the poor thing—what does she signify? A pitiful creature, no more than a turkey-hen, the Lord forgive us! But when it comes to pregnancy, to child birth—why, her life then actually hangs by a hair. That's when the Days of Atonement come upon her. And what do we poor things have for the salvation of our souls? Only the Pentateuch. And really, a fine fellow Zorech is—he won't even wear the ritual fringed vest. After all, there are just three rites left for us women to perform: the Benediction of Dough, the observance of certain purificatory periods, and the Benediction of Candles. The Benediction of Dough—well, it's not so very fearsome; one can always attend to it; that also goes for the Benediction of Candles—all one has to do is get everything ready for the Sabbath on Friday, by noon. But when it comes to . . . you know . . . how can one guard oneself? If your glance," said the mother, "should fall on . . . the spot where his glance fell, if your breath should mingle with his, you're done for! Lilith snatches up that glance, she blows that breath up on high, straight to the very Throne of the All-Highest, and fans the matter into a real judicial storm . . . and right off women in childbirth and little children start dying off . . ."

Miriam realized that she had sinned more than once on both these

*During menstruation women are even forbidden to hand anything directly to their husbands, according to the orthodox Jewish religious rules.—*Translator*.

things her mother had mentioned. And each time, after sinning thus anew, she had been unable to fall asleep because of her dread that her soul would go up on high and, on its own initiative, make an entry of the new transgression.

It had once so happened that a temporary session of the circuit court had been held in the little town. The whole populace had come running to look on, as if at a miracle. Miriam had also gone to see the trial. This had happened shortly after her wedding, when one is attracted by all sorts of novelties. She had beheld three judges, the prosecutor, the court clerk, and the man on trial. She had not understood just what was being said, but she had seen the defendant keel over as if he had been struck by lightning, when a sentence to hard labor has been pronounced. From then on she had dreaded the judgment of Heaven. On this spot the Prosecutor would be delivering his speech, stammering a little, while over there Satan himself would appear on the scene. Satan would be spewing black fire, and boiling pitch would be pouring out of his mouth. Come, what did a sentence to hard labor amount to! In the other world the stentorian decision would be *kaph-hakal!** She would be sentenced to roasting, to burning!

"How the soul will swoon then!" Miriam pondered. She was seized by tremors while the pain in her chest turned to pricking needles.

Zorech did not as much as suspect all this. In his presence Miriam's mother kept silent. But Miriam, whenever he was around, was an altogether different person—gay, joyous. But then, when was he ever home? On Friday evening, on the Sabbath. All week long he was taken up with business—he had no time to be sitting home. Even at night there was no rest. Long Serel could not fall asleep for hours; she fussed, paced the room, read aloud the whole of the Prayer Before Sleep, as well as the Confessional. Now and then Zorech gnashed his teeth, but did not say anything. Only once had he said something rude to his mother-in-law, and Miriam had all but wept her eyes out then. He wouldn't indulge in any more foolish things like that now; he might gnash his teeth, but he wouldn't say anything any more.

About the admonitions delivered by his mother-in-law, he knew nothing. He could see that Miriam was growing paler and paler, and becoming even thinner; he would see her clutching at her breast and gasping for breath. And he would smile gaily in expectation of a joyous event. At times he had the fleeting thought that he ought to call in a doctor, but he had not done so and was afraid even to hint at it—afraid of frightening Miriam. For some time back she had begun getting frightened by all sorts of things,

*The torment wherein the sinner is tossed from one end of the world to the other.—*Translator*.

especially at night—the mewing of a cat, the barking of a dog out in the street. If she heard a knock on a door somewhere, or some rustle, she would start shaking all over and then cry out—and first thing you knew she'd be lying there barely breathing, practically in a faint! If he were to bring in a doctor she would, God forbid, become ill in earnest.

He had often led the conversation around to this matter: "What is wrong with you, Miriam? What's hurting you?"

"When you're home," she would answer him with a feeble smile, "I feel fine. I do hope nobody puts the evil eye on us!"

She was horribly afraid of the evil eye—there were not a few things in her life some people might find enviable! When, on Sabbath after dinner Zorech dozed off, she would often tiptoe up to him, ever so quietly, and puff at him lightly. For if it was summer, the window was open—and many a thing might befall him; some passerby might put the evil eye on him! It seemed to her that everybody must envy her, that there was nobody better or more goodlooking than her Zorech—no, not even if you were to crisscross all Poland in search of his like!

There just wouldn't be a thing to say against him (she reflected), if only he were stricter about observing . . . *that* one point; just a little stricter, at least! But again, he was a man, after all (as her mother said) and he had all of 613 religious observances to follow. So that point was of no great importance to him!

Zorech maintained that she was ailing, but she stubbornly denied it. If only he were to stay home—stay home all the time! He would listen to her and smile. Did he at all surmise the real reason for her ill health? But as for complaining against her mother—that was something she would never do; he would never find out what suffering she had to go through when he was away from home.

However, on the evening we are now picturing, it would be Sabbath soon; Zorech could leave now—let him go to the synagogue. On the Sabbath Miriam was not afraid, and on that day her mother always refrained from delivering any admonitions for her benefit. On the Sabbath our mother is a kindhearted mamma!

"Miriam, dear," said her mother after Zorech had left, "it's the Sabbath today; wash yourself, dress up. When, after the service, your husband enters the room with the angels you must run to meet him with a joyous mien, with glowing eyes, in peace and amity and with all good wishes. For that you will be found worthy—"

"Of a good kiss from Zorech," Miriam finished, laughing.

This ending was not particularly after the mother's heart, but then it was the Holy Sabbath already and she refrained from uttering any harsh word. She sat down to the Old Testament, put on her spectacles and began to read aloud.

Miriam had often listened attentively to her mother reading—some of the stories were much to her liking. During previous readings, her laugh had rung out like a little silver bell when she heard how Abraham, as a youth had smashed the stone idols of old Terah; or she had become all a-quiver: would Isaac surmise that it was Jacob who brought him his meal and not Esau? Tears had come to her eyes over Jacob's encountering Rachel at the well, and she had felt a deadly hatred toward Laban for having duped Jacob. There, let somebody try to fool her Zorech! She had been all on edge during that reading but had calmed down when Jacob got both Leah and Rachel as wives; after all, she knew that these events all occurred long before the days of Rabbi Gershon's forbidding a multiplicity of wives.

Today's scheduled reading, however, was only about gift-offerings. All sorts of objects for the inner temple were brought. This held but little interest for Miriam; she was tired and wanted to sleep. Her head drooped; her eyelids closed . . . she dozed off. A kind, charming smile appeared on her face; it became slightly flushed.

"Miriam!" her mother's voice suddenly awoke her.

"What is it, Mamma dear? I'm listening."

"No, I didn't mean that—"

"What then?"

"According to my reckoning . . . do you understand, my daughter—*it* is due today—"

"It isn't time yet, Mamma dear!"

"Watch out, daughter—don't make any mistake!"

Miriam again fell into a doze; the mother went on and on reading about the plates of silver and the silver spoons. And then she awakened her daughter again.

Alas—*it* had already happened!

"What a pity," said Serel. "The Sabbath is spoiled. But, perhaps you're not quite certain? . . ."

She sighed and again plunged into her reading. Miriam fell asleep, but her little face was no longer covered with a rosy blush; the smile no longer appeared on her rosebud lips.

In the meanwhile Zorech had finished his prayers and was in a hurry to leave the synagogue, lest someone detain him. He crossed the street at a run. When he reached his door he stood still and listened closely to what was going on within the room. His mother-in-law was reading; while Miriam, as absorbed in the stories as always, must be listening. He wanted to give her a pleasant surprise by appearing suddenly.

He opened the door quietly. His mother-in-law failed to hear him; Miriam was asleep. At a single leap he was by her side and kissed her, with holiday greetings.

"You Godless sinner!" Serel cried out.

Miriam lost consciousness. They had ever so hard a time bringing her to. The holiday was spoiled. . . .

•

"A Woman's Wrath"

The tiny room is as somber as the poverty within its four walls. There is an orphaned hook sticking out of the ceiling, bereft of its big brass lamp. An enormous, lopsided oven, girt with an apron of coarse sacking, is sadly facing the blackened hearth, which harbors an overturned pot and a broken spoon. This tinny creature has found an honorable death, having fallen in the fight against yesterday's dried up porridge.

The handsomest piece of furniture in the room is a tall bed with torn curtains, through the holes of which bare pillows peep out, their eyes bleary with feathers. There is a cradle, where one can see the large red head of a sleeping baby; near by a tin trunk, its lock hanging open—next come a table and three stools. All this furniture had once been painted red; now the roomful is a dirty gray. Add a wardrobe, a water-cask, a slop-pail, a poker, and a coal shovel and you will see there isn't room for one more pin.

And yet, there are two people—a man and a woman.

The woman is middle-aged, sitting on the trunk that takes up all the room there is between the bed and the cradle. To her right is the only window, with its greenish pane; to her left, the table. She knits a stocking and rocks the cradle with her foot as she listens attentively to the man, who is seated at the table reading the Talmud. He reads in a choppy and nervous chant. Some of the words are mumbled, others are drawn out; some he blurts out in one breath, others he skips over altogether; certain passages are lovingly emphasized, others are read by rote, until they sound like peas rolling out of a sack. And all the while he never sits still: now he snatches his bandanna out of his pocket, which at one time had been red and whole, rubbing his nose and wiping the perspiration from his face and forehead; then he will drop the bandanna on his lap and start twisting his ritual locks, or twitching his grizzled goatee. Now he has plucked a hair from it, which he places on the folio volume before him, and takes to slapping his knees.

Aha—he has found the bandanna again! He seizes it, pops one corner of it into his mouth and begins chewing it, at the same time crossing and recrossing his legs.

And all this while his pale forehead is crisscrossed with wrinkles; deep furrows lie across the bridge of his nose—his elongated eyelids all but vanish under the overhanging skin of his forehead. Suddenly he imagines that he has felt a stabbing pain in his chest and smites it with his right hand; he snatches a pinch of snuff and begins to sway still more, until his voice rings out and the stool under him groans.

The baby sleeps through all this: he has become used to such concerts. As for his wife who has aged so prematurely, she sits there and cannot get her fill of rejoicing over her spouse. She does not take her eyes off him, and is on the alert for every sound of his voice. From time to time she sighs, as she reflects: If he were only as good for this world as he is for the *other*, things would be fine and bright for her even here—yes, even here! Oh, well (she consoles herself), whom will you ever find who is worthy of tasting both repasts?

She listens still more attentively. Her wrinkled face is also changing from moment to moment; she, too, is nervous.

Just now immeasurable gratification had suffused her face—so much delight had she derived from his Torah. But suddenly she recalls that today is already Thursday, that there isn't a copper for the Sabbath—and the glow of Paradise on her face grows dimmer, until the smile disappears altogether. Then she glances through the green window and takes a look at the sun. There isn't as much as a spoonful of hot water in the house. The knitting needles stop; a somber shadow overcasts her face. She glances at the baby: by now his sleep is uneasy—he will be waking soon. The baby is ailing, yet there isn't a drop of milk for him. By this time the shadow on her face has turned into a cloud; her knitting needles begin to shake, and bob up and down. When she remembers that Easter is almost here, that the candlesticks and her earrings are in pawn, that the trunk is empty and the brass lamp has been sold—the knitting needles begin to dance at a deathly speed; the cloud turns to lead; lightning flashes in her small gray eyes, which one can barely glimpse under her headkerchief.

But *he* still sits there and reads on. He does not perceive that a storm is about to break—that she has let the stocking fall out of her hands, that she is beginning to crack her gaunt fingers while her forehead wrinkles in pain, one eye closing while the other is regarding him with such murderous keenness that, were he to notice it, he would be chilled to the bone with terror. He does not perceive how her livid lips quiver, how her jaws work as if in an ague as she restrains herself with all her might. But the storm is about to break and the least little thing will bring it bursting from her lips.

And this does happen.

He is reading: "*Shma minei—tloss* . . ." and translates the passage in a long-drawn-out chant: "Therefore, it follows hence—" He is about to say "Thirdly—" but the word *follows* suffices. Her long-aching heart seizes on the word; it falls like a spark of gunpowder. Her much-enduring patience explodes. The unfortunate word opens all the sluices and shatters all restraints. Frenziedly she leaps toward her husband with foam-flecked lips, ready to scratch his eyes out.

"It *follows*, you say—it *follows*, does it? Ah, my God, if you would only *follow* along with it!" she screams in a hoarse voice. "Yes, yes," she goes on, hissingly, "it will be Passover soon . . . today is Thursday . . . the baby is ailing . . . and there isn't a drop of milk in the house!"

She is all out of breath; her flabby bosom is heaving; sparks fly from her eyes.

He seems to be petrified. Jumping up from the stool, pale, gasping in fright, he begins retreating toward the door. They stand facing each other—his eyes glassy with fright, hers blazing in wrath. He soon notices that because of her rancor she has not control over her tongue or her hands. His eyes narrow more and more. Popping a corner of his bandanna in his mouth he moves back a little more, and mutters, breathing with difficulty:

"Listen, you woman—do you know the meaning of *bitul Toirah*—do you know what it means to hinder one's husband in studying the Torah—eh? Always harping about earnings, eh? There, who provides for the fowl of the air? Still no faith in God! Temptation everywhere—everywhere concern over *this* world only. . . . You are a stupid woman—and a malicious one! Not to let one's husband study—why, hell is the punishment meted out for that!"

She is silent and he grows bolder. Her face is becoming ever paler, she is trembling more and more, and the more she trembles and the paler she grows, the firmer and louder does his voice sound:

"Hell! Everlasting flames! You'll be hung by your tongue—you'll receive all the four punishments of the Supreme Tribunal!"

She is still silent; her face is as white as chalk. He feels that he is not acting right, that he ought not to torture her thus, that this is dishonest, but by now he is no longer able to hold himself in check. All the rancor that had been lurking in his soul is now poured forth without restraint.

"*Skilo*! There, do you know what that means?"—and his voice becomes thunderous. "It means being cast into a pit and stoned to death . . . *Sreifo*!" he goes on—and is amazed at his own daring. "That means having a spoonful of molten, boiling lead poured down your throat. *Hereg*: that means having your head lopped off by a sword—like this!"—and he waves his hand in a circle about his neck. "And now we come to *chenek*—that's strangulation—do you hear? Strangulation! *Bitul Toirah*—you understand? All this for *bitul Toirah!*"

His very heart contracts with pity for his victim, but then, this is the first time he has ever gained the upper hand. This intoxicates him. Such a foolish woman! Up to now he hadn't known at all that one could throw such a scare into her.

"There, that's what *bitul Toirah* means!" he cries out once more—and then falls abruptly silent: after all, she may come to herself and grab the broom! He dashes back to the table, slams the folio volume shut and dashes out of the room.

"I'm going to the synagogue!" he calls out to her, by now in a gentler tone and shuts the door behind him.

The shouts and the slamming of the door have awakened the ailing baby. He slowly raises his heavy lids; his face, yellow as wax, becomes distorted, and a wheezing breath issues through his tiny nose.

She, however, seems petrified. She is still beside herself as she stands there and does not hear the baby crying.

"Aha!" escapes from her sunken breast at last in a voice hoarse and strangled. "There's no place for me either in *this* world or the *next*—They'll hang me, says he; they'll use boiling pitch and molten lead on me, he says. *Bitul Toirah*! Nothing matters—to *me* nothing matters!"—and there is a gurgling in her tortured breast. "Starvation *here* . . . nothing to wear . . . no candlesticks . . . nothing at all . . . the baby is starved . . . not a drop of milk. . . . But over *there* I'll be hanged—hanged by the tongue. *Bitul Toirah*, says he. So they'll hang me—" and she breaks into laughter, despairing and shrill. "Very well, let me be hanged, but let it be here, right now! Nothing matters—why wait?"

The baby breaks into still louder crying, but she hears nothing.

"A rope, a rope!" she cries out, and her wandering eyes search all the corners. "Where is one to get a rope? May he fail to find even my bones! Just as long as I get out of this hellish place. Let him know what's what! Let *him* become a mother—let him! Let me perish! One can die but one death—the end is the same. Let there be an end, once and for all! Give me a rope!"—the last word escapes her like a call for help in a fire.

She recalls where the rope is lying . . . yes, under the oven: they were thinking of using it to hold the oven together through the winter: it must still be there. She dashes to the oven and finds the rope. Oh, joy—she has found a treasure! She glances toward the ceiling—the hook is right there. All one has to do is to scramble up on the table. She scrambles up on it. But, from her vantage point, she sees that the baby is on his feet, that he is leaning over the edge of the cradle, wanting to clamber out. There, he'll fall at any moment!

"Mamma!" the baby barely manages to utter faintly—his throat is none too strong. A fresh outburst of rage seizes her.

She drops the rope, jumps down from the table, dashes over to the baby, tosses his little head back on the pillow and shouts malevolently:

"Monster! He won't even let me hang myself! Won't let me hang myself in peace, even! He wants to be suckled, now—to be suckled! Oh, it is poison you will be sipping from my breast! Poison! There, you glutton!" she gasps and thrusts her withered nipple in the baby's mouth. "There, sip away—torture me!"

Sholem Aleichem

Sholem Rabinovitch, born in 1859 in Pereyaslev, Ukraine, was one of the founders of modern Yiddish literature and became the most widely read and cherished Yiddish author of all time under the pseudonym "Sholem Aleichem." Sholem Aleichem, like Peretz and Asch, blended a thorough grounding in Jewish texts with sophisticated literary interests. Stylistically, however, the three authors vary widely. If Asch specializes in the sweeping historical panorama and Peretz in the elegantly spare and deceptively simple narrative, Sholem Aleichem bubbles over: his brilliantly humorous and inventive stories are a cornucopia of colorful characters and details of Eastern European Jewish life. His warmth was reportedly evident not only in his writing but in his reading of his stories as well; an immensely popular reader, Sholem Aleichem traveled around the world reading from his works. He lived in Kiev until the 1905 pogrom, stayed in New York from 1905 to 1907, returned to Geneva and European travels until 1914, and then returned to New York, where he died in 1916.

Sholem Aleichem is perhaps best known for his tales of Tevye the dairyman, which were originally written and published serially, beginning in 1894, over a span of many years. Americans are familiar with the Tevye stories through their adaptation as a hit Broadway musical and movie, *Fiddler on the Roof.* Himself the father of a household of daughters, Sholem Aleichem was, according to his daughters, an attentive, involved, proud, and loving parent. In Sholem Aleichem's classic, "Hodel," Hodel is Tevye's favorite daughter because of her sincere devotion to the prophetic goals of socialism—as Tevye understands them—although Tevye, with characteristic skepticism, has little hope of their ever being fulfilled. In Hodel—named for Sholem Aleichem's beloved grandmother—Tevye has more than met his match; he feels, he says, like a chicken who has given birth to a free-swimming duck. The feminine connotations of egg-laying and tending, as well as the humorous female imagery of the hen, are significant and tell us much about both Tevye's powerlessness in the face of worldwide change and his nurturing attitude toward his daughter.

•

"Hodel"

You look, Mr. Sholom Aleichem, as though you were surprised that you hadn't seen me for such a long time. You're thinking that Tevye has aged all at once, his hair has turned gray.

Ah, well, if you only knew the troubles and heartaches he has endured of late! How is it written in our Holy Books? "Man comes from dust, and to dust he returns." Man is weaker than a fly, and stronger than iron. Whatever plague there is, whatever trouble, whatever misfortune—it never misses me. Why does it happen that way? Maybe because I am a simple soul who believes everything that everyone says. Tevye forgets that our wise men have told us a thousand times: "Beware of dogs . . ."

But I ask you, what can I do if that's my nature? I am, as you know, a trusting person, and I never question God's ways. Whatever He ordains is good. Besides, if you do complain, will it do you any good? That's what I always tell my wife. "Golde," I say, "you're sinning. We have a *midrash*—"

"What do I care about a *midrash*?" she says. "We have a daughter to marry off. And after her two more are almost ready. And after these two, three more—may the evil eye spare them!"

"Tut," I say. "What's that? Don't you know, Golde, that our sages have thought of that also? There is a *midrash* for that too—"

But she doesn't let me finish. "Daughters to be married off," she says, "are a stiff *midrash* in themselves."

Try to explain something to a woman!

Where does that leave us? Oh yes, with a houseful of daughters, bless the Lord, each one prettier than the next. It may not be proper for me to praise my own children, but I can't help hearing what the whole world calls them, can I? Beauties, every one of them! And especially Hodel, the one that comes after Tzeitl, who, you remember, fell in love with the tailor. And Hodel—how can I describe her to you? Like Esther in the Bible, "of beautiful form and fair to look upon." And as if that weren't bad enough, she has to have brains too. She can write and she can read—Yiddish and Russian both. And books she swallows like dumplings. You may be wondering how a daughter of Tevye happens to be reading books when her father deals in butter and cheese? That's what I'd like to know myself.

But that's the way it is these days. Look at these lads who haven't got a pair of pants to their name, and still they want to study! Ask them, "What are you studying? Why are you studying?" They can't tell you. It's their nature, just as it's a goat's nature to jump into gardens. Especially since they aren't even allowed in the schools. "Keep off the grass!" read all the signs as far as they're concerned. And yet you ought to see how they go after it! And who are they? Workers' children. Tailors' and cobblers', so help me God! They go away to Yehupetz or to Odessa, sleep in garrets, eat what Pharoah ate during the plagues—frogs and vermin—and for months on end do not see a piece of meat before their eyes. Six of them can make a banquet on a loaf of bread and a herring. Eat, drink, and be merry! That's the life!

Well, one of that band had to lose himself in our corner of the world. I used to know his father—he was a cigarette-maker and as poor as a man could be. But that is nothing against the young fellow. For if Rabbi Jochanan wasn't too proud to mend boots, what is wrong with having a father who makes cigarettes? There is only one thing I can't understand: why should a pauper like that be so anxious to study? True, to give the devil his due, the boy has a good head on his shoulders, an excellent head. Pertschik, his name was, but we called him Feferel—Peppercorn. And he looked like a peppercorn, little, dark, dried up, and homely, but full of confidence and with a quick, sharp tongue.

Well, one day I was driving home from Boiberik, where I had got rid of my load of milk and butter and cheese, and as usual I sat lost in thought, dreaming of many things, of this and that, and of the rich people of Yehupetz who had everything their own way while Tevye, the *shlimazel*, and his wretched little horse slaved and hungered all their days. It was summer, the sun was hot, the flies were biting, on all sides the world stretched endlessly. I felt like spreading out my arms and flying!

I lift up my eyes, and there on the road ahead of me I see a young man trudging along with a package under his arm, sweating and panting. "Rise, O Yokel the son of Flekel, as we say in the synagogue," I called out to him. "Climb into my wagon and I'll give you a ride. I have plenty of room. How is it written? 'If you see the ass of him that hateth thee lying under its burden, thou shalt forbear to pass it by.' Then how about a human being?"

At this the *shlimazel* laughs and climbs into the wagon.

"Where might the young gentleman be coming from?" I ask.

"From Yehupetz."

"And what might a young gentleman like you be doing in Yehupetz?" I ask.

"A young gentleman like me is getting ready for his examinations."

"And what might a young gentleman like you be studying?"

"I only wish I knew!"

"Then why does a young gentleman like you bother his head for nothing?"

"Don't worry, Reb Tevye. A young gentleman like me knows what he's doing."

"So, if you know who *I* am, tell me who *you* are!"

"Who am I? I'm a man."

"I can see that you're not a horse. I mean, as we Jews say, *whose* are you?"

"Whose should I be but God's?"

"I know that you're God's. It is written, 'All living things are His.' I mean, whom are you descended from? Are you from around here or from Lithuania?"

"I am descended," he says, "from Adam, our father. I *come* from right around here. You know who we are."

"Well then, who is your father? Come, tell me."

"My father," he says, "was called Pertschik."

I spat with disgust. "Did you have to torture me like this all that time? Then you must be Pertschik the cigarette-maker's son!"

"Yes, that's who I am. Pertschik the cigarette-maker's son."

"And you go to the university?"

"Yes, the university."

"Well," I said, "I'm glad to hear it. Man and fish and fowl—you're all trying to better yourselves! But tell me, my lad, what do you live on, for instance?"

"I live on what I eat."

"That's good," I say. "And what do you eat?"

"I eat anything I can get."

"I understand," I say. "You're not particular. If there is something to eat, you eat. If not, you bite your lip and go to bed hungry. But it's all worth while as long as you can attend the university. You're comparing yourself to those rich people of Yehupetz—"

At these words Pertschik bursts out, "Don't you dare compare me to them! They can go to hell as far as I care!"

"You seem to be somewhat prejudiced against the rich," I say. "Did they divide your father's inheritance among themselves?"

"Let me tell you," says he, "it may well be that you and I and all the rest of us have no small share in *their* inheritance."

"Listen to me," I answer. "Let your enemies talk like that. But one thing I can see: you're not a bashful lad. You know what a tongue is for. If you have the time, stop at my house tonight and we'll talk a little more. And if you come early, you can have supper with us too."

Our young friend didn't have to be asked twice. He arrived at the right moment—when the borscht was on the table and the knishes were baking in the oven. "Just in time!" I said. "Sit down. You can say grace or not, just as you please. I'm not God's watchman; I won't be punished for your sins." And as I talk to him I feel myself drawn to the fellow somehow; I don't know why. Maybe it's because I like a person one can talk to, a person who can understand a quotation and follow an argument about philosophy or this or that or something else. That's the kind of person I am.

And from that evening on our young friend began coming to our house almost every day. He had a few private students, and when he was through giving his lessons he'd come to our house to rest up and visit for a while. What the poor fellow got for his lessons you can imagine for yourself, if I tell you that the very richest people used to pay their tutors three rubles a month; and besides their regular duties they were expected to read telegrams for them, write out addresses, and even run errands at times. Why not? As the passage says, "If you eat bread you have to earn it." It was lucky for him that most of the time he ate with us. For this he used to give my daughters lessons too. One good turn deserves another. And in this way he almost became a member of the family. The girls saw to it that he had enough to eat and my wife kept his shirts clean and his socks mended. And it was at this time that we changed his Russian name of Pertschik to Feferel. And it can truthfully be said that we all came to love him as though he were one of us, for by nature he was a likable young man, simple, straightforward, generous. Whatever he had he shared with us.

There was only one thing I didn't like about him, and that was the way he had of suddenly disappearing. Without warning he would get up and go off; we would look around: no Feferel. When he came back I would ask, "Where were you, my fine-feathered friend?" And he wouldn't say a word. I don't know how you are, but as for me, I dislike a person with secrets. I like a person to be willing to tell what he's been up to. But you can say this for him: when he did start talking, you couldn't stop him. He poured out everything. What a tongue he had! "Against the Lord and against His anointed; let us break their bands asunder." And the main thing was to break the bands. He had the wildest notions, the most peculiar ideas. Everything was upside down, topsy-turvy. For instance, according to his way of thinking, a poor man was far more important than a rich one, and if he happened to be a worker too, then he was really the brightest jewel in the diadem! He who toiled with his hands stood first in his estimation.

"That's good," I say, "but will that get you any money?"

At this he becomes very angry and tries to tell me that money is the root of all evil. Money, he says, is the source of all falsehood, and as long as money amounts to something, nothing will ever be done in this world in the spirit of justice. And he gives me thousands of examples and illustrations that make no sense whatever.

"According to your crazy notions," I tell him, "there is no justice in the fact that my cow gives milk and my horse draws a load." I didn't let him get away with anything. That's the kind of man Tevye is. But my Feferel can argue too. And how he can argue! If there is something on his mind he comes right out with it.

One evening we were sitting on my stoop talking things over, discussing philosophic matters, when he suddenly says, "Do you know, Reb Tevye, you have very fine daughters."

"Is that so?" say I. "Thanks for telling me. After all, they have someone to take after."

"The oldest one especially is a very bright girl. She's all there!"

"I know without your telling me," say I. "The apple never falls very far from the tree."

I glowed with pride. What father isn't happy when his children are praised? How should I have known that from such an innocent remark would grow such fiery love?

Well, one summer twilight I was driving through Boiberik, going from villa to villa with my goods, when someone stopped me. I looked up and saw that it was Ephraim the matchmaker. And Ephraim, like all matchmakers, was concerned with only one thing—arranging marriages. So when he saw me here in Boiberik he stopped me.

"Excuse me, Reb Tevye," he says, "I'd like to tell you something."

"Go ahead," I say, stopping my horse, "as long as it's good news."

"You have," says he, "a daughter."

"I have," I answer, "seven daughters."

"I know," says he. "I have seven too."

"Then together," I tell him, "we have fourteen."

"But joking aside," he says, "here is what I have to tell you. As you know, I am a matchmaker; and I have a young man for you to consider, the very best there is, a regular prince. There's not another like him anywhere."

"Well," I say, "that sounds good enough to me. But what do you consider a prince? If he's a tailor or a shoemaker or a teacher, you can keep him. I'll find my equal or I won't have anything. As the *midrash* says—"

"Ah, Reb Tevye," says he, "you're beginning with your quotations already! If a person wants to talk to you he has to study up first. But better listen to the sort of match Ephraim has to offer you. Just listen and be quiet."

And then he begins to rattle off all his client's virtues. And it really sounds like something. First of all, he comes from a very fine family. And that is very important to me, for I am not just a nobody either. In our family you will find all sorts of people—spotted, striped, and speckled, as the Bible says. There are plain, ordinary people, there are workers, and there are property owners. Secondly, he is a learned man who can read small print as well as large; he knows all the commentaries by heart. And that is certainly not a small thing either, for an ignorant man I hate even worse than pork itself. To me an unlettered man is worse, a thousand times worse, than a hoodlum. You can go around bareheaded, you can even walk on your head if you like, but if you know what Rashi and the others have said, you are a man after my own heart. And on top of everything, Ephraim tells me, this man of his is as rich as can be. He has his own carriage drawn by two horses so spirited that you can see a vapor rising from them. And that I don't object to either. Better a rich man than a poor one! God Himself must hate a poor man, for if He did not, would He have made him poor?

"Well," I ask, "what more do you have to say?"

"What more can I say? He wants me to arrange a match with you. He is dying, he's so eager. Not for you, naturally, but for your daughter. He wants a pretty girl."

"He is dying? Then let him go on dying. And who is this treasure of yours? What is he? A bachelor? A widower? Is he divorced? What's wrong with him?"

"He is a bachelor," said Ephraim. "Not so young any more, but he's never been married."

"And what is his name, may I ask?"

But this he wouldn't tell me. "Bring the girl to Boiberik, and then I'll tell you."

"Bring her? That's the way one talks about a horse or a cow that's being brought to market. Not a girl!"

Well, you know what these matchmakers are. They can talk a stone wall into moving. So we agreed that early next week I would bring my daughter to Boiberik. And, driving home, all sorts of wonderful thoughts came to me, and I imagined my Hodel riding in a carriage drawn by spirited horses. The whole world envied me, not so much for the carriage and horses as for the good deeds I accomplished through my wealthy daughter. I helped the needy with money—let this one have twenty-five rubles, that one fifty, another a hundred. How do we say it? "Other people have to live too." That's what I think to myself as I ride home in the evening, and I whip my horse and talk to him in his own language.

"Hurry, my little horse," I say, "move your legs a little faster and you'll get your oats that much sooner. As the Bible says, 'If you don't work, you don't eat.'"

Suddenly I see two people coming out of the woods—a man and a woman. Their heads are close together and they are whispering to each other. Who could they be? I wonder, and I look at them through the dazzling rays of the setting sun. I could swear the man was Feferel. But whom was he walking with so late in the day? I put up my hand and shield my eyes and look closely. Who was the damsel? Could it be Hodel? Yes, that's who it was! Hodel! So? So that's how they'd been studying their grammar and reading their books together? Oh, Tevye, what a fool you are!

I stop the horse and call out, "Good evening! And what's the latest news of the war? How do you happen to be out here this time of the day? What are you looking for, the day before yesterday?"

At this they stop, not knowing what to do or say. They stand there, awkward and blushing, with their eyes lowered. Then they look up at me, I look at them, and they look at each other.

"Well," I say, "you look as if you hadn't seen me in a long time. I am the same Tevye as ever; I haven't changed by a hair."

I speak to them half angrily, half jokingly. Then my daughter, blushing harder than ever, speaks up.

"Father, you can congratulate us."

"Congratulate you?" I say. "What's happened? Did you find a treasure buried in the woods? Or were you just saved from some terrible danger?"

"Congratulate us," says Feferel this time. "We're engaged."

"What do you mean, engaged?"

"Don't you know what engaged means?" says Feferel, looking me straight in the eyes. "It means that I'm going to marry her and she's going to marry me."

I look him back in the eyes and say, "When was the contract signed? And why didn't you invite me to the ceremony? Don't you think I have a slight interest in the matter?" I joke with them and yet my heart is breaking. But Tevye is not a weakling. He wants to hear everything out. "Getting married," I say, "without matchmakers, without an engagement feast?"

"What do we need matchmakers for?" says Feferel. "We arranged it between ourselves."

"So?" I say. "That's one of God's wonders! But why were you so silent about it?"

"What was there to shout about?" says he. "We wouldn't have told you now either, but since we have to part soon, we decided to have the wedding first."

This really hurt. How do they say it? It hurt to the quick. Becoming engaged without my knowledge—that was bad enough, but I could stand it. He loves her, she loves him—that I'm glad to hear. But getting married? That was too much for me.

The young man seemed to realize that I wasn't too well pleased with the news. "You see, Reb Tevye," he offered, "this is the reason: I am about to go away."

"When are you going?"

"Very soon."

"And where are you going?"

"That I can't tell you. It's a secret."

What do you think of that? A secret! A young man named Feferel comes into our lives—small, dark, homely, disguises himself as a bridegroom, wants to marry my daughter and then leave her—and he won't even say where he's going! Isn't that enough to drive you crazy?

"All right," I say. "A secret is a secret. But explain this to me, my friend. You are a man of such—what do you call it?—integrity; you wallow in justice. So tell me, how does it happen that you suddenly marry Tevye's daughter and then leave her? Is that integrity? Is that justice? It's lucky that you didn't decide to rob me or burn my house down!"

"Father," says Hodel, "you don't know how happy we are now that we've told you our secret. It's like a weight off our chests. Come, Father, kiss me."

And they both grab hold of me, she on one side, he on the other, and they begin to kiss and embrace me, and I to kiss them in return. And in their great excitement they begin to kiss each other. It was like going to a play. "Well," I say at last, "maybe you've done enough kissing already? It's time to talk about practical things."

"What, for instance?" they ask.

"For instance," I say, "the dowry, clothes, wedding expenses, this, that, and the other—"

"We don't need a thing," they tell me. "We don't need anything. No this, no that, no other."

"Well then, what do you need?" I ask.

"Only the wedding ceremony," they tell me.

What do you think of that! Well, to make a long story short, nothing I said did any good. They went ahead and had their wedding, if you want to call it a wedding. Naturally it wasn't the sort that I would have liked. A quiet little wedding—no fun at all. And besides, there was a wife I had to do something about. She kept plaguing me: what were they in such a hurry about? Go try to explain their haste to a woman. But don't worry. I invented a story—"great, powerful, and marvelous," as the Bible says, about a rich aunt in Yehupetz, an inheritance, all sorts of foolishness.

And a couple of hours after this wonderful wedding I hitched up my horse and wagon and the three of us got in, that is, my daughter, my son-in-law, and I, and off we went to the station at Boiberik. Sitting in the wagon, I steal a look at the young couple, and I think to myself, What a great and powerful Lord we have and how cleverly He rules the world. What strange and fantastic beings He has created. Here you have a new young couple, just hatched; he is going off, the Good Lord alone knows where, and is leaving her behind—and do you see either one of them shed a tear, even for appearance's sake? But never mind—Tevye is not a curious old woman. He can wait. He can watch and see.

At the station I see a couple of young fellows, shabbily dressed, down at the heels, coming to see my happy bridegroom off. One of them is dressed like a peasant and wears his blouse like a smock over his trousers. The two whisper together mysteriously for several minutes. Look out, Tevye, I say to myself. You have fallen among a band of horse thieves, pickpockets, housebreakers, or counterfeiters.

Coming home from Boiberik, I can't keep still any longer and tell Hodel what I suspect. She bursts out laughing and tries to assure me that they are very honest young men, honorable men, who were devoting their lives to the welfare of humanity; their own private welfare meant nothing to them. For instance, the one with his blouse over his trousers was a rich man's son. He had left his parents in Yehupetz and wouldn't take a penny from them.

"Oh," said I, "that's just wonderful. An excellent young man! All he needs, now that he has his blouse over his trousers and wears his hair long, is a harmonica, or a dog to follow him, and then he would really be a beautiful sight!" I thought I was getting even with her for the pain she and this new husband of hers had caused me. But did she care? Not at all! She pretended not to understand what I was saying. I talked to her about Feferel and she answered me with "the cause of humanity" and "workers" and other such talk.

"What good is your humanity and your workers," I say, "if it's all a secret? There is a proverb: 'Where there are secrets, there is knavery.' But tell me the truth now. Where did he go, and why?"

"I'll tell you anything," she says, "but not that. Better don't ask. Believe me, you'll find out yourself in good time. You'll hear the news—and maybe very soon—and good news at that."

"Amen," I say. "From your mouth into God's ears! But may our enemies understand as little about it as I do."

"That," says she, "is the whole trouble. You'll never understand."

"Why not?" say I. "Is it so complicated? It seems to me that I can understand even more difficult things."

"These things you can't understand with your brain alone," she says. "You have to feel them, you have to feel them in your heart."

And when she said this to me, you should have seen how her face shone and her eyes burned. Ah, those daughters of mine! They don't do anything halfway. When they become involved in anything it's with their hearts and minds, their bodies and souls.

Well, a week passed, then two weeks—five—six—seven—and we heard nothing. There was no letter, no news of any kind. "Feferel is gone for good," I said and glanced over at Hodel. There wasn't a trace of color in her face. And at the same time she didn't rest at all; she found something to do every minute of the day, as though trying to forget her troubles. And she never once mentioned his name, as if there never had been a Feferel in the world.

But one day when I came home from work I found Hodel going about with her eyes swollen from weeping. I made a few inquiries and found out that someone had been to see her, a long-haired young man who had taken her aside and talked to her for some time. Ah! That must have been the young fellow who had disowned his rich parents and pulled his blouse down over his trousers.

Without further delay I called Hodel out into the yard and bluntly asked her, "Tell me, daughter, have you heard from him?"

"Yes."

"Where is he, your predestined one?"

"He is far away."

"What is he doing there?"

"He is serving time."

"Serving time?"

"Yes."

"Why? What did he do?"

She doesn't answer me. She looks me straight in the eyes and doesn't say a word.

"Tell me, dear daughter," I say, "according to what I can understand, he is not serving for a theft. So if he is neither a thief nor a swindler, why is he serving? For what good deeds?"

She doesn't answer. So I think to myself, If you don't want to, you don't have to. He is your headache, not mine. But my heart aches for her. No matter what you say, I'm still her father.

Well, it was the evening of *Hashono Rabo*. On a holiday I'm in the habit of resting, and my horse rests too. As it is written in the Bible: "Thou shalt rest from thy labors and so shall thy wife and thine ass." Besides, by that time of the year there is very little for me to do in Boiberik. As soon as the holidays come and the *shofar* sounds, all the summer villas close down and Boiberik becomes a desert. At that season I like to sit at home on my own stoop. To me it is the finest time of the year. Each day is a gift from heaven. The sun no longer bakes like an oven but caresses with a heavenly softness. The woods are still green, the pines give out a pungent smell. In my yard stands the *succeh*—the booth I have built for the holiday, covered with branches, and around me the forest looks like a huge *succeh* designed for God himself. Here, I think, God celebrates His holiday, here and not in town, in the noise and tumult where people run this way and that, panting for breath as they chase after a small crust of bread, and all you hear is money, money, money.

As I said, it is the evening of *Hashono Rabo*. The sky is a deep blue and myriads of stars twinkle and shine and blink. From time to time a star falls through the sky, leaving behind it a long green band of light. This means that someone's luck has fallen. I hope it isn't my star that is falling, and somehow Hodel comes to mind. She has changed in the last few days, has come to life again. Someone, it seems, has brought her a letter from him, from over there. I wish I knew what he had written, but I won't ask. If she won't speak, I won't either. Tevye is not a curious old woman. Tevye can wait.

And as I sit thinking of Hodel, she comes out of the house and sits down near me on the stoop. She looks cautiously around and then whispers, "I have something to tell you, Father. I have to say good-by to you, and I think it's for always."

She spoke so softly that I could barely hear her, and she looked at me in a way that I shall never forget.

"What do you mean, good-by for always?" I say to her and turn my face aside.

"I mean I am going away early tomorrow morning, and possibly we shall never see each other again."

"Where are you going, if I may be so bold as to ask?"

"I am going to him."

"To him? And where is he?"

"He is still serving, but soon they'll be sending him away."

"And you're going there to say good-by to him?" I ask, pretending not to understand.

"No. I am going to follow him," she says. "Over there."

"There? Where is that? What do they call the place?"

"We don't know the exact name of the place, but we know that it's far—terribly, terribly far."

And she speaks, it seems to me, with great joy and pride, as though he had done something for which he deserved a medal. What can I say to her? Most fathers would scold a child for such talk, punish her, even beat her maybe. But Tevye is not a fool. To my way of thinking, anger doesn't get you anywhere. So I tell her a story.

"I see, my daughter, as the Bible says, 'Therefore shalt thou leave thy father and mother'—for a Feferel you are ready to forsake your parents and go off to a strange land, to some desert across the frozen wastes, where Alexander of Macedon, as I once read in a storybook, once found himself stranded among savages . . ."

I speak to her half in fun and half in anger, and all the time my heart weeps. But Tevye is no weakling; I control myself. And Hodel doesn't lose her dignity either; she answers me word for word, speaking quietly and thoughtfully. And Tevye's daughters can talk.

And though my head is lowered and my eyes are shut, still I seem to see her—her face is pale and lifeless like the moon, but her voice trembles. Shall I fall on her neck and plead with her not to go? I know it won't help. Those daughters of mine—when they fall in love with somebody, it is with their heads and hearts, their bodies and souls.

Well, we sat on the doorstep a long time—maybe all night. Most of the time we were silent, and when we did speak it was in snatches, a word here, a word there. I said to her, "I want to ask you only one thing: did you ever hear of a girl marrying a man so that she could follow him to the ends of the earth?" And she answered, "With him I'd go anywhere." I pointed out how foolish that was. And she said, "Father, you will never understand." So I told her a little fable, about a hen that hatched some ducklings. As soon as the ducklings could move they took to the water and swam, and the poor hen stood on shore, clucking and clucking.

"What do you say to that, my daughter?"

"What can I say?" she answered. "I am sorry for the poor hen; but just because she stood there clucking, should the ducklings have stopped swimming?"

There is an answer for you. She's not stupid, that daughter of mine.

But time does not stand still. It was beginning to get light already, and within the house my old woman was muttering. More than once she had called out that it was time to go to bed, but, seeing that it didn't help, she stuck her head out of the window and said to me, with her usual benediction, "Tevye, what's keeping you?"

"Be quiet, Golde," I answered. "Remember what the Psalm says: 'Why are the nations in an uproar, and why do the peoples mutter in vain?' Have you forgotten that it's *Hashono Rabo* tonight? Tonight all our fates are decided and the verdict is sealed. We stay up tonight. Listen to me, Golde, you light the samovar and make some tea while I get the horse and wagon ready. I am taking Hodel to the station in the morning." And once more I make up a story about how she has to go to Yehupetz, and from there farther on, because of the same old inheritance. It is possible, I say, that she may have to stay there through the winter and maybe the summer too, and maybe even another winter; and so we ought to give her something to take along—some linen, a dress, a couple of pillows, some pillow slips, and things like that.

And as I give these orders I tell her not to cry. "It's *Hashono Rabo,* and on *Hashono Rabo* one mustn't weep. It's a law." But naturally they don't pay any attention to me, and when the time comes to say good-by they all start weeping—their mother, the children, and even Hodel herself. And when she came to say good-by to her older sister Tzeitl (Tzeitl and her husband spend their holidays with us), they fell on each other's necks and you could hardly tear them apart.

I was the only one who did not break down. I was firm as steel—though inside I was more like a boiling samovar. All the way to Boiberik we were silent, and when we came near the station I asked her for the last time to tell me what it was that Feferel had really done. If they were sending him away there must have been a reason. At this she became angry and swore by all that was holy that he was innocent. He was a man, she insisted, who cared nothing about himself. Everything he did was for humanity at large, especially for those who toiled with their hands—that is, the workers.

That made no sense to me. "So he worries about the world," I told her. "Why doesn't the world worry a little about him? Nevertheless, give him my regards, that Alexander of Macedon of yours, and tell him I rely on his honor—for he is a man of honor, isn't he?—to treat my daughter well. And write to your old father sometimes."

When I finish talking she falls on my neck and begins to weep. "Good-by, Father," she cries. "Good-by! God alone knows when we shall see each other again."

Well, that was too much for me. I remembered this Hodel when she was still a baby and I carried her in my arms, I carried her in my arms. . . . Forgive me, Mr. Sholom Aleichem, for acting like an old woman. If you only knew what a daughter she is! If you could only see the letters she writes! Oh, what a daughter . . .

And now let's talk about more cheerful things. Tell me, what news is there about the cholera in Odessa?

Sholem Asch

Born in Kutno, Poland, in 1880, Sholem Asch received a traditional Orthodox Jewish education. He went to Warsaw in 1899, where he became a great reader of European literature, including German, Russian, and Polish fiction and drama. Although Asch began his literary career by writing in Hebrew, he soon turned to writing in his own distinctive mode of Yiddish, which draws heavily on Germanic style. His writing was influenced by European literature, not only in style but in subject matter and imagery as well; his novels often include gritty, realistic pictures of urban life, detailed and affectionate descriptions of rural nature, unflinching explorations of twisted human psychology, and universalistic and Christological themes.

Asch came to the United States in 1920. Five years later he returned to Europe, living in France while he wrote his trilogy, *Three Cities*. This panoramic novel captures the sweeping impact of the Russian revolution upon European and Russian Jewry through the experiences of several emancipated Jewish families. Early in the 1930s, Asch settled in the United States, although he continued to travel abroad for readings of his fiction. The author of numerous novels, Sholem Asch died in 1957.

Along with elements derived from European literature, Asch's novels are steeped in Jewish themes and concerns. He provides the apotheosis of the sympathetically drawn Woman of Valor, Rachel-Leah Hurwitz in *Three Cities*, the heroine of the trilogy's middle book, *Warsaw*. Rachel-Leah's husband, a former Talmudic scholar, has lost his religious faith and has become a secular-humanist scholar and teacher and a Polish nationalist. Young yeshiva boys who run away from home go to the Hurvitzes' home in Warsaw to study with Hurvitz, and Rachel-Leah looks after them. Clever, resourceful, and energetic, she finds her husband's students food, clothing, and employment; looks after her own little ones; and also tends to impoverished families in the neighborhood. Despite the relentless grime of the urban tenement in which they live, Rachel-Leah's home is joyously clean, and she herself is artlessly beautiful and radiant, "young looking, elastic in her movements and as fresh in her appearance as a country girl." Asch's prose shimmers with admiration.

Although Rachel-Leah's primary task is to enable the spiritual world of men, she accomplishes her goals not through passiveness and reticence but through intelligence, assertiveness, and a truly impressive time-management system. Furthermore, she maintains her own inner spiritual life, as Asch shows the reader in several intimate vignettes.

•

"Soldier in an Army of Mothers"

(excerpt)

"No, Pessie, it isn't money this time." Frau Hurvitz screamed into her ear through the shawl. "Do you happen to have room in your place for a poor young man that's come up from the country to study?"

"What? What is that?" demanded old Pessie, drawing the shawl aside and taking a huge plug of cotton-wool out of her ear.

"Room for a night's lodging!"

"Room? For the night? No, my dear." Old Pessie shrugged her shoulders as if it were useless to waste words on such a question, and to explain her shrug she waved her muff towards the surrounding herring-barrels and gherkin-casks.

Nor was there any room to spare at the leather-dresser's. In the first place the teacher's wife had begun to appear politically suspect to him, and in the second place his whole store-cellar was already occupied by the Talmud school from the second story; the scholars slept at night on his hides and so guarded them from thieves.

Benjamin the baker was a jolly fellow. He was always powdered white with flour and there was always a friendly smile on his lips. And he had long had a weakness for the teacher's wife. Benjamin the baker was a handsome fellow; but what good does that do one when one is always white from top to toe and one's black beard looks like a devil's brush in the midst of all that whiteness?

"O, Pani Hurvitz! You're a sight for sore eyes!" The baker made an elegant bow and scraped his foot. "Clear that dough away; let the lady have a seat!" he shouted to his apprentice as Rachel-Leah entered, and with his floury white overall he zealously dusted the chair on which the dough-tub had been standing.

"Benjamin, my friend, have you any place where a young man could sleep who has just come up from the country and has nowhere to go?" Frau Hurvitz asked with a smile that she knew would make the baker do whatever she wanted.

"There's nothing I wouldn't do for you, Pani Hurvitz!" replied Benjamin, putting his black beard to rights with a floury hand. "Would he care to sleep on the flour-sacks here? There are three people sleeping there already, my own two apprentices and another apprentice who can't be put up in his own place. But I don't mind if a fourth comes in, and I can let him have a dough-tub for a pillow." The gallant baker twirled his mustache and his black eyes shot amorous glances at Frau Hurvitz.

Rachel-Leah regarded the flour-sacks that were strewn with all manner of tattered and filthy bed-covers, shook her head and quitted the bakery without so much as a look at the handsome Benjamin. The apprentice burst out laughing behind her and delightedly scratched his curly red poll with his floury fingers.

Next door to the bakery was the establishment where Velvel the flesh-curer made his sausages. The whole courtyard trembled before him. His expression was always sinister: thick brows gloomed above his eyes, his bushy mustache, to which drops were always clinging, drooped morosely, and his eyes furtively avoided meeting anybody's look. Velvel always muttered to himself as if his conscience were secretly tormenting him. In his ragged blood-stained woolen waistcoat, with his chopping-knife in his hand, he looked like a bandit or some wild charcoal-burner just come from the forest. His children had early quitted their father's home: the sons had been thrown out, and the daughters, handsome wenches with thick black plaits of hair, full-bosomed and broad-hipped, had vanished of their own accord and were living, the devil knew why (so said Velvel), in the Argentine. For several years now gifts of money and cards wishing him luck had arrived from the Argentine every New Year's day. He laid the money and the cards (which he took to be another kind of money, since whatever came through the post was "money" to him) in his safe untouched, in their envelopes; for Velvel the sausage-maker had no need of money; he needed nothing in the world but his work. From six in the morning until late at night he chopped away at the enormous sides of meat that the butcher delivered to him properly sprinkled and stamped with the Kosher-mark of the Rabbinate. This Kosher-stamp had been already the cause of much scandal. The Rabbinate had several times pronounced his sausages to be *trefe,* for it had little confidence in his methods of preparation, and Velvel had rushed to the Community House and driven home with his rough fists the superiority of his "Kosher" wares. And now, whenever the butcher brought him a side of meat with the Kosher-stamp on it, he dragged it out into the courtyard and shouted at the top of his voice: "There's the Kosher-stamp for you, and devil take all of you!"

Velvel had no idea that breakfast or dinner could consist of anything but smoked meat; he fed entirely on the left-overs from his sausages. Thus he labored from one Sabbath to the next, and his only relaxation was a sleep on Sabbath afternoon. In summer he would put on his top boots, and together with his wife Neche, who was round and fat as a barrel and the only person he feared, since she did not scruple to box his ears for him, he would set out on foot for the citadel of Makatov near the Jewish Hospital, throw himself on the sunbleached grass, lay his head on Neche's lap and sleep undisturbed by the yells of playing boys and squabbling girls right through the summer afternoon until the evening. Then he would waken, make a wry face and say: "Neche, let's go home, I have a bad taste in my mouth." In winter he took his nap beside his wife near the stove. Neche, who could read Yiddish, would open the Women's Bible and read her husband the chapter about Noah and the Ark. If Velvel interrupted her with an occasional belch, she would reprove him: "Velvel, you might at least show some respect for Noah."

"You're right, Neche," Velvel would sigh, oppressed by the thought that he was doomed to go to hell and had no chance of salvation. In utter dejection he would hide his hard head in Neche's full bosom and soon begin to snore; it never took long for Neche to follow his example. . . .

The only tenant in the building who was not afraid of the sausage-maker was Frau Hurvitz, and Velvel himself had a kind of respect for her. He knew that she was a woman who deserved to be respected, and whenever she made a collection for the consumptive cigarette-maker on the fourth story he would bring her of his own accord a juicy bit of meat, a piece from the breast such as he never allowed himself even on a Sabbath. When he saw her quitting the bakery in a hurry he came out to the threshold of his shop. The shop door was always open and emitted such a fog of steam that nothing could be seen of the interior, and in this cloud of steam the sausage-maker, in his ragged woolen waistcoat and blood-stained apron, with his shirt-sleeves rolled up and his chopping-knife in one hand, now waited for Frau Hurvitz. But when she hastened past without looking at him he called out sulkily: "What's this? Have the Jews disowned me? Is my house *trefe?* Why are you leaving me out if you're making a collection? Come in and I'll give you a bit of meat."

"No, Velvel," responded Frau Hurvitz, "I'm only looking for a lodging for a poor young man."

"For one that learns things?"

"Of course! Do you think I would be running round like this for the sake of an idler?"

Velvel scratched his head and shouted through the steam: "Neche, Neche, come here!"

The flabby mass that loomed up in the fog took shape as a woman when presently it emerged into the faint light of the doorway; a woman in a flowered dimity petticoat, with red stockings drawn over shapeless and swollen legs, and, instead of a head-shawl, a handkerchief tied round her enormous neck to supplement her chemise. One might have thought that she had just come from the wash-tub, but as a matter of fact she had been helping her husband to smoke the sausages that he sent out to cheap lodging-houses.

"What is it?" asked Neche, wiping the sweat from her massive face with her neckerchief.

"Do you want to do a good deed? Then take in a poor Talmud student as a lodger; the teacher's wife has one to give away," said Velvel, indicating Frau Hurvitz.

Neche's smoke-inflamed eyes regarded her husband with amazement.

"Eh, Velvel, have you begun to think of good deeds? When did this fit come over you?"

"Can't I do a good deed if I want to? Is the leather-dresser the only man that's allowed some credit? I want to earn myself a good place in the next world as well as everybody else," growled Velvel.

"It's hell-fire you deserve in the next world, for you eat without saying grace and without washing," retorted Neche; then she turned to Frau Hurvitz: "I'm afraid it can't be done. Where could he sleep? In the oven, beside the sausages? We have to sleep in the smoke ourselves."

"And I'll show you that I can do a good deed! Just a minute, Pani Hurvitz," shouted the sausage-maker, whose pride had been wounded by his wife's words. "Just you wait a minute! . . . There, that's a sausage made of the best meat off the breast; take it and give it to the sick woman on the fourth floor. Let her have something good for once! Her brats keep nosing round here all day like dogs trying to snatch a bone or a bit of sausage-skin."

"Velvel, have you gone crazy? A whole sausage! Some bones for soup would be enough."

"No, a whole sausage, and a piece of rib-beef as well! I want to be a decent Jew! I want to have some credit for good deeds!" screamed Velvel in a voice as pitiable as if he were being knifed. . . .

The whole tenement knew the consumptive cigarette-maker on the fourth floor. For every now and then the desperate shrieks of her children could be heard echoing through the house: "Mother's dying!" But that had been going on for several years and people had got used to it. On several occasions the house had subscribed money to send the sick woman to

Otvock; but it's ill work filling a bottomless sack, and so she was still there, fading away, and every year, as she lay in bed spitting blood, she became a mother again and bore another child. Her husband was a ne'er-do-well who was supposed to be an excellent Talmud scholar; by profession he was a watchmaker but never got a job, and so he made cigarettes which the children sold on the quiet since they had no government stamp. Frau Hurvitz knew the family very well. Whenever the sick woman grew a little worse the children came rushing to the teacher's wife on the first floor: "Mother's dying." And then Frau Hurvitz would throw on her shawl and hurry up to the fourth floor.

Having received such an unexpected and lavish gift for the invalid—due entirely to the fact that Velvel had lost his head and remembered the next world—Frau Hurvitz ran upstairs to give her the sausage and the piece of beef. She found the sick woman in bed as usual; from the elevation, wearing her embroidered marriage-cap and with the characteristic red patches on her cheeks, she governed a troop of naked or half-naked children, one smaller than the other, who filled the tiny room, which was further cramped by a broad, heavy, carved cupboard, a remnant of the marriage outfit. The husband was not at home; he was out looking for odd jobs. But traces of his activity were visible, for on the table that stood in the middle of the room lay a large heap of tobacco. That did not hinder the children from eating at the table; they dabbled their crusts and spilt the coffee-dregs into the tobacco. The smaller children's toys were also bedded in the tobacco, filthy rag dolls that had been made by their mother.

The consumptive woman lay in bed and unceasingly chewed pieces of orange rind. When Frau Hurvitz entered the children grew quieter and the hubbub in the narrow room subsided a little. More and more little heads popped up from every corner; like hungry mice they were drawn out of their burrows by the smell of the sausage under Frau Hurvitz's arm.

"Here's something for you! Just fancy, Velvel the sausage-maker sent this up for you. Well, Gitel, how are things going?"

"Long may you live, Pani Hurvitz, for the goodliness of your heart! What should I do without you?

The invalid stretched out a pale skinny arm, eagerly grabbed the sausage and hid it under the blankets.

"But why put it away? Give the children a bit," said Frau Hurvitz, moved by the greedy look in the wide, wondering eyes of the children, who had gradually surrounded their mother's bed.

"In a minute, yes . . . but surely something should be saved for later . . ." stammered the invalid in embarrassment. "Go and play, children, go away, children," she concluded, in a weak voice.

But the children did not budge from the bed-side. If they weren't to have any sausage to eat they wanted at least to enjoy the satisfying odor of it.

"Give them all a bit now! You, my boy, bring me a knife," commanded Frau Hurvitz.

Then she divided the sausage among the children, much to the chagrin of the mother, who had to watch her booty vanishing piece by piece.

"They've just had something to eat. They should be thankful, and so should I, for they've just had something to eat. They're not hungry at all—isn't that so, children?" The mother stretched out her hand for the butt-end of the sausage. Her agitation brought on such a severe fit of coughing that she seemed to be on the point of dying.

This affliction of their mother's, an ordinary occurrence in their lives, did not interfere in the least with the children's enjoyment of the unusual tit-bit. Frau Hurvitz attended to the invalid. But the spasm of coughing grew so alarming that she was at her wit's end to know what to do. At that point Sheindel, the oldest girl, came to her assistance; still munching the delicious sausage she went coolly to the water-tap with a matter-of-fact air and brought a glass of water; she clutched the sausage in one hand and between bites held the glass of water with the other to the mouth of her mother, who was half-suffocated and weak with coughing.

Frau Hurvitz was alarmed and shocked. But the sick woman seemed to think nothing of the incident. When she felt a little better she merely turned in a matter-of-fact way to her visitor: "I'm glad you've come in, Frau Hurvitz; I was just going to send for you." Then she lowered her voice and whispered, with a shamed but pleased smile on her fever-flushed face: "Do you know, I think I'm near my time; it won't be more than a day or two now."

Frau Hurvitz stiffened: "What? And you in this state? How long is this kind of thing going to go on?"

"How can I help it? We're only sinful mortals after all." The sick woman smiled coquettishly. But the smile outlined with painful sharpness the bony skull beneath the drawn skin of her face. . . .

Frau Hurvitz was not a woman to be deterred by obstacles. What she once undertook to do she carried out to the end. And so she was determined now that the young Talmudist who had fled from the provinces and knocked at her door should remain in Warsaw.

As she descended the stairs after visiting the consumptive woman she paused for a moment and reviewed in her mind all the neighbors, acquaintances, and friends whom she had previously persuaded to take in young country students. She soon gave up, however, for there was not a friend of hers on whom she had not already landed somebody.

On her way home she looked in on Henoch the joiner, not because she counted on his having room for a lodger, but because she needed his help. Henoch was a good friend of hers and she thought highly of him; he often helped her in very delicate negotiations of which mention will be made later. Besides, the joiner's workshop was in the part of the building where the invalid lived, and so within convenient reach.

The following was the domestic interior she beheld as she entered. Henoch the joiner was standing almost up to his neck in a turbulent sea of shavings and hammering away at a plank. But the hammering could scarcely be heard for the shrieking and yelling of a swarm of children of all ages who were playing about among the shavings. Near the open door stood a cradle over which Jochebed, the carpenter's wife, was bending with her naked breasts hanging down like udders, while from the cradle came a smacking, sucking sound. While she nursed her infant in this fashion Jochebed evidently found it quite easy to carry on at the same time a conversation with a loving couple sitting enlaced on a rumpled bed in the corner; the feminine partner in this alliance was her own sister, a source of shame to Henoch, who suspected her of following an ancient and none too honorable profession; and indeed the reek of cheap perfume and toilet-soap which emanated from her told its own story. Beside her sat a youth wearing the typical Warsaw cap with its patent leather peak. They were both eating pumpkin seeds out of a paper bag, and the floor around them was strewn with the husks. The conversation seemed to be about marriage; for as Frau Hurvitz came in Jochebed, stooping still lower over the cradle, was making a remark that obviously referred to some difference of opinion on the subject: "My sister's quite right in not wanting to get married. Why should she be such a fool? What advantage does one get, God help us, from being married? Nothing but *this* . . ."—and she indicated the cradle.

"And anyhow, do you think I don't know what he's after?" interrupted her sister. "He may talk about marriage but it's something else he means. I can't bear that kind of hypocrisy. If *that's* what you're after, you should say it right out and not try to bamboozle me with all this talk of marriage!"

Henoch the carpenter took no part in the discussion. He liked neither his wife's sister with her cheap perfumes nor the youth who was courting her; he regarded both of them with suspicion. So he withdrew into the middle of his shavings and worked with redoubled energy.

"Just look at him working himself to death!" cried out Jochebed, still bending over the cradle. "You would think to see him that I must be rolling in money and getting the best of everything. But with all his hammering and planing he doesn't bring in enough to give us a decent meal once a week on the Sabbath. . . ."

Henoch remained unruffled. He wiped his dirty, sweat-bedewed forehead and ran his plane furiously over the plank so that it screeched.

But Frau Hurvitz's arrival was now remarked and the discussion broke off. Jochebed rose from her stooping position and covered her bosom with her blouse. The couple shifted a little apart from each other. Henoch stopped working, left his work-bench, and came forward to the cradle beside the door where Frau Hurvitz was standing, the only part of the room that was well lighted.

"Oh, it's the teacher's wife!" cried Henoch with obvious pleasure, loosening shavings from his hair and beard.

"Yes, Henoch, I was just passing and looked in. Any news?"

"What news could there be? Everything's all right so long as there's some work to be had and a bit of something to eat. What else does one want?"

Frau Hurvitz liked Henoch; in all the neighborhood he was the only man who never complained and was always good-humored and cheerful.

"There's one man at least who's pleased with life! You never grumble, Henoch."

"Why should I? And if I did have cause to grumble—what would that matter? The world wouldn't come to an end: I should still go on living. So why grumble?"

"Dogs in the gutter go on living, too!" broke in his wife. "Of course he's quite content so long as he has his plane and a bit of bread and a book to read from his Union! And once he's buried in a book there's not a word to be got out of him—the devil knows what can be in these books! What does he care if his children have nothing to put in their bellies but potatoes, until they're all blown up? What does he care if winter's coming on and they haven't a rag to their backs?"

"Well, my dear, now you've brought out all your grievances; and to listen to you one would think the world was coming to an end. But meanwhile you have a roof over your head and a loaf of bread in the cupboard; there are plenty of people who haven't as much."

"What a comfort—to be told that there are people who haven't as much! Why don't you tell me about the people who live in fine houses and walk on Persian carpets and eat meat every day?"

Henoch calmly fished shavings out of his thick dark beard and replied with a smile: "Now, now, my dear, don't get excited. The palaces and the Persian carpets and the chicken broth will all come some fine day. Let Pani Hurvitz get a word in edgeways. She hasn't taken the trouble to come here for nothing . . ."

"Oh, it's nothing particular; I only looked in because I was passing. But tell me, Henoch, do you know by any chance where I could get a lodging for a poor young man who's come up from the country to study?"

"A lodging for a poor young man . . ." repeated Henoch. "If there's no room elsewhere, why not here? It could be managed. We could sweep the shavings away at night and put an extra bed behind the work-bench. A bed doesn't take up much room, does it, Jochebed?"

"And where are we to put Surele and Avreymel and Moyshle and the two littlest ones? Where do you think we could put a bed? On top of your head?"

"No, Henoch, you really haven't room for anybody. I wasn't thinking of you, but perhaps you might know of somebody willing to let out a bed?" asked Frau Hurvitz. "Of course it would have to be cheap, for the stranger's no Rothschild, but we could pay something amongst us."

"Half a minute, Pani Hurvitz, I have an idea; I'll run up and see Motche in the factory. If you need a bed you need a bed, and something must be done about it." And Henoch rushed away.

"Just look at him, how quick he can run! If he would only take half as much trouble for his own family as he does for strangers!" Jochebed shouted after him.

But neither Henoch nor Frau Hurvitz heard a word; they were already out through the door.

"Probably some *trefe* fellow," said the youth, cuddling in beside Jochebed's sister again. "And if he gets into trouble nothing will happen to *her*, you bet. Nothing ever happens to well-off people; but Henoch'll be put into jug. And I'd like to know who would lift a finger to help him?"

"Why did you let him do it?" demanded Jochebed's sister.

"How could I help it? That's just the sort of thing I've got to put up with. . . ."

The handbag factory was a story higher than the joiner's workshop. Motche, also called "the hunchback," was chief cutter-out there. He was a master of his craft and had, as the phrase ran in his profession, a "golden hand"; he knew how to cut out the leather so that not a square inch was wasted. For that reason he was cherished by his employer, all the more so as other factories were always trying to tempt him away. Motche was anything but handsome. Reared in the most bitter poverty, he had a deformed shoulder caused by a bad fall in childhood; hence his nickname. But Motche was obsessed by a devouring passion for handsome women with dark hair and large dark eyes—he called them "gypsies." And since in actual life he had little chance of meeting any, he had cut out of illustrated papers and advertisements all the pictures of such women that he could find, Amazons from the circus, dancers, lion-tamers, and these he had pinned to the wall above his cutting-bench; while he worked he would cast an admiring glance on them from time to time and heave a gentle sigh. His physical weakness made him want to pose as a strong character, and everything risky and dangerous attracted him. He belonged to a secret political organization and whenever he got the chance undertook dangerous commissions that might easily have cost him his life. Without employing the most elementary precautions, he would quite openly carry about or distribute revolutionary proclamations; in his lodgings he kept compromising documents and gave shelter to suspected members of his party. The more dangerous an enterprise, the more strongly he was tempted to test his strength on it. His recklessness had made him notorious in the party and among the working classes; everybody knew him, and anybody needing help turned at once to Motche: he did all that was required of him openly and under the very noses of the police. In this way he had endangered both his comrades and the party itself more than once.

Henoch briefly informed Motche that there was a job to be done. A simple member of the party rank and file, he was naive enough to believe that some important personage must be in question if the teacher's wife, who was so highly respected by the party, herself took the trouble of seeking a lodging for him. This conviction of Henoch's was at once apparent to the hunchback, who laid down his work and came downstairs to where Frau Hurvitz was waiting. He listened to her with close attention, but was extremely disappointed to learn that this time it was not a conspiratorial "job," and that the man for whom the teacher's wife wanted a lodging was not a political personage.

"I have lodgings, of course, but I need them for party purposes. I'm really sorry not to be able to help you this time. But in this case I can do nothing," he said, very gravely. "Tell me, was it the Shachliner who sent you?"

"No."

"Without instructions from the Shachliner I can do nothing."

Frau Hurvitz's hopes had sunk almost to zero; she feared that the Shachliner would yet be able to crow over her. But she was resolved not to surrender: "The young man must stay in Warsaw, even if the Shachliner has to stand on his head! But where am I to find a bed for him?" Once more she mentally reviewed the whole house from roof to cellar; she simply had to find a lodging for the stranger even if she had to keep him in the school for the night and so risk her husband's teaching license. . . . "And I won't stop till I've got lessons for him, too, and a new shirt into the bargain!"

But it was from an unexpected quarter that help finally came, from a direction Frau Hurvitz had never even thought of.

As she was going upstairs to her own flat, completely absorbed in the problem of the young man's lodging, she met Pan Kviatkovski coming down from the second story. Pan Kviatkovski was the sole Gentile tenant in the whole building. Why he had ever come here and what made him go on staying in a Jewish tenement scarcely remarkable for cleanliness were questions that no one could answer. His door was the only one in the building over which hung a holy picture and on which the three letters K. M. B., representing the names of the Three Holy Kings, were chalked every year. These letters filled the hearts of the Jewish tenants with a dull fear, as if they had been symbols of the Inquisition. Pan Kviatkovski was a "nature doctor" and cured people with herbs. Whole trains of countrywomen in their bright village costumes climbed daily up the stairs to the "doctor," carrying baskets filled with country products such as eggs, butter and fowls with which they paid the "Pan" for his medical advice and decoctions. The Jewish tenants were always eager to investigate these covered baskets and often asked: "Anything for sale?" But they were always met by a firm refusal which they accepted with a sigh, envying the doctor's good fortune. . . .

Naturally they all felt a great respect for their only Christian neighbor. Mothers made their daughters sweep the stairs, not so much for the sake of cleanliness as on Pan Kviatkovski's account: "Be quick now, the Goy will be downstairs in a minute," was the usual formula. . . . Pan Kviatkovski's own attitude to his Jewish neighbors was somewhat singular. He was often, indeed usually, very affable, courteously returned greetings and even stopped to gossip with a great display of Yiddish. When he was in a particularly good mood he peppered his Yiddish with Hebrew words that he had picked up somewhere or other and used with humorous exaggeration and without knowing what they meant. But now and then, without any reason, Pan Kviatkovski suddenly turned "cross" towards his neighbors, and then he would go downstairs scowling with his brows knit and his mustache bristling, ignoring every salutation and growling in his beard: "Lousy Jews!"

The Jews called this mood "the Pan's bad fit" and, whenever it came over him they avoided him, until suddenly without any reason his behavior would alter again, and just as abruptly as he had turned against the Jews he once more made friends with them. The Pan's bad fit always evoked the same remark from the Jews: "The worm's gnawing him."

Pan Kviatkovski showed more respect for the teacher's wife than for any of the other Jewish tenants. She was the only person with whom he talked Polish, a sign that he regarded her as an equal. And yet Frau Hurvitz was not certain when she met him now whether Pan Kviatkovski was in his "good" or his "cross" mood, and did not know whether to greet him or pretend she did not see him. But Pan Kviatkovski stopped of his own accord, swept his hat from his graying head and inquired with a smile: "Why so deep in thought, dear madam? Has anything happened?"

"Nothing has happened, but there's so much distress in the building, Pan Kviatkovski."

"Ah yes. Yes, there's a great deal of poverty among you as well as among us. Why don't you apply to me sometimes if help is needed? You only look to your own people to relieve distress, but am I not a neighbor, too? I like to be on good terms with all my neighbors whether they are Jews or Gentiles."

"On the contrary, your help is always most welcome, Pan Kviatkovski!—Can you by any chance take in a poor young man who has come up from the country to study and has nowhere to sleep?" asked Frau Hurvitz, more in jest than in earnest.

"Why not? I have plenty of room. Bring him to me; he can both lodge and board in my house. There's only the two of us, myself and my housekeeper, and the flat's large enough. Why not?"

Frau Hurvitz could not recover from her amazement: "Are you joking, or do you mean it, Pan Kviatkovski?"

"Joking?" cried Pan Kviatkovski, so deeply offended and so red with anger that Frau Hurvitz became alarmed. "Do you think I would permit myself to joke on such a subject? You are looking for a lodging for a poor fellow who wants to study, and you think I would joke about that? Do you fancy I'm incapable of understanding?—But that's just like you Jews; you think that nobody but yourselves has any fellow-feeling, and that you're the only people who help others—nobody else is allowed a look in! But we must all help each other, we must help everybody all round—not in the narrow way you set about it. You Jews turn only to your own people and never think of the others."

"Who says so? On the contrary, it was *I* who asked *you,* Pan Kviatkovski. And if you are willing to do it, my very best thanks to you! The young man is very respectable; he has run away from fanatical parents and wants to be a student in Warsaw."

"Bring him upstairs at once, then. I'll go back now and have a bed set up for him. He can have his meals with me, too. Our country needs educated people; the more intelligence we have the stronger we'll become. And you Yiddishers have good heads on you," he added in Yiddish jargon. "I'll teach him Polish myself. Bring him right up, Frau Hurvitz. I'll go up and tell my housekeeper." And Pan Kviatkovski ran upstairs again to his flat.

Frau Hurvitz stood for a moment quite struck dumb. She could hardly believe what she had heard. Then full of joy and pride she entered her kitchen.

The Shachliner stuck his goatee round the door of the "High School" and his eyes danced mockingly: "Well, Frau Hurvitz—have you found a bed for your young man?"

"Just to spite you, you Lithuanian, I have—and not only a lodging, but board and lessons as well! You come with me, young man," commanded

Frau Hurvitz. She took the Talmudist by the hand like a child and dragged him and his bundle wrapped in newspaper upstairs to Pan Kviatkovski. . . .

After Frau Hurvitz had thus absolved her public duties and established the young Talmudist in his quarters, she turned to the domestic tasks that awaited her. The chief meal of the day had now to be prepared, and Rachel-Leah betook herself to her cooking-pots. This she did with the energy and swiftness that characterized all her actions and were even more in evidence than usual on this day, after such a successful morning.

A couple of hours later the whole family was assembled round the table and Solomon Hurvitz made ready to instruct his children in the science of food values. He was always learning or teaching something; but, since it was too dark in the room now to read a book either privately or aloud, he applied his time to telling his children how much iron there was in turnips and how much albumen in lentils. The teacher liked imparting information to other people and drew no distinction between his pupils, his children and perfect strangers whom he had never seen before.

The early dusk of the brief autumn day was already darkening the room. The weather had taken a turn for the worse, and the children, who had set out in brilliant sunshine that morning, had come back wet through and plastered with snow and mud. David and Sosha had to take off their damp shoes and sit at table in their stockings. The conversation inevitably turned to the urgent necessity for galoshes, and that depressed everybody, for it reminded them how near the winter was. The father behaved as if he had not heard a word, but the mother pursued in her thoughts plans of all kinds.

There was always some guest at Rachel-Leah's table and she had a unique skill in apportioning the food so that it always sufficed. She was sitting now as usual before the large dish, thinking out contrivances and at the same time ladling out portions; to one plate she added something, from another she removed something, according to the age and appetite of the recipient. Of course the newcomer had been invited to share the meal. He seemed to have been born under a lucky star, that young man, for he had won Frau Hurvitz's sympathy from the very first and the fact that she had found a lodging for him in such an unlikely quarter invested him with extra distinction not only in her eyes, but in the eyes of everybody else. It was almost as if they gave him credit for the fact that Pan Kviatkovski had suddenly gone mad and taken in a young Jew as a lodger. The guest, however, was a handsome youngster as well; unlike his predecessors, who had mostly been small and ill-formed, he was of a tall straight figure and had well-cut features of a provincial simplicity, beautiful large dark eyes and a soft down on his cheeks that looked like a continuation of his side curls and gave him a soft youthful charm. But what chiefly recommended him to Frau Hurvitz was the superior cleanliness of his garments, which in that respect were unlike those of all the young men who had previously turned up from the provinces. He wore the traditional caftan, but it was spotlessly clean. His shirt showing beneath his prominent Adam's apple was decently ironed. And the satin ribbon that he wore, in the Chassidic manner, instead of a tie, was smooth and neatly knotted round his neck. It could be seen that this young man came out of no poor family, and even in a house so democratic as the teacher's this fact did not fail to make an impression. The attention of everybody was centered on the stranger. And since Frau Hurvitz had managed to procure a lodging and all kinds of extra privileges for him in such an extraordinary manner, the teacher and even the Shachliner were reconciled to the idea of his staying in Warsaw, and all were curious to know more about him.

"Why do you want to study?" asked the teacher.

The visitor, who obviously found himself in such company for the first time in his life, and had to endure the additional ordeal of sitting at the same table with strange girls, blushed to the roots of his hair. The girls, observing his blush, nudged each other under the table and bent low over their plates to hide their smiles from their father. But the young man soon recovered his composure: staring at his plate like a schoolboy he answered with unexpected assurance: "I want to be an author."

This answer surprised and excited the company. The master of the house laid down his fork, took off his glasses, polished them thoroughly with his handkerchief so that he might examine the speaker better, and asked: "You want to be an author?"

"Yes, I want to write," replied the young man with conviction.

"What do you want to write?" the teacher went on with his cross-examination.

"I've written a drama already and I've brought it with me to read to literary men."

"A drama?"

"Yes, a drama in four acts."

"Have you studied the rules of dramatic construction?" inquired the astonished teacher.

"Rules? Are there rules? No, I haven't studied them."

"You haven't studied the rules and yet you have written a drama?"

"As you see," returned the young man, waving one hand as if he were displaying an ox standing before him in the market.

"Have you read the literature of classical drama?"—the teacher's voice became as severe as if he were examining a pupil.

"Classical drama? What's that?" asked the young man, growing red.

Everybody smiled. Sosha could no longer restrain herself and burst out laughing, until a glare from her father silenced her.

"I mean Shakespeare, for instance. Have you read Shakespeare?" the teacher continued.

"I've heard of him, but I've never read him."

"Do you know Moliere? Have you read Moliere?"

"Moliere? Who's he? I don't understand—must I read all that before writing a drama? What has that got to do with it?" asked the candidate in surprise.

Once more Sosha lost control of herself. Her elder sister pinched her under the table to silence her. The teacher paused in his cross-examination, and his expression betrayed profound sorrow and misgiving. The young man divined that he had said the wrong thing; he blushed still more in his confusion; but his shy embarrassment won him the others' sympathy.

"Tell me, young man, have you ever been in a theater? Have you ever even seen a theater?" The teacher took up his catechism again.

"Yes, a Jewish theatrical company once came to our town and I looked in through a hole in the tent."

Sosha burst out laughing again. The guest sat as if on hot coals and did not know where to look. His guardian angel rescued him: "Look here, what do you mean by jumping on a stranger like that? Hasn't he come to study in Warsaw just because he doesn't know all these things? You should be trying to help him," cried Frau Hurvitz, and as a kind of compensation for all his humiliations she transferred a piece of meat from her own plate to his.

"Eat it up, young man. You'll have the laugh of them all one day."

The master of the house brought this painful scene to a close: "There's nothing to laugh at. All our talented men have begun like that. We have no schools. The synagogue is all the university we have. I am very interested in your drama, young man, and I beg you to read it to me whenever you have time."

These words rehabilitated the guest before the whole company and Rachel-Leah cried triumphantly: "Aha, see that, now!"

But the meal could not be prolonged, for various members of the family had to go out again. The teacher had afternoon lessons to give in private houses. Helene, too, gave private lessons and so had no free time to herself, a fact that vexed her mother. But living was dear and the family was large. The school brought in very little, for it was mainly attended by poor children from the neighborhood whose parents could afford to pay only half-fees, and even to get these it cost much trouble and many fruitless journeys. True, a committee of rich Jewish ladies who moved in Polish circles privately supported the school, because it was the only place where poor Jewish children could learn the officially proscribed Polish language, which Herr Hurvitz taught them in secret; but the support of these ladies, like that given by most charitable committees, was moral rather than material. The committee was prodigal of good advice only. The chief patroness of the school, Frau Dr. Silberstein, appeared every Monday and Thursday to examine the children in Polish, and fate ordained that many a time while she was actually in the building the Russian inspector, who kept a sharp eye on the school because of its suspected Polish sympathies, made a flying raid on it and cross-examined the children to find out if they were learning Polish and had Polish text-books. But whenever an actual problem cropped up, such as how to pay the rent or get coal for the winter, the committee was never of any real use; Frau Hurvitz was kept trotting round from one lady to the next, and as usual it was on her shoulders that the whole burden fell.

Yet it would be a mistake to assume that all the worries, her own and other people's, with which Frau Hurvitz contended had furrowed her face or aged her prematurely. The contrary seemed to be the case; the more she had to do the higher rose her energy, strength and spirit. The inexhaustible reserve of nervous force that was stored in her—presumably an inheritance from generations of peasant ancestors—made her young-looking, elastic in her movements and as fresh in her appearance as a country girl. When she went downstairs the whole house knew her step, for it was unmistakable; the stairs quivered under her tread and yet she always flew whether going up or down. Although she was over forty she looked like a woman of thirty. Sorrow and care had not boxed her proud figure. Full-bosomed and ripe, she advanced like a soldier in an army of mothers, knowing her duty and her own value. She radiated courage, energy and self-confidence; it was as if destiny had challenged her to come out and do battle. The more difficult her circumstances the greater her strength and the more lightly she shouldered her burdens. It must be admitted that when her eldest son, the hope of the family, was imprisoned as a political criminal, Frau Hurvitz looked on the verge of breaking down, and for some time her health actually suffered. She, who had never been ill, began to complain of headaches and pains in her legs. But that lasted only while she was fighting for her son's release; as soon as she was convinced that nothing could be done she returned to her daily round, and was shortly in command of herself once more and as young and fresh as ever. To be quite honest, her clear-cut face showed a few furrows after her son's misfortune, and round the column of her neck three deep rings had appeared; but the furrows only gave a tender, sorrowing look to her muscular features, while her gray eyes, which had previously gleamed like those of some wild animal ready to spring now had a gentle, contemplative, mildly resigned expression that suggested a film of tears over the eyeballs. This mild look and the furrows of maternal sorrow scored round her neck formed a remarkable contrast to the proud straightness of her figure. It was as if her body lived a life of its own as far as the neck; it was controlled throughout by a unified force of will that brooked no obstacles.

Frau Hurvitz knew exactly what she had to do at every moment of her life. There was always new labor awaiting her. As soon as her husband and the children were out of the house she turned up her sleeves and set to washing dishes; she poured a pan of hot water into the large basin, threw in soap and soda, and began to scour her pots, her dishes, her knives and forks, with the same energy that flowed from her at all times like sap from a mighty tree.

But Rachel-Leah could not wash dishes mechanically; she dreamed to herself as she did so.

Her spirit was far away as she stood there with sleeves rolled up and hands plunged into the soapy lye. Her imagination drew glorious pictures. Where nobody else could see anything remarkable Rachel-Leah's eye perceived a light that irradiated all things with its golden beams; she saw everything through transforming spectacles. The simple, unsullied faith within her made her see things and happenings not as they actually were but in a kind of perspective, as if from the vantage ground of a higher reality. And in her fantasy the young Talmudist whom she had found at her door became a great and renowned man, and she was proud to have helped him. Just as she was firmly convinced that her husband was the greatest scholar in the world, that her children would be eminent, and that the Shachliner, whom she called a "renegade" and a "Lithuanian thief," would yet make his mark and become famous, so she now began to believe in the young stranger's future (her imagination made no distinction here between her own children and strangers). And while she was scouring her pots and plates sheer joy illumined her face, and an endless, incomprehensible happiness flowed through her because she had been able to help such a promising young man. She looked forward with great expectations to his future.

From her maternal forbears she had inherited the firm belief that men were born for the higher aims of life that lay beyond the trivial round of petty cares; the ordinary tasks of daily existence fell to women, but men lived to create spiritual worlds, spiritual values that guaranteed eternal life and the eternal meaning of the universe. For Rachel-Leah these spiritual values had once been embodied in the study of the Torah and a belief in heaven, but since she had followed her husband into apostasy she attached her faith to the new values of culture and progress, to a belief in a brighter future on earth that was bound to come as soon as humanity shed its stupidities and no longer submitted to slavery. She had heard much about this future from the Shachliner and the other young men who came in every

Friday evening. And in her opinion women were intended to help men in the struggle towards that brighter future—just as her mother and her mother's mother had helped their men to secure immortality in the other world and a share in paradise.

It was already dark in the kitchen. A film of raindrops obscured the window that looked out on the courtyard. The large room adjoining the kitchen, by day dining-room, study and family sitting-room, by night the children's bedroom, was now half-lit by the milky glow of a lamp, within whose circle David was sitting doing his home tasks for school before going to his evening job. He, too, had to earn his own keep and school clothes; every evening from five to seven he read aloud to a blind man. It was now getting so dark in the kitchen that Rachel-Leah could not see the dishes, and she remembered the lamp in the big room (she was too thrifty to light a second lamp). So she called to her son:

"David, bring the lamp in here! You can work at the kitchen table, I've wiped it clean."

David came in with the lamp and his lesson-book. When he saw that his mother was washing dishes he asked in amazement:

"Are you doing the washing up? Where's the concierge? Doesn't she come in to do that every day?"

"What an idea! The concierge indeed! As if I can't do it myself! We can easily use the extra shillings for something else. Don't say anything to your father, do you hear?"

"Well, why can't Sosha help you? Isn't she in?"

"I don't want her to ruin her hands doing housework, so I've sent her out to see a friend of hers."

"Let me help you then, mother; give me a shot at it."

"Go away; you have your lessons to do."

"I've only to learn a little bit of Caesar, and I know it already."

"I'll do the washing, all the same, but you can dry. There's a dish-cloth."

In the middle of operations, however, Rachel-Leah made a discovery.

"For goodness' sake, just look at that hole in your trousers! And it's no time since I bought them for you." She indicated the seat of her son's trousers.

David was pulled up short in a dramatic sentence from the "Bellum civile." Awkwardly he stuttered out something about an "accident" and then cried wrathfully:

"How can I help it if they get torn? Trousers are just like that; they always get torn. Cast-iron trousers haven't been invented yet."

"That's the kind you would need! Cloth trousers are evidently not much use to you. Come here, my learned scholar, and let me mend that hole."

She left her dishes, fished a work-basket out of the drawer of the kitchen-table and threaded a needle with the stoutest cotton she could find; then dropping on one knee she set to work on the trousers of her son, who did not allow this attack on his hind-quarters to interrupt him in the recitation of Caesar's heroic deeds. Rachel-Leah's face was radiant with pride for a moment as she listened to the mysterious syllables rolled out by her son, but soon she was paying little heed to Caesar for she was thinking: "All kinds of things are invented, but why has nobody ever invented untearable cloth for trousers?" And while she was meditating on this relevant question she noticed that the boy's pockets were crammed to bursting.

"What's all this?" she asked, feeling his coat-pockets.

"Nothing at all . . . something I mustn't tell you." David reddened with embarrassment.

But his mother's hand pounced like lightning and extracted a thick bundle of revolutionary pamphlets.

"This is the last straw!" cried Rachel-Leah. "You too? What do you think is to become of me?" she added despairingly.

"Mother, please don't tell father. I only brought them here for tonight; I have to pass them on to somebody tomorrow."

"Have I to keep my mouth shut as well? To have one son lying in prison is enough—and now *you're* at it, too? Can't you wait at least until you've finished school?" Rachel-Leah was calming down a little.

"I only took them to oblige a comrade. I promise you, mother, I'll pass them all on tomorrow."

"You haven't the slightest idea how to manage things like this, you greenhorn. How are you going to carry them in your torn clothes? Look, just look here, they're sticking right out of your pockets; a blind man couldn't help seeing them. Hand them over! The next thing I'll have to put up with is hearing you've been arrested in the street. There are police-spies at every corner!"

With that she emptied her son's pockets of the pamphlets, seized a newly washed pot and crammed the papers into it, then laid a sheet of paper on top, shook over that a bowlful of peeled potatoes that were ready for next day's dinner and set the whole on the stove.

David laughed. "What are you after? Are you going to boil the pamphlets?"

"Boiling isn't enough for them, I'm going to roast them! I'm going to burn them to cinders! Don't let me catch you bringing things like that into the house again, you greenhorn. You can keep that kind of thing for later on, or else I'll tell your father. As sure as I'm a living woman, as sure as I stand here I'll tell your father!"

"Then I'll tell my father that you've been swearing again." (The teacher, who never stopped trying to educate his own wife, was at much pains to break Rachel-Leah of her habit of swearing.) "And I'll tell him, too, that you've been washing up the dishes yourself!"

"Will you hold your tongue, you greenhorn?"

"If you don't tell, neither will I. One good turn deserves another—" The boy ran off laughing, for it was time to go to his evening job.

"Stop! . . . Why are you flying off without your galoshes? Do you want to catch cold again? It's raining and your shoes are leaking."

"How can I put on galoshes? The ones I had are all torn."

"Come here a minute. There—I bought a pair second-hand at the market." With these words she threw a parcel at her son.

"Galoshes! Where did you get the cash for them?"

"Never you mind. Put them on and clear out at once."

The evening hours between five and seven, since her husband and her children were then out of the house, belonged entirely to Frau Hurvitz. The chief meal of the day was over, the dishes were washed up, and now the time for relaxation and dreaming came for the housewife, and she resented any interruption of it. It was reserved for one of two of her favorite occupations; scrubbing the floor or taking a bath. On this occasion she did both. Cleanliness was an obsession with her; as a girl in her country village she had been accustomed to see everything in the house shining, and to this custom she adhered all her life, honoring it even more now than she had done formerly. To scrub the floor was for her a kind of pleasant recreation, in a sense an escape from the troubles of the day, and whenever her burdens grew too heavy, whenever necessity pinched her too hard, Rachel-Leah betook herself to this favorite occupation.

She slipped off her shoes and stockings, dipped a cloth in a basin of soapy water, and on all fours crawled round the room, wringing out the cloth from time to time and scrubbing the floor thoroughly with a zeal that showed her pleasure in the job. The wet cloth traveled into every corner of the large dining-room, under the beds and the chests, and no crevice, however securely hidden, escaped its attentions. Rachel-Leah suffered no one to interrupt her; it was as if she were doing priestly service in a sanctuary; no one either could or dared enter the house; and if the Messiah Himself had knocked at the door, He would have had to wait until all the floors in the flat had been wiped with that wet cloth. Then every window was thrown open—summer and winter alike—to let the floors dry more quickly. After the scrubbing, yellow sand was strewn all over, and then no one dared to stir out of the kitchen, and it was in the kitchen that the teacher and the Shachliner had to fight out their battles over a glass of tea until the large room was dry and ready to receive its guests in a fitting manner.

When she had finished with the floors Rachel-Leah took herself in hand.

She loved nothing so much as soap and water, and so not only her own body but everything that pertained to her had to make the acquaintance of soap and water pretty frequently. From time immemorial it had been an established law in the Hurvitzes' house that every member of the family had to face a tub of soapy water on Friday evening. The mistress of the house divided each victim into two halves; first the top half was dealt with, from the head to the middle, and then the lower half from the middle downwards. She made no distinction of age or of sex amongst her family: Friday's bath was obligatory. But in the middle of the week it might occur to Rachel-Leah to examine the ears of her children or the backs of their necks. And these attentions were not confined to her own family; she had even made it a law that every young man from the provinces who came to seek instruction from her husband should first of all face the tub of soapy water—to say nothing of her own lodgers, over whom she exercised a strict supervision. She would appear unexpectedly in the "High School" with a basin of hot water and a piece of yellow soap, and issue the command: "You must all take a wash, or else I'll have to come and wash you myself." It was the Shachliner who suffered most, for whenever Rachel-Leah was at odds with him or whenever he said anything of which she disapproved, she would call out, not matter who was present: "Herr Lithuanian, wouldn't you like to have a bath? As sure as I'm a living woman, there's a large kettle of boiling water ready."

But she loved most of all to apply soap and water to her own person. A bath was a kind of reward for the toils of the day and aroused in her new reserves of energy and courage. She locked and bolted the door, threw off her frock and underwear, and standing naked in the great tub poured water from a ladle over her supple athletic body. And just as thoroughly as she had previously scoured her pots, her dishes and floors, she now washed every portion of her own body with a hard loofah dipped in soap and soda. Her beautifully modeled back with all its hollows and dimples arched itself like a well-strung bow: her spine was as slim and delicate in its articulations as the backbone of a fish. Energetically and with great contentment she labored over the whole of her supple body from the breasts to the wide hips, nor did she forget to scour her strong and rounded knees. Every touch of the loofah left a red mark behind as if her blood had been awakened from sleep, as if it had been summoned from its farthest retreat and now was trying to burst through her transparent white skin.

But today was a special occasion, for Rachel-Leah washed not only her body but her hair as well. After such a day of trouble and running to-and-fro, it was a great comfort to her to wash her hair. Still naked, with her skin prickling into goose-flesh after her bath, she stood before a basin of warm rain-water and rinsed her long hair in it, squeezing out the soap;

then she tossed her locks apart and poured the rain-water luxuriously over her head. A childlike innocence beamed from her face and her whole body at that moment, as if it were blessings that were being showered on her head. The dreams of her youth rose up again; green dells of her childhood, cool streams in which she had bathed as a girl, secret glades in fragrant spring woods; all lived again in her memory while she poured the lukewarm rain-water over her head. The sins of the intervening years were washed away, the sins of poverty and encroaching age; and Rachel-Leah quitted the wash-basin fresh and purified, as if newborn.

She sat drying her hair by the hot tiled stove in the sitting-room; she felt relaxed and drowsy in the green dressing-gown that had been made from her wedding frock. All the chairs and tables had lesson-books of some kind lying on them. But the floor was scrubbed white and strewn with yellow sand; so Rachel-Leah sat by the stove drinking tea in great content, newborn, purified, comforted; as happy as a child.

This was the sole hour of the day when Rachel-Leah heard her own heart, the sole point at which she became aware of her own life. It was the Sabbath hour of her day, the hour in which she dried her hair and drank tea by the milky light of the table lamp. As a shepherd passes in review his well-tended flocks, Rachel-Leah now reviewed her days and her dreams. . . . Long-forgotten and buried maiden dreams that had been shrouded in the darkness of the past rose and hovered as if in sunlight before her eyes; summer-green meadows, murmuring brooks, secret sensations, shadowy longings; almost bloodless and bodiless, they drifted before her, floated off and vanished. Following these came more sharply defined memories and actions more clearly retained in her mind. . . .

Frau Hurvitz did not lament her destiny; on the contrary she was content. Could she have lived her life over again she would have taken the same path, the path she was now retracing in memory. . . . The first year after her marriage, when her husband had not been much in evidence. And then the children. . . . Her thoughts lingered with her eldest son, her child of sorrow, her darling. She remembered him as a nursling, when she was living in her father-in-law's house and was homesick because she did not care much for the new house into which she had been admitted; she liked neither her husband's parents nor their unfamiliar customs. She was regarded with suspicion because she could not adapt herself to their severe piety; locks of her hair would keep straggling out from beneath her marriage wig and hood, and she was always being caught in the breach of some observance or other. Her mother-in-law always had some fault to find with her and lectured her unceasingly. Her father-in-law grumbled at her beneath his breath. Even her husband had seemed a stranger. She had longed for escape, for her home, her village, the inn her parents kept, the country girls and country youths. Her only comfort was the infant she nursed at her bosom. . . . Then the whole course of her son's life unrolled itself; she saw him as a child playing, then as a school-boy in school uniform, with long trousers and a bulky satchel of text-books. What a trouble it had always been to find the money for his school-fees! What palpitations she had had over his examinations, wondering whether he would get "excellent" or not! She saw him shoot up: oh God! why did he grow so quickly? She did not want him to grow up; he should have remained a child, a little child, as when he lay at her breast. . . .

Her eyes longed to sate themselves with the sight of her son. Where was he now? Alone, pacing up and down a gloomy cell. Or he might have been already sent to Siberia! Alone, and no one beside him. Was he yearning for her as she for him? If only the door would open, if only he would come in! Not tall and grown-up, alien and belonging to an alien world, as he had been in his last phase, but once more a child as in those days when he got his first pair of shoes. . . . Rachel-Leah remembered those shoes; it had pained her to throw them away when they became too small, for they still kept the shape of his little feet. She remembered how she used to hold him naked in her arms and bathe his small smooth body, how she used to hold him to her and give him the breast. The joy and sorrow of motherhood shook her; she had no wish but to hold him in her arms again and lay his little face, his open, warm little mouth, on her bosom. . . .

She did not know that tears were running down her cheeks. Her heart ached; her soul was empty. She yearned for something, she did not herself know what. It was not her husband she missed; she had a timid respect for him and looked up to him as beyond her reach; she took him for granted and never yearned for him, since he was always present, always above her head like a roof. It was something else she yearned for, something she had lost and no longer possessed, something that would never return again.

There came a knock at the door. "They're home already," murmured Rachel-Leah, still absorbed in her dreams. Involuntarily she asked herself which of them it could be; her husband? David? Perhaps Helene?

The knock was repeated.

"In a minute, in a minute," called Rachel-Leah imploringly, as if she were begging not to be recalled to the waking world. Then she rose slowly and opened the door. A man stood there who was a complete stranger and yet curiously familiar. He seemed to be known to her, an old friend, and yet she could not remember who he was.

"Don't you remember me, Madame Hurvitz? I'm Mirkin," said the stranger shyly, twisting his cap of Persian lambskin.

"Mirkin? Mirkin?" said she to herself in bewilderment.

"Yes. I hope I'm not disturbing you? I'm on my way through Warsaw and took the liberty of calling on you. You were once so good as to invite me," said Mirkin, somewhat disconcerted by her lack of recognition.

"Mirkin? Mirkin?" murmured Frau Hurvitz again, as if in a dream. She was not surprised to see him standing there so unexpectedly, for she had the feeling that she was dreaming.

"Come in, come in. . . . Please sit down . . . here, beside me. I'm all alone in the house; they're all out."

She led him into the room and set him beside her at the table without remembering that she had only her dressing-gown on and that her damp hair was hanging loose. Mirkin was at a loss. He felt he had arrived at the wrong moment. The woman was acting so queerly: was she half-asleep? Her state struck him as uncanny: "Perhaps I'd better come at another time? I'm sure I'm disturbing you."

"No, no, not at all—I'm very glad you've come, very glad indeed. Will you have some tea with me?"

Still as if in a dream she went into the kitchen and poured tea for Mirkin into a coarse bowl such as she gave her children; then she brought the bowl into the sitting-room and set it on the table.

Mirkin did not know whether to accept it or not. "Now, tell me, how are you getting on? Where have you been all this while? It was high time you came . . ." she said, as if to herself, as if it were not a living man who sat there but a vision.

More and more disconcerted Mirkiri said timidly: "I'm on my way to the frontier, and so I took the liberty of looking you up."

"You're on your way to the frontier? But why need you go farther? One of them has gone already, and now the other is going, too. . . . Why must you go? Stay here with us. Why must you wander about all alone? It's a shame, and you such a child!"

With these words she stretched out her hand and began to stroke Mirkin's hair maternally, as if she were hypnotized.

Mirkin sat motionless and white as death. He did not know whether this scene was real or a dream. He saw clearly enough that the woman beside him did not know what she was doing and was acting as if under some spell; once she woke up she would be ashamed of her conduct. He wanted to get up quietly and slip from the room, but her words, the smile that shone through her tears, the caressing movements of her hands, so affected him that he, too, sank under the spell; he felt that he was dreaming, and his head dropped lower and lower. . . .

How long this trance lasted who can tell? Frau Hurvitz suddenly started up as if out of a dream: "Who's this?" She lifted the head that was resting on her bosom and gazed with bewilderment into Mirkin's eyes: "Mirkin? Oh, it's you, is it? The assistant to the Petersburg advocate! I didn't know you were here! Where on earth have I been? My God, what have I been doing? I must have been dreaming!" She smiled in embarrassment. "It was you who came in, then? But look at the state I'm in! Excuse me, I must go and dress myself at once; my husband and children will be here in a moment!"

She forced the blenching Mirkin, who had jumped up in alarm, into his chair again and fled into the adjoining bedroom.

Chaim Grade

Born in Vilna, Lithuania, in 1910, Chaim Grade emigrated in 1948 to the United States and settled in New York, where he lived until his death in 1982. He is the author of numerous award-winning works of both prose and poetry in Yiddish. Grade's gently realistic, shrewdly observed characterizations of both men and women are evident in such acclaimed works as *The Yeshiva*, *The Agunah*, and the collection of novellas, *Rabbis and Wives*. The characters whom he treats as "touchstones," admirably human, are men and women who blend sincere piety with generosity of spirit and a kind of innate balance; frequently, Grade's touchstone characters do not achieve material success in the pages of the novel, despite their appealing qualities.

In *My Mother's Sabbath Days*, Grade's mother is the touchstone of the memoir. An impoverished woman who lives with her family in a smoky, unhealthy room behind a printing shop, she sells withered fruit in the marketplace to provide for her family. Despite her difficult existence, however, she displays integrity and fairness and cares deeply about other human beings—sometimes to the point of slighting her own needs and the needs of her son. She is modest, but she has an underlying sense of self-esteem, which enables her to contradict men more educated than she. Her fine character traits, including convincingly portrayed dignity and generosity, evoke admiration in widely varying personality types, from a pious, rather rigid rabbi to his irreligious, Zionist son.

•

"Mother Vella and Her In-Laws"

(excerpt)

Amidst a clear and bustling Wednesday, our street suddenly grows as still as on a Sabbath afternoon, when the householders take a nap before returning to the synagogue. The shopkeepers stand in front of their stores and stare with amazement at the gate, where Vella the fruit-vendor is speaking to a tall Jew with a golden-blond beard who carries a large tallith-bag under his arm.

"The Rabbi is her future in-law—the father of her son's betrothed," explains Shaya the grain merchant to Ḥatzkel the grocer. "The Rabbi has come to look for his son, who ran away from the yeshiva to become a ḥalutz."

"What a misfortune! What a misfortune!" Ḥatzkel smacks his lips. "The Rabbi clearly has little joy of his children. His daughter has picked herself a husband who's fit to be a rabbi's son-in-law as I am to be governor of a province. And as if that weren't enough, his son has become a ḥalutz."

"That's surely no tragedy," says Shaya. "You really think any blessings-mumbler is better than a ḥalutz?"

"It's easy to see you're a Zionist," growls Ḥatzkel. "You sound just like all the Zionist small-fry around here—'a blessings-mumbler.' When the son of a rabbi joins up with those freethinkers the kibbutzniks, then there's real cause to weep and lament."

"Vilna isn't like your Warsaw, swarming and teeming with Hassidim with their little hats," the grain merchant warns the grocer. "In Vilna we detest the Agudah fanatics like pork. You hear, Reb Ḥatzkel?"

While the two shopkeepers carry on their quarrel in low voices, my mother is speaking with great deference to my future father-in-law:

"Let the Rabbi not be angry with me; it wasn't my doing. They met and became engaged. And when your daughter left for Warsaw because she wanted to get experience in a hospital there, my son followed."

The Rabbi does not look directly at the woman, but he listens attentively to what she is saying. His daughter has written him that she did not want to say anything about her fiance, since whatever she considered to be his virtues her father would regard as faults; but she went on to say that her fiance's mother was the finest woman she had ever met. Judging by her manner of speaking, the Rabbi thinks to himself, the mother does indeed seem to be a truly fine woman, and he answers with a smile:

"There's no need to justify yourself. As far as the mother is concerned, I have no objections at all to this match. My doubts concern your son: He might have asked me whether I'm willing to have him as a son-in-law. The excuse he might wish to offer, that my daughter herself didn't ask my permission, is no excuse at all. And if your son were really concerned about my family, he would have tried to persuade my boy to return home."

"How could my son have done that, when he himself has abandoned the study of Torah?" asks my mother.

'For these things I weep,' reflects the Rabbi. Whose example could the son of my old age follow—his older brothers'? So I thought to myself: My daughter will marry a Torah scholar who will bring her back to the right path, and perhaps he will even be able to influence his youngest brother-in-law. But instead my daughter has chosen "one who has fallen away." And perhaps, indeed, she chose him just because he is a former yeshiva student and she wants his help in tearing herself away from home, from Faith and Tradition.

Nonetheless, feeling that this pious woman at the gate has herself already suffered quite enough on her son's account, he does not wish to cause her further grief.

"You must be lonely since the young couple went away?" he asks with a furrowed brow, and sighs as though he were thinking of his own wife, one at home.

"A little lonely," admits my mother. "But when your son comes for the Sabbath, then I'm happy. He says the Kiddush for me."

"My son says the Kiddush for you?" The Rabbi is astonished. "When I went to see him in his kibbutz, he said nothing about that. So then, he hasn't yet become a complete unbeliever. Perhaps the Almighty may yet help me persuade him to return to his studies." He confides in the fruit-vendor as he would in his wife. "Well, I'll go back to the inn now to have breakfast. And while I'm here in Vilna, I must pay my respects to the city's rabbis and also buy a book or two."

The future father-in-law is silent a moment, shifts his tallith-bag to his left arm, and, with his right hand, strokes his golden beard. In a tone of thoughtful deliberation he says: "You say my son comes to you every Friday evening?"

"He stays with me for the entire Sabbath and sleeps in my son's bed."

"It would be better," the Rabbi murmurs, "if I could speak with him privately and not in the kibbutz, where it's so hard for him to tear himself away from his friends," Raising his heavy eyebrows, he looks directly at the fruit-seller. "How would it be, in-law, if I were to come to you this Friday evening?"

"If the Rabbi trusts in my kashruth," replies Mother, disconcerted by his addressing her as "in-law," "it would be an honor I would never have thought myself worthy of receiving from the Almighty."

"Would God I could trust my children's kashruth as much as I can trust yours," says the Rabbi with a smile.

"Regarding your children's piety I cannot speak," replies my mother, plucking up courage. "But as for their goodness and decency, I can vouch for your son and your daughter more than for myself."

"And can you vouch for your son's character as well?" he asks sternly, as though examining a witness in his rabbinical court.

"Concerning my son—let others speak," says my mother, bowing her head.

My daughter is fortunate in her choice of a mother-in-law, reflects the Rabbi as he walks off. God grant she be equally fortunate in her choice of a husband.

Not even for Passover has my mother ever prepared more carefully than for this Sabbath. How it would actually turn out, however, she could never have imagined.

The Rabbi has already been seated at the table for an hour, but his son has yet to arrive. Mother has remembered just in time that a pious Jew must not remain alone in the same room with a woman, especially at night, so she has opened wide the door to the second room and also left open the door to the courtyard. She herself has remained in the front room, the dimly lit workshop, from which she continually peers into the inner room at the Rabbi, sitting in silence. At last he calls to her:

"In-law, please forgive me for spoiling your Sabbath. I'm waiting for my son. He's already established his title to reciting the Kiddush for you—" the Rabbi smiles bitterly—"but it seems he won't be coming tonight."

"I'm really surprised." Mother approaches the doorway to the inner room. "He always comes for the Sabbath. I told the Rabbi the absolute truth."

"Of course, of course," he mumbles, somewhat impatiently. "I've been to see him once more at the kibbutz. Again I tried to argue with him and his only answer was: 'No, I don't want to go back.' Then, when I told him I'd be having dinner here tonight, he said nothing. At the time I didn't realize that that meant he wouldn't come. Now I begin to understand: he doesn't want to listen to any more pleading. Nu, we must go ahead and wash for the meal."

Mother brings in a pitcher of water, a bowl and a towel, and then returns to the dark smithy. "She is a saintly woman," thinks the Rabbi. "She doesn't want to stay in the same room with me because of the prohibition against 'seclusion.' She's overworked and worn out, pour soul yet she won't sit down to eat with me. But if I should leave, she'd be even more upset. She has prepared everything for me and my son." He rises and, in a quavering voice, chants the Kiddush:

"On the sixth day . . ."

Mother stands on the threshold, her gaze fixed reverently on the Rabbi: The Divine Presence rests upon him; the holiness of the Torah shines from his countenance. Lord of the Universe, how had she ever become worthy of hearing such a great scholar recite the Kiddush in the smithy that was her home? Nonetheless, her joy is incomplete. For herself, nothing would be too hard to do for the Rabbi, yet his own son has refused to give him even the joy and satisfaction of joining him for dinner. The young man is a quiet, gentle soul such as one hardly ever finds among young people today, and still he is causing his father grief. It would seem, then, that this entire rabbinical family is, in its quiet way stubborn.

Throughout the meal the Rabbi chews on a single mouthful and stares at the bookcase that faces him. He takes out a book, leafs through it, puts it down, and draws out a second one. In this way, a pile of books with worn leather bindings grows steadily beside him. Suddenly remembering that the mistress of the house has gone to great pains to prepare the meal for him, he tastes one dish, then another, but then pushes the plates away. He grows more and more uneasy and agitated, and angry at himself for desecrating the sanctity of the Sabbath with his unhappiness; he begins to drum on the table with his fingers, to bite his lips, to look all about with flashing eyes, as though he were sitting at his own table at home and resting his severely disapproving gaze on his rebellious children.

"At the very moment I told my son I would be here, he made up his mind not to come." His face turned crimson with wrath. "Whose books are these?"

"My husband's, peace be upon him."

"And has your son ever looked into them?"

"When he was younger, he used to study them at night. But now—"

"Now he reads modern novels." Seething with anger, the Rabbi finishes the sentence. "It's no wonder, then. When one starts with books like these, one ends with forbidden books."

"Are these, then, bad books?" asks my mother, astonished and hurt—her late husband, peace be upon him, had treasured them all his life as the apple of his eye.

"They are not bad books," replies the Rabbi, somewhat more calmly. "They are works of speculation, of philosophy. A mature person, one past forty, may look into them, provided he has already studied a great deal of Torah and is an upright Jew. In that case they will do no harm. That is to say, even then they may cause one to stray from the right path, but the danger is not as great. But when a mere youngster tries to ascend to the heavens on them, he will fall as one falls from a crooked staircase, into the deepest abyss. The atheists of our time think they are wiser, not only than pious Jews, but even than the enlightened thinkers of the past. And today's youth have already divested themselves of every trace of faith and Tradition."

"May the Rabbi forgive me, but my husband used to study these same books even when he was old. He never exchanged them for new ones."

"That's just it," the father-in-law-to-be shouts angrily. "Because your husband was already old and sick, he wasn't able to run as far and as fast as your son!" But then he quickly catches himself. "How can one compare the generations of old to those of today? In any case, what right do I have to complain about your son? Is my son any better? . . . Well," he concludes wearily, his voice drained of life, "it's time to say the Grace After Meals."

Mother does not dare point out that he hasn't eaten anything. She brings in to him the "last water," preliminary to saying Grace. The Rabbi moistens his fingers, strokes his forehead with his wet hand as though trying to calm his turbulent thoughts, closes his eyes, and begins to sway to and fro. He recites Grace very rapidly, virtually swallowing the words; my mother—still standing on the other side of the threshold, and listening for the end of the initial blessing so she might respond "Amen"—strives in vain to hear the concluding words. Suddenly the Rabbi stops dead and, as if lost in thought, begins to stammer, repeats a particular verse with intense concentration, and then starts to sway again, even more fervently. He is seeking to banish the thoughts that have become entangled with the verses of his prayer, but they give him no peace.

"The Merciful One, He shall rule over us forever and ever . . ." And what of Your promise, Master of Creation, that whenever three successive generations of a family devote themselves to the study of Torah, the Torah shall cleave to that family forever and ever? Were not my ancestors truly righteous men and great rabbis? Yet, the question is not really a question. The words of our Sages are holy. For, when a guest returns to his customary inn but is refused admittance, he departs and seeks lodgings elsewhere. The Torah came to my sons, but they would not admit her into their hearts. . . .

"The Merciful One, He shall be blessed in the heavens and on earth . . ." My only daughter did not want to marry a scholar from the Mir Yeshiva and has chosen, instead, a writer of heresy and ungodliness. Now she's in Warsaw with him, and my relatives there shrug their shoulders; they read the newspapers, but they say they've never heard of him. Only she believes that one day he will attain fame, in the realm of impurity. Neither Torah nor fame—wherein then is he worthier in her eyes than a young man from the Yeshiva of Lomza or of Mir? Who knows whether he's not God forbid, one of those whose head never bears tefillin? Perhaps I made a mistake when I didn't go to see him and exact a promise that he would at least observe the Sabbath and pray with tefillin.

"The Merciful One! He shall be praised through all generations . . ." As for my three older sons, no use even thinking about them. One has gone across the ocean, the second across the Mediterranean to the Land of Israel, and the third, still in Warsaw, is also going to the Holy Land. The only one who remained with me was the youngest, and I nurtured him as the apple of my eye. He is the quietest, the finest of all my children—my "child of delights." " 'He shall be our comfort,' " I said to myself. But now the spirit of folly has entered into him as well—he has become a ḥalutz. Oh Master Of All Creation, this is not the halutz of whom it is written: "and let the ḥalutz pass on before the Ark of the Lord. . . ." The halutzim of today, in their free-thinking settlements in the Holy Land, do not observe the Sabbath, they eat food that is not kosher, and their young people care nothing at all for the laws of family purity. And it is these whom my youngest son has made his comrades! He even turns to me and says: "I'm surprised, father, that you should be against the resettling of the Land of Israel. That is, after all, one of the greatest of the commandments of the Torah." He, the righteous one, wants to speed the coming of the Messiah, and of all the six hundred and thirteen precepts of the Law, he accepts only this one—to dwell in the Land of Israel.

"The Merciful One! He shall lead us with dignity to our land." One of my sons is already there, the second one, from Warsaw, is preparing to go, and now the child of my old age is setting out on the same journey. What, then, am I doing here? For whose sake am I maintaining my rabbinate—for my future son-in-law? And how long must I continue to deal with my congregants, exhorting them to be pious, bearing the moral responsibility for them? In the World-to-Come I shall be held to account not only for my own children but for my town, for the entire community. But how can I be a guardian for others when I have been unable to safeguard my own house? And how long shall I continue to make of the Torah "a spade wherewith to dig," to live off my piety? My wife cannot bear having to earn our livelihood from her sale of yeast and my fees for supervising the slaughterers. She dreams of living an independent life in the Holy Land and raising poultry. Perhaps if my children hadn't witnessed how a rabbi is obliged to live off the community, they would not have fled my house. And perhaps, if I live there too, my sons will not cut themselves off entirely from tradition—they will not want to grieve their father. And my youngest won't be able to throw it up to me that he fulfills the commandment of "dwelling in the Land of Israel," while I do not. Immediately after the Sabbath I shall, with God's help, go back home and begin selling off our belongings. I shall go to the Land of Israel and fulfill all those precepts that pertain directly to our Holy Land . . . "The Merciful One! He shall grant us a day which is wholly Sabbath, wholly a day of rest, for life eternal . . ."

A few days later, the Rabbi stood once again at the gate, his tallith-bag under his arm, and spoke to the fruit-vendor:

"I have decided to leave my pulpit and go to the Holy Land. My rebbetzin has long wanted to give up being a rebbetzin, but I always thought, 'The children . . .' Now Heaven has given me a sign that I have reasoned falsely. May it be the Almighty's will, blessed be He, that with His help—." His voice was choked, and he drew his bushy eyebrows together so that no tears would fall on his golden beard. "May it be His will that my daughter walk in her mother's way, and that your son will turn to his mother's way. I beg you, in-law, keep an eye on my youngest. I see that he is attached to you. And just because you are not a rebbetzin, but simply a hard-working woman who is yet meticulously faithful and devout, just for that reason you may be able to influence him more than I have, with all my illustrious ancestry and all the sacred learning to which I have devoted my life, without hope of reward, as the Creator of the Universe knows."

Had my mother not been standing at the gate, she would have wept aloud; but she did not wish the neighbors to come running. Trembling, she asks:

"Will the Rabbi, then, not wait for his daughter's wedding?"

"My daughter's wedding?" The Rabbi furrows his brow, as though he has totally forgotten this matter. "She never asked me whether I wanted this match, so why would she need me at the wedding? No, I shall not postpone my departure for the Land of Israel for that, and my wife, may she live and be well, will agree with me."

The bride's father coughs hard, as though he were trying to change his voice. Angry red patches appear on his cheeks, and in the stern tones of a presiding judge he cries out:

"Write to your son that you order him, by virtue of the honor and respect he owes you as his mother—and I shall write the same to my daughter—to get married at once. It is already more than a year since their betrothal."

With a silent nod of the head, he walks quickly away. He dares not stay longer, even to say good-bye, lest his anger overwhelm him and he bring still more sorrow to this poor downtrodden woman. Tall and erect of bearing, the large tallith-bag under his arm, the Rabbi strides down the street without noticing the unknown shopkeepers who stand at the entrances of their stores and gaze deferentially after him.

Mother remains standing at the gate, her head bowed low; she does not even feel the tears that are quietly streaming down her face. With a start she comes to herself, and begins to run after the Rabbi. She wants to ask him to give his rebbetzin a message: to plead with her not to resent the fact that she, the rebbetzin, would not be present at her own daughter's wedding, while she, the fruit-seller, would be there at her son's wedding.

But then Mother realizes how foolish it would be to run after him with such a message. And even if she were to ask the rebbetzin's forgiveness, would that ease her pain?

She feels a pang in her heart. A thought begins to take shape in her mind, a thought that frightens her. She bends over her baskets, rearranges her merchandise, calls out to customers; but the thought grows steadily stronger. She turns to the wall and talks to herself:

"That would really be best: let them get married in Warsaw. The girl has many relatives there, and I will give my son my blessing from a distance. Here the whole town would be talking: 'The bride's parents left for the Land of Israel before the wedding. That just goes to show how little this match was to their liking.' And how will I feel when the bride, standing under the canopy, looks at me with eyes filled with tears: her parents aren't there on her day of joy—only I, the mother of the groom. It's possible that my son would not agree to it; he knows, after all, that I've been waiting all my life for his wedding. At the slightest excuse I've always said, over and over, 'May I live to see you under the wedding canopy.' 'And now, Mother,' he'll probably write, 'you're not going to be there?' Then I'll answer him: 'Foolish boy. True, the Almighty heard my prayers and I've lived to your wedding day. But where could I possibly put up guests? What sort of festive meal could I offer? What sort of table could I set for the poor? What musicians could I hire? And on the other hand, the trip to Warsaw would be too difficult for me. Trains always make me dizzy. And what kind of impression will I make on my Warsaw in-laws, when I can't even understand the way Polish Jews speak?' . . . It's just my good luck—" Mother laughs to herself as the tears stream from her eyes—"it's just my good luck that the Rebbetzin is going away. How would a simple woman like me even talk to such an in-law?". . . .

"Mother Vella."

That is what Moshele, the Rabbi's son, calls her.

"Moshele, don't call me 'Mother,'" she pleads with him. "You have a mother, may she live to a hundred and twenty. Your mother in the Land of Israel will be upset if she hears about it."

He listens with a smile in his soft, dreamy eyes behind their large glasses, and continues to call her "Mother Vella."

Since the departure of his father the Rabbi, Moshele has resumed his weekly Sabbath visits to her smithy. Of the Friday evening when his father had waited for him and he had not come, he never says a word, and so Mother never speaks of it, either.

And what, indeed, is there to ask about? She sees clearly that the Rabbi and his son are as alike as two drops of water. Both are stiff-necked and stubborn. Because his daughter had chosen a mate without asking his consent, the father refused to meet his future son-in-law; Moshele, having made up his mind to become a ḥalutz, had stayed away that Friday evening to avoid a lecture from his father. The same personality the same build, the same expression. The father is a tall man with a golden beard, and Moshele, may no evil eye fall upon him, is a tree in a forest. His delicate young face sprouts a silky, dark-blond beard; he looks like one of those young Russians of a bygone day who wore peasant shirts, let their hair grow long, and ate no meat.

Moshele arrives before sunset on Fridays and helps her take in her baskets. On the day before the Sabbath, she always sets out a great deal of merchandise, so that when candle-lighting time approaches, she has to make at least ten trips back and forth to put everything away. For some years her Chaimka had helped her, but when he left for Warsaw with his betrothed, she had thought to herself, Well, I'll just have to drag it all in alone, just as she had done when he was still studying at the yeshiva. But she had been younger and stronger then. So now the Almighty has sent her a Moshele. Normally he walks with the slow, measured steps of his father the Rabbi, but when he is carrying the baskets, he races like a storm-wind. He tries to move all the remaining baskets from the gate to the house before she has managed to carry in the first two.

Since he became a truck gardener in Soltaniszki, he has been coming to see her on Thursday evening, right after he finishes work. And on Friday morning, when she returns from the wholesale market, she finds her baskets at the gate, her scale hung in place, and Moshele already selling her wares to the housewives.

The first time this happened she could not believe her eyes. She stood speechless for several minutes, watching the Rabbi's son act the vendor. Only now did she understand why, the evening before, he had been asking about the prices she charged for her fruits and vegetables. At the time she had thought he was simply curious—after all, he himself was a truck gardener; now it was clear that he had carefully planned this out in advance.

"Moshele," she said, "what are you doing? Your parents will be very angry with me when they hear about this."

"On the contrary, they'll be pleased," he answered in his calm and deliberate manner. "Since I'm going to the Land of Israel to live on a kibbutz, it's important for me to know how to sell produce."

"But is this proper for you, a rabbi's son? Even my son never did it while he was a yeshiva student."

"But now your son would be doing it. Or he would go to the market, with you, while I would be selling. It wouldn't do to make him the seller—he's too much of a hothead," said Moshele with a smile.

She had to laugh: though her son was older, Moshele was by far the steadier of the two. Which was why, she realized, no matter how hard she tried she could never dissuade him from his intention of becoming her assistant.

As a vendor he presents a curious spectacle. The women all stand gaping around him, unable to make sense of it all. The nobility and goodness shining in his face attest clearly to his fine breeding, to a family background of the highest distinction; and yet, quite puzzlingly at odds with this impression are the simple attire and sun-tanned features that bespeak a life of outdoor labor in the fields. And so the women stand about with open mouths, their gaze fixed more on him than on what they are buying. To any customer who decides to haggle, objecting perhaps that "The vegetables should be cheaper now that it's summer," he answers, quite calmly: "That can't be. I work for a truck farmer, and I know that vegetables haven't gone down in price."

Mother asks him whom he works for, since she knows all the farmers. But when he tells her his employer's name, she is dismayed. It is someone she has known for years, a man far removed from any gentleness or refinement, and, indeed, as hard as steel—no one has ever been able to bargain so much as a groschen off his price.

Moshele, she knows, keeps things to himself; he will tell her nothing of his life on the farm. She too, therefore, remains silent—as he has made his plans, so she also now has a plan.

The following Monday morning she seeks out the farmer from Soltaniszki at the wholesale market. She finds him standing atop a large wagon laden with open sacks of potatoes, red tomatoes, yellow carrots, young red radishes grown in hothouses, larger white radishes, heads of cabbage, and cauliflower, squash, and other vegetables. He is besieged by fruit-and-vegetable women trying to bargain with him, but, hard and obdurate as ever, he refuses to yield an inch, and at last the women go off in search of more tender-hearted dealers. She, however, does not haggle with him this time; she makes her purchases, sends them off to her gate with a woman-porter, and lingers around the marketplace until the Soltaniszki gardener has sold all his produce. Then she returns and questions him about his worker, Moshele.

He, however, knows nothing of any Moshele. He has, he says, got lots of goyim working for him, both men and girls, and also some Jewish roughnecks and girls; pushing his cap to one side, he moves to start up his already fed horses.

She entreats him to wait just a moment more. She tells him that Moshele is the youngest brother of her son's fiance, that he comes from a small town and is preparing to go to the Land of Israel.

"Oh, the ḥalutz!" says the farmer, as he seats himself on the coach-box; and he begins to laugh so hard he seems ready to burst.

She interprets this as meaning that Moshele is a poor worker, and pleads with the farmer to take pity on the boy: he is a rabbi's son, and not used to such hard physical labor.

"Not at all, he's a very good worker," says the farmer; if not, he wouldn't have kept him on—he has no use for freeloaders. The fact that the fellow is a rabbi's son isn't worth an onion to him, and he doesn't care either where he's planning to go—to the Arabs in Palestine, or the black Africans, or the "little red Jews" over the border. He's laughing about something else entirely.

And the truck farmer proceeds to tell Mother a tale that makes the day go dark before her eyes.

The crew that works for him are all young, and the hot blood seethes in their veins. Any free moment they get, the goyim take a roll in the tall grass with the sweating shiksas, in the fields, in the forests round about, between the hothouses, or wherever they find a likely spot. There's a saying for it: "Where even swine won't bed down, Love will." And the Jewish louts and their girls don't lag behind the goyim. But this ḥalutz, with his short little beard, never hangs around with the rest. When the sweaty shiksas caught sight of him, handsome lad that he is, they tried to get something going with him. And the Jewish girls didn't keep their distance either. But he escaped from them to where the pepper grows, and that just made them all the crazier about him.

The farmer claps himself resoundingly on the brow:

"You say he's a rabbi's son? That's right—the peasant girls do call him the Rabbi."

Mother wrings her hands: she was used to hearing such stories bandied about concerning ordinary young fellows—but that they should dare to pester Moshele, a rabbi's son?

"Woman, the whole world doesn't spend its time in fasting and prayer!" The truck farmer laughs in her lace.

"But you, you yourself are a decent man, after all," says Mother. "You have grown children of your own. See to it that the others don't torment the Rabbi's son so. Try to imagine that it's not I, the fruit-peddler, who plead for him, but his father the Rabbi himself."

"Don't upset yourself so, woman," says the gardener. "The ḥalutz can hold the fort quite well by himself. Bit by bit the whole crew has learned to respect him, and now nobody starts up with him. I'll tell you more: when he walks by, the shiksas stop giggling and move away from their fellows, just as if one of their own priests were passing by. Woman, Soltaniszki has been turned into a synagogue!"

The farmer slaps his forehead again:

"But I really am a pig! When the ḥalutz first came to me, we agreed that, until he knew his work, he wouldn't get a kopeck in wages—only his food and a place to sleep. Now he knows the work better than any ten of the peasants, but he's never said a word about the money. This week I'll pay him his full wages. That's the way I am: If I say I'll take something, I'll take it. But if I say I'll give, then I—just say it." Laughing, he cracks his whip and drives on.

Master of the Universe, what kind of person is he, this Moshele? my mother reflects on her way back from the market. To stay at home in his parents' house—that he doesn't want. To study in a yeshiva—also not. But to be a field hand for a truck farmer—that he wants. Go argue with him, he's got a will of iron! He's been visiting me every Sabbath, yet I've never had the slightest idea of the humiliations he's been suffering in Soltaniszki all week long.

The following Thursday night, when Moshele appears as usual, she scrutinizes him intensely . . . nothing. He is as calm and serene as ever, like a senior yeshiva student come home for a holiday or festival. His expression offers no clue as to whether the farmer has told him of his meeting with her. Well then, she thinks, I'll keep quiet too.

He brings her merchandise into the house, joins her at dinner, begins to leaf through a book, and then, still immersed in reading, says to her as though speaking of the most ordinary, routine matter:

"Mother Vella, today I got my wages. Here, take this toward your Sabbath expenses." And with that he hands her a roll of bills, wound into a tight ball so as to appear smaller than it actually is.

"Don't be angry, Moshele, but you're acting like a child. How can I take money from you? Aren't your sister and my son engaged to be married? Do you still think of me as a stranger?"

"Very well, then"—he takes back the money—"I just won't come to you for the Sabbath any more."

This really frightens her. Moshele, she knows, is not one to make empty threats; what he says, he means. If even his father the Rabbi couldn't make him change his mind, she certainly won't be able to. Hastily she says;

"All right, Moshele, I'll take two zlotys from you, but keep the rest for yourself. No one should be without money—especially not a young man."

After midnight, when Moshele is already asleep, she is still in the kitchen preparing for the Sabbath. "A son!" she thinks. She had had no labor pains at his birth, nor had she suffered the travails of rearing him—and yet the Almighty has sent her a son. Since her own son went off to Warsaw, his bed has been occupied by a diamond, a heart of light, a golden head. Her only fear is that her great joy might be accounted a sin. Far away in the Land of Israel, his real mother is pining away with longing for her youngest child, while she, a stranger, has been vouchsafed so much joy.

She picks up the kitchen lamp, passes through the workshop, and walks into the back room. She has come to fetch something, but cannot remember what . . . no, she doesn't really need anything—she has come only to take a look at Moshele asleep.

He lies stretched out on his back, his strong arms under his head. His fresh, full lips are partly open and he is breathing quietly. His thick and curly hair merges into the hair of his silky beard, and his tanned neck seems made of bronze. No wonder the girls like him, she thinks, and sighs deeply. Her own son tosses about in his sleep, awakens ten times a night at the merest rustle, and rises in the morning exhausted.

Perhaps because of her deep sigh, or because she has not adequately shaded the light of the lamp with her hand and it has flashed into his face, Moshele opens his eyes—so quietly one might suspect he has all the while only been pretending to be asleep. He looks at her and smiles:

"Mother Vella."

"We have a great-grandchild whose name is Moshele, too," she says, overcome by confusion. "My husband's oldest son's name was Moïsey. Sad to say, he died while my husband was still alive. When Moïsey's son, Aronchik, grew up, he married and his son was given the name Moshele. Aronchik himself doesn't give us much joy, he's a Bolshevik, but his little boy is a splendid child. All Mosheles are just splendid," she says with a quiet, bashful laugh, and leaves the room.

"I've really become senile," she murmurs to herself. She cannot forgive herself for having disturbed Moshele's sleep. . . .

The farmer from Soltaniszki, in the heat of a vigorous dispute with a group of women, shouted across the length and breadth of the market square:

"Go to the ḥalutz—the brother of Vella's son's fiance—and he'll tell you I've paid him every groschen that was due him, just as much as I pay the louts who work for me every season. The ḥalutz won't tell you any lies—he's a rabbi's son, and he chased away all the shiksas who were after him. I don't lay claim to anything that belongs to others, but I don't want other people claiming what is mine."

Temporarily, the peddler women left off cursing "the swine" who wouldn't lower his prices by so much as a groschen, in order to question him about the rabbi's son and the shiksas. Laden with this news as with heavy baskets of merchandise, they spread and trumpeted it about among the neighborhood shopkeepers.

"What did I tell you?" cried Ḥatzkel the grocer, resuming his argument with Shaya the grain merchant. "Aren't they real Jeroboams? The ḥalutzim, I mean. To take a rabbi's son, talk him into leaving home, and ship him off, as if to Siberia, to Soltaniszki outside of Vilna, where he has to dig the earth with his nose and cope with shiksas."

"That's true," agrees the grain merchant. "If the ḥalutz runs away from the shiksas, he'll surely run away from the Arabs."

"That's what I've been saying all along," exclaims the grocer triumphantly. "Who is it they're sending off to drain the swamps, who? Who is it they're sending to break up rocks, who? A rabbi's son?"

"Then who will do it, Reb Ḥatzkel? Will you? Will I?"

"Whoever wants to! But not the children of good families. It's a fine state of affairs when the sons and daughters of rabbis, of wealthy families, live twenty to a room in the kibbutz in the charity houses, and roam about the city looking for work in a tannery or a sawmill. Just the other day a couple of youngsters came into my shop, one with a saw and the other an ax over his shoulder, to ask whether I might want a cord of wood sawed and chopped. The kibbutzniks want to become 'hewers of wood and drawers of water,' like the Gibeonites."

I've got better things to do than stand here jabbering away with this simpleton, thinks the grain-dealer to himself. It's all well and good for Ḥatzkel, he's already declared bankruptcy several times, so he's got something put away for a rainy day. But I don't even have anyone to declare bankruptcy against.

The grain merchant sighs, and dashes off in quest of a little business.

. . . . It is Friday afternoon and Mother is at her stand, surrounded by customers. She speaks with restraint to even the stubbornest hagglers among them, because Moshele is standing at the gate and about him, as always, is an air of serenity and peace, like the radiance of the Sabbath candles. Mother's face already mirrors her joy at the prospect of spending the entire Sabbath day together with Moshele.

Suddenly a large open wagon, loaded with cartons, appears. Seated on the coach-box is a young giant, who drives the big brown horse directly into the narrow gateway.

"Wait!" shouts my mother as she hastily begins to dismantle her stand. But the teamster does not wait, and urges the horse forward. One wagon-wheel catches onto the stand, dragging it along and causing two baskets full of fruit to tumble off and spill their contents. With an anguished cry

Mother throws herself under the wagon to pick up her wares. She struggles to pull free the braided baskets now entangled in the wheels. The driver hears her wail and comes to a halt. Moshele, who has also rushed forward to help take the stand apart, now abandons it to pull Mother out from under the wagon.

"It's borrowed goods, it's the wholesaler's money!" she moans, perspiring and disheveled, and feels in her apron for the few apples she has managed to pick up from the cobblestones; but they are crushed, and disintegrate in her hands like gruel, "My blood, my labor, my Sabbath!" she cries out, clapping her hands to her head in despair and letting her rescued goods fall back onto the street.

The teamster climbs down from his seat, grasps the horse's bridle, and starts to pull the wagon into the courtyard.

"Murderer!" Mother throws herself upon him with clenched fists. "Don't move the wagon, let me take my goods away first!"

The tall, broad-shouldered youth looks down at the tiny slip of a woman with green eyes burning with rage and yellowish foam on her lips threatening him with tightly clenched fists—and he bursts into raucous laughter:

"Oi, I'm done for now." His laughter doubles him up, as though he has been seized by a stomach cramp. "Look who's attacking me!" From his open mouth loud guffaws roll out like claps of thunder, as he turns back to the horse. "You really think I'll waste half a day, and on Friday to boot, waiting for you to take your garbage away?"

But because of the baskets entangled in the wheels, and the narrowness of the gate, the horse cannot move. The overloaded wagon begins to shake and a full, square box falls off, striking Mother on the shoulder.

Mother utters a single scream; then, numb with pain, falls silent. She seems about to collapse, but Moshele catches her and she hangs limply in his arms.

"Vella, Mother Vella, what is it?" he cries out.

"My shoulder," she groans feebly, unable to utter another word.

"She needs cold compresses," calls out Lisa, widow of Alterka the goose-dealer, who has run out from her shop.

Lisa and Moshele take hold of Mother under the arms and lift her. The pain from the sudden twist in her shoulder revives her:

"Don't carry me, I'll walk by myself Moshele, you stay here with the merchandise, it isn't paid for yet."

Barely able to walk, she is led away by Lisa. There is a buzzing in her brain, an echoing sound in her ears, a dizziness before her eyes.

In the meantime a crowd has gathered at the gate. A shopkeeper takes courage and begins to berate the wagoner:

"You have the heart of a Cossack. Other drivers wait until the woman has had a chance to take away her stand, but you drove straight at her. You nearly killed her. It was just lucky it was only a cardboard box."

"Let her not stand in the gate when she sees that someone is driving in," shouts the teamster. "And as for you, get out of the way, unless you want me to twist your shoulder. I'll do a better job of it than the cardboard box. Giddy-up!"

"You were told to wait, so wait until I've taken away all the baskets!" Moshele rushes at the driver, who is again pulling the horse by its bridle.

By now the driver is exasperated; everyone is telling him what to do. Enraged, he looks up to see before him a pious young bookworm with spectacles and a beard.

The ḥalutz, tall and slender, looks like a deer whose back this wild ox of a teamster could break with one blow: so the neighbors are thinking as they stand watching with bated breath, afraid to interfere.

The wagon driver senses the fear he is arousing in the onlookers. Leisurely he turns to the young man who is facing him, pale and tense but composed.

"Hey, you there—are you going to hit me?"

He reaches out, grabs Moshele's cap by the brim, and pulls it down over his entire face to the chin.

Moshele pushes the cap back up on his head, slowly takes off his glasses, and furrows his brow exactly like his father the Rabbi when he is deciding which book to consult for the correct solution to some difficult ritual problem. But suddenly he jumps up and pulls the pole from which the scale is suspended out of the ring that holds it.

"Oho!" The wagoner moves further inside the gate and positions himself close to the wall. "Look at the tough guy! He's got an iron pipe and I've only got my bare hands."

Moshele glares at him darkly and throws away the pole. At almost the same instant he grabs the fellow by his bearlike paws and with his bent head smashes into the wagoner's jaw, like a soccer player leaping into the air to bounce the ball off his skull. The wagoner's teeth are knocked together; he lets out a howl and, leaning back against the wall for support, lifts one knee and rams it into Moshele's stomach. Moshele doubles over, releasing the driver's hands. The driver seizes him by his full, curly hair and pushes his head down, down, like a butcher twisting a steer's head by the horns until the animal falls to the ground with a roar of pain.

Moshele, his lips clenched tight, utters no sound. He cannot free his head, and his neck is strained to the bursting point. Now from below he jabs his fists, like hammers of iron, up into the teamster's bloated face. Then, getting a grip on his beefy neck, he slams the driver's head against the wall, again and again. Only now does the driver let go of Moshele's hair; grunting like a wild boar, he kicks out at his opponent. A leg outstretched like a heavy log sends Moshele sprawling, but he pulls the burly driver down with him as he falls, and the two of them go rolling together over the paving stones.

The bystanders, who have been watching in silence since the fight began, break all at once into passionate yelling and screaming. They rejoice to see the loutish teamster getting his comeuppance. Still afraid to become directly involved themselves, they encourage the Rabbi's son with shouts and cheers:

"Give him a good thrashing!"

"Give him what David gave Goliath. Let him know that God still rules the world."

"Give it to him like a ḥalutz, like a true ḥalutz!"

"Beat him with the strength of the Torah, with the power of your father the Rabbi!"

"Moshele!"

A scream rends the heavens. My mother, inside the house, has heard the uproar and her heart has not misled her. With her last ounce of strength she runs across the courtyard, closely followed by Lisa.

Moshele, as though he was the only one to hear my mother's cry amid all the noise and commotion, jumps nimbly up from the pavement and seizes the iron he has just thrown away. Mother, seeing his swollen face, throws herself upon him and embraces him.

"Moshele, take pity upon your dear parents," she pleads with him, trembling and drawing him close to herself. "Look, my child, calm yourself—" It is as if, in her distraction, she were addressing her own son. "Come inside the house. Never mind about the merchandise and the money. God has punished me for making such a fuss about my spilled apples. It's nearly time to light the Sabbath candles. Moshele . . ."

He is silent. One of his arms enfolds my mother, the other holds the metal pole. His watchful, suspicious gaze closely follows the movements of the driver, now rising slowly and clumsily from the cobbled pavement. Suddenly Mother turns to face the bully, keeping Moshele protectively behind her.

"You don't have God in your heart," she wails. "May you have the kind of Sabbath that I will have because of you."

The shopkeepers surround Moshele and Mother to shield them, and now begin to berate the teamster without fear:

"You boor, don't you dare raise your hand against a rabbi's son. His father will put a curse on you!"

"I'll call the police. There's still justice in this world."

"You'll drop dead before you get another load from us. We'd rather give our business to a goy than a murderer like you."

But the driver has no intention of resuming the fight. He wipes his big face and looks with astonishment at his palms, which are also smeared with blood. Who has given him such a beating—was it really that pious bookworm with the eyeglasses and the beard? He vents his wrath upon the horse, which has all this time been standing in the gate with ears pointed, as though savoring the spectacle of his master, who whipped him regularly, being trounced. The wagoner strikes the animal across the muzzle:

"Carrion, what are you blinking your goggle-eyes for? Giddy-up you bag of bones, may you drop dead!"

Moshele takes my mother home, and the neighbors bring in what is left of her merchandise. They find the ḥalutz standing in the smithy with sleeves rolled up, soaking pieces of cloth in a pot filled with water. He wrings them out with his strong hands and hands them to Lisa. Lisa places the cloths on Mother's shoulder, which is shivering with successive waves of heat and cold.

The neighbors now gather in a circle in the courtyard to talk. So astonished are they by what has just taken place that they even forget to bemoan my mother's suffering.

"That wagoner must have been drunk, or he would never have let a youngster beat him to a pulp. . . ."

"He's no youngster, that one, he's a regular tough nut. He gave it to the driver with his head coming up from below, like a real underworld thug."

"No, a thug leaves no marks when he beats someone, but he squashed the wagoner's nose."

"A Napoleon!" exclaims Ḥatzkel the grocer.

"Well, what do you say now?" the grain merchant taunts the grocer. "This was a sign to you from the heavens, Reb Ḥatzkel: Don't talk like Ḥassidim from Warsaw, with their little hats. And don't talk like the Lubavitcher Ḥassidim in Oppatov's Synagogue. The Messiah is indeed the Messiah, but until he comes, you have to know how to fight back."

"That a rabbi's son should have such strength and courage," marvels Ḥatzkel. "That's fine, very fine."

"And you were moaning and groaning over him!" scoffs the grain merchant. "He may have run away from the shiksas, but as for the Arabs, that's different! They'll be running away from him. It's his kind we need in the Land of Israel—just his kind." . . .

Thursday evening. Mother is standing in the kitchen and rushing to finish preparing the Sabbath meals before Moshele arrives.

Two Thursday nights earlier, Moshele had placed the lamp upon the workbench, directly facing the open door of the kitchen, rested his elbows on the screw-vise, and begun to read a book.

She had been puzzled: Moshele always sat in the other room with his head buried in a book, ruining his shining eyes with constant reading, just as his father did studying the holy books; but why, tonight, has he gone into the workshop and started reading standing up? Perhaps so she should not feel lonely while working in the kitchen? She had peeled the potatoes, mixed together all the ingredients of the cholent, and blown up the fire in the oven. And all the while Moshele had kept turning the pages and reading.

One half-hour passed, then another. The summer night is short, and she knew that early in the morning Moshele would set up her baskets at the gate and begin to sell her merchandise, until she herself returned from the market. At last, unable to restrain herself any longer, she asked:

"Moshele, why aren't you going to bed? Usually at this time you're asleep already."

"And why don't you go to bed?" he replied.

"At my age one doesn't sleep so well any more," she said, with a light laugh.

"Then I won't go either," he said.

More time passed, but he did not move from the spot, just as if this were quite customary. She had no wish to scold him as she might have her own son, but his behavior was upsetting her very much. What a youngster will think of! This has been her way for many years, ever since she became a fruit-vendor. Neither her husband, peace be upon him, nor her son, may the Almighty grant him long life, had ever succeeded in persuading her to go to sleep on Thursday night.

"I see, Moshele—" she tried to argue with him—"that you're on strike against me. But I still have to stuff a chicken-neck with flour and fat, to peel the carrots, and to grate the horseradish for the fish."

"It isn't necessary," Moshele said sternly and closed his book, as though he already knew that, whatever her show of resistance, she was about to give in.

"To tell you the truth, Moshele," she said, "I never really know which dishes you like and which you don't. You thank me equally for all of them."

"I like all the dishes, Mother Vella," he answered. "Everything you cook is good and tasty, just like my mother's cooking at home. But if you won't go to bed, then I won't go either, and next week I won't come at all. I know that for yourself alone you wouldn't be staying up all night."

Whereupon, without another word, she quickly moved the pots inside the oven onto the glowing coals, closed the oven door, and immediately went to bed. She understood quite well that if Moshele said something, he meant it.

While she was lying on her bed and Moshele, facing her, was on her son's bed, he told her a story of his student days at the yeshiva:

"Every Thursday night the yeshiva students held a 'mishmor'—that means they stayed up all night to study. But then the rosh yeshiva forbade this practice. 'I realize now,' he said, 'that instead of becoming more diligent students, as you imagine, you are really wasting time and studying less. On Thursday the day is disrupted because you're already preparing for mishmor. On Friday and on the Sabbath you cannot study because you've been up all night for the mishmor. And on Thursday night itself you do study, but some of the time you're dozing as you stand at your lecterns.' "

This story, she realized, was Moshele's attempt to apologize for having insisted upon having his way. And, after all, he was right: On Thursday nights she could hardly stand on her feet, and tasks that should have required no more than an hour took her three hours. On Fridays she would stand at the gate exhausted and befuddled, not even hearing what her customers were saying, and immediately after the Kiddush Friday evening she would fall asleep with her head resting on the edge of the table. She herself didn't eat and neither did Moshele, for, not wanting to wake her, he would wait for her to rouse herself to serve the second course.

But why hasn't he yet come tonight, when it is already so late. Usually on Thursday evenings, Moshele arrived in time to help her take in her baskets, and his failure to show up must mean that something, God forbid, has happened to him. Ever since the box fell on her shoulder, he has never permitted her to carry the baskets herself. Perhaps he has fallen ill and is running a fever from standing for so many hours with head bent under the sun? A youngster alone, far from home, sleeping in a barn together with the peasants. And here she's been rushing to finish her work before he came. What will she do now for the remainder of the night? She won't be able to close her eyes even for a minute anyway. As soon as dawn begins to break, she'll run to the market to wait for the farmer from Soltaniszki . . . Praised be the Almighty! She hears the door being opened. It's he, it's his walk—but why is he entering so very quietly? She takes the lamp from the kitchen and goes into the workshop to help light his way, so he won't hurt himself stumbling over some piece of iron lying about. She finds him carrying a heavy sack.

"Good evening, Mother Vella. The work at Soltaniszki has come to an end now, so I had to settle accounts with the owner and say good-bye to my friends. That's why I'm so late. I brought along all my things."

"So from now on you'll be staying with me all the time!" she cries out joyfully, but regrets her words immediately. It's ridiculous to ask this of him, she thinks. After all, he owes her nothing.

Moshele gazes at her silently, solemnly, but she is so overjoyed at seeing him safe and unhurt that she doesn't notice this; she does not even realize that her hard, work-worn fingers are stroking his thick, curly hair:

"Oh Moshele, how perspired you are—" She wipes the sweat from his forehead. "I just didn't know what to think, because it was so late and you weren't here yet. I received a letter from my son today, he writes that he and your sister will soon be coming home. Moshele, go and eat."

He sits down at the table to read for himself the letter from Warsaw. Mother brings in her finest delicacies: a portion of fish, a hot meatball, a bowl of soup. For her own son she has never served a Sabbath meal on Thursday nights—he had to wait until after the Kiddush on Friday evening. But Moshele is hardly more than a child! And, to please him still further, she says:

"I've nearly finished all my work, and you won't need to go on strike again. Why don't you eat, Moshele?"

"How is your shoulder?" He rouses himself abruptly from his reverie and begins to eat. But my mother senses that this is not what he meant to say, and he is obviously forcing himself to eat.

"The Almighty be thanked," she answers, "the shoulder is completely healed. But I haven't fully come to myself yet since you had the fight with that wagon driver."

She feels the urge to scold him once more for having started up with that ruffian of a teamster, but she remains silent. From his deeply wrinkled forehead she can tell that he has something important to say to her and is trying to decide how to begin.

"Mother Vella," he says at last, in a strangely altered voice, "I'm leaving for the Land of Israel."

He begins to shift uneasily on his chair, displeased with himself for not having broken this news more gradually and gently to Mother Vella.

She remains seated, her hands stiff in her lap, unable to breathe. Moshele, as though he has expected this, adds hastily:

"You did know, Mother Vella, that I was working in Soltaniszki only in order to prepare myself for joining a kibbutz in the Land of Israel, and I promised my father that I would go there as soon as I finished my training."

"For whom now will I prepare the Sabbath?" she murmurs to herself.

"Your son and my sister will soon be returning home"—Moshele hastens to comfort her—"then you'll have someone to prepare the Sabbath for again, and you won't be lonely."

"But my son and your sister will be living by themselves, somewhere else!" she says with a stiff smile, her tears rolling down.

"Oh, Mother Vella—" Moshele shakes his head—"don't you need to live for yourself? You're always looking for someone to love and to sacrifice yourself for."

Mother gazes at his full, warm, half-open lips, now trembling, and regains her composure: Moshele, after all, is going to the sacred Land of the Patriarchs, and his own parents are already there. His mother has surely been yearning for him quite long enough, his father has even given up the rabbinate in order to be together with him, and their only daughter is remaining here, with her, Vella's, own son; how, then, does she dare to ask that Moshele also stay here, to help her carry her baskets?

To make him forget the foolish words she has uttered, she begins in a cheerful tone, to tell a tale:

"Our eldest son, Moïsey, was also a Zionist. If only Moïsey's son, Aronchik, were like his father and like you, may you be granted long life, his mother wouldn't have to tremble now, day and night, at the thought of his being arrested again. But Aronchik always laughed at his Uncle Issak, the pharmacist, who used to tell my son when he was still a baby to go to the Land of Israel to drain the swamps."

"Aronchik was right to laugh at his uncle," says Moshele with a smile. "One should go oneself, not tell others to go."

"Our neighbor, Reb Boruḥel, may he keep away from the living also wanted to go to the Land of Israel, to die," says Mother, increasingly disturbed by her inability to control her agitation, "but his wife, my partner, Blumele, only wanted to go to her children in Argentina. But in the end both of them, poor souls, remained in Vilna, in the cemetery in Zarecze."

"A pity," says Moshele regretfully. "Of course it's better to go to the Land of Israel to live and to work. But if someone at least wants to go there to die, it's a sign that he would have wanted to live there, too, but didn't have the strength to carry it through."

Mother sees that Moshele is trying to help her distract herself. Anger at herself rises in her, and with trembling hands she takes a small canvas bag from her purse:

"Moshele, every week you gave me two zlotys out of your wages. I didn't want to argue with you because you said that if I didn't take the money, you wouldn't come to me for the Sabbath. So I took the money and put it aside. Now that you're about to leave on such a long and difficult journey, I beg of you: take back your money and use it to help pay for whatever you need."

"Mother Vella—" Moshele pulls a bundle of bills from his pocket—"I, too, didn't want to argue with you. You didn't want to take the money you had coming to you, so I held on to it. But I had no use for it—all week long I ate and slept in Soltaniszki. Now that I'm going away, I want to give it to you. My father is sending me the money I need for the trip."

Mother feels a choking sensation in her throat—if only she could hide away in some corner, where she might weep over her prayerbook.

"Moshele, you shame me."

Moshele gazes at her in astonishment and pushes the coins she has taken from her bag into one heap with his paper zlotys.

"Well, then, Mother Vella," he says calmly, "we'll buy a gift together for your son and my sister."

"Moshele, are you leaving right after the Sabbath?"

"No, Mother Vella. I'll wait until my sister returns from Warsaw."

"Moshele, when you write a letter to us from the Land of Israel, don't address me as 'Mother Vella.' Your mother, the Rebbetzin, might resent it. I beg your mother not to be angry at me because her daughter hasn't married into the sort of comfort and wealth that she deserves. If it were in my power, I would treat your sister like a princess."

She draws a deep breath, as though to fill the emptiness in her heart. Bands of light creep over the walls of the smithy. The dark blue in the window grows lighter and lighter—Moshele has forgotten to remind Mother Vella to go to bed. He sits silent and sad, his head resting on both his hands.

Isaac Bashevis Singer

One of the most prolific Yiddish writers, Isaac Bashevis Singer was born in Leoncin, Poland, in 1904, the son and grandson of rabbis who expected him to follow in the line of religious scholars. Singer grew up in Warsaw and Bilgoray. He was influenced by the success of his older brother, I. J. Singer, who achieved prominence as a Yiddish novelist, to become a writer himself. Singer, who made his home base in New York from 1935 until his death in 1991, achieved both great popular and great critical success among Yiddish readers and perhaps even more so among his English-speaking reading audience, winning many prizes, including the 1978 Nobel Prize for Literature.

Singer's work provides difficult problems for feminist readers. On one hand, especially when writing about Eastern European settings, he is capable of creating interesting, unexpected, strong, and multifaceted Jewish women. Black Dobie in Singer's "The Spinoza of Market Street" (1961), for example, is a tough, aging survivor of coarse urban street life. Illustrating the Yiddish proverb, "An old maid who gets married becomes a young wife," Black Dobie brings the surprise of passion, health, and vitality into the last years of an otherworldly philosopher. On the other hand, especially in his writings about contemporary environments, Singer's women are often described very unsympathetically as sexually voracious and perverse, stupid, or manipulative. Sexual appetite in modern women is depicted by Singer in great detail and with a palpable sense of revulsion. Most egregiously, the protagonist of the novel *Shosha* rejects adult, sexually active women who might be seen as his appropriate counterparts and marries a physically and emotionally immature child-woman, whom his sister characterizes as "a board with a hole."

Nevertheless, we have in "Yentl the Yeshiva Boy" and other stories in the Old World milieu rather impressive depictions of believable and likable women. "Yentl" is quite a sympathetic and sensitive portrayal of the woman whose intellectual passions make her marginal to normative shtetl life. She dreads above all things the possibility that she may be forever locked into the domestic dreariness of wifely and motherly roles. In her psychological and physical wanderings, she enters a murky, androgynous existence, from which, it seems likely, she may never emerge.

•

"Yentl the Yeshiva Boy"

I

After her father's death, Yentl had no reason to remain in Yanev. She was all alone in the house. To be sure, lodgers were willing to move in and pay rent; and the marriage brokers flocked to her door with offers from Lublin, Tomashev, Zamosc. But Yentl didn't want to get married. Inside her, a voice repeated over and over: "No!" What becomes of a girl when the wedding's over? Right away she starts bearing and rearing. And her mother-in-law lords it over her. Yentl knew she wasn't cut out for a woman's life. She couldn't sew, she couldn't knit. She let the food burn and the milk boil over; her Sabbath pudding never turned out right, and her hallah dough didn't rise. Yentl much preferred men's activities to women's. Her father, Reb Todros, may he rest in peace, during many bedridden years had studied Torah with his daughter as if she were a son. He told Yentl to lock the doors and drape the windows, then together they pored over the Pentateuch, the Mishnah, the Gemara, and the Commentaries. She had proved so apt a pupil that her father used to say:

"Yentl—you have the soul of a man."

"So why was I born a woman?"

"Even Heaven makes mistakes."

There was no doubt about it, Yentl was unlike any of the girls in Yanev—tall, thin, bony, with small breasts and narrow hips. On Sabbath afternoons, when her father slept, she would dress up in his trousers, his fringed garment, his silk coat, his skullcap, his velvet hat, and study her reflection in the mirror. She looked like a dark, handsome young man. There was even a slight down on her upper lip. Only her thick braids showed her womanhood—and if it came to that, hair could always be shorn. Yentl conceived a plan and day and night she could think of nothing else. No, she had not been created for the noodle board and the pudding dish, for chattering with silly women and pushing for a place at the butcher's block. Her father had told her so many tales of yeshivas, rabbis, men of letters! Her head was full of Talmudic disputations, questions and answers, learned phrases. Secretly, she had even smoked her father's long pipe.

Yentl told the dealers she wanted to sell the house and go to live in Kalish with an aunt. The neighborhood women tried to talk her out of it, and the marriage brokers said she was crazy, that she was more likely to make a good match right here in Yanev. But Yentl was obstinate. She was in such a rush that she sold the house to the first bidder, and let the furniture go for a song. All she realized from her inheritance was one hundred and forty rubles. Then late one night in the month of Av, while Yanev slept, Yentl cut off her braids, arranged sidelocks at her temples, and dressed herself in her father's clothes. Packing underclothes, phylacteries, and a few books into a straw suitcase, she started off on foot for Lublin.

On the main road, Yentl got a ride in a carriage that took her as far as Zamosc. From there, she again set out on foot. She stopped at an inn along the way, and gave her name there as Anshel, after an uncle who had died. The inn was crowded with young men journeying to study with famous rabbis. An argument was in progress over the merits of various yeshivas, some praising those of Lithuania, others claiming that study was more intensive in Poland and the board better. It was the first time Yentl had ever found herself alone in the company of young men. How different their talk was from the jabbering of women, she thought, but she was too shy to join in. One young man discussed a prospective match and the size of the dowry, while another, parodying the manner of a Purim rabbi, declaimed a passage from the Torah, adding all sorts of lewd interpretations. After a while, the company proceeded to contests of strength. One pried open another's fist; a second tried to bend a companion's arm. One student, dining on bread and tea, had no spoon and stirred his cup with his penknife.

Presently, one of the group came over to Yentl and poked her in the shoulder. "Why so quiet? Don't you have a tongue?"

"I have nothing to say."

"What's your name?"

"Anshel."

"You *are* bashful. A violet by the wayside."

And the young man tweaked Yentl's nose. She would have given him a smack in return, but her arm refused to budge. She turned white. Another student, slightly older than the rest, tall and pale, with burning eyes and a black beard, came to her rescue.

"Hey, you, why are you picking on him?"

"If you don't like it, you don't have to look."

"Want me to pull your sidelocks off?"

The bearded young man beckoned to Yentl, then asked where she came from and where she was going. Yentl told him she was looking for a yeshiva, but wanted a quiet one. The young man pulled at his beard.

"Then come with me to Bechev."

He explained that he was returning to Bechev for his fourth year. The yeshiva there was small, with only thirty students, and the people in the town provided board for them all. The food was plentiful and the housewives darned the students' socks and took care of their laundry. The Bechev rabbi, who headed the yeshiva, was a genius. He could pose ten questions and answer all ten with one proof. Most of the students eventually found wives in the town.

"Why did you leave in the middle of the term?" Yentl asked.

"My mother died. Now I'm on my way back."

"What's your name?"

"Avigdor."

"How is it you're not married?"

The young man scratched his beard. "It's a long story."

"Tell me."

Avigdor covered his eyes and thought a moment. "Are you coming to Bechev?"

"Yes."

"Then you'll find out soon enough anyway. I was engaged to the only daughter of Alter Vishkower, the richest man in town. Even the wedding date was set when suddenly they sent back the engagement contract."

"What happened?"

"I don't know. Gossips, I guess, were busy spreading tales. I had the right to ask for half the dowry, but it was against my nature. Now they're trying to talk me into another match, but the girl doesn't appeal to me."

"In Bechev, yeshiva boys look at women?"

"At Alter's house, where I ate once a week, Hadass, his daughter, always brought in the food . . ."

"Is she good-looking?"

"She's blond."

"Brunettes can be good-looking too."

"No."

Yentl gazed at Avigdor. He was lean and bony with sunken cheeks. He had curly sidelocks so black they appeared blue, and his eyebrows met across the bridge of his nose. He looked at her sharply with the regretful shyness of one who has just divulged a secret. His lapel was rent, according to the custom for mourners, and the lining of his gaberdine showed through. He drummed restlessly on the table and hummed a tune. Behind the high furrowed brow his thoughts seemed to race. Suddenly he spoke:

"Well, what of it. I'll become a recluse, that's all."

II

It was strange, but as soon as Yentl—or Anshel—arrived in Bechev, she was allotted one day's board a week at the house of that same rich man, Alter Vishkower, whose daughter had broken off her betrothal to Avigdor.

The students at the yeshiva studied in pair, and Avigdor chose Anshel for a partner. He helped her with the lessons. He was also an expert swimmer and offered to teach Anshel the breast stroke and how to tread water, but she always found excuses for not going down to the river. Avigdor suggested that they share lodgings, but Anshel found a place to sleep at the house of an elderly widow who was half blind. Tuesdays, Anshel ate at Alter Vishkower's and Hadass waited on her. Avigdor always asked many questions: "How does Hadass look? Is she sad? Is she gay? Are they trying to marry her off? Does she ever mention my name?" Anshel reported that Hadass upset dishes on the tablecloth, forgot to bring the salt, and dipped her fingers into the plate of grits while carrying it. She ordered the servant girl around, was forever engrossed in storybooks, and changed her hairdo every week. Moreover, she must consider herself a beauty, for she was always in front of the mirror, but, in fact, she was not that good-looking.

"Two years after she's married," said Anshel, "she'll be an old bag."

"So she doesn't appeal to you?"

"Not particularly."

"Yet if she wanted you, you wouldn't turn her down."

"I can do without her."

"Don't you have evil impulses?"

The two friends, sharing a lectern in a corner of the study house, spent more time talking than learning. Occasionally Avigdor smoked, and Anshel, taking the cigarette from his lip, would have a puff. Avigdor liked baked flatcakes made with buckwheat, so Anshel stopped at the bakery every morning to buy one, and wouldn't let him pay his share. Often Anshel did things that greatly surprised Avigdor. If a button came off Avigdor's coat, for example, Anshel would arrive at the yeshiva the next day with needle and thread and sew it back on. Anshel bought Avigdor all kinds of presents: a silk handkerchief, a pair of socks, a muffler. Avigdor grew more and more attached to this boy, five years younger than himself, whose beard hadn't even begun to sprout.

Once Avigdor said to Anshel: "I want you to marry Hadass."

"What good would that do *you*?"

"Better you than a total stranger."

"You'd become my enemy."

"Never."

Avigdor liked to go for walks through the town and Anshel frequently joined him. Engrossed in conversation, they would go off to the water mill, or to the pine forest, or to the crossroads where the Christian shrine stood. Sometimes they stretched out on the grass.

"Why can't a woman be like a man?" Avigdor asked once, looking up at the sky.

"How do you mean?"

"Why couldn't Hadass be just like you?"

"How like me?"

"Oh—a good fellow."

Anshel grew playful. She plucked a flower and tore off the petals one by one. She picked up a chestnut and threw it at Avigdor. Avigdor watched a ladybug crawl across the palm of his hand.

After a while he spoke up: "They're trying to marry me off."

Anshel sat up instantly. "To whom?"

"To Feitl's daughter, Peshe."

"The widow?"

"That's the one."

"Why should you marry a widow?"

"No one else will have me."

"That's not true. Someone will turn up for you."

"Never."

Anshel told Avigdor such a match was bad. Peshe was neither good-looking nor clever, only a cow with a pair of eyes. Besides, she was bad luck, for her husband died in the first year of their marriage. Such women were husband-killers. But Avigdor did not answer. He lit a cigarette, took a deep puff, and blew out smoke rings. His face had turned green.

"I need a woman. I can't sleep at night."

Anshel was startled. "Why can't you wait until the right one comes along?"

"Hadass was my destined one."

And Avigdor's eyes grew moist. Abruptly he got to his feet. "Enough lying around. Let's go."

After that, everything happened quickly. One day Avigdor was confiding his problem to Anshel, two days later he became engaged to Peshe, and brought honey cake and brandy to the yeshiva. An early wedding date was set. When the bride-to-be is a widow, there's no need to wait for a trousseau. Everything is ready. The groom, moreover, was an orphan and no one's advice had to be asked. The yeshiva students drank the brandy and offered their congratulations. Anshel also took a sip, but promptly choked on it.

"Oy, it burns!"

"You're not much of a man," Avigdor teased.

After the celebration, Avigdor and Anshel sat down with a volume of the Gemara, but they made little progress, and their conversation was equally slow. Avigdor rocked back and forth, pulled at his beard, muttered under his breath.

"I'm lost," he said abruptly.

"If you don't like her, why are you getting married?"

"I'd marry a she-goat."

The following day Avigdor did not appear at the study house. Feitl the leather dealer belonged to the Hasidim and he wanted his prospective son-in-law to continue his studies at the Hasidic prayer house. The yeshiva students said privately that though there was no denying the widow was short and round as a barrel, her mother the daughter of a dairyman, her father half an ignoramus, still the whole family was filthy with money. Feitl was part-owner of a tannery; Peshe had invested her dowry in a shop that sold herring, tar, pots and pans, and was always crowded with peasants. Father and daughter were outfitting Avigdor and had placed orders for a fur coat, a cloth coat, a silk kapote, and two pair of boots. In addition, he had received many gifts immediately, things that had belonged to Peshe's first husband: the Vilna edition of the Talmud, a gold watch, a Hanukkah candelabra, a spice box. Anshel sat alone at the lectern.

On Tuesday when Anshel arrived for dinner at Alter Vishkower's house, Hadass remarked: "What do you say about your partner—back in clover, isn't he?"

"What did you expect—that no one else would want him?"

Hadass reddened. "It wasn't my fault. My father was against it."

"Why?"

"Because they found out a brother of his had hanged himself."

Anshel looked at her as she stood there—tall, blond, with a long neck, hollow cheeks, and blue eyes, wearing a cotton dress and a calico apron. Her hair, fixed in two braids, was flung back over her shoulders. A pity I'm not a man, Anshel thought.

"Do you regret it now?" Anshel asked.

"Oh, yes!"

Hadass fled from the room. The rest of the food, meat dumplings and tea, was brought in by the servant girl. Not until Anshel had finished eating and was washing her hands for the Final Blessings did Hadass reappear.

She came up to the table and said in a smothered voice: "Swear to me you won't tell him anything. Why should he know what goes on in my heart!"

Then she fled once more, nearly falling over the threshold.

III

The head of the yeshiva asked Anshel to choose another study partner, but weeks went by and still Anshel studied alone. There was no one in the yeshiva who could take Avigdor's place. All the others were small, in body and in spirit. They talked nonsense, bragged about trifles, grinned oafishly, behaved like shnorrers. Without Avigdor the study house seemed empty. At night Anshel lay on her bench at the widow's, unable to sleep. Stripped of gaberdine and trousers, she was once more Yentl, a girl of marriageable age, in love with a young man who was betrothed to another. Perhaps I should have told him the truth, Anshel thought. But it was too late for that. Anshel could not go back to being a girl, could never again do without books and a study house. She lay there thinking outlandish thoughts that brought her close to madness. She fell asleep, then awoke with a start. In her dream she had been at the same time a man and a woman, wearing both a woman's bodice and a man's fringed garment. Yentl's period was late and she was suddenly afraid . . . who knew? In *Medrash Talpioth* she had read of a woman who had conceived merely through desiring a man. Only now did Yentl grasp the meaning of the Torah's prohibition against wearing the clothes of the other sex. By doing so one deceived not only others but also oneself. Even the soul was perplexed, finding itself incarnate in a strange body.

At night Anshel lay awake; by day she could scarcely keep her eyes open. At the houses where she had her meals, the women complained that the youth left everything on his plate. The rabbi noticed that Anshel no longer paid attention to the lectures but stared out the window lost in private thoughts. When Tuesday came, Anshel appeared at the Vishkower house for dinner. Hadass set a bowl of soup before her and waited, but Anshel was so disturbed she did not even say thank you. She reached for a spoon but let it fall.

Hadass ventured a comment: "I hear Avigdor has deserted you."

Anshel awoke from her trance. "What do you mean?"

"He's no longer your partner."

"He's left the yeshiva."

"Do you see him at all?"

"He seems to be hiding."

"Are you at least going to the wedding?"

For a moment Anshel was silent as though missing the meaning of the words. Then he spoke: "He's a big fool."

"Why do you say that?"

"You're beautiful, and the other one looks like a monkey."

Hadass blushed to the roots of her hair. "It's all my father's fault."

"Don't worry. You'll find someone who's worthy of you."

"There's no one I want."

"But everyone wants you . . ."

There was a long silence. Hadass' eyes grew larger, filling with the sadness of one who knows there is no consolation.

"Your soup is getting cold."

"I, too, want you."

Anshel was astonished at what she had said. Hadass stared at her over her shoulder.

"What are you saying!"

"It's the truth."

"Someone might be listening."

"I'm not afraid."

"Eat the soup. I'll bring the meat dumplings in a moment."

Hadass turned to go, her high heels clattering. Anshel began hunting for beans in the soup, fished one up, then let it fall. Her appetite was gone; her throat had closed up. She knew very well she was getting entangled in evil, but some force kept urging her on. Hadass reappeared, carrying a platter with two meat dumplings on it.

"Why aren't you eating?"

"I'm thinking about you."

"What are you thinking?"

"I want to marry you."

Hadass made a face as though she had swallowed something.

"On such matters, you must speak to my father."

"I know."

"The custom is to send a matchmaker."

She ran from the room, letting the door slam behind her. Laughing inwardly, Anshel thought: "With girls I can play as I please!" She sprinkled salt on the soup and then pepper. She sat there lightheaded. What have I done? I must be going mad. There's no other explanation . . . She forced herself to eat, but could taste nothing. Only then did Anshel remember that it was Avigdor who had wanted her to marry Hadass. From her confusion, a plan emerged; she would exact vengeance for Avigdor, and at the same time, through Hadass, draw him closer to herself. Hadass was a virgin: what did she know about men? A girl like that could be deceived for a long time. To be sure, Anshel too was a virgin but she knew a lot about such matters from the Gemara and from hearing men talk. Anshel was seized by both fear and glee, as a person is who is planning to deceive the whole community. She remembered the saying: "The public are fools." She stood up and said aloud: "Now I'll really start something."

That night Anshel didn't sleep a wink. Every few minutes she got up for a drink of water. Her throat was parched, her forehead burned. Her brain worked away feverishly of its own volition. A quarrel seemed to be going on inside her. Her stomach throbbed and her knees ached. It was as if she had sealed a pact with Satan, the Evil One who plays tricks on human beings, who sets stumbling blocks and traps in their path. By the time Anshel fell asleep, it was morning. She awoke more exhausted than before. But she could not go on sleeping on the bench at the widow's. With an effort she rose and, taking the bag that held her phylacteries, set out for the study house. On the way whom should she meet but Hadass's father. Anshel bade him a respectful good morning and received a friendly greeting in return. Reb Alter stroked his beard and engaged her in conversation:

"My daughter Hadass must be serving you left-overs. You look starved."

"Your daughter is a fine girl, and very generous."

"So why are you so pale?"

Anshel was silent for a minute. "Reb Alter, there's something I must say to you."

"Well, go ahead, say it."

"Reb Alter, your daughter pleases me."

Alter Vishkower came to a halt. "Oh, does she? I thought yeshiva students didn't talk about such things."

His eyes were full of laughter.

"But it's the truth."

"One doesn't discuss these matters with the young man himself."

"But I'm an orphan."

"Well . . . in that case the custom is to send a marriage broker."

"Yes . . ."

"What do you see in her?"

"She's beautiful . . . fine . . . intelligent . . ."

"Well, well, well . . . Come along, tell me something about your family."

Alter Vishkower put his arm around Anshel and in this fashion the two continued walking until they reached the courtyard of the synagogue.

IV

Once you say "A," you must say "B." Thoughts lead to words, words lead to deeds. Reb Alter Vishkower gave his consent to the match. Hadass's mother Freyda Leah held back for a while. She said she wanted no more Bechev yeshiva students for her daughter and would rather have someone from Lublin or Zamosc; but Hadass gave warning that if she were shamed publicly once more (the way she had been with Avigdor) she would throw herself into the well. As often happens with such ill-advised matches, everyone was strongly in favor of it—the rabbi, the relative, Hadass's girl friends. For some time the girls of Bechev had been eyeing Anshel longingly, watching from their windows when the youth passed by on the street. Anshel kept his boots well polished and did not drop his eyes in the presence of women. Stopping in at Beila the baker's to buy a *pletzl*, he joked with them in such a worldly fashion that they marveled. The women agreed there was something special about Anshel: his sidelocks curled like nobody else's and he tied his neck scarf differently; his eyes, smiling yet distant, seemed always fixed on some faraway point. And the fact that Avigdor had become betrothed to Feitl's daughter Peshe, forsaking Anshel, had endeared him all the more to the people of the town. Alter Vishkower had a provisional contract drawn up for the betrothal, promising Anshel a bigger dowry, more presents, and an even longer period of maintenance than he had promised Avigdor. The girls of Bechev threw their arms around Hadass and congratulated her. Hadass immediately began crocheting a sack for Anshel's phylacteries, a hallah cloth, a matzoh bag. When Avigdor heard the news of Anshel's betrothal, he came to the study house to offer his congratulations. The past few weeks had aged him. His beard was disheveled, his eyes were red.

He said to Anshel: "I knew it would happen this way. Right from the beginning. As soon as I met you at the inn."

"But it was you who suggested it."

"I know that."

"Why did you desert me? You went away without even saying goodbye."

"I wanted to burn my bridges behind me."

Avigdor asked Anshel to go for a walk. Though it was already past Succoth, the day was bright with sunshine. Avigdor, friendlier than ever, opened his heart to Anshel. Yes, it was true, a brother of his had succumbed to melancholy and hanged himself. Now he too felt himself near the edge of the abyss. Peshe had a lot of money and her father was a rich man, yet he couldn't sleep nights. He didn't want to be a storekeeper. He couldn't forget Hadass. She appeared in his dreams. Sabbath night when her name occurred in the Havdala prayer, he turned dizzy. Still it was good that Anshel and no one else was to marry her . . . At least she would fall into decent hands. Avigdor stooped and tore aimlessly at the shriveled grass. His speech was incoherent, like that of a man possessed.

Suddenly he said: "I have thought of doing what my brother did."

"Do you love her *that* much?"

"She's engraved in my heart."

The two pledged their friendship and promised never again to part. Anshel proposed that, after they were both married, they should live next door or even share the same house. They would study together every day, perhaps even become partners in shop.

"Do you want to know the truth?" asked Avigdor. "It's like the story of Jacob and Benjamin: my life is bound up in your life."

"Then why did you leave me?"

"Perhaps for that very reason."

Though the day had turned cold and windy, they continued to walk until they reached the pine forest, not turning back until dusk when it was time for the evening prayer. The girls of Bechev, from their posts at the windows, watched them going by with their arms round each other's shoulders and so engrossed in conversation that they walked through puddles and piles of trash without noticing. Avigdor looked pale, disheveled, and the wind whipped one sidelock about; Anshel chewed his fingernails. Hadass, too, ran to the window, took one look, and her eyes filled with tears.

Events followed quickly. Avigdor was the first to marry. Because the bride was a widow, the wedding was a quiet one, with no musicians, no wedding jester, no ceremonial veiling of the bride. One day Peshe stood beneath the marriage canopy, the next she was back at the shop, dispensing tar with greasy hands. Avigdor prayed at the Hasidic assembly house in his new prayer shawl. Afternoons, Anshel went to visit him and the two whispered and talked until evening. The date of Anshel's wedding to Hadass was set for the Sabbath in Hanukkah week, though the prospective father-in-law wanted it sooner. Hadass had already been betrothed once. Besides, the groom was an orphan. Why should he toss about on a makeshift bed at the widow's when he could have a wife and home of his own?

Many times each day Anshel warned herself that what she was about to do was sinful, mad, an act of utter depravity. She was entangling both Hadass and herself in a chain of deception and committing so many transgressions that she would never be able to do penance. One lie followed another. Repeatedly Anshel made up her mind to flee Bechev in time, to put an end to this weird comedy that was more the work of an imp than a human being. But she was in the grip of a power she could not resist. She grew more and more attached to Avigdor, and could not bring herself to destroy Hadass's illusory happiness. Now that he was married, Avigdor's desire to study was greater than ever, and the friends met twice each day: in the mornings they studied the Gemara and the Commentaries, in the afternoon the Legal Codes with their glosses. Alter Vishkower and Feitl the leather dealer were pleased and compared Avigdor and Anshel to David and Jonathan. With all the complications, Anshel went about as though drunk. The tailor took her measurements for a new wardrobe and she was forced into all kinds of subterfuge to keep them from discovering she was not a man. Though the imposture had lasted many weeks, Anshel still could not believe it: How was it possible? Fooling the community had become a game, but how long could it go on? And in what way would the truth come to the surface? Inside, Anshel laughed and wept. She had turned into a sprite brought into the world to mock people and trick them. I'm wicked, a transgressor, a Jeroboam ben Nabat, she told herself. Her only justification was that she had taken all these burdens upon herself because her soul thirsted to study Torah.

Avigdor soon began to complain that Peshe treated him badly. She called him an idler, a shlemiel, just another mouth to feed. She tried to tie him to the store, assigned him tasks for which he hadn't the slightest inclination, begrudged him pocket money. Instead of consoling Avigdor, Anshel goaded him against Peshe. She called his wife an eyesore, a shrew, a miser, and said that Peshe had no doubt nagged her first husband to death and would Avigdor also. At the same time, Anshel enumerated Avigdor's virtue: his height and manliness, his wit, his erudition.

"If I were a woman and married to you," said Anshel, "I'd know how to appreciate you."

"Well, but you aren't . . ."

Avigdor sighed.

Meanwhile, Anshel's wedding date drew near.

On the Sabbath before Hanukkah, Anshel was called to the pulpit to read from the Torah. The women showered her with raisins and almonds. On the day of the wedding Alter Vishkower gave a feast for the young men. Avigdor sat as Anshel's right hand. The bridegroom delivered a Talmudic discourse, and the rest of the company argued the points, while smoking cigarettes and drinking wine, liqueurs, tea with lemon or raspberry jam. Then followed the ceremony of veiling the bride, after which the bridegroom was led to the wedding canopy that had been set up at the side of the synagogue. The night was frosty and clear, the sky full of stars. The musicians struck up a tune. Two rows of girls held lighted tapers and braided wax candles. After the wedding ceremony the bride and groom broke their fast with golden chicken broth. Then the dancing began and the announcement of the wedding gifts, all according to custom. The gifts were many and costly. The wedding jester depicted the joys and sorrows that were in store for the bride. Avigdor's wife, Peshe, was one of the guests but, though she was bedecked with jewels, she still looked ugly in a wig that sat low on her forehead, wearing an enormous fur cape, and with traces of tar on her hand that no amount of washing could ever remove. After the virtue dance the bride and groom were led separately to the marriage chamber. The wedding attendants instructed the couple in the proper conduct and enjoined them to "be fruitful and multiply."

At daybreak Anshel's mother-in-law and her band descended upon the marriage chamber and tore the bedsheets from beneath Hadass to make sure the marriage had been consummated. When traces of blood were discovered, the company grew merry and began kissing and congratulating the bride. Then, brandishing the sheet, they flocked outside and danced a kosher dance in the newly fallen snow. Anshel had found a way to deflower the bride. Hadass in her innocence was unaware that things weren't quite as they should have been. She was already deeply in love with Anshel. It is commanded that the bride and groom remain apart for seven days after the first intercourse. The next day Anshel and Avigdor took up the study of the Tractate on Menstruous Women. When the other men had departed and the two were left to themselves in the synagogue, Avigdor shyly questioned Anshel about his night with Hadass. Anshel gratified his curiosity and they whispered together until nightfall.

V

Anshel had fallen into good hands. Hadass was a devoted wife and her parents indulged their son-in-law's every wish and boasted of his accomplishments. To be sure, several months went by and Hadass was still not with child, but no one took it to heart. On the other hand, Avigdor's lot grew steadily worse. Peshe tormented him and finally would not give him enough to eat and even refused him a clean shirt. Since he was penniless, Anshel again brought him a daily buckwheat cake. Because Peshe was too busy to cook and too stingy to hire a servant, Anshel asked Avigdor to dine at his house. Reb Alter Vishkower and his wife disapproved, arguing that it was wrong for the rejected suitor to visit the house of his former fiancee. The town had plenty to talk about. But Anshel cited precedents to show that it was not prohibited by the Law. Most of the townspeople sided with Avigdor and blamed Peshe for everything. Avigdor soon began pressing Peshe for a divorce, and, because he did not want to have a child by such a fury, he acted like Onan, or, as the Gemara translates it: he threshed on the inside and cast his seed without. He confided in Anshel, told him how Peshe came to bed unwashed and snored like a buzz saw, of how she was so occupied with the cash taken in at the store that she babbled about it even in her sleep.

"Oh, Anshel, how I envy you," he said.

"There's no reason for envying me."

"You have everything. I wish your good fortune were mine—with no loss to you, of course."

"Everyone has troubles of his own."

"What sort of troubles do *you* have? Don't tempt Providence."

How could Avigdor have guessed that Anshel could not sleep at night and thought constantly of running away? Lying with Hadass and deceiving her had become more and more painful. Hadass's love and tenderness shamed her. The devotion of her mother- and father-in-law and their hopes for a grandchild were a burden. On Friday afternoons all of the townspeople went to the baths and every week Anshel had to find a new excuse. But this was beginning to awake suspicions. There was talk that Anshel must have an unsightly birthmark, or a rupture, or perhaps was not properly circumcised. Judging by the youth's years, his beard should certainly have begun to sprout, yet his cheeks remained smooth. It was already Purim, and Passover was approaching. Soon it would be summer. Not far from Bechev there was a river where all the yeshiva students and young men went swimming as soon as it was warm enough. The lie was swelling like an abscess and one of these days it must surely burst. Anshel knew she had to find a way to free herself.

It was customary for the young men boarding with their in-laws to travel to nearby cities during the half-holidays in the middle of Passover week. They enjoyed the change, refreshed themselves, looked around for business opportunities, bought books or other things a young man might need. Bechev was not far from Lublin and Anshel persuaded Avigdor to make the journey with her at her expense. Avigdor was delighted at the prospect of being rid for a few days of the shrew he had at home. The trip by carriage was a merry one. The fields were turning green; storks, back from the warm countries, swooped across the sky in great arcs. Streams rushed toward the valley. The birds chirped. The windmills turned. Spring flowers were beginning to bloom in the fields. Here and there a cow was already grazing. The companions, chatting, ate the fruit and little cakes that Hadass had packed, told each other jokes, and exchanged confidences until they reached Lublin. There they went to an inn and took a room for two. In the journey, Anshel had promised to reveal an astonishing secret to Avigdor in Lublin. Avigdor had joked: what sort of secret could it be? Had Anshel discovered a hidden treasure? Had he written an essay? By studying the Cabala, had he created a dove?

Now they entered the room and while Anshel carefully locked the door, Avigdor said teasingly: "Well, let's hear your great secret."

"Prepare yourself for the most incredible thing that ever was."

"I'm prepared for anything."

"I'm not a man but a woman," said Anshel. "My name isn't Anshel, it's Yentl."

Avigdor burst out laughing. "I knew it was a hoax."

"But it's true."

"Even if I'm a fool, I won't swallow this."

"Do you want me to show you?"

"Yes."

"Then I'll get undressed."

Avigdor's eyes widened. It occurred to him that Anshel might want to practice pederasty. Anshel took off the gaberdine and the fringed garment, and threw off her underclothes. Avigdor took one look and turned first white, then fiery red. Anshel covered herself hastily.

"I've done this only so that you can testify at the courthouse. Otherwise, Hadass will have to stay a grass widow."

Avigdor had lost his tongue. He was seized by a fit of trembling. He wanted to speak, but his lips moved and nothing came out. He sat down quickly, for his leg would not support him.

Finally he murmured: "How is it possible? I don't believe it!"

"Should I get undressed again?"

"No!"

Yentl proceeded to tell the whole story: how her father, bedridden, had studied Torah with her; how she had never had the patience for women and their silly chatter; how she had sold the house and all the furnishings, left the town, made her way disguised as a man to Lublin, and on the road met Avigdor. Avigdor sat speechless, gazing at the storyteller. Yentl was by now wearing men's clothes once more.

Avigdor spoke: "It must be a dream."

He pinched himself on the cheek.

"It isn't a dream."

"That such a thing should happen to me!"

"It's all true."

"Why did you do it? *Nu,* I'd better keep still."

"I didn't want to waste my life on a baking shovel and a kneading trough."

"And what about Hadass—why did you do that?"

"I did it for your sake. I knew that Peshe would torment you and at our house you would have some peace."

Avigdor was silent for a long time. He bowed his head, pressed his hands to his temples, shook his head. "What will you do now?"

"I'll go away to a different yeshiva."

"What? If you had only told me earlier, we could have . . ."

Avigdor broke off in the middle.

"No—it wouldn't have been good."

"Why not?"

"I'm neither one nor the other."

"What a dilemma I'm in!"

"Get a divorce from that horror. Marry Hadass."

"She'll never divorce me and Hadass won't have me."

"Hadass loves you. She won't listen to her father again."

Avigdor stood up suddenly but then sat down. "I won't be able to forget you. Ever . . ."

VI

According to the Law, Avigdor was now forbidden to spend another moment alone with Yentl; yet dressed in the gaberdine and trousers, she was again the familiar Anshel.

They resumed their conversation on the old footing: "How could you bring yourself to violate the commandment every day: 'A woman shall not wear that which pertaineth to a man'?"

"I wasn't created for plucking feathers and chattering with females."

"Would you rather lose your share in the world to come?"

"Perhaps . . ."

Avigdor raised his eyes. Only now did he realize that Anshel's cheeks were too smooth for a man's, the hair too abundant, the hands too small. Even so he could not believe that such a thing could have happened. At any moment he expected to wake up. He bit his lips, pinched his thigh. He was seized by shyness and could not speak without stammering. His friendship with Anshel, their intimate talk, their confidences, had been turned into a sham and delusion. The thought even occurred to him that Anshel might be a demon. He shook himself as to cast off a nightmare; yet that power which knows the difference between dream and reality told him it was all true. He summoned up his courage. He and Anshel could never be strangers to one another, even though Anshel was in fact Yentl . . .

He ventured a comment: "It seems to me that the witness who testifies for a deserted woman may not marry her, for the Law calls him "a party to the affair."

"What? That didn't occur to me!"

"We must look it up in Eben Ezer."

"I'm not even sure that the rules pertaining to a deserted woman apply in this case," said Anshel in the manner of a scholar.

"If you don't want Hadass to be a grass widow, you must reveal the secret to her directly."

"That I can't do."

"In any event, you must get another witness."

Gradually the two went back to their Talmudic conversation. It seemed strange at first to Avigdor to be disputing holy writ with a woman, yet before long the Torah had reunited them. Though their bodies were different, their souls were of one kind. Anshel spoke in a singsong, gesticulated with her thumb, clutched her sidelocks, plucked at her beardless chin, made all the customary gestures of a yeshiva student. In the heat of argument she even seized Avigdor by the lapel and called him stupid. A great love for Anshel took hold of Avigdor, mixed with shame, remorse, anxiety. If I had only known this before, he said to himself. In his thoughts he likened Anshel (or Yentl) to Bruria, the wife of Reb Meir, and to Yalta, the wife of Reb Nachman. For the first time he saw clearly that this was what he had always wanted: a wife whose mind was not taken up with material things . . . His desire for Hadass was gone now, and he knew he would long for Yentl, but he dared not say so. He felt hot and knew that his face was burning. He could no longer meet Anshel's eyes. He began to enumerate Anshel's sins and saw that he too was implicated, for he had sat next to Yentl and had touched her during her unclean days. Nu, and what could be said about her marriage to Hadass? What a multitude of transgressions there! Wilful deception, false vows, misrepresentation!—Heaven knows what else.

He asked suddenly: "Tell the truth, are you a heretic?"

"God forbid!"

"Then how could you bring yourself to do such a thing?"

The longer Anshel talked, the less Avigdor understood. All Anshel's explanations seemed to point to one thing: she had the soul of a man and the body of a woman. Anshel said she had married Hadass only in order to be near Avigdor.

"You could have married me," Avigdor said.

"I wanted to study the Gemara and Commentaries with you, not darn your socks!"

For a long time neither spoke. Then Avigdor broke the silence: "I'm afraid Hadass will get sick from all this, God forbid!"

"I'm afraid of that, too."

"What's going to happen now?"

Dusk fell and the two began to recite the evening prayer. In his confusion Avigdor mixed up the blessings, omitted some and repeated others. He glanced sideways at Anshel, who was rocking back and forth, beating her breast, bowing her head. He saw her, eyes closed, lift her face to Heaven, as though beseeching: You, Father in Heaven, know the truth . . . When their prayers were finished, they sat down on opposite chairs, facing one another yet a good distance apart. The room filled with shadows. Reflections of the sunset, like purple embroidery, shook on the wall opposite the window. Avigdor again wanted to speak but at first the words, trembling on the tip of his tongue, would not come.

Suddenly they burst forth: "Maybe it's still not too late? I can't go on living with that accursed woman . . . You . . ."

"No, Avigdor, it's impossible."

"Why?"

"I'll live out my time as I am . . ."

"I'll miss you. Terribly."

"And I'll miss you."

"What's the sense of all this?"

Anshel did not answer. Night fell and the light faded. In the darkness they seemed to be listening to each other's thoughts. The Law forbade Avigdor to stay in the room alone with Anshel, but he could not think of her just as a woman. What a strange power there is in clothing, he thought.

But he spoke of something else: "I would advise you simply to send Hadass a divorce."

"How can I do that?"

"Since the marriage sacraments weren't valid, what difference does it make?"

"I suppose you're right."

"There'll be time enough later for her to find out the truth."

The maidservant came in with a lamp, but as soon as she had gone, Avigdor put it out. Their predicament and the words which they must speak to one another could not endure light. In the blackness Anshel related all the particulars. She answered all Avigdor's questions. The clock struck two, and still they talked. Anshel told Avigdor that Hadass had never forgotten him. She talked of him frequently, worried about his health, was sorry—though not without a certain satisfaction—about the way things had turned out with Peshe. "She'll be a good wife," said Anshel. "I don't even know how to bake a pudding."

"Nevertheless, if you're willing . . ."

"No, Avigdor. It wasn't destined to be . . ."

VII

It was all a great riddle to the town: the messenger who arrived bringing Hadass the divorce papers; Avigdor's remaining in Lublin until after the holidays; his return to Bechev with slumping shoulders and lifeless eyes as if he had been ill. Hadass took to her bed and was visited by the doctor three times a day. Avigdor went into seclusion. If someone ran across him by chance and addressed him, he did not answer. Peshe complained to her parents that Avigdor paced back and forth smoking all night long. When he finally collapsed from sheer fatigue, in his sleep he called out the name of an unknown female—Yentl. Peshe began talking of a divorce. The town thought Avigdor wouldn't grant her one or would demand money at the very least, but he agreed to everything.

In Bechev the people were not used to having mysteries stay mysteries for long. How can you keep secrets in a little town where everyone knows what's cooking in everyone else's pots? Yet, though there were plenty of persons who made a practice of looking through keyholes and laying an ear to shutters, what happened remained an enigma. Hadass lay in her bed and wept. Chanina the herb doctor reported that she was wasting away. Anshel had disappeared without a trace. Reb Alter Vishkower sent for Avigdor and he arrived, but those who stood straining beneath the window couldn't catch a word of what passed between them. Those individuals who habitually pry into other people's affairs came up with all sorts of theories, but not one of them was consistent.

One party came to the conclusion that Anshel had fallen into the hands of Catholic priests and had been converted. That might have made sense. But where could Anshel have found time for the priests, since he was always studying in the yeshiva? And apart from that, since when does an apostate send his wife a divorce?

Another group whispered that Anshel had cast an eye on another woman. But who could it be? There were no love affairs conducted in Bechev. And none of the young women had recently left town—neither a Jewish woman nor a Gentile one.

Somebody else offered the suggestion that Anshel had been carried away by evil spirits, or was even one of them himself. As proof he cited the fact that Anshel had never come either to the bathhouse or to the river. It is well known that demons have the feet of geese. Well, but had Hadass never seen him barefoot? And who ever heard of a demon sending his wife a divorce? When a demon marries a daughter of mortals, he usually lets her remain a grass widow.

It occurred to someone else that Anshel had committed a major transgression and gone into exile in order to do penance. But what sort of transgression could it have been? And why had he not entrusted it to the rabbi? And why did Avigdor wander about like a ghost?

The hypothesis of Tevel the musician was closest to the truth. Tevel maintained that Avigdor had been unable to forget Hadass and that Anshel had divorced her so that his friend would be able to marry her. But was such friendship possible in this world? And in that case, why had Anshel divorced Hadass even before Avigdor divorced Peshe? Furthermore, such a thing can be accomplished only if the wife has been informed of the arrangement and is willing, yet all signs pointed to Hadass's great love for Anshel, and in fact she was ill from sorrow.

One thing was clear to all: Avigdor knew the truth. But it was impossible to get anything out of him. He remained in seclusion and kept silent with an obstinacy that was a reproof to the whole town.

Close friends urged Peshe not to divorce Avigdor, though they had severed all relations and no longer lived as man and wife. He did not even, on Friday night, perform the kiddush blessing for her. He spent his nights either at the study house or at the widow's where Anshel had found lodgings. When Peshe spoke to him he didn't answer, but stood with bowed head. The tradeswoman Peshe had no patience for such goings-on. She needed a young man to help her out in the store, not a yeshiva student who had fallen into melancholy. Someone of that sort might even take it into his head to depart and leave her deserted. Peshe agreed to a divorce.

In the meantime, Hadass had recovered, and Reb Alter Vishkower let it be known that a marriage contract was being drawn up. Hadass was to marry Avigdor. The town was agog. A marriage between a man and a woman who had once been engaged and their betrothal broken off was unheard of. The wedding was held on the first Sabbath after Tishe b'Av, and included all that is customary at the marriage of a virgin: the banquet for the poor, the canopy before the synagogue, the musicians, the wedding jester, the virtue dance. Only one thing was lacking: joy. The bridegroom stood beneath the marriage canopy, a figure of desolation. The bride had recovered from her sickness, but had remained pale and thin. Her tears fell into the golden chicken broth. From all eyes the same question looked out: why had Anshel done it?

After Avigdor's marriage to Hadass, Peshe spread that rumor that Anshel had sold his wife to Avigdor for a price, and that the money had been supplied by Alter Vishkower. One young man pondered the riddle at great length until he finally arrived at the conclusion that Anshel had lost his beloved wife to Avigdor at cards, or even on a spin of the Hanukkah dreidl. It is a general rule that when the grain of truth cannot be found, men will swallow great helpings of falsehood. Truth itself is often concealed in such a way that the harder you look for it, the harder it is to find.

Not long after the wedding, Hadass became pregnant. The child was a boy and those assembled at the circumcision could scarcely believe their ears when they heard the father name his son Anshel.

Dislocation and Survival in Immigrant America

Abraham Cahan

Abraham Cahan, born in 1860, in Podberezy near Vilna, often called the Jerusalem of Lithuania, was educated in various Hebrew schools, a yeshiva, and the Vilna Teachers Institute, a government-sponsored school for Jewish teachers in which Yiddish was prohibited. In 1881 he broke away from traditional Judaism and moved toward socialism, joining an underground anti-Czarist group. When he realized that his life was in danger, he joined a group of emigrés and landed in America on June 6, 1882, barely escaping the vicious pogroms then shaking Eastern European Jewry.

Once in America, Cahan quickly became a leader among the Russian Jewish Socialists and intellectuals. A true Renaissance man, he helped organize the first Jewish tailors union in 1884 and continued to take an active role in American Jewish socialist efforts. In addition, as a radical editor, he co-edited the first, albeit short-lived, Jewish-language Socialist weekly, called *Neie Tzeit*, in 1886. He founded the *Jewish Daily Forward* in 1877 and served as its senior editor from 1903 to 1951. In addition to his political and editorial activities, Cahan was an English fiction writer from the 1890s until 1917, largely writing stories and novels about the accommodation and acculturation of immigrant Jews in America. He gave up the daily running of the *Daily Forward* only after suffering a stroke in 1946, but he continued to write, review, and speak out, authoring his last book review in 1948. Cahan died in 1951.

Cahan's insights into the psychology of both women and men are shrewd and sympathetic. Gitl is described as a woman of average looks and intelligence, a sweet but initially not very resilient or resourceful soul who is for a long time overwhelmed by the cultural upheaval of emigration. Her husband, Yekl, is a shallow, mediocre lout; he is swept away by the charms of Mamie, a pretty, sullen, older, Americanized Jewish woman. At first, Gitl wants nothing in the world but to regain her husband's affection and to see her little son eat and grow strong. Eventually, however, Gitl begins to regain her sense of self-esteem and direction, thanks partially to the attentions of an overbearing landlady and a kindly, gentle, intellectual boarder.

•

"Gitl Learns It's Not Easy Being Green" (excerpt)

It was early in the afternoon of Gitl's second Wednesday in the New World. Jake, Bernstein and Charley, their two boarders, were at work. Yossele was sound asleep in the lodgers' double bed, in the smallest of the three tiny rooms which the family rented on the second floor of one of a row of brand-new tenement houses. Gitl was by herself in the little front room which served the quadruple purpose of kitchen, dining room, sitting room, and parlor. She wore a skirt and a loose jacket of white Russian calico, decorated with huge gay figures, and her dark hair was only half covered by a bandana of red and yellow. This was Gitl's compromise between her conscience and her husband. She panted to yield to Jake's demands completely, but could not nerve herself up to going about "in her own hair, like a Gentile woman." Even the expostulations of Mrs. Kavarsky—the childless middle-aged woman who occupied with her husband the three rooms across the narrow hallway—failed to prevail upon her. Nevertheless Jake, succumbing to Mrs. Kavarsky's annoying solicitations, had bought his wife a cheap high-crowned hat, utterly unfit to be worn over her voluminous wig, and even a corset. Gitl could not be coaxed into accompanying them to the store; but the eloquent neighbor had persuaded Jake that her presence at the transaction was not indispensable after all.

"Leave it to me," she said; "I know what will become her and what won't. I'll get her a hat that will make a Fifth Avenue lady of her, and you shall see if she does not give in. If she is then not *satetzfiet* to go with her own hair, *vell!*" What then would take place Mrs. Kavarsky left unsaid.

The hat and the corset had been lying in the house now three days, and the neighbor's predictions had not yet come true, save for Gitl's prying once or twice into the pasteboard boxes in which those articles lay, otherwise unmolested, on the shelf over her bed.

The door was open. Gitl stood toying with the knob of the electric bell, and deriving much delight from the way the street door latch kept clicking under her magic touch two flights above. Finally she wearied of her diversion, and shutting the door she went to take a look at Yossele. She found him fast asleep, and, as she was retracing her steps through her own and Jake's bedroom, her eye fell upon the paper boxes. She got up on the edge of her bed and, lifting the cover from the hatbox, she took a prolonged look at its contents. All at once her face brightened up with temptation. She went to fasten the hallway door of the kitchen on its latch, and then regaining the bedroom shut herself in. After a lapse of some ten or fifteen minutes she re-emerged, attired in her brown holiday dress in which she had first confronted Jake on Ellis Island, and with the tall black straw hat on her head. Walking on tiptoe, as though about to commit a crime, she crossed over to the looking glass. Then she paused, her eyes on the door, to listen for possible footsteps. Hearing none she faced the glass. "Quite a *panenke!*"* she thought to herself all aglow with excitement, a smile, at once shamefaced and beatific, melting her features. She turned to the right then to the left, to view herself in profile, as she had seen Mrs. Kavarsky do, and drew back a step to ascertain the effect of the corset. To tell the truth, the corset proved utterly impotent against the baggy shapelessness of the Povodye garment. Yet Gitl found it to work wonders, and readily pardoned it for the very uncomfortable sensation which it caused her. She viewed herself again and again, and was in a flutter both of ecstasy and alarm when there came a timid rap on the door. Trembling all over, she scampered on tiptoe back into the bedroom, and after a little she returned in her calico dress and bandana kerchief. The knock at the door had apparently been produced by some peddler or beggar, for it was not repeated. Yet so violent was Gitl's agitation that she had to sit down on the haircloth lounge for breath and to regain composure.

"What is it they call this?" she presently asked herself gazing at the bare boards of the floor. "Floor!" she recalled, much to her self-satisfaction. "And that?" she further examined herself as she fixed her glance on the ceiling. This time the answer was slow in coming, and her heart grew faint. "And what was it Yekl called that?"—transferring her eyes to the window. "Veen—neev—veenda," she at last uttered exultantly. The evening before she had happened to call it *fentzter*, in spite of Jake's repeated corrections.

"Can't you say *veenda?*" he had growled. "What a peasant head! Other greenhornsh learn to speak American *shtyle* very fast; and she—one might tell her the same word eighty thousand times, and it is *nu used.*"

"*Es is of'n veenda mein ich,*"† she hastened to set herself right.

She blushed as she said it, but at the moment she attached no importance to the matter and took no more notice of it. Now, however, Jake's tone of voice, as he had rebuked her backwardness in picking up American Yiddish, came back to her and she grew dejected.

*A young noblewoman.

†It is on the window, I mean to say.

She was getting used to her husband, in whom her own Yekl and Jake the stranger were by degrees merging themselves into one undivided being. When the hour of his coming from work drew near she would every little while consult the clock and become impatient with the slow progress of its hands; although mixed with this impatience there was a feeling of apprehension lest the supper, prepared as it was under culinary conditions entirely new to her, should fail to please Jake and the boarders. She had even become accustomed to address her husband as Jake without reddening in the face; and, what is more, was getting to tolerate herself being called by him Goitie (Gertie)—a word phonetically akin to Yiddish for Gentile. For the rest she was too inexperienced and too simple-hearted naturally to comment upon his manner toward her. She had not altogether overcome her awe of him, but as he showed her occasional marks of kindness she was upon the whole rather content with her new situation. Now, however, as she thus sat in solitude, with his harsh voice ringing in her ears and his icy look before her, a feeling of suspicion darkened her soul. She recalled other scenes where he had looked and spoken as he had done the night before. "He must hate me! A pain upon me!" she concluded with a fallen heart. She wondered whether his demeanor toward her was like that of other people who hated their wives. She remembered a woman of her native village who was known to be thus afflicted, and she dropped her head in a fit of despair. At one moment she took a firm resolve to pluck up courage and cast away the kerchief and the wig; but at the next she reflected that God would be sure to punish her for the terrible sin so that instead of winning Jake's love the change would increase his hatred for her. It flashed upon her mind to call upon some "good Jew" to pray for the return of his favor, or to seek some old Polish beggar woman who could prescribe a love potion. But then, alas! who knows whether there are in this terrible America any good Jews or beggar women with love potions at all! Better she had never known this "black year" of a country! Here everybody says she is green. What an ugly word to apply to people! She had never been green at home, and here she had suddenly become so. What do they mean by it, anyhow? Verily, one might turn green and yellow and gray while young in such a dreadful place. Her heart was wrung with the most excruciating pangs of homesickness. And as she thus sat brooding and listlessly surveying her new surroundings—the iron stove, the stationary washtubs, the window opening vertically, the fire escape, the yellowish broom with its painted handle—things which she had never dreamed of at her birthplace—these objects seemed to stare at her haughtily and inspired her with fright. Even the burnished cup of the electric bell knob looked contemptuously and seemed to call her "Greenhorn! greenhorn!" "Lord of the world! Where am I?" she whispered with tears in her voice.

The dreary solitude terrified her, and she instinctively rose to take refuge at Yossele's bedside. As she got up, a vague doubt came over her whether she should find there her child at all. But Yossele was found safe and sound enough. He was rubbing his eyes and announcing the advent of his famous appetite. She seized him in her arms and covered his warm cheeks with fervent kisses which did her aching heart good. And by-and-by, as she admiringly watched the boy making savage inroads into a generous slice of rye bread she thought of Jake's affection for the child; whereupon things began to assume a brighter aspect, and she presently set about preparing supper with a lighter heart, although her countenance for some time retained its mournful woebegone expression.

Meanwhile Jake sat at his machine merrily pushing away at a cloak and singing to it some of the popular American songs of the day.

The sensation caused by the arrival of his wife and child had nearly blown over. Peltner's dancing school he had not visited since a week or two previous to Gitl's landing. As to the scene which had greeted him in the shop after the stirring news had first reached it, he had faced it out with much more courage and got over it with much less difficulty than he had anticipated.

"Did I ever tell you I was a *tzingle man*?" he laughingly defended himself though blushing crimson, against his shopmates' taunts. "And am I obliged to give you a *report* whether my wife has come or not? You are not worth mentioning her name to, *anyhoy*."

The boss then suggested that Jake celebrate the event with two pints of beer, the motion being seconded by the presser, who volunteered to fetch the beverage. Jake obeyed with alacrity, and if there had still lingered any trace of awkwardness in his position it was soon washed away by the foaming liquid.

As a matter of fact, Fanny's embarrassment was much greater than Jake's. The stupefying news was broken to her on the very day of Gitl's arrival. After passing a sleepless night she felt that she could not bring herself to face Jake in the presence of her other shopmates, to whom her feelings for him were an open secret. As luck would have it, it was Sunday, the beginning of a new working week in the metropolitan Ghetto, and she went to look for a job in another place.

Jake at once congratulated himself upon her absence and missed her. But then he equally missed the company of Mamie and of all the other dancing-school girls, whose society and attentions now more than ever seemed to him necessities of his life. They haunted his mind day and night; he almost never beheld them in his imagination except as clustering together with his fellow-cavaliers and making merry over him and his wife; and the vision pierced his heart with shame and jealousy. All his achievements seemed wiped out by a sudden stroke of ill fate. He thought himself a martyr, an innocent exile from a world to which he belonged by right; and he frequently felt the sobs of self-pity mounting to his throat. For several minutes at a time, while kicking at his treadle, he would see, reddening before him, Gitl's bandana kerchief and her prominent gums, or hear an un-American piece of Yiddish pronounced with Gitl's peculiar lisp—that very lisp, which three years ago he used to mimic fondly, but which now grated on his nerves and was apt to make his face twitch with sheer disgust, insomuch that he often found a vicious relief in mocking that lisp of hers audibly over his work. But can it be that he is doomed for life? No! no! he would revolt, conscious at the same time that there was really no escape. "Ah, may she be killed, the horrid greenhorn!" he would gasp to himself in a paroxysm of despair. And then he would bewail his lost youth, and curse all Russia for his premature marriage. Presently, however, he would recall the plump, spunky face of his son who bore such close resemblance to himself to whom he was growing more strongly attached every day, and who was getting to prefer his company to his mother's; and thereupon his heart would soften toward Gitl, and he would gradually feel the qualms of pity and remorse, and make a vow to treat her kindly. "Never min'," he would at such instances say in his heart, "she will *oyshgreen** herself and I shall get used to her. She is a—*shight* better than all the dancing-school girls." And he would inspire himself with respect for her spotless purity, and take comfort in the fact of her being a model housewife, undiverted from her duties by any thoughts of balls or picnics. And despite a deeper consciousness which exposed his readiness to sacrifice it all at any time, he would work himself into a dignified feeling as the head of a household and the father of a promising son, and soothe himself with the additional consolation that sooner or later the other fellows of Joe's academy would also be married.

On the Wednesday in question Jake and his shopmates had warded off a reduction of wages by threatening a strike, and were accordingly in high feather. And so Jake and Bernstein came home in unusually good spirits. Little Joey—for such was Yossele's name now—with whom his father's plays were for the most part of an athletic character, welcomed Jake by a challenge for a pugilistic encounter, and the way he said "Coom a fight!" and held out his little fists so delighted Mr. Podkovnik, Sr., that upon ordering Gitl to serve supper he vouchsafed a fillip on the tip of her nose.

While she was hurriedly setting the table, Jake took to describing to Charley his employer's defeat. "You should have seen how he looked, the

*A verb coined from the Yiddish *oys*, "out," and the English *green*, and signifying to cease being green.

cockroach!" he said. "He became as pale as the wall and his teeth were chattering as if he had been shaken up with fever, *'pon my void*. And how quiet he became all of a sudden, as if he could not count two! One might apply him to an ulcer, so soft was he—ha-ha-ha!" he laughed, looking to Bernstein, who smiled assent.

At last supper was announced. Bernstein donned his hat, and did not sit down to the repast before he had performed his ablutions and whispered a short prayer. As he did so Jake and Charley interchanged a wink. As to themselves, they dispensed with all devotional preliminaries, and took their seats with uncovered heads. Gitl also washed her fingers and said the prayer, and as she handed Yossele his first slice of bread she did not release it before he had recited the benediction.

Bernstein, who, as a rule, looked daggers at his meal, this time received his plate of *borshtch**—his favorite dish—with a radiant face; and as he ate he pronounced it a masterpiece, and lavished compliments on the artist.

"It's a long time since I tasted such a borshtch! Simply a vivifier! It melts in every limb!" he kept rhapsodizing, between mouthfuls. "It ought to be sent to the Chicago Exposition. The misses would get a medal."

"A *regely* European borshtch!" Charley chimed in. "It is worth ten cents a spoonful, *'pon mine vort!*"

"Go away! You are only making fun of me," Gitl declared, beaming with pride. "What is there to be laughing at? I make it as well as I can," she added demurely.

"Let him who is laughing laugh with teeth," jested Charlie. "I tell you it is a—" The remainder of the sentence was submerged in a mouthful of the vivifying semi-liquid.

"*Alla right*!" Jake bethought himself. "*Charge* him ten *shent* for each spoonful. Mr. Bernstein, you shall be kind enough to be the *bookkeeper*. But if you don't pay, Chollie, I'll get out a *tzommesh* [summons] from *court*."

Whereat the little kitchen rang with laughter, in which all participated except Bernstein. Even Joey, or Yossele joined in the general outburst of merriment. Otherwise he was busily engaged cramming borshtch into his mouth, and, in passing, also into his nose, with both his plump hands for a pair of spoons. From time to time he would interrupt operations to make a wry face and, blinking his eyes, to lisp out rapturously, "Sour!"

"Look—may you live long—do look; he is laughing, too!" Gitl called attention to Yossele's bespattered face. "To think of such a crumb having as much sense as that!" She was positive that he appreciated his father's witticism, although she herself understood it but vaguely.

"May he know evil no better than he knows what he is laughing at,"

*A sour soup of cabbage and beets.

Jake objected, with a fatherly mien. "What makes you laugh, Joey?" The boy had no time to spare for an answer, being too busy licking his emptied plate. "Look at the soldier's appetite he has, *de feller*! Joey, hoy you like de borshtch! Alla right?" Jake asked in English.

"Awrr-ra rr-right!" Joey pealed out his sturdy rustic r's, which he had mastered shortly before taking leave of his doting grandmother.

"See how well he speaks English?" Jake said, facetiously.

"A —— *shight* better than his mamma, *anyvay*."

Gitl, who was in the meantime serving the meat, colored but took the remark in good part.

"*I tell ye* he is growing to be Presdent 'Nited States," Charlie interposed.

"*Greenhorn*, that you are! A president must be American born," Jake explained, self-consciously. "Ain't it, Mr. Bernstein?"

"It's a pity, then, that he was not born in this country," Bernstein replied, his eye envyingly fixed now on Gitl, now at the child, on whose place she was at this moment carving a piece of meat into tiny morsels. "*Vell*, if he cannot be a president of the United States, he may be one of a synagogue, so he is a president."

"Don't you worry for his sake," Gitl put in, delighted with the attention her son was absorbing. "He does not need to be a pesdent; he is growing to be a rabbi; don't be making fun of him." And she turned her head to kiss the future rabbi.

"Who is making fun?" Bernstein demurred. "I wish I had a boy like him."

"Get married and you will have one," said Gitl, beamingly.

"*Shay*, Mr. Bernstein, how about your *shadchen?*"* Jake queried. He gave a laugh, but forthwith checked it, remaining with an embarrassed grin on his face, as though anxious to swallow the question. Bernstein blushed to the roots of his hair, and bent an irate glance on his plate, but held his peace.

His reserved manner, if not his superior education, held Bernstein's shopmates at a respectful distance from him, and, as a rule, rendered him proof against their badinage, although behind his back they would indulge an occasional joke on his inferiority as a workman, and—while they were at it—on his dyspepsia, his books, and staid, methodical habits. Recently, however, they had got wind of his clandestine visits to a marriage broker's, and the temptation to chaff him on the subject had proved resistless, all the more so because Bernstein, whose leading foible was his well-controlled vanity, was quick to take offence in general, and on this matter in particular. As to Jake, he was by no means averse to having a laugh at somebody

*A matrimonial agent.

else's expense; but since Bernstein had become his boarder he felt that he could not afford to wound his pride. Hence his regret and anxiety at his allusion to the matrimonial agent.

After supper Charlie went out for the evening, while Bernstein retired to their little bedroom. Gitl busied herself with the dishes, and Jake took to romping about with Joey and had a hearty laugh with him. He was beginning to tire of the boy's company and to feel lonesome generally, when there was a knock at the door.

"Coom in!" Gitl hastened to say somewhat coquettishly, flourishing her proficiency in American manners, as she raised her head from the pot in her hands.

"Coom in!" repeated Joey.

The door flew open, and in came Mamie, preceded by a cloud of cologne odors. She was apparently dressed for some occasion of state, for she was powdered and straight-laced and resplendent in a waist of blazing red, gaudily trimmed, and with puff sleeves, each wider than the vast expanse of white straw, surmounted with a whole forest of ostrich feathers, which adorned her head. One of her gloved hands held the huge hoop-shaped yellowish handle of a blue parasol.

"Good-evenin', Jake!" she said, with ostentatious vivacity.

"Good-evenin', Mamie!" Jake returned, jumping to his feet and violently reddening, as if suddenly pricked. "Mish Fein, my vife! My vife, Mish Fein!"

Miss Fein made a stately bow, primly biting her lip as she did so. Gitl, with the pot in her hands, stood staring sheepishly, at a loss what to do.

"Say 'I'm glyad to meech you,'" Jake urged her, confusedly.

The English phrase was more than Gitl could venture to echo.

"She is still *green*," Jake apologized for her, in Yiddish.

"*Never min'*, she will soon *oysgreen* herself," Mamie remarked, with patronizing affability.

"The *lada* is an acquaintance of mine," Jake explained bashfully, his hand feeling the few days' growth of beard on his chin.

Gitl instinctively scented an enemy in the visitor, and eyed her with an uneasy gaze. Nevertheless she mustered a hospitable air, and drawing up the rocking chair, she said, with shamefaced cordiality: "Sit down; why should you be standing? You may be seated for the same money."

In the conversation which followed Mamie did most of the talking. With a nervous volubility often broken by an irrelevant giggle, and violently rocking with her chair, she expatiated on the charms of America, prophesying that her hostess would bless the day of her arrival on its soil, and went off in ecstasies over Joey. She spoke with an overdone American accent in the dialect of the Polish Jews, affectedly Germanized and profusely interspersed with English, so that Gitl, whose mother tongue was Lithuanian Yiddish, could scarcely catch the meaning of one half of her flood of garrulity. And as she thus rattled on, she now examined the room, now surveyed Gitl from head to foot, now fixed her with a look of studied sarcasm, followed by a side glance at Jake, which seemed to say, "Woe to you, what a rag of a wife yours is!" Whenever Gitl ventured a timid remark, Mamie would nod assent with dignified amiability, and thereupon imitate a smile, broad yet fleeting, which she had seen performed by some uptown ladies.

Jake stared at the lamp with a faint simper, scarcely following the caller's words. His head swam with embarrassment. The consciousness of Gitl's unattractive appearance made him sick with shame and vexation, and his eyes carefully avoided her bandana, as a culprit schoolboy does the evidence of his offence.

"You mush vant you tventy-fife dollars," he presently nerved himself up to say in English, breaking an awkward pause.

"I should cough!" Mamie rejoined.

"In a coupel a veeksh, Mamie, as sure as my name is Jake."

"In a couple o' veeks! No, sirree! I mus' have my money at oncet. I don' know vere you vill get it, dough. Vy, a married man!"—with a chuckle. "You got a —— of a lot o' t'ings to pay for. You took de foinitsha by a custom peddler, ain' it? But what a —— do I care? I vant my money. I voiked hard enough for it."

"Don' shpeak English. She'll t'ink I don' knu vot ve shpeakin'," he besought her, in accents which implied intimacy between the two of them and a common aloofness from Gitl.

"Vot d'I care vot she t'inks? She's your vife, ain' it? Vell, she mus' know ev'ryt'ing. Dot's right! A husban' dass'n't hide not'ink from his vife!"—with another chuckle and another look of deadly sarcasm at Gitl. "I can say de same in Jewish—"

"Shurr-r up, Mamie!" he interrupted her, gaspingly.

"Don'tch you like it, lump it! A vife mus'n't be skinned like a strange lady, see?" she pursued inexorably. "O'ly a strange goil a feller might bluff dot he ain' married, and skin her out of tventy-five dollars." In point of fact, he had never directly given himself out for a single man to her. But it did not even occur to him to defend himself on that score.

"Mamie! Ma-a-mie! Shtop! I'll pay you ev'ry shent. Shpeak Jewesh, pleashe!" he implored, as if for life.

"You'r' afraid of her? Dot's right! Dot's right! Dot's nice! All religious peoples is afraid of deir vifes. But vy didn' you say you vas married from de sta't, an' dot you vant money to send for dem?" she tortured him, with a lingering arch leer.

"For Chrish' shake, Mamie!" he entreated her, wincingly.

"Shtop to shpeak English, an' shpeak shomet'ing differench. I'll shee you—vere can I shee you?"

"You von't come by Joe no more?" she asked, with sudden interest and even solicitude.

"You t'ink indeed I'm 'frait? If I vanted I can gu dere more ash I ushed to gu dere. But vere can I findsh you?"

"I guess you know vere I'm livin', don'ch you? So kvick you forget? Vot a sho't mind you got! Vill you come? Never min', I know you are only bluffin', an' dot's all."

"I'll come, ash sure ash I leev."

"Vill you? All right. But if you don' come an' pay me at least ten dollars for a sta't, you'll see!"

In the meanwhile Gitl, poor thing, sat pale and horror-struck. Mamie's perfumes somehow terrified her. She was racked with jealousy and all sorts of suspicions, which she vainly struggled to disguise. She could see that they were having a heated altercation, and that Jake was begging about something or other, and was generally the under dog in the parley. Ever and anon she strained her ears in the effort to fasten some of the incomprehensible sounds in her memory, that she might subsequently parrot them over to Mrs. Kavarsky, and ascertain their meaning. But alas! the attempt proved futile; "never min'" and "all right" being all she could catch.

Mamie concluded her visit by presenting Joey with the imposing sum of five cents.

"What do you say? Say 'danks, sir!'" Gitl prompted the boy.

"Shay 't'ank you, ma'am!'" Jake overruled her. "'Shir' is said to a gentlemarn."

"Good-night!" Mamie sang out, as she majestically opened the door.

"Good-night!" Jake returned, with a burning face.

"Goot-night!" Gitl and Joey chimed in duet.

"Say 'cull again!'"

"Cullye gain!"

"Good-night!" Mamie said once more, as she bowed herself out of the door with what she considered an exquisitely "tony" smile.

The guest's exit was succeeded by a momentary silence. Jake felt as if his face and ears were on fire.

"We used to work in the same shop," he presently said.

"Is that the way a seamstress dresses in America?" Gitl inquired. "It is not for nothing that it is called the golden land," she added, with timid irony.

"She must be going to a ball," he explained, at the same moment casting a glance at the looking glass.

The word "ball" had an imposing ring for Gitl's ears. At home she had heard it used in connection with the sumptuous life of the Russian or Polish nobility, but had never formed a clear idea of its meaning.

"She looks a veritable *panenke,*" she remarked, with hidden sarcasm. "Was she born here?"

"*Nu,* but she has been very long here. She speaks English like one American born. We are used to speak in English when we talk *shop*. She came to ask me about a *job*."

Gitl reflected that with Bernstein Jake was in the habit of talking shop in Yiddish, although the boarder could even read English books, which her husband could not do.

Anzia Yezierska

Anzia Yezierska, born in a mud hut in Plinsk on the Russian–Polish border in 1885, emigrated to the Lower East Side at age fifteen. She worked in a sweatshop by day and attended school by night in order to learn to read and write in English. She studied "domestic science" at Columbia University and married an attorney, but she did not find herself happy with either enterprise. After a second unsuccessful marriage, which produced a child, Louise (Henrikson), Yezierska gave her four-year-old daughter to the child's father to raise; Yezierska did maintain a relationship with her daughter, however, which became stronger as they grew older. In 1917 she developed a short romance with John Dewey, who appears in several stories as the elegant, older, well-educated gentile suitor. Yezierska, who devoted most of her adult life to writing, won a Hollywood contract on the basis of some of her early work but found living in California unconducive to her creative craft. She returned to New York and, although she never really found a niche in which she felt comfortable, continued writing even in her later years. Yezierska died in 1970.

Reading Yezierska's short stories and novels is a little like sitting inside a pressure cooker with no relief. She expertly captures the intense intergenerational conflicts that erupted in many immigrant Jewish families. Although Yezierska's stories typically leave characters still raw and hurting and issues still unresolved, her characters are lively and believable, and her insights often skillfully blend humor and pathos.

Hanneh Breineh, in "The Fat of the Land," is almost the diametric opposite of Asch's Rachel-Leah. She is scarcely able to deal with the demands of her family in the abject poverty of her environment. She has the kind of personality, furthermore, that sees the black cloud above every silver lining, and she manages time and again to snatch defeat from the jaws of victory. Hanneh Breineh is a masterful creation, a very effective antidote both to the stereotype of the supercompetent "Jewish mother" and to the nostalgic American Jewish tendency to sentimentalize the immigrant slums of New York's Lower East Side. Moreover, the story brilliantly depicts the hunger of second-generation American Jews to become "real" Americans, often crudely rejecting parents whom they perceived as standing in the way of their progress to a better life.

•

"The Fat of the Land"

In an air-shaft so narrow that you could touch the next wall with your bare hands, Hanneh Breineh leaned out and knocked on her neighbor's window.

"Can you loan me your wash-boiler for the clothes?" she called.

Mrs. Pelz threw up the sash.

"The boiler? What's the matter with yours again? Didn't you tell me you had it fixed already last week?"

"A black year on him, the robber, the way he fixed it! If you have no luck in this world, then it's better not to live. There I spent out fifteen cents to stop up one hole, and it runs out another. How I ate out my gall bargaining with him he should let it down to fifteen cents! He wanted yet a quarter, the swindler. Gottuniu! My bitter heart on him for every penny he took from me for nothing!"

"You got to watch all those swindlers, or they'll steal the whites out of your eyes," admonished Mrs. Pelz. "You should have tried out your boiler before you paid him. Wait a minute till I empty out my dirty clothes in a pillowcase; then I'll hand it to you."

Mrs. Pelz returned with the boiler and tried to hand it across to Hanneh Breineh, but the soapbox refrigerator on the window sill was in the way.

"You got to come in for the boiler yourself," said Mrs. Pelz.

"Wait only till I tie my Sammy on to the highchair he shouldn't fall on me again. He's so wild that ropes won't hold him."

Hanneh Breineh tied the child in the chair, stuck a pacifier in his mouth, and went in to her neighbor. As she took the boiler Mrs. Pelz said:

"Do you know Mrs. Melker ordered fifty pounds of chicken for her daughter's wedding? And such grand chickens! Shining like gold! My heart melted in me just looking at the flowing fatness of those chickens."

Hanneh Breineh smacked her thin, dry lips, a hungry gleam in her sunken eyes.

"Fifty pounds!" she gasped. "It ain't possible. How do you know?"

"I heard with my own ears. I saw them with my own eyes. And she said she will chop up the chicken livers with onions and eggs for an appetizer, and then she will buy twenty-five pounds of fish, and cook it sweet shtrudels on pure chicken fat."

"Some people work themselves up in the world," sighed Hanneh Breineh. "For them is America flowing with milk and honey. In Savel, Mrs. Melker used to get shriveled up from hunger. She and her children used to live on potato-peelings and crusts of dry bread picked out from the barrels; and in America she lives to eat chicken, and apple shtrudels soaking in fat."

"The world is a wheel always turning," philosophized Mrs. Pelz. "Those who were high go down low, and those who've been low go up higher. Who will believe me here in America that in Poland I was a cook in a banker's house? I handled ducks and geese every day. I used to bake coffeecake with cream so thick you could cut it with a knife."

"And do you think I was a nobody in Poland?" broke in Hanneh Breineh, tears welling in her eyes as the memories of her past rushed over her. "But what's the use of talking? In America money is everything. Who cares who my father or grandfather was in Poland? Without money I'm a living dead one. My head dries out worrying how to get for the children the eating a penny cheaper."

Mrs. Pelz wagged her head, a gnawing envy contracting her features.

"Mrs. Melker had it good from the day she came," she said, begrudgingly. "Right away she sent all her children to the factory, and she began to cook meat for dinner every day. She and her children have eggs and buttered rolls for breakfast each morning like millionaires."

A sudden fall and a baby's scream, and the boiler dropped from Hanneh Breineh's hands as she rushed into her kitchen, Mrs. Pelz after her. They found the highchair turned on top of the baby.

"Gewalt! Save me! Run for a doctor!" cried Hanneh Breineh, as she dragged the child from under the highchair. "He's killed! He's killed! My only child! My precious lamb!" she shrieked as she ran back and forth with the screaming infant.

Mrs. Pelz snatched little Sammy from the mother's hands.

"Meshugeneh! What are you running around like a crazy, frightening the child? Let me see. Let me tend to him. He ain't killed yet." She hastened to the sink to wash the child's face, and discovered a swelling lump on his forehead. "Have you a quarter in your house?" she asked.

"Yes, I got one," replied Hanneh Breineh, climbing on a chair. "I got to keep it on a high shelf where the children can't get it."

Mrs. Pelz seized the quarter Hanneh Breineh handed down to her.

"Now pull your left eyelid three times while I'm pressing the quarter, and you'll see the swelling go down."

Hanneh Breineh took the child again in her arms, shaking and cooing over it and caressing it.

"Ah-ah-ah, Sammy! Ah-ah-ah-ah, little lamb! Ah-ah-ah, little bird! Ah-ah-ah-ah, precious heart! Oh, you saved my life; I thought he was killed," gasped Hanneh Breineh, turning to Mrs. Pelz. "Oi-i!" she sighed, "a mother's heart! Always in fear over her children. The minute anything happens to them all life goes out of me. I lose my head and I don't know where I am anymore."

"No wonder the child fell," admonished Mrs. Pelz. "You should have a red ribbon or red beads on his neck to keep away the evil eye. Wait. I got something in my machine-drawer."

Mrs. Pelz returned, bringing the boiler and a red string, which she tied about the child's neck while the mother proceeded to fill the boiler.

A little later Hanneh Breineh again came into Mrs. Pelz's kitchen, holding Sammy in one arm and in the other an apronful of potatoes. Putting the child down on the floor, she seated herself on the unmade kitchen-bed and began to peel the potatoes in her apron.

"Woe to me!" sobbed Hanneh Breineh. "To my bitter luck there ain't no end. With all my other troubles, the stove got broke. I lighted the fire to boil the clothes, and it's to get choked with smoke. I paid rent only a week ago, and the agent don't want to fix it. A thunder should strike him! He only comes for the rent, and if anything has to be fixed, then he don't want to hear nothing.

"Why comes it to me so hard?" went on Hanneh Breineh, the tears streaming down her cheeks. "I can't stand it no more. I came in to you for a minute to run away from my troubles. It's only when I sit myself down to peel potatoes or nurse the baby that I take time to draw a breath, and beg only for death."

Mrs. Pelz, accustomed to Hanneh Breineh's bitter outbursts, continued her scrubbing.

"Ut!" exclaimed Hanneh Breineh, irritated at her neighbor's silence, "what are you tearing up the world with your cleaning? What's the use to clean up when everything only gets dirty again?"

"I got to shine up my house for the holidays."

"You've got it so good nothing lays on your mind but to clean your house. Look on this little bloodsucker," said Hanneh Breineh, pointing to the wizened child, made prematurely solemn from starvation and neglect. "Could anybody keep that brat clean? I wash him one minute, and he is dirty the minute after." Little Sammy grew frightened and began to cry. "Shut up!" ordered the mother, picking up the child to nurse it again. "Can't you see me take a rest for a minute?"

The hungry child began to cry at the top of its weakened lungs.

"Na, na, you glutton." Hanneh Breineh took out a dirty pacifier from her pocket and stuffed it into the baby's mouth. The grave, pasty-faced infant shrank into a panic of fear, and chewed the nipple nervously, clinging to it with both his thin little hands.

"For what did I need yet the sixth one?" groaned Hanneh Breineh, turning to Mrs. Pelz. "Wasn't it enough five mouths to feed? If I didn't have this child on my neck, I could turn myself around and earn a few cents." She wrung her hands in a passion of despair. "Gottuniu! The earth should only take it before it grows up!"

"Shah! Shah!" reproved Mrs. Pelz. "Pity yourself on the child. Let it grow up already so long as it is here. See how frightened it looks on you." Mrs. Pelz took the child in her arms and petted it. "The poor little lamb! What did it done you should hate it so?"

Hanneh Breineh pushed Mrs. Pelz away from her.

"To whom can I open the wounds of my heart?" she moaned. "Nobody has pity on me. You don't believe me, nobody believes me until I'll fall down like a horse in the middle of the street. Oi weh! Mine life is so black for my eyes! Some mothers got luck. A child gets run over by a car, some fall from a window, some burn themselves up with a match, some get choked with diphtheria; but no death takes mine away."

"God from the world, stop cursing!" admonished Mrs. Pelz. "What do you want from the poor children? Is it their fault that their father makes small wages? Why do you let it all out on them?" Mrs. Pelz sat down beside Hanneh Breineh. "Wait only till your children get old enough to go to the shop and earn money," she consoled. "Push only through those few years while they are yet small; your sun will begin to shine; you will live on the fat of the land, when they begin to bring you in the wages each week."

Hanneh Breineh refused to be comforted.

"Till they are old enough to go to the shop and earn money they'll eat the head off my bones," she wailed. "If you only knew the fights I got by each meal. Maybe I gave Abe a bigger piece of bread than Fanny. Maybe Fanny got a little more soup in her plate than Jake. Eating is dearer than diamonds. Potatoes went up a cent on a pound, and milk is only for millionaires. And once a week, when I buy a little meat for the Sabbath, the butcher weighs it for me like gold, with all the bones in it. When I come to lay the meat out on a plate and divide it up, there ain't nothing to it but bones. Before, he used to throw me in a piece of fat extra or a piece of lung, but now you got to pay for everything, even for a bone to the soup."

"Never mind; you'll yet come out from all your troubles. Just as soon as your children get old enough to get their working papers the more children you got, the more money you'll have."

"Why should I fool myself with the false shine of hope? Don't I know it's already my black luck not to have it good in this world? Do you think American children will right away give everything they earn to their mother?"

"I know what is with you the matter," said Mrs. Pelz. "You didn't eat yet today. When it is empty in the stomach, the whole world looks black. Come, only let me give you something good to taste in the mouth; that will freshen you up." Mrs. Pelz went to the cupboard and brought out the saucepan of gefullte fisch that she had cooked for dinner and placed it on the table in front of Hanneh Breineh. "Give a taste my fish," she said, taking one slice on a spoon, and handing it to Hanneh Breineh with a piece of bread. "I wouldn't give it to you on a plate because I just cleaned up my house, and I don't want to dirty up more dishes."

"What, am I a stranger you should have to serve me on a plate yet!" cried Hanneh Breineh, snatching the fish in her trembling fingers.

"Oi weh! How it melts through all the bones!" she exclaimed, brightening as she ate. "May it be for good luck to us all!" she exulted, waving aloft the last precious bite.

Mrs. Pelz was so flattered that she even ladled up a spoonful of gravy.

"There is a bit of onion and carrot in it," she said, as she handed it to her neighbor.

Hanneh Breineh sipped the gravy drop by drop, like a connoisseur sipping wine.

"Ah-h-h! A taste of that gravy lifts me up to heaven!" As she disposed leisurely of the slice of onion and carrot she relaxed and expanded and even grew jovial. "Let us wish all our troubles on the Russian Czar! Let him burst with our worries for rent! Let him get shriveled with our hunger for bread! Let his eyes dry out of his head looking for work!

"Shah! I'm forgetting from everything," she exclaimed, jumping up. "It must be eleven or soon twelve, and my children will be right away out of school and fall on me like a pack of wild wolves. I better quick run to the market and see what cheaper I can get for a quarter."

Because of the lateness of her coming, the stale bread at the nearest bakeshop was sold out, and Hanneh Breineh had to trudge from shop to shop in search of the usual bargain, and spent nearly an hour to save two cents.

In the meantime the children returned from school, and, finding the door locked, climbed through the fire-escape, and entered the house through the window. Seeing nothing on the table, they rushed to the stove. Abe pulled a steaming potato out of the boiling pot, and so scalded his fingers that the potato fell to the floor, whereupon the three others pounced on it.

"It was my potato," cried Abe, blowing his burned fingers, while with the other hand and his foot he cuffed and kicked the three who were struggling on the floor. A wild fight ensued, and the potato was smashed under Abe's foot amid shouts and screams. Hanneh Breineh, on the stairs, heard the noise of her famished brood, and topped their cries with curses and invective.

"They are here already, the savages! They are here already to shorten my life! They heard you all over the hall, in all the houses around!"

The children disregarding her words, pounced on her market-basket, shouting ravenously: "Mamma, I'm hungry! What more do you got to eat?"

They tore the bread and herring out of Hanneh Breineh's basket and devoured it in starved savagery, clamoring for more.

"Murderers!" screamed Hanneh Breineh, goaded beyond endurance. "What are you tearing from me my flesh? From where should I steal to give you more? Here I had already a pot of potatoes and a whole loaf of bread and two herrings, and you swallowed it down in the wink of an eye. I have to have Rockefeller's millions to fill your stomachs."

All at once Hanneh Breineh became aware that Benny was missing. "Oi weh!" she burst out, wringing her hands in a new wave of woe, "where is Benny? Didn't he come home yet from school?"

She ran out into the hall, opened the grime-coated window, and looked up and down the street, but Benny was nowhere in sight.

"Abe, Jake, Fanny, quick, find Benny!" entreated Hanneh Breineh, as she rushed back into the kitchen. But the children, anxious to snatch a few minutes' play before the school-call, dodged past her and hurried out.

With the baby on her arm, Hanneh Breineh hastened to the kindergarten.

"Why are you keeping Benny here so long?" she shouted at the teacher as she flung open the door. "If you had my bitter heart, you would send him home long ago and not wait till I got to come for him."

The teacher turned calmly and consulted her record-cards.

"Benny Safron? He wasn't present this morning."

"Not here?" shrieked Hanneh Breineh. "I pushed him out myself he should go. The children didn't want to take him, and I had no time. Woe is me! Where is my child?" She began pulling her hair and beating her breast as she ran into the street.

Mrs. Pelz was busy at a pushcart, picking over some spotted apples, when she heard the clamor of an approaching crowd. A block off she recognized Hanneh Breineh, her hair disheveled, her clothes awry, running toward her with her yelling baby in her arms, the crowd following.

"Friend mine," cried Hanneh Breineh, falling on Mrs. Pelz's neck, "I lost my Benny, the best child of all my children." Tears streamed down her red, swollen eyes as she sobbed. "Benny! mine heart, mine life! Oi-i-i!"

Mrs. Pelz took the frightened baby out of the mother's arms.

"Still yourself a little! See how you're frightening your child."

"Woe to me! Where is my Benny? Maybe he's killed already by a car. Maybe he fainted away from hunger. He didn't eat nothing all day long. Gottuniu! Pity yourself on me!"

She lifted her hands full of tragic entreaty.

"People, my child! Get me my child! I'll go crazy out of my head! Get me my child, or I'll take poison before your eyes!"

"Still yourself a little!" pleaded Mrs. Pelz.

"Talk not to me!" cried Hanneh Breineh, wringing her hands. "You're having all your children. I lost mine. Every good luck comes to other people. But I didn't live yet to see a good day in my life. Mine only joy, mine Benny, is lost away from me."

The crowd followed Hanneh Breineh as she wailed through the street, leaning on Mrs. Pelz. By the time she returned to her house the children were back from school; but seeing that Benny was not there, she chased them out in the street, crying:

"Out of here, you robbers, gluttons! Go find Benny!" Hanneh Breineh crumpled into a chair in utter prostration. "Oi weh! he's lost! Mine life; my little bird; mine only joy! How many nights I spent nursing him when he had the measles! And all that I suffered for weeks and months when he had the whooping-cough! How the eyes went out of my head till I learned him how to walk, till I learned him how to talk! And such a smart child! If I lost all the others, it wouldn't tear me so by the heart."

She worked herself up into such a hysteria, crying, and tearing her hair, and hitting her head with her knuckles, that at last she fell into a faint. It took some time before Mrs. Pelz, with the aid of neighbors, revived her.

"Benny, mine angel!" she moaned as she opened her eyes.

Just then a policeman came in with the lost Benny.

"Na, na, here you got him already!" said Mrs. Pelz. "Why did you carry on so for nothing? Why did you tear up the world like a crazy?"

The child's face was streaked with tears as he cowered, frightened and forlorn. Hanneh Breineh sprang toward him, slapping his cheeks, boxing his ears, before the neighbors could rescue him from her.

"Woe on your head!" cried the mother. "Where did you lost yourself? Ain't I got enough worries on my head than to go around looking for you? I didn't have yet a minute's peace from that child since he was born!"

"See a crazy mother!" remonstrated Mrs. Pelz, rescuing Benny from another beating. "Such a mouth! With one breath she blesses him when he is lost, and with the other breath she curses him when he is found."

Hanneh Breineh took from the windowsill a piece of herring covered with swarming flies, and putting it on a slice of dry bread, she filled a cup of tea that had been stewing all day, and dragged Benny over to the table to eat.

But the child, choking with tears, was unable to touch the food.

"Go eat!" commanded Hanneh Breineh. "Eat and choke yourself eating!"

"Maybe she won't remember me no more. Maybe the servant won't let me in," thought Mrs. Pelz, as she walked by the brownstone house on Eighty-Fourth Street where she had been told Hanneh Breineh now lived. At last she summoned up enough courage to climb the steps. She was all out of breath as she rang the bell with trembling fingers. "Oi weh! even the outside smells riches and plenty! Such curtains! And shades on all windows like by millionaires! Twenty years ago she used to eat from the pot to the hand, and now she lives in such a palace."

A whiff of steam-heated warmth swept over Mrs. Pelz as the door opened, and she saw her old friend of the tenements dressed in silk and diamonds like a being from another world.

"Mrs. Pelz, is it you!" cried Hanneh Breineh, over-joyed at the sight of her former neighbor. "Come right in. Since when are you back in New York?"

"We came last week," mumbled Mrs. Pelz, as she was led into a richly carpeted reception-room.

"Make yourself comfortable. Take off your shawl," urged Hanneh Breineh.

But Mrs. Pelz only drew her shawl more tightly around her, a keen sense of her poverty gripping her as she gazed, abashed by the luxurious wealth that shone from every corner.

"This shawl covers up my rags," she said, trying to hide her shabby sweater.

"I'll tell you what; come right into the kitchen," suggested Hanneh Breineh. "The servant is away for this afternoon, and we can feel more comfortable there. I can breathe like a free person in my kitchen when the girl has her day out."

Mrs. Pelz glanced about her in an excited daze. Never in her life had she seen anything so wonderful as a white-tiled kitchen, with its glistening porcelain sink and the aluminum pots and pans that shone like silver.

"Where are you staying now?" asked Hanneh Breineh, as she pinned an apron over her silk dress.

"I moved back to Delancey Street, where we used to live," replied Mrs. Pelz, as she seated herself cautiously in a white enameled chair.

"Oi weh! What grand times we had in that old house when we were neighbors!" sighed Hanneh Breineh, looking at her old friend with misty eyes.

"You still think on Delancey Street? Haven't you more high-class neighbors uptown here?"

"A good neighbor is not to be found every day," deplored Hanneh Breineh. "Uptown here, where each lives in his own house, nobody cares if the person next door is dying or going crazy from loneliness. It ain't any-thing like we used to have it in Delancey Street, when we could walk into one another's rooms without knocking, and borrow a pinch of salt or a pot to cook in."

Hanneh Breineh went over to the pantry-shelf.

"We are going to have a bite right here on the kitchen-table like on Delancey Street. So long there's no servant to watch us we can eat what we please."

"Oi! How it waters my mouth with appetite, the smell of the herring and onion!" chuckled Mrs. Pelz, sniffing the welcome odors with greedy pleasure.

Hanneh Breineh pulled a dishtowel from the rack and threw one end of it to Mrs. Pelz.

"So long there's no servant around, we can use it together for a napkin. It's dirty, anyhow. How it freshens up my heart to see you!" she rejoiced as she poured out her tea into a saucer. "If you would only know how I used to beg my daughter to write for me a letter to you; but these American children, what is to them a mother's feelings?"

"What are you talking!" cried Mrs. Pelz. "The whole world rings with you and your children. Everybody is envying you. Tell me how began your luck?"

"You heard how my husband died with consumption," replied Hanneh Breineh. "The five hundred dollars lodge money gave me the first lift in life, and I opened a little grocery store. Then my son Abe married himself to a girl with a thousand dollars. That started him in business, and now he has the biggest shirtwaist factory on West Twenty-Ninth Street."

"Yes, I heard your son had a factory." Mrs. Pelz hesitated and stammered; "I'll tell you the truth. What I came to ask you—I thought maybe you would beg your son Abe if he would give my husband a job."

"Why not?" said Hanneh Breineh. "He keeps more than five hundred hands. I'll ask him if he should take in Mr. Pelz."

"Long years on you, Hanneh Breineh! You'll save my life if you could only help my husband get work."

"Of course my son will help him. All my children like to do good. My daughter Fanny is a milliner on Fifth Avenue, and she takes in the poorest girls in her shop and even pays them sometimes while they learn the trade." Hanneh Breineh's face lit up, and her chest filled with pride as she enumerated the successes of her children. "And my son Benny he wrote a play on Broadway, and he gave away more than a hundred free tickets for the first night."

"Benny? The one who used to get lost from home all the time? You always did love that child more than all the rest. And what is Sammy your baby doing?"

"He ain't a baby no longer. He goes to college and quarterbacks the football team. They can't get along without him.

"And my son Jake, I nearly forgot him. He began collecting rent in Delancey Street, and now he is boss of renting the swellest apartment-houses on Riverside Drive."

"What did I tell you? In America children are like money in the bank," purred Mrs. Pelz, as she pinched and patted Hanneh Breineh's silk sleeve. "Oi weh! How it shines from you! You ought to kiss the air and dance for joy and happiness. It is such a bitter frost outside; a pail of coal is so dear, and you got it so warm with steam heat. I had to pawn my feather bed to have enough for the rent, and you are rolling in money."

"Yes, I got it good in some ways, but money ain't everything," sighed Hanneh Breineh.

"You ain't yet satisfied?"

"But here I got no friends," complained Hanneh Breineh.

"Friends?" queried Mrs. Pelz. "What greater friend is there on earth than the dollar?"

"Oi! Mrs. Pelz; if you could only look into my heart! I'm so choked up! You know they say a cow has a long tongue, but can't talk." Hanneh Breineh shook her head wistfully, and her eyes filmed with inward brooding. "My children give me everything from the best. When I was sick, they got me a nurse by day and one by night. They bought me the best wine. If I asked for dove's milk, they would buy it for me; but—but—I can't talk myself out in their language. They want to make me over for an American lady, and I'm different." Tears cut their way under her eyelids with a pricking pain as she went on: "When I was poor, I was free, and could holler and do what I like in my own house. Here I got to lie still like a mouse under a broom. Between living up to my Fifth-Avenue daughter and keeping up with the servants, I am like a sinner in the next world that is thrown from one hell to another." The doorbell rang, and Hanneh Breineh jumped up with a start.

"Oi weh! It must be the servant back already!" she exclaimed, as she tore off her apron. "Oi weh! Let's quickly put the dishes together in a dishpan. If she sees I eat on the kitchen table, she will look on me like the dirt under her feet."

Mrs. Pelz seized her shawl in haste.

"I better run home quick in my rags before your servant sees me."

"I'll speak to Abe about the job," said Hanneh Breineh, as she pushed a bill into the hand of Mrs. Pelz, who edged out as the servant entered.

"I'm having fried potato lotkes special for you, Benny," said Hanneh Breineh, as the children gathered about the table for the family dinner given in honor of Benny's success with his new play. "Do you remember how you used to lick the fingers from them?"

"Oh, mother!" reproved Fanny. "Any one hearing you would think we were still in the pushcart district."

"Stop your nagging, sis, and let ma alone," commanded Benny, patting his mother's arm affectionately. "I'm home only once a month. Let her feed me what she pleases. My stomach is bomb-proof."

"Do I hear that the President is coming to your play?" said Abe, as he stuffed a napkin over his diamond-studded shirt-front.

"Why shouldn't he come?" returned Benny. "The critics say it's the greatest antidote for the race hatred created by the war. If you want to know, he is coming tonight; and what's more, our box is next to the President's."

"Nu, mammeh," sallied Jake, "did you ever dream in Delancey Street that we should rub sleeves with the President?"

"I always said that Benny had more head than the rest of you," replied the mother.

As the laughter died away, Jake went on:

"Honor you are getting plenty; but how much mezummen does this play bring you? Can I invest any of it in real estate for you?"

"I'm getting ten per cent royalties of the gross receipts," replied the youthful playwright.

"How much is that?" queried Hanneh Breineh.

"Enough to buy up all your fish-markets in Delancey Street," laughed Abe in good-natured raillery at his mother.

Her son's jest cut like a knife-thrust in her heart. She felt her heart ache with the pain that she was shut out from their successes. Each added triumph only widened the gulf. And when she tried to bridge this gulf by asking questions, they only thrust her back upon herself.

"Your fame has even helped me get my hat trade solid with the Four Hundred," put in Fanny. "You bet I let Mrs. Van Suyden know that our box is next to the President's. She said she would drop in to meet you. Of course she let on to me that she hadn't seen the play yet, though my designer said she saw her there on the opening night."

"Oh, Gosh, the toadies!" sneered Benny. "Nothing so sickens you with success as the way people who once shoved you off the sidewalk come crawling to you on their stomachs begging you to dine with them."

"Say, that leading man of yours he's some class!" cried Fanny. "That's the man I'm looking for. Will you invite him to supper after the theater?"

The playwright turned to his mother.

"Say, ma," he said laughingly, "how would you like a real actor for a son-in-law?"

"She should worry," mocked Sam. "She'll be discussing with him the future of the Greek drama. Too bad it doesn't happen to be Warfield, or mother could give him tips on the 'Auctioneer.' "

Jake turned to his mother with a covert grin.

"I guess you'd have no objection if Fanny got next to Benny's leading man. He makes at least fifteen hundred a week. That wouldn't be such a bad addition to the family, would it?"

Again the bantering tone stabbed Hanneh Breineh. Everything in her began to tremble and break loose.

"Why do you ask me?" she cried, throwing her napkin into her plate. "Do I count for a person in this house? If I'll say something, will you even listen to me? What is to me the grandest man that my daughter could pick out? Another enemy in my house! Another person to shame himself from me!" She swept in her children in one glance of despairing anguish as she rose from the table. "What worth is an old mother to American children? The President is coming tonight to the theater, and none of you asked me to go." Unable to check the rising tears, she fled toward the kitchen and banged the door.

They all looked at one another guiltily.

"Say, sis," Benny called out sharply, "what sort of frame-up is this? Haven't you told mother that she was to go with us tonight?"

"Yes—I—" Fanny bit her lips as she fumbled evasively for words. "I asked her if she wouldn't mind my taking her some other time."

"Now you have made a mess of it!" fumed Benny, "Mother'll be too hurt to go now."

"Well, I don't care," snapped Fanny. "I can't appear with mother in a box at the theater. Can I introduce her to Mrs. Van Suyden? And suppose your leading man should ask to meet me?"

"Take your time, sis. He hasn't asked yet," scoffed Benny.

"The more reason I shouldn't spoil my chances. You know mother. She'll spill the beans that we come from Delancey Street the minute we introduce her anywhere. Must I always have the black shadow of my past trailing after me?"

"But have you no feelings for mother?" admonished Abe.

"I've tried harder than all of you to do my duty. I've *lived* with her." She turned angrily upon them. "I've borne the shame of mother while you bought her off with a present and a treat here and there. God knows how hard I tried to civilize her so as not to have to blush with shame when I take her anywhere. I dressed her in the most stylish Paris models, but Delancey Street sticks out from every inch of her. Whenever she opens her mouth, I'm done for. You fellows had your chance to rise in the world because a man is free to go up as high as he can reach up to; but I, with all my style and pep, can't get a man my equal because a girl is always judged by her mother."

They were silenced by her vehemence, and unconsciously turned to Benny.

"I guess we all tried to do our best for mother," said Benny, thoughtfully. "But wherever there is growth, there is pain and heartbreak. The trouble with us is that the ghetto of the Middle Ages and the children of the twentieth century have to live under one roof, and—"

A sound of crashing dishes came from the kitchen, and the voice of Hanneh Breineh resounded through the diningroom as she wreaked her pent-up fury on the helpless servant.

"Oh, my nerves! I can't stand it any more! There will be no girl again for another week!" cried Fanny.

"Oh, let up on the old lady," protested Abe. "Since she can't take it out on us any more, what harm is it if she cusses the servants?"

"If you fellows had to chase around employment agencies, you wouldn't see anything funny about it. Why can't we move into a hotel that will do away with the need of servants altogether?"

"I got it better," said Jake, consulting a notebook from his pocket. "I have on my list an apartment on Riverside Drive where there's only a small kitchenette; but we can do away with the cooking, for there is a dining service in the building."

The new Riverside apartment to which Hanneh Breineh was removed by her socially ambitious children was for the habitually active mother an empty desert of enforced idleness. Deprived of her kitchen, Hanneh Breineh felt robbed of the last reason for her existence. Cooking and marketing and puttering busily with pots and pans gave her an excuse for living and struggling and bearing up with her children. The lonely idleness of Riverside Drive stunned all her senses and arrested all her thoughts. It gave her that choked sense of being cut off from air, from life, from everything warm and human. The cold indifference, the each-for-himself look in the eyes of the people about her were like stinging slaps in the face. Even the children had nothing real or human in them. They were starched and stiff miniatures of their elders.

But the most unendurable part of the stifling life on Riverside Drive was being forced to eat in the public diningroom. No matter how hard she tried to learn polite table manners, she always found people staring at her, and her daughter rebuking her for eating with the wrong fork or guzzling the soup or staining the cloth.

In a fit of rebellion Hanneh Breineh resolved never to go down to the public diningroom again, but to make use of the gas-stove in the kitchenette to cook her own meals. That very day she rode down to Delancey Street and purchased a new market-basket. For some time she walked among the haggling pushcart venders, relaxing and swimming in the warm waves of her old familiar past.

A fish-peddler held up a large carp in his black, hairy hand and waved it dramatically:

"Women! Women! Fourteen cents a pound!"

He ceased his raucous shouting as he saw Hanneh Breineh in her rich attire approach his cart.

"How much?" she asked, pointing to the fattest carp.

"Fifteen cents, lady," said the peddler, smirking as he raised his price.

"Swindler! Didn't I hear you call fourteen cents?" shrieked Hanneh Breineh, exultingly, the spirit of the penny chase surging in her blood. Diplomatically, Hanneh Breineh turned as if to go, and the fisherman seized her basket in frantic fear.

"I should live; I'm losing money on the fish, lady," whined the peddler. "I'll let it down to thirteen cents for you only."

"Two pounds for a quarter, and not a penny more," said Hanneh Breineh, thrilling again with the rare sport of bargaining, which had been her chief joy in the good old days of poverty.

"Nu, I want to make the first sale for good luck." The peddler threw the fish on the scale.

As he wrapped up the fish, Hanneh Breineh saw the driven look of worry in his haggard eyes, and when he counted out the change from her dollar, she waved it aside. "Keep it for your luck," she said, and hurried off to strike a new bargain at a pushcart of onions.

Hanneh Breineh returned triumphantly with her purchases. The basket under her arm gave forth the old, homelike odors of herring and garlic, while the scaly tail of a four-pound carp protruded from its newspaper wrapping. A gilded placard on the door of the apartment-house proclaimed that all merchandise must be delivered through the trade entrance in the rear; but Hanneh Breineh with her basket strode proudly through the marble-paneled hall and rang nonchalantly for the elevator.

The uniformed hall-man, erect, expressionless, frigid with dignity, stepped forward:

"Just a minute, madam. I'll call a boy to take up your basket for you."

Hanneh Breineh, glaring at him, jerked the basket savagely from his hands. "Mind your own business!" she retorted. "I'll take it up myself. Do you think you're a Russian policeman to boss me in my own house?"

Angry lines appeared on the countenance of the representative of social decorum.

"It is against the rules, madam," he said, stiffly.

"You should sink into the earth with all your rules and brass buttons. Ain't this America? Ain't this a free country? Can't I take up in my own house what I buy with my own money?" cried Hanneh Breineh, reveling in the opportunity to shower forth the volley of invectives that had been suppressed in her for the weeks of deadly dignity of Riverside Drive.

In the midst of this uproar Fanny came in with Mrs. Van Suyden. Hanneh Breineh rushed over to her, crying:

"This bossy policeman won't let me take up my basket in the elevator."

The daughter, unnerved with shame and confusion, took the basket in her white-gloved hand and ordered the hall-boy to take it around to the regular delivery entrance.

Hanneh Breineh was so hurt by her daughter's apparent defense of the hall-man's rules that she utterly ignored Mrs. Van Suyden's greeting and walked up the seven flights of stairs out of sheer spite.

"You see the tragedy of my life?" broke out Fanny, turning to Mrs. Van Suyden.

"You poor child! You go right up to your dear, old lady mother, and I'll come some other time."

Instantly Fanny regretted her words. Mrs. Van Suyden's pity only roused her wrath the more against her mother.

Breathless from climbing the stairs, Hanneh Breineh entered the apartment just as Fanny tore the faultless millinery creation from her head and threw it on the floor in a rage.

"Mother, you are the ruination of my life! You have driven away Mrs. Van Suyden, as you have driven away all my best friends. What do you think we got this apartment for but to get rid of your fish smells and your brawls with the servants? And here you come with a basket on your arm as if you just landed from steerage! And this afternoon, of all times, when Benny is bringing his leading man to tea. When will you ever stop disgracing us?"

"When I'm dead," said Hanneh Breineh, grimly. "When the earth will cover me up, then you'll be free to go your American way. I'm not going to make myself over for a lady on Riverside Drive. I hate you and all your swell friends. I'll not let myself be choked up here by you or by that hall-boss policeman that is higher in your eyes than your own mother."

"So that's your thanks for all we've done for you?" cried the daughter.

"All you've done for me!" shouted Hanneh Breineh. "What have you done for me? You hold me like a dog on a chain! It stands in the Talmud; some children give their mothers dry bread and water and go to heaven for it, and some give their mother roast duck and go to Gehenna because it's not given with love."

"You want me to love you yet?" raged the daughter. "You knocked every bit of love out of me when I was yet a kid. All the memories of childhood I have is your ever-lasting cursing and yelling that we were gluttons."

The bell rang sharply, and Hanneh Breineh flung open the door.

"Your groceries, ma'am," said the boy.

Hanneh Breineh seized the basket from him and with a vicious fling sent it rolling across the room, strewing its contents over the Persian rugs and inlaid floor. Then seizing her hat and coat, she stormed out of the apartment and down the stairs.

Mr. and Mrs. Pelz sat crouched and shivering over their meager supper when the door opened, and Hanneh Breineh in fur coat and plumed hat charged into the room.

"I come to cry out to you my bitter heart," she sobbed. "Woe is me! It is so black for my eyes!"

"What is the matter with you, Hanneh Breineh?" cried Mrs. Pelz in bewildered alarm.

"I am turned out of my own house by the brass-buttoned policeman that bosses the elevator. Oi-i-i-i! Weh-h-h-h! What have I from my life? The whole world rings with my son's play. Even the President came to see it, and I, his mother, have not seen it yet. My heart is dying in me like in a prison," she went on wailing. "I am starved out for a piece of real eating. In that swell restaurant is nothing but napkins and forks and lettuce-leaves. There are a dozen plates to every bite of food. And it looks so fancy on the plate, but it's nothing but straw in the mouth. I'm starving, but I can't swallow down their American eating."

"Hanneh Breineh," said Mrs. Pelz, "you are sinning before God. Look on your fur coat; it alone would feed a whole family for a year. I never had yet a piece of fur trimming on a coat, and you are in fur from the neck to the feet. I never had yet a piece of feather on a hat, and your hat is all feathers."

"What are you envying me?" protested Hanneh Breineh. "What have I from all my fine furs and feathers when my children are strangers to me?

All the fur coats in the world can't warm up the loneliness inside my heart. All the grandest feathers can't hide the bitter shame in my face that my children shame themselves from me."

Hanneh Breineh suddenly loomed over them like some ancient, heroic figure of the Bible condemning unrighteousness.

"Why should my children shame themselves from me? From where did they get the stuff to work themselves up in the world? Did they get it from the air? How did they get all their smartness to rise over the people around them? Why don't the children of born American mothers write my Benny's plays? It is I, who never had a chance to be a person, who gave him the fire in his head. If I would have had a chance to go to school and learn the language, what couldn't I have been? It is I and my mother and my mother's mother and my father and father's father who had such a black life in Poland; it is our choked thoughts and feelings that are flaming up in my children and making them great in America. And yet they shame themselves from me!"

For a moment Mr. and Mrs. Pelz were hypnotized by the sweep of her words. Then Hanneh Breineh sank into a chair in utter exhaustion. She began to weep bitterly, her body shaking with sobs.

"Woe is me! For what did I suffer and hope on my children? A bitter old age—my end. I'm so lonely!"

All the dramatic fire seemed to have left her. The spell was broken. They saw the Hanneh Breineh of old, ever discontented, ever complaining even in the midst of riches and plenty.

"Hanneh Breineh," said Mrs. Pelz, "the only trouble with you is that you got it too good. People will tear the eyes out of your head because you're complaining yet. If I only had your fur coat! If I only had your diamonds! I have nothing. You have everything. You are living on the fat of the land. You go right back home and thank God that you don't have my bitter lot."

"You got to let me stay here with you" insisted Hanneh Breineh. "I'll not go back to my children except when they bury me. When they will see my dead face, they will understand how they tried killed me."

Mrs. Pelz glanced nervously at her husband. They barely had enough covering for their one bed; how could they possibly lodge a visitor?

"I don't want to take up your bed," said Hanneh Breineh. "I don't care if I have to sleep on the floor or on the chairs, but I'll stay here for the night."

Seeing that she was bent on staying, Mr. Pelz prepared to sleep by putting a few chairs next to the trunk, and Hanneh Breineh was invited to share the rickety bed with Mrs. Pelz.

The mattress was full of lumps and hollows. Hanneh Breineh lay cramped and miserable, unable to stretch out her limbs. For years she had been accustomed to hair mattresses and ample woolen blankets, so that though she covered herself with her fur coat, she was too cold to sleep. But worse than the cold were the creeping things on the wall. And as the lights were turned low, the mice came through the broken plaster and raced across the floor. The foul odors of the kitchen-sink added to the night of horrors.

"Are you going back home?" asked Mrs. Pelz, as Hanneh Breineh put on her hat and coat the next morning.

"I don't know where I'm going," she replied, as she put a bill into Mrs. Pelz's hand.

For hours Hanneh Breineh walked through the crowded ghetto streets. She realized that she no longer could endure the sordid ugliness of her past, and yet she could not go home to her children. She only felt that she must go on and on.

In the afternoon a cold, drizzling rain set in. She was worn out from the sleepless night and hours of tramping. With a piercing pain in her heart she at last turned back and boarded the subway for Riverside Drive. She had fled from the marble sepulcher of the Riverside apartment to her old home in the ghetto; but now she knew that she could not live there again. She had outgrown her past by the habits of years of physical comforts, and these material comforts that she could no longer do without choked and crushed the life within her.

A cold shudder went through Hanneh Breineh as she approached the apartment-house. Peering through the plate glass of the door she saw the face of the uniformed hallman. For a hesitating moment she remained standing in the drizzling rain, unable to enter, and yet knowing full well that she would have to enter.

Then suddenly Hanneh Breineh began to laugh. She realized that it was the first time she had laughed since her children had become rich. But it was the hard laugh of bitter sorrow. Tears streamed down her furrowed cheeks as she walked slowly up the granite steps.

"The fat of the land!" muttered Hanneh Breineh, with a choking sob as the hallman with immobile face deferentially swung open the door—"the fat of the land!"

Henry Roth

Henry Roth has fascinated critics because his first, superb novel, *Call It Sleep*, was not succeeded by another full-length book until fifty years after its publication (*Shifting Landscapes: A Composite, 1915–1987*, 1987). Clearly, the first novel was written out of Roth's own deeply felt experience. He was born in Tysmentitsa, near Lemberg, Galicia, in 1906. His mother brought him to New York when he was eighteen months old, where they reunited with Roth's father, who had gone to America in preparation for his family's arrival. Roth's parents were troubled with a variety of marital problems, causing feelings of anxiety in young Roth that were only exacerbated when the family moved uptown to Harlem in 1914. Roth was favored by his mother but sensed his father's disapproval.

Roth's career as a writer was suggested and encouraged by a freshman English teacher in New York's City College and by Eda Lou Walton, a gentile New York University professor and poet with whom he later developed a romantic relationship. Estranged from his family and from Judaism, Roth began writing a first-person sketch of his own life in the summer of 1930. More than three years later, Roth finished the novel *Call It Sleep*. In the summer of 1938, Roth went to Yaddo, an artists' colony at Saratoga Springs, New York, where he met Muriel Parker, a young composer whom he later married. He held a series of diverse but unsatisfying jobs in New York, in Cambridge, Massachusettes, and in Montville, Maine. In the mid-1950s, when Roth was suffering from depression, *Call It Sleep* was rediscovered by the American literary critical world and by a large reading public as well. It has been reissued several times since then and is considered to be one of the outstanding American novels of the twentieth century. Recently, Roth has become reidentified with Jewish peoplehood, largely through the State of Israel, although he has few if any ties with diaspora Judaism.

Call It Sleep is a unique, compelling, and moving novel about a dysfunctional family that is profoundly stressed by the dislocations of immigration. The protagonist, David Schearl, is a young boy who must cope simultaneously with the mean streets of the immigrant Lower East Side of New York and the even meaner moods of his paranoiac, abusive father. His mother, Genya, married the possibly patricidal Albert as a form of penance to her family for her earlier affair with a gentile organist in her Eastern European village. Albert is ignorant of the details of Genya's earlier life, but he suspects that David may not be his legitimate son; in jealous outbursts he sometimes turns savagely on the boy. Albert's vicious, unpredictable temper causes him to lose job after job, further increasing the sense of instability in the family. Genya, who is totally confused by the English-speaking culture outside the few streets that comprise her world, is a tower of strength in the home, pacifying and calming her husband and providing her young son with an island of peace, love, and sanity. Her volatile and forthright younger sister Bertha, who emigrates somewhat later, provides an effective foil for the cautiousness, gentleness, and half-hidden sensuality of the remakable Genya.

•

"Genya's Boy on an Island" (excerpt)

Friday. Rain. The end of school. He could stay home now, stay home and do nothing, stay near his mother the whole afternoon. He turned from the window and regarded her. She was seated before the table paring beets. The first cut into a beet was like lifting a lid from a tiny stove. Sudden purple under the peel; her hands were stained with it. Above her blue and white checkered apron her face bent down, intent upon her work, her lips pressed gravely together. He loved her. He was happy again.

His eyes roamed about the kitchen: the confusion of Friday afternoons. Pots on the stove, parings in the sink, flour smeared on the rolling pin, the board. The air was warm, twined with many odors. His mother rose, washed the beets, drained them, set them aside.

"There!" she said. "I can begin cleaning again."

She cleared the table, washed what dishes were soiled, emptied out the peelings that cluttered the sink into the garbage can. Then she got down on all fours and began to mop the floor. With knees drawn up, David watched her wipe the linoleum beneath his chair. The shadow between her breasts, how deep! How far it—No! No! Luter! When he looked! That night! Mustn't! Mustn't! Look away! Quick! Look at—look at the linoleum there, how it glistened under a thin film of water.

"Now you'll have to sit there till it dries," she cautioned him, straightening up and brushing back the few wisps of hair that had fallen over her cheek. "It will only be a few minutes." She stooped, walked backward to the steps, trailing the mop over her footprints, then went into the frontroom.

Left alone, he became despondent again. His thoughts returned to Luter. He would come again this evening. Why? Why didn't he go away. Would they have to run away every Thursday? Go to Yussie's house? Would he have to play with Annie again? He didn't want to. He never wanted to see her again. And he would have to. The way he did this afternoon beside the carriages. The black carriage with the window. Scared. The long box. Scared. The cellar. No! No!

"Mama!" he called out.

"What is it, my son?"

"Are you going to—to sleep inside?"

"Oh, no. Of course not! I'm just straightening my hair a little."

"Are you coming in here soon?"

"Why yes. Is there anything you want?"

"Yes."

"In just a moment."

He waited impatiently for her to appear. In a little while she came out. She had changed her dress and combed her hair. She spread a frayed clean towel out on the parlor steps and sat down.

"I can't come over unless I have to," she smiled. "You're on an island. What is it you want?"

"I forgot," he said lamely.

"Oh, you're a goose!"

"It has to dry," he explained. "And I have to watch it."

"And so I do too, is that it? My, what a tyrant you'll make when you're married!"

David really didn't care what she thought of him just as long as she sat there. Besides, he did have something to ask her, only he couldn't make up his mind to venture it. It might be too unpleasant. Still no matter what her answer would be, no matter what be found out, he was always safe near her.

"Mama, did you ever see anyone dead?"

"You're very cheerful to-day!"

"Then tell me." Now that he had launched himself on this perilous sea, he was resolved to cross it. "Tell me," he insisted.

"Well," she said thoughtfully, "The twins who died when I was a little girl I don't remember. My grandmother though, she was the first I really saw and remember. I was sixteen then."

"Why did she die?"

"I don't know. No one seemed to know."

"Then why did she die?"

"What a dogged questioner you are! I'm sure she had a reason. But do you want to know what I think?"

"Yes!" eagerly.

His mother took a deep breath, lifted a finger to arouse an already fervent attention. "She was very small, my grandmother, very frail and delicate. The light came through her hands like the light through a fan. What has that to do with it? Nothing. But while my grandfather was very pious, she only pretended to be—just as I pretend, may God forgive us both. Now long ago, she had a little garden before her house. It was full of sweet flowers in the summertime, and she tended it all by herself. My grandfather, stately Jew, could never understand why she should spend a whole spring morning watering the flowers and plucking off the dead leaves, and snipping here and patting there, when she had so many servants to do it for her. You would hardly believe how cheap servants were in those days—my grandfather had five of them. Yes, he would fret when he saw her working in the garden and say it was almost irreligious for a Jewess of her rank—she was rich then remember—the forests hadn't been cut"—

"What forests?"

"I've told you about them—the great forests and the lumber camps. We were rich while the forests were there. But after they were cut and the lumber camps moved away, we grew poor. Do you understand? And so my grandfather would fret when he saw her go dirtying her hands in the soil like any peasant's wife. But my grandmother would only smile at him—I can still see her bent over and smiling up at him—and say that since she had no beautiful beard like his to stroke, what harm could there be in getting a little dirt on her hands. My grandfather had a beard that turned white early; he was very proud of it. And once she told him that she was sure the good Lord would not be angry at her if she did steal a little from Esau's heritage—the earth and the fields are Esau's heritage—since Esau himself, she said, was stealing from Isaac on every side—she meant all the new stores that were being opened by the other gentiles in our town. What could my grandfather do? He would laugh and call her a serpent. Now wait! Wait! I'm coming to it." She smiled at his impatience.

"As she grew older, she grew very strange. Shall I tell you what she used do? When autumn came and everything had died—"

"Died? Everything?" David interrupted her.

"Not everything, little goose. The flowers. When they died she didn't want to leave the house. Wasn't that strange? She stayed for days and days in her large living room—it had crystal chandeliers. You wouldn't believe how quietly she would sit—not seeing the servants, hardly hearing what was said—and her hands folded in her lap—so. Nor could my grandfather, though he begged her to come out, ever make her. He even went to ask a great Rabbi about it—it was no use. Not till the first snow fall, did she willingly leave the house again."

"Why?"

"Here is the answer. See if you can find it. When I came to visit her once on a day in late autumn, I found her sitting very quietly, as usual, in her large arm-chair. But when I was about to take my coat off, she said, keep it on, Genya, darling, there is mine on the chair in the corner. Will you get it for me, child?

"Well, I stood still staring at her in surprise. Her coat? I thought. Was she really of her own accord going out and in Autumn? And then for the first time I noticed that she was dressed in her prettiest Sabbath clothes—a dark shimmering satin—very costly. I can see her yet. And on her head—she had never let them cut her hair—she had set a broad round comb with rows of pearls in it—the first present my grandfather had ever given her. It was like a pale crown. And so I fetched her coat and helped her put it on. Where are you going, grandmother? I asked. I was puzzled. In the garden, she said, in the garden. Well, an old woman must have her way, and into the garden we went. The day was very grey and full of winds, whirling, strong winds that could hold the trees down like a hand. Even us it almost blew about and it was cold. And I said to her, Grandmother, isn't it too cold out here? Isn't the wind too strong? No, her coat was warm, so she said. And then she said a very strange thing. Do you remember Petrush Kolonov? I wasn't sure. A goy, she said, a clod. He worked for your grandfather many years. He had a neck like a tree once, but he grew old and crooked at last. And when he grew so old he couldn't lift a faggot, he would sit on a stone and look at the mountains. This was my grandmother talking, you understand?"

David couldn't quite follow these threads within threads, but nodded. "Why did he sit?" he asked, afraid that she might stop talking.

She laughed lightly. "That same question has been asked by three generations. You. Myself. My grandmother. He had been a good drudge this Petrush, a good ox. And when my grandmother asked him, Petrush, why do you sit like a keg and stare at the mountains, his only answer was, my teeth are all gone. And that's the story my grandmother told me while we walked. You look puzzled," she laughed again.

He was indeed, but she didn't explain.

"And so we walked and the leaves were blowing. Shew-w-w! How they lifted, and one blew against her coat, and while the wind held it there, you know, like a finger, she lifted it off and crumbled it. And then she said suddenly, come let us turn back. And just as we were about to go in she sighed so that she shivered—deep—the way one sighs just before sleep—and she dropped the bits of leaves she was holding and she said, it is wrong being the way I am. Even a leaf grows dull and old together! Together! You understand? Oh, she was wise! And we went inside."

His mother stopped, touched the floor to see if it was dry. Then she rose and went to the stove to push the seething beet soup from where it had been over the heat of the coals to the cooler end of the stove.

"And now the floor is dry," she smiled, "I'm liberated."

But David felt cheated, even resentful. "You—you haven't told me anything!" he protested. "You haven't even told me what happened?"

"Haven't I?" She laughed. "There's hardly anything more to tell. She died the winter of that same year, before the snow fell." She stared at the rain beating against the window. Her face sobered. The last wink of her eyelids before she spoke was the slowest. "She looked so frail in death, in her shroud—how shall I tell you, my son? Like early winter snow. And I thought to myself even then, let me look deeply into her face for surely she will melt before my eyes." She smiled again. "Have I told you enough now?"

He nodded. Without knowing why, her last words stirred him. What he had failed to grasp as thought, her last gesture, the last supple huskiness of her voice conveyed. Was it in his heart this dreamlike fugitive sadness dwelled, or did it steep the feathery air of the kitchen? He could not tell. But if only the air were always this way, and he always here alone with his mother. He was near her now. He was part of her. The rain outside the window set continual seals upon their isolation, upon their intimacy, their identity. When she lifted the stove lid, the rosy glow that stained her wide brow warmed his own body as well. He was near her. He was part of her. Oh, it was good being here. He watched her every movement hungrily.

She threw a new white table cloth over the table. It hovered like a cloud in air and settled slowly. Then she took down from the shelf three brass candlesticks and placed them in the center of whiteness, then planted candles into each brass cup.

"Mama."

"Yes?"

"What do they do when they die?"

"What?" she repeated. "They are cold; they are still. They shut their eyes in sleep eternal years."

Eternal years. The words echoed in his mind. Raptly, he turned them over and over as though they had a lustre and shape of their own. *Eternal years*.

His mother set the table. Knives ringing faintly, forks, spoons, side by side. The salt shaker, secret little vessel of dull silver, the pepper, greyish-brown eye in the shallow glass, the enameled sugar bowl, headless shoulders of silver tongs leaning above the rim.

"Mama, what are eternal years?"

His mother sighed somewhat desperately, lifted her eyes a moment then dropped them to the table, her gaze wandered thoughtfully over the dishes and silverware. Then her eyes brightened. Reaching toward the sugar bowl she lifted out the tongs, carefully pinched a cube of sugar, and held it up before his eyes.

"This is how wide my brain can stretch," she said banteringly. "You see? No wider. Would you ask me to pick up a frozen sea with these narrow things? Not even the ice-man could do it." She dropped the tongs back into the bowl. "The sea to this—"

"But—" David interrupted, horrified and bewildered. "But when do they wake up, mama?"

She opened her two palms in a gesture of emptiness. "There is nothing left to waken."

"But sometime, mama," he urged.

She shook her head.

"But sometime."

"Not here, if anywhere. They say there is a heaven and in heaven they waken. But I myself do not believe it. May God forgive me for telling you this. But it's all I know. I know only that they are buried in the dark earth and their names last a few more lifetimes on their gravestones."

The dark. In the dark earth. Eternal years. It was a terrible revelation. He stared at her fixedly. Picking up a cloth that lay on the washtub, she went to the oven, flipped the door open, drew out a pan. The warmth and odor of new bread entered his being as through a rigid haze of vision. She spread out a napkin near the candlesticks, lifted the bread out of the pan and placed it on the square of linen.

"I still have the candles to light," she murmured sitting down, "and my work is done. I don't know why they made Friday so difficult a day for women."

—Dark. In the grave. Eternal years . . .

Rain in brief gusts seething at the window . . . The clock ticked too briskly. No, never. It wasn't sometime . . . In the dark.

Slowly the last belated light raveled into dusk. Across the short space of the kitchen, his mother's face trembled as if under sea, grew blurred. Flecks, intricate as foam, swirled in the churning dark—

—Like popcorn blowing in that big window in that big candystore. Blowing and settling. That day. Long ago.

His gaze followed the aimless flux of light that whirled and flickered in the room, troubling the outline of door and table.

—Snow it was, grey snow. Tiny bits of paper, floating from the window, that day. Confetti, a boy said. Confetti, he said. They threw it down on those two who were going to be married. The man in the tall, black shiny hat, hurrying. The lady in white laughing, leaning against him, dodging the confetti, winking it out of her eyes. Carriages waiting. Confetti on the step, on the horses. Funny. Then they got inside, both laughing. Confetti. Carriages.

—Carriages!

—The same!

—This afternoon! When the box came out! Carriages.

—Same!

—Carriages—!

"Dear God!" exclaimed his mother. "You startled me! What makes you leap that way in your chair? This is the second time today!"

"They were the same," he said in a voice of awe. It was solved now. He saw it clearly. Everything belonged to the same dark. Confetti and coffins.

"What were the same?"

"The carriages!"

"Oh, child!" she cried with amused desperation. "God alone knows what you're dreaming about now!" She rose from her chair, went over to the wall where the matchbox hung. "I had better light these candles before you see an angel."

The match rasped on the sandpaper, flared up, making David aware of how dark it had become.

One by one she lit the candles. The flame crept tipsily up the wick, steadied, mellowed the steadfast brass below, glowed on each knot of the crisp golden braid of the bread on the napkin. Twilight vanished, the kitchen gleamed. Day that had begun in labor and disquiet, blossomed now in candlelight and sabbath.

With a little, deprecating laugh, his mother stood before the candles, and bowing her head before them, murmured through the hands she spread before her face the ancient prayer for the Sabbath . . .

The hushed hour, the hour of tawny beatitude . . .

•

"Two Sisters" (excerpt)

On a clear Sunday afternoon in July, David and his aunt set out together toward the Third Avenue Elevated. They were going to the Metropolitan

Museum. Sweat runneled his aunt's cheeks, hung down from her chin, fell sometimes, spotting the bosom of her green dress. With her handkerchief, she slapped at the beads viciously as though they were flies and cursed the heat. When they reached the elevated, David was compelled to ask innumerable people what the right train was, and during the whole trip, she sent him forward to plague the conductor.

At 86th Street, they got off and after further inquiry walked west toward Fifth Avenue. The further they got from Third Avenue, the more aloof grew the houses, the more silent the streets. David began to feel uneasy at his aunt's loud voice and Yiddish speech both of which seemed out of place here.

"Hmm!" she marveled in resounding accents. "Not a single child on the street. Children, I see, are not in style in this portion of America." And after gaping about her. "Bah! It is quiet as a forest here. Who would want to live in these houses? You see that house?" She pointed at a red brick structure. "Just such a house did Baron Kobelien have, with just such shades. He was an old monster, the Baron, may he rot away! His eyes were rheumy, and his lips munched as though he were chewing a cud. He had a back as crooked as his soul." And in the role of the Baron, she tottered onto Fifth Avenue.

Before them stood a stately white-stone edifice set in the midst of the green park.

"That must be it," she said. "So they described it to me at the shop."

But before they crossed the street she decided to take her bearings and cautioned David to remember a certain brown-stone house with gabled roofs and iron railings before it. Thus assured of a certain return, they hurried across the avenue and stopped again at the foot of a flight of broad stairs that led up to a door. A number of people were going in.

"Whom shall we ask to make sure we are right?"

A short distance from the building stood a peanut-vender with his cart and whistling box. They walked over to him. He was a lean, swarthy fellow with black mustaches and bright eyes.

"Ask him!" she ordered.

"Is dat a museum?"

"Dotsa duh musee," he flickered his eyebrows at her while he spoke. "You go inna straight," he pushed out his chest and hips, "you come out all tire."

David felt his arm clutched; his aunt hurried him away.

"Kiss my arse," she flung over her shoulder in Yiddish; "What did that black worm say?"

"He said it was a museum."

"Then let's go in. The worst we can get is a kick in the rear."

His aunt's audacity scared him quite a bit, but there was nothing to do except follow her up the stairs. Ahead of them, a man and woman were on the point of entering the door. His aunt pressed his arm and whispered hastily. "Those two people! They seem knowing. We'll follow them till they come out again, else we'll surely be lost in this stupendous castle!"

The couple before them passed through a turn-stile. David and his aunt did likewise. The others turned to the right and entered a room full of grotesque granite figures seated bolt upright upon granite thrones. They followed in their wake.

"We must look at things with only one eye," she cautioned him, "the other must always be on them."

And keeping to this plan, wherever their two unwitting guides strolled, his aunt and he tagged along behind. Now and then, however, when she was particularly struck by some piece of sculpture, they allowed their leaders to draw so far ahead that they almost lost them. This happened once when she stood gawking at the spectacle of a stone wolf suckling two infants.

"Woe is me!" Her tone was loud enough for the guard to knit his brows at her. "Who would believe it—a dog with babies! No! It could not have been!"

David had to pluck her dress several times and remind her that their companions had disappeared before she could tear herself away.

Again, when they arrived before an enormous marble figure seated on an equally huge horse, her aunt was so overcome that her tongue hung out in awe. "This is how they looked in the old days," she breathed reverently. "Gigantic they were, Moses and Abraham and Jacob, and the others in the earth's youth. Ai!" Her eyes bulged.

"They're going, Aunt Bertha," he warned. "Hurry, They're going away!"

"Who? Oh, may they burst! Won't they ever stop a moment! But come! We must cleave to them like mire on a pig!"

In this fashion, hours seemed to go by. David was growing weary. Their quarry had led them past miles and miles of armor, tapestries, coins, furniture and mummies under glass, and still they showed no sign of flagging. His aunt's interest in the passing splendors had long since worn off and she was beginning to curse her guides heartily.

"A plague on you," she muttered every time those walking ahead stopped to glance into a show case. "Haven't you crammed your eyes full yet! Enough!" She waved her sopping handkerchief. "May your heart burn the way my feet are burning!"

At last the man ahead of them stopped to tell one of the uniformed guards something. Aunt Bertha halted abruptly. "Hoorrah! He's complaining about our following him! God be praised! Let them kick us out now. That's all I ask!"

But alas, such was not the case; the guards paid no attention to them, but seemed instead to be giving the others directions of some kind.

"They're leaving now," she said with a great sigh of relief. "I'm sure he's telling them how to get out. What a fool I was not to have had you ask him myself. But who would have known! Come, we may as well follow them out, since we've followed them in."

Instead of leaving, however, the man and woman, after walking a short distance, separated, one going into one door and one into another.

"Bah!" Her rage knew no bounds. "Why they're only going to pee. Ach! I follow no longer. Ask that blockhead in uniform, how one escapes this jungle of stone and fabric."

The guard directed them, but his directions were so involved that in a short space they were lost again. They had to ask another and still another. It was only by a long series of inquiries that they finally managed to get out at all.

"Pheh!" she spat on the stairs as they went down. "May a bolt shatter you to bits! If I ever walk up those stairs again, I hope I give birth to a pair of pewter twins!" And she yanked David toward their landmark.

His mother and father were home when they entered. His aunt sprawled into a chair with a moan of fatigue.

"You look as though you've stumbled into every corner of the world!" His mother seated him on her knee. "Where have you led the poor child, Bertha?"

"Led?" she groaned. "Where was I led you mean? We were fastened to a he and a she-devil with a black power in their legs. And they dragged us through a wilderness of man's work. A wilderness I tell you! And now I'm so weary, my breast seems empty of its heart!"

"Why didn't you leave when you had seen enough?"

She laughed weakly. "That place wasn't made for leaving. Ach, green rump that I am, the dirt of Austria is still under my toe-nails and I plunge into museums." She buried her nose under her arm-pit. "Phew, I reek!"

As always, when she indulged herself in some coarse expression or gesture, his father grimaced and tapped his foot.

"It serves you right," he said abruptly.

"Humph!" she tossed her head sarcastically.

"Yes!"

"And why?" Irritation and weariness were getting the better of her.

"A raw jade like yourself ought learn a little more before she butts into America."

"My cultivated American!" she drawled, drawing down the corners of her under lip in imitation of the grim curve on the face of her brother-in-law. "How long is it since you shit on the ocean?"

"Chops like those," he glowered warningly, "deserve to drop off."

"That's what I say, but they're not mine."

The ominous purple vein began to throb on his temple. "To me you can't talk that way," his eyelids grew heavy. "Save that fishwives' lip for your father, the old glutton!"

"And you, what have you—"

"Bertha!" his mother broke in warningly. "Don't!"

Aunt Bertha's lips quivered rebelliously a moment and she reddened as though she had throttled a powerful impulse to blurt out something.

"Come, you're all worn out," continued his mother gently. "Why don't you lie down for a little space while I make you some dinner."

"Very well," she answered and flounced out of the room. . . .

"Here is a man," Aunt Bertha said vehemently to her sister, "who drives a milk wagon and mingles with peddlars and truckmen, who sits at a horse's tail all morning long, and yet when I say—what! When I say nothing! Nothing at all!—he begins to tap his feet or rustle his newspaper as though an ague were upon him! Did anyone ever hear of the like? He's as squeamish as a newly-minted nun. One is not even permitted to fart when he's around!"

"You're making the most of Albert's absence, aren't you?" his mother asked.

"And why not? I don't have much opportunity to speak my mind when he's around. And what's more, it won't hurt your son to know what I think of all fathers. His father he knows. A sour spirit. Gloomy. The world slapped him on both chins and so everyone he meets must suffer. But my father, the good Reb Benjamin Krollman, was this way." And she began to shake and mumble rapidly and look furtively around and draw closer to herself a figment praying shawl. "His praying was an excuse for his laziness. As long as he prayed he didn't have to do anything else. Let Genya or his wife take care of the store, he had to take care of God. A pious Jew with a beard—who dared ask more of him? Work? God spare him! He played the lotteries!"

"Why do you say that?" his mother objected. "No one can blame father because he was pious. Well, he lacked business sense, but he tried to do his best."

"Tried? Don't defend him. I've just left him and I know. If I remember grandfather he worked till the cancer stretched him out—after grandmother died. And he was seventy then. But father—God keep him from cancer—he was old at forty—Ai! Ai!" She switched with characteristic suddenness into mimicry. "Ai! Unhappy! Ai! My back, my bones! Slivers of death have lodged in me! Ai! There are dots before my eyes! Is that you, Bertha? I can't see. Ai! Groaning about the house as though he already stank for earth—God forbid! And not a grey hair in his head. But let one of us get in his road—Ho! Ho! He was suddenly spry as a colt! And could he shower blows? Tireless! Like a bandmaster's his stick would wave."

His mother sighed and then laughed acknowledging defeat.

"It was mother's fault too," Aunt Bertha added warningly as if giving her an object lesson. "A wife should have driven a man like that, not coddled him, not pampered him to ruin. Soft and meek, she was." Aunt Bertha became soft and meek. "She let herself be trampled on. Nine children she bore him beside the twins that died between your birth and mine. She's grey now. You'd weep to see her. Bloodless as a rag in the weather. You wouldn't know her. Still trailing after him. Still saving him the dainties—the breast and giblets of the hen, the middle of herrings, the crispest rolls! Do you remember how he would stretch out over the table, pawing each roll, pumping it in his glutton's haste to feel how soft it was? And then hide away the new-baked cake from the rest of us? His nose was in every pot. But whenever you saw him—" she broke off, stretched out her hands in a gesture of injured innocence—"What have I eaten today? What? An age-old crust, a glass of coffee. I tremble with hunger. Bah!"

"I sometimes don't think he could help it. There were so many mouths to feed. It must have frightened him."

"Well, whose fault was it? Not mother's certainly. Why even when she was ailing he—" And at this point she did what she often did in her speech—finish her sentence in Polish, a language David had come to hate because he couldn't understand it.

"Tell me, would you go back to Austria if you had the money?"

"Never!"

"No?"

"Money I'd send them," Aunt Bertha asserted flatly. "But go home—never! I'm too glad I escaped. And why should I go home? To quarrel?"

"Not even to see mother?"

"God pity her more than any. But what good would my seeing her do her? Or me? It would only give me grief. No! Neither her, nor father, nor Yetta, nor Adolf, nor Herman, nor even Saul, the baby, though God knows I was fond of him. You see I'm one who doesn't yearn for the home land."

"You haven't been here long enough," said his mother. "One grapples this land at first closer to one's self than it's worth."

"Closer than it's worth? Why? True I work like a horse and I stink like one with my own sweat. But there's life here, isn't there? There's a stir here always. Listen! The street! The cart! High laughter! Ha, good! Veljish was still as a fart in company. Who could endure it? Trees! Fields! Again trees! Who can talk to trees? Here at least I can find other pastimes than sliding down the gable on a roof!"

"I suppose you're right," his mother laughed at her vehemence. "It appears to me that you'll grow from green to yellow in this land years before I do. Yes, there are other pastimes here than—" She broke off, flinched even though she laughed. "That sliver of wood in your flesh! Dear God you were rash!"

"It was nothing! Nothing!" Aunt Bertha chuckled lightly. "My rump has forgotten it long ago! But that should prove to you that I'm better off here than I was there. Anyone is! That quiet was enough to spring the brain!"

His mother shook her head noncommittally.

"What? No?" Aunt Bertha mistook her gesture. "Can you say no?" She began counting on her fingers. "Ha-a-d A-Adolf come here as a boy, would he have to run away to the lumber camps and gotten a rupture that big? Ha? A-And Yetta-a. She could have found a better husband than that idiot tailor she's married to. He finds diamonds in the road, I tell you, and loses them before he gets home. He sees children falling into the frozen river and not a child in the village is missing. Awful! Awful! And Herman and that peasant wench. And the peasant looking for him with an ax. You don't see that in this land! Fortunate for him anyway that he fled to Strij in time, and fortunate too that it wasn't Russia. There might have been a pogrom! There was nothing to do and so they went mad, and because they were mad they did whatever came into their heads. That's how I was, and if you want to know, my dear, close-mouthed sister, as quiet and gentle as you were," her tone became sly—"there was still, well a rumor of some sort. Someone, something—er—done. But only a rumor!" she added hastily. "A lie of course!"

His mother turned abruptly toward the window, and her own irrelevant words crossed her sister's before the other and finished—"Look, Bertha! That new automobile. What a pretty blue! Wouldn't you like to be rich enough to own one?"

Aunt Bertha made a face, but came over and looked down. "Yes. What a grinder it has in front of it. Like a hand-organ, no? Do you remember when we saw our first one on the new road in Veljish—the black one?" The least bit of resentment crept into her voice. "You eternal close-mouth, when will that secret be weaned?"

Something about their tones and expressions, so curiously guarded in both stirred David's curiosity. But since their conversation on that score went no further, he could only wonder in a vague and transient way what his mother had done, and hope that another time would reveal the meaning. . . .

Hostilities between Aunt Bertha and David's father were rapidly reaching the breaking point. David was sure that something would happen soon if Aunt Bertha did not curb her over-ready tongue. He marveled at her rashness.

On that Saturday night Aunt Bertha had arrived home bearing a large cardboard box. She was later tonight than usual and had delayed the supper almost an hour. The fast had not helped to put David's father in an amiable frame of mind. He had been grumbling before she came, and now, though she was washing her face and hands with as great dispatch as possible, he could not restrain a testy—

"Hurry up. You'll never wash that stench off!"

To which Aunt Bertha made no other reply than to bob her ample buttocks in his general direction. Glaring furiously at her back, he said nothing, but savagely toyed with the table knife in his hands.

Aunt Bertha at length straightened up, and apparently unconscious of the rage she had put him in, began drying herself.

"I suppose you've been shopping," said her sister amiably, setting the food on the table.

"Indeed I have," she seated herself. "I'm coming up in the world."

"What did you buy?"

"Bargains of course!" his father broke in contemptuously. He seemed to have been waiting for just this opportunity. "The storekeeper who couldn't lift the head from her shoulders without her knowing it might as well close up shop!"

"Is that so?" she retorted sarcastically. "Speak for yourself! I don't spend my life hunting for rusty horseshoes. That gramophone you bought in the summer—Ha! Ha! Mute and motionless as the day before creation."

"Hold your tongue!"

"Your noodles and cheese are growing cold," said David's mother. "Both of you!"

There was a pause while everyone ate. From time to time, Aunt Bertha cast her eyes happily at the cardboard box resting on the chair.

"Apparel?" asked his mother discreetly.

"What else? Half the country's goods!"

His mother smiled at his aunt's fervor.

"Blessed is this golden land," she let herself be carried away by enthusiasm. "Such beautiful things to wear!"

"Much good that does you," said his father over a forkful of noodles.

"Albert!" his wife protested.

Aunt Bertha abruptly stopped eating. "Who was speaking to you? Go snarl up your own wits! You're one person I don't have to please."

"To please me, the Lord need grant you a new soul."

"To spite you, I'd stay just as I am!" She tossed her head scornfully, "I'd sooner have a pig admire me."

"No doubt he would."

"Tell me, dear Bertha," said her sister desperately. "What did you buy?"

"Oh, a parcel of rags! With what I earn what else can I buy?" Then brightening a little. "I'll show them to you."

Casting a hasty glance at her husband, David's mother put up a restraining hand, but too late. Aunt Bertha had seized a table knife and was already cutting the strings off the box.

"Are we having dinner or going to a fair?" he asked.

"Perhaps a little later—" suggested his mother.

"Not at all," Aunt Bertha said with vindictive cheerfulness. "Let him gorge himself if he wants to. My appetite can wait." And she whipped open the box.

Lifting out first one article of woman's wear and then another—a corset cover, a petticoat, stockings—she commented blithely on each and quoted its price. Finally, she brought into view a pair of large white drawers and turned them over admiringly in her hands. David's father abruptly shoved his chair around to cut them from his field of vision.

"Aren't they beautiful?" she chattered on. "See the lace at the bottom. And so cheap. Only twenty cents. I saw such small ones in the store. Some poor women have no buttocks at all!" Then she giggled, "When I hold them at a distance upside down this way they look like peaks in Austria."

"Yes, yes," said his mother apprehensively.

"Ha! Ha!" She went on entirely enchanted by the charm of her purchase. "But what can I do? I *am* fat below. But isn't it a miracle? Twenty cents, and I can wear what only a baroness in Austria could wear. And so convenient and so neatly cut—these buttons here. See how this drops down! The newest style, he told me. Do you remember the drawers we wore in Austria—into the stockings? Winter and Summer my legs looked like a gypsy's accordion."

But David's father could restrain himself no longer.

"Put those things away!" he rapped out.

Aunt Bertha drew back startled. Then narrowed her eyes and thrust out stubborn lips. "Don't shout at me!"

"Put those away!" He banged his fist on the table so that the dishes danced and the yellow noodles cast their long necks over the rim of the platters.

"Please, Bertha!" her sister implored, "You know how—"

"Do you side with him too?" She interrupted her. "I'll put them away when I please! I'm not his slave!"

"Are you going to do what I say?"

Aunt Bertha clapped one hand to her hip, "When I please! It's time you knew what women wore on their bottoms."

"I'll ask you once more, you vile slut," he shoved his chair back and rose in slow wrath.

David began to cry.

"Let me go!" Aunt Bertha pushed back her sister who had interposed herself. "Is he so pious, he can't bear to look at a pair of drawers? Does he piss water as mortals do, or only the purest of vegetable oil?"

His father advanced on her. "I'm pleading with you as with Death!" He always said that at moments of intense anger. His voice had taken on that thin terrific hardness that meant he was about to strike. "Will you put them away?"

"Make me!" she screamed and waved the drawers like a goad in his very eyes.

Before she could recoil, his long arm had swept out, and with a bark of rage, he plucked the drawers from her. A moment later, he had ripped them in two. "Here, you slut!" he roared. "Here are your peaks!" And he flung them in her face.

Raging with fury, Aunt Bertha leapt at him with clawing fingers. The flat thrust of his palm against her bosom sent her reeling to the wall. He turned on his heel, and his eyeballs glaring in demonic rage, he tore his hat and coat from a peg near the door and stalked out.

Aunt Bertha dropped into a chair and began weeping loudly and hysterically. Her sister, her own eyes filling with tears, tried to comfort her.

"Madman! Mad!" came his aunt's stifled words. "Savage beast!" She picked up the drawers at her feet and wrung them in the frenzy of her anguish. "My new drawers! What did he have against them? May his head be cloven as they are! Oh!" The tears streamed down her cheeks. Stray strands of her red hair parted on her clammy brow and nose.

David's mother stroked her shoulders soothingly.

"Hush, dear sister! Don't weep so, child! You'll break your heart!"

Aunt Bertha only lamented the more, "Why did I ever set foot on this stinking land? Why did I ever come here? Ten hours a day in a smothering shop—paper flowers! Rag flowers! Ten long hours, afraid to pee too often because the foreman might think I was shirking. And now when I've bought with the sweat of my brow a little of what my heart desires, that butcher rends it. Ai!"

"I tried to save you, sister. You must know what he's like by now. Listen to me, I have some money, I'll buy you a new pair."

"Oh! Woe is me!"

"And even the ones you have there may be mended."

"May his heart be broken as mine is, they'll never be mended."

"Look, they're torn exactly at the seam."

"What?" Aunt Bertha opened grief stricken eyes. She stared at the drawers a moment and then jumped frenziedly from her chair. "He threw them at me too, dashed them in my face. He flung me to the wall! I'm not going to stay here another minute! I'll not endure it another minute. I'm going to pack my things! I'm going!" She made for the door.

David's mother hastened after her. "Wait," she pleaded, "where will you run at this time of night? Please, I beg you!"

"I'll go anywhere! What did I leave Europe for if not to escape that tyrant of a father. And this is what I came to—a madman! May a trolley-car crack his bones! Slaughter him, Almighty God!" And she ran weeping loudly into her bedroom.

David's mother followed her sadly. . . .

Although Aunt Bertha did not move out of their house as she had threatened to do, the next day and the next, there was no exchange of communication between her and David's father. Dinners at night were eaten in silence, and if either of them required anything of the other, David or his mother were impressed as intermediaries. However after several nights of this embarrassing constraint, Aunt Bertha's self-imposed shackles grew too much for her. Quite suddenly one evening, she broke them.

"Pass me the herring jar," she muttered—this time directly at her brother-in-law.

His face darkened when she spoke, but sullenly though he did it, he nevertheless did push the herring jar toward her.

Thus an armistice was signed and relations, if not cordial, were at least established. And thereafter, as much as it was possible for her, Aunt Bertha kept her peace.

"He's a mad dog," she told her sister. "He has to run. There's nothing to do but keep out of his way."

And she did for many months.

Tillie Olsen

Tillie Olsen was born in 1913, the second child of seven, to Jewish immigrants who had fled Russia after the 1905 rebellion. Her father worked as a farmer, painter, paperhanger, and packinghouse worker and became the state secretary of the Nebraska Socialist party. Like her father, Olsen worked hard yet made time for political action: she was an active member of the Young Communist League while employed as a trimmer in a slaughterhouse, a power-press operator, a hash slinger, a mayonnaise jar capper, a checker in a warehouse. Olsen never graduated from high school.

In 1933, Olsen moved from the Great Plains states to California. Both as a single woman and after she married a printer and raised their three daughters, Olsen continued her political activities and worked in a series of menial jobs. She was enabled to devote herself to writing when she won a Stanford University creative writing fellowship in 1956–1957; however, from 1957 to 1959 she had to return to regular employment and was "silenced" as a writer. This literary silence was broken by a 1959 Ford Foundation grant, which allowed her to complete *Tell Me a Riddle*. Its publication in 1961 earned her a myriad of distinguished awards and fellowships, which gave her the impetus and means to keep writing. Among other works she has published since that time, her book of essays, *Silences*, explores the literary tragedy of writers who, like herself, have been inhibited by class and gender.

Tell Me a Riddle, reprinted here in its entirety, is surely one of the most extraordinary novellas ever written by an American Jewish woman. The characters of the protagonist, Eva; her husband, David; and her children and their spouses are revealed subtly, in layers, with all of their ambivalences intact. The complexity of human personality and behavior provides one text to this piece of fiction; the cultural and familial suppression of female individuality provides another.

Special attention is paid to the mysteries of memory: Eva, as a bitter, desperately ill old woman, remembers only certain aspects of her years as a young mother; Vivi, the most maternal of her daughters, remembers other aspects entirely. Both of them are remembering truthfully, but the truth is larger than either of them can grasp. Similarly, Eva's hatred of Jewish religious ritual is steeped in her own angry memories of the rigid pieties of her childhood; she also holds the Jewish religion as somehow responsible for the savagery of Russian pogroms and the Nazi extermination of Europe's Jews. In rejecting formal religion, Eva is in her own mind rejecting the artificial barriers that divide one human being from another—and yet her implacable hatred of religion prevents her from understanding her daughter Hannah's Sabbath candles, which represent to the young mother a circle of peace, joy, and familial affection.

Although *Tell Me a Riddle* is surely heart-wrenching, it achieves in its final pages a hopeful resolution: whereas nothing can ever undo the tragic waste of human potential that results from the mistakes of the past, the characters are shown growing and changing even in old age and under extreme conditions. Olsen reveals how men and women, parents and children can cannibalize each other; she also reveals how they can develop a deeper understanding and capacity for unselfishness.

•

"Tell Me a Riddle"

"THESE THINGS SHALL BE"

I

For forty-seven years they had been married. How deep back the stubborn, gnarled roots of the quarrel reached, no one could say—but only now, when tending to the needs of others no longer shackled them together, the roots swelled up visible, split the earth between them, and the tearing shook even to the children, long since grown.

Why now, why now? wailed Hannah.

As if when we grew up weren't enough, said Paul.

Poor Ma. Poor Dad. It hurts so for both of them, said Vivi. They never had very much; at least in old age they should be happy.

Knock their heads together, insisted Sammy; tell 'em: you're too old for this kind of thing; no reason not to get along now.

Lennie wrote to Clara: They've lived over so much together; what could possibly tear them apart?

Something tangible enough.

Arthritic hands, and such work as he got, occasional. Poverty all his life, and there was little breath left for running. He could not, could not turn away from this desire: to have the troubling of responsibility, the fretting with money, over and done with; to be free, to be carefree where success was not measured by accumulation, and there was use for the vitality still in him.

There was a way. They could sell the house, and with the money join his lodge's Haven, cooperative for the aged. Happy communal life, and was he not already an official; had he not helped organize it, raise funds, served as a trustee?

But she—would not consider it.

"What do we need all this for?" he would ask loudly, for her hearing aid was turned down and the vacuum was shrilling. "Five rooms" (pushing the sofa so she could get into the corner) "furniture" (smoothing down the rug) "floors and surfaces to make work. Tell me, why do we need it?" And he was glad he could ask in a scream.

"Because I'm use't."

"Because you're use't. This is a reason, Mrs. Word Miser? Used to can get unused!"

"Enough unused I have to get used to already. . . . Not enough words?" turning off the vacuum a moment to hear herself answer. "Because soon enough we'll need only a little closet, no windows, no furniture, nothing to make work, but for worms. Because now I want room. . . . Screech and blow like you're doing, you'll need that closet even sooner. . . . Ha, again!" for the vacuum bag wailed, puffed half up, hung stubbornly limp. "This time fix it so it stays; quick before the phone rings and you get too important-busy."

But while he struggled with the motor, it seethed in him. Why fix it? Why have to bother? And if it can't be fixed, have to wring the mind with how to pay the repair? At the Haven they come in with their own machines to clean your room or your cottage; you fish, or play cards, or make jokes in the sun, not with knotty fingers fight to mend vacuums.

Over the dishes, coaxingly: "For once in your life, to be free, to have everything done for you, like a queen."

"I never liked queens."

"No dishes, no garbage, no towel to sop, no worry what to buy, what to eat."

"And what else would I do with my empty hands? Better to eat at my own table when I want, and to cook and eat how I want."

"In the cottages they buy what you ask, and cook it how you like. *You* are the one who always used to say: better mankind born without mouths and stomachs than always to worry for money to buy, to shop, to fix, to cook, to wash, to clean."

"How cleverly you hid that you heard. I said it then because eighteen hours a day I ran. And you never scraped a carrot or knew a dish towel sops. Now—for you and me—who cares? A herring out of a jar is enough. But when *I* want, and nobody to bother."

And she turned off her ear button, so she would not have to hear.

But as *he* had no peace, juggling and rejuggling the money to figure: how will I pay for this now?; prying out the storm windows (there they take care of this); jolting in the streetcar on errands (there I would not have to ride to take care of this or that); fending the patronizing relatives just back from Florida (at the Haven it matters what one is, not what one can afford), he gave *her* no peace.

"Look! In their bulletin. A reading circle. Twice a week it meets."

"Haumm," her answer of not listening.

"A reading circle. Chekhov they read that you like, and Peretz. Cultured people at the Haven that you would enjoy."

"Enjoy!" She tasted the word. "Now, when it pleases you, you find a reading circle for me. And forty years ago when the children were morsels and there was a Circle, did you stay home with them once so I could go? Even once? You trained me well. I do not need others to enjoy. Others!" Her voice trembled. "Because you want to be there with others. Already it makes me sick to think of you always around others. Clown, grimacer, floormat, yesman, entertainer, whatever they want of you."

And now it was he who turned on the television loud so he need not hear.

Old scar tissue ruptured and the wounds festered anew. Chekhov indeed. She thought without softness of that young wife, who in the deep night hours while she nursed the current baby, and perhaps held another in her lap, would try to stay awake for the only time there was to read. She would feel again the weather of the outside on his cheek when, coming late from a meeting, he would find her so, and stimulated and ardent, sniffing her skin, coax: "I'll put the baby to bed, and you—put the book away, don't read, don't read."

That had been the most beguiling of all the "don't read, put your book away" her life had been. Chekhov indeed!

"Money?" She shrugged him off. "Could we get poorer than once we were? And in America, who starves?"

But as still he pressed:

"Let me alone about money. Was there ever enough? Seven little ones—for every penny I had to ask—and sometimes, remember, there was nothing. But always *I* had to manage. Now *you* manage. Rub your nose in it good."

But from those years she had had to manage, old humiliations and terrors rose up, lived again, and forced her to relive them. The children's need-ings; that grocer's face or this merchant's wife she had had to beg credit from when credit was a disgrace; the scenery of the long blocks walked around when she could not pay; school coming, and the desperate going over the old to see what could yet be remade; the soups of meat bones begged "for-the-dog" one winter. . . .

Enough. Now they had no children. Let *him* wrack his head for how they would live. She would not exchange her solitude for anything. *Never again to be forced to move to the rhythms of others.*

For in this solitude she had won to a reconciled peace.

Tranquillity from having the empty house no longer an enemy, for it stayed clean—not as in the days when it was her family, the life in it, that had seemed the enemy: tracking, smudging, littering, dirtying, engaging her in endless defeating battle—and on whom her endless defeat had been spewed.

The few old books, memorized from rereading; the pictures to ponder (the magnifying glass superimposed on her heavy eyeglasses). Or if she wishes, when he is gone, the phonograph, that if she turns up very loud and strains, she can hear: the ordered sounds and the struggling.

Out in the garden, growing things to nurture. Birds to be kept out of the pear tree, and when the pears are heavy and ripe, the old fury of work, for all must be canned, nothing wasted.

And her one social duty (for she will not go to luncheons or meetings) the boxes of old clothes left with her, as with a life-practised eye for finding what is still wearable within the worn (again the magnifying glass superimposed on the heavy glasses) she scans and sorts—this for rag or rummage, that for mending and cleaning, and this for sending away.

Being able at last to live within, and not move to the rhythms of others, as life had forced her to: denying; removing; isolating; taking the children one by one; then deafening, half-blinding—and at last, presenting her solitude.

And in it she had won to a reconciled peace.

Now he was violating it with his constant campaigning: *Sell the house and move to the Haven.* (You sit, you sit—there too you could sit like a stone.) He was making of her a battleground where old grievances tore. (Turn on your ear button—I am talking.) And stubbornly she resisted—so that from wheedling, reasoning, manipulation, it was bitterness he now started with.

And it came to where every happening lashed up a quarrel.

"I will sell the house anyway," he flung at her one night. "I am putting it up for sale. There will be a way to make you sign."

The television blared, as always it did on the evenings he stayed home, and as always it reached her only as noise. She did not know if the tumult was in her or outside. Snap! she turned the sound off. "Shadows," she whispered to him, pointing to the screen, "look, it is only shadows." And in a scream: "Did you say that you will sell the house? Look at me, not at that. I am no shadow. You cannot sell without me."

"Leave on the television. I am watching."

"Like Paulie, like Jenny, a four-year-old. Staring at shadows. *You cannot sell the house.*"

"I will. We are going to the Haven. There you would not hear the television when you do not want it. I could sit in the social room and watch. You could lock yourself up to smell your unpleasantness in a room by yourself—for who would want to come near you?"

"No, no selling." A whisper now.

"The television is shadows. Mrs. Enlightened! Mrs. Cultured! A world comes into your house—and it is shadows. People you would never meet in a thousand lifetimes. Wonders. When you were four years old, yes, like Paulie, like Jenny, did you know of Indian dances, alligators, how they use bamboo in Malaya? No, you scratched in your dirt with the chickens and thought Olshana was the world. Yes, Mrs. Unpleasant, I will sell the house, for there better can we be rid of each other than here."

She did not know if the tumult was outside, or in her. Always a ravening inside, a pull to the bed, to lie down, to succumb.

"Have you thought maybe Ma should let a doctor have a look at her?" asked their son Paul after Sunday dinner, regarding his mother crumpled on the couch, instead of, as was her custom, busying herself in Nancy's kitchen.

"Why not the President too?"

"Seriously, Dad. This is the third Sunday she's lain down like that after dinner. Is she that way at home?"

"A regular love affair with the bed. Every time I start to talk to her."

Good protective reaction, observed Nancy to herself. The workings of hos-til-ity.

"Nancy could take her. I just don't like how she looks. Let's have Nancy arrange an appointment."

"You think she'll go?" regarding his wife gloomily. "All right, we have to have doctor bills, we have to have doctor bills." Loudly: "Something hurts you?"

She startled, looked to his lips. He repeated: "Mrs. Take It Easy, something hurts?"

"Nothing. . . . Only you."

"A woman of honey. That's why you're lying down?"

"Soon I'll get up to do the dishes, Nancy."

"Leave them, Mother, I like it better this way."

"Mrs. Take It Easy, Paul says you should start ballet. You should go to see a doctor and ask: how soon can you start ballet?"

"A doctor?" she begged. "Ballet?"

"We were talking, Ma," explained Paul, "you don't seem any too well. It would be a good idea for you to see a doctor for a checkup."

"I get up now to do the kitchen. Doctors are bills and foolishness, my son. I need no doctors."

"At the Haven," he could not resist pointing out, "a doctor is *not* bills. He lives beside you. You start to sneeze, he is there before you open up a Kleenex. You can be sick there for free, all you want."

"Diarrhea of the mouth, is there a doctor to make you dumb?"

"Ma. Promise me you'll go. Nancy will arrange it."

"It's all of a piece when you think of it," said Nancy, "the way she attacks my kitchen, scrubbing under every cup hook, doing the inside of the oven so I can't enjoy Sunday dinner, knowing that half-blind or not, she's going to find every speck of dirt. . . ."

"Don't, Nancy, I've told you—it's the only way she knows to be useful. What did the *doctor* say?"

"A real fatherly lecture. Sixty-nine is young these days. Go out, enjoy life, find interests. Get a new hearing aid, this one is antiquated. Old age is sickness only if one makes it so. Geriatrics, Inc."

"So there was nothing physical."

"Of course there was. How can you live to yourself like she does without there being? Evidence of a kidney disorder, and her blood count is low. He gave her a diet, and she's to come back for follow-up and lab work. . . . But he was clear enough: Number One prescription—start living like a human being. . . . When I think of your dad, who could really play the invalid with that arthritis of his, as active as a teenager, and twice as much fun. . . ."

"You didn't tell me the doctor says your sickness is in you, how you live." He pushed his advantage. "Life and enjoyments you need better than medicine. And this diet, how can you keep it? To weigh each morsel and scrape away each bit of fat, to make this soup, that pudding. There, at the Haven, they have a dietician, they would do it for you."

She is silent.

"You would feel better there, I know it," he says gently. "There there is life and enjoyments all around."

"What is the matter, Mr. Importantbusy, you have no card game or meeting you can go to?"—turning her face to the pillow.

For a while he cut his meetings and going out, fussed over her diet, tried to wheedle her into leaving the house, brought in visitors:

"I should come to a fashion tea. I should sit and look at pretty babies in clothes I cannot buy. This is pleasure?"

"Always you are better than everyone else. The doctor said you should go out. Mrs. Brem comes to you with goodness and you turn her away."
"Because *you* asked her to, she asked me."

"They won't come back. People you need, the doctor said. Your own cousins I asked; they were willing to come and make peace as if nothing had happened. . . ."
"No more crushers of people, pushers, hypocrites, around me. No more in *my* house. You go to them if you like."

"Kind he is to visit. And you, like ice."
"A babbler. All my life around babblers. Enough!"

"She's even worse, Dad? Then let her stew a while," advised Nancy. "You can't let it destroy you; it's a psychological thing, maybe too far gone for any of us to help."

So he let her stew. More and more she lay silent in bed, and sometimes did not even get up to make the meals. No longer was the tongue-lashing inevitable if he left the coffee cup where it did not belong, or forgot to take out the garbage or mislaid the broom. The birds grew bold that summer and for once pocked the pears, undisturbed.

A bellyful of bitterness and every day the same quarrel in a new way and a different old grievance the quarrel forced her to enter and relive. And the new torment: I am not really sick, the doctor said it, then why do I feel so sick?

One night she asked him: "You have a meeting tonight? Do not go. Stay . . . with me."

He had planned to watch "This Is Your Life," but half sick himself from the heavy heat, and sickening therefore the more after the brooks and woods of the Haven, with satisfaction he grated:

"Hah, Mrs. Live Alone And Like It wants company all of a sudden. It doesn't seem so good the time of solitary when she was a girl exile in Siberia. 'Do not go. Stay with me.' A new song for Mrs. Free As A Bird. Yes, I am going out, and while I am gone chew this aloneness good, and think how you keep us both from where if you want people, you do not need to be alone."

"Go, go. All your life you have gone without me."

After him she sobbed curses he had not heard in years, old-country curses from their childhood: Grow, oh shall you grow like an onion, with your head in the ground. Like the hide of a drum shall you be, beaten in life, beaten in death. Oh shall you be like a chandelier, to hang, and to burn. . . .

She was not in their bed when he came back. She lay on the cot on the sun porch. All week she did not speak or come near him; nor did he try to make peace or care for her.

He slept badly, so used to her next to him. After all the years, old harmonies and dependencies deep in their bodies; she curled to him, or he coiled to her, each warmed, warming, turning as the other turned, the nights a long embrace.

It was not the empty bed or the storm that woke him, but a faint singing. *She* was singing. Shaking off the drops of rain, the lightning riving her lifted face, he saw her so; the cot covers on the floor.

"This is a private concert?" he asked. "Come in, you are wet."

"I can breathe now," she answered; "my lungs are rich." Though indeed the sound was hardly a breath.

"Come in, come in." Loosing the bamboo shades. "Look how wet you are." Half helping, half carrying her, still faint-breathing her song.

A Russian love song of fifty years ago.

He had found a buyer, but before he told her, he called together those children who were close enough to come. Paul, of course, Sammy from New Jersey, Hannah from Connecticut, Vivi from Ohio.

With a kindling of energy for her beloved visitors, she arrayed the house, cooked and baked. She was not prepared for the solemn after-dinner conclave, they too probing in and tearing. Her frightened eyes watched from mouth to mouth as each spoke.

His stories were eloquent and funny of her refusal to go back to the doctor; of the scorned invitations; of her stubborn silence or the bile "like a Niagara"; of her contrariness: "If I clean it's no good how I cleaned; if I don't clean, I'm still a master who thinks he has a slave."

(Vinegar he poured on me all his life; I am well marinated; how can I be honey now?)

Deftly he marched in the rightness for moving to the Haven; their money from social security free for visiting the children, not sucked into daily needs and into the house; the activities in the Haven for him; but mostly the Haven for *her:* her health, her need of care, distraction, amusement, friends who shared her interests.

"This does offer an outlet for Dad," said Paul; "he's always been an active person. And economic peace of mind isn't to be sneezed at, either. I could use a little of that myself."

But when they asked: "And you, Ma, how do you feel about it?" could only whisper:

"For him it is good. It is not for me. I can no longer live between people."

"You lived all your life *for* people," Vivi cried.

"Not with." Suffering doubly for the unhappiness on her children's faces.

"You have to find some compromise," Sammy insisted. "Maybe sell the house and buy a trailer. After forty-seven years there's surely some way you can find to live in peace."

"There is no help, my children. Different things we need."

"Then live alone!" He could control himself no longer. "I have a buyer for the house. Half the money for you, half for me. Either alone or with me to the Haven. You think I can live any longer as we are doing now?"

"Ma doesn't have to make a decision this minute, however you feel, Dad," Paul said quickly, "and you wouldn't want her to. Let's let it lay a few months, and then talk some more."

"I think I can work it out to take Mother home with me for a while," Hannah said. "You both look terrible, but especially you, Mother. I'm going to ask Phil to have a look at you."

"Sure," cracked Sammy. "What's the use of a doctor husband if you can't get free service out of him once in a while for the family? And absence might make the heart . . . you know."

"There was something after all," Paul told Nancy in a colorless voice. "That was Hannah's Phil calling. Her gall bladder. . . . Surgery."

"Her *gall* bladder. If that isn't classic. 'Bitter as gall'—talk of psychosom—"

He stepped closer, put his hand over her mouth, and said in the same colorless, plodding voice. "We have to get Dad. They operated at once. The cancer was everywhere, surrounding the liver, everywhere. They did what they could . . . at best she has a year. Dad . . . we have to tell him."

2

Honest in his weakness when they told him, and that she was not to know. "I'm not an actor. She'll know right away by how I am. Oh that poor woman. I am old too, it will break me into pieces. Oh that poor woman. She will spit on me: 'So my sickness was how I live.' Oh Paulie, how she will be, that poor woman. Only she should not suffer. . . . I can't stand sickness. Paulie, I can't go with you."

But went. And play-acted.

"A grand opening and you did not even wait for me. . . . A good thing Hannah took you with her."

"Fashion teas I needed. They cut out what tore in me; just in my throat something hurts yet. . . . Look! so many flowers, like a funeral. Vivi called, did Hannah tell you? And Lennie from San Francisco, and Clara; and Sammy is coming." Her gnome's face pressed happily into the flowers.

It is impossible to predict in these cases, but once over the immediate effects of the operation, she should have several months of comparative well-being.

The money, where will come the money?

Travel with her, Dad. Don't take her home to the old associations. The other children will want to see her.

The money, where will I wring the money?

Whatever happens, she is not to know. No, you can't ask her to sign papers to sell the house; nothing to upset her. Borrow instead then after. . . .

I had wanted to leave you each a few dollars to make life easier, as other fathers do. There will be nothing left now. (Failure! you and your "business is exploitation." Why didn't you make it when it could be made?—Is that what you're thinking, Sammy?)

Sure she's unreasonable, Dad—but you have to stay with her; if there's to be any happiness in what's left of her life, it depends on you.

Prop me up, children, think of me, too. Shuffled, chained with her, bitter woman. No Haven, and the little money going. . . . How happy she looks, poor creature.

The look of excitement. The straining to hear everything (the new hearing aid turned full). Why are you so happy, dying woman?

How the petals are, fold on fold, and the gladioli color. The autumn air.

Stranger grandsons, tall above the little gnome grandmother, the little spry grandfather. Paul in a frenzy of picture-taking before going. She, wandering the great house. Feeling the books; laughing at the maple shoemaker's bench of a hundred years ago used as a table. The ear turned to music.

"Let us go home. See how good I walk now." "One step from the hospital," he answers, "and she wants to fly. Wait till Doctor Phil says."

"Look—the birds too are flying home. Very good Phil is and will not show it, but he is sick of sickness by the time he comes home."

"Mrs. Telepathy, to read minds," he answers; "read mine what it says: when the trunks of medicines become a suitcase, then we will go."

The grandboys, they do not know what to say to us. . . . Hannah, she runs around here, there, when is there time for herself? Let us go home. Let us go home.

Musing; gentleness—*but for the incidents of the rabbi in the hospital, and of the candles of benediction.*

Of the rabbi in the hospital:

Now tell me what happened, Mother.

From the sleep I awoke, Hannah's Phil, and he stands there like a devil in a dream and calls me by name. I cannot hear. I think he prays. Go away, please, I tell him, I am not a believer. Still he stands, while my heart knocks with fright.

You scared *him,* Mother. He thought you were delirious.

Who sent him? Why did he come to me?

It is a custom. The men of God come to visit those of their religion they might help. The hospital makes up the list for them—race, religion—and you are on the Jewish list.

Not for rabbis. At once go and make them change. Tell them to write: Race, human; Religion, none.

And of the candles of benediction:

Look how you have upset yourself, Mrs. Excited Over Nothing. Pleasant memories you should leave.

Go in, go back to Hannah and the lights. Two weeks I saw candles and said nothing. But she asked me.

So what was so terrible? She forgets you never did, she asks you to light the Friday candles and say the benediction like Phil's mother when she visits. If the candles give her pleasure, why shouldn't she have the pleasure?

Not for pleasure she does it. For emptiness. Because his family does. Because all around her do.

That is not a good reason too? But you did not hear her. For heritage, she told you. For the boys, from the past they should have tradition.

Superstition! From our ancestors, savages, afraid of the dark, of themselves: mumbo words and magic lights to scare away ghosts.

She told you: how it started does not take away the goodness. For centuries, peace in the house it means.

Swindler! does she look back on the dark centuries? Candles bought instead of bread and stuck into a potato for a candlestick? Religion that stifled and said: in Paradise, woman, you will be the footstool of your husband, and in life—poor chosen Jew—ground under, despised, trembling in cellars. And cremated. And cremated.

This is religion's fault? You think you are still an orator of the 1905 revolution? Where are the pills for quieting? Which are they?

Heritage. How have we come from our savage past, how no longer to be savages—this to teach. To look back and learn what humanizes—this to teach. To smash all ghettos that divide us—not to go back, not to go back—this to teach. Learned books in the house, will humankind live or die, and she gives to her boys—superstition.

Hannah that is so good to you. Take your pill, Mrs. Excited For Nothing, swallow.

Heritage! But when did I have time to teach? Of Hannah I asked only hands to help.

Swallow.

Otherwise—musing; gentleness.

Not to travel. To go home.

The children want to see you. We have to show them you are as thorny a flower as ever.

Not to travel.

Vivi wants you should see her new baby. She sent the tickets—airplane tickets—a Mrs. Roosevelt she wants to make of you. To Vivi's we have to go.

A new baby. How many warm, seductive babies. She holds him stiffly, *away* from her, so that he wails. And a long shudder begins, and the sweat beads on her forehead.

"Hush, shush," croons the grandfather, lifting him back. "You should forgive your grandmamma, little prince, she has never held a baby before, only seen them in glass cases. Hush, shush."

"You're tired, Ma," says Vivi. "The travel and the noisy dinner. I'll take you to lie down."

(A long travel from, to, what the feel of a baby evokes.)

In the airplane, cunningly designed to encase from motion (no wind, no feel of flight), she had sat severely and still, her face turned to the sky through which they cleaved and left no scar.

So this was how it looked, the determining, the crucial sky, and this was how man moved through it, remote above the dwindled earth, the concealed human life. Vulnerable life, that could scar.

There was a steerage ship of memory that shook across a great, circular sea: clustered, ill human beings; and through the thick-stained air, tiny fretting waters in a window round like the airplane's—sun round, moon round. (The round thatched roofs of Olshana.) Eye round—like the smaller window that framed distance the solitary year of exile when only her eyes could travel, and no voice spoke. And the polar winds hurled themselves across snows trackless and endless and white—like the clouds which had closed together below and hidden the earth.

Now they put a baby in her lap. Do not ask me, she would have liked to beg. Enough the worn face of Vivi, the remembered grandchildren. I cannot, cannot. . . .

Cannot what? Unnatural grandmother, not able to make herself embrace a baby.

She lay there in the bed of the two little girls, her new hearing aid turned full, listening to the sound of the children going to sleep, the baby's fretful crying and hushing, the clatter of dishes being washed and put away. They thought she slept. Still she rode on.

It was not that she had not loved her babies, her children. The love—the passion of tending—had risen with the need like a torrent; and like a torrent drowned and immolated all else. But when the need was done—oh the power that was lost in the painful dimming back and drying up of what still surged, but had nowhere to go. Only the thin pulsing left that could not quiet, suffering over lives one felt, but could no longer hold nor help.

On that torrent she had borne them on their own lives, and the riverbed was desert long years now. Not there would she dwell, a memoried wraith. Surely that was not all, surely there was more. Still the springs, the springs were in her seeking. Somewhere an older power that beat for life. Somewhere coherence, transport, meaning. If they would but leave her in the air now stilled of clamor, in the reconciled solitude, to journey on.

And they put a baby in her lap. Immediacy to embrace, and the breath of *that* past: warm flesh like this that had claims and nuzzled away all else and with lovely mouths devoured; hot-living like an animal—intensely and now; the turning maze; the long drunkenness; the drowning into needing and being needed. Severely she looked back—and the shudder seized her again, and the sweat. Not that way. Not there, not now could she, not yet. . . .

And all that visit, she could not touch the baby.

"Daddy, is it the . . . sickness she's like that?" asked Vivi. "I was so glad to be having the baby—for her. I told Tim, it'll give her more happiness than anything, being around a baby again. And she hasn't played with him once."

He was not listening. "Aahh little seed of life, little charmer," he crooned,

"Hollywood should see you. A heart of ice you would melt. Kick, kick. The future you'll have for a ball. In 2050 still kick. Kick for your grandaddy then."

Attentive with the older children; sat through their performances (command performance; we command you to be the audience); helped Ann sort autumn leaves to find the best for a school program; listened gravely to Richard tell about his rock collection, while her lips mutely formed the words to remember: *igneous*, *sedimentary*, *metamorphic*; looked for missing socks, books, and bus tickets; watched the children whoop after their grandfather who knew how to tickle, chuck, lift, toss, do tricks, tell secrets, make jokes, match riddle for riddle. (Tell me a riddle, Grammy. I know no riddles, child.) Scrubbed sills and woodwork and furniture in every room; folded the laundry; straightened drawers; emptied the heaped baskets waiting for ironing (while he or Vivi or Tim nagged: You're supposed to rest here, you've been sick) but to none tended or gave food—and could not touch the baby.

After a week she said: "Let us go home. Today call about the tickets."

"You have important business, Mrs. Inahurry? The President waits to consult with you?" He shouted, for the fear of the future raced in him. "The clothes are still warm from the suitcase, your children cannot show enough how glad they are to see you, and you want home. There is plenty of time for home. We cannot be with the children at home."

"Blind to around you as always: the little ones sleep four in a room because we take their bed. We are two more people in a house with a new baby, and no help."

"Vivi is happy so. The children should have their grandparents a while, she told to me. I should have my mommy and daddy. . . ."

"Babbler and blind. Do you look at her so tired? How she starts to talk and she cries? I am not strong enough yet to help. Let us go home."

(To reconciled solitude.)

For it seemed to her the crowded noisy house was listening to her, listening for her. She could feel it like a great ear pressed under her heart. And everything knocked: quick constant raps: let me in, let me in. How was it that soft reaching tendrils also became blows that knocked?

C'mon, Grandma, I want to show you. . . .

Tell me a riddle, Grandma. *(I know no riddles.)*

Look, Grammy, he's so dumb he can't even find his hands. (Dody and the baby on a blanket over the fermenting autumn mould.)

I made them—for you. (Ann) (Flat paper dolls with aprons that lifted on scalloped skirts that lifted on flowered pants; hair of yarn and great ringed questioning eyes.)
Watch me, Grandma. (Richard snaking up the tree, hanging exultant, free, with one hand at the top. Below Dody hunching over in pretend-cooking.)
(Climb too, Dody, climb and look.)
Be my nap bed, Grammy. (The "No!" too late.)
Morty's abandoned heaviness, while his fingers ladder up and down her hearing-aid cord to his drowsy chant: eentsiebeentsiespider. (Children trust.)
It's to start off your own rock collection, Grandma.
That's a trilobite fossil, 200 million years old (millions of years on a boy's mouth) and that one's obsidian, black glass.

Knocked and knocked.

Mother, I *told* you the teacher said we had to bring it back all filled out this morning. Didn't you even ask Daddy? Then tell *me* which plan and I'll check it: evacuate or stay in the city or wait for you to come and take me away. (Seeing the look of straining to hear.) It's for Disaster, Grandma. *(Children trust.)*

Vivi in the maze of the long, the lovely drunkenness. The old old noises: baby sounds; screaming of a mother flayed to exasperation; children quarreling; children playing; singing; laughter.

And Vivi's tears and memories, spilling so fast, half the words not understood.

She had started remembering out loud deliberately, so her mother would know the past was cherished, still lived in her.

Nursing the baby: My friends marvel, and I tell them, oh it's easy to be such a cow. I remember how beautiful my mother seemed nursing my brother, and the milk just flows. . . . Was that Davy? It must have been Davy. . . .

Lowering a hem: How did you ever . . . when I think how you made everything we wore . . . Tim, just think, seven kids and Mommy sewed everything . . . do I remember you sang while you sewed? That white dress with the red apples on the skirt you fixed over for me, was it Hannah's or Clara's before it was mine?

Washing sweaters: Ma, I'll never forget, one of those days so nice you washed clothes outside; one of the first spring days it must have been.

The bubbles just danced while you scrubbed, and we chased after, and you stopped to show us how to blow our own bubbles with green onion stalks . . . you always . . . .

"Strong onion, to still make you cry after so many years," her father said, to turn the tears into laughter.

While Richard bent over his homework: Where is it now, do we still have it, the Book of Martyrs? It always seemed so, well—exalted, when you'd put it on the round table and we'd all look at it together; there was even a halo from the lamp. The lamp with the beaded fringe you could move up and down; they're in style again, pulley lamps like that, but without the fringe. You know the book I'm talking about, Daddy, the Book of the Martyrs, the first picture was a bust of Spartacus . . . Socrates? I wish there was something like that for the children, Mommy, to give them what you . . . . (And the tears splashed again.)

(What I intended and did not? Stop it, daughter, stop it, leave that time. And he, the hyprocrite, sitting there with tears in his eyes—it was nothing to you then, nothing.)

. . . The time you came to school and I almost died of shame because of your accent and because I knew you knew I was ashamed; how could I? . . . Sammy's harmonica and you danced to it once, yes you did, you and Davy squealing in your arms. . . . That time you bundled us up and walked us down to the railway station to stay the night 'cause it was heated and we didn't have any coal, that winter of the strike, you didn't think I remembered that, did you, Mommy? . . . How you'd call us out to see the sunsets. . . .

Day after day, the spilling memories. Worse now, questions, too. Even the grandchildren: Grandma, in the olden days, when you were little . . . .

It was the afternoons that saved.

While they thought she napped, she would leave the mosaic on the wall (of children's drawings, maps, calendars, pictures, Ann's cardboard dolls with their great ringed questioning eyes) and hunch in the girls' closet on the low shelf where the shoes stood, and the girls' dresses covered.

For that while she would painfully sheathe against the listening house, the tendrils and noises that knocked, and Vivi's spilling memories. Sometimes it helped to braid and unbraid the sashes that dangled, or to trace the pattern on the hoop slips.

Today she had jacks and children under jet trails to forget. Last night, Ann and Dody silhouetted in the window against a sunset of flaming manmade clouds; of jet trail, their jacks ball accenting the peaceful noise of dinner being made. Had she told them, yes she had told them of how they played jacks in her village though there was no ball, no jacks. Six stones, round and flat, toss them out, the seventh on the back of the hand, toss, catch and swoop up as many as possible, toss again. . . .

Of stones (repeating Richard) there are three kinds: earth's fire jetting; rock of layered centuries; crucibled new out of the old (*igneous, sedimentary, metamorphic*). But there was that other—frozen to black glass, never to transform or hold the fossil memory . . . (let not my seed fall on stone). There was an ancient man who fought to heights a great rock that crashed back down eternally—eternal labor, freedom, labor . . . (stone will perish, but the word remain). And you, David, who with a stone slew, screaming: Lord, take my heart of stone and give me flesh.

Who was screaming? Why was she back in the common room of the prison, the sun motes dancing in the shafts of light, and the informer being brought in, a prisoner now, like themselves. And Lisa leaping, yes, Lisa, the gentle and tender, biting at the betrayer's jugular. Screaming and screaming.

No, it is the children screaming. Another of Paul and Sammy's terrible fights?

In Vivi's house. Severely: you are in Vivi's house.

Blows, screams, a call: "Grandma!" For her? Oh please not for her. Hide, hunch behind the dresses deeper. But a trembling little body hurls itself beside her—surprised, smoothered laughter, arms surround her neck, tears rub dry on her cheek, and words too soft to understand whisper into her ear (Is this where you hide too, Grammy? It's my secret place, we have a secret now).

And the sweat beads, and the long shudder seizes.

It seemed the great ear pressed inside now, and the knocking. "We have to go home," she told him, "I grow ill here."

"It's your own fault, Mrs. Bodybusy, you do not rest, you do too much." He raged, but the fear was in his eyes. "It was a serious operation, they told you to take care. . . . All right, we will go to where you can rest."

But where? Not home to death, not yet. He had thought to Lennie's, to Clara's; beautiful visits with each of the children. She would have to rest first, be stronger. If they could but go to Florida—it glittered before him, the never-realized promise of Florida. California: of course. (The money, the money, dwindling!) Los Angeles first for sun and rest, then to Lennie's in San Francisco.

He told her the next day. "You saw what Nancy wrote: snow and wind back home, a terrible winter. And look at you—all bones and a swollen belly. I called Phil: he said: 'A prescription, Los Angeles sun and rest.'"

She watched the words on his lips. "You have sold the house," she cried, "that is why we do not go home. That is why you talk no more of the

Haven, why there is money for travel. After the children you will drag me to the Haven."

"The Haven! Who thinks of the Haven any more?

Tell her, Vivi, tell Mrs. Suspicious: a prescription, sun and rest, to make you healthy. . . . And how could I sell the house without *you?*"

At the place of farewells and greetings, of winds of coming and winds of going, they say their good-byes.

They look back at her with the eyes of others before them: Richard with her own blue blaze; Ann with the nordic eyes of Tim; Morty's dreaming brown of a great-grandmother he will never know; Dody with the laughing eyes of him who had been her springtide love (who stands beside her now); Vivi's, all tears.

The baby's eyes are closed in sleep.

Good-bye, my children.

3

It is to the back of the great city he brought her, to the dwelling places of the cast-off old. Bounded by two lines of amusement piers to the north and to the south, and between a long straight paving rimmed with black benches facing the sand—sands so wide the ocean is only a far fluting.

In the brief vacation season, some of the boarded stores fronting the sands open, and families, young people and children, may be seen. A little tasselled tram shuttles between the piers, and the lights of roller coasters prink and tweak over those who come to have sensation made in them.

The rest of the year it is abandoned to the old, all else boarded up and still; seemingly empty, except the occasional days and hours when the sun, like a tide, sucks them out of the low rooming houses, casts them onto the benches and sandy rim of the walk—and sweeps them into decaying enclosures once again.

A few newer apartments glint among the low bleached squares. It is in one of these Lennie's Jeannie has arranged their rooms. "Only a few miles north and south people pay hundreds of dollars a month for just this gorgeous air, Grandaddy, just this ocean closeness."

She had been ill on the plane, lay ill for days in the unfamiliar room. Several times the doctor came by-left medicine she would not take. Several times Jeannie drove in the twenty miles from work, still in her Visiting Nurse uniform, the lightness and brightness of her like a healing.

"Who can believe it is winter?" he asked one morning. "Beautiful it is outside like an ad. Come, Mrs. Invalid, come to taste it. You are well enough to sit in here, you are well enough to sit outside. The doctor said it too."

But the benches were encrusted with people, and the sands at the sidewalk's edge. Besides, she had seen the far ruffle of the sea: "there take me," and though she leaned against him, it was she who led.

Plodding and plodding, sitting often to rest, he grumbling. Patting the sand so warm. Once she scooped up a handful, cradling it close to her better eye; peered, and flung it back. And as they came almost to the brink and she could see the glistening wet, she sat down, pulled off her shoes and stockings, left him and began to run. "You'll catch cold," he screamed, but the sand in his shoes weighed him down—he who had always been the agile one—and already the white spray creamed her feet.

He pulled her back, took a handkerchief to wipe off the wet and the sand. "Oh no," she said, "the sun will dry," seized the square and smoothed it flat, dropped on it a mound of sand, knotted the kerchief corners and tied it to a bag—"to look at with the strong glass" (for the first time in years explaining an action of hers)—and lay down with the little bag against her cheek, looking toward the shore that nurtured life as it first crawled toward consciousness the millions of years ago.

He took her one Sunday in the evil-smelling bus, past flat miles of blister houses, to the home of relatives. Oh what is this? she cried as the light began to smoke and the houses to dim and recede. Smog, he said, everyone knows but you. . . . Outside he kept his arms about her, but she walked with hands pushing the heavy air as if to open it, whispered: who has done this? sat down suddenly to vomit at the curb and for a long while refused to rise.

One's age as seen on the altered face of those known in youth. Is this they he has come to visit? This Max and Rose, smooth and pleasant, introducing them to polite children, disinterested grandchildren, "the whole family, once a month on Sundays. And why not? We have the room, the help, the food."

Talk of cars, of houses, of success: this son that, that daughter this. And *your* children? Hastily skimped over, the intermarriages, the obscure work—"my doctor son-in-law, Phil"—all he has to offer. She silent in a corner. (Car-sick like a baby, he explains.) Years since he has taken her to visit anyone but the children, and old apprehensions prickle: "no incidents," he silently begs, "no incidents." He itched to tell them. "A very sick woman," significantly, indicating her with his eyes, "a very sick woman." Their restricted faces did not react. "Have you thought maybe she'd do better at Palm Springs?" Rose asked. "Or at least a nicer section of the beach, nicer people, a pool." Not to have to say "money" he said instead: "would she have sand to look at through a magnifying glass?" and went on, detail after detail, the old habit betraying of parading the queerness of her for laughter.

After dinner—the others into the living room in men- or women-clusters, or into the den to watch TV—the four of them alone. She sat close to him, and did not speak. Jokes, stories, people they had known, beginning of reminiscence, Russia fifty-sixty years ago. Strange words across the Duncan Phyfe table: *hunger; secret meetings; human rights; spies; betrayals; prison; escape*—interrupted by one of the grandchildren: "Commercial's on; any Coke left? Gee, you're missing a real hair-raiser." And then a granddaughter (Max proudly: "Look at her, an American queen") drove them home on her way back to U.C.L.A. No incident—except that there had been no incidents.

The first few mornings she had taken with her the magnifying glass, but he would sit only on the benches, so she rested at the foot, where slatted bench shadows fell, and unless she turned her hearing aid down, other voices invaded.

Now on the days when the sun shone and she felt well enough, he took her on the tram to where the benches ranged in oblongs, some with tables for checkers or cards. Again the blanket on the sand in the striped shadows, but she no longer brought the magnifying glass. He played cards, and she lay in the sun and looked towards the waters; or they walked—two blocks down to the scaling hotel, two blocks back—past chili-hamburger stands, open-doored bars, Next-to-New and perpetual rummage sale stores.

Once, out of the aimless walkers, slow and shuffling like themselves, someone ran unevenly towards them, embraced, kissed, wept: "dear friends, old friends." A friend of *hers,* not his: Mrs. Mays who had lived next door to them in Denver when the children were small.

Thirty years are compressed into a dozen sentences; and the present, not even in three. All is told: the children scattered; the husband dead; she lives in a room two blocks up from the sing hall—and points to the domed auditorium jutting before the pier. The leg? phlebitis; the heavy breathing? that, one does not ask. She, too, comes to the benches each day to sit. And tomorrow, tomorrow, are they going to the community sing? Of course he would have heard of it, everybody goes—the big doings they wait for all week. They have never been? She will come to them for dinner tomorrow and they will all go together.

So it is that she sits in the wind of the singing, among the thousand various faces of age.

She had turned off her hearing aid at once they came into the auditorium—as she would have wished to turn off sight.
One by one they streamed by and imprinted on her—and though the savage zest of their singing came voicelessly soft and distant, the faces still roared—the races densened the air—chorded into
children-chants, mother-croons, singing of the chained love serenades, Beethoven storms, mad Lucia's scream drunken joy-songs, keens for the dead, work-singing

> *while from floor to balcony to dome a bare-footed fore-covered little girl threaded the sound-thronged tumult, danced her ecstasy of grimace to flutes that scratched at a cross-roads village wedding.*

Yes, faces became sound, and the sound became faces; and faces and sound became weight—pushed, pressed—

"Air"—her hands claw his.

"Whenever I enjoy myself. . . ." Then he saw the gray sweat on her face. "Here. Up. Help me, Mrs. Mays," and they support her out to where she can gulp the air in sob after sob.

"A doctor, we should get for her a doctor."

"Tch, it's nothing," says Ellen Mays, "I get it all the time. You've missed the tram; come to my place. Fix your hearing aid, honey . . . close . . . tea. My view. See, she *wants* to come. Steady now, that's how." Adding mysteriously: "Remember your advice, easy to keep your head above water, empty things float. Float."

The singing a fading march for them, tall woman with a swollen leg, weaving little man, and the swollen thinness they help between.

The stench in the hall: mildew? decay? "We sit and rest then climb. My gorgeous view. We help each other and here we are."

The stench along into the slab of room. A washstand for a sink, a box with oilcloth tacked around for a cupboard, a three-burner gas plate. Artificial flowers, colorless with dust. Everywhere pictures foaming: wedding, baby, party, vacation, graduation, family pictures. From the narrow couch under a slit of window, sure enough the view: lurching rooftops and a scallop of ocean heaving, preening, twitching under the moon.

"While the water heats. Excuse me . . . down the hall." Ellen Mays has gone.

"You'll live?" he asks mechanically, sat down to feel his fright; tried to pull her alongside.

She pushed him away. "For air," she said; stood clinging to the dresser. Then, in a terrible voice:

After a lifetime of room. Of many rooms.

Shhh.

You remember how she lived. Eight children. And now one room like a coffin.

She pays rent!

Shrinking the life of her   into one room   like a coffin   Rooms and rooms like this   I lie on the quilt and hear them talk

Please, Mrs. Orator-without-Breath.

Once you went for coffee   I walked   I saw   A Balzac   a Chekhov to write it   Rummage Alone   On scraps

Better old here than in the old country!

On scraps   Yet they sang like   like   Wondrous! *Humankind   one has to believe*   So strong for what? To rot   not grow?

Your poor lungs beg you. They sob between each word.

Singing.   Unused   the life in them. She   in this poor room   with her pictures   Max   You   The children   Everywhere   unused the life   And who has meaning?   Century after century   still all in us   not   to grow?

Coffins, rummage, plants: sick woman. Oh lay down. We will get for you the doctor.

"And when will it end. Oh, *the end.*" *That* nightmare thought, and this time she writhed, crumpled against him, seized his hand (for a moment again the weight, the soft distant roaring of humanity) and on the strangled-for breath, begged: "Man . . . we'll destroy ourselves?"

And looking for answer—in the helpless pity and fear for her (for *her*) that distorted his face—she understood the last months, and knew that she was dying.

4

"Let us go home," she said after several days.

"You are in training for a cross-country run? That is why you do not even walk across the room? Here, like a prescription Phil said, till you are stronger from the operation. You want to break doctor's orders?"

She saw the fiction was necessary to him, was silent; then: "At home I will get better. If the doctor here says?"

"And winter? And the visits to Lennie and to Clara? All right," for he saw the tears in her eyes, "I will write Phil, and talk to the doctor."

Days passed. He reported nothing. Jeannie came and took her out for air, past the boarded concessions, the hooded and tented amusement rides, to the end of the pier. They watched the spent waves feeding the new, the gulls in the clouded sky; even up where they sat, the wind-blown sand stung.

She did not ask to go down the crooked steps to the sea.

Back in her bed, while he was gone to the store, she said: "Jeannie, this doctor, he is not one I can ask questions. Ask him for me, can I go home?"

Jeannie looked at her, said quickly: "Of course, poor Granny. You want your own things around you, don't you? I'll call him tonight. . . . Look, I've something to show you," and from her purse unwrapped a large cookie, intricately shaped like a little girl. "Look at the curls—can you hear me well, Granny?—and the darling eyelashes. I just came from a house where they were baking them."

"The dimples, there in the knees," she marveled, holding it to the better light, turning, studying, "like art. Each singly they cut, or a mold?"

"Singly," said Jeannie, "and if it is a child only the mother can make them. Oh Granny, it's the likeness of a real little girl who died yesterday—Rosita. She was three years old. *Pan del Muerto*, the Bread of the Dead. It was the custom in the part of Mexico they came from."

Still she turned and inspected. "Look, the hollow in the throat, the little cross necklace. . . . I think for the mother it is a good thing to be busy with such bread. You know the family?"

Jeannie nodded. "On my rounds. I nursed. . . . Oh Granny, it is like a party; they play songs she liked to dance to. The coffin is lined with pink velvet and she wears a white dress. There are candles. . . ."

"In the house?" Surprised, "They keep her in the house?"

"Yes," said Jeannie, "and it is against the health law. The father said it would be sad to bury her in this country; in Oaxaca they have a feast night with candles each year; everyone picnics on the graves of those they loved until dawn."

"Yes, Jeannie, the living must comfort themselves." And closed her eyes.

"You want to sleep, Granny?"

"Yes, tired from the pleasure of you. I may keep the Rosita? There stand it, on the dresser, where I can see; something of my own around me."

In the kitchenette, helping her grandfather unpack the groceries, Jeannie said in her light voice:

"I'm resigning my job, Grandaddy."

"Ah, the lucky young man. Which one is he?"

"Too late. You're spoken for." She made a pyramid of cans, unstacked, and built again.

"Something is wrong with the job?"

"With me. I can't be"—she searched for the word—"What they call professional enough. I let myself feel things. And tomorrow I have to report a family. . . ." The cans clicked again. "It's not that, either. I just don't know what I want to do, maybe go back to school, maybe go to art school. I thought if you went to San Francisco I'd come along and talk it over with Momma and Daddy. But I don't see how you can go. She wants to go home. She asked me to ask the doctor."

The doctor told her himself. "Next week you may travel, when you are a little stronger." But next week there was the fever of an infection, and by the time that was over, she could not leave the bed—a rented hospital bed that stood beside the double bed he slept in alone now.

Outwardly the days repeated themselves. Every other afternoon and evening he went out to his newfound cronies, to talk and play cards. Twice a week, Mrs. Mays came. And the rest of the time, Jeannie was there.

By the sickbed stood Jeannie's FM radio. Often into the room the shapes of music came. She would lie curled on her side, her knees drawn up, intense in listening (Jeannie sketched her so, coiled, convoluted like an ear), then thresh her hand out and abruptly snap the radio mute—still to lie in her attitude of listening, concealing tears.

Once Jeannie brought in a young Marine to visit, a friend from high-school days she had found wandering near the empty pier. Because Jeannie asked him to, gravely, without self-consciousness, he sat himself cross-legged on the floor and performed for them a dance of his native Samoa.

Long after they left, a tiny thrumming sound could be heard where, in her bed, she strove to repeat the beckon, flight, surrender of his hands, the fluttering footbeats and his low plaintive calls.

Hannah and Phil sent flowers. To deepen her pleasure, he placed one in her hair. "Like a girl," he said, and brought the hand mirror so she could see. She looked at the pulsing red flower, the yellow skull face; a desolate, excited laugh shuddered from her, and she pushed the mirror away—but let the flower burn.

The week Lennie and Helen came, the fever returned. With it the excited laugh, and incessant words. She, who in her life had spoken but seldom and then only when necessary (never having learned the easy, social uses of words), now in dying, spoke incessantly.

In a half-whisper: "Like Lisa she is, your Jeannie. Have I told you of Lisa who taught me to read? Of the highborn she was, but noble in herself. I was sixteen; they beat me; my father beat me so I would not go to her. It was forbidden, she was a Tolstoyan. At night, past dogs that howled, terrible dogs, my son, in the snows of winter to the road, I to ride in her carriage like a lady, to books. To her, life was holy, knowledge was holy, and she taught me to read. They hung her. Everything that happens one must try to understand why. She killed one who betrayed many. Because of betrayal, betrayed all she lived and believed. In one minute she killed, before my eyes (there is so much blood in a human being, my son), in prison with me. All that happens, one must try to understand.

"The name?" Her lips would work. "The name that was their pole star; the doors of the death houses fixed to open on it; I read of it my year of penal servitude. Thuban!" very excited. "Thuban, in ancient Egypt the pole star. Can you see, look out to see it, Jeannie, if it swings around *our* pole star that seems to *us* not to move.

"Yes, Jeannie, at your age my mother and grandmother had already buried children . . . yes, Jeannie, it is more than oceans between Olshana and you . . . yes, Jeannie, they danced, and for all the bodies they had they might as well be chickens, and indeed, they scratched and flapped their arms and hopped.

"And Andrei Yefimitch, who for twenty years had never known of it and never wanted to know, said as if he wanted to cry: but why my dear friend this malicious laughter?" Telling to herself half-memorized phrases from her few books. "Pain I answer with tears and cries, baseness with indignation, meanness with repulsion . . . for life may be hated or wearied of, but never despised."

Delirious: "Tell me, my neighbor, Mrs. Mays, the pictures never lived, but what of the flowers? Tell them who ask: no rabbis, no ministers, no priests, no speeches, no ceremonies: ah, false—let the living comfort themselves. Tell Sammy's boy, he who flies, tell him to go to Stuttgart and see where Davy has no grave. And what? . . . And what? where millions have no graves—save air."

In delirium or not, wanting the radio on; not seeming to listen, the words still jetting, wanting the music on. Once, silencing it abruptly as of old, she began to cry, unconcealed tears this time. "You have pain, Granny?" Jeannie asked.

"The music," she said, "still it is there and we do not hear; knocks, and our poor human ears too weak. What else, what else we do not hear?"

Once she knocked his hand aside as he gave her a pill, swept the bottles from her bedside table: "no pills, let me feel what I feel," and laughed as on his hands and knees he groped to pick them up.

Nighttimes her hand reached across the bed to hold his.

A constant retching began. Her breath was too faint for sustained speech now, but still the lips moved:

When no longer necessary   to injure others
Pick   pick pick   Blind Chicken
As a human being   responsibility

"David!" imperious, "Basin!" and she would vomit, rinse her mouth, the wasted throat working to swallow, and begin the chant again.

She will be better off in the hospital now, the doctor said.

He sent the telegrams to the children, was packing her suitcase, when her hoarse voice startled. She had roused, was pulling herself to sitting.

"Where now?" she asked. "Where now do you drag me?"

"You do not even have to have a baby to go this time," he soothed, looking for the brush to pack. "Remember, after Davy you told me—worthy to have a baby for the pleasure of the ten day rest in the hospital?"

"Where now? Not home yet?" Her voice mourned. "Where *is* my home?"

He rose to ease her back. "The doctor, the hospital," he started to explain, but deftly, like a snake, she had slithered out of bed and stood swaying, propped behind the night table.

"Coward," she hissed, "runner."

"You stand," he said senselessly.

"To take me there and run. Afraid of a little vomit."

He reached her as she fell. She struggled against him, half slipped from his arms, pulled herself up again.

"Weakling," she taunted, "to leave me there and run. Betrayer. All your life you have run."

He sobbed, telling Jeannie. "A Marilyn Monroe to run for her virtue. Fifty-nine pounds she weighs, the doctor said, and she beats at me like a Dempsey. Betrayer, she cries, and I running like a dog when she calls; day and night, running to her, her vomit, the bedpan. . . ."

"She needs you, Grandaddy," said Jeannie. "Isn't that what they call love? I'll see if she sleeps, and if she does, poor worn-out darling, we'll have a party, you and I: I brought us rum babas."

They did not move her. By her bed now stood the tall hooked pillar that held the solutions—blood and dextrose—to feed her veins. Jeannie moved down the hall to take over the sickroom, her face so radiant, her grandfather asked her once: "you are in love?" (Shameful the joy, the pure overwhelming joy from being with her grandmother; the peace, the serenity that breathed.) "My darling escape," she answered incoherently, "my darling Granny"—as if that explained.

Now one by one the children came, those that were able. Hannah, Paul,

Sammy. Too late to ask: and what did you learn with your living, Mother, and what do we need to know?

Clara, the eldest, clenched:

Pay me back, Mother, pay me back for all you took from me. Those others you crowded into your heart. The hands I needed to be for you, the heaviness, the responsibility.

Is this she? Noises the dying make, the crablike hands crawling over the covers. The ethereal singing.

She hears that music, that singing from childhood; forgotten sound—not heard since, since . . . And the hardness breaks like a cry: Where did we lose each other, first mother, singing mother?

Annulled: the quarrels, the gibing, the harshness between; the fall into silence and the withdrawal.

I do not know you, Mother. Mother, I never knew you.

Lennie, suffering not alone for her who was dying, but for that in her which never lived (for that which in him might never live). From him too, unspoken words: *good-bye Mother who taught me to mother myself.*

Not Vivi, who must stay with her children; not Davy, but he is already here, having to die again with *her* this time, for the living take their dead with them when they die.

Light she grew, like a bird, and, like a bird, sound bubbled in her throat while the body fluttered in agony. Night and day, asleep or awake (though indeed there was no difference now) the songs and the phrases leaping. And he, who had once dreaded a long dying (from fear of himself, from horror of the dwindling money) now desired her quick death profoundly, for *her* sake. He no longer went out, except when Jeannie forced him; no longer laughed, except when in the bright kitchenette, Jeannie coaxed his laughter (and she, who seemed to hear nothing else, would laugh too, conspiratorial wisps of laughter).

Light, like a bird, the fluttering body, the little claw hands, the beaked shadow on her face; and the throat, bubbling, straining.

He tried not to listen, as he tried not to look on the face in which only the forehead remained familiar, but trapped with her the long nights in that little room, the sounds worked themselves into his consciousness, with their punctuation of death swallows, whimpers, gurglings.

Even in reality (swallow) *life's lack of it*
Slaveships   deathtrains   clubs   eeenough
The bell   summon what enables

78,000 in one minute (whisper of a scream) *78,000 human beings we'll destroy ourselves?*

"Aah, Mrs. Miserable," he said, as if she could hear, "all your life working, and now in bed you lie, servants to tend, you do not even need to call to be tended, and still you work. Such hard work it is to die? Such hard work?"

The body threshed, her hand clung in his. A melody, ghost-thin, hovered on her lips, and like a guilty ghost, the vision of her bent in listening to it, silencing the record instantly he was near. Now, heedless of his presence, she floated the melody on and on.

"Hid it from me," he complained, "how many times you listened to remember it so?" And tried to think when she had first played it, or first begun to silence her few records when he came near—but could reconstruct nothing. There was only this room with its tall hooked pillar and its swarm of sounds.

No man one except through others
Strong with the not yet in the now
Dogma dead war dead one country

"It helps, Mrs. Philosopher, words from books? It helps?" And it seemed to him that for seventy years she had hidden a tape recorder, infinitely microscopic, within her, that it had coiled infinite mile on mile, trapping every song, every melody, every word read, heard, and spoken—and that maliciously she was playing back only what said nothing of him, of the children, of their intimate life together.

"Left us indeed, Mrs. Babbler," he reproached, "you who called others babbler and cunningly saved your words. A lifetime you tended and loved, and now not a word of us, for us. Left us indeed? Left me."

And he took out his solitaire deck, shuffled the cards loudly, slapped them down.

Lift high banner of reason (tatter of an orator's voice) *justice freedom light*

Humankind life worthy capacities
Seeks (blur of shudder) *belong human being*

"Words, words," he accused, "and what human beings did you seek around you, Mrs. Live Alone, and what humankind think worthy?"

Though even as he spoke, he remembered she had not always been isolated, had not always wanted to be alone (as he knew there had been a voice before this gossamer one; before the hoarse voice that broke from silence to lash, make incidents, shame him—a girl's voice of eloquence that spoke their holiest dreams). But again he could reconstruct, image, nothing of what had been before, or when, or how, it had changed.

Ace, queen, jack. The pillar shadow fell, so, in two tracks; in the mirror depths glistened a moonlike blob, the empty solution bottle. And it worked in him: *of reason and justice and freedom . . . Dogma dead*: he remembered the full quotation, laughed bitterly. "Hah, good you do not know what you say; good Victor Hugo died and did not see it, his twentieth century."

Deuce, ten, five. Dauntlessly she began a song of their youth of belief:

These things shall be, a loftier race
than e'er the world hath known shall rise
with flame of freedom in their souls
and light of knowledge in their eyes

King, four, jack "In the twentieth century, hah!"

They shall be gentle, brave and strong
to spill no drop of blood, but dare
all . . .

on earth and fire and sea and air

"To spill no drop of blood, hah! So, cadaver, and you too, cadaver Hugo, 'in the twentieth century ignorance will be dead, dogma will be dead, war will be dead, and for all humankind one country—of fulfilment?' Hah!"

And every life (long strangling cough) *shall*
be a song

The cards fell from his fingers. Without warning, the bereavement and betrayal he had sheltered—compounded through the years—hidden even from himself—revealed itself,

uncoiled,
released,
sprung

and with it the monstrous shapes of what had actually happened in the century. A ravening hunger or thirst seized him. He groped into the kitchenette, switched on all three lights, piled a tray—"you have finished your night snack, Mrs. Cadaver, now I will have mine." And he was shocked at the tears that splashed on the tray.

"Salt tears. For free. I forgot to shake on salt?"

Whispered: "Lost, how much I lost."

Escaped to the grandchildren whose childhoods were childish, who had never hungered, who lived unravaged by disease in warm houses of many rooms, had all the school for which they cared, could walk on any street, stood a head taller than their grandparents, towered above—beautiful skins, straight backs, clear straightforward eyes. "Yes, you in Olshana," he said to the town of sixty years ago, "they would be nobility to you."

And was this not the dream then, come true in ways undreamed? he asked.

And are there no other children in the world? he answered, as if in her harsh voice.

And the flame of freedom, the light of knowledge?

And the drop, to spill no drop of blood?

And he thought that at six Jeannie would get up and it would be his turn to go to her room and sleep, that he could press the buzzer and she would come now; that in the afternoon Ellen Mays was coming, and this time they would play cards and he could marvel at how rouge can stand half an inch on the cheek; that in the evening the doctor would come, and he could beg him to be merciful, to stop the feeding solutions, to let her die.

To let her die, and with her their youth of belief out of which her bright, betrayed words foamed; stained words, that on her working lips came stainless.

Hours yet before Jeannie's turn. He could press the buzzer and wake her to come now; he could take a pill, and with it sleep; he could pour more brandy into his milk glass, though what he had poured was not yet touched.

Instead he went back, checked her pulse, gently tended with his knotty fingers as Jeannie had taught.

She was whimpering; her hand crawled across the covers for his. Compassionately he enfolded it, and with his free hand gathered up the cards again. Still was there thirst or hunger ravening in him.

That world of their youth—dark, ignorant, terrible with hate and disease—how was it that living in it, in the midst of corruption, filth, treachery, degradation, they had not mistrusted man nor themselves; had believed so beautifully, so . . . falsely?

"Aaah, children," he said out loud, "how we believed, how we belonged." And he yearned to package for each of the children, the grandchildren, for everyone, *that joyous certainty, that sense of mattering, of moving and being moved, of being one and indivisible with the great of the past, with all that freed, ennobled.* Package it, stand on corners, in front of stadiums and on crowded beaches, knock on doors, give it as a fabled gift.

"And why not in cereal boxes, in soap packages?" he mocked himself. "Aah. You have taken my senses, cadaver."

Words foamed, died unsounded. Her body writhed; she made kissing motions with her mouth. (Her lips moving as she read, poring over the Book of the Martyrs, the magnifying glass superimposed over the heavy eyeglasses.) *Still she believed?* "Eva!" he whispered. "Still you believed? You lived by it? These Things Shall Be?"

"One pound soup meat" she answered distinctly, "one soup bone."

"My ears heard you. Ellen Mays was witness: 'Humankind . . . one has to believe.' " Imploringly: "Eva!"

"Bread, day-old." She was mumbling. "Please, in a wooden box . . . for kindling. The thread, hah, the thread breaks. Cheap thread"—and a gurgling, enormously loud, began in her throat.

"I ask for stone; she gives me bread—day-old." He pulled his hand away, shouted: "Who wanted questions? Everything you have to wake?" Then dully, "Ah, let me help you turn, poor creature."

Words jumbled, cleared. In a voice of crowded terror:

"Paul, Sammy, don't fight.

"Hannah, have I ten hands?

"How can I give it, Clara, how can I give it if I don't have?"

"You lie," he said sturdily, "there was joy too." Bitterly: "Ah how cheap you speak of us at the last."

As if to rebuke him, as if her voice had no relationship with her flailing body, she sang clearly, beautifully, a school song the children had taught her when they were little; begged:

"Not look   my hair   where they cut. . . ."

(The crown of braids shorn.) And instantly he left the mute old woman poring over the Book of the Martyrs; went past the mother treading at the sewing machine, singing with the children; past the girl in her wrinkled prison dress, hiding her hair with scarred hands, lifting to him her awkward, shamed, imploring eyes of love; and took her in his arms, dear, personal, fleshed, in all the heavy passion he had loved to rouse from her.

"Eva!"

Her little claw hand beat the covers. How much, how much can a man stand? He took up the cards, put them down, circled the beds, walked to the dresser, opened, shut drawers, brushed his hair, moved his hand bit by bit over the mirror to see what of the reflection he could blot out with each move, and felt that at any moment he would die of what was unendurable. Went to press the buzzer to wake Jeannie, looked down, saw on Jeannie's sketch pad the hospital bed, with *her;* the double bed alongside, with him; the tall pillar feeding into her veins, and their hands, his and hers, clasped, feeding each other. And as if he had been instructed he went to his bed, lay down, holding the sketch (as if it could shield against the monstrous shapes of loss, of betrayal, of death) and with his free hand took hers back into his.

So Jeannie found them in the morning.

That last day the agony was perpetual. Time after time it lifted her almost off the bed, so they had to fight to hold her down. He could not endure and left the room; wept as if there never would be tears enough.

Jeannie came to comfort him. In her light voice she said: Grandaddy, Grandaddy don't cry. She is not there, she promised me. On the last day, she said she would go back to when she first heard music, a little girl on the road of the village where she was born. She promised me. It is a wedding and they dance, while the flutes so joyous and vibrant tremble in the air. Leave her there, Grandaddy, it is all right. She promised me. Come back, come back and help her poor body to die.

For two of that generation
Seevya and Genya
Infinite, dauntless, incorruptible
Death deepens the wonder

The Evolution of Literary Types

The "Jewish Mother" and the "Jewish American Princess"

Herman Wouk

Herman Wouk was born in 1915 and raised in New York. He received his B.A. degree from Columbia in 1934, the same year he received the Fox Prize. He was variously employed as a radio writer, a script writer for comedian Fred Allen, and later as a consultant to the U.S. Treasury Department. He served in the U.S. Naval Reserve for four years, 1942–1946. Although Wouk has taught on college campuses, for most of his working life he has been a full-time and highly successful writer, producing numerous popular novels. Several of Wouk's novels, such as the Pulitzer Prize–winning *The Caine Mutiny*, *Marjorie Morningstar*, and *The Winds of War*, have exercised a broad influence on American culture both as books and in their dramatized forms in film and television.

Herman Wouk's 1955 novel, *Marjorie Morningstar*, popularized the idea that Jewish mothers train their daughters to look for materialistic success and to regard men as potential tickets to security and status. Indeed, the definitive description of the Jewish princess has undoubtedly been Noel Airman's depiction of "Shirley," the Jewish daughter, "all tricked out to appear gay and girlish and carefree, but with a terrible threatening solid dullness jutting through, like the gray rocks under the spring grass in Central Park." Marjorie herself, however, the "good little Jewish beauty" whom Wouk created, is much more substantive than the shallow, materialistic creature Airman describes.

Wouk uses the characters of the glittering but worthless Airman and of another Jewish girl, Marcia Zelenko, as foils for Marjorie. Among the novel's primary strengths, in fact, are its perfectly rendered relationships between Marjorie and her mother, on the one hand, and her best friend, Zelenko, on the other. Ostensibly a free-spirited bohemian type, Zelenko claims to disdain security and materialism, and her attitudes, which are much like Airman's, influence Marjorie for a long time. Wouk very effectively reveals both the shallowness of Airman and Zelenko and the reasons that a girl like Marjorie would find them attractive. The reader catches on earlier than Marjorie does that Zelenko, in her own life, grabs precisely for security and materialism, although she continues to advise Marjorie to disdain security and to take chances. Similarly, the reader realizes far before Marjorie does that her mother is probably the person who understands her best and who often functions as her best and most supportive friend.

•

"Marjorie's Conversations with Mother" (excerpt)

Mrs. Morgenstern had eaten breakfast several hours earlier with her husband, who was unable to sleep once the day dawned, Sunday or not. Calculating the time it would take her daughter to shower and dress, she placed herself at the breakfast table again a few seconds before Marjorie came out of her room. In her hand was a cup of steaming coffee. She was not lying in wait to grill Marjorie. Surely she was entitled to an extra cup of coffee on Sunday morning.

"Hello, Mother dear." Marjorie draped her jacket on the arm of a chair.

Mrs. Morgenstern put down her coffee. "My God."

"My God what?" Marjorie dully dropped into the chair.

"That sweater, Marjorie."

"What about it? Don't you like the color?" She knew what her mother didn't like. She had spent the last few minutes at the mirror worrying about the sweater. It perfectly matched her British boots and breeches and tweed jacket, and the russet band on her perky hat—all new, all being worn for the first time. It had looked charming in the shop, that cat-smooth russet cashmere, and the size was correct. But the fit was snug; mighty snug. Marjorie knew that a pretty girl in a tight sweater created a commotion. It was very vexing, she thought, and so silly; in the South Seas nobody would think twice about it. She had decided to brave it out. Her mother might not like the sweater, but Sandy Goldstone probably would.

"Marjorie, people will think—I don't know what they'll think."

"I'm a big girl, Mama."

"That's just what's bothering me, dear."

"Mom, for your information girls don't ride horses in pink quilted housecoats that make them look like tubs. They wear sweaters."

Mrs. Morgenstern, short and stout, was wearing a pink quilted housecoat. But this kind of argumentation was standard between them; she took no offense. "Well, Papa will never let you out of the house. Is that all you're having for breakfast? Black coffee? You'll be a nervous wreck by the time you're twenty-one. Have a bun, at least.—Who was at the dance?"

"The junior class of Columbia College, Mama, about two hundred and fifty boys, with girls."

"Anybody we know?"

"No."

"How can you say that? Wasn't Rosalind Green there?"

"Of course she was."

"Well, we know her." Marjorie said nothing. "How is it you're going riding? I thought your lessons were on Tuesday."

"I just decided to go today."

"Who with?"

"Billy Ehrmann."

"How come you're wearing your new riding habit?"

"Why not? Spring is here."

"You don't have to impress Billy Ehrmann."

"Well, I've got to start wearing it sometime."

"Yes, once you've learned to ride. But what's the point, just for a lesson in the armory?"

Here Mrs. Morgenstern was driving to a material point. Marjorie had been taking the armory lessons in a borrowed old habit of an El Dorado neighbor, Rosalind Green. Her mother had bought her the new outfit on the understanding that she wasn't to wear it until she graduated to the bridle paths of the park. Marjorie could lie to her mother cheerfully, and with a good conscience, but she had several minor lies going, and it seemed a weariness to take on another. "Mom, I'm not going to the armory. We're going riding in the park."

"What? You've only had three lessons. You're not ready. You'll fall off the horse and break your neck."

"That'll be something to look forward to." The girl put her cup down with a clink and poured more coffee.

"Marjorie, I am not going to let you go riding in the park with that fat clumsy Billy Ehrmann. He probably can't ride any better than you."

"Mother, please. We're riding with two other couples and a groom. We'll be safer than in the armory."

"Who are the others?"

"Well, there's Rosalind and Phil."

"Who else?"

"Oh, some fraternity brothers of theirs." Marjorie was determined to let her mother know nothing whatever about Sandy Goldstone.

"Who?"

"Oh, some fellow. I don't know his name. I know he's a very good rider."

"How do you know that, if you don't even know his name?"

"For heaven's sake, Mom! Billy and Phil said so."

"Was he at the dance? Did you meet him there?"

"I think maybe I did. I don't know. I met a hundred boys."

"Is he a good dancer?"

"I don't know."

"Where does he live?"

"Mom, I'm late. I said I don't know the boy—"

The telephone rang, and with immense relief Marjorie sprang into the foyer. "Hello?"

"Hello, pooch."

The proprietary nickname and the old twangy voice brought the usual pleasurable warmth to Marjorie, mingled this time with a dim feeling of guilt. "Oh—hello, George, how are you?"

"What's the matter? Did I wake you up?"

"No, George. Matter of fact, I was just going out, so excuse me if—"

"Out?"

"Just out in the park. Riding."

"Well, well. Riding in Central Park. You'll be joining the Junior League next."

"Don't be funny."

"Well, how was the Columbia dance?"

"It was miserable, thanks." Her mother, she saw, had come to the doorway of the dining room and was openly listening to the conversation. Marjorie made her tone more affectionate. "I never realized how young a crowd of college juniors could look and act."

"Well, sure, how old can they be?" said George with a relieved lift in his voice. "Nineteen, average. Less, some of them. I warned you you'd be bored stiff." George Drobes was twenty-two, and a graduate of City College. "Well, pooch, when am I going to see you?"

"I don't know."

"Today?"

"I've got a ton of homework, dear."

"But you say you're going riding."

"Just for an hour. Then I'll be at the desk all day, really, George."

"Take off another hour."

"Dear, I'd love to—it's just such a long trip from the Bronx down here, just for an hour—"

"I'm not doing anything. It's Sunday. It's been almost two weeks—Look, I'd just about decided to go to the art museum anyway. I've got the car. I'll drop by. If you feel like it, we'll go for a drive in the country. If you don't, why I'll just go on to the museum."

"Well—"

"See you about one or so, okay, pooch?"

"All right, George, sure. Love to see you." She hung up.

"What's the matter between you and George all of a sudden?" said Mrs. Morgenstern with pleasure.

"Absolutely nothing. Mother, I wonder whether you know that people don't usually listen to other people's phone conversations?"

"I'm not people. I'm your mother. You don't have anything to hide from me, do you?"

"There's a thing called privacy, that's all."

"I hope the great love isn't beginning to cool off."

"It certainly is not!"

"I haven't seen him in such a long time. Does he still have that red nose?"

"He does not have a red nose."

"Bronx Park East is a long way from Central Park West," said Mrs. Morgenstern with a majestic sigh. Marjorie made for the door. "Listen, Marjorie, don't be foolish. The first time in the park anything can happen. Don't wear the new outfit."

Marjorie's hand was on the doorknob. "Clothes don't do anybody any good hanging in the closet." She opened the door. "Goodbye, Mom. I won't be home for lunch."

"Where will you eat?"

"Tavern on the Green."

"Listen," said Mrs. Morgenstern, "Billy's friend, this fellow who's such a good rider, will like you just as well in the other outfit."

Marjorie's heart sank. "I can't imagine what you're talking about, Mom. Goodbye."

Her exit, which she made with a fine airy wave of the hand, was spoiled as soon as she closed the door. She had no money. The stable was at Sixty-sixth Street, and she was late. She had to go back in and ask her mother for taxi fare. "Well, I'm glad I'm still good for something in your life," said Mrs. Morgenstern, "even if it's only money. What's happened to your allowance this week?"

"Mom, you know my allowance only runs from Saturday to Saturday."

The mother was fumbling in a large black patent-leather purse. "It's a good thing your father's business doesn't run from Saturday to Saturday."

"Might as well give me the rest of my allowance, Mom. Then I won't have to trouble you again."

"No trouble, I assure you." Mrs. Morgenstern drew another dollar and a half from the purse. She always managed, thought Marjorie, to make the payment of the allowance a triumph. Marjorie often felt that she would go hungry and barefoot rather than ask for her allowance again. A hundred times she had planned to gain independence by writing short stories, or tutoring, or getting a weekend job as a salesgirl. These plans usually sprouted just before she had to ask for her allowance, and tended to wither right after she got it.

"Thank you, Mother," she said, remotely cool and formal as she accepted the money.

At this moment her father came into the hallway, carrying the Sunday *Times* in a disordered sheaf under his arm. He wore a red silk smoking jacket in which he looked uncomfortable. Marjorie kissed him. "Morning, Dad. Sorry I've got to run."

The father said, "Horseback . . . Can't you find something less dangerous than horseback, Margie? People get killed riding horseback."

"Don't worry. Marjorie will come back in one piece.'Bye."

•

"Marsha's Advice" (excerpt)

The mother opened the door of the bedroom carefully. Marsha lay face down on the bed, under the picture of Mrs. Michaelson. She said in a strange voice, grainy and dry, "I just want to talk to Marjorie, Tonia. You can go along."

"Marsha dear, I'll do anything—"

"I'm perfectly okay. I'm wonderful. Goodbye."

Mrs. Zelenko shrugged at Marjorie and went out. When the door closed Marsha sat up, clutching Marjorie's handkerchief. Her eyes were moist and reddish. The little white hat was askew over one ear. "Have you ever been closed in on by a herd of bellowing buffalo? My dear cousins were beginning to oppress me. I had to get rid of them, or jump out of the window. And I couldn't do that. Think what the rain would do to this sweet little hat. Twenty-seven dollars shot to hell." She laughed. "Well, la Morningstar, are you nervous? I'm not. Calmest bride you ever heard of. Well? Sit down, for heaven's sake, don't stand there looking at me."

Marjorie sat by her on the bed.

Marsha said, "What time is it?"

"Twenty past six."

"Ten minutes, hey? Just time for one more cigarette." She took a crumpled pack from the bed, lit one, and inhaled with a hiss. "My last cigarette as a free girl. Next one I smoke will be smoked by Mrs. Michaelson." She gestured with the cigarette toward the picture of Lou's mother. "That was her name, too. Mrs. Michaelson. Could anything be queerer? The old girl must be turning over in her grave like a cement mixer."

"Marsha, don't say such things. You'll make a wonderful wife for Lou."

Marsha looked at her with unnaturally wide eyes. "Why is it, I wonder, that I was destined never to have anything I really wanted?"

With a catch in her voice, Marjorie said, "Look, dear, when the time comes for me to take the fatal step I'll probably have an attack of the dismals twice as bad as this—"

"It doesn't seem to me I've ever wanted so much. A friend, a good job, a fellow—" Marsha made strange sharp sounds like a cough; but she wasn't coughing. She seemed to be laughing. She put her arms around Marjorie, pressing her tight, and she cried desperately. The straw of her hat scratched Marjorie's cheek.

It was very hot and uncomfortable to be hugged by Marsha, but there was nothing to do but pat her shoulder and murmur soothing words. "I'm so alone, darling," Marsha sobbed. "So absolutely alone. You'll never know what it means. I've always been alone. So alone, so damned alone. And now I'll always be alone. Forever, till I die."

Marjorie started to cry too, yet she resented this sudden closeness with Marsha, and tried to fight down her pity. She felt that Marsha was taking advantage of her. "Don't go on like that. Good Lord, I thought you were such a tough bird. You're going to be very happy and you know it. Stop crying, Marsha, you've got me doing it. We'll both ruin our faces. There's nothing to cry about. You should be very happy."

Marsha withdrew from her and sat bowed on the edge of the bed, crying and crying. Marjorie took away the cigarette that was burning down in her fingers, and crushed it. After a minute or so Marsha blew her nose and sighed. "Ye gods, I needed that. I feel five thousand per cent better." She got up and began to work on her face at the mirror. "I've been fighting it off and fighting it off. How could I cry with those fat gloating harpies around, my sweet maids of honor? Thanks, dear, you saved my life."

Marjorie said, "Well, live and learn. I'd have bet you'd be the last girl in the world to get maidenly hysterics. I guess we're all human."

Marsha turned on her. White powder smudged around her eyes gave her a clown-like look. "What the hell! Don't you suppose I have feelings? Do you think I'm a lizard or something?"

"Darling, it's perfectly natural—"

"Oh, sure. Natural for everybody except Marsha Zelenko, hey? The girl with the rubber heart. Listen, kid, when it comes to insensitivity, you're the world's champion for weight and size." She blinked and shook her head. "Oh, look, I don't want to be mean. I'm all in a stew, you've got to forgive me—" She dabbed at her face with the powder puff. "But the hell with it, I'm going to tell you something, Marjorie, even if you never speak to me again. Lou didn't invite Noel Airman tonight. I did."

Marjorie said, "Frankly, I surmised as much. I wish you wouldn't give it another thought, that's all."

Marsha faced her, lipstick in hand. "Just like that. Don't give it another thought. Have you any idea how infuriating it is to me to think of you discarding Noel Airman? How on earth can you do it? That's what I keep asking myself. Where do you get the willpower? What runs in your veins, anyway—ammonia? It isn't blood, that's for sure. You're madly in love with the man. He loves you the way he's never loved any girl and probably never will. Do you know what I'd have given for one hour of such a love affair? With such a man? My eyes."

"Marsha, it really isn't—"

"I know, I know, I know, it really isn't any of my damned business. What do I care? I've got to say this or I'll explode. I'll probably never see you after tonight. I know all too well what you must think of my marrying Lou Michaelson—"

"I like Lou, Marsha, I swear I do, you're being hysterical—"

"I like him, too. I'm marrying him because life only lasts so long, and I'm damned tired. I could kiss his hands for being willing to take over, and be good to me, and let me relax, and give my folks what they want. I don't have a Noel Airman in love with me. If I had I'd follow him like a dog. I'd support him. I'd ask him to walk on me every morning, just to feel the weight of his shoes. Oh, Marjorie, you fool, you fool, don't you know that you'll be dead a long long time? That you'll be old and dried up and sick a long long time? You've got all of God's gold at your feet, all He ever gives anybody in this filthy world, youth and good looks and a wonderful lover, and you kick it all aside like garbage just because Noel doesn't go to synagogue twice a day or something. I tell you, you're the fool of fools, Marjorie. You'll die screaming curses at yourself. That is, if you're not too withered and stupid by then to realize what you did to yourself when you were young and alive and pretty and had your chance—"

Marjorie, her breath all but knocked out by the sudden attack, gasped, "You're just crazy, that's all. Noel doesn't care two hoots about me, and—"

"Oh, shut up, he's *insane* about you!"

"All right, and if he is, what do you want me to do—sleep with him like all his other trollops? And then let him kick me out when he's had all he wants?"

"YES, goddamn you, YES! If you're not woman-enough to hold him, all you deserve is to be kicked out. What do you think he is, one of your puking little temple dates? He's a MAN. If you can make him marry you, okay. And if you can't, that's your tough luck! Find out what he's like. Let him find out what you're like. *Live* your life, you poor boob. I'll tell you a great big secret, Marjorie dear—*there's no hell*. You won't burn. Nothing will happen to you, except you'll pile up a thousand memories to warm you when you're an old crock. And what's more, if you've got what it takes you'll snag yourself a husband—a bloody Prince Charming of a husband, not only witty and good-looking but rich and famous, which Noel Airman is damn well going to be. . . . Lord, look at you. You're staring at me as though I had horns and a tail. All right, *don't* listen to me. Do as you damn please. What do I care? Go to your temple dances and marry Sammy Lefkowitz, the brassiere manufacturer's son. It's probably all you deserve."

The knocking at the door had been going on for several seconds, but Marjorie, transfixed, had been unable to interrupt. Now it turned to pounding, and Mrs. Zelenko's indistinct voice called, "Marsha, Marsha dear, for heaven's sake, it's past six-thirty!"

"Oh God." Marsha whirled to the mirror. "Go out there, sugar bun. Keep them at bay, will you? Just for two minutes while I do something about these red holes I've got for eyes."

"Sure I will." Marjorie hesitated, and said to Marsha's back, "Good luck, Marsha. God bless you."

Marsha turned, looked forlornly at her, caught her in her arms, and kissed her. "Oh baby, baby darling. Forget it, forget everything I said. Goodbye, sugar bun. I can't tell you why I've always loved you, and why I fuss so over you. I should have had a brother or a sister. I've had nobody. You'll be all right no matter what you do, I'm sure. You're God's favorite, Marjorie Morningstar. Go along with you."

Marjorie slipped out through the door, and held off the fretting mother and cousins until Marsha called, "Okay, Marge, let the firing squad in." They brushed past her, twittering angrily and anxiously.

Philip Roth

Born in 1933 to middle-class Jewish parents whom he himself has described as loving and normal, Philip Roth grew up in Newark, New Jersey, and attended Weequahic High School and Rutgers University from 1950 to 51. He received his B.A. degree from Bucknell University, where he edited the literary magazine, in 1954, graduating magna cum laude and Phi Beta Kappa. Only one year after his college graduation, his story "The Contest for Aaron Gold" was published in *Epock* and anthologized in Martha Foley's *Best American Short Stories*. That same year Roth earned his M.A. degree at Chicago University. He pursued a Ph.D. in Chicago University's English department until 1957, when he left school to become a film/television reviewer for *The New Republic*. The novella *Goodbye, Columbus* came out in 1959, launching Roth's career as a much-discussed writer of American Jewish fiction. His disastrous marriage to Margaret Williams, from 1958 to 1966, provided him with plot materials for several pieces of fiction and memoirs. Roth has taught at the Writers' Workshop of the University of Iowa, Princeton, the State University of New York at Stony Brook, and the University of Pennsylvania, among other schools and has won numerous literary awards. For many years he has lived in England with actress Claire Bloom.

Perhaps more effectively than any other American Jewish writer, Philip Roth captures the quintessential spirit of American Jewish life in the 1940s, 1950s, and 1960s. His witty narratives and lively dialogue pierce to the center of the quasi-assimilated, deeply ambivalent male American Jewish psyche at midcentury. He has outraged and offended Jewish readers across the country, not because he is—as some have accused—a "self-hating Jew" but because his depictions of character and incident often cut so close to the bone of actual experience.

Roth's depictions of female characters are another matter entirely. He has been one of the most influential American Jewish writers to create and maintain the literary stereotypes of the overprotective Jewish mother and her spoiled, materialistic daughter. On one level, Roth's female characters reflect—albeit in distorted form—a sociological phenomenon in the lives of both Jewish and non-Jewish women. After the national traumas of the economic depression and World War II, the majority of American women—not just Jewish women—did not work outside the home while their children were growing up; consequently, the vast majority of American girls did not prepare for or pursue careers. Even college was often seen as a species of finishing school for middle-class American girls, both Jewish and non-Jewish, rather than an occupational training ground. Both mothers and daughters were thus freed to use their considerable intellectual and verbal talents for non-labor force–related activities.

In the novels and short stories of Philip Roth, Jewish women use their skills to tame and terrorize the men in their lives. In all of his extensive *oeuvre*, Roth has yet to produce one multifaceted, believable, and likable Jewish woman. Thus, in *Goodbye, Columbus,* Roth creates a touchingly sympathetic portrait of a little black boy who loves Gauguin's paintings; every Jewish woman in the novella, on the other hand, is domineering, materialistic, shallow, and obsessed with food preparation, consumption, and storage. Chief among the offenders is Brenda Patimkin, the protagonist's significant other, heiress to the Patimkin plumbing fortune. Brenda and her little sister Julie have been trained from childhood on to manipulate the people around them so that they may gratify every personal whim. It is no wonder that Neal—who has already illustrated his moral superiority through his friendship with the little boy—finally tires of Brenda's games.

Portnoy's Complaint takes the attack on Jewish womanhood one step further. In its pages, Sophie Ginsky Portnoy, the Jewish mother par excellence, is a force-feeding, predatorially inquisitive, seductive tyrant. She threatens little Alexander Portnoy with a bread knife because he isn't eating enough and then reports the incident to her lady friends, who sympathize with her difficult situation. She tries to squelch the youthful Alex's forays into the outside world by threatening him with polio and paralysis. She follows the adolescent Alex to the bathroom door and demands a complete report on the products of his efforts within. She hikes up her skirt in front of the adult Alex to adjust her garterbelt and stockings and then chides him for blushing. Coincidentally, she also gives Alex poetic introductions to the world of nature, listens intently and encouragingly to his early intellectual efforts, and tries to transmit a love for Jewish tradition. Nevertheless, poor Alex is traumatized by his mother and can retain his manhood only through world-class levels of masturbation and by cavorting with and humiliating nubile gentile women.

Roth's savagely funny portraits of American Jewish women were, notoriously, of seminal importance. They have served as inspiration both to other writers and dramatists and to generations of American Jewish men, who still like to cite them as "evidence" about the characters and personalities of American Jewish women.

•

"Princess Brenda Fixes Life"

(excerpt from *Goodbye, Columbus*)

Suddenly it was nine o'clock and everything was scurrying. Wobbly-heeled girls revolved through the doors of the telephone building across the way, traffic honked desperately, policeman barked, whistled, and waved motorists to and fro. Over at St. Vincent's Church the huge dark portals swung back and those bleary-eyes that had risen early for Mass now blinked at the light. Then the worshipers had stepped off the church steps and were racing down the streets towards desks, filing cabinets, secretaries, bosses, and—if the Lord had seen fit to remove a mite of harshness from their lives—to the comfort of airconditioners pumping at their windows. I got up and crossed over to the library, wondering if Brenda was awake yet.

The pale cement lions stood unconvincing guard on the library steps, suffering their usual combination of elephantiasis and arteriosclerosis, and I was prepared to pay them as little attention as I had for the past eight months were it not for a small colored boy who stood in front of one of them. The lion had lost all of its toes the summer before to a safari of juvenile delinquents, and now a new tormentor stood before him, sagging a little in his knees, and growling. He would growl, low and long, drop back, wait, then growl again. Then he would straighten up, and, shaking his head, he would say to the lion, "Man, you's a coward . . ." Then, once again, he'd growl.

The day began the same as any other. From behind the desk on the main floor, I watched the hot high-breasted teen-age girls walk twitchingly up the wide flight of marble stairs that led to the main reading room. The stairs were an imitation of a staircase somewhere in Versailles, though in their toreador pants and sweaters these young daughters of Italian leather-workers, Polish brewery hands, and Jewish furriers were hardly duchesses. They were not Brenda either, and any lust that sparked inside me through the dreary day was academic and time-passing. I looked at my watch occasionally, thought of Brenda, and waited for lunch and then for after lunch, when I would take over the Information Desk upstairs and John McKee, who was only twenty-one but wore elastic bands around his sleeves, would march starchily down the stairs to work assiduously at stamping books in and out. John McRubberbands was in his last year at Newark State Teachers College where he was studying at the Dewey Decimal System in preparation for his lifework. The library was not going to be my lifework, I knew it. Yet, there had been some talk—from Mr. Scapello, an old eunuch who had learned somehow to disguise his voice as a man's—that when I returned from my summer vacation I would be put in charge of the Reference Room, a position that had been empty ever since that morning when Martha Winney had fallen off a high stool in the Encyclopedia Room and shattered all those frail bones that come together to form what in a woman half her age we would call the hips.

I had strange fellows at the library and, in truth, there were many hours when I never quite knew how I'd gotten there or why I stayed. But I did stay and after a while waited patiently for that day when I would go into the men's room on the main floor for a cigarette and, studying myself as I expelled smoke into the mirror, would see that at some moment during the morning I had gone pale, and that under my skin, as under McKee's and Scapello's and Miss Winney's, there was a thin cushion of air separating the blood from the flesh. Someone had pumped it there while I was stamping out a book, and so life from now on would be not a throwing off, as it was for Aunt Gladys, and not a gathering in, as it was for Brenda, but a bouncing off, a numbness. I began to fear this, and yet, in my muscleless devotion to my work, seemed edging towards it, silently, as Miss Winney used to edge up to the Britannica. Her stool was empty now and awaited me.

Just before lunch the lion tamer came wide-eyed into the library. He stood still for a moment, only his fingers moving, as though he were counting the number of marble stairs before him. Then he walked creepily about on the marble floor, snickering at the clink of his taps and the way his little noise swelled up to the vaulted ceiling. Otto, the guard at the door, told him to make less noise with his shoes, but that did not seem to bother the little boy. He clacked on his tiptoes, high, secretively, delighted at the opportunity Otto had given him to practice this posture. He tiptoed up to me.

"Hey," he said, "where's the heart section?"

"The what?" I said.

"The heart section. Ain't you got no heart section?"

He had the thickest sort of southern Negro dialect and the only word that came clear to me was the one that sounded like heart.

"How do you spell it?" I said.

"*Heart*. Man, pictures. Drawing books. Where you got them?"

"You mean art books? Reproductions?"

He took my polysyllabic word for it. "Yea, they's them."

"In a couple places," I told him. "Which artist are you interested in?"

The boy's eyes narrowed so that his whole face seemed black. He started backing away, as he had from the lion. "All of them . . ." he mumbled.

"That's okay," I said. "You go look at whichever ones you want. The next flight up. Follow the arrow to where it says Stack Three. You remember that? Stack Three. Ask somebody upstairs."

He did not move; he seemed to be taking my curiosity about his taste as a kind of poll-tax investigation. "Go ahead," I said, slashing my face with a smile, "right up there . . ."

And like a shot he was scuffling and tapping up towards the heart section.

After lunch I came back to the in-and-out desk and there was John McKee, waiting, in his pale blue slacks, his black shoes, his barbercloth shirt with the elastic bands, and a great knit tie, green, wrapped into a Windsor knot, that was huge and jumped when he talked. His breath smelled of hair oil and his hair of breath and when he spoke, spittle cobwebbed the corners of his mouth. I did not like him and at times had the urge to yank back on his armbands and slingshoot him out past Otto and the lions into the street.

"Has a little Negro boy passed the desk? With a thick accent? He's been hiding in the art books all morning. You know what those boys *do* in there."

"I saw him come in, John."

"So did I. Has he gone *out* though."

"I haven't noticed. I guess so."

"Those are very expensive books."

"Don't be so nervous, John. People are supposed to touch them."

"There is touching," John said sententiously, "and there is touching. Someone should check on him. I was afraid to leave the desk here. You know the way they treat the housing projects we give them."

"*You* give them?"

"The city. Have you seen what they do at Seth Boyden? They threw *beer* bottles, those big ones, on the *lawn*. They're taking over the city."

"Just the Negro sections."

"It's easy to laugh, you don't live near them. I'm going to call Mr. Scapello's office to check the Art Section. Where did he ever find out about art?"

"You'll give Mr. Scapello an ulcer, so soon after his egg-and-pepper sandwich. I'll check, I have to go upstairs anyway.

"You know what they do in there," John warned me.

"Don't worry, Johnny, *they're* the ones who'll get warts on their dirty little hands."

"Ha ha. Those books happen to cost—"

So that Mr. Scapello would not descend upon the boy with his chalky fingers, I walked up the three flights to Stack Three, past the receiving room where rheumy-eyed Jimmy Boylen, our fifty-one-year-old boy, unloaded books from a cart; past the reading room, where bums off Mulberry Street slept over *Popular Mechanics*; past the smoking corridor where damp-browed summer students from the law school relaxed, some smoking, others trying to rub the colored dye from their tort texts off their fingertips; and finally, past the periodical room, where a few ancient ladies who'd been motored down from Upper Montclair now huddled in their chairs, pince-nezing over yellowed, fraying society pages in old old copies of the Newark *News*. Up on Stack Three I found the boy. He was seated on the glass-brick floor holding an open book in his lap, a book, in fact, that was bigger than his lap and had to be propped up by his knees. By the light of the window behind him I could see the hundreds of spaces between the hundreds of tiny black corkscrews that were his hair. He was very black and shiny, and the flesh of his lips did not so much appear to be a different color as it looked to be unfinished and awaiting another coat. The lips were parted, the eyes wide, and even the ears seemed to have a heightened receptivity. He looked ecstatic—until he saw me, that is. For all he knew I was John McKee.

"That's okay," I said before he could even move, "I'm just passing through. You read."

"Ain't nothing *to* read. They's pictures."

"Fine." I fished around the lowest shelves a moment, playing at work.

"Hey, mister," the boy said after a minute, "where is this?"

"Where is what?"

"Where is these pictures? These people, man, they sure does look cool. They ain't no yelling or shouting here, you could just see it."

He lifted the book so I could see. It was an expensive large-sized edition of Gauguin reproductions. The page he had been looking at showed an 8½ X 11 print, in color, of three native women standing knee-high in a rose-colored stream. It *was* a silent picture, he was right.

"That's Tahiti. That's an island in the Pacific Ocean."

"That ain't no place you could go, is it? Like a ree-*sort*?"

"You could go there, I suppose. It's very far. People live there . . ."

"Hey, *look*, look here at this one." He flipped back to a page where a young brown-skinned maid was leaning forward on her knees, as though to dry her hair. "Man," the boy said, "that's the fuckin life." The euphoria of his diction would have earned him eternal banishment from the Newark Public Library and its branches had John or Mr. Scapello—or, God forbid, the hospitalized Miss Winney—come to investigate.

"Who took these pictures?" he asked me.

"Gauguin. He didn't take them, he painted them. Paul Gauguin. He was a Frenchman."

"Is he a white man or a colored man?"

"He's white."

"Man," the boy smiled, chuckled almost, "I knew that. He don't *take* pictures like no colored men would. He's a good picture taker . . . *Look, look,* look here at this one. Ain't that the fuckin *life?*"

I agreed it was and left.

Later I sent Jimmy Boylen hopping down the stairs to tell McKee that everything was all right. The rest of the day was uneventful. I sat at the Information Desk thinking about Brenda and reminding myself that that evening I would have to get gas before I started up to Short Hills, which I could see now, in my mind's eye, at dusk, rose-colored, like a Gauguin stream.

When I pulled up to the Patimkin house that night, everybody but Julie was waiting for me on the front porch: Mr. and Mrs., Ron, and Brenda, wearing a dress. I had not seen her in a dress before and for an instant she did not look like the same girl. But that was only half the surprise. So many of those Lincolnesque college girls turn out to be limbed for shorts alone. Not Brenda. She looked, in a dress, as though she'd gone through life so attired, as though she'd never worn shorts, or bathing suits, or pajamas, or anything but that pale linen dress. I walked rather bouncingly up the lawn, past the huge weeping willow, towards the waiting Patimkins, wishing all the while that I'd had my car washed. Before I'd even reached them, Ron stepped forward and shook my hand, vigorously, as though he hadn't seen me since the Diaspora. Mrs. Patimkin smiled and Mr. Patimkin grunted something and continued twitching his wrists before him, then raising an imaginary golf club and driving a ghost of a golf ball up and away towards the Orange Mountains, that are called Orange, I'm convinced, because in that various suburban light that's the *only* color they do not come dressed in.

"We'll be right back," Brenda said to me. "You have to sit with Julie. Carlota's off."

"Okay," I said.

"We're taking Ron to the airport."

"Okay."

"Julie doesn't want to go. She says Ron pushed her in the pool this afternoon. We've been waiting for you, so we don't miss Ron's plane. Okay?"

"Okay."

Mr. and Mrs. Patimkin and Ron moved off, and I flashed Brenda just the hint of a glare. She reached out and took my hand a moment.

"How do you like me?" she said.

"You're great to baby-sit for. Am I allowed all the milk and cake I want?"

"Don't be angry, baby. We'll be right back." Then she waited a moment, and when I failed to deflate the pout from my mouth, she gave *me* a glare, no hints about it. "I *meant* how do you like me in a dress!" Then she ran off towards the Chrysler, trotting in her high heels like a colt.

When I walked into the house, I slammed the screen door behind me.

"Close the other door too," a little voice shouted. "The air-conditioning."

I closed the other door, obediently.

"Neil?" Julie called.

"Yes."

"Hi. Want to play five and two?"

"No."

"Why not?"

I did not answer.

"I'm in the television room," she called.

"Good."

"Are you supposed to stay with me?"

"Yes."

She appeared unexpectedly through the dining room. "Want to read a book report I wrote?"

"Not now."

"What do you want to do?" she said.

"Nothing, honey. Why don't you watch TV?"

"All right," she said disgustedly, and kicked her way back to the television room.

For a while I remained in the hall, bitten with the urge to slide quietly out of the house, into my car, and back to Newark, where I might even sit in the alley and break candy with my own. I felt like Carlota; no, not even as comfortable as that. At last I left the hall and began to stroll in and out of rooms on the first floor. Next to the living room was the study, a small knotty-pine room jammed with cater-cornered leather chairs and a complete set of *Information Please Almanacs*. On the wall hung three colored photo-paintings; they were the kind which, regardless of the subjects, be they vital or infirm, old or youthful, are characterized by bud-cheeks, wet lips, pearly teeth, and shiny, metallized hair. The subjects in this case were Ron, Brenda, and Julie at about ages fourteen, thirteen, and two. Brenda had long auburn hair, her diamond-studded nose, and no glasses; all combined to make her look a regal thirteen-year-old who'd just gotten smoke in her eyes. Ron was rounder and his hairline was lower, but that love of spherical objects and lined courts twinkled in his boyish eyes. Poor little

Julie was lost in the photo-painter's Platonic idea of childhood; her tiny humanity was smothered somewhere back of gobs of pink and white.

There were other pictures about, smaller ones, taken with a Brownie Reflex before photo-paintings had become fashionable. There was a tiny picture of Brenda on a horse; another of Ron in bar mitzvah suit, *yamalkah*, and *tallas*; and two pictures framed together—one of a beautiful, faded woman, who must have been, from the eyes, Mrs. Patimkin's mother, and the other of Mrs. Patimkin herself, her hair in a halo, her eyes joyous and not those of a slowly aging mother with a quick and lovely daughter.

I walked through the archway into the dining room and stood a moment looking out at the sporting goods tree. From the television room that winged off the dining room, I could hear Julie listening to *This Is Your Life*. The kitchen, which winged off the other side, was empty, and apparently, with Carlota off, the Patimkins had had dinner at the club. Mr. and Mrs. Patimkin's bedroom was in the middle of the house, down the hall, next to Julie's, and for a moment I wanted to see what size bed those giants slept in—I imagined it wide and deep as a swimming pool—but I postponed my investigation while Julie was in the house, and instead opened the door in the kitchen that led down to the basement.

The basement had a different kind of coolness from the house, and it had a smell, which was something the upstairs was totally without. It felt cavernous down there, but in a comforting way, like the simulated caves children make for themselves on rainy days, in hall closets, under blankets, or in between the legs of dining room tables. I flipped on the light at the foot of the stairs and was not surprised at the pine paneling, the bamboo furniture, the ping-pong table, and the mirrored bar that was stocked with every kind and size of glass, ice bucket, decanter, mixer, swizzle stick, shot glass, pretzel bowl—all the bacchanalian paraphernalia, plentiful, orderly, and untouched, as it can be only in the bar of a wealthy man who never entertains drinking people, who himself does not drink, who, in fact, gets a fishy look from his wife when every several months he takes a shot of schnapps before dinner. I went behind the bar where there was an aluminum sink that had not seen a dirty glass, I'm sure, since Ron's bar mitzvah party, and would not see another, probably, until one of the Patimkin children was married or engaged. I would have poured myself a drink—just as a wicked wage for being forced into servantry—but I was uneasy about breaking the label on a bottle of whiskey. You had to break a label to get a drink. On the shelf back of the bar were two dozen bottles—twenty-three to be exact—of Jack Daniels, each with a little booklet tied to its collared neck informing patrons how patrician of them it was to drink the stuff. And over the Jack Daniels were more photos: there was a blown-up newspaper photo of Ron palming a basketball in one hand like a raisin; under the picture it said, "*Center,* Ronald Patimkin, Millburn High School, 6′ 4″, 217 pounds." And there was another picture of Brenda on a horse, and next to that, a velvet mounting board with ribbons and medals clipped to it: Essex County Horse Show 1949, Union County Horse Show 1950, Garden State Fair 1952, Morristown Horse Show 1953, and so on—all for Brenda, for jumping and running or galloping or whatever else young girls receive ribbons for. In the entire house I hadn't seen one picture of Mr. Patimkin.

The rest of the basement, back of the wide pine-paneled room, was gray cement walls and linoleum floor and contained innumerable electrical appliances, including a freezer big enough to house a family of Eskimos. Beside the freezer, incongruously, was a tall old refrigerator; its ancient presence was a reminder to me of the Patimkin roots in Newark. This same refrigerator had once stood in the kitchen of an apartment in some four-family house, probably in the same neighborhood where I had lived all my life, first with my parents and then, when the two of them went wheezing off to Arizona, with my aunt and uncle. After Pearl Harbor the refrigerator had made the move up to Short Hills; Patimkin Kitchen and Bathroom Sinks had gone to war: no new barracks was complete until it had a squad of Patimkin sinks lined up in its latrine.

I opened the door of the old refrigerator; it was not empty. No longer did it hold butter, eggs, herring in cream sauce, ginger ale, tuna fish salad, an occasional corsage—rather it was heaped with fruit, shelves swelled with it, every color, every texture, and hidden within, every kind of pit. There were greengage plums, black plums, red plums, apricots, nectarines, peaches, long horns of grapes, black, yellow, red, and cherries, cherries flowing out of boxes and staining everything scarlet. And there were melons—cantaloupes and honeydews—and on the top shelf, half of a huge watermelon, a thin sheet of wax paper clinging to its bare red face like a wet lip. Oh Patimkin! Fruit grew in their refrigerator and sporting goods dropped from their trees!

I grabbed a handful of cherries and then a nectarine, and I bit right down to its pit.

"You better wash that or you'll get diarrhea."

Julie was standing behind me in the pine-paneled room. She was wearing *her* Bermudas and *her* white polo shirt which was unlike Brenda's only in that it had a little dietary history of its own.

"What?" I said.

"They're not washed yet," Julie said, and in such a way that it seemed to place the refrigerator itself out-of-bounds, if only for me.

"That's all right," I said, and devoured the nectarine and put the pit in my pocket and stepped out of the refrigerator room, all in one second. I still didn't know what to do with the cherries. "I was just looking around," I said.

Julie didn't answer.

"Where's Ron going?" I asked, dropping the cherries into my pocket, among my keys and change.

"Milwaukee."

"For long?"

"To see Harriet. They're in love."

We looked at each other for longer than I could bear. "Harriet?" I asked.

"Yes."

Julie was looking at me as though she were trying to look behind me, and then I realized that I was standing with my hands out of sight. I brought them around to the front, and, I swear it, she did peek to see if they were empty.

We confronted one another again; she seemed to have a threat in her face.

Then she spoke. "Want to play ping-pong?"

"God, yes," I said, and made for the table with two long, bounding steps. "You can serve."

Julie smiled and we began to play.

I have no excuses to offer for what happened next. I began to win and I liked it.

"Can I take that one over?" Julie said. "I hurt my finger yesterday and it just hurt when I served."

"No."

I continued to win.

"That wasn't fair, Neil. My shoelace came untied. Can I take it—"

"No."

We played, I ferociously.

"Neil, you leaned over the table. That's illegal—"

"I didn't lean and it's not illegal."

I felt the cherries hopping among my nickels and pennies.

"Neil, you gypped me out of a point. You have nineteen and I have eleven—"

"Twenty and *ten*," I said. "Serve!"

She did and I smashed my return past her—it zoomed off the table and skittered into the refrigerator room.

"You're a cheater!" she screamed at me. "You cheat!" Her jaw was trembling as though she carried a weight on top of her pretty head. "I *hate* you!" And she threw her racket across the room and it clanged off the bar, just as, outside, I heard the Chrysler crushing gravel in the driveway.

"The game isn't over," I said to her.

"You cheat! And you were stealing fruit!" she said, and ran away before I had my chance to win.

Later that night, Brenda and I made love, our first time. We were sitting on the sofa in the television room and for some ten minutes had not spoken a word to each other. Julie had long since gone to a weepy bed, and though no one had said anything to me about her crying, I did not know if the child had mentioned my fistful of cherries, which, some time before, I had flushed down the toilet.

The television set was on and though the sound was off and the house quiet, the gray pictures still wiggled at the far end of the room. Brenda was quiet and her dress circled her legs, which were tucked back beneath her. We sat there for some while and did not speak. Then she went into the kitchen and when she came back she said that it sounded as though everyone was asleep. We sat a while longer, watching the soundless bodies on the screen eating a silent dinner in someone's silent restaurant. When I began to unbutton her dress she resisted me, and I like to think it was because she knew how lovely she looked in it. But she looked lovely, my Brenda, anyway, and we folded it carefully and held each other close and soon there we were, Brenda falling, slowly but with a smile, and me rising.

How can I describe loving Brenda? It was so sweet, as though I'd finally scored that twenty-first point.

When I got home I dialed Brenda's number, but not before my aunt heard and rose from her bed.

"Who are you calling at this hour? The doctor?"

"No."

"What kind phone calls, one o'clock at night?"

"Shhh!" I said.

"He tells *me* shhh. Phone calls one o'clock at night, we haven't got a big enough bill," and then she dragged herself back into the bed, where with a martyr's heart and bleary eyes she had resisted the downward tug of sleep until she'd heard my key in the door.

Brenda answered the phone.

"Neil?" she said.

"Yes," I whispered. "You didn't get out of bed, did you?"

"No," she said, "the phone is next to the bed."

"Good. How is it in bed?"

"Good. Are you in bed?"

"Yes," I lied, and tried to right myself by dragging the phone by its cord as close as I could to my bedroom.

"I'm in bed with you," she said.

"That's right," I said, "and I'm with you."

"I have the shades down, so it's dark and I don't see you."

"I don't see you either."

"That was so nice, Neil."

"Yes. Go to sleep, sweet, I'm here," and we hung up without goodbyes. In the morning, as planned, I called again, but I could hardly hear Brenda or myself for that matter, for Aunt Gladys and Uncle Max were going on a Workmen's Circle picnic in the afternoon, and there was some trouble about grape juice that had dripped all night from a jug in the refrigerator and by morning had leaked out onto the floor. Brenda was still in bed and so could play our game with some success, but I had to pull down all the shades of my senses to imagine myself beside her. I could only pray our nights and mornings would come, and soon enough they did. . . .

Over the next week and a half there seemed to be only two people in my life: Brenda and the little colored kid who liked Gauguin. Every morning before the library opened, the boy was waiting; sometimes he seated himself on the lion's back, sometimes under his belly, sometimes he just stood around throwing pebbles at his mane. Then he would come inside, tap around the main floor until Otto stared him up on tiptoes, and finally headed up the long marble stairs that led to Tahiti. He did not always stay to lunch time, but one very hot day he was there when I arrived in the morning and went through the door behind me when I left at night. The next morning, it was, that he did not show up, and as though in his place, a very old man appeared, white, smelling of Life Savers, his nose and jowls showing erupted veins beneath them. "Could you tell me where I'd find the art section?"

"Stack Three," I said.

In a few minutes, he returned with a big brown-covered book in his hand. He placed it on my desk, withdrew his card from a long moneyless billfold and waited for me to stamp out the book.

"Do you want to take this book *out?*" I said.

He smiled.

I took his card and jammed the metal edge into the machine; but I did not stamp down. "Just a minute," I said. I took a clipboard from under the desk and flipped through a few pages, upon which were games of battleship and tick-tack-toe that I'd been playing through the week with myself. "I'm afraid there's a hold on this book."

"A what?"

"A hold. Someone's called up and asked that we hold it for them. Can I take your name and address and drop a card when it's free . . ."

And so I was able, not without flushing once or twice, to get the book back in the stacks. When the colored kid showed up later in the day, it was just where he'd left it the afternoon before.

As for Brenda, I saw her every evening and when there was not a night game that kept Mr. Patimkin awake and in the TV room, or a Hadassah card party that sent Mrs. Patimkin out of the house and brought her in at unpredictable hours, we made love before the silent screen. One muggy, low-skied night Brenda took me swimming at the club. We were the only ones in the pool, and all the chairs, the cabanas, the lights, the diving boards, the very water seemed to exist only for our pleasure. She wore a blue suit that looked purple in the lights and down beneath the water it flashed sometimes green, sometimes black. Late in the evening a breeze came up off the golf course and we wrapped ourselves in one huge towel, pulled two chaise longues together, and despite the bartender, who was doing considerable pacing back and forth by the bar window, which overlooked the pool, we rested side by side on the chairs. Finally the bar light itself flipped off, and then, in a snap, the lights around the pool went down and out. My heart must have beat faster, or something, for Brenda seemed to guess my sudden doubt—*we should go,* I thought.

She said: "That's okay."

It was very dark, the sky was low and starless, and it took a while for me to see, once again, the diving board a shade lighter than the night, and to distinguish the water from the chairs that surrounded the far side of the pool.

I pushed the straps of her bathing suit down but she said no and rolled an inch away from me, and for the first time in the two weeks I'd known her she asked me a question about me.

"Where are your parents?" she said.

"Tucson," I said. "Why?"

"My mother asked me."

I could see the life guard's chair now, white almost.

"Why are you still here? Why aren't you with them?" she asked.

"I'm not a child any more, Brenda," I said, more sharply than I'd intended. "I just can't go wherever my parents are."

"But then why do you stay with your aunt and uncle?"

"They're not my parents."

"They're better?"

"No. Worse. I don't *know* why I stay with them."

"Why?" she said.

"Why don't I know?"

"Why do you stay? You do know, don't you?"

"My job, I suppose. It's convenient from there, and it's cheap, and it pleases my parents. My aunt's all right really . . . Do I really have to explain to your mother why I live where I do?"

"It's not for my mother. I want to know. I wondered why you weren't with your parents, that's all."

"Are you cold?" I asked.

"No."

"Do you want to go home?"

"No, not unless you do. Don't you feel well, Neil?"

"I feel all right," and to let her know that I was still me, I held her to me, though that moment I was without desire.

"Neil?"

"What?"

"What about the library?"

"Who wants to know that?"

"My father," she laughed.

"And you?"

She did not answer a moment. "And me," she said finally.

"Well, what about it? Do I like it? It's okay. I sold shoes once and like the library better. After the Army they tried me for a couple months at Uncle Aaron's real estate company—Doris' father—and I like the library better than that . . ."

"How did you get a job *there*?"

"I worked there for a little while when I was in college, then when I quit Uncle Aaron's, oh, I don't know . . ."

"What did you take in college?"

"At Newark Colleges of Rutgers University I majored in philosophy. I am twenty-three years old. I—"

"Why do you sound nasty again?"

"Do I?"

"Yes."

I didn't say I was sorry.

"Are you planning on making a career of the library?"

"Bren, I'm not planning anything. I haven't planned a thing in three years. At least for the year I've been out of the Army. In the Army I used to plan to go away weekends. I'm—I'm not a planner." After all the truth I'd suddenly given her, I shouldn't have ruined it for myself with that final lie. I added, "I'm a liver."

"I'm a pancreas," she said.

"I'm a—"

And she kissed the absurd game away; she wanted to be serious.

"Do you love me Neil?"

I did not answer.

"I'll sleep with you whether you do or not, so tell me the truth."

"That was pretty crude."

"Don't be prissy," she said.

"No, I mean a crude thing to say about me."

"I don't understand," she said, and she didn't, and that she didn't pained me; I allowed myself the minor subterfuge, however, of forgiving Brenda her obtuseness. "Do you?" she said.

"No."

"I want you to."

"What about the library?"

"What about it?" she said.

Was it obtuseness again? I thought not—and it wasn't, for Brenda said, "When you love me, there'll be nothing to worry about."

"Then of course I'll love you." I smiled.

"I know you will," she said. "Why don't you go in the water, and I'll wait for you and close my eyes, and when you come back you'll surprise me with the wet. Go ahead."

"You like games, don't you?"

"Go ahead. I'll close my eyes."

I walked down to the edge of the pool and dove in. The water felt colder than it had earlier, and when I broke through and was headed blindly down I felt a touch of panic. At the top again, I started to swim the length of the pool and then turned at the end and started back, but suddenly I was sure that when I left the water Brenda would be gone. I'd be alone in this damn place. I started for the side and pulled myself up and ran to the chairs and Brenda was there and I kissed her.

"God," she shivered, "You didn't stay long."

"I know."

"My turn," she said, and then she was up and a second later I heard a little crack of water and then nothing. Nothing for quite a while.

"Bren," I called softly, "are you all right?" but no one answered.

I found her glasses on the chair beside me and held them in my hands. "Brenda?"

Nothing.

"Brenda?"

"No fair calling," she said and gave me her drench self. "Your turn," she said.

This time I stayed below the water for a long while and when I surfaced again my lungs were ready to pop. I threw my head back for air and above me saw the sky, low like a hand pushing down, and I began to swim as though to move out from under its pressure. I wanted to get back to Brenda, for I worried once again—and there was no evidence, was there?—that if I stayed away too long she would not be there when I returned. I wished that I had carried her glasses away with me, so she would have to wait for me to lead her back home. I was having crazy thoughts, I knew, and yet they did not seem uncalled for in the darkness and strangeness of that place. Oh how I wanted to call out to her from the pool, but I knew she would not answer and I forced myself to swim the length a third time, and then a fourth, but midway through the fifth I felt a weird fright again, had momentary thoughts of my own extinction, and that time when I came back I held her tighter than either of us expected.

"Let go, let go," she laughed, "my turn—"

"But Brenda—"

But Brenda was gone and this time it seemed as though she'd never come back. I settled back and waited for the sun to dawn over the ninth hole, prayed it would if only for the comfort of its light, and when Brenda finally returned to me I would not let her go, and her cold wetness crept into me somehow and made me shiver. "That's it, Brenda. Please, no more games," I said, and then when I spoke again I held her so tightly I almost dug my body into hers, "I love you," I said, "I do."

So the summer went on. I saw Brenda every evening: we went swimming, we went for walks, we went for rides, up through the mountains so far and so long that by the time we started back the fog had begun to emerge from the trees and push out into the road, and I would tighten my hands on the wheel and Brenda would put on her glasses and watch the white line for me. And we would eat—a few nights after my discovery of the fruit refrigerator Brenda led me to it herself. We would fill huge soup bowls with cherries, and in serving dishes for roast beef we would heap slices of watermelon. Then we would go up and out the back doorway of the basement and onto the back lawn and sit under the sporting-goods tree, the light from the room the only brightness we had out there. All we would hear for a while were just the two of us spitting pits. "I wish they would take root overnight and in the morning there'd just be watermelons and cherries."

"If they took root in this yard, sweetie, they'd grow refrigerators and Westinghouse preferred. I'm not being nasty," I'd add quickly, and Brenda would laugh, and say she felt like a greengage plum, and I would disappear down into the basement and the cherry bowl would now be a greengage plum bowl, and then a nectarine bowl, and then a peach bowl, until, I have to admit it, I cracked my frail bowel, and would have to spend the following night, sadly, on the wagon. And then too we went out for corned beef sandwiches, pizza, beer and shrimp, ice cream sodas, and hamburgers. We went to the Lions Club Fair one night and Brenda won a Lions Club ashtray by shooting three baskets in a row. And when Ron came home from Milwaukee we went from time to time to see him play basketball in the semi-pro summer league, and it was those evenings that I felt a stranger with Brenda, for she knew all the players' names, and though for the most part they were gawky-limbed and dull, there was one named Luther Ferrari who was neither, and whom Brenda had dated for a whole year in high school. He was Ron's closest friend and I remembered his name from the Newark *News*: he was one of the great Ferrari brothers, All State all of them in at least two sports. It was Ferrari who called Brenda Buck, a nickname which apparently went back to her ribbon-winning days. Like Ron, Ferrari was exceedingly polite, as though it were some affliction of those over six feet three; he was gentlemanly towards me and gentle towards Brenda, and after a while I balked when the suggestion was made that we go to see Ron play. And then one night we discovered that at eleven o'clock the cashier of the Hilltop Theatre went home and the manager disappeared into his office, and so that summer we saw the last quarter of at least fifteen movies, and then when we were driving home—driving Brenda home, that is—we would try to reconstruct the beginnings of the films. Our favorite last quarter of a movie was *Ma and Pa Kettle in the City*, our favorite fruit, greengage plums, and our favorite, our only, people, each other. Of course we ran into others from time to time, some of Brenda's friends, and occasionally, one or two of mine. One night in August we even went to a bar out on Route 6 with Laura Simpson Stolowitch and her fiance but it was a dreary evening. Brenda and I seemed untrained in talking to others, and so we danced a great deal, which we realized was one thing we'd never done before. Laura's boyfriend drank stingers pompously and Simp—Brenda wanted me to call her Stolo but I didn't—Simp drank a tepid combination of something like ginger ale and soda. Whenever we returned to the table, Simp would be talking about "the dance" and her fiancé about "the film," finally Brenda asked him "Which film?" and then we danced till closing time. And when we went back to Brenda's we filled a bowl with cherries which we carried into the room and ate sloppily for a while; and later, on the sofa, we loved each other and when I moved from the darkened room to the bathroom I could always feel cherry pits against my bare soles. At home, undressing for the second time that night, I would find red marks on the undersides of my feet.

And how did her parents take all of this? Mrs. Patimkin continued to smile at me and Mr. Patimkin continued to think I ate like a bird. When invited to dinner I would, for his benefit, eat twice what I wanted, but the truth seemed to be that after he'd characterized my appetite that first time, he never really bothered to look again. I might have eaten ten times my normal amount, have finally killed myself with food, he would still have considered me not a man but a sparrow. No one seemed distressed by my presence, though Julie had cooled considerably; consequently, when Brenda suggested to her father that at the end of August I spend a week of my vacation at the Patimkin house, he pondered a moment, decided on the five iron, made his approach shot, and said yes. And when she passed on to her mother the decision of Patimkin Sink, there wasn't much Mrs. Patimkin could do. So, through Brenda's craftiness, I was invited.

On that Friday morning that was to be my last day of work, my Aunt Gladys saw me packing my bag and she asked where I was going. I told her. She did not answer and I thought I saw awe in those red-rimmed hysterical eyes—I had come a long way since that day she'd said to me on the phone, "Fancy-shmancy."

"How long you going, I should know how to shop I wouldn't buy too much. You'll leave me with a refrigerator full of milk it'll go bad it'll stink up the refrigerator—"

"A week," I said.

"A *week*?" she said. "They got room for a week?"

"Aunt Gladys, they don't live over the store."

"I lived over a store I wasn't ashamed. Thank God we always had a roof. We never went begging in the streets," she told me as I packed the Bermudas I'd just bought, "and your cousin Susan we'll put through college, Uncle Max should live and be well. We didn't send her away to camp for August, she doesn't have shoes when she wants them, sweaters she doesn't have a drawerful—"

"I didn't say anything, Aunt Gladys."

"You don't get enough to eat here? You leave over sometimes I show your Uncle Max your plate it's a shame. A child in Europe could make a four-course meal from what you leave over."

"Aunt Gladys." I went over to her. "I get everything I want here. I'm just taking a vacation. Don't I deserve a vacation?"

She held herself to me and I could feel her trembling. "I told your mother I would take care of her Neil she shouldn't worry. And now you go running—"

I put my arms around her and kissed her on the top of her head. "C'mon," I said, "you're being silly. I'm not running away. I'm just going away for a week, on a vacation."

"You'll leave their telephone number God forbid you should get sick."

"Okay."

"Millburn they live?"

"Short Hills. I'll leave the number."

"Since when do Jewish people live in Short Hills? They couldn't be real Jews believe me."

"They're real Jews," I said.

"I'll see it I'll believe it." She wiped her eyes with the corner of her apron, just as I was zipping up the sides of the suitcase. "Don't close the bag yet. I'll make a little package with some fruit in it, you'll take with you."

"Okay, Aunt Gladys," and on the way to work that morning I ate the orange and the two peaches that she'd put in a bag for me.

A few hours later Mr. Scapello informed me that when I returned from my vacation after Labor Day, I would be hoisted up onto Martha Winney's stool. He himself, he said, had made the same move some twelve years ago, and so it appeared that if I could manage to maintain my balance I might someday be Mr. Scapello. I would also get an eight-dollar increase in salary which was five dollars more than the increase Mr. Scapello had received years before. He shook my hand and then started back up the long flight of marble stairs, his behind barging against his suit jacket like a hoop. No sooner had he left my side than I smelled spearmint and looked up to see the old man with veiny nose and jowls.

"Hello, young man," he said pleasantly. "Is the book back?"

"What book?"

"The Gauguin. I was shopping and I thought I'd stop by to ask. I haven't gotten the card yet. It's two weeks already."

"No," I said, and as I spoke I saw that Mr. Scapello had stopped midway up the stairs and turned as though he'd forgotten to tell me something. "Look," I said to the old man, "it should be back any day." I said it with a finality that bordered on rudeness, and I alarmed myself, for suddenly I saw what would happen: the old man making a fuss, Mr. Scapello gliding down the stairs, Mr. Scapello scampering up to the stacks, Scapello scandalized, Scapello profuse, Scapello presiding at the ascension of John McKee to Miss Winney's stool. I turned to the old man, "Why don't you leave your phone number and I'll try to get a hold of it this afternoon—" but my attempt at concern and courtesy came too late, and the man growled some words about public servants, a letter to the Mayor, snotty kids, and left the library, thank God, only a second before Mr. Scapello returned to my desk to remind me that everyone was chipping in for a present for Miss Winney and that if I liked I should leave a half dollar on his desk during the day.

After lunch the colored kid came in. When he headed past the desk for the stairs, I called over to him. "Come here," I said. "Where are you going?"

"The heart section."

"What book are you reading?"

"That Mr. Go-again's book. Look, man, I ain't doing nothing wrong. I didn't do *no* writing in *any*thing. You could search me—."

"I know you didn't. Listen, if you like that book so much why don't you please take it home? Do you have a library card?"

"No, sir, I didn't take *nothing*."

"No, a library card is what we give to you so you can take books home.

Then you won't have to come down here every day. Do you go to school?"

"Yes, sir. Miller Street School. But this here's summertime. It's okay I'm not in school. I ain't *supposed* to be in school."

"I know. As long as you go to school you can *have* a library card. You could take the book home."

"What you keep telling me take that book home for? At home somebody dee-*stroy* it."

"You could hide it someplace, in a desk—"

"Man," he said, squinting at me, "why don't you want me to come round here?"

"I didn't say you shouldn't."

"I *likes* to come here. I likes them stairs."

"I like them too," I said. "But the trouble is that someday somebody's going to take that book out."

He smiled. "Don't you worry," he said to me. "Ain't nobody done that yet," and he tapped off to the stairs and Stack Three.

Did I perspire that day! It was the coolest of the summer, but when I left work in the evening my shirt was sticking to my back. In the car I opened my bag, and while the rush-hour traffic flowed down Washington Street, I huddled in the back and changed into a clean shirt so that when I reached Short Hills I'd look as though I was deserving of an interlude in the suburbs. But driving up Central Avenue I could not keep my mind on my vacation, or for that matter on my driving: to the distress of pedestrians and motorists, I ground gears, overshot crosswalks, hesitated at green and red lights alike. I kept thinking that while I was on vacation that jowly bastard would return to the library, that the colored kid's book would disappear, that my new job would be taken away from me, that, in fact my old job—but then why should I worry about all that: the library wasn't going to be *my* life. . . .

"Ron's getting married!" Julie screamed at me when I came through the door. "Ron's getting married!"

"Now?" I said.

"Labor Day! He's marrying Harriet, he's marrying Harriet." She began to sing it like a jump-rope song, nasal and rhythmic. "I'm going to be a sister-in-law!"

"Hi," Brenda said, "I'm going to be a sister-in-law."

"So I hear. When did it happen?"

"This afternoon he told us. They spoke long distance for forty minutes last night. She's flying here next week, and there's going to be a *huge* wedding. My parents are flittering all over the place. They've got to arrange everything in about a day or two. And my father's taking Ron in the business—but he's going to have to start at two hundred a week and then work himself up. That'll take till October."

"I thought he was going to be a gym teacher."

"He was. But now he has responsibilities . . ."

And at dinner Ron expanded on the subject of responsibilities and the future.

"We're going to have a boy," he said, to his mother's delight, "and when he's about six months old I'm going to sit him down with a basketball in front of him, and a football, and a baseball, and then whichever one he reaches for, that's the one we're going to concentrate on."

"Suppose he doesn't reach for any of them," Brenda said.

"Don't be funny, young lady," Mrs. Patimkin said.

"I'm going to be an aunt," Julie sang, and she stuck her tongue out at Brenda.

"When is Harriet coming?" Mr. Patimkin breathed through a mouthful of potatoes.

"A week from yesterday."

"Can she sleep in my room?" Julie cried. "*Can* she?"

"No, the guest room—" Mrs. Patimkin began, but then she remembered me—with a crushing side glance from those purple eyes, and said, "Of course."

Well, I did eat like a bird. After dinner my bag was carried—by me—up to the guest room which was across from Ron's room and right down the hall from Brenda. Brenda came along to show me the way.

"Later," she said.

"Can we? Up here?"

"I think so," she said. "Ron sleeps like a log."

"Can I stay the night?"

"I don't know."

"I could get up early and come back in here. We'll set the alarm."

"It'll wake everybody up."

"I'll remember to get up. I can do it."

"I better not stay up here with you too long," she said. "My mother'll have a fit. I think she's nervous about your being here."

"So am I. I hardly know them. Do you think I should really stay a whole week?"

"A whole week? Once Harriet gets here it'll be so chaotic you can probably stay two months."

"You think so?"

"Yes."

"Do you want me to?"

"Yes," she said, and went down the stairs so as to ease her mother's conscience.

I unpacked my bag and dropped my clothes into a drawer that was empty except for a packet of dress shields and a high school yearbook. In the middle of my unpacking, Ron came clunking up the stairs.

"Hi," he called into my room.

"Congratulations," I called back. I should have realized that any word of ceremony would provoke a handshake from Ron; he interrupted whatever it was he was about to do in his room, and came into mine.

"Thanks." He pumped me. "Thanks."

Then he sat down on my bed and watched me as I finished unpacking. I have one shirt with a Brooks Brothers label and I let it linger on the bed a while; the Arrows I heaped in the drawer. Ron sat there rubbing his forearm and grinning. After a while I was thoroughly unsettled by the silence.

"Well," I said, "that's something."

He agreed, to *what* I don't know.

"How does it feel?" I asked, after another longer silence.

"Better, Ferrari smacked it under the boards."

"Oh. Good," I said. "How does getting married feel?"

"Ah, okay, I guess."

I leaned against the bureau and counted stitches in the carpet.

Ron finally risked a journey into language. "Do you know anything about music?" he asked.

"Something, yes."

"You can listen to my phonograph if you want."

"Thanks, Ron. I didn't know you were interested in music."

"Sure. I got all the Andre Kostelanetz records ever made. You like Mantovani? I got all of him too. I like semi-classical a lot. You can hear my Columbus record if you want . . ." he dwindled off. Finally he shook my hand and left.

Downstairs I could hear Julie singing. "I'm going to be an a-a-aunt," and Mrs. Patimkin saying to her, "No, honey, you're going to be a sister-in-law. Sing that sweetheart," and then I heard Brenda's voice joining hers, singing, "We're going to be an a-a-aunt," and then Julie joined that, and finally Mrs. Patimkin called to Mr. Patimkin, "Will you make her stop encouraging her . . ." and soon the duet ended.

And then I heard Mrs. Patimkin again. I couldn't make out the words but Brenda answered her. Their voices grew louder; finally I could hear perfectly. "I need a houseful of company at a time like this?" It was Mrs. Patimkin. "I asked you, Mother." "You asked your father. I'm the one you should have asked first. He doesn't know how much extra work this is for me . . ."

"My God, Mother, you'd think we didn't have Carlota and Jenny." "Carlota and Jenny can't do everything. This is not the Salvation Army!" "What the hell does that mean?" "Watch your tongue, young lady. That may be very well for your college friends." "Oh, *stop* it, Mother!" "Don't raise your voice to me. When's the last time you lifted a finger to help around here?" "I'm not a slave . . . I'm a daughter." "You ought to learn what a day's work means." "Why?" Brenda said. *"Why?"* "Because you're lazy," Mrs. Patimkin answered, "and you think the world owes you a living." "Whoever said *that*?" "You ought to earn some money and buy your own clothes." "Why? Good God, Mother, Daddy could live off the stocks alone, for God's sake. What are you complaining about?" "When's the last time you washed the dishes!" "Jesus Christ!" Brenda flared, "Carlota washes the dishes!" "Don't Jesus Christ me!" "Oh, Mother!" and Brenda was crying. "Why the hell are you like this!" "That's it," Mrs. Patimkin said "cry in front of your company . . ." "My *company* . . ." Brenda wept, "why don't you go yell at him too . . . why is everyone so nasty to me . . ."

From across the hall I heard Andre Kostelanetz let several thousand singing violins loose on "Night and Day." Ron's door was open and I saw he was stretched out, colossal, on his bed; he was singing along with the record. The words belonged to "Night and Day," but I didn't recognize Ron's tune. In a minute he picked up the phone and asked the operator for a Milwaukee number. While she connected him, he rolled over and turned up the volume on the record player, so that it would carry the nine hundred miles west.

I heard Julie downstairs. "Ha ha, Brenda's crying, ha ha, Brenda's crying."

And then Brenda was running up the stairs. "Your day'll come, you little bastard!" she called.

"*Brenda*!" Mrs. Patimkin called.

"*Mommy*!" Julie cried. "Brenda cursed at me!"

"What's going *on* here!" Mr. Patimkin shouted.

"You call *me*, Mrs. P?" Carlota shouted.

And Ron, in the other room, said, "Hello, Har, I told them . . ."

I sat down on my Brooks Brothers shirt and pronounced my own name out loud.

"Goddam her!" Brenda said to me as she paced up and down my room.

"Bren, do you think I should go—"

"Shhh . . ." She went to the door of my room and listened. "They're going visiting, thank God."

"Brenda—"

"Shhh . . . They've gone."

"Julie too?"

"Yes," she said. "Is Ron in his room? His door is closed."

"He went out."

"You can't hear anybody move around here. They all creep around in *sneakers*. Oh Neil."

"Bren, I asked you, maybe I should just stay through tomorrow and then go."

"Oh, it isn't you she's angry about."

"I'm not helping any."

"It's Ron, really. That he's getting married just has her flipped. And me. Now with that goody-good Harriet around she'll just forget I ever exist."

"Isn't that okay with you?"

She walked off to the window and looked outside. It was dark and cool; the trees rustled and flapped as though they were sheets that had been hung out to dry. Everything outside hinted at September, and for the first time I realized how close we were to Brenda's departure for school.

"Is it, Bren?" but she was not listening to me.

She walked across the room to a door at the far end of the room. She opened it.

"I thought that was a closet," I said.

"Come here."

She held the door back and we leaned into the darkness and could hear the strange wind hissing in the eaves of the house.

"What's in here?" I said.

"Money."

Brenda went into the room. When the puny sixty-watt bulb was twisted on, I saw that the place was full of old furniture—two wing chairs with hair-oil lines at the back, a sofa with a paunch in its middle, a bridge table, two bridge chairs with their stuffing showing, a mirror whose backing had peeled off, shadeless lamps, lampless shades, a coffee table with a cracked glass top, and a pile of rolled up shades.

"What is this?" I said.

"A storeroom. Our old furniture."

"How old?"

"From Newark," she said. "Come here." She was on her hands and knees in front of the sofa and was holding up its paunch to peek beneath.

"Brenda, what the hell are we doing here? You're getting filthy."

"It's not here."

"What?"

"The money. I told you."

I sat down on a wing chair, raising some dust. It had begun to rain outside, and we could smell the fall dampness coming through the vent that was outlined at the far end of the storeroom. Brenda got up from the floor and sat down on the sofa. Her knees and Bermudas were dirty and when she pushed her hair back she dirtied her forehead. There among the disarrangement and dirt I had the strange experience of seeing us, *both* of us, placed among disarrangement and dirt: we looked like a young couple who had just moved into a new apartment; we had suddenly taken stock of our furniture, finances, and future, and all we could feel any pleasure about was the clean smell of outside, which reminded us we were alive, but which, in a pinch, would not feed us.

"What money?" I said again.

"The hundred-dollar bills. From when I was a little girl . . ." and she breathed deeply. "When I was little and we'd just moved from Newark, my father took me up here one day. He took me into this room and told me that if anything should ever happen to him, he wanted me to know where there was some money that I should have. He said it wasn't for anybody else but me, and that I should never tell anyone about it, not even Ron. Or my mother."

"How much was it?"

"Three hundred-dollar bills. I'd never seen them before. I was nine, around Julie's age. I don't think we'd been living here a month. I remember I used to come up here about once a week, when no one was home but Carlota, and crawl under the sofa and make sure it was still here. And it always was. He never mentioned it once again. Never."

"Where is it? Maybe someone stole it."

"I don't know, Neil. I suppose he took it back."

"When it was gone," I said, "my God, didn't you tell him? Maybe Carlota—"

"I never knew it was gone, until just now. I guess I stopped looking at one time or another . . . And then I forgot about it. Or just didn't think about it. I mean I always had enough, I didn't need this. I guess one day *he* figured I wouldn't need it."

Brenda paced up to the narrow, dustcovered window and drew her initials on it.

"Why did you want it now?" I said.

"I don't know . . ." she said and went over and twisted the bulb off.

I didn't move from the chair and Brenda, in her tight shorts and shirt, seemed naked standing there a few feet away. Then I saw her shoulders shaking. "I wanted to find it and tear it up in little pieces and put the goddam pieces in her purse! If it was there, I swear it, I would have done it."

"I wouldn't have let you, Bren."

"Wouldn't you have?"

"No."

"Make love to me, Neil. Right now."

"Where?"

"Do it! *Here*. On this cruddy cruddy cruddy sofa."

And I obeyed her.

The next morning Brenda made breakfast for the two of us. Ron had gone off to his first day of work—I'd heard him singing in the shower only an hour after I'd returned to my own room; in fact, I had still been awake when the Chrysler had pulled out of the garage, carrying boss and son down to the Patimkin works in Newark. Mrs. Patimkin wasn't home either; she had taken her car and had gone off to the Temple to talk to Rabbi Kranitz about the wedding. Julie was on the back lawn playing at helping Carlota hang the clothes.

"You know what I want to do this morning?" Brenda said. We were eating a grapefruit, sharing it rather sloppily, for Brenda couldn't find a paring knife, and so we'd decided to peel it down like an orange and eat the segments separately.

"What?" I said.

"Run," she said. "Do you ever run?"

"You mean on a track? God, yes. In high school we had to run a mile every month. So we wouldn't be Momma's boys. I think the bigger your lungs get the more you're supposed to hate your mother."

"I want to run," she said, "and I want you to run. Okay?"

"Oh, Brenda . . ."

But an hour later, after a breakfast that consisted of another grapefruit, which apparently is all a runner is supposed to eat in the morning, we had driven the Volkswagen over to the high school, behind which was a quarter-mile track. Some kids were playing with a dog out in the grassy center of the track, and at the far end, near the woods, a figure in white shorts with slits in the side, and no shirt, was twirling, twirling, and then flinging a shot put as far as he could. After it left his hand he did a little eagle-eyed tap dance while he watched it arch and bend and land in the distance.

"You know," Brenda said, "you look like me. Except bigger."

We were dressed similarly, sneakers, sweat socks, khaki Bermudas, and sweat shirts, but I had the feeling that Brenda was not talking about the accidents of our dress—if they were accidents. She meant, I was sure, that I was somehow beginning to look the way she wanted me to. Like herself.

"Let's see who's faster," she said, and then we started along the track. Within the first eighth of a mile the three little boys and their dog were following us. As we passed the corner where the shot putter was, he waved at us; Brenda called "Hi!" and I smiled, which, as you may or may not know, makes one engaged in serious running feel inordinately silly. At the quarter mile the kids dropped off and retired to the grass, the dog turned and started the other way, and I had a tiny knife in my side. Still I was abreast of Brenda, who as we started on the second lap, called "Hi!" once again to the lucky shot putter, who was reclining on the grass now, watching us, and rubbing his shot like a crystal ball. Ah, I thought, there's the sport.

"How about us throwing the shot put?" I panted.

"After," she said, and I saw beads of sweat clinging to the last strands of hair that shagged off her ear. When we approached the half mile Brenda suddenly swerved off the track onto the grass and tumbled down; her departure surprised me and I was still running.

"Hey, Bob Mathias," she called, "let's lie in the sun . . ."

But I acted as though I didn't hear her and though my heart pounded in my throat and my mouth was dry as a drought, I made my legs move, and swore I would not stop until I'd finished one more lap. As I passed the shot putter for the third time, I called "Hi!"

She was excited when I finally pulled up alongside of her. "You're good," she said. My hands were on my hips and I was looking at the ground and sucking air—rather, air was sucking me, I didn't have much to say about it.

"Uh-huh," I breathed.

"Let's do this every morning," she said. "We'll get up and have two grapefruit, and then you'll come out here and run. I'll time you. In two weeks you'll break four minutes, won't you, sweetie? I'll get Ron's stop watch." She was so excited—she'd slid over on the grass and was pushing my socks up against my wet ankles and calves. She bit my kneecap.

"Okay," I said.

"Then we'll go back and have a real breakfast."

"Okay."

"You drive back," she said, and suddenly she was up and running ahead of me, and then we were headed back in the car.

And the next morning, my mouth still edgy from the grapefruit segments, we were at the track. We had Ron's stop watch and a towel for me, for when I was finished.

"My legs are a little sore," I said.

"Do some exercises," Brenda said. "I'll do them with you."

She heaped the towel on the grass and together we did deep knee bends, and sit-ups, and push-ups, and some high-knee raising in place. I felt overwhelmingly happy.

"I'm just going to run a half today, Bren. We'll see what I do . . ." and I heard Brenda click the watch, and then when I was on the far side of the track, the clouds trailing above me like my own white, fleecy tail, I saw that Brenda was on the ground, hugging her knees, and alternately checking the watch and looking out at me. We were the only ones there, and it all reminded me of one of those scenes in race-horse movies, where an old trainer like Walter Brennan and a young handsome man clock the beautiful girl's horse in the early Kentucky morning, to see if it really is the fastest two-year-old alive. There were differences all right—one being simply that at the quarter mile Brenda shouted out to me, "A minute and fourteen seconds," but it was pleasant and exciting and clean and when I was finished Brenda was standing up and waiting for me. Instead of a tape to break I had Brenda's sweet flesh to meet, and I did, and it was the first time she said that she loved me.

We ran—I ran—every morning, and by the end of the week I was running a 7:02 mile, and always at the end there was the little click of the watch and Brenda's arms.

At night, I would read in my pajamas, while Brenda, in her room, read, and we would wait for Ron to go to sleep. Some nights we had to wait longer than others, and I would hear the leaves swishing outside, for it had grown cooler at the end of August, and the air-conditioning was turned off at night and we were all allowed to open our windows. Finally Ron would be ready for bed. He would stomp around his room and then he would come to the door in his shorts and T-shirt and go into the bathroom where he would urinate loudly and brush his teeth. After he brushed his teeth I would go in to brush mine. We would pass in the hall and I would give him a hearty and sincere "Good-night." Once in the bathroom, I would spend a moment admiring my tan in the mirror; behind me I could see Ron's jock straps hanging out to dry on the Hot and Cold knobs of the shower. Nobody ever questioned their tastefulness as adornment, and after a few nights I didn't even notice them.

While Ron brushed his teeth and I waited in my bed for my turn, I could hear the record player going in his room. Generally, after coming in from basketball, he would call Harriet—who was now only a few days away from us—and then would lock himself up with *Sports Illustrated* and Mantovani; however, when he emerged from his room for his evening toilet, it was not a Mantovani record I would hear playing, but something else, apparently what he'd once referred to as his Columbus record. I *imagined* that was what I heard, for I could not tell much from the last moments of sound. All I heard were bells moaning evenly and soft patriotic music behind them, and riding over it all, a deep kind of Edward R. Murrow gloomy voice: "*And so goodbye, Columbus,*" the voice intoned, ". . . *goodbye, Columbus* . . . *goodbye* . . ." Then there would be silence and Ron would be back in his room; the light would switch off and in only a few minutes I would hear him rumbling down into that exhilarating, restorative, vitamin-packed sleep that I imagined athletes to enjoy.

One morning near sneaking-away time I had a dream and when I awakened from it, there was just enough dawn coming into the room for me to see the color of Brenda's hair. I touched her in her sleep, for the dream had unsettled me: it had taken place on a ship, an old sailing ship like those you see in pirate movies. With me on the ship was the little colored kid from the library—I was the captain and he my mate, and we were the only crew members. For a while it was a pleasant dream; we were anchored in the harbor of an island in the Pacific and it was very sunny. Up on the beach there were beautiful bare-skinned Negresses, and none of them moved; but suddenly *we* were moving our ship, out of the harbor, and the Negresses moved slowly down to the shore and began to throw leis at us and say "Goodbye, Columbus . . . goodbye, Columbus . . . goodbye . . ." and though we did not want to go, the little boy and I, the boat was moving and there was nothing we could do about it, and he shouted at me that it was my fault and I shouted it was his for not having a library card, but we were wasting our breath, for we were further and further from the island, and soon the natives were nothing at all. Space was all out of proportion in the dream, and things were sized and squared in no way I'd ever seen before, and I think it was that more than anything else that steered me into consciousness. I did not want to leave Brenda's side that morning, and for a while I played with the little point at the nape of her neck, where she'd had her hair cut. I stayed longer than I should have, and when finally I returned to my room I almost ran into Ron who was preparing for his day at Patimkin Kitchen and Bathroom Sinks.

•

"Jewish Mother Par Excellence"

(excerpt from *Portnoy's Complaint*)

It was my mother who could accomplish anything, who herself had to admit that it might even be that she was actually too good. And could a small child with my intelligence, with my powers of observation, doubt that this was so? She could make jello, for instance, with sliced peaches *hanging* in it, peaches just *suspended* there, in defiance of the law of gravity. She could bake a cake that tasted like a banana. Weeping, suffering, she grated her own horseradish rather than buy the *pishachs* they sold in a bottle at the delicatessen. She watched the butcher, as she put it, "like a hawk," to be certain that he did not forget to put her chopped meat through the kosher grinder. She would telephone all the other women in the building drying clothes on the back lines—called even the divorced *goy* on the top floor one magnanimous day—to tell them rush, take in the laundry, a drop of rain had fallen on our windowpane. What radar on that woman! And this is *before* radar! The energy on her! The thoroughness! For mistakes she checked my sums; for holes, my socks; for dirt, my nails, my neck, every seam and crease of my body. She even dredges the furthest recesses of my ears by pouring cold peroxide into my head. It tingles and pops like an earful of ginger ale, and brings to the surface, in bits and pieces, the hidden stores of yellow wax, which can apparently endanger a person's hearing. A medical procedure like this (crackpot though it may be) takes time, of course. It takes effort to be sure—but where health and cleanliness are concerned, germs and bodily secretions, she will not spare herself and sacrifice others. She lights candles for the dead—others invariably forget, she religiously remembers, and without ever the aid of a notation or the calendar. Devotion is just in her blood. She seems to be the only one, she says, who when she goes to the cemetery has "the common sense," "the ordinary common decency," to clear the weeds from the graves of our relatives. The first bright day of spring, and she has moth-proofed everything wool in the house, rolled and bound the rugs, and dragged them off to my father's trophy room. She is never ashamed of her house: a stranger could walk in and open any closet, any drawer, and she would have nothing to be ashamed of. You could even eat off her bathroom floor, if that should ever become necessary. When she loses at mah-jongg she takes it like a sport, not-like-the-others-whose-names-she-could-mention-but-she-won't-not-even-Tilly-Hochman-it's-too-petty-to-even-talk-about-let's-just-forget-she-even-brought-it-up. She sews, she knits, she darns—she irons better even than the *schvartze,* to whom, of all her friends who each possess a piece of this grinning childish black old lady's hide, she alone is good. "I'm the only one who's good to her. I'm the only one who gives her a whole can of tuna for lunch, and I'm not talking *dreck*, either. I'm talking Chicken of the Sea, Alex. I'm sorry, I can't be a stingy person. Excuse me, but I can't live like that, even if it is 2 for 49. Esther Wasserberg leaves twenty-five cents in nickels around the house when Dorothy comes, and counts up afterwards to see it's all there. Maybe I'm too good," she whispers to me, meanwhile running scalding water over the dish from which the cleaning lady has just eaten her lunch, alone like a leper, "but I couldn't do a thing like that." Once Dorothy chanced to come back into the kitchen while my mother was still standing over the faucet marked H, sending torrents down upon the knife and fork that had passed between the *schvartze*'s thick pink lips. "Oh, you know how hard it is to get mayonnaise off silverware these days, Dorothy," says my nimble-tongued mother—and thus, she tells me later, by her quick thinking, has managed to spare the colored woman's feelings.

When I am bad I am locked out of the apartment. I stand at the door hammering and hammering until I swear I will turn over a new leaf. But what is it I have done? I shine my shoes every evening on a sheet of last night's newspaper laid carefully over the linoleum; afterward I never fail to turn securely the lid on the tin of polish, and to return all the equipment to where it belongs. I roll the toothpaste tube from the bottom, I brush my teeth in circles and never up and down, I say "Thank you," I say "You're welcome," I say "I beg your pardon," and "May I." When Hannah is ill or out before supper with her blue tin can collecting for the Jewish National Fund, I voluntarily and out of my turn set the table, remembering always knife and spoon on the right, fork on the left, and napkin to the left of the fork and folded into a triangle. I would never eat *milchiks* off a *flaishedigeh* dish, never, never, never. Nonetheless, there is a year or so in my life when not a month goes by that I don't do something so inexcusable that I am told to pack a bag and leave. But what could it possibly be? Mother, it's me, the little boy who spends whole nights before school begins beautifully lettering in Old English script the names of his subjects on his colored course dividers, who patiently fastens reinforcements to a term's worth of three-ringed paper, lined and unlined both. I carry a comb and a clean hankie; never do my knicker stockings drag at my shoes, I see to that; my homework is completed weeks in advance of the assignment—let's face it, Ma, I am the smartest and neatest little boy in the history of my school! Teachers (as you know, as they have told you) go home happy to their husbands because of me; so what is it I have done? Will someone with the answer to that question please stand up! I am so awful she will not have me in her house *a minute longer*. When I once called my sister a cocky-doody, my mouth was immediately washed with a cake of brown laundry soap; this I understand. But banishment? What can I possibly have done!

Because she is good she will pack a lunch for me to take along, but then out I go, in my coat and my galoshes, and what happens is not her business.

Okay, I say, if that's how you feel! (For I have the taste for melodrama too—I am not in this family for nothing.) I don't need a bag of lunch! I don't need anything!

I don't love you any more, not a little boy who behaves like you do. I'll live alone here with Daddy and Hannah, says my mother (a master really at phrasing things just the right way to kill you). Hannah can set up the mah-jongg tiles for the ladies on Tuesday night. We won't be needing you any more.

Who cares! And out the door I go, into the long dim hallway. Who cares!

I will sell newspapers on the streets in my bare feet. I will ride where I want on freight cars and sleep in open fields, I think—and then it is enough for me to see the empty milk bottles standing by our welcome mat, for the immensity of all I have lost to come breaking over my head. "I hate you!" I holler, kicking a galosh at the door; "you stink!" To this filth, to this heresy booming through the corridors of the apartment building where she is vying with twenty other Jewish women to be the patron saint of self-sacrifice, my mother has no choice but to throw the double-lock on our door. This is when I start to hammer to be let in. I drop to the doormat to beg forgiveness for my sin (which is what again?) and promise her nothing but perfection for the rest of our lives, which at that time I believe will be endless.

Then there are the nights I will not eat. My sister, who is four years my senior, assures me that what I remember is fact: I would refuse to eat, and my mother would find herself unable to submit to such willfulness—and such idiocy. And unable to for my own good. She is only asking me to do something *for my own good*—and still I say *no*? Wouldn't she give me the food out of her own mouth, don't I know that by now?

But I don't want the food from her mouth. I don't even want the food from my plate—that's the point.

Please! a child with my potential! my accomplishments! my future!—all the gifts God has lavished upon me, of beauty, of brains, am I to be allowed to think I can just starve myself to death for no good reason in the world?

Do I want people to look down on a skinny little boy all my life, or to look up to a man?

Do I want to be pushed around and made fun of, do I want to be skin and bones that people can knock over with a sneeze, or do I want to command respect? Which do I want to be when I grow up, weak or strong, a success or a failure, a man or a mouse?

I just don't want to eat, I answer.

So my mother sits down in a chair beside me with a long bread knife in her hand. It is made of stainless steel, and has little sawlike teeth. Which do I want to be, weak or strong, a man or a mouse?

Doctor, *why*, why oh why oh why oh why does a mother pull a knife on her own son? I am six, seven years old, how do I know she really wouldn't use it? What am I supposed to do, try bluffing her out, at seven? I have no complicated sense of strategy, for Christ's sake—I probably don't even weigh sixty pounds yet! Someone waves a knife in my direction, I believe there is an intention lurking somewhere to draw my blood! Only *why*? What can she possibly be thinking in *her brain*? How crazy can she possibly be? Suppose she had let me win—what would have been lost? Why a *knife*, why the threat of *murder*, why is such total and annihilating victory necessary—when only the day before she set down her iron on the ironing board and *applauded* as I stormed around the kitchen rehearsing my role as Christopher Columbus in the third-grade production of *Land Ho!* I am the star actor of my class, they cannot put a play on without me. Oh, once they tried, when I had my bronchitis, but my teacher later confided in my mother that it had been decidedly second-rate. Oh *how,* how can she spend such glorious afternoons in that kitchen, polishing silver, chopping liver, threading new elastic in the waistband of my little jockey shorts—and feeding me all the while my cues from the mimeographed script, playing Queen Isabella to my Columbus, Betsy Ross to my Washington, Mrs. Pasteur to my Louis—how can she rise with me on the crest of my genius during those dusky beautiful hours after school, and then at night, because I will not eat some string beans and a baked potato, point a bread knife at my heart?

And why doesn't my father stop her? . . .

Look, she is probably not the happiest person in the world either. She was once a tall stringbean of a girl whom the boys called "Red" in high school. When I was nine and ten years old I had an absolute passion for her high school yearbook. For a while I kept it in the same drawer of exotica, my stamp collection.

> *Sophie Ginsky the boys call "Red,"*
> *She'll go far with her big brown eyes and her clever head.*

And that was my mother!

Also, she had been secretary to the soccer coach, an office pretty much without laurels in our own time, but apparently the post for a young girl to hold in Jersey City during the First World War. So I thought, at any rate, when I turned the pages of her yearbook, and she pointed out to me her dark-haired beau, who had been captain of the team, and today, to quote Sophie, "the biggest manufacturer of mustard in New York." "And I could have married him instead of your father," she confided in me, and more than once. I used to wonder sometimes what that would have been like for my momma and me, invariably on the occasions when my father took us to dine out at the corner delicatessen. I look around the place and think, "We would have manufactured all this mustard." I suppose she must have had thoughts like that herself.

"He eats French fries," she says, and sinks into a kitchen chair to Weep Her Heart Out once and for all. "He goes after school with Melvin Weiner and stuffs himself with French-fried potatoes. Jack, you tell him, I'm only his mother. Tell him what the end is going to be. Alex," she says passionately, looking to where I am edging out of the room, "*tateleh,* it begins with diarrhea, but do you know how it ends? With a sensitive stomach like yours, do you know how it finally ends? *Wearing a plastic bag to do your business in!*"

Who in the history of the world has been least able to deal with a woman's tears? My father. I am second. He says to me, "You heard your mother. Don't eat French fries with Melvin Weiner after school."

"Or ever," she pleads.

"Or ever," my father says.

"Or hamburgers out," she pleads.

"Or hamburgers out," he says.

"Hamburgers," she says bitterly, just as she might say *Hitler*, "where they can put anything in the world in that they want—and *he* eats them. Jack, make him promise, before he gives himself a terrible *tsura*, and it's too late."

"I *promise*!" I scream. "I *promise*!" and race from the kitchen—to where? Where else.

I tear off my pants, furiously I grab that battered battering ram to freedom, my adolescent cock, even as my mother begins to call from the other side of the bathroom door. "Now this time don't flush. Do you hear me, Alex? I have to see what's in that bowl!"

Doctor, do you understand what I was up against? My wang was all I really had that I could call my own. You should have watched her at work during polio season! She should have gotten medals from the March of Dimes! Open your mouth. Why is your throat red? Do you have a headache you're not telling me about? You're not going to any baseball game, Alex, until I see you move your neck. Is your neck stiff? Then why are you moving it that way? You ate like you were nauseous, are you nauseous? Well, you ate like you were nauseous. I don't want you drinking from the drinking fountain in that playground. If you're thirsty wait until you're home. Your throat is sore, isn't it? I can tell how you're swallowing. I think maybe what you are going to do, Mr. Joe Di Maggio, is put that glove away and lie down. I am not going to allow you to go outside in this heat and run around, not with that sore throat, I'm not. I want to take your temperature. I don't like the sound of this throat business one bit. To be very frank, I am actually beside myself that you have been walking around all day with a sore throat and not telling your mother. Why did you keep this a secret? Alex, polio doesn't know from baseball games. It only knows from iron lungs and crippled forever! I don't want you running around, and that's final. Or eating hamburgers out. Or mayonnaise. Or chopped liver. Or tuna. Not everybody is careful the way your mother is about spoilage. You're used to a spotless house, you don't begin to know what goes on in restaurants. Do you know why your mother when we go to the Chink's will never sit facing the kitchen? Because I don't want to see what goes on back there. Alex, you must wash everything, is that clear? Everything! God only knows who touched it before you did.

Look, am I exaggerating to think it's practically miraculous that I'm ambulatory? The hysteria and the superstition! The watch-its and the be-carefuls! You mustn't do this, you can't do that—hold it! don't you're breaking an important law! *What* law? *Whose* law? They might as well have had plates in their lips and rings through their noses and painted themselves blue for all the human sense they made! Oh, and the *milchiks* and *flaishiks* besides, all those *meshuggeneh* rules and regulations on top of their own private craziness! It's a family joke that when I was a tiny child I turned from the window out of which I was watching a snowstorm, and hopefully asked, "Momma, do we believe in winter?" Do you get what I'm *saying?* I was raised by Hottentots and Zulus! I couldn't even contemplate drinking a glass of milk with my salami sandwich without giving serious offense to God Almighty. Imagine then what my conscience gave me for all that jerking off! The guilt, the fears—the terror bred into my bones! What in their world was not charged with danger, dripping with germs, fraught with peril? Oh, where was the gusto, where was the boldness and courage? Who filled these parents of mine with such a fearful sense of life? My father, in his retirement now, has really only one subject into which he can sink his teeth, the New Jersey Turnpike. "I wouldn't go on that thing if you paid me. You have to be out of your mind to travel on that thing—it's Murder Incorporated, it's a legalized way for people to go out and get themselves killed—" Listen, you know what he says to me three times a week on the telephone—and I'm only counting when I pick it up, not the total number of rings I get between six and ten every night. "Sell that car, will you? Will you do me a favor and sell that car so I can get a good night's sleep? Why you have to have a car in that city is beyond my comprehension. Why you want to pay for insurance and garage and upkeep I don't even begin to understand. But then I don't understand yet why you even want to live by yourself over in that jungle. What do you pay those robbers again for that two-by-four apartment? A penny over fifty dollars a month and you're out of your mind. Why you don't move back to North Jersey is a mystery to me—why you prefer the noise and the crime and the fumes—"

And my mother, she just keeps whispering. *Sophie whispers on!* I go for dinner once a month, it is a struggle requiring all my guile and cunning and strength, but I have been able over all these years, and against imponderable odds, to hold it down to once a month: I ring the bell, she opens the door, the whispering promptly begins! "Don't ask what kind of day I had with him yesterday." So I don't. "Alex," *sotto voce* still, "when he has a day like that you don't know what a difference a call from you would make." I nod. "And, Alex"—and I'm nodding away, you know—it doesn't cost anything, and it may even get me through—"next week is his birthday. That Mother's Day came and went without a card, *plus* my birthday, those things don't bother me. But he'll be sixty-six, Alex. That's not a baby, Alex—that's a landmark in a life. So you'll send a card. It wouldn't kill you."

Doctor, these people are incredible! These people are unbelievable! These two are the outstanding producers and packagers of guilt in our time! They render it from me like fat from a chicken! "Call, Alex. Visit, Alex. Alex, keep us informed. Don't go away without telling us, please, not again. Last time you went away you didn't tell us, your father was ready to phone the police. You know how many times a day he called and got no answer? Take a guess, how many?" "Mother," I inform her, from between my teeth, "if I'm dead they'll smell the body in seventy-two hours, I assure you!" "Don't *talk* like that! God *forbid!*" she cries. Oh, and now she's got the beauty, the one guaranteed to do the job. Yet how could I expect otherwise? Can I ask the impossible of my own mother? "Alex, to pick up a phone is such a simple thing—how much longer will we be around to bother you anyway?"

Doctor Spielvogel, this was my life, my only life, and I'm living it in the middle of a Jewish joke! I am the son in the Jewish joke—*only it ain't no joke!* Please, who crippled us like this? Who made us so morbid and hysterical and weak? Why, why are they screaming still, "Watch out! Don't do it! Alex—*no!*" and why, alone on my bed in New York, why am I still hopelessly beating my meat? Doctor, what do you call this sickness I have? Is this the Jewish suffering I used to hear so much about? Is this what has come down to me from the pogroms and the persecution? from the mockery and abuse bestowed by the goyim over these two thousand lovely years? Oh my secrets, my shame, my palpitations, my flushes, my sweats! The way I respond to the simple vicissitudes of human life! Doctor, I can't stand any more being frightened like this over nothing! Bless me with manhood! Make me brave! Make me strong! Make me whole! Enough being a nice Jewish boy, publicly pleasing my parents while privately pulling my putz! Enough! . . . .

Of course around the house I saw less of his sexual apparatus than I did of her erogenous zones. And once I saw her menstrual blood . . . saw it shining darkly up at me from the worn linoleum in front of the kitchen sink. Just two red drops over a quarter of a century ago, but they glow still in that icon of her that hangs, perpetually illuminated, in my Modern Museum of Gripes and Grievances (along with the box of Kotex and the nylon stockings, which I want to come to in a moment). Also in this icon is an endless dripping of blood down through a drain-board into a dishpan. It is the blood she is draining from the meat so as to make it kosher and fit for consumption. Probably I am confusing things—I sound like a son of the House of Atreus with all this talk of blood—but I see her standing at the sink salting the meat so as to rid it of its blood, when the attack of "women's troubles" sends her, with a most alarming moan, rushing off to her bedroom. I was no more than four or five, and yet those two drops of blood that I beheld on the floor of her kitchen are visible to me still . . . as is the box of Kotex . . . as are the stockings sliding up her legs . . . as is—need I even say it?—the bread knife with which my own blood would be threatened when I refuse to eat my dinner. That knife! *That knife!* What gets me is that she herself did not even consider the use of it anything to be ashamed of, or particularly reticent about. From my bed I hear her babbling about her problems to the women around the mah-jongg game: *My Alex is suddenly such a bad eater I have to stand over him with a knife.* And none of them apparently finds this tactic of hers at all excessive. I have to stand over him with a knife! And not one of those women gets up from the mah-jongg table and walks out of her house! Because in their world, that is the way it is with bad eaters—you have to stand over them *with a knife!*

It was years later that she called from the bathroom, Run to the drugstore! bring a box of Kotex! immediately! And the panic in her voice. Did I run! And then at home again, breathlessly hand the box to the white fingers that extended themselves at me through a narrow crack in the bathroom door . . . Though her menstrual troubles eventually had to be resolved by surgery, it is difficult nevertheless to forgive her for having sent me on that mission of mercy. Better she should have bled herself out on our cold bathroom floor, better *that*, than to have sent an eleven-year-old boy in hot pursuit of sanitary napkins! Where was my sister, for Christ's sake? Where was her own emergency supply? Why was this woman so grossly insensitive to the vulnerability of her own little boy—on the one hand so insensitive to my shame, and yet on the other, so attuned to my deepest desires!

. . . I am so small I hardly know what sex I am, or so you would imagine. It is early in the afternoon, spring of the year Four. Flowers are standing up in purple stalks in the patch of dirt outside our building. With the windows flung open the air in the apartment is fragrant, soft with the season—and yet electric too with my mother's vitality: she has finished the week's wash and hung it on the line; she has baked a marble cake for our dessert tonight, beautifully bleeding—there's that blood again! there's that knife again!—anyway expertly bleeding the chocolate in and out of the vanilla, an accomplishment that seems to me as much of a miracle as getting those peaches to hang there suspended in the shimmering mold of jello. She has done the laundry and baked the cake; she has scrubbed the kitchen and bathroom floors and laid them with newspaper; she has of course dusted; needless to say, she has vacuumed; she has cleared and washed our luncheon dishes and (with my cute little assistance) returned them to their place in the *milchiks* cabinet in the pantry—and whistling like a canary all the morning through, a tuneless melody of health and joy, of heedlessness and self-sufficiency. While I crayon a picture for her, she showers—and now in the sunshine of her bedroom, she is dressing to take me downtown. She sits on the edge of the bed in her padded bra and her girdle, rolling on her stockings and chattering away. Who is Mommy's good little boy? Who is the best little boy a mommy ever had? Who does Mommy love more than anything in the whole wide world? I am absolutely punchy with delight, and meanwhile follow in their tight, slow, agonizingly delicious journey up her legs the transparent stockings that give her flesh a hue of stirring dimensions. I sidle close enough to smell the bath powder on her throat—also to appreciate better the elastic intricacies of the dangling straps to which the stockings will presently be hooked (undoubtedly with a flourish of trumpets). I smell the oil with which she has polished the four gleaming posts of the mahogany bedstead, where she sleeps with a man who lives with us at night and on Sunday afternoons. My father they say he is. On my finger-tips, even though she has washed each one of those little piggies with a warm wet cloth, I smell my lunch, my tuna fish salad. Ah, it might be cunt I'm sniffing. Maybe it is! Oh, I want to growl with pleasure. Four years old, and yet I sense in my blood—uh-huh, again with the blood—how rich with passion is the moment, how dense with possibility. This fat person with the long hair whom they call my sister is away at school. This man, my father, is off somewhere making money, as best he is able. These two are gone, and who knows, maybe I'll be lucky, maybe they'll never come back . . . In the meantime, it is afternoon, it is spring, and for me and me alone a woman is rolling on her stockings and singing a song of love. Who is going to stay with mommy forever and ever? *Me*. Who is it who goes with Mommy wherever in the whole wide world Mommy goes? *Why me, of course. What a silly question—but don't get me wrong, I'll play the game!* Who had a nice lunch with Mommy, who goes downtown like a good boy on the bus with Mommy, who goes into the big store with Mommy . . . and on and on and on . . . so that only a week or so ago, upon my safe return from Europe, Mommy had this to say—

"Feel."

"What?"—even as she takes my hand in hers and draws it toward her body—"Mother—"

"I haven't gained five pounds," she says, "since you were born. Feel," she says, and holds my stiff fingers against the swell of her hips, which aren't bad . . .

And the stockings. More than twenty-five years have passed (the game is supposed to be over!), but Mommy still hitches up the stockings in front of her little boy. Now, however, he takes it upon himself to look the other way when the flag goes fluttering up the pole—and out of concern not just for his own mental health. That's the truth, I look away not for me but for the sake of that poor man, my father! Yet what preference does Father really have? If there in the living room their grown-up little boy were to tumble all at once onto the rug with his mommy, what would Daddy do? Pour a bucket of boiling water on the raging, maddened couple? Would he draw *his* knife—or would he go off to the other room and watch television until they were finished? "What are you looking away—?" asks my mother, amused in the midst of straightening her seams. "You'd think I was a twenty-one-year-old girl; you'd think I hadn't wiped your backside and kissed your little tushy for you all those years. Look at him"—this to my father, in case he hasn't been giving a hundred percent of his attention to the little floor show now being performed—"look, acting like his own mother is some sixty-year-old beauty queen."

Real Women

Jewish Mothers and Daughters Explore New Paths

Bernard Malamud

Bernard Malamud was a second-generation American, born in Brooklyn in 1914 to Russian Jewish immigrants who ran a "Mom-and-Pop" grocery store. He attended City College of New York and received his master's degree from Columbia College. He spent several years working for the Census Bureau in Washington, then returned to New York, married an Italian-American woman, and taught high school English. In the meantime, he had begun publishing short stories, many of which focused on New York City ethnic groups, such as Italians, Jews, and African Americans. Malamud became one of the most celebrated and widely read American Jewish authors, publishing more than half a dozen novels and scores of short stories. For many years he taught in Bennington College in Vermont, and he also spent several years teaching at Harvard University. He died in 1983. Together with Saul Bellow and Philip Roth, Malamud has generally been considered one of the triumvirate of the most accomplished midtwentieth-century American Jewish writers.

In *The Assistant*, the Bober family, Malamud's archetypecal lower-class Jews, are secularized but are deeply committed to education, self-discipline, gentleness, and human decency. They are true Jews, in Malamud's vision, because their suffering gives them empathy for other unfortunate souls. Indeed, in Malamud's fiction the development of empathy is the providential raison d'être for Jewish suffering: all poor people suffer, but the "Jewish heart" makes suffering into a humanizing rather than a dehumanizing experience. The novel's protagonist, Frank Alpine, an Italian drifter with a troubled past, represents the underclass of poor, undereducated ethnic Americans, who often blunder into destructive behavior through lack of both self-control and sense of direction.

Alpine becomes Morris's grocery assistant, insinuates himself thoroughly into the family's life, and falls desperately in love with Helen. To Malamud, the union between Helen and Frank is not the ethnic betrayal that it seems to Ida but the opportunity for Jewish idealism to be transmitted to another foundering human being. Malamud portrays each character with insight and sensitivity. His portrait of Helen, as she struggles to find and maintain her own moral guidelines, is especially fine. Surprisingly, there are few women as carefully developed as Helen in Malamud's later fiction.

•

"Helen's Search" (excerpt)

Helen felt herself, despite the strongest doubts, falling in love with Frank. It was a dizzying dance, she didn't want to. The month was cold—it often snowed—she had a rough time, fighting hesitancies, fears of a disastrous mistake. One night she dreamed their house had burned down and her poor parents had nowhere to go. They stood on the sidewalk, wailing in their underwear. Waking, she fought an old distrust of the broken-faced stranger, without success. The stranger had changed, grown unstrange. That was the clue to what was happening to her. One day he seemed unknown, lurking at the far end of an unlit cellar; the next he was standing in sunlight, a smile on his face, as if all she knew of him and all she didn't, had fused into a healed and easily remembered whole. If he was hiding anything, she thought, it was his past pain, his orphanhood and consequent suffering. His eyes were quieter, wiser. His crooked nose fitted his face and his face fitted him. It stayed on straight. He was gentle, waiting for whatever he awaited with a grace she respected. She felt she had changed him and this affected her. That she had willed to stay free of him made little difference now: She felt tender to him, wanted him close by. She had, she thought, changed in changing him.

After she had accepted his gift of a book their relationship had subtly altered. What else, if whenever she read in her Shakespeare, she thought of Frank Alpine, even heard his voice in the plays? Whatever she read, he crept into her thoughts; in every book he haunted the words, a character in a plot somebody else had invented, as if all associations had only one end. He was, to begin with, everywhere. So, without speaking of it, they met again in the library. That they were meeting among books relieved her doubt, as if she believed, what possible wrong can I do among books, what possible harm can come to me here?

In the library he too seemed surer of himself—though once they were on their way home he became almost remote, strangely watchful, looking back from time to time as though they were being followed, but who or what would follow them? He never took her as far as the store; as before, by mutual consent, she went on ahead, then he walked around the block and entered the hall from the other way so he wouldn't have to go past the grocery window and possibly be seen coming from the direction she had come from. Helen interpreted his caution to mean he sensed victory and didn't want to endanger it. It meant he valued her more than she was altogether sure she wanted to be.

Then one night they walked across a field in the park and turned to one another. She tried to awaken in herself a feeling of danger, but danger was dulled, beyond her, in his arms, pressed against him, responsive to his touch, she felt the cold ebb out of the night, and a warmth come over her. Her lips parted—she drew from his impassioned kiss all she had long desired. Yet at the moment of sweetest joy she felt again the presence of doubt, almost a touch of illness. This made her sad. The fault was her. It meant she still could not fully accept him. There were still signals signaling no. She had only to think of them and they would work in her, pinching the nerves. On their way home she could not forget the first happiness of their kiss. But why should a kiss become anxiety? Then she saw that his eyes were sad, and she wept when he wasn't looking. Would it never come spring?

She stalled love with arguments, only to be surprised at their swift dissolution; found it difficult to keep her reasons securely nailed down, as they were before. They flew up in the mind, shifted, changed, as if something had altered familiar weights, values, even experience. He wasn't, for instance, Jewish. Not too long ago this was the greatest barrier, her protection against ever taking him seriously; now it no longer seemed such an urgently important thing—how could it in times like these? How could anything be important but love and fulfillment? It had lately come to her that her worry he was a gentile was less for her own sake than for her mother and father. Although she had only loosely been brought up as Jewish she felt loyal to the Jews, more for what they had gone through than what she knew of their history or theology—loved them as a people, thought with pride of herself as one of them; she had never imagined she would marry anybody but a Jew. But she had recently come to think that in such unhappy times—when the odds were so high against personal happiness—to find love was miraculous, and to fulfill it as best two people could was what really mattered. Was it more important to insist a man's religious beliefs be exactly hers (if it was a question of religion), or that the two of them have in common ideals, a desire to keep love in their lives, and to preserve in every possible way what was best in themselves? The less difference among people, the better; thus she settled it for herself yet was dissatisfied for those for whom she hadn't settled it.

But her logic, if it was logic, wouldn't decide a thing for her unhappy parents once they found out what was going on. With Frank enrolled in college maybe some of Ida's doubts of his worth as a person might wither away, but college was not the synagogue, a B.A. not a bar mitzvah; and her mother and even her father with his liberal ideas would insist that Frank had to be what he wasn't. Helen wasn't at all sure she could handle them if it ever came to a showdown. She dreaded the arguments, their tear-stained pleas and her own misery for taking from the small sum of peace they had in the world, adding to the portion of their unhappiness. God knows they had had enough of that. Still, there was just so much time to live, so little of youth among the years; one had to make certain heartbreaking choices. She foresaw the necessity of upholding her own, enduring pain yet keeping to her decisions. Morris and Ida would be grievously hurt, but before too long their pain would grow less and perhaps leave them; yet she could not help but hope her own children would someday marry Jews.

And if she married Frank, her first job would be to help him realize his wish to be somebody. Nat Pearl wanted to be "somebody," but to him this meant making money to lead the life of some of his well-to-do friends at law school. Frank, on the other hand, was struggling to realize himself as a person, a more worthwhile ambition. Though Nat had an excellent formal education, Frank knew more about life and gave the impression of greater potential depth. She wanted him to become what he might, and conceived a plan to support him through college. Maybe she could even see him through a master's degree, once he knew what he wanted to do. She realized this would mean the end of her own vague plans for going to day college, but that was really lost long ago, and she thought she would at last accept the fact once Frank had got what she hadn't. Maybe after he was working, perhaps as an engineer or chemist, she could take a year of college just to slake her thirst. By then she would be almost thirty, but it would be worth postponing having a family to give him a good start and herself a taste of what she had always wanted. She also hoped they would be able to leave New York. She wanted to see more of the country. And if things eventually worked out, maybe Ida and Morris would someday sell the store and come to live near them. They might all live in California, her parents in a little house of their own where they could take life easy and be near their grandchildren. The future offered more in the way of realizable possibilities, Helen thought, if a person dared take a chance with it. The question was, did she?

She postponed making any important decision. She feared most of all the great compromise—she had seen so many of the people she knew settle for so much less than they had always wanted. She feared to be forced to choose beyond a certain point, to accept less of the good life than she had hungered for, appreciably less—to tie up with a fate far short of her ideals. That she mustn't do, whether it meant taking Frank or letting him go. Her constant fear, underlying all others, was that her life would not turn out as she had hoped, or would turn out vastly different. She was willing to change, make substitutions, but she would not part with the substance of her dreams. Well, she would know by summertime what to do. In the meantime Frank went every third night to the library and there she was. But when the old-maid librarian smiled knowingly upon them, Helen felt embarrassed, so they met elsewhere. They met in cafeterias, movie houses, the pizza place—where it was impossible to say much, or hold him or be held. To talk they walked, to kiss they hid.

Frank said he was getting the college bulletins he had written for, and around May he would have a transcript of his high school record sent to whichever place they picked for him to go. He showed he knew she had plans for him. He didn't say much more, for he was always afraid the old jinx would grab hold of him if he opened his mouth a little too wide.

At first he waited patiently. What else was there to do? He had waited and was still waiting. He had been born waiting. But before long, though he tried not to show it, he was beginning to be fed up with his physical loneliness. He grew tired of the frustrations of kissing in doorways, a cold feel on a bench in the park. He thought of her as he had seen her in the bathroom, and the memory became a burden. He was the victim of the sharp edge of his hunger. So he wanted her to the point where he thought up schemes for getting her into his room and in bed. He wanted satisfaction, relief, a stake in the future. She's not yours till she gives it to you, he thought. That's the way they all are. It wasn't always true, but it was true enough. He wanted an end to the torment of coming to a boil, then thank you, no more. He wanted to take her completely.

They met more often now. At a bench on the Parkway, on street corners—in the wide windy world. When it rained or snowed, they stepped into doorways, or went home.

He complained one night, "What a joke. We leave the same warm house to meet out in the cold here."

She said nothing.

"Forget it," Frank said, looking into her troubled eyes, "we will take it the way it is."

"This is our youth," she said bitterly.

He wanted then to ask her to come to his room but felt she wouldn't, so he didn't ask.

One cold, starry night she led him through the trees in the park near where they usually sat, onto a broad meadow where on summer nights lovers lay in the grass.

"Come on and sit down on the ground for a minute," Frank urged, "there's nobody here now."

But Helen wouldn't.

"Why not?" he asked.

"Not now," she said.

She realized, though he later denied it, that the situation had made him impatient. Sometimes he was moody for hours. She worried, wondering what rusty wound their homelessness had opened in him.

One evening they sat alone on a bench on the parkway, Frank with his arm around her; but because they were so close to home Helen was jumpy and moved away whenever somebody passed by.

After the third time Frank said, "Listen, Helen, this is no good. Some night we will have to go where we can be inside."

"Where?" she asked.

"Where do you say?"

"I can't say anything Frank. I don't know."

"How long is this going to keep up like this?"

"As long as we like," she said, smiling faintly, "or as long as we like each other."

"I don't mean it that way. What I am talking about is not having any place private to go to."

She answered nothing.

"Maybe some night we ought to sneak up to my room," he suggested. "We could do it easy enough—I don't mean tonight but maybe Friday, after Nick and Tessie go to the show and your mother is down in the store. I bought a new heater and the room keeps warm. Nobody will know you are there. We would be alone for once. We have never been alone that way."

"I couldn't," Helen said.

"Why?"

"Frank, I can't."

"When will I get a chance to put my arms around you without being an acrobat?"

"Frank," said Helen, "there's one thing I wish to make clear to you. I won't sleep with you now, if that's what you mean. It'll have to wait till I am really sure I love you, maybe till we're married, if we ever are."

"I never asked you to," Frank said. "All I said was for you to come up to my room so we could spend the time more comfortable, not you bucking away from me every time a shadow passes."

He lit a cigarette and smoked in silence.

"I'm sorry." After a minute she said, "I thought I ought to tell you how I feel on this subject. I was going to sometime anyway."

They got up and walked, Frank gnawing his wound.

A cold rain washed the yellow slush out of the gutters. It rained drearily for two days. Helen had promised to see Frank on Friday night but she didn't like the thought of going out in the wet. When she came home from work, and got the chance, she slipped a note under his door, then went down. The note said that if Nick and Tessie did go to the movies, she would try to come up to his room for a while.

At half past seven Nick knocked on Frank's door and asked him if he wanted to go to the pictures. Frank said no, he thought he had seen the picture that was playing. Nick said good-by and he and Tessie, bundled in raincoats and carrying umbrellas, left the house. Helen waited for her mother to go down to Morris, but Ida complained that her feet hurt, and said she would rest. Helen then went down herself, knowing Frank would hear her on the stairs and figure something had gone wrong. He would understand she could not go up to see him so long as anyone might hear her.

But a few minutes later, Ida came down, saying she felt restless upstairs. Helen then said she intended to drop in on Betty Pearl and might go along with her to the dressmaker who was making her wedding things.

"It's raining," said Ida.

"I know, Mama," Helen answered, hating her deceit.

She went up to her room, got her hat and coat, rubbers and an umbrella; then walked down, letting the door bang, as if she had just left the house. She quietly opened it and went on tiptoe up the stairs.

Frank had guessed what was going on and opened his door to her quick tap. She was pale, obviously troubled, but very lovely. He held her hard and could feel her heartbeat against his chest.

She will let me tonight, he told himself.

Helen was still uneasy. It took her a while to quiet her conscience for having lied to her mother. Frank had put out the light and tuned in the radio to soft dance music; now he lay on the bed, smoking. For a time she sat awkwardly in his chair, watching the glow of his cigarette, and when not that, the drops of lit rain on the window, reflecting the street light. But after he had rubbed his butt into an ash tray on the floor, Helen stepped out of her shoes and lay down beside him on the narrow bed, Frank moving over to the wall.

"This is more like it," he sighed.

She lay with closed eyes in his arms, feeling the warmth of the heater like a hand on her back. For a minute she half-dozed, then woke to his kisses. She lay motionless, a little tense, but when he stopped kissing her, relaxed. She listened to the quiet sound of the rain in the street, making it in her mind into spring rain, though spring was weeks away; and within the rain grew all sorts of flowers; and amid the spring flowers, in this flowering dark—a sweet spring night—she lay with him in the open under new stars and a cry rose to her throat. When he kissed her again, she responded with passion.

"Darling."

"I love you, Helen, you are my girl."

They kissed breathlessly, then he undid the buttons of her blouse. She sat up to unhook her brassiere but as she was doing it, felt his fingers under her skirt.

Helen grabbed his hand. "Please, Frank. Let's not get that hot and bothered."

"What are we waiting for, honey?" He tried to move his hand but her legs tightened and she swung her feet off the bed.

He pulled her back, pressing her shoulders down. She felt his body trembling on hers and for a fleeting minute thought he might hurt her; but he didn't.

She lay stiff, unresponsive on the bed. When he kissed her again she didn't move. It took a while before he lay back. She saw by the reflected glow of the heater how unhappy he looked.

Helen sat on the edge of the bed, buttoning her blouse.

His hands covered his face. He said nothing but she could feel his body shivering on the bed.

"Christ," he muttered.

"I'm sorry," she said softly. "I told you I wouldn't."

Five minutes passed. Frank slowly sat up. "Are you a virgin, is that what's eating you?"

"I'm not," she said.

"I thought you were," he said, surprised. "You act like one."

"I said I wasn't."

"Then why do you act like one? Don't you know what it does to people?"

"I'm people."

"Then why do you do it for?"

"Because I believe in what I'm doing."

"I thought you said you weren't a virgin?"

"You don't have to be a virgin to have ideals in sex."

"What I don't understand is if you did it before, what's the difference if we do it now?"

"We can't, just because I did," she said, brushing her hair back. "That's the point. I did it and that's why I can't with you now. I said I wouldn't, that night on the Parkway."

"I don't get it," Frank said.

"Loving should come with love."

"I said I love you, Helen, you heard me say it."

"I mean I have to love you too. I think I do but sometimes I'm not sure."

He fell again into silence. She listened absent-mindedly to the radio but nobody was dancing now.

"Don't be hurt, Frank."

"I'm tired of that," he said harshly.

"Frank," said Helen, "I said I slept with somebody before and the truth of it is, if you want to know, I'm sorry I did. I admit I had some pleasure, but after, I thought it wasn't worth it, only I didn't know at the time I would feel that way, because at the time I didn't know what I wanted. I suppose I felt I wanted to be free, so I settled for sex. But if you're not in love sex isn't being free, so I made a promise to myself that I never would any more unless I really fell in love with somebody. I don't want to dislike myself. I want to be disciplined, and you have to be too if I ask it. I ask it so I might someday love you without reservations."

"Crap," Frank said, but then, to his surprise, the idea seized him. He thought of himself as disciplined, then wished he were. This seemed to him like an old and faraway thought, and he remembered with regret and strange sadness how often he had wished for better control over himself, and how little of it he had achieved.

He said, "I didn't mean to say what I just now did, Helen."

"I know," she answered.

"Helen," he said huskily, "I want you to know I am a very good guy in my heart."

"I don't think otherwise."

"Even when I am bad I am good."

She said she thought she knew what he meant.

They kissed, again and again. He thought there were a whole lot worse things than waiting for something that was going to be good once he got it.

Helen lay back on the bed and dozed, awaking when Nick and Tessie came into their bedroom, talking about the movie they had seen. It was a love story and Tessie had liked it very much. After they undressed and got into bed their double bed creaked. Helen felt bad for Frank but Frank did not seem to feel bad. Nick and Tessie soon fell asleep. Helen, breathing lightly, listened to their heavy breathing, worrying how she was going to get down to her floor, because if Ida was awake she would hear her on the stairs. But Frank said in a low voice that he would carry her to the vestibule, then she could go up after a few minutes, as if she had just come home from some place.

She put on her coat, hat and rubbers, and was careful to remember her umbrella. Frank carried her down the stairs. There were only his slow, heavy steps going down. And not long after they had kissed good night and he had gone for a walk in the rain, Helen opened the hall door and went up.

Then Ida fell asleep.

Thereafter Helen and Frank met outside the house. . . .

One dark and windy night when Helen left the house late, Ida followed her through the cold streets and across the plaza into the interior of the deserted park, and saw her meet Frank Alpine. There, in an opening between a semicircle of tall lilac shrubs and a grove of dark maples, were a few benches, dimly lit and private, where they liked to come to be alone. Ida watched them sitting together on one of the benches, kissing. She dragged herself home and went upstairs, half-dead. Morris was asleep and she didn't want to wake him, so she sat in the kitchen, sobbing.

When Helen returned and saw her mother weeping at the kitchen table, she knew Ida knew, and Helen was both moved and frightened.

Out of pity she asked, "Mama, why are you crying?"

Ida at last raised her tear-stained face and said in despair, "Why do I cry? I cry for the world. I cry for my life that it went away wasted. I cry for you."

"What have I done?"

"You have killed me in my heart."

"I've done nothing that's wrong, nothing I'm ashamed of."

"You are not ashamed that you kissed a goy?"

Helen gasped. "Did you follow me, Mama?"

"Yes," Ida wept.

"How could you?"

"How could you kiss a goy?"

"I'm not ashamed that we kissed."

She still hoped to avoid an argument. Everything was unsettled, premature.

Ida said, "If you marry such a man your whole life will be poisoned."

"Mama, you'll have to be satisfied with what I now say. I have no plans to marry anybody."

"What kind plans you got then with a man that he kisses you alone in a place where nobody can find you in the park?"

"I've been kissed before."

"But a goy, Helen, an Italyener."

"A man, a human being like us."

"A man is not good enough. For a Jewish girl must be a Jew."

"Mama, it's very late. I don't wish to argue. Let's not wake papa."

"Frank is not for you. I don't like him. His eyes don't look at a person when he talks to them."

"His eyes are sad. He's had a hard life."

"Let him go and find someplace a shikse that he likes, not a Jewish girl."

"I have to work in the morning. I'm going to bed."

Ida quieted down. When Helen was undressing she came into her room. "Helen," she said, holding back her tears, "the only thing I want for you is the best. Don't make my mistake. Don't make worse and spoil your whole life, with a poor man that he is only a grocery clerk which we don't know about him nothing. Marry somebody who can give you a better life, a nice professional boy with a college education. Don't mix up now with a stranger. Helen, I know what I'm talking. Believe me, I know." She was crying again.

"I'll try my best," Helen said.

Ida dabbed at her eyes with a handkerchief. "Helen, darling, do me one favor."

"What is it? I am very tired."

"Please call up Nat tomorrow. Just to speak to him. Say hello, and if he asks you to go out with him, tell him yes. Give him a chance."

"I gave him one."

"Last summer you enjoyed so much with him. You went to the beach, to concerts. What happened?"

"Our tastes are different," Helen said wearily.

"In the summer you said your tastes were the same."

"I learned otherwise."

"He is a Jewish boy, Helen, a college graduate. Give him another chance."

"All right," said Helen, "now will you go to sleep?"

"Also don't go no more with Frank. Don't let him kiss you, it's not nice."

"I can't promise."

"Please, Helen."

"I said I'd call Nat. Let that be an end of it now. Good night, Mama."

"Good night," Ida said sadly.

Though her mother's suggestion depressed her, Helen called Nat from her office the next day. He was cordial, said he had bought a secondhand car from his future brother-in-law and invited her to go for a drive.

She said she would sometime.

"How about Friday night?" Nat asked.

She was seeing Frank on Friday. "Could you make it Saturday?"

"I happen to have an engagement Saturday, also Thursday—something doing at the law school."

"Then Friday is all right." She agreed reluctantly, thinking it would be best to change the date with Frank, to satisfy her mother.

When Morris came up for his nap that afternoon Ida desperately begged him to send Frank away at once.

"Leave me alone on this subject ten minutes."

"Morris," she said, "last night I went out when Helen went, and I saw she met Frank in the park, and they kissed each the other."

Morris frowned. "He kissed her?"

"Yes."

"She kissed him?"

"I saw with my eyes."

But the grocer, after thinking about it, said wearily, "So what is a kiss? A kiss is nothing."

Ida said furiously, "Are you crazy?"

"He will go away soon," he reminded her. "In the summer."

Tears sprang into her eyes. "By summer could happen here ten times a tragedy."

"What kind tragedy you expecting—murder?"

"Worse," she cried.

His heart turned cold, he lost his temper. "Leave me alone on this subject, for God's sakes."

"Wait," Ida bitterly warned.

Seymour Epstein

Seymour Epstein was born in New York in 1917 and was educated in the New York City public school system, later attending City College and New York University. He served in the U.S. Army Air Corps during World War II and worked as a factory manager in New York for ten years following the war. He taught creative writing at the New School for Social Research and began to publish short stories in the late 1950s. The author of numerous novels and short stories, Epstein has also been a professor of contemporary literature and creative writing at the University of Denver in Colorado. In addition to other literary awards he has received, Epstein's novel *Leah* won him the Edward Lewis Wallant Memorial Book Award.

Epstein's writing blends a perfectly crafted literary style with cool, honest realism and carefully developed characters. Epstein places the title character in *Leah* in the office of a business that is sliding downhill. Caught between labor and management, Leah sympathizes with the human frailties and exigencies of all parties, trying wearily to find some high ground of moral coherence to which she can cling. This confusion is echoed in Leah's personal life: her charming, dynamic father, Max, has long since abandoned her supposedly unimaginative, rigid mother, Bertha. Moreover, the men who pursue Leah each seem to reveal dismaying flaws—especially in comparison with her father.

Exhausted and nearing collapse, Leah allows Bertha to nurture her. Returning to a forgotten mode in which her mother was the dependable source of warmth and comfort, Leah gains the emotional strength to confront realities about her father—and ultimately about herself—that she had previously denied. Half-consciously, Leah had accepted Max's rejection of Bertha as a person incapable of giving and receiving love; she had applied his standards to herself as well. Leah relearns to love both Bertha and her own female self; this self-love frees Leah from Max's selfish demands and empowers her to respond to the one suitor capable of loving and nurturing her in return.

•

"Leah Rediscovers Her Mother"

(excerpt)

Leah curled in the armchair with the wobbly arm. Bertha sat in the other armchair, drawing from a heavy paper shopping bag the skein of wool she fed dextrously into the sweater-in-progress. Illumination in the room came from old-fashioned wall fixtures whose arms curved upward into electrical sockets, each of which sported an indestructible bulb of helical design. Against the pale blue, institutional wall, the light given off induced the same kind of heavy-eyed dullness which follows big meals or prolonged boredom. Leah reached up and switched on the floor lamp near her chair.

"Don't you remember?" Bertha asked, taking up the conversation begun in the kitchen, over dinner.

"How could I remember?" Leah returned. "How old was I?"

"Nine," Bertha said.

Leah was surprised. "Are you sure of that?" she asked.

"I went in the hospital the middle of October," Bertha stated with certitude, "I came out two weeks later, on a Wednesday. I remember very well. That Friday was your birthday. Nine."

Leah examined her nails, pushing at the cuticle on one finger with the nail of another. She had no recollection of the event, had always assumed it had happened on the far side of that zone where all events were either forgotten or immured like decorative scenes in a solid block of clear crystal—visible but unreachable. While she was still a child, the reply had always been the same: "*We couldn't have any more.*" Later she learned of an operation.

"I always thought I was much younger," she said.

"You were nine," Bertha repeated.

Nine. . . She could have been surrounded by brothers and sisters, lives she had conjured so often that learning of their denied birth added an obituary note to her remembered longing.

"So what stopped you?" she asked her mother.

Bertha counted her stitches, a sullen and embarrassed flush heightening her natural color. "Did you ever ask *him?*" was her retort.

"What was there to ask?"

Bertha shrugged. She said: "You always had so much to say to each other, I thought he might have told you something."

"Well, he didn't tell me *something*. You tell me."

Bertha's concentration on her knitting intensified. This conversation, begun after the meal and continued amid the splash and clatter of dishes, was not at all to Bertha's liking. True, she had started it, hoping perhaps that a word here and a grimace there would charm her meaning into full-blown existence, like a genie out of a bottle; but it hadn't, and now she was faced with the uncomfortable necessity of giving a proper name to things.

"It isn't always the wife's doing," she said cryptically.

"You mean Max didn't want any more children?" Leah asked coaxingly. She knew only too well how easily Bertha might slip into that stone fortress where she was both jailer and jailed. "Was it his decision?"

"It wasn't mine," said Bertha.

"Why?"

"Ask him."

"Ma, I'm not talking to him. I'm talking to *you*. You were just complaining that I never wanted to talk to you. Here we are talking about something that concerns the both of us, and you tell me to ask him. Why should I ask him? Why shouldn't you tell me?"

"Why shouldn't I tell you?" said Bertha. "Because it wasn't my doing. He was the one who—"

"Who what?"

"Who decided."

"All right," Leah said. "He decided. *How* did he decide? Did he discuss it with you? Did he give you any reasons?"

Bertha kept her eyes riveted to the flying needles. "Reasons!" she echoed scornfully. "Who could understand his reasons? Did he ever talk sense? Riddles! And do you think I remember after all these years?" Rapidly she twisted the skein of wool around one finger, as if to close off an artery. But the artery remained open. Blood flowed, nourishing memory. "What does it mean when a husband tells a wife that he isn't like other men? As if I didn't know! Whatever would fly into his head, that's what would come out of his mouth. . . . 'Children should come from joy. When there's no joy, there should be no children.' A liar! When a man is afraid to tell one big lie, he makes up a lot of little ones. One day it was not joy; the next it was something else."

"Like what?" Leah asked, feeling weightless and strange, as she sometimes did when smoking a cigarette on an empty stomach.

"Who knows?" said Bertha. "Words. He didn't want to be like other men. He didn't want to creep in the subway every morning with his head down, like an animal. Life! An expert on life! Life should be this, life should be that, life should be books, life should be friendship. . . . Get up a minute, I want to measure across the shoulders."

Leah got up. Bertha held the sweater against her back.

"A little more, and I can begin the sleeves," Bertha decided.

Leah returned to her chair. She looked at her mother. "And what did you say to all of that?" she asked.

"What did I say?" Bertha's habit of repeating questions was but one of the heavy, plodding mannerisms that would make a white welt of fury in Max's mouth. *("What kind of maniac are you? Can't you answer a question without repeating the question? A typical* moujik! *Feet in mud, and brains in mud!")* "I didn't say a word," Bertha replied. "Not—one—word. Why? I should have said something? I haven't got any pride?"

Leah was silent. Her thoughts skirted around the flanks of Max's decision and Bertha's pride. If the decision had been Max's then the precautions must have been his, too. Bertha would never. Not in a million years. Not on this earth. Bertha and her stone fortress. God alone knew what provisions she had stored there to sustain her all these years. Leah's curiosity was greater than her caution.

"Do you mean he used something?"

Bertha blushed agonizingly. . . . *We are mother and daughter*, Leah thought. *I am a middle-aged woman, and this stranger is my mother*. . . . "I'm surprised at you," Bertha said, stiff with admonition. "It's nothing to be discussed. What difference does it make?"

"It might have made a lot of difference." Leah spoke her thought aloud. "You didn't have so much to share. The one good thing you had was probably spoiled."

Drunken soldiery couldn't have left Bertha's holy places more ravaged. Icons were ripped from the walls, tabernacles overturned, bawdy songs sung in the choir stall. But even the horror of desecration has its limits; and beyond the limits perhaps even a sneaking contempt for mysteries so easily invaded and casually wrecked.

"Things were spoiled long before," she said.

True!

"It was never any good," Leah said.

"I know, Leah," Bertha retorted, her voice rising above mere concurrence. "From the very beginning, *he* told me it was no good; and from the moment you were old enough to listen to him, *you* told me it was no good. If people want a thing to be no good, it'll be no good. They'll see to it that it's no good."

Hopeless, hopeless, hopeless! Bertha's pathos lay in her belief that a little more good will, a little more effort, would have made it good. And her saving as well. She could never see the hopelessness, and consequently she would never believe the finality. Leah looked at her mother. A premonitory tic of compassion twitched somewhere within the settled order of old hostilities and envies.

Bertha was a beauty. Drowning in rage and frustration, Max would never deny it. They had married in this country, a pair of greenhorns, each slain by the other's attractiveness. In answer to the oft-put question of Why? they had said the same thing in different ways: Who knew?

Leah could believe it. Even to this day, Bertha retained her high, fresh color, and the long, gorgeous hair she braided and coiled on her head like a diadem. New in the country, out for a husband, shrewd enough in her way, and knowing full well how to value her gifts, she could, in the radiant ambience of youth, appear in whatever guise would ensnare her heart's desire. Yes, Max was a little funny in his ways, talked a blue streak, wrote crazy poems to her, but he was young, young—and, oh, so handsome! Besides, he had a trade. A cutter in the fur industry. Respectable. Solid. Let them but marry, and she would take care of the rest. Max's heart fell like a ripe apple, shattering and scattering its seeds on the unsuspected concrete of her nature. In six months, they both knew.

The conflict was made legend by the long retelling of simple themes. Max flirted with other women. Max swore that it was not flirtation; that it was a manner, a way of being, an attribute as natural as the color of his eyes. Bertha said no—did he think she was blind? Everybody saw. What would people think of her? Max bit his knuckle and cried out that people would think she was what she was, a stupid peasant! How could they think otherwise? Every time she exhibited her mind it was caked with mud and cow dung. . . . Patiently, in those rare moments of conciliation and hope, Max would explain: "There are many ways of life. Some people want to walk a straight line to the grave, looking neither left nor right, doing their work, eating, looking up once a year at the Thing they call God, and down at their shoes the rest of the year. When they throw dirt on the face of such a man, he can rest content that he knows what his shoes look like. Other people—yes, like me!—I'm not ashamed of it!—don't care what their shoes look like, hate the straight line, love to wander off the straight path and discover things . . ."

"I ever stopped you from taking a walk?" Bertha asked.

She wanted Max to join the local synagogue, to show some respect. Max said he sought God in his own way. Bertha said fine, good, so there's no harm in joining the temple. It's one more place to look. . . .

Life, life—life should have a savor. Life should be a prism of beautiful colors. For years Max was flung like a shuttlecock from Woodlawn to West Twenty-eighth, carrying a different-colored thread on each flight. Bertha knitted monochrome sweaters.

When Max began to write, Bertha was confirmed in her suspicion of an unbalanced mind. Would a sane man sit night after night in the kitchen, writing? Writing what! What? . . . She was fearful of the activity for a reason she couldn't explain to herself or anyone else. And she was right to be fearful. Like the fairy-tale mill that ground out salt, Max began to grind out words until the legal-size, yellow pages covered Bertha, marriage and all.

"Are you still in the same place?" Bertha asked.

"Of course," Leah replied. "Do you think I would have moved without telling you about it?"

"It's none of my business," Bertha said, "but just out of curiosity, how much rent do you pay there?"

Leah told her. Bertha reared back a little. "So much?" she exclaimed. "For one room?"

"It's not exactly one room," Leah said. "I mean, there's a kitchen, a bathroom, a foyer—"

"This I call one room," Bertha said, her tone edged with the caution and criticism which preceded all her explorations into her daughter's private life. But Leah thought she detected something else—a real purpose this time, instead of the usual straw-man query for the knockdown riposte. "I had no idea you paid such a rent," Bertha continued, shaking her head. "Can you afford it?"

Leah gave a little snort of laughter. "If I couldn't afford it, I wouldn't be there very long."

"Everybody who lives in Manhattan pays such rents?"

Leah cocked her head to one side. "Ma, what are you getting at?" she asked. "If you're trying to find out from me what Max is paying for rent, I can't tell you. I won't say I don't know, that would be a lie, but I feel that's strictly his business. Believe me, it isn't exorbitant. It's considerably less than I pay."

"Leah," said Bertha, "one thing puzzles me. After all, I'm in the world now, I meet people, talk to them—I never hear children call their parents by their first name. They say 'my mother,' 'my father,' 'Pa,' 'Ma'—different ways, but never by their first name. Is this something modern?"

"I don't call you Bertha," Leah said.

"Not to my face. I'm not speaking of me."

"Max?" Leah asked. Bertha was silent. "Why does it bother you?" Leah asked, concealing a smile.

"I'm sitting here trying to remember when it began," Bertha said. "*Who* began? Did he ask you to call him Max? Did you begin by yourself?"

"I don't remember," Leah replied, rummaging around in her mind for some clue. "It goes back—God, I don't know how long—*years*—since I was old enough to talk. It was either Max or Pa. Why do you ask?"

Bertha said: "A child calls a parent what the parent wants to be called. He must have wanted you to call him by his first name."

"And? So? Supposing he did? It's not such an uncommon practice."

"I'm just saying."

"*What* are you saying?"

"He must have had a reason," Bertha said.

Leah awoke to the astonishing possibility that Bertha (Bertha!) was leading toward a prepared point rather than coming upon it accidentally, as she usually did, in her random fashion. Incredible! Maybe this Dr. Fox was every bit the magician Bertha claimed he was.

"What do you think his reason could be?" she asked.

"I know what the reason is," Bertha retorted. "*You'll* laugh."

"You can depend on it, I won't laugh," Leah promised.

"He wanted a friend," Bertha declared. "He wanted someone who would under*stand* him. Someone to take from . . . Call me Max, not Papa, because from a Papa you expect things. Not from me. With a father, there's a mother. A mother is a wife. But I have no wife. *You* be my wife. You be my wife, and my daughter, and my friend. With *two* children, this wouldn't be so good. Yes, it's possible you can take a daughter away from mother—but suppose there's a brother? A sister? Not so good. You already have a family here. It wouldn't be so—so—"

"Exclusive," Leah supplied.

Bertha looked up from her knitting. "Yes," she said. "I see you know."

"If things were that simple," Leah said.

"What simple? You call that simple?"

"I mean," said Leah, "that people don't plan things in that way. Forty years later it looks as if they did—but they didn't."

"Don't be so sure," Bertha said.

"I'm not sure of anything," Leah said, looking away.

"I'll make some more coffee," Bertha said.

"Please don't bother," Leah said. She looked at her watch. "I'll be leaving soon."

"What's the sense?" Bertha argued, dropping her knitting paraphernalia into the bag. "You have a half a mile to walk to the subway from here. In the morning the buses run regular; you'll take a bus in the morning."

"I can't," Leah said, immediately resigned to the protocol of a well-worn routine. "I want to change my clothes, take a shower—"

"You can't take a shower here?"

"I have some things at home I'll have to bring to the office tomorrow," Leah lied, and immediately wondered why she had lied, why she didn't stay, why the prospect of sleeping in the bed she had slept in for twenty-one years filled her with such spectral horror.

"I don't see the sense in the whole thing," Bertha remarked on cue.

"In what thing?"

"Why you should be living there, paying such rent . . . Leah, I don't want to go into the past; I don't want to go into the future; right now I'm talking about. You pay a ridiculous rent for one room. I pay less for five rooms. I ask you, what's the sense?"

Leah sighed. She arose, touching her hand to her hair. "We had this argument fifteen years ago," she said.

"That was fifteen years ago," Bertha pointed out. "You had a different reason. I had a different reason. We won't go into that. Now I'm talking plain common sense. The money you could save. For that money you could buy yourself a wardrobe. You could—"

"My God!" Leah cried, in a kind of Alice-in-Wonderland amazement. She spread her arms and waved her hands to simulate the flow of beneficence. "Suddenly everybody wants to take care of me! They want me to have clothes. . . . what's the matter, do I look shabby or something?"

Bertha closed her eyes at the nonsense. She opened them. "I can't force you," she said.

"Ma, I couldn't," Leah apologized. "It's nice of you to want me, but it just wouldn't work."

"You're seeing someone?" Bertha asked.

Her conjecture sidling in through the side door that way was irresistible. Leah laughed, then said: "As a matter of fact, I am. I was introduced to a nice chap over the weekend. At Bunny's."

"You still see Bunny?"

Leah nodded.

"This girl has always been a very good friend to you," Bertha said. "What's his name?"

"Dave. Dave Kahn."

"He's nice?"

"He's nice."

"You'll see him again?"

"Yes."

"Well—I'm glad. If you would like, one evening, you haven't got anything particular to do, you can bring him to dinner."

"We'll see," said Leah.

The same drizzle which had accompanied Leah on her way to Bertha's still saturated the air. It was like walking in a warm cloud. Tomorrow, she thought, it will probably be freezing again. Snow.

She was wearing her cloth coat and a pair of plastic rain boots. Her feet felt uncomfortably warm. The street lamps revealed impacted hillocks of ice lying on the grounds of the high school, on the north side of the building, where ice would probably remain until the first extended spell of warmth. Only once, in all the years she had walked this route from home to subway, had she ever been approached. A haunted-looking young man whom she had seen before on the station platform, sometimes on the train, had followed her a distance, catching up with a few running steps, the words beginning to tumble from his lips, his own terror an emetic, and the messy eruption the result of whatever poison of loneliness or fear was rotting his guts.

". . . *I-know-you'll-think-this-is-funny-my-coming-up-to-you-this-way-talking-to-you-but-sometimes-you-see-a-person-for-a-long-time-and-you-know-if-you-could-just-get-to-speak* . . ."

She walking faster and faster (there was no one else in sight), running at last, and he not even attempting to keep up with her, but standing in one place, babbling, his voice receding until she reached the corner, where she turned, taking one last frightened look to see him standing in deep blue twilight, like one of those stark figures seen in the mural paintings of depression artists. And that was how he remained in her memory, a figure congealed out of the sulphurous fog of the war years, jabbering the perfect soliloquy of solitude.

Call me Max—

Truly she couldn't recall that he had ever asked to be called by his first name. But she knew that a child will experiment with a parent's name, delighting in the contrast of so small a sound against so large an identity; and if the experiment provokes reciprocal delight, then what greater delight but to repeat it again and again, until the name has absorbed all the color and complexity to make it fit.

You be my wife, and my daughter, and my friend—

Nothing is simple. One could as soon draw a line in the ocean as assign a sure motive. What Max did he did because he was Max. Bertha had her fortress. And she had her thirteen-, or fourteen-, or fifteen-year-old troubles. She was no beauty. Whatever she did have was a long time in ripening, while the Thelma Kirsches and Shirley Samuels welled like water in the arid climate of adolescence.

Birds of a feather . . .

Vivian Carter, the English girl, was another such bony mutt. They did their homework together, at Vivian's house. The tricky hypotenuse and Abbe Sieyes. Oh, the Necco wafers! And the peanut brittle! And the evenings when she had come home to find Max sitting on a bench near the apartment house, waiting.

"A fight?"

"*Come*," he said. *"We'll walk. We'll have an ice cream soda."*

They walked to the candy store and had ice cream sodas. Syrup-sweet smell of the candy store; and then out into the park where spring was distilling another sweetness from the earth and trees. Max talked.

Did she think for one minute that he didn't know what she was feeling, what was going on in her mind? He knew. Any human being who survives the anguish of being young deserves only the best that life can offer. The best? Love. Love and respect. He would shock her. Yes. Perhaps this was not what a father should tell his daughter, but life was not that long nor conventions that binding that a person need submit indefinitely to unhappiness.

He wanted her to grow, upstairs, in the head; the rest would take care of itself. He would have her understand why mankind guards and cherishes its few sacred flames. What have all the thousands of years left us? Some stones, some colors, some words, some music. Naturally, a young person thinks that other things are more important—and for a time they are—he wouldn't deny this—but if he gave her nothing else, he would give her this, and she should bear it well in mind: keep a place apart for Leah and for value. He knew what was coming for her. He could already feel the pressure in her, this terrible pressure to give everything away, this ruinous extravagance of youth. Don't. That was his advice. Give other things. He would not counsel her to be indiscreet—that, too, had its penalties—but when she had learned discretion, then he would say to be careful not to fling everything after her heart and her body. Keep value apart, and a little corner that is Leah and no one else. And when she did admit someone to these sacred precincts, she must be very, very careful how he uses it. If he tramples on it with big muddy feet, and laughs, and shrugs his shoulders, and says he's got something better, then cast him out. Cast him out and shut the door! He hasn't got anything better. *This* he would implore her not to be fooled about. But if she did admit someone, and he treated what he found with at least consideration, if not understanding, then here was the possibility of love. . . .

The long walks and the long talks. The syrup-sweet smell of candy stores and street lamps wreathed in young spring leaves. Max gave her this while Bertha sat in her fortress.

Leah entered the dark, sepulchral arcade which housed the staircase leading to the elevated, and as she did so it came to her, mildly, like the turning up of a light, that this evening, Bertha Rubel, in her own way and for the first time in her life, had made a competitive bid for the one child she and her incomprehensible husband had so unequally shared. . . .

Things end, and the people who are involved with one in that ending lose the continuity of their lives. Leah took with her into the subway that evening a vision of Tom Williams propped against the shipping room table—distant, ominous, taciturn. Harry was already assuming the posture of prosperous despair.

She would see them both again, doubtlessly many times, but they were no longer connected to the as yet unlived time which made their futures contingent on her own. They had slipped into the past, and it was there that they added a dragging weight of regret. For good or ill, their presences had measured off a portion of her life, and it was this portion-made-past that added to the oppression of the crowded subway car, the shocks of the day, and the irritating sense of something forgotten.

Besides all of which, Leah was getting one of her ice-tong headaches, the kind that hooked one pincer into the right side of her neck and the other into her right temple. By the time she arrived home, it would be dug inches deep and contemptuous of aspirin. . . . And what was it she'd forgotten? . . . She couldn't remember, and she couldn't care less at this point. Whatever it was, it couldn't relieve her present discomfort, and that's all that counted. . . . Dear God, only Penn Station! Half a continent of weariness to go! And if that animal at her back didn't get his great wad of a stomach away, she would turn around and sear the flesh from his fat, stupid face with a blow-torch of a scream. . . . *No! . . . Oh, dear God! . . . Bertha*!

The fuse of forgetfulness had burned down and exploded as the doors of the subway rattled open at Times Square. Leah pushed her way out, and then cursed herself for an idiot as she stood on the platform. Why on earth had she gotten off the train? She should have stayed on, gone home, called Bertha, explained the situation, gone to bed. She could still do that, of course, but the reflex act of getting off the train, while being a hideous mistake, was also the first nudge toward undertaking the long, exhausting trek to the Bronx. Leah remained rooted to the spot, hoping in a dim way that some mute emissary of kindness would come along and pick her up, ailing cat that she was, and carry her to a warm, soft, dark corner where she would sleep for years.

Sighing, she turned and began to walk toward the steps that would take her to the shuttle, that would take her to the East Side train, that would take her to Bertha. She recalled Bertha's unprecedented wail of sorrow, and the only impossibility that remained was *not* going.

"You're late."

"I got hung up at the office."

"I hope the dinner isn't spoiled."

Leah closed her eyes. "Ma, I'm afraid—"

"You aren't hungry?"

"I've got a splitting headache. I really don't know if I can. . . . What did you prepare?"

"I made the rolled cabbage," Bertha said. "I prepared it last night."

Bertha's supreme dish was rolled cabbage. Her own preparation composed of ground meat, rice, raisins, spices. Leah, an indifferent eater, had always praised Bertha's rolled cabbage—and that she had prepared it tonight was a votive offering to so many things that even with her brutalized head and recoiling stomach, Leah didn't have the heart to refuse.

"I'll try," she said.

"I don't want you to force yourself to eat if you don't feel like it," Bertha said. "Your body knows what it needs and what it doesn't need."

Curled up in the armchair, Leah looked across at her mother in surprise. This liberality was again something new. Bertha had always taken the uncompromising view that a meal prepared was a meal to be eaten. Leah could remember the occasion when Max arose from his chair in the living room, strode into the kitchen, and smashed a plate of food against the wall. The gravy splattered against the whiteness and dotted here and there with clinging bits of potatoes and meat looked like a collage of his fury. (*"All right! Are you satisfied now? Are you convinced I don't feel like eating?"*) Bertha had badgered him for an hour, reminding him that the food was on the table, that it was getting ice cold, that it was a sin to throw out good food. . . .

"I think it would be best if I waited," Leah said. "I really don't think I could eat right now."

"Then don't," said Bertha. "I'll put it in the refrigerator. It'll keep."

"Thank you," Leah said, relieved.

"From what have you got a headache?" Bertha asked.

"I don't know. . . . I had a rotten day. My boss is going out of business. I'll have to look for a new job." She spoke with her eyes closed.

"Tension," Bertha pronounced.

Leah opened her eyes. The ice tongs bit deeper, twisted malevolently. Buds of nausea opened in her stomach.

"What?" she asked.

"Probably from tension," Bertha repeated. "How come he's losing his business? I thought you had such a secure job there."

"I thought so, too. Things happen."

"So how are you going to live? I mean, without an income—"

"I don't think I'll have any trouble finding another job," Leah said.

"Of course not," Bertha quickly affirmed. "But it takes a little time. Weeks, maybe. I was thinking, maybe, in the meantime, you might want to give up your apartment."

Leah cupped one hand around the back of her neck. She massaged. With the tips of her fingers she pressed against the quarter-sized torture terminal. She could well imagine what she looked like. Her headache face drained away to the color of Roquefort. Bertha looked like health incarnate. A Rubens woman. Hefty, high color, and hair braided with feminine craft.

"Are you very lonely by yourself?" Leah asked her mother. The question was a crowbar pried between the base blocks of Bertha's fortress. In all the years of siege, Bertha had always considered herself self-sufficient; but now that the aggressor was no longer at the gate she knew that it was not her own perseverance that had made her situation bearable, but the beloved presence of the aggressor himself.

"Lonely?" she repeated, Bertha-fashion. "I have plenty to do during the day. It's only when I come home in the evening, I get—confused. It's a funny thing—cooking, for example—would you believe it, I can't cook for one. I'm so used to using so many eggs, so much flour, butter—you know? Everything comes out wrong. . . . Leah, I want him to come home."

"He won't, Ma," Leah said. "He won't. I can't make him. You can't make him."

"How do you know? He told you so?"

"Yes."

Bertha sat beautifully straight on the sofa, her hands in her lap. She looked more proud and lovely than Leah had ever seen her. Her eyes glittered with tears that willingly confessed her heartbreak, although they were not yet, and probably never would be, tears that confessed her understanding.

"What did I do to him that was so terrible?" she asked.

"Whatever you did to him, it can't be undone," Leah said, seizing this afflicted moment to make plain what had to be made plain, what she had hoped time and not words would make plain. She said: "Ma, he's better off, and you're better off like this."

Slowly Bertha shook her head. "No," she declared serenely, "he's not better off."

For all the world, a Victorian heroine prepared to wait until delusion had played its part, and the errant lover would finally realize his mistake. Bertha believed this. Leah could see that she did. Not in those terms, perhaps, but in the invincible certainty that Max was wallowing in the degradation of unwashed socks bilious with a diet of cafeteria food, shamefaced in a society which abjured his illicit bachelorhood. As surely as Max had never ascribed a penny's worth of value to Bertha's proprieties, so surely did Bertha cling to them as the final arbiters of happiness.

Max (Bertha had decided) could never be happy separated from the decencies as she defined them. That Max had never been happy *with* them was his pose, a peculiarity this man had affected for forty years and still had not overcome. And if this blindness was no more than a simple refusal to see, then Bertha's tragedy would be no greater than the range of her vision; but socks and meals and conjugality were the artifacts she had fashioned out of her love. She loved Max fully, but in her fashion, and it was her fashion that had finished Max. And now here was Bertha with her heart as heavy as a melon, and with no Max to love. The pity and hopelessness of it made Leah groan.

"Your head hurts so bad?" Bertha asked.

"It's making me sick," Leah said, taking refuge in her head.

"Will you let me help you?" Bertha said.

"Help me? How?"

"How? That's what I do all day; I help people with backaches, with headaches. . . . You and your father never believed in it, but I wish you could hear what people say to Dr. Fox, even to me. . . . I won't give you a real adjustment, but you'll see if I don't help you. Come—harm it can't do, and it might help."

"But what are you going to do?"

"A little manipulation, a little massage—you'll see."

"Here?" Leah asked.

"Wait," said Bertha, getting up.

She disappeared into her bedroom and returned in a few seconds wheeling before her the kind of contraption used in hospitals to take patients to surgery.

"Where on earth did you get that?" Leah asked, astonished.

"Where? I had it for almost a year already."

"You bought it?"

"Doctor Fox had an extra one, an old one. He didn't need it, so he let me have it."

"But what do you use it for?"

Bertha spread a snowy sheet over the leather padding. "Occasionally," she said, "I do a little work here."

"In the house?"

"In the evening, sometimes. Weekends."

"Isn't there some law against using residential apartments for business?" Leah asked.

"Who has to know?" said Bertha. "Why, do you think I can live on what your father gives me?"

"How much *does* he give you?"

"I'm lucky if it pays the rent. What he gives me! . . . The whole thing is so ridiculous—I'm paying rent; you're paying rent; he's paying rent. . . . Leah, come here . . ."

"Ma, what are you going to do?" Leah demanded suspiciously. She didn't trust this business. A doctor friend had once warned her against the bone-setters. No particular harm, he had said, but if you've really got something wrong they can make it worse.

"What are you afraid of, I'm going to hurt you? Just a little massage. Take off your things."

The queer look of the contraption in the living room, the shroud-like, asceptic sheet—in a bizarre way it was very fascinating, very inviting. With her head being hammered to bits, she was ready to submit to voodoo, cupping, or euthanasia.

"Everything?" Leah asked.

"Everything if you'll be more comfortable. Just the top will be enough."

Leah stripped completely. Bertha went to the linen closet and got another sheet, which she silently handed to Leah.

"What's this for?" Leah asked.

"To wrap around."

Leah couldn't be sure that Bertha had actually avoided looking at her, but certainly she hadn't taken the occasion to have a good look at what had become of the body she had borne. Unquestionably she looked at other women's bodies all day, so it was unlikely that a puritan modesty had made her turn away. No, not modesty. And how long was it since Bertha had last seen her daughter's body? Fifteen years? Twenty? Leah couldn't remember. She guessed that it was what had happened in all those years that Bertha did not want to look upon; the unimaginable rites that had been performed on her daughter's body, none of which had resulted in marriage, and therefore shameful as much for its failure as for its immorality.

"On the table," Bertha directed. "On your stomach. Make yourself comfortable. I'll get the mineral oil."

Bertha was gone for another few seconds, returning with a bottle of mineral oil and a small hand towel for herself. She pulled the sheet away from the upper half of Leah's body. "So," she said, arranging Leah's arms, head. "I want you to relax," Bertha ordered in a firm, professional voice. "Completely. I can see you're all tensed up." Bertha put her hand on Leah's neck, a firm, practiced hand, on the very spot that was scooping up pain by the bucketful. "All tensed up," Bertha murmured, like a diagnostician looking at X rays. "I want you to sink in, let yourself fall in—sink here—" touching Leah in the small of the back—"and here—now here—here—close your eyes like you're going to sleep—that's right, now you're relaxing a little." Admonitory click of the tongue. "Such tension . . . all right . . ."

Bertha poured mineral oil into the palms of her hands; she began below the rib casing on Leah's right side. Her touch was gentle yet firm. She soothed the flesh while miraculously finding the hidden network of nerves and muscles connected to the central source of that punishing pain. She traced its course along the spine, to the base of the neck, laterally over to that pulsating node of misery, behind the ear, down again, gently, gently—

until Leah felt herself go all goose-pimply with a thrill of utter submission. To be so completely and skillfully discovered caught her up and sent her rolling weightlessly in a long sea-well of deliciousness.

And where had Bertha learned this? How had Bertha accumulated all this knowledge in her hands? Leah could remember the time, some years ago, when Bertha had suffered an excruciating sacro attack, and a friend had urged her to go to "Dr." Fox, the healer, the magical layer-on of hands. Dr. Fox (Leah had seen his picture on a little monograph which bore the title "What Doctors Won't Tell You"), who wore a spotless white jacket, who had a forearm like a caveman's club, and who preached a new gospel with the simple-minded fervor of a monomaniac. If ever there was a born disciple for a Dr. Fox, it was Bertha Rubel. And Dr. Fox must have sensed the true calling in Bertha. He needed an assistant; so many patients and more coming all the time; he offered to teach her, gave her books . . .

"Ma, that feels wonderful!" Leah moaned sinkingly. "Does it really do any good?"

"Don't you feel better?"

"Oh—yes! . . . Is—is what you're doing chiropracty?"

"—tic," Bertha corrected.

"—tic," Leah said, smiling. "What does it mean?" (Her words rolled like glass beads on brown velvet.) "Something about bones?"

"From the Greek," Bertha explained promptly. "It means to do by hand—a hand doing. All I'm doing is just massage; no manipulation at all. For a real adjustment, you have to catch the vertebra."

Leah almost giggled. . . . *Vertebra* . . . *Adjustment* . . . Who would ever think to hear such words from Bertha!

"Tell me about it," Leah encouraged, finding a kind of narcotic bliss even in the sound of Bertha's voice.

"It's very simple," Bertha said. "In chiropractic, we depend on the intelligence of the spinal column—" (Leah's mouth, eyes, her very blood expanded in amazement.) "We" (We!) "look to the nervous system for the cause of all disease. You see, diseases and inflammations come about because something interrupts the parts of the body. By manipulating we correct the interruption. A vertebral subluxation—"

"A wha-a-a-t?" Leah yelped.

"A subluxation—"

Pink doves fluttering from Bertha's mouth couldn't have been more unbelievable! That marvelous, improbable word spoken by Bertha Rubel in all seriousness was the down-hill-rolling object that began the snowball of Leah's laughter. It started slowly, as all good, devastating snowballs will, and then began to gather momentum. It caught up things nearest at hand; this crazy table; Bertha's subluxation (soob-looks-ay-shun, it sounded like); Bertha handing her a sheet and averting her eyes . . . and as her laughter grew larger, became more encompassing, it caught up more and more of recent days, of people, of events, until everything took on a cartoon-like comicality as it all went end-over-ending in the giant accumulation, arms and expressions and objects splayed out in the mad, rushing, comic reel.

Self-perpetuating, it whipped itself on. Leah imagined herself walking into this room and witnessing this scene, and this added fresh impetus to her laughter. She thought of Harry Bloch and his petulant disappointment that the cozy little affair he had so vividly foreseen and was ready to pay for with fine restaurants, orchestra seats, and assurances of lifelong security was just not going to materialize, and this suddenly seemed as tragical as a two-year-old wetting his pants. She saw Max brooding down on "Alhambra" New York from the tower of the meat-king's widow, and she could hear Donald Duck quacking in the background. She had a vision of two mice running around, chasing their tails, and even this (with a spasm of loathing) became very funny. She thought of Dave Kahn scouring ladies' magazines to find not naked women, but tearful wretches lifting their faces to be kicked or spat upon or God-knows-what. She thought of Ed Bernstein with his chick-fuzz hair and grubby fingers holding a fat, phallic cigar, and she writhed on the table. She thought of Irving sawing away at his fiddle, playing beautiful Beethoven and apostrophizing about novelists who should solve the problems they pose. . . . If only—if only she could somehow get *herself* in the scene, be rolling right in there with the rest of them, so that she could from this moment on see the wholeness of the joke and spend the rest of her life laughing. . . .

"Subluxation?" Bertha queried. "Is that what you're laughing at?"

Leah contracted into a fist of soundless, painful hysteria. "I . . . oh . . . you . . . oh . . . !"

It subsided at last, and Leah lay gasping, blanking out her mind whenever some new turn of ludicrousness threatened. "I wasn't laughing at you," she said weakly. "It was that word. . . . I don't know . . . it just struck me . . ."

"How does your head feel?" Bertha asked.

"Better," Leah replied. "Oh, so much better! But you must be tired. That's enough."

"You don't want any more?"

"You must be tired," Leah said again, making the point, because, truthfully, she did want more. It felt so rapturously healing when Bertha plied her expert thumb in that bruised corner of her neck. And when Bertha assured her that she was not tired, that this was nothing compared to some of the massages she gave, Leah gave in and allowed herself to be rocked toward a downy, gray peace.

"That's enough," she said at last, and gathered the sheet round her body and wondered what in the world would happen now. Was she expected to get dressed? Eat a hearty meal? Go home?

"Now," said Bertha, settling the matter, "I'm going to fill a hot sitz bath" (laughter jiggled; Leah bit her lip) "and I want you to soak in it for a good half-hour. Then, if you feel like it, you'll have a bite to eat. Then you'll go right to sleep."

"Here?" Leah asked.

"Where then? You'll go out after a hot bath? Of course you'll sleep here. I'll give you a nightgown, and you'll sleep in your own bed."

The logic and inevitability were so overwhelming that Leah didn't even make a token protest. Something in her still deplored the idea, but the alternative was so much more deplorable that she could offer a sound argument to the vintage fear within her. She wasn't "coming home"; she was merely acting rationally in a situation that called for rational action.

So Leah took her sitz bath, which Bertha made scaldingly hot and laced with Epsom salts. After the bath it was decided that something light to eat was in order. The rolled cabbage was out of the question. A couple of poached eggs on toast and a cup of tea. Leah agreed. First-rate. Light and nourishing. And, as she discovered while eating, delicious. After, Leah went to her old room, in which there had been some rearrangement, but which was essentially as she had left it about a decade and a half ago. Her high school diploma, books (she spied on one of the shelves the ancient, Morocco-bound Shakespeare with the brown silk ribbon), the hook-on lamp on the headboard of the bed, the round, mahogany night table with the tiny drawers and ballet legs.

She was wearing one of Bertha's pink nightgowns. At the door of the room, Leah turned and looked at Bertha, who was flushed and a trifle moist from all the exertions and preparations. It was impossible to know what she was feeling, so well did she disguise it behind the fuss and practicality. "I'll rinse out your stockings," she said to Leah. "By morning they'll be dry. If you want, you can take my . . . I don't know if they'll fit . . ."

Leah leaned across and kissed Bertha on the cheek. "Thank you, dear," she said. "You've been very, very sweet to me tonight."

Bertha gave out a pantomime of deprecation involving head, shoulders, eyes, lips. Wonderful, she seemed to say. What's wonderful? A massage? Eggs? She nodded, turned away. "I'll rinse your stockings," she repeated in her confusion. "Tomorrow they'll be dry."

Incredible that after all these years her body should recognize in the matrix of this bed a configuration it had known before. Tired as she was, Leah had feared that the effects of her old bed, this room, the possibility of queer evocations might result in a sleepless night. But she had no sooner touched her head to the pillow than she knew she was safe. Sleep crowded into her skull instantly, filling it so thoroughly that no sudden gust of thought or treachery of nerves could contend with it.

She had it so securely, Leah thought, that she could risk toying with the few minutes of consciousness left to her. Hazily she tried to recall what her life had been like, what state of being prevailed for her when she had last retired to this bed. She could remember that it was a time of crisis. She had made known her intention to move, to be on her own, weeks before, and accusations of depravity and betrayal emanated from Bertha's fortress in silent waves. But this was not what Leah sought. Instead, she would have liked, before sleep swirled in, to catch a glimpse of some lost brightness, to catch the flavor or some lost desolation that had been her companion on one of those many kaleidoscopic journeys before sleep.

She could remember incidents, but they were flat and stillborn, recording only time and place. But what of all those turbid, troubled nightsongs of longing? What of the scent of privet flowers? What of the green, dusty taste of privet leaves crushed between her teeth on summer nights when her heart ballooned and threatened to burst and scatter her lovesick, life-sweet fragments along the dark stones of the reservoir? What of the taste of harsh, sour wine . . . ?

Who had said that? A boy. Tall. Quoting Baudelaire. Tall and morose and as sick as she with the malaise of being young. Yes. But what was his name? She could see his face, but the face had no name. That was lost. Utterly.

They had walked around the reservoir, conversation draining from the sores of their adolescent sickness, thinking themselves bright, entertaining, entertained, while beneath the talk they languished and died. . . . Then? . . . Then he had walked with her into the hall of the apartment house, and there, in that dank, furtive recess beneath the staircase he had closed his eyes and had fallen toward her like someone toppling from a cliff, bruising her lips with his blind hunger for pressure, pressing and pressing his swollen, suffering manhood against her until his breathing became a thick, ecstatic cry—and then he had fled.

And she had climbed the steps to the apartment, entering the darkened rooms, making straight for the kitchen, sitting down in the darkness and pressing her burning face to the cool enamel of the kitchen table, and heard Max shuffle through the rooms, into the foyer, at the doorway of the kitchen, and then the light. . . . Drunk and dizzy with her own drugged blood, she had looked up at him, and could see that he saw, could see on his creased, knowing face the half-sick longing for privet sweetness. . . .

Oh, Max, it was gone for you then, and it's gone for me now, the time of privet sweetness. Only days and days. How have you endured all the dead days? Soon you will be dead, and then I will be dead, and all that we knew of privet sweetness will be lowered into earth on clever, canvas straps. Nothing . . . nothing . . .

A bubble of terror rose in Leah's mind. Quickly she punctured it . . . let sleep swirl in. . . .

. . . *This*, then, was the place; *this* was the time—walking on a dark, chilly side street toward the house of the unknown woman her father intended to marry because she would pay for the publication of his book, and give him a fairyland view of the city at night, and probably tell him what she had told him ever since she was old enough to understand how badly he needed the words: *"Max, you are wonderful! Max, you are gifted! Max, I will help you!"*

And where was Leah? No promontory, the dream finished, and the rest of her life to weep in.

Liar! Thief! You have stolen years from me! Where shall I go now? What shall I do? Falsifier! You told me there were values! You old job lot! You merchant!

"Why are you doing it, Max?" she asked.

"Heh?" he said, lowering his head into the wind.

"Why do you want to marry Irma Singer?"

"Oh, that again?"

"This time I want an answer."

Max raised his head and looked sideways at her, compelled by her voice. "Why does a man—even an old one—marry a woman?"

"Because he loves her."

"Then you have your answer."

"And do you love Irma Singer?"

"Please, Leah—"

"All you have to do is say yes."

He wagged his head in mock indignation, hoping this police interrogation would soon reveal itself for a jest.

"And if I won't say?" he asked.

"Then you won't marry her," said Leah.

"Who will forbid it?"

"I will."

"Leah—what is the matter with you?"

"I am the one to persuade Bertha," she said. "And if I persuade her, I shall have to make it up to her for the rest of her life. I'm entitled to an answer."

Max stopped in his tracks. They were at the corner of Columbus Avenue. He squinted through wind-teared eyes at his daughter. Fear was in his eyes. Leah knew what it was that he feared. He was no less a victim of his thievery and falsification than she. He was an old man now. He did not have her strength. Perhaps she could endure the cruelty of confession; he could not. He had always depended on her for a wise and gentle mendacity. She was tearing at a terrible responsibility like a heedless child. She must be careful.

"Why do you want to hurt me?" he pleaded. "Why do you choose such a time! *Dushenka*, why don't you wait? Why don't you wait until you meet Irma? You will see. She is a fine woman, clever, a sense of humor—"

"Don't bribe me!" Leah shouted at her father. "I have a mother!"

Her words were overheard by a passing man, an intern, young, his coat collar turned up, his white, neck-high hospital jacket showing through the V of his coat. Leah could read in his wise, city-bred eyes the annotation of a scene he would later describe to his wife, sweetheart, friends; one of those comic reckonings played out on the city streets; an old duffer who no longer had his young love to keep him warm. . . .

For an instant Leah saw Max stripped of the mantle of seriousness that had always protected him, and her heart almost died. No, whatever he had done, whatever he planned to do, he had always exalted her above all women. He had always loved her. That had been honest. His *dushenka*. His soul. He must never know contempt from her.

Leah wept hot tears into her gloved hands. She moved away from the open corner into the concealment of a building. Max followed her. He put his arms around her, rocking her, murmuring, "What is it that you want me to say? I like Irma. She likes me. Listen, sweet girl, it is possible to live with someone you like, much more possible than to live with someone you have ceased to love. I have thought so many things. I say let us help ourselves in the ways that we can. Love? *You* I love. Haven't I always?" . . . and Max went on, crooningly, until Leah could control herself with a quavering intake of breath.

And Max was right. There was no accountability. Only life—and one must grope toward that through whatever passages remain.

"All right," she said, taking his arm and continuing on toward Central Park West. "Everything will be fine."

Grace Paley

Grace Paley, born in the Bronx in 1922, grew up in a socialist, politically vibrant environment with parents who had been exiled from their native countries for political activities. Her father, a physician, artist, and talented storyteller, was a strong figure in her development. Paley began her career as a poet, studying with W. H. Auden and others at the New School for Social Research, Hunter College, and New York University. However, her literary output was small during most of her first marriage, which lasted from 1942 to 1962; for the bulk of that marriage, she was absorbed in the responsibilities of motherhood, along with some work as a typist. At the end of the 1950s, she launched into a second phase of life, in which her energies were devoted to political activism and to writing. She began to publish distinctive pieces of short fiction both in magazines and in collections, which gained a loyal, initially small but steadily growing following among both critics and discriminating readers. Paley has received several literary grants and fellowships; many consider her to be one of the country's most skilled living short-story writers. She has taught at Columbia and Syracuse universities and various writers' workshops. Currently, she teaches at Sarah Lawrence College.

Paley's short stories are distinguished by their unique style: the action, delineated in a deliberately understated, often ironic tone, is studded with brief internal monologues and memory flashbacks that have the verbal connective tissue stripped away. The result is an elliptical, economical syntax that demands a level of reader involvement more typical of poetry. Her people and their surroundings are definitively urban; their spoken dialogue is absolutely in character, sometimes hesitant, sometimes staccato, sometimes irrepressibly loquacious, feisty, and searching. The flavor of her fiction, even when it deals with heartbreaking themes, is good-natured and resilient without ever being sullied by false sentiment. It is a combination her admirers find irresistible and her detractors sometimes find cryptic and confusing.

Faith Darwin Asbury is the quintessential Paley protagonist. A woman drawn in lust and camaraderie to men and in intense friendships to women, Faith often wavers between the loyalties she feels she owes to other women and the delights she finds in the arms of her favorite lovers. In the two stories reprinted here, Faith wrestles with her political, intellectual, and affectional selves, with personal freedom and familial love and responsibility.

•

"Dreamers in a Dead Language"

The old are modest, said Philip. They tend not to outlive one another.

That's witty, said Faith, but the more you think about it, the less it means.

Philip went to another table where he repeated it at once. Faith thought a certain amount of intransigence was nice in almost any lover. She said, Oh well, O.K. . . .

Now, why at that lively time of life, which is so full of standing up and lying down, *why* were they thinking and speaking sentences about the old.

Because Faith's father, one of the resident poets of the Children of Judea, Home for the Golden Ages, Coney Island Branch, had written still another song. This amazed nearly everyone in the Green Coq, that self-mocking tavern full of artists, entrepreneurs, and working women. In those years, much like these, amazing poems and grizzly tales were coming from the third grade, from the first grade in fact, where the children of many of the drinkers and talkers were learning creativity. But the old! This is very interesting, said some. This is too much, said others. The entrepreneurs said, Not at all—watch it—it's a trend.

Jack, Faith's oldest friend, never far but usually distant, said, I know what Philip means. He means the old are modest. They tend not to outlive each other by too much. Right, Phil?

Well, said Philip, you're right, but the mystery's gone.

In Faith's kitchen, later that night, Philip read the poem aloud. His voice had a timbre which reminded her of evening, maybe nighttime. She had often thought of the way wide air lives and moves in a man's chest. Then it's strummed into shape by the short-stringed voice box to become a wonderful secondary sexual characteristic.

Your voice reminds me of evening too, said Philip.

This is the poem he read:

> *There is no rest for me since love departed*
> *no sleep since I reached the bottom of the sea*
> *and the end of this woman, my wife.*
> *My lungs are full of water. I cannot breathe.*
> *Still I long to go sailing in spring among realities.*
> *There is a young girl who waits in a special time and place*
> *to love me, to be my friend and lie beside me all through the night.*

Who's the girl? Philip asked.

Why, my mother of course.

You're sweet, Faith.

Of course it's my mother, Phil. My mother, young.

I think it's a different girl entirely.

No, said Faith. It has to be my mother.

But Faith, it doesn't matter who it is. What an old man writes poems about doesn't really matter.

Well, goodbye, said Faith. I've known you one day too long already.

O.K. Change of subject, smile, he said. I really am *crazy* about old people. Always have been. When Anita and I broke up, it was those great Sundays playing chess with her dad that I missed most. They don't talk to me, you know. People take everything personally. I don't, he said. Listen, I'd love to meet your daddy *and* your mom. Maybe I'll go with you tomorrow.

We don't say mom, we don't say daddy. We say mama and papa, when in a hurry we say pa and ma.

I do too, said Philip. I just forgot myself. How about I go with you tomorrow. Damn it, I don't sleep. I'll be up all night. I can't stop cooking. My head. It's like a percolator. Pop! pop! Maybe it's my age, prime of life, you know. Didn't I hear that the father of your children, if you don't mind my mentioning it, is doing a middleman dance around your papa?

How about a nice cup of Sleepytime tea?

Come on Faith, I asked you something.

Yes.

Well, I could do better than he ever dreams of doing. I know—on good terms—more people. Who's that jerk know? Four old maids in advertising, three Seventh Avenue models, two fairies in TV, one literary dyke . . .

Philip . . .

I'm telling you something. My best friend is Ezra Kalmback. He made a fortune in the great American Craft and Hobby business—he can teach a four-year-old kid how to make an ancient Greek artifact. He's got a system and the equipment. That's how he supports his other side, the ethnic, you know. They publish these poor old dreamers in one dead language—or another. Hey! How's that! A title for your papa. "Dreamer in a Dead Language." Give me a pen. I got to write it down. O.K. Faith, I give you that title free of charge, even if you decide to leave me out.

Leave you out of what? she asked. Stop walking up and down. This room is too small. You'll wake the kids up. Phil, why does your voice get so squeaky when you talk business? It goes higher and higher. Right now you're above high C.

He had been thinking printing costs and percentage. He couldn't drop his answer more than half an octave. That's because I was once a pure-thinking English major—but alas, I was forced by bad management, the thoughtless begetting of children, and the vengeance of alimony into low practicality.

Faith bowed her head. She hated the idea of giving up the longed-for night in which sleep, sex, and affection would take their happy turns. What will I do, she thought. How can you talk like that to me Philip? Vengeance . . . you really stink Phil. Me. Anita's old friend. Are you dumb? She didn't want to hit him. Instead her eyes filled with tears.

What'd I do now? he asked. Oh, I know what I did. I know exactly.

What poet did you think was so great when you were pure?

Milton, he said. He was surprised. He hadn't known till asked that he was lonesome for all that Latin moralizing. You know, Faith, Milton was of the party of the devil, he said. I don't think I am. Maybe it's because I have to make a living.

I like two poems, said Faith, and except for my father's stuff, that's all I like. This was not necessarily true, but she was still thinking with her strict offended face. I like, *Hail to thee blithe spirit bird thou never wert,* and I like, *Oh what can ail thee knight at arms alone and palely loitering*. And that's all.

Now listen Philip, if you ever see my folks, if I ever bring you out there, don't mention Anita Franklin—my parents were crazy about her, they thought she'd be a Ph.D. medical doctor. Don't let on you were the guy who dumped her. In fact, she said sadly, don't even tell me about it again.

Faith's father had been waiting at the gate for about half an hour. He wasn't bored. He had been discussing the slogan "Black Is Beautiful" with Chuck Johnson, the gatekeeper. Who thought it up, Chuck?

I couldn't tell you, Mr. Darwin. It just settled on the street one day, there it was.

It's brilliant, said Mr. Darwin. If we could've thought that one up, it would've saved a lot of noses, believe me. You know what I'm talking about?

Then he smiled. Faithy! Richard! Anthony! You said you'd come and you came. Oh oh, I'm not sarcastic—it's only a fact. I'm happy. Chuck, you remember my youngest girl? Faithy, this is Chuck in charge of coming and going. Richard! Anthony! say hello to Chuck. Faithy, look at me, he said.

What a place! said Richard.

A castle! said Tonto.

You are nice to see your grandpa, said Chuck. I bet he been nice to you in his day.

Don't mention day. By me it's morning. Right Faith? I'm first starting out.

Starting out where? asked Faith. She was sorry so much would have to happen before the true and friendly visit.

To tell you the truth, I was talking to Ricardo the other day.

That's what I thought, what kind of junk did he fill you up with?

Faith, in the first place don't talk about their father in front of the boys. Do me the favor. It's a rotten game. Second, probably you and Ricardo got the wrong chemistry.

Chemistry? The famous scientist. Is that his idea? How's his chemistry with you? Huh?

Well, he talks.

Is Daddy here? asked Richard.

Who cares? said Tonto, looking at his mother's face. We don't care much, do we Faith?

No no, said Faith. Daddy isn't here. He just spoke to Grandpa, remember I told you about Grandpa writing that poetry. Well, Daddy likes it.

That's a little better, Mr. Darwin said.

I wish you luck Pa, but you ought to talk to a few other people. I could ask someone else—Ricardo is a smart operator, I know. What's he planning for you?

Well Faithy, two possibilities. The first a little volume, put out in beautiful vellum, maybe something like vellum, you know, *Poems from the Golden Age* . . . You like that?

Ugh! said Faith.

Is this a hospital? asked Richard.

The other thing is like this. Faithy, I got dozens of songs, you want to call them songs. You could call them songs or poems, whatever, I don't know. Well, he had a good idea, to put out a book also with some other people here—a series—if not a book. Keller for instance is no slouch when it comes to poetry, but he's more like an epic poet, you know . . . When Israel was a youth, then I loved . . . it's a first line, it goes on a hundred pages at least. Madame Nazdarova, our editor from *A Bessere Zeit*—did you meet her?—she listens like a disease. She's a natural editor. It goes in her ear one day. In a week you see it without complications, no mistakes, on paper.

You're some guy, Pa, said Faith. Worry and tenderness brought her brows together.

Don't wrinkle up so much, he said.

Oh shit! said Faith.

Is this a hospital? asked Richard.

They were walking toward a wall of wheelchairs that rested in the autumn sun. Off to the right under a great-leaf linden a gathering of furious arguers were leaning—every one of them—on aluminum walkers.

Like a design, said Mr. Darwin. A beautiful sight.

Well, is this a hospital? Richard asked.

It looks like a hospital, I bet, sonny. Is that it?

A little bit, Grandpa.

A lot, be honest. Honesty, my grandson, is one of the best policies.

Richard laughed. Only one, huh Grandpa.

See, Faithy, he gets the joke. Oh, you darling kid. What a sense of humor! Mr. Darwin whistled for the joy of a grandson with a sense of humor. Listen to him laugh, he said to a lady volunteer who had come to read very loud to the deaf.

I have a sense of humor too Grandpa, said Tonto.

Sure sonny, why not. Your mother was a constant entertainment to us. She could take jokes right out of the air for your grandma and me and your aunt and uncle. She had us in stitches, your mother.

She mostly laughs for company now, said Tonto, like if Philip comes.

Oh, he's so melodramatic, said Faith, pulling Tonto's ear. What a lie . . .

We got to fix that up, Anthony. Your mama's a beautiful girl. She should be happy. Let's think up a good joke to tell her. He thought for about twelve seconds. Well, O.K. I got it. Listen:

There's an old Jew. He's in Germany. It's maybe '39, '40. He comes around to the tourist office. He looks at the globe. They got a globe there. He says, Listen, I got to get out of here. Where you suggest, Herr Agent, I should go? The agency man also looks at the globe. The Jewish man says, Hey, how about here? He points to America. Oh, says the agency man, sorry, no, they got finished up with their quota. Ts, says the Jewish man, so how about here? He points to France. Last train left already for there, too bad, too bad. Nu, then to Russia? Sorry, absolutely nobody they let in there at the present time. A few more places . . . the answer is always, port is closed. They got already too many, we got no boats . . . So finally the poor Jew, he's thinking he can't go anywhere on the globe, also he also can't stay where he is, he says oi, he says ach! he pushes the globe away, disgusted. But he got hope. He says, So this one is used up, Herr Agent. Listen—you got another one?

Oh, said Faith, what a terrible thing. What's funny about that? I hate that joke.

I get it, I get it, said Richard. Another globe. There is no other globe. Only one globe, Mommy? He had no place to go. On account of that old Hitler. Grandpa, tell it to me again. So I can tell my class.

I don't think it's so funny either, said Tonto.

Pa, is Hegel-Shtein with Mama? I don't know if I can take her today. She's too much.

Faith, who knows? You're not the only one. Who can stand her? One person, your mama, the saint, that's who. I'll tell you what—let the boys come with me. I'll give them a quick rundown on the place. You go upstairs. I'll show them wonderful sights.

Well, O.K. . . . will you go with Grandpa, boys?

Sure, said Tonto. Where'll you be?

With Grandma.

If I need to see you about anything, said Richard, could I?

Sure, sonny boys, said Mr. Darwin. Any time you need your mama say the word, one, two, three, you got her. O.K.? Faith, the elevator is over there by that entrance.

Christ, I know where the elevator is.

Once, not paying attention, rising in the gloom of her troubles, the elevator door had opened and she'd seen it—the sixth-floor ward.

Sure—the incurables, her father had said. Then to comfort her: Would you believe it, Faithy? Just like the world, the injustice. Even here, some of us start on the top. The rest of us got to work our way up.

Ha ha, said Faith.

It's only true, he said.

He explained that incurable did not mean near death necessarily, it meant, in most cases, just too far from living. There were, in fact, thirty-year-old people in the ward, with healthy hearts and satisfactory lungs. But they lay flat or curved by pain, or they were tied with shawls into wheel-chairs. Here and there an old or middle-aged parent came every day to change the sheets or sing nursery rhymes to her broken child.

The third floor, however, had some of the characteristics of a hotel—that is, there were corridors, rugs, and doors, and Faith's mother's door was, as always, wide open. Near the window, using up light and the curly shadow of hanging plants, Mrs. Hegel-Shtein was wide awake, all smiles and speedy looks, knitting needles and elbows jabbing the air. Faith kissed her cheek for the awful sake of her mother's kindness. Then she sat beside her mother to talk and be friends.

Naturally, the very first thing her mother said was: The boys? She looked as though she'd cry.

No no, Ma, I brought them, they're with Pa a little.

I was afraid for a minute . . . This gives us a chance . . . So, Faithy, tell me the truth. How is it? A little better? The job helps?

The job . . . ugh. I'm buying a new typewriter, Ma. I want to work at home. It's a big investment, you know, like going into business.

Faith! Her mother turned to her. Why should you go into business? You could be a social worker for the city. You're very good-hearted, you always worried about the next fellow. You should be a teacher, you could be off in the summer. You could get a counselor job, the children would go to camp.

Oh, Ma . . . oh, damn it! . . . said Faith. She looked at Mrs. Hegel-Shtein, who, for a solid minute, had not been listening because she was counting stitches.

What could I do, Faithy? You said eleven o'clock.

Now it's one. Am I right?

I guess so, said Faith. There was no way to talk. She bent her head down to her mother's shoulder. She was much taller and it was hard to do. Though awkward, it was necessary. Her mother took her hand—pressed it to her cheek. Then she said, Ach! what I know about this hand . . . the way it used to eat applesauce, it didn't think a spoon was necessary. A very backward hand.

Oh boy, cute, said Mrs. Hegel-Shtein.

Mrs. Darwin turned the hand over, patted it, then dropped it. My goodness! Faithy. Faithy, how come you have a boil on the wrist. Don't you wash?

Ma, of course I wash. I don't know. Maybe it's from worry, anyway it's not a boil.

Please don't tell me worry. You went to college. Keep your hands clean. You took biology. I remember. So wash.

Ma. For godsakes. I know when to wash.

Mrs. Hegel-Shtein dropped her knitting. Mrs. Darwin, I don't like to interfere, only it so happens your little kiddie is right. Boils on the wrist is the least from worry. It's a scientific fact. Worries what start long ago don't come to a end. You didn't realize. Only go in and out, in and out the heart a couple hundred times something like gas. I can see you don't believe me. Stubborn Celia Darwin. Sickness comes from trouble. Cysts, I got all over inside me since the Depression. Where the doctor could put a hand, Cyst! he hollered. Gallbladder I have since Archie married a fool. Slow blood, I got that when Mr. Shtein died. Varicose veins, with *hemorrhoids* and a crooked neck, I got when Mr. Shtein got social security and retired. For him that time nervousness from the future come to an end. For me it first began. You know what is responsibility? To keep a sick old man alive. Everything like the last supper before they put the man in the electric chair. Turkey. Pot roast. Stuffed kishkas, kugels all kinds, soups without an end. Oi, Faithy, from this I got arthritis and rheumatism from top to bottom. Boils on the wrist is only the beginning.

What you mean is, Faith said, what you mean is—life has made you sick.

If that's what I mean, that's what I mean.

Now, said Mr. Darwin, who was on his way to the roof garden with the boys. He had passed the room, stopped to listen; he had a comment to make. He repeated: Now! then continued, That's what I got against modern times. It so happens you're in the swim, Mrs. H. Psychosomatic is everything nowadays. You don't have a cold that you say, I caught it on the job from Mr. Hirsh. No siree, you got your cold nowadays from your wife, whose health is perfect, she just doesn't think you're so handsome. It might turn out that to her you were always a mutt. Usually then you get hay fever for life. Every August is the anniversary of don't remind me.

All right, said Mrs. Darwin, the whole conversation is too much. My own health doesn't take every lopsided idea you got in your head, Sid. Meanwhile, wash up a little bit extra anyway, Faith, all right? A favor.

O.K. Ma, O.K., said Faith.

What about me? said Mr. Darwin, when will I talk to my girl? Faithy, come take a little walk.

I hardly sat down with Mama yet.

Go with him, her mother said. He can't sit. Mr. Pins and Needles. Tell her, Sid, she has to be more sensible. She's a mother. She doesn't have the choice.

Please don't tell me what to tell her, Celia. Faithy, come. Boys, stay here, talk to your grandma. Talk to her friend.

Why not, boys. Mrs. Hegel-Shtein smiled and invited them. Look it in the face: old age! Here it comes, ready or not. The boys looked, then moved close together, their elbows touching.

Faith tried to turn back to the children, but her father held her hand hard. Faithy, pay no attention. Let Mama take care. She'll make it a joke. She has presents for them. Come! We'll find a nice tree next to a bench. One thing this place got is trees and benches. Also, every bench is not just a bench—it's a dedicated bench. It has a name.

From the side garden door he showed her. That bench there, my favorite, is named Jerome (Jerry) Katzoff, six years old. It's a terrible thing to die young. Still, it saves a lot of time. Get it? That wonderful circular bench there all around that elm tree (it should live to be old) is a famous bench named Sidney Hillman. So you see we got benches. What we do *not* have here, what I am suffering from daily, is not enough first-class books. Plenty of best sellers, but first-class literature? . . . I bet you're surprised. I wrote the manager a letter. "Dear Goldstein," I said. "Dear Goldstein, Are we or are we not the People of the Book? I admit by law we're a little non sectarian, but by and large we are here living mostly People of the Book. Book means mostly to you Bible, Talmud, etc., probably. To me, and to my generation, idealists all, book means BOOKS. Get me? Goldstein, how about putting a little from Jewish Philanthropies into keeping up the reputation for another fifty years. You could do it single-handed, adding very little to the budget. Wake up, brother, while I still got my wits."

That reminds me, another thing, Faithy. I have to tell you a fact. People's brains, I notice, are disappearing all around me. Every day.

Sit down a minute. It's pressing on me. Last one to go is Eliezer Heligman. One day I'm pointing out to him how the seeds, the regular germinating seeds of Stalinist anti-Semitism, existed not only in clockwork, Russian pogrom mentality, but also in the everyday attitude of even Mensheviks to Zionism. He gives me a big fight, very serious, profound, fundamental. If I weren't so sure I was right, I would have thought I was wrong. A couple of days later I pass him, under this tree resting on this exact bench. I sit down also. He's with Mrs. Grund, a lady well known to be in her second, maybe third, childhood at least.

She's crying. Crying. I don't interfere. Heligman is saying, Madame Grund, you're crying. Why?

My mother died, she says.

Ts, he says.

Died. Died. I was four years old and my mother died.

Ts, he says.

Then my father got me a stepmother.

Oi, says Heligman. It's hard to live with a stepmother. It's terrible. Four years old to lose a mother.

I can't stand it, she says. All day. No one to talk to. She don't care for me, that stepmother. She got her own girl. A girl like me needs a mother.

Oi, says Heligman, a mother, a mother. A girl surely needs a mother.

But not me, I ain't got one. A stepmother I got, no mother.

Oi, says Heligman.

Where will I get a mother from? Never.

Ach, says Heligman. Don't worry, Madame Grund darling, don't worry. Time passes. You'll be healthy, you'll grow up, you'll see. Soon you'll get married, you'll have children, you'll be happy.

Heligman, oi, Heligman, I say, what the hell are you talking about?

Oh, how do you do, he says to me, a passing total stranger. Madame Grund here, he says, is alone in the world, a girl four years old, she lost her mother. (Tears are in his disappearing face.) But I told her she wouldn't cry forever, she'll get married, she'll have children, her time will come, her time will come.

How do you do yourself, Heligman, I say. In fact, goodbye, my dear friend, my best enemy, Heligman, forever goodbye.

Oh Pa! Pa! Faith jumped up. I can't stand your being here.

Really? Who says *I* can stand it?

Then silence.

He picked up a leaf. Here you got it. Gate to Heaven. Ailanthus. They walked in a wide circle in the little garden. They came to another bench: Dedicated to Theodor Herzl Who Saw the Light if Not the Land / In Memory of Mr. and Mrs. Johannes Mayer 1958. They sat close to one another.

Faith put her hand on her father's knee. Papa darling, she said.

Mr. Darwin felt the freedom of committed love. I have to tell the truth. Faith, it's like this. It wasn't on the phone. Ricardo came to visit us. I didn't want to talk in front of the boys. Me and your mother. She was in a state of shock from looking at him. She sent us out for coffee. I never realized he was such an interesting young man.

He's not so young, said Faith. She moved away from her father—but not more than half an inch.

To me he is, said Mr. Darwin. Young. Young is just not old. What's to argue. What you know, *you* know. What I know, *I* know.

Huh! said Faith. Listen, did you know he hasn't come to see the kids. Also, he owes me a chunk of dough.

Aha, money! Maybe he's ashamed. He doesn't have money. He's a man. He's probably ashamed. Ach, Faith, I'm sorry I told you anything. On the subject of Ricardo, you're demented.

Demented? Boy oh boy, I'm demented. That's nice. You have a kind word from Ricardo and I'm demented.

Calm down, Faithy, please. Can't you lead a more peaceful life? Maybe you call some of this business down on yourself. That's a terrible neighborhood. I wish you'd move.

Move? Where? With what? What are you talking about?

Let's not start that again. I have more to say. Serious things, my dear girl, compared to which Ricardo is a triviality. I have made a certain decision. Your mother isn't in agreement with me. The fact is, I don't want to be in this place anymore. I made up my mind. Your mother likes it. She thinks she's in a nice quiet kibbutz, only luckily Jordan is not on one side and Egypt is not on the other. She sits. She knits. She reads to the blind. She gives a course in what you call needlepoint. She organized the women. They have a history club, Don't Forget the Past. That's the real name, if you can believe it.

Pa, what are you leading up to?

Leading. I'm leading up to the facts of the case. What you said is right. This: I don't want to be here, I told you already. If I don't want to be here, I have to go away. If I go away, I leave Mama. If I leave Mama, well, that's terrible. But, Faith, I can't live here anymore. Impossible. It's not my life. I don't feel old. I never did. I was only sorry for your mother—we were close companions. She wasn't so well, to bother with the housework like she used to. Her operation changed her . . . well, you weren't in on that trouble. You were already leading your private life . . . well, to her it's like the Grand Hotel here, only full of *landsmen*. She doesn't see Hegel Shtein, a bitter, sour lady. She sees a colorful matriarch, full of life. She doesn't see the Bissel twins, eighty-four years old, tragic, childish, stinking from urine. She sees wonderful! A whole lifetime together, brothers! She doesn't see, ach! Faithy, she plain doesn't see!

So?

So Ricardo himself remarked the other day, You certainly haven't the appearance of an old man, in and out, up and down the hill, full of ideas.

It's true. . . . Trotsky pointed out, the biggest surprise that comes to a man is old age. O.K. That's what I mean, I don't feel it. Surprise. Isn't that interesting that he had so much to say on every subject. Years ago I didn't have the right appreciation of him. Thrown out the front door of history, sneaks in the window to sit in the living room, excuse me, I mean I do not feel old. DO NOT. In any respect. You understand me, Faith?

Faith hoped he didn't really mean what she understood him to mean.

Oh yeah, she said. I guess. You feel active and healthy. That's what you mean?

Much more, much more. He sighed. How can I explain it to you, my dear girl. Well, this way. I have certainly got to get away from here. This is the end. This is the last station. Right?

Well, right . . .

The last. If it were possible, the way I feel suddenly toward life, I would divorce your mother.

Pa! . . . Faith said. Pa, now you're teasing me.

You, the last person to tease, a person who suffered so much from changes. No. I would divorce your mother. That would be honest.

Oh, Pa, you wouldn't really, though. I mean you wouldn't.

I wouldn't leave her in the lurch, of course, but the main reason—I won't, he said. Faith, you know why I won't. You must've forgot. Because we were never married.

Never married?

Never married. I think if you live together so many years it's almost equally legal as if the rabbi himself lassoed you together with June roses.

Still, the problem is thorny like the rose itself. If you never got married, how can you get divorced?

Pa, I've got to get this straight. You are planning to leave Mama.

No, no, no. I plan to go away from here. If she comes, good, although life will be different. If she doesn't, then it must be goodbye.

Never married, Faith repeated to herself. Oh . . . well, how come?

Don't forget, Faithy, we were a different cut from you. We were idealists.

Oh, *you* were idealists . . . Faith said. She stood up, walking around the bench that honored Theodore Herzl. Mr. Darwin watched her. Then she sat down again and filled his innocent ear with the real and ordinary world.

Well, Pa, you know I have three lovers right this minute. I don't know which one I'll choose to finally marry.

What? Faith . . .

Well, Pa, I'm just like you, an idealist. The whole world is getting more idealistic all the time. It's so idealistic. People want only the best, only perfection.

You're making fun.

Fun? What fun? Why did Ricardo get out? It's clear: an idealist. For him somewhere, something perfect existed. So I say, That's right. Me too. Me too. Somewhere for me perfection is flowering. Which of my three lovers do you think I ought to settle for, a high-class idealist like me. *I* don't know.

Faith. Three men, you sleep with three men. I don't believe this.

Sure. In only one week. How about that?

Faithy. Faith. How could you do a thing like that? My God, how? Don't tell your mother. I will never tell her. Never.

Why, what's so terrible, Pa? Just what?

Tell me. He spoke quietly. What for? Why you do such things for them? You have no money, this is it. Yes, he said to himself, the girl has no money.

What are you talking about?

. . . Money.

Oh sure, they pay me all right. How'd you guess? They pay me with a couple of hours of their valuable time. They tell me their troubles and why they're divorced and separated, and they let me make dinner once in a while. They play ball with the boys in Central Park on Sundays. Oh sure, Pa, I'm paid up to here.

It's not that I have no money, he insisted. You have only to ask me. Faith, every year you are more mixed up than before. What did your mother and me do? We only tried our best.

It sure looks like your best was lousy, said Faith. I want to get the boys. I want to get out of here. I want to get away now.

Distracted, and feeling pains in her jaws, in her right side, in the small infection on her wrist, she ran through the Admitting Parlor, past the library, which was dark, and the busy arts-and-crafts studio. Without a glance, she rushed by magnificent, purple-haired, black-lace-shawled Madame Elena Nazdarova, who sat at the door of the Periodical Department editing the prize-winning institutional journal *A Bessere Zeit*. Madame Nazdarova saw Mr. Darwin, breathless, chasing Faith, and called, Ai, Darwin . . . no love poems this month? How can I go to press?

Don't joke me, don't joke me, Mr. Darwin said, hurrying to catch Faith. Faith, he cried, you go too fast.

So. Oh boy! Faith said, stopping short on the first-floor landing to face him. You're a young man, I thought. You and Ricardo ought to get a nice East Side pad with a separate entrance so you can entertain separate girls.

Don't judge the world by yourself. Ricardo had his trouble with you. I'm beginning to see the light. Once before I suggested psychiatric help. Charlie is someone with important contacts in the medical profession.

Don't mention Charlie to me. Just don't. I want to get the boys. I want to go now. I want to get out of here.

Don't tell your mother is why I run after you like a fool on the stairs. She had a sister who was also a bum. She'll look at you and she'll know. She'll know.

Don't follow me, Faith yelled.

Lower your voice, Mr. Darwin said between his teeth. Have pride, do you hear me?

Go away, Faith whispered, obedient and frantic.

Don't tell your mother.

Shut up! Faith whispered.

The boys are down playing Ping-Pong with Mrs. Reis. She kindly invited them. Faith, what is it? you look black, her mother said.

Breathless, Mr. Darwin gasped, Crazy, crazy like Sylvia, your crazy sister.

Oh her. Mrs. Darwin laughed, but took Faith's hand and pressed it to her cheek. What's the trouble, Faith? Oh yes, you are something like Sylvie. A temper. Oh, she had life to her. My poor Syl, she had zest. She died in front of the television set. She didn't miss a trick.

Oh, Ma, who cares what happened to Sylvie?

What exactly is the matter with you?

A cheerful man's face appeared high in the doorway. Is this the Darwin residence?

Philip leaned into the small room. His face was shy and determined, which made him look as though he might leave at any moment. I'm a friend of Faith's, he said. My name is Mazzano. I really came to talk to Mr. Darwin about his work. There are lots of possibilities.

You heard something about me? Mr. Darwin asked. From who?

Faithy, get out the nice china, her mother said.

What? asked Faith.

What do you mean what? What, she repeated, the girl says what.

I'm getting out of here, Faith said. I'm going to get the boys and I'm getting out.

Let her go, Mr. Darwin said.

Philip suddenly noticed her. What shall I do? he asked. What do you want me to do?

Talk to him, I don't care. That's what you want to do. Talk. Right? She thought, This is probably a comedy, this crummy afternoon. Why?

Philip said, Mr. Darwin, your songs are beautiful.

Goodbye, said Faith.

Hey, wait a minute, Faith. Please.

No, she said.

On the beach, the old Brighton Beach of her childhood, she showed the boys the secret hideout under the boardwalk, where she had saved the scavenged soda-pop bottles. Were they three cents or a nickel? I can't remember, she said. This was my territory. I had to fight for it. But a boy named Eddie helped me.

Mommy, why do they live there? Do they have to? Can't they get a real apartment? How come?

I think it's a nice place, said Tonto.

Oh shut up, you jerk, said Richard.

Hey boys, look at the ocean. You know you had a great-grandfather who lived way up north on the Baltic Sea, and you know what, he used to skate, for miles and miles and miles along the shore, with a frozen herring in his pocket.

Tonto couldn't believe such a fact. He fell over backwards into the sand. A frozen herring! He must've been a crazy nut.

Really Ma? said Richard. Did you know him? he asked.

No, Richie, I didn't. They say he tried to come. There was no boat. It was too late. That's why I never laugh at that story Grandpa tells.

Why does Grandpa laugh?

Oh Richie, stop for godsakes.

Tonto, having hit the sand hard, couldn't bear to get up. He had begun to build a castle. Faith sat beside him on the cool sand. Richard walked down to the foamy edge of the water to look past the small harbor waves, far out, as far as the sky. Then he came back. His little mouth was tight and his eyes worried. Mom, you have to get them out of there.

It's your mother and father. It's your responsibility. Come on, Richard, they like it. Why is everything my responsibility, every goddamn thing?

It just is, said Richard. Faith looked up and down the beach. She wanted to scream, Help!

Had she been born ten, fifteen years later, she might have done so, screamed and screamed.

Instead, tears made their usual protective lenses for the safe observation of misery.

So bury me, she said, lying flat as a corpse under the October sun.

Tonto immediately began piling sand around her ankles. Stop that! Richard screamed. Just stop that, you stupid jerk. Mom, I was only joking.

Faith sat up. Goddamn it, Richard, what's the matter with you? Everything's such a big deal. I was only joking too. I mean, bury me only up to here, like this, under my arms, you know, so I can give you a good whack every now and then when you're too fresh.

Oh, Ma . . . said Richard, his heart eased in one long sigh. He dropped to his knees beside Tonto, and giving her lots of room for wiggling and whacking, the two boys began to cover most of her with sand.

Vivian Gornick

Like the other authors in this chapter, Vivian Gornick was raised as a New Yorker, born in 1935 into the urban Jewish socialist milieu prevalent at the time, receiving her B.A. degree from City College of New York and her M.A. from New York University. She taught English at several colleges in New York but really emerged into the public eye through her work as a staff writer for the *Village Voice* and through her ground-breaking books on feminist social commentary, beginning with *Women in Sexist Society: Studies in Power and Powerlessness* (edited with Barbara Moran) in 1972. Through both extensive political activity and her writing, Gornick is widely regarded as one of the guiding spirits of the contemporary feminist movement. Within these books, her occasional critiques of traditional Jewish attitudes toward women have been scathingly negative and arguably polemical.

Gornick's one memoir/novel, *Fierce Attachments*, represents a departure both in subject matter and in style from her discursive works. In it, a middle-aged protagonist and her aging mother confront the past: both remember the years when the daughter grew up in a Bronx apartment building, oppressed first by her mother's excessive romanticization of the married state and later by her mother's pathologically prolonged widow's grieving. Locked in seemingly unbreakable bonds of love and resentment, mother and daughter struggle to forgive each other and to come to terms with their own personal failures and mistakes as well.

•

"The Burning Bond" (excerpt)

My relationship with my mother is not good, and as our lives accumulate it often seems to worsen. We are locked into a narrow channel of acquaintance, intense and binding. For years at a time there is an exhaustion, a kind of softening, between us. Then the rage comes up again, hot and clear, erotic in its power to compel attention. These days it is bad between us. My mother's way of "dealing" with the bad times is to accuse me loudly and publicly of the truth. Whenever she sees me she says, "You hate me. I know you hate me." I'll be visiting her and she'll say to anyone who happens to be in the room—a neighbor, a friend, my brother, one of my nieces—"She hates me. What she has against me I don't know, but she hates me." She is equally capable of stopping a stranger on the street when we're out walking and saying, "This is my daughter. She hates me." Then she'll turn to me and plead, "What did I do to you, you should hate me so?" I never answer. I know she's burning and I'm glad to let her burn. Why not? I'm burning, too.

But we walk the streets of New York together endlessly. We both live in lower Manhattan now, our apartments a mile apart, and we visit best by walking. My mother is an urban peasant and I am my mother's daughter. The city is our natural element. We each have daily adventures with bus drivers, bag ladies, ticket takers, and street crazies. Walking brings out the best in us. I am forty-five now and my mother is seventy-seven. Her body is strong and healthy. She traverses the island easily with me. We don't love each other on these walks, often we are raging at each other, but we walk anyway.

Our best times together are when we speak of the past.

I'll say to her, "Mom, remember Mrs. Kornfeld? Tell me that story again," and she'll delight in telling me the story again. (It is only the present she hates; as soon as the present becomes the past, she immediately begins loving it.) Each time she tells the story it is both the same and different because each time I'm older, and it occurs to me to ask a question I didn't ask the last time around.

The first time my mother told me that her uncle Sol had tried to sleep with her I was twenty-two and I listened silently: rapt and terrified. The background I knew by heart. She was the youngest of eighteen children, eight of whom survived into adult life. (Imagine. My grandmother was pregnant for twenty years.) When the family came to New York from Russia, Sol, my grandmother's youngest brother and the same age as her own oldest child (her mother had also been pregnant for twenty years), came along with them.

My mother's two oldest brothers had preceded the family by some years, had gone to work in the rag trade, and had rented a cold-water flat on the Lower East Side for all eleven of them: bathroom in the hall, coal stove in the kitchen, a train of dark cubbyhole inner rooms. My mother, then a ten-year-old child, slept on two chairs in the kitchen, because my grandmother took in a boarder.

Sol had been drafted into the army during the First World War and sent to Europe. When he returned to New York my mother was sixteen years old and the only child left at home. So here he comes, a glamorous stranger, the baby niece he left behind now womanly and dark-eyed, with glossy brown hair cut in a stylish bob and a transforming smile, all of which she pretends she doesn't know how to use (that was always my mother's style: outrageous coquettishness unhampered by the slightest degree of self-consciousness), and he begins sleeping in one of those cubbyholes two walls away from her, with the parents snoring loudly at the farthest end of the apartment.

"One night," my mother said, "I jumped up from sleep, I don't know why, and I see Sol is standing over me. I started to say, 'What is it?' I thought something was wrong with my parents, but then he looked so funny I thought maybe he was sleepwalking. He didn't say a word to me. He picked me up in his arms and he carried me to his bed. He laid us both down on the bed, and he held me in his arms, and he began to stroke my body. Then he lifted my nightgown and he began to stroke my thigh. Suddenly he pushed me away from him and said, 'Go back to your bed.' I got up and went back to my bed. He never spoke one word about what happened that night, and I didn't either."

The second time I heard the story I was thirty. She repeated it nearly word for word as we were walking up Lexington Avenue somewhere in the Sixties. When she came to the end I said to her, "And you didn't say anything to him, throughout the whole time?" She shook her head no. "How come, Ma?" I asked. Her eyes widened, her mouth pursed. "I don't know," she puzzled. "I only know I was very scared." I looked at her, as she would say, funny. "Whatsamatter?" she said. "You don't like my answer?" "No," I protested, "it's not that. It just seems odd not to have uttered a sound, not to have indicated your fears at all."

The third time she told the story I was nearly forty. We were walking up Eighth Avenue, and as we neared Forty-second Street I said to her, "Ma, did it ever occur to you to ask yourself why you remained silent when Sol made his move?" She looked quickly at me. But this time she was wise to me. "What are you getting at?" she asked angrily. "Are you trying to say I liked it? Is that what you're getting at?" I laughed nervously, gleefully. "No, Ma, I'm not saying that. I'm just saying it's odd that you didn't make a sound." Again, she repeated that she had been very frightened. "Come off it," I said sharply. "You are disgusting!" she raged at me in the middle of the street. "My brilliant daughter. I should send you to college for another two degrees you're so brilliant. I wanted my uncle to rape me, is that it? A new thought!" We didn't speak for a month after that walk. . . .

It's a cloudy afternoon in April, warm and gray, the air sweet with new spring. The kind of weather that induces nameless stirrings in unidentifiable parts. As it happens, it is also the anniversary of the Warsaw Ghetto uprising. My mother wants to attend the annual memorial meeting at Hunter College. She has asked me to come with her. I've refused, but I've agreed to walk her up Lexington Avenue to the school. Now, as we walk, she recounts an adventure she had yesterday on the street.

"I was standing on the avenue," she tells me, "waiting for the light to change, and a little girl, maybe seven years old, was standing next to me. All of a sudden, before the light changed, she stepped out into the street. I pulled her back onto the sidewalk and I said to her, 'Darling, never never cross on the red. Cross only on the green.' The kid looks at me with real pity in her face and she says, 'Lady, you've got it all upside down.'"

"That kid's not gonna make it to eight," I say.

"Just what I was thinking." My mother laughs.

We're on Lexington in the lower Forties. It's a Sunday. The street is deserted, its shops and restaurants closed, very few people out walking.

"I must have a cup of coffee," my mother announces.

My mother's wishes are simple but they are not negotiable. She experiences them as necessities. Right now she must have a cup of coffee. There will be no sidetracking of this desire she calls a need until the cup of steaming liquid is in her hand being raised to her lips.

"Let's walk over to Third Avenue," I say. "There should be something open there." We cross the street and head east.

"I was talking to Bella this morning," my mother says on the other side of the avenue, shaking her head from side to side. "People are so cruel! I don't understand it. She has a son, a doctor, you should pardon me, he is so mean to her. I just don't understand. What would it hurt him, he'd invite his mother out for a Sunday to the country?"

"The country? I thought Bella's son works in Manhattan."

"He lives in Long Island."

"Is that the country?"

"It isn't West End Avenue!"

"Okay, okay, so what did he do now?"

"It isn't what he did now, it's what he does always. She was talking to her grandchild this morning and the kid told her they had a lot of people over yesterday afternoon, what a nice time they all had eating on the porch. You can imagine how Bella felt. She hasn't been invited there in months. Neither the son nor his wife have any feeling for her."

"Ma, how that son managed to survive having Bella for a mother, much less made it through medical school, is something for Ripley, and you know it."

"She's his mother."

"Oh, God."

"Don't 'oh, God' me. That's right. She's his mother. Plain and simple. She went without so that he could have."

"Have what? Her madness? Her anxiety?"

"Have life. Plain and simple. She gave him his life."

"That was all a long time ago, Ma. He can't remember that far back."

"It's uncivilized he shouldn't remember!"

"Be that as it may. It cannot make him want to ask her to sit down with his friends on a lovely Saturday afternoon in early spring."

"He should do it whether he wants to or not. Don't look at me like that. I know what I'm talking about."

We find a coffee shop on Third Avenue, an upwardly mobile greasy spoon, all plastic wood, vinyl leather, tin-plated chandeliers with candle-shaped bulbs burning in the pretentiously darkened afternoon.

"All right?" my mother says brightly to me.

If I said, "Ma, this place is awful," she'd say, "My fancy daughter. I was raised in a cold-water flat with the toilet in the hall but this isn't good enough for you. So okay, you pick the place," and we'd go trudging on up Third Avenue. But I nod yes, sit down with her in a booth by the window, and prepare to drink a cup of dreadful coffee while we go on with our weighty conversation about children and parents.

"Hot," my mother says to the heavy-lidded, black-haired waiter approaching our table very slowly. "I want my coffee hot."

He stares at her with so little expression on his face that each of us is sure he has not understood. Then he turns toward me only his eyebrows inquiring. My mother puts her hand on his arm and cocking her head to one side smiles extravagantly at him. "Where are you from?" she asks.

"Ma," I say.

Holding the waiter fast between her fingers, she repeats, "Where?"

The waiter smiles. "Greek," he says to her. "I Greek."

"Greek," she says, as though assessing the value of the nationality he has offered her. "Good. I like Greeks. Remember. Hot. I want my coffee hot." He bursts out laughing. She's right. She knows what she's talking about. It's I who am confused in the world, not she.

Business over, she settles back into the argument. "It's no use. Say what you will, children don't love their parents as they did when I was young."

"Ma, do you really believe that?"

"I certainly do! My mother died in my sister's arms, with all her children around her. How will I die, will you please tell me? They probably won't find me for a week. Days pass. I don't hear from you. Your brother I see three times a year. The neighbors? Who? Who's there to check on me? Manhattan is not the Bronx, you know."

"Exactly. That's what this is all about. Manhattan is not the Bronx. Your mother didn't die in her daughter's arms because your sister loved her more than we love you. Your sister hated your mother, and you know it. She was there because it was her duty to be there, and because she lived around the corner all her married life. It had nothing to do with love. It wasn't a better life, it was an immigrant life, a working-class life, a life from another century."

"Call it what you want," she replies angrily, "it was a more human way to live."

We are silent. The waiter comes with the coffee. She has the cup in her hands before he has fully turned away.

She sips, looks scornfully after his retreating back. "You think it's hot?" she says. "It's not hot."

"Call him back."

She pushes the air away with her hand. "Forget it. I'll drink it as it is, the devil won't take me." Clearly the conversation is depressing her.

"Well, all I can say is, if he wasn't her son Bella would never lay eyes on him again."

"That makes two of them, doesn't it? He certainly wouldn't lay eyes on her again if she wasn't his mother, would he?"

My mother gazes steadily at me across the table. "So what are you saying, my brilliant daughter?"

"I'm saying that nowadays love has to be earned. Even by mothers and sons."

Her mouth falls open and her eyes deepen with pity. What I have just said is so retarded she may not recover the power of speech. Then, shaking her head back and forth, she says, "I'll tell you like the kid told me, 'Lady, you've got the whole thing upside down.'"

At this moment the waiter passes by carrying a pot of steaming coffee. My mother's hand shoots out, nearly unbalancing him. "Is that hot?" she demands. "This wasn't hot." He shrugs, stops, pours coffee into her cup. She drinks greedily and nods grudgingly. "It's hot." Satisfaction at last.

"Let's go," she says, standing up, "it's getting late."

We retrace our steps and continue on up Lexington Avenue. The air is sweeter than before, warmer, fuller, with a hint of rain now at its bright gray edge. Delicious! A surge of expectation rises without warning in me but, as usual, does not get very far. Instead of coming up straight and clear it twists about, turns inward, and quickly stifles itself to death; a progress with which I am depressingly familiar. I glance sideways at my mother. I must be imagining this, but it seems to me her face reflects the same crazy journey of detoured emotion. There is color in her cheek, but her eye is startled and her mouth pulled downward. What, I wonder, does she see when she looks at me? The mood of the day begins to shift dangerously.

We're in the Fifties. Huge plate-glass windows filled with color and design line the avenue. What a relief it's Sunday, the stores are closed, no decisions to make. We share an appreciation of clothes, my mother and I, of looking nice in clothes, but we cannot bear to shop, either of us. We're always wearing the same few articles of clothing we have each picked hastily from the nearest rack. When we stand as we do now, before a store window, forced to realize there are women who dress with deliberation, we are aware of mutual disability, and we become what we often are: two women of remarkably similar inhibitions bonded together by virtue of having lived within each other's orbit nearly all their lives. In such moments the fact that we are mother and daughter strikes an alien note. I know it is precisely because we *are* mother and daughter that our responses are mirror images, yet the word filial does not seem appropriate. On the contrary, the idea of family, of our being family, of family *life* seems altogether puzzling: an uncertainty in her as well as in myself. We are so used to thinking of ourselves as a pair of women, ill-starred and incompetent (she widowed, me divorced), endlessly unable to get family life for themselves. Yet, as we stand before the store window, "family life" seems as much a piece of untested fantasy in her as it is in me. The clothes in the window make me feel we have both been confused the whole of our lives about who we are, and how to get there.

Suddenly, I am miserable. Acutely miserable. A surge of defeat passes through me. I feel desolated, without direction or focus, all my daily struggles small and disoriented. I become speechless. Not merely silent, but speechless. My mother sees that my spirits have plunged. She says nothing. We walk on, neither of us speaking.

We arrive at Sixty-ninth Street, turn the corner, and walk toward the entrance to the Hunter auditorium. The doors are open. Inside, two or three hundred Jews sit listening to the testimonials that commemorate their unspeakable history. These testimonials are the glue that binds. They remind and persuade. They heal and connect. Let people make sense of themselves. The speeches drone on. My mother and I stand there on the sidewalk, alone together, against the sound of culture-making that floats out to us. "We are a cursed people," the speaker announces. "Periodically we are destroyed, we struggle up again, we are reborn. That is our destiny."

The words act like adrenaline on my mother. Her cheeks begin to glow. Tears brighten her eyes. Her jawline grows firm. Her skin achieves muscle tone. "Come inside," she says softly to me, thinking to do me a good turn. "Come. You'll feel better."

I shake my head no. "Being Jewish can't help me anymore," I tell her.

She holds tightly to my arm. She neither confirms nor denies my words, only looks directly into my face. "Remember," she says. "You are my daughter. Strong. You must be strong."

"Oh Ma!" I cry, and my frightened greedy freedom-loving life wells up in me and spills down my soft-skinned face, the one she has given me. . . .

It rained earlier in the day and now, at one in the afternoon, for a minute and a half, New York is washed clean. The streets glitter in the pale spring sunlight. Cars radiate dust-free happiness. Storefront windows sparkle mindlessly. Even people look made anew.

We're walking down Eighth Avenue into the Village. At the corner of Eighth and Greenwich is a White Tower hamburger joint, where a group of derelicts in permanent residence entertain visiting out-of-towners from Fourteenth Street, Chelsea, even the Bowery. This afternoon the party on the corner, often raucous, is definitely on the gloomy side, untouched by weather renewal. As we pass the restaurant doors, however, one gentleman detaches from the group, takes two or three uncertain steps, and bars our way. He stands, swaying, before us. He is black, somewhere between twenty-five and sixty. His face is cut and swollen, the eyelids three-quarters shut. His hair is a hundred filthy matted little pigtails, his pants are held up by a piece of rope, his shoes are two sizes too large, the feet inside them bare. So is his chest, visible beneath a grimy tweed coat that swings open whenever he moves. This creature confronts us, puts out his hand palm up, and speaks.

"Can you ladies let me have a thousand dollars for a martini?" he inquires.

My mother looks directly into his face. "I know we're in an inflation," she says, "but a thousand dollars for a martini?"

His mouth drops. It's the first time in God knows how long that a mark has acknowledged his existence. "You're beautiful," he burbles at her. "Beautiful."

"Look on him," she says to me in Yiddish. "Just look on him."

He turns his bleary eyelids in my direction. "Whad-she-say?" he demands. "Whad-she-say?"

"She said you're breaking her heart," I tell him.

"She-say-that?" His eyes nearly open. "She-say-that?"

I nod. He whirls at her. "Take me home and make love to me," he croons, and right there in the street, in the middle of the day, he begins to bay at the moon. "I need you," he howls at my mother and doubles over, his fist in his stomach. "I need you."

She nods at him. "I need too," she says dryly. "Fortunately or unfortunately, it is not you I need." And she propels me around the now motionless derelict. Paralyzed by recognition, he will no longer bar our progress down the street.

We cross Abingdon Square and walk into Bleecker Street.

The gentrified West Village closes around us, makes us not peaceful but quiet. We walk through block after block of antique stores, gourmet shops, boutiques, not speaking. But for how long can my mother and I not speak?

"So I'm reading the biography you gave me," she says. I look at her, puzzled, and then I remember. "Oh!" I smile in wide delight. "Are you enjoying it?"

"Listen," she begins. The smile drops off my face and my stomach contracts. That "listen" means she is about to trash the book I gave her to read. She is going to say, "What. What's here? What's here that I don't already know? I lived through it. I know it all. What can this writer tell me that I don't already know? Nothing. To you it's interesting, but to me? How can this be interesting to me?"

On and on she'll go, the way she does when she thinks she doesn't understand something and she's scared, and she's taking refuge in scorn and hypercriticality.

The book I gave her to read is a biography of Josephine Herbst, a thirties writer, a stubborn willful raging woman grabbing at politics and love and writing, in there punching until the last minute.

"Listen," my mother says now in the patronizing tone she thinks conciliatory. "Maybe this is interesting to you, but not to me. I lived through all this. I know it all. What can I learn from this? Nothing. To you it's interesting. Not to me."

Invariably, when she speaks so, my head fills with blood and before the sentences have stopped pouring from her mouth I am lashing out at her. "You're an ignoramus, you know nothing, only a know-nothing talks the way you do. The point of having lived through it, as you say, is only that the background is familiar, so the book is made richer, not that you could have written the book. People a thousand times more educated than you have read and learned from this book, but you can't learn from it?" On and on I would go, thoroughly ruining the afternoon for both of us.

However, in the past year an odd circumstance has begun to obtain. On occasion, my head fails to fill with blood. I become irritated but remain calm. Not falling into a rage, I do not make a holocaust of the afternoon. Today, it appears, one of those moments is upon us. I turn to my mother, throw my left arm around her still solid back, place my right hand on her upper arm, and say, "Ma, if this book is not interesting to you, that's fine. You can say that." She looks coyly at me, eyes large, head half-turned; now she's interested. "But don't say it has nothing to teach you. That there's nothing here. That's unworthy of you, and of the book, and of me. You demean us all when you say that." Listen to me. Such wisdom. And all of it gained ten minutes ago.

Silence. Long silence. We walk another block. Silence. She's looking off into that middle distance. I take my lead from her, matching my steps to hers. I do not speak, do not press her. Another silent block.

"That Josephine Herbst," my mother says. "She certainly carried on, didn't she?"

Relieved and happy, I hug her. "She didn't know what she was doing either, Ma, but yes, she carried on."

"I'm jealous," my mother blurts at me. "I'm jealous she lived her life, I didn't live mine."

Mama went to work five weeks after my father died. He had left us two thousand dollars. To work or not to work was not a debatable question. But it's hard to imagine what would have happened if economic necessity had not forced her out of the house. As it was, it seemed to me that she lay on a couch in a half-darkened room for twenty-five years with her hand across her forehead murmuring, "I can't." Even though she could, and did.

She pulled on her girdle and her old gray suit, stepped into her black suede chunky heels, applied powder and lipstick to her face, and took the subway downtown to an employment agency where she got a job clerking in an office for twenty-eight dollars a week. After that, she rose each morning, got dressed and drank coffee, made out a grocery list for me, left it together with money on the kitchen table, walked four blocks to the subway station, bought the Times, read it on the train, got off at Forty-second Street, entered her office building, sat down at her desk, put in a day's work, made the trip home at five o'clock, came in the apartment door, slumped onto the kitchen bench for supper, then onto the couch where she instantly sank into a depression she welcomed like a warm bath. It was as though she had worked all day to earn the despair waiting faithfully for her at the end of her unwilling journey into daily life.

Weekends, of course, the depression was unremitting.

A black and wordless pall hung over the apartment all of Saturday and all of Sunday. Mama neither cooked, cleaned, nor shopped. She took no part in idle chatter: the exchange of banalities that fills a room with human presence, declares an interest in being alive. She would not laugh, respond, or participate in any of the compulsive kitchen talk that went on among the rest of us: me, my aunt Sarah, Nettie, my brother. She spoke minimally, and when she did speak her voice was uniformly tight and miserable, always pulling her listener back to a proper recollection of her "condition." If she answered the phone her voice dropped a full octave when she said hello; she could not trust that the caller would otherwise gauge properly the abiding nature of her pain. For five years she did not go to a movie, a concert, a public meeting. She worked, and she suffered.

Widowhood provided Mama with a higher form of being.

In refusing to recover from my father's death she had discovered that her life was endowed with a seriousness her years in the kitchen had denied her. She remained devoted to this seriousness for thirty years. She never tired of it, never grew bored or restless in its company, found new ways to keep alive the interest it deserved and had so undeniably earned.

Mourning Papa became her profession, her identity, her persona. Years later, when I was thinking about the piece of politics inside of which we had all lived (Marxism and the Communist Party), and I realized that people who worked as plumbers, bakers, or sewing-machine operators had thought of themselves as thinkers, poets, and scholars because they were members of the Communist Party, I saw that Mama had assumed her widowhood in much the same way. It elevated her in her own eyes, made of her a spiritually significant person, lent richness to her gloom and rhetoric to her speech. Papa's death became a religion that provided ceremony and doctrine. A woman-who-has-lost-the-love-of-her-life was now her orthodoxy: she paid it Talmudic attention.

Papa had never been so real to me in life as he was in death. Always a somewhat shadowy figure, benign and smiling, standing there behind Mama's dramatics about married love, he became and remained what felt like the necessary instrument of her permanent devastation. It was almost as though she had lived with Papa in order that she might arrive at this moment. Her distress was so all-consuming it seemed ordained. For me, surely, it ordered the world anew.

The air I breathed was soaked in her desperation, made thick and heady by it, exciting and dangerous. Her pain became my element, the country in which I lived, the rule beneath which I bowed. It commanded me, made me respond against my will. I longed endlessly to get away from her, but I could not leave the room when she was in it. I dreaded her return from work, but I was never not there when she came home. In her presence anxiety swelled my lungs (I suffered constrictions of the chest and sometimes felt an iron ring clamped across my skull), but I locked myself in the bathroom and wept buckets on her behalf. On Friday I prepared myself for two solid days of weeping and sighing and the mysterious reproof that depression leaks into the air like the steady escape of gas when the pilot light is extinguished. I woke up guilty and went to bed guilty and on weekends the guilt accumulated into low-grade infection.

She made me sleep with her for a year, and for twenty years afterward I could not bear a woman's hand on me. Afraid to sleep alone, she slung an arm across my stomach, pulled me toward her, fingered my flesh nervously, inattentively. I shrank from her touch: she never noticed. I yearned toward the wall, couldn't get close enough, was always being pulled back. My body became a column of aching stiffness. I must have been excited. Certainly I was repelled.

For two years she dragged me to the cemetery every second or third Sunday morning. The cemetery was in Queens. This meant taking three buses and traveling an hour and fifteen minutes each way. When we climbed onto the third bus she'd begin to cry. Helplessly, I would embrace her. Her cries would grow louder. Inflamed with discomfort, my arm would stiffen around her shoulder and I would stare at the black rubber floor. The bus would arrive at the last stop just as she reached the verge of convulsion.

"We have to get off, Ma," I'd plead in a whisper.

She would shake herself reluctantly (she hated to lose momentum once she'd started on a real wail) and slowly climb down off the bus. As we went through the gates of the cemetery, however, she'd rally to her own cause. She would clutch my arm and pull me across miles of tombstones (neither of us ever seemed to remember the exact location of the grave), stumbling like a drunk, lurching about and shrieking: "Where's Papa? Help me find Papa! They've lost Papa. Beloved! I'm coming. Wait, only wait, I'm coming!" Then we would find the grave and she would fling herself across it, arrived at last in a storm of climactic release. On the way home she was a rag doll. And I? Numb and dumb, only grateful to have survived the terror of the earlier hours.

One night when I was fifteen I dreamed that the entire apartment was empty, stripped of furniture and brilliantly whitewashed, the rooms gleaming with sun and the whiteness of the walls. A long rope extended the length of the apartment, winding at waist-level through all the rooms. I followed the rope from my room to the front door. There in the open doorway stood my dead father, gray-faced, surrounded by mist and darkness, the rope tied around the middle of his body. I laid my hands on the rope and began to pull, but try as I might I could not lift him across the threshold. Suddenly my mother appeared. She laid her hands over mine and began to pull also. I tried to shake her off, enraged at her interference, but she would not desist, and I did so want to pull him in I said to myself, "All right, I'll even let her have him, if we can just get him inside."

For years I thought the dream needed no interpretation, but now I think I longed to get my father across the threshold not out of guilt and sexual competition but so that I could get free of Mama. My skin crawled with her. She was everywhere, all over me, inside and out. Her influence clung, membrane-like, to my nostrils, my eyelids, my open mouth. I drew her into me with every breath I took. I drowsed in her etherizing atmosphere, could not escape the rich and claustrophobic character of her presence, her being, her suffocating suffering femaleness.

I didn't know the half of it.

One afternoon, in the year of the dream, I was sitting with Nettie. She was making lace, and I was drinking tea. She began to dream out loud. "I think you'll meet a really nice boy this year," she said. "Someone older than yourself. Almost out of college. Ready to get a good job. He'll fall in love with you, and soon you'll be married."

"That's ridiculous," I said sharply.

Nettie let her hands, with the lace still in them, fall to her lap. "You sound just like your mother," she said softly. . . .

The years are coming up thickly . . . forty-six, forty-seven, forty-eight . . . There is no past now, only the ongoing present . . . seventy-eight, seventy-nine, eighty. Eighty. My God, my mother is eighty. We stand still, looking at each other. She shrugs her shoulder and sits down on the couch in her living room.

She came to my house this afternoon. We had a drink, then went out to dinner in the neighborhood, then I walked her home. She made coffee and we talked, looked at pictures, some old (America, 1941), some older (Russia, 1913), and we read together from a batch of letters we have dipped into fifty times in my life; letters written to her in 1922 by one Noah Shecter, formerly a professor of literature in Rumania and at the time of the letter-writing manager of the bakery where my mother worked as a bookkeeper. The letters are remarkable: nineteenth-century romantic fantasy written by a lonely man living in the Bronx with an unintellectual wife and three needy children, his head filled with Ibsen, Gorki, Mozart, writing his heart out each night at midnight to a vain brown-eyed empty vessel of receptivity (my eighteen-year-old mother) who would read these impassioned outpourings at eight in the morning before she went off to work to see the man who had written them stiff and formal in a high starched collar, looking like Franz Kafka in the insurance company. Now, sixty years later, I hold these hundreds of yellowed sheets covered with thickly scrawled European handwriting, the black ink long ago turned brown, and read of Noah Shecter's midnight desperation that my mother should understand how full his heart is, just having seen Ibsen's Brand performed in a Fourteenth Street theater, and how necessary it is that he let her know how well the actors captured the essential meaning of this very great play. The letters and the pictures surround us (I see her as she must have looked when she first read them)—fragments, scraps, tales told and retold of the life lived and the life unlived. Especially the one unlived.

A sad, silent weight hangs about my mother all evening. She looks very pretty tonight—soft white hair, soft smooth skin, the wrecked face looking wonderfully whole again—but the years are dragging inside her, and in her eyes I see the confusion, the persistent confusion.

"A lifetime gone by," she says quietly.

My pain is so great I dare not feel it. "Exactly," I say evenly. "Not lived. Just gone by."

The softness in her face hardens into definition. She looks at me and, with iron in her voice, says in Yiddish, "So you'll write down: From the beginning it was all lost."

We sit together then, silent, not embroiled with each other, two women only staring into the obscurity of all that lost life. My mother looks neither young nor old, only deeply absorbed by the terribleness of what she is seeing. I do not know how I look to her.

We always walked, she and I. We don't always walk now. We don't always argue, either. We don't always do any of the things we always did. There is no always anymore. The fixed patterns are beginning to break up. This breakup has its own pleasures and surprises. In fact, surprise is now the key word between us. We cannot depend on change, but we can depend on surprise. However, we cannot always depend on surprise either. This keeps us on our toes.

I come to see her one night with an old friend of mine, a man who grew up with me, someone we've both known for thirty years. I say known advisedly. This man is something of a lunatic. An inspired lunatic, to be sure, but a lunatic nonetheless. He, like Davey Levinson, is educated in a vacuum, and he speaks a kind of imaginative gibberish. It is the only way he knows how to get through the ordinary anxiety of the ordinary day.

We are having coffee and cake. I am eating too much cake. I am, in fact, wolfing down the cake. My mother is getting crazy watching me. She cries, "Stop it! For God's sake, stop eating like that. Don't you care at all that you'll gain two pounds and hate yourself tomorrow? Where's your motivation?"

My friend, sitting at the table beside me, his head thrust forward and down and twisted to the side, looking at her like the madman that he is, starts going on nonsensically about motivation. "You know, of course, that motivation is life," he says. "Life itself. Taken from the Latin *motus*, it means to move, set in motion, engage . . ."

My mother looks at him. I can see in her face that she does not understand the construction of these sentences. She feels put down: if she doesn't understand something she is being told she is stupid. Her expression becomes one of glittering scorn. "You think you're telling me something I don't know?" she says. "You think I was born yesterday?" No surprise here.

One week later I'm sitting in her apartment drinking tea with her, and from out of nowhere she says to me, "So tell me about your abortion." She knows I had an abortion when I was thirty, but she has never referred to it. I, in turn, know she had three abortions during the Depression, but I never mention them, either. Now, suddenly . . . Her face is unreadable. I don't know what has stirred the inquiry and I don't know what to tell her. Should I tell her the truth or . . . ? What the hell. The truth. "I had an abortion with my legs up against the wall in an apartment on West Eighty-eighth Street, with Demerol injected into my veins by a doctor whose consulting room was the corner of Fifty-eighth Street and Tenth Avenue." She nods at me as I speak, as though these details are familiar, even expected. Then she says, "I had mine in the basement of a Greenwich Village nightclub, for ten dollars, with a doctor who half the time when you woke up you were holding his penis in your hand." I look at her in admiration. She has matched me clause for clause, and raised the ante with each one. We both burst out laughing at the same moment. Surprise.

Yet another night I am sitting at her table and we are talking of the time she went to work when I was eight years old. This is a story I never tire of hearing.

"What made you decide to do it, Ma? I mean, why that time rather than any other?"

"I always wanted to work, always. God, how I loved having my own money in my pocket! It was the middle of the war, you threw a stone you got seven jobs, I couldn't resist."

"So what did you do?"

"I read the want ads one morning and I got dressed, took the subway downtown, and applied for a job. In ten minutes I had it. What was the name of that company? I've forgotten it now."

"Angelica Uniform Company," I instantly supply.

"You remember!" She smiles beatifically at me. "Look at that. She remembers. I can't remember. She remembers."

"I am the repository of your life now, Ma."

"Yes, you are, you are. Let's see now. Where were we?"

"You went downtown and got the job."

"Yes. So I came home and told Papa, 'I have a job.'"

"How did he respond?"

"Badly. Very badly. He didn't want me to work. He said, 'No other wife in the neighborhood works, why should you work.' I said, 'I don't care what any other wife in the neighborhood does, I want to work.'" She stares into this memory, shaking her head. Her voice falters. "But it was no good, no good. I didn't last long."

"Eight months," I say.

"Yes, eight months."

"Why, Ma? Why only eight months?"

"Papa was miserable. He kept saying to me, 'The children need you.'"

"That was silly," I interrupt. "I remember being *excited* that you were working. I loved having a key around my neck, and rushing home every afternoon to do things that made it easier for you."

"Then he said, 'You're losing weight.'"

"You were twenty pounds overweight. It was *great* that you were losing weight."

"What can I tell you?" she says to me. "Either you were going to make a hell in the house or you were going to be happy. I wanted to be happy. He didn't want me to work. I stopped working."

We are quiet together for a while. Then I say, "Ma, if it was now, and Papa said he didn't want you to work, what would you do?"

She looks at me for a long moment. She is eighty years old. Her eyes are dim, her hair is white, her body is frail. She takes a swallow of her tea, puts down the cup, and says calmly, "I'd tell him to go fuck himself."

Real surprise.

We're in the Lincoln Center library for a Saturday afternoon concert. We've arrived late and all the seats are taken. We stand in the darkened auditorium leaning against the wall. I start to worry. I know my mother cannot stand for two and a half hours. "Let's go," I whisper to her. "Sh-h-h," she says, pushing the air away with her hand. I look around. In the aisle seat next to me is a little boy, tossing about on his seat. Beside him his young mother. Next to her another little boy, and next to him the husband and father. The woman lifts the little boy in the aisle seat onto her lap and motions my mother to sit down. My mother leans over, gives the woman her most brilliant smile, and says coyly, "When you'll be eighty, and you'll want a seat at a concert, I'll come back and give you one." The woman is charmed. She turns to her husband to share her pleasure. Nothing doing. He stares balefully at my mother. Here is one Jewish son who hasn't forgotten. His response pulls me up short, reminds me of how seductive my mother has always been, how unwilling she is to part with this oldest trick of the trade, how dangerous and untrustworthy is this charm of hers.

On and on it goes. My apartment is being painted. I spend two nights on her couch. Whenever I sleep over I like to make the coffee in the morning, because she has gotten used to weak coffee and I like mine strong. Meanwhile, she has become convinced that her weak coffee is the correct way to make coffee, and although she has said to me, "All right, you don't like my coffee, make it yourself," she stands over me in the kitchen and directs me to make it as she makes it.

"It's enough already," she says as I spoon coffee into the pot.

"No, it's not," I say.

"It is. For God's sake, enough!"

"Look for yourself, Ma. See how far short of the measuring line it is?"

She looks. The evidence is indisputable. There is not enough coffee in the pot. She turns away from me, the flat edge of her hand cutting the air in that familiar motion of dismissal.

"Ah, leave me alone," she says in deep trembling disgust.

I stare at her retreating back. That dismissiveness of hers: it will be the last thing to go. In fact, it will never go. It is the emblem of her speech, the idiom of her being, that which establishes her in her own eyes. The dismissal of others is to her the struggle to rise from the beasts, to make distinctions, to know the right and the wrong of a thing, to not think it unimportant, ever, that the point be made. Suddenly her life presses on my heart.

Anne Richardson Roiphe

Born into a casually Jewish New York family on Christmas day in 1935, Anne Roiphe's professional relationship with Jewish topics has undergone a 180-degree turn. Roiphe, who received her B.A. degree from Sarah Lawrence College, established her reputation by writing witty books that articulated the conflicts implicit in the feminine mystique; one of the best-known was *Up the Sandbox* (1972), a humorous exposé of the angst in a young mother's restricted life. She also wrote, and continues to write, articles promoting feminist causes, such as abortion rights and equal-responsibility parenting. However, a *New York Times* op-ed piece that Roiphe authored, probably without too much forethought, on being an assimilated Jew at Christmas time, aroused so much furor and reader response that Roiphe found herself reevaluating her own relationship with Judaism. Discovering that her knowledge base was woefully inadequate, Roiphe began to study Jewish texts in earnest. She soon began to write both about her own voyage of discovery and also about Jews, both knowledgeable and assimilated, in American Jewish environments; one product of her voyage of self-discovery is her nonfiction book *Generation without Memory: A Jewish Journey in Christian America* (1981).

Lovingkindness is a product of Roiphe's recent Jewish interests as well as a perceptive exploration of the emotional underpinnings of mother–daughter relationships. American Jewish parents sometimes say they might feel more comfortable having a child marry an Episcopalian than marrying a Hassidic Jew; the characters in Roiphe's novel do both. Annie, the protagonist, holds vehement beliefs in individual freedom and secular Western humanism that are tantamount to fanatical religious convictions. Those convictions are challenged when her daughter Andrea, after passing through a series of drugs and experimental life-styles, becomes a docile and obedient daughter of Israel in an ultra-Orthodox community in Jerusalem. Andrea's defection to Orthodox Judaism is, in Annie's eyes, virtually an apostasy into an alien culture. However, Annie subsequently genuinely searches her soul and sees that her daughter's needs and perceptions differ from hers. She becomes, perhaps for the first time, her daughter's genuine enabler and advocate.

•

"Mothers and Daughters Make Their Own Myth" (excerpt)

I remember Andrea at the beach the summer I was writing my book on the spinsters of New England. She was brown and long-legged, and on the rainy days she sat at the kitchen table and drew pictures of crabs and clams, seaweed and butterflies. She would lean her head down over the paper and her legs would bang against the kitchen chair and I hung all her drawings in the house. I tacked them up on the pine walls and I taped them on the refrigerator door. They were elaborate crayonings with shadows and layers. If I leaned over and kissed her while she worked, she would brush me aside as if a fly had settled on her cheek. That was the summer she sold lemonade at the edge of the boardwalk with her friends and the summer she read all thirty-four volumes of Nancy Drew. That was the summer she and her friends made up plays. Each performance contained a wicked witch who was burnt, melted down, crushed in the garbage disposal or killed by a falling star. Andrea would announce the play, her cheeks flushed, her lips trembling. There would be illustrated programs placed on the seats of each adult. We clapped, we called for encores. We laughed in the right places. The plays rarely lasted longer than four minutes, but they were hours in the preparation. The audience was satisfied, eager for more, amazed by each devise of plot or costume.

I watched her at the edge of the ocean, laughing that laugh that mingles joy with terror as the waves came up over her ankles as she ran back and forth like a sandpiper at dusk. That was the August when thousands or perhaps it was millions of starfish washed up on the sand and were drying in the sun. Andrea organized a crew to pick up the starfish and toss them back into the waves so that they could live longer. The children worked long hours at the rescue of the starfish, filled buckets and buckets with pink pulsing forms who had no words to thank, no brain to register salvation. I tried to explain to Andrea that all the beach was made of dead creatures, that nature was indifferent to the particular forms it had created and was willing to let each go in turn in service to another. Andrea did not believe me. She felt each starfish had a right, had a purpose, had a destiny of its own. Only a two-day storm that shifted currents of the sea, bringing an end to the starfish harvest, stopped the frenzied efforts of the children, tight-lipped, combing the shoreline in defiance of the natural order.

In the mornings I would wake up with her body resting against mine. She smelled of salt and sun. Once in her hair I found a tiny shell. I gave her the shell and told her to keep it in a safe place so it could bring her luck. Later that day she found a large clamshell polished clean in the sun. She gave it to me and said it would bring me luck. I still have it by my bedside. It used to serve as an ashtray and then when I gave up smoking, because Andrea begged me, I kept it. Who knows exactly what brings you luck?

Andrea found a stick in the dunes. It had been the home and the sustenance of some life form that had left markings along the dried-out curve; curious indentations, like Sanskrit, like cuneiform, like the hieroglyphics of a dwarfed species. Andrea told me that the stick was a message from the dolphins, who wished to contact us to improve human life. I watched her hold the stick in her hands and wave it at the fish in the sea. "I have your message, I have your message," she shouted at the white froth that rolled up the wet beach. Her nose had freckled and burnt and peeled, and she had taken off the top of her bathing suit because she didn't need it anyway. As the wind blew up off the sea I scanned the horizon for sharks the way I always did when I felt that my happiness must be exposing me to immediate peril.

That was the summer I felt sorry for the spinsters of New England. I tried not to let my pity slip onto the page. I wanted to present these women of the nineteenth century who devoted themselves to good works, to the library, to the hospital, to the church, to their sisters' families, to their elderly bedridden parents, as heroines of a new order, like woodchucks announcing the coming spring. I tried to present their lives as knit of stern ideals, proper behavior, repression to the right degree. I tried to see them as the freest members of their icy social order, but every time I would look at Andrea, asleep in her bed, Nancy Drew on her pillow, red-and-white sneakers on the floor, I would grieve for my straight-backed upright ladies, who had missed the brightest bondage of them all.

My grandfather had come from Bratslav to New York some years before the century turned. He had been a young man willing to work hard, and a pushcart with trousers soon became a loft with twenty girls sewing seams, which in turn metamorphosed into a factory and then two factories and a sales force and an office with secretaries and switchboards. His sons, who had gone to college before entering the business, spoke without an accent and they wore no beards and they went bareheaded through the streets and they played golf on Saturday and laughed at the old man and his black coat and his hat and the curls that hung down beside his cheeks and all the things he wouldn't do because it was forbidden and all the things he would do because it was bidden. A common tale of old ways lost and new ways taken, of the young striking out for new territory and the old beginning the journey but not completing it, of centuries of clashing, of the enlightenment wooing, of Hellenism seducing, of possessions undreamed of in the old town where the door handle on the Mikvah was constantly coming off in the hands that turned it. When they moved the firm to its new office building in the garment center amid the sounds of jazz and jive and honking horns and racks of clothing bumping steel frames one against another, they made the old man chairman of the board and sent him down to Florida to live. I saw him on his occasional trips to New York. My mother did not want him coming in the elevator and standing in the lobby of our building. We would visit him at his sister's in Long Island. "I should have gone to Palestine instead of to New York. I was a fool, a young fool," he said to me. "Look what has become of you, my family, in New York," he said. "In Palestine they have brought Rabbi Nachman's chair, piece by piece, and put it in its place, where he will come after the Messiah." There were tears in his eyes. "In Bratslav I personally knew the Bratslav Hasidim, who told the stories told to their fathers by the famous Rabbi Nachman. I knew those men who remembered those stories as well as I know the hand in front of my face.

"Better stories than your 'Lone Ranger,' better than your 'Inner Sanctum,' and much better than your 'Dr. Christian.' Those were stories that made the stars come into your mouth so you could taste them."

A story could do that? My grandfather, who died one winter in Miami wearing his black coat and his black hat and his tallis in his single room on the beachfront where I had never been but imagined him sometimes staring out the window at the pelicans diving into the turquoise waters, believed that a story could do that. "Tell me a story," I had said.

"No." He had stared at me as at a newly discovered stain on the tablecloth. "Not for you."

I had been named Annie after my dead grandmother, Ann. My grandmother's picture was in a jade frame near my mother's bed, a plump woman whose pineapple-sized breasts strain forward against a string of pearls at her throat. Her lips are parted; the photographer asks, she obliges. Her hair is a cap of white curls and her cheeks are full as if stuffed with chocolate. And in her eyes, memories of soft sheets and embroidered napkins held close and treasured. My mother lights a gray wax candle that fills a thick milky glass and places it beneath this picture each year at the anniversary of her mother's death. The doctors chasing a malignancy through the membranes and the tissues had set my grandmother's bones on fire by using excessive radiation . . . a new toy whose limits were in 1935 only a matter of opinion. Often I thought of the bones smoldering like the late-night logs of a campfire, glowing embers, occasional sparks and light that flickered in the shadows. My mother told me that she had gone to a fortune-teller who read the cards at the Palm Court of the Plaza Hotel, and under the fronds, sitting at a table near the violinist, the fortune-teller had said that if a special tea was brewed and brought to the invalid's bedside, health would be restored. My mother dipped into her jewelry box and brought out diamond earrings and gold bracelets and purchased the tea, which proved less than effective. Which is why I, born several weeks after the funeral, was given the name Annie, an unpromising plain name with no reference to art or literature or lineage, no historical reference, except perhaps to Anne Boleyn, who had not pleased and lost her head, an alien association anyway for a child whose relatives took their history in the collective rather than the individual form, a people for whom historical events were rarely spectator sports. The name Annie was an odd choice. I had a Hebrew name but my mother forgot what it was; like my appendix, it served no function and was excised.

I sat on the carpet outside the door to my mother's room, in the dark hallway beside the linen closet whose shelves held the monogrammed sheets, the lace tablecloths, the lace-edged guest towels, the pillowcases of silk, the bedcovers fringed with gold thread. I would sit waiting for the maid to bring my mother her breakfast on a tray, a tray complete with a rose in a china vase, the morning paper and a pink napkin in which nested rolls and toast. I often waited several hours as my mother slept on and the kitchen maid scrubbed the bathtubs and the cook ordered dinner from the market and my nanny wrote long letters home to her relatives in Bavaria. In the hallway I waited, still and silent. Even after I had learned to read, in that hallway I did not read. I needed all my energy to wait, to will her awake, to will the door to open, the maid to come, the window blinds to be pulled and my mother to sit up in bed and let the smell of sweat and perfume, the smell of nail polish, cold cream and nicotine, the smell of sleep and dreams, of tissues aging and stretching, of stomach gas and waste and face powder and body powder to mix and float out the door into the hallway and let me in. The hallway was decorated with red velvet wallpaper with indentations of vines that climbed from ceiling to floor. I would lie on the carpet and put my face next to the crack at the bottom of the door. I would just see the morning light that was seeping into the room beneath the heavy drapes. I could see the base of my mother's bed and the flowered ruffle of her spread as it brushed against the floor. I could stay in that position a long time. I learned patience. I learned how to still the beating of my heart and the twitching of my limbs. I learned how to float with time as if on a raft in a becalmed sea. My mother's late sleeping habit had the effect of teaching me how to lie like a lizard waiting for a passing fly. It also taught me how to love through a closed door.

My mother woke each morning with puffed eyes. The night had been disappointing. Her lace nightgown, the satin bed jacket, would be all askew. Her painted fingernails would be chipped. She would reach for her Camels before she rang for the maid. On the floor would be the solitaire game she had played to bring on sleep. Aces and king, fours and fives, hearts and diamonds, were slung about carelessly as if she hadn't spent hours trying to make the order come out right, as if she hadn't held on to the shiny pictures of sailboats or cats that decorated the deck in her hand and stroked them up and down, to give them luck before dealing out each hand. In the morning on her way to the bathroom my mother stepped on her cards as if they were no more than drops of light reflected from her mirror.

Sometimes she would let me in the bathroom with her. I would sit on the toilet as she soaped in the tub. A small woman with soft folds all over her body, her legs were waxed, her hair was set twice a week. There were thousands of bottles of creams on the sink and still she always looked rumpled, her mascara had a way of running down her cheeks like mourners caught in summer rain. There was always some lipstick on her teeth and she had certain complaints she was more than willing to share with me. They usually concerned my meticulous father, who had a predilection for attractive women, good clothes and fine leather attache cases. Despite the fact he had married an heiress whose family company had put his name on the annual report, he had regrets of his own . . . or else why were his lips drawn into such a tight line, why were his hooded eyes always turning away, why did he sit silently at the dinner table and why was he always polishing his shoes and going off for long walks or staying late hours at his club, where women were not permitted past the outer vestibule? My father had a hundred white handkerchiefs with his monogram on each. His shirts were perfectly starched and his ties were of dark blue silk. He had a camel's hair coat that was so soft that if a child put her head near the pockets she might expect to hear the heartbeat of the animal who had given his skin. My father stood straight and tall and he had a cable-knit tennis sweater and his whites were always pressed.

Every few months he would succumb to headaches. He would lie in the library in his purple dressing gown with the maroon velvet collar. The shades would be down, the drapes drawn and the room still. Get out, he would yell if anyone came to the door.

He was not a free man this known, unknown fact—of his obligations to others, of his more humble past, where passage on the boat had been steerage, where he had been cast among the peasants and the Jews by a blind and dumb fate—disturbed his sleep. Rue drilled through his brain as if looking for buried treasure and the result was headache, banging, pulsating, nerve-crumpling headache. When it was over he would get dressed, shower and go off to his office. His eyes remained chips of stone, hidden under his heavy lids, slanted as if a roving Mongol had violated a Jewish maiden on the slopes of Odessa generations earlier.

Sometimes I would stand at the window of my room. Gretchen, my nanny, would be knitting silently. It was war time and she was worried about her relatives, who lived in the villages outside of Munich. It was possible they were hungry or cold, and she knitted them scarves and mittens and prayed for them each Sunday at the Church of Our Lady of Perpetual Mercy in Yorkville. In the evening light, I could see a reflection of the room in the window. My chair, my table, everything painted with red hearts and little birds, were duplicated exactly in the mirror image. Beyond the reflection the awnings on Park Avenue stood like the guards at Buckingham Palace as the streetlights went from green to red and back, and under the avenue the hidden trains rumbled on their tracks, headed to Harlem, to the place at Ninety-sixth Street when they would rise from the depths and roar past the gray-faced tenements toward escape. As I stood there transfixed between the real room and its echo in the window, I had a feeling that began low in the stomach and settled like a handcuff on the heart that I could fall between the two. The hearts on the wallpaper in both rooms would begin to spin and I would hold myself very tight because I knew that Gretchen did not like fancy. I must manage to stay on the safe side of the reflection, in the right room, the one with a real floor, by my wit, by my skills at discriminating between illusion and reality. Even the best of carpeting could cover an immense hole. I walked carefully.

Dear Andrea, Changing your name will not change who you are or where you come from. It is a superficial gesture, like dyeing your hair blue or fixing your nose; I realize you never had nose surgery but you must by now be learning that changing the surface has very little effect on the substance. Your name for better or worse has been with you since the first moments of your birth. It was given to you with only the best intentions and I find among the impossible things you have done in your short life, and I will not list them all here, the new naming among the most absurd, unfriendly and peculiar. I don't recognize the name Sarai, I don't accept you as Sarai and I will not. If you really are on a new turn of life that involves honoring your mother, then you will immediately change your name back to the one that I selected when you were no more than plasma and glue. Does it bother you that I am the one who gave the name? Does this fact compromise your most precious independence? Most people in the world carry on with the name given at birth and most certainly do not feel yoked to the previous generation like beasts in the field forced to plow the same row over and over again. I am not trying to control you. I wasn't trying to hold something over you at your birth, either. The hospital staff insisted on having something to print on the birth certificate and you were unable at the time to give them your opinions.

I can understand your interest in things Jewish. I have talked to many of my friends and it seems that a lot of young people are discovering their roots in the cultures and civilizations of the past. However, your grandparents were not the religious sort. They stopped going to synagogue as soon as they were old enough to defy the old man and his old-fashioned expectations. They did not think that a friendly force from the heavens had paid his passage over or protected him from the rapists and thugs in the czar's army. They spoke Yiddish, yes, but they were anxious that the next generation speak only the president's English. Don't have pictures in your head of a grandpa weaving over the Talmud, shoulders wraped in tallis, dust on his skullcap. That is somebody else's picture (mine in fact, and I don't go all to pieces over it, either). Your grandfather, my father, wanted money. He wanted to be respected in the new world. He wanted to own fine silver and jewels. He wanted security; a lot of security. He wasn't heroic or particularly gifted in spiritual matters. He didn't waste his time at the corner shul entreating, pleading, promising, feeling guilty and unworthy. Your great-grandfather had a loyalty, yes, to a town and some Hasidim who told strange stories, and he was pious enough but not so pious that he didn't start the business that his sons carried on. What is the point of going back two generations, sliding down the historical ladder, slamming doors of opportunity behind you, as if someone hadn't struggled hard and long to open those doors for you? My father, who had no patience with mystics and babblers in foreign tongues, would hardly be overcome with joy to see you poring over old books with cryptic sayings by sages so long dead that they can be misquoted at will. Your religious roots are so distant they might as well be with Abraham in the desert, or Adam in the Garden, a connection, yes, but not a particularly personal one. By those standards you are also related to the ichthyosaurus. You are not feeling under any compulsion to exercise your prehistoric wings, are you?

I doubt the sincerity of your religious impulse. Are you sure you just don't want someone to tell you what to do? Don't you really think that those laws that determine what you can eat with what, when you can eat and what you say before and after, what belongs together, what should be separated, are infringements on your natural choices? Don't you determine for yourself your own personal ethical behavior? Is lobster really an immoral creature of the deep? Do you really need the opinions of other centuries on your dining table? Don't you feel weighted down, free spirit that thou wert, refusing to learn algebra, refusing to be home at midnight, refusing to eat anything but Hostess cupcakes? Has someone done a lobotomy on you? Did you take so many drugs that you can no longer stand alone without your strings being pulled? Who are you, anyway? Love, Mother.

I reread the letter and realized it was less than persuasive. It was simply angry. Was anger all right in this situation? Would it cause me to lose more than I could gain? Why did I feel betrayed? Why had Andrea always made me feel abandoned? I decided not to send the letter, to rewrite another day, to wait patiently and hear more. I tried to picture her by the Damascus gate, standing among the tourists, changing money with Arab boys, clutching handfuls of silver earrings and ropes of colored beads. I tried to imagine her near the white stones of the city wall looking up at the Mount of Olives across the ravines of graves, tombs that seemed to fall or crumble all about the mountainside as if the natives didn't know that death should be discreet, hidden, placed in orderly rows in distant suburbs or behind shrubbery on highways that led to airports. Andrew once told me she wanted to be cremated to save the land for the living. It was a blithe statement from one who didn't intend to die, but there at the yeshiva they would teach her that cremation was impure, against the law, might prevent the remains from gathering together and rising when the Messiah finally arrived. Was it possible that Andrea, who only a short while ago believed that sexual restraint was a disease against which one needed frequent innoculations, could turn into one of those pious women in long dress with high neck and long sleeves, with a scarf tied over her hair, with eyes demurely downcast, in sensible shoes with laces and thick stockings? Andrea wore red spike heels when I last had seen her. I had remarked that they looked like she was working the street. She had told me that I had lost touch with reality and belonged in an institution where they would mash up my food and take away my television privileges if I didn't behave. I loved that about Andrea: the sass, the rudeness, that was her gift. I liked the way she spoke up for herself. She was never conned by our ordinary ways of nodding back and forth. Once, when she first turned punk and shaved the back of her head and put on an old man's coat whose lining followed her like her shadow, she met me at a conference I was attending at the Roosevelt Hotel. We were going to the dentist together. (Some activities require support.) I told her I was embarrassed by how she looked. People on their lunch breaks were staring at us. She told me with her fake pout that she understood my feelings perfectly, there were parts of town, around Sixth Street and Avenue C, where she would be mortified to be walking with me. My wool coat with the beaver collar, my gray flannel suit, would be so out of it everyone would turn around to gape. Any child who understands cultural relativism can't be all bad. I kissed her on the spot and she pretended not to be pleased she had pleased me.

My mother had taught me to spit if I saw a nun on the street because without some magic I too might become a disappointed woman. My mother must have thought virginity was catching and we were in the midst of a chastity epidemic. But I used reason as my prophylactic. As I sallied forth out of the house I examined each superstition carefully on its own terms. This had left me with the normal dread of the unknown, the drift of those who cannot forgive God for the condition of life and so banish Him to the outer fringes of consciousness, where He becomes defanged, declawed, hollowed out and incapable of causing fear and trembling; also incapable of curing fear and trembling. My mother, on the other hand, wore the dress that had brought her luck at the canasta table yesterday to today's game. She never encouraged the evil eye by boasting about her winnings, she avoided black cats, walking under ladders, using the number thirteen and she always had the manicurist paint her nails from left to right because she had never yet become terminally ill on a day on which she painted her nails in the correct direction. Considering that some peoples have cut out the hearts of their enemies as sacrifices to their gods, a little directional nail painting seems harmless enough. Could Andrea believe in the evil eye?

Eventually a letter came:

Dear Mother, I am planning to stay longer at the Yeshiva Rachel. I hope that you will be pleased that I am studying hard. I am certain that I belong here where our people came after years of wandering in the desert to fulfill their part of the covenant. I too am under the covenant, it embraces me and folds me in its truths tenderly. I am your daughter, grateful at last that you gave me life, although you could have brought me up closer to Gd and more in harmony with the soul of Israel. I suppose you were distracted and fooled by the seeming cleverness of the material world, by the seducers and the betrayers who promised you truth through clever media and wicked images. I'm sure you did your best and meant well. I forgive you for your mistakes. I still have hopes of making you proud of me. I remember all the times you told me not to be afraid of dogs, of thunder, of the hamster who had died in his cage. You comforted me and one day I hope I can comfort you. Love, Sarai.

I read the letter several times. I finally tore it up, but not before I had unintentionally memorized it. It intruded on my thoughts; unwanted and unbidden it would rise to remind me of Andrea and her newest predicament even as I was working on an essay. Even when I went out to dinner with friends and even as I lay in my bed at night trying to find a comfortable position that would leave me free of Andrea and able to sleep peacefully.

Once I had hurt my lower back and was forced into bed for several weeks. I had hired a housekeeper but she left at six o'clock. One night I called out to Andrea, who was watching television in the living room, for a glass of water. "Later," said Andrea, "in the commercial."

After a half hour I called out again. She didn't answer me. She was talking on the telephone. "Andrea," I screamed, "help me." There was no answer. I got out of bed and crawled along the floor slowly. I could feel my hair damp at the back of my neck. I could smell the nightgown I had been wearing too many days in a row.

I found Andrea curled up by the phone. She put one hand over the mouthpiece. "Do you want your water in a bowl or a glass?" she asked.

I had frightened her by not standing up, I had frightened her by needing her. My thirst was gone. . . .

When Andrea was four we went to Washington on a peace march. We left on the seven A.M. Metroliner from Pennsylvania Station. Andrea slept in the seat beside me most of the way down. I talked strategy with the women in the row behind me, gentle-eyed political experts who wore peasant blouses with embroidered flowers and sensible shoes for the day's outing. Andrea wore a T-shirt with a peace sign on the front and a dove on the back. I had joined a group called Mothers for Peace and we had a flag crayoned by an older child that said "War No More" and showed a flower being stamped under a boot. Some teenagers were carrying our flag and in the Metroliner they jumped up and went from car to car unfurling their message.

I had to carry Andrea on my shoulders because the walk from the railroad station to the steps of the Senate was beyond her. She was heavy. The day was hot. I stopped to get her an ice cream, which then dripped down my neck. We lost my friends, who had moved ahead in what became a river of people descending from buses coming in from all the tributary side streets. Marshals with bands around their arms kept waving people forward. We stood next to an old black woman who was there with her church choir. The group sang as they marched. "Swing low, sweet chariot, coming for to carry me home . . ." Andrea sang with them and the old lady gave me a tissue to wipe the ice cream off Andrea's face. I looked back down the avenue and saw a million people swaying in the heat, their bodies floating slowly over the pavement.

"Judgment Day," I heard somebody say.

"No more war," shouted Andrea.

"You tell 'em, sweetheart," a voice answered.

I lifted Andrea down and held her in my arms with her legs wrapped around my waist. "Remember everything about today," I said to Andrea. "We are ending the war." I could feel her heart beating against my shirt.

Later, in front of the Capitol, we listened to the speeches. Andrea looked for four-leaf clovers beneath the knees and legs of all the seated, sprawled people, who were clapping, chanting, singing at various moments. I found the Mothers for Peace group. I found my friends sitting on a blanket in the hot sun. I sat down, my legs and arms tired, my face flushed and perspiration stains under my arms. We talked of napalm and body counts and massacres small and large, and we passed around a Thermos of apple juice. We inhaled deeply and breathed in the sweet smell of pot that rose from several yards away. Children were wrestling on the grass. Two little Chinese girls were dressing up their Barbie doll, who had on a ball gown. I looked for Andrea, who had been right behind me. I couldn't see her.

I stood up. The voice on the microphone set up on a platform right at the bottom of the Senate steps droned out a list of movie stars who had joined the peace movement. The crowd, now exhausted from the speeches, applauded each name politely, like a summer breeze in a field. "Andrea," I called out. "Andrea." I raised my voice, but the chatter, the speaker, an airplane overhead, dwarfed my voice. "Andrea!" I screamed.

My friends jumped to their feet. "Andrea," they called, as if a dog or cat or sacred cow had been lost, each moving off our blanket in another direction.

People were packed thick on the hill; below, one could see the crowds waving flags on Pennsylvania Avenue. The line of humanity, looking like a column of multicolored ants, stretched out into infinity. Litter baskets were overflowing with cartons of juice, soda cans, potato-chip wrappers. On the side of the slope the portable toilets stood with lines in front of them. Far off beyond vision the rows of buses stood like obedient behemoths, their drivers drinking beer in the shade.

"Andrea!" I saw a child with red hair and a T-shirt with a peace sign, but I knew instantly that the child was not Andrea. "God," I screamed, but it was a curse, not a prayer. I grew still and quiet as if I were a deer in a forest and the hunter had his sights trained at my flank. I waited in the eye of the storm, quiet, without feeling. Dread erased all pictures in my mind. It cut off all words and thoughts. I froze. There was Andrea sitting on someone else's blanket; a boy with a Magic Marker was drawing peace signs on her arm.

"No," she said when I pulled her toward me. "I want to stay here."

I slapped her on the face. Everyone around stared at me. "God," I said; it was still a curse.

On the Metroliner back to New York, I apologized to Andrea. I explained I had been scared. She sat in my lap and put her head on my shoulder, and playing with a strand of her hair and fingering my stained and sweaty blouse, she fell asleep. I held her gently as the train swayed from side to side, as it passed through the tunnel, as it rattled past Baltimore row houses where laundry still hung from balconies, as it sped through the dairy farms of New Jersey and past the factories of Newark and the bridges that crossed the swamplands at the side of the Hudson River. I held her all the way home.

"We ain't gonna practice war no more," I sang into her ear.

"No," I said as we rode up the elevator, "you don't have to take a bath tonight."

"Did you go on peace marches with your mother?" she asked me.

"No," I said, "but I saved tin cans, and I knitted a square for a blanket my class sent overseas."

"What?" she asked, but fell asleep before I had to explain.

My Friend Nancy, who had written a book called *The Gender Blues*, an exploration of depression in women, asked me to meet her for lunch. Before the waiter had brought the rolls she leaned across the table, her long arms reaching for the silver chain I wore around my neck. "You know why women are told to buy cosmetics, new cosmetics, better cosmetics, different-colored cosmetics, all the time? It's because of the oil industry. Don't be naive"—she noticed my incredulous expression—"do you know how much oil is used in every lipstick, every dab of blush, each swipe of eyeliner? The economic powers in this country want us to keep on buying. If we stopped—if for one moment each woman in America looked in the mirror and said, 'I like myself just the way I am. George doesn't put pancake on his nose every morning and he looks fine'—if *Vogue* put on its cover a model with a perfectly scrubbed face, do you know how many businesses would scream, how much behind-the-scenes pressure would be applied? Quickly, 'They' in the advertising industry would take *Vogue* off the newsstands and bum it in a great bonfire on Madison Avenue. Do you think, in your wildest dreams of a new golden age of equality, justice, and liberation for all, they wouldn't make ash out of a model whose face mocked their pocketbooks with her own natural skin?"

"Who is They?" I asked. My friend Nancy had lost her dear friend of five years to a younger woman and was not sounding altogether all right.

"They"—she waved her hand around the room in an inclusive gesture—"They are the ones who prevent women's books from being well reviewed. They are the ones who make sure that if a woman is elected to political office she's either too old or too ugly to inspire imitation."

"Are They the ones who also killed Karen Silkwood?" I smiled at her.

"You know what I mean"—she glared at me impatiently—"you agree, I'm sure that They allowed women into the job market when the economy was booming and there was a need for more workers especially at the lower levels; when the first whiff of recession comes along out will go the women, back to the kitchens, where, the press will suddenly be saying, they wanted to be all the time, poor things, driven from their hearth by unfeeling feminists who slipped value confusion into their morning cereal. You know that's the way it's going to be. As soon as They need us at home buying things in the supermarket, making an audience for the daytime soaps so we can listen to the ads and run out and buy some more, as soon as that happens, off with our measly jobs, back to the washing machine, that shining white altar of each home. Every women's magazine is going to discover the virtue of the large family that buys many boxes of Pampers and thousands of shoes that are outgrown in three weeks."

"But Nancy," I said, "I don't believe in your They. They are us, all of us together, and that includes you and me." I was feeling foolish about the antiwrinkle cream I had just purchased for twenty-five dollars, even though I suspected it would work only on deposed Rumanian princesses who had affairs with well-known Hollywood actors and would prove ineffective on the skin of New York City feminists who had bad dreams about rabbis who lived in the eighteenth century and were best known for their interest in things divine, not those of the flesh. Before the coffee arrived, Nancy told me that her son had taken a job as a nurse's aide. I remembered when she wanted him to be a district attorney and put rapists behind bars.

"If you don't believe they are undermining us," said Nancy, "then why are you so undermined?"

I shrugged.

LETTER RECEIVED: Dear Mrs. Annie Johnson, Your daughter, Andrea Johnson, has joined us at the Yeshiva Rachel. She has asked me to write to you so that you can take your rightful share in her new life. Several months ago I found your daughter in the Plaza outside the Hilton Hotel. She was sitting on the grass with her backpack beside her. She looked disheveled and confused. There was an odor in her clothes and no doubt she had not found the opportunity to cleanse herself for a considerable time. I struck up a conversation with her and encouraged her to return with me to our yeshiva, where she has remained ever since. Surely the One Above must have been looking out for your daughter and arranged this meeting. She told us of her very sad experiences at home, the early death of her non-Jewish father and your struggles to bring her up. She speaks of you with respect and affection. We believe that she is not a bad girl but one who has responded with understandable sensitivity and pain to the conditions of life outside the covenant. We have enabled her to understand that the world of the modern machine, the world of the jumping pictures on the television screen, the newest fashions and the latest sound, has not and cannot bring peace to her troubled soul. This is because your daughter is a very special person with a deep spiritual thirst. She has been reaching for the path, longing for the path, her entire life. Her inability to conform to your expectations was a sign of her real nature struggling to assert itself, searching in vain among the cleverness of the world for the truth that would nurture and cherish her, the place for her to dwell in righteousness and holiness. It is here among us. Each day she changes into an increasingly contented, useful and virtuous woman. Her progress has been remarkable. Her eyes are clear, her thoughts are ordered. She has demonstrated good learning skills and a true compassion and understanding of others. Under the direction of my wife she has adopted some important personal hygienic habits as well as our rudimentary expectations of a Jewish woman. We have taken care of some necessary dental matters and are instructing her by example in matters of modesty and devotion. Each day she settles into her self and we see her grow and become ready to take on increasingly complicated chores and responsibilities. She is truly a jewel in the treasure house of the Jewish people.

We know that her father was not Jewish. In America we know many women such as yourself became undone, mistook the stranger for the liberator and became blinded to the truth within. We are completely unconcerned about the religious affiliation of her father, for us he was no more than the physical convenience that enabled this precious soul to find breath. We count her as one of ours because her mother is Jewish. However, we would appreciate some proof of your original status. It would save your daughter from the additional effort, which she is quite willing to make, of a formal conversion. Perhaps you have a birth certificate with your maiden name on it? A letter from your rabbi will do. If you are at present unaffiliated, and I understand from Sarai that this is so, a letter from the rabbi of your parents would be acceptable. Perhaps you have some other living relatives who could vouch for you. They must be male and we need at least three of them. I hope that you will want to support your daughter in her return to a life within the people, a life dedicated to the will of the One Above. Your daughter is now living with the Halacha, the holy laws that give shape and purpose to human life. Your daughter is no longer cut off, a dangling spit of flesh and bone; now she is engaged with us in the effort to bring together the king and the queen, the spirit and the power, so that the Messiah can walk on the streets of Jerusalem and the Garden of the Lord one day open its gate and welcome us all.

Your daughter, Sarai, is a valued recruit in the army of Hashem. We extend our congratulations to you. K'lal Israel, all of Israel, rejoices when a daughter has opened her eyes and seen that the frivolity, the carnal delights of the world, have nothing more to offer her. K'lal Israel rejoices when she opens her heart to Him Who will hear her and bring her true sight as she repents and returns to righteousness. Holy is His name.

Your daughter has taken a Hebrew name, as befits a child of this place. She has chosen the name Sarai, the mother of us all. Sarah, who like your daughter waited a long time for the visit of the angel and whose goodness and piety has inspired generations of women to gentle acts of service in the pursuit of a pure body and soul, to keep the laws of the food, to keep the laws of physical separation, of immersion, of cleanliness. We felt that Sarai would be an especially appropriate name for your child because she seemed so in need of mothering and Sarah was the mother of the entire Jewish people. We have found in your daughter the capacities (stillborn in the secular world) to one day be a mother to herself and then in time to be a mother to her children, guiding them in the ways of Torah. It will give you joy, I am certain, to learn that Sarai now laughs with her friends, learns to cook and to pray, and when she is ready we will help her find a husband so that she can increase the numbers of the House of Israel and live with honor among us for the rest of her days.

I have written many of these letters and have been visited by many parents and so I am aware that this is difficult for you. In your cities our light has dimmed, been replaced by the incessant whine of the new. We must seem alien and frightening to someone who has not heard His voice. Our ways are the old ways that have accompanied us throughout this pause between creation and redemption. We ask you to trust us, do not fear for your daughter, do not pressure her to return to a world where she wandered without place, like a seed that cannot find the earth and remains in the belly of the wind, sterile and hard. Such a child as yours needs time for healing, for rising up, for returning. In coming to Jerusalem, in sitting in the park outside the Hilton Hotel, she put herself in the way of the One Who will continue to embrace her as the days spin out, lengthening the distance from her error-filled past as she forgets what must be forgotten.

We would be most happy to have you visit us in Jerusalem and see for yourself the peace and sanctity that reside here with us. Our ways will seem less strange to you if you spend some time among our people. We will house you with one of our English-speaking families, who will welcome you as a lost relative and show you every consideration. As you consider all this, remember your daughter whirling about this globe, afraid of the night, clutching at men as if they could save her from the daily bruising she endured. This was not her fault. She is not a failure. She is a spiritual child who was destined to ascend to higher levels, whose soul was uncomfortable in the fleshpots, in the marketplaces of Sodom. We value her and she has come to value herself. As Gd will call all of His creatures to Him at the end of time, so He has called your child now and she has heeded the voice. We thank you for the gift of your daughter and hope to have the necessary documents in our hands promptly. Sincerely, Rabbi Joshua Cohen.

Contemporary Soldier Women in a Changing World

Gloria Goldreich

Gloria Goldreich was born in 1934 into a Zionistic, strongly Jewish family in the Bronx. She graduated from Brandeis University with a B.A. degree in European civilization and did graduate work in Jewish history at the Hebrew University in Jerusalem. She describes herself as being "unilaterally committed to Israel's security and survival," and in her essays and public speaking she tries to combat what she sees as "the harsh, negative response to Israel by many in the intellectual community." Goldreich says that she tries to incorporate many literary "layers" in her books, and she takes pride in crafting her books carefully. She is also pleased that, because of their strong historical content, they can serve an educational function for readers.

Goldreich is best known to the American reading public through her popular multigenerational sagas, such as *Leah's Journey* (1979), winner of the National Jewish Book Award for Fiction, which take their Jewish heroines from intensely Jewish Old World environments through struggle, adventure, and eventual romantic fulfillment in the United States. Readers report being impressed with the fact that the heroines of Goldreich sagas are strong, independent women who cope with seemingly insurmountable obstacles on their own. She has written many short stories and critical essays for periodicals as diverse as *Commentary*, *Redbook*, and *Ms.* and is currently working on a new novel, which deals with women's friendships.

In Goldreich's novel *Four Days*, both the protagonist, Ina, and her mother, Shirley, are survivors of a Nazi concentration camp. However, Ina's subconscious allows her to remember almost nothing of her nightmare childhood, even after extensive analysis, while Shirley has every detail of the experience burned indelibly into her conscious memory. In the camp, Shirley kept Ina alive through heroic, never-flagging efforts of alertness, will, cleverness, and instinct. Thin, pale, indomitable, Ina's Holocaust mother was a fierce angel of life. After liberation from the camp and emigration to the United States, however, Shirley seems to live out each detail of her days in reaction to the evil years. If she was obsessed with Ina and survival in the camps, in the United States she throws herself into business, surrounds herself with luxury, and seems almost cool to her daughter. In a telling vignette, Ina notes, "Shirley Cherne remembered every thing. Every incident and every odor. *Pishachs and dreck*. Urine and Shit. The stench pursued her. . . . In the Cherne household the bathrooms sparkled, the water in the toilets swirled bluely, the towels were changed each day, and plants grew on lucite shelves." Shirley's reaction goes deeper: she is unable to bring herself ever to change a grandchild's diaper, declaring that she has already encountered enough excrement in her life. Goldreich explores the ways in which the mother–daughter relationship, always complex, is further complicated in the families of Holocaust survivors and their children.

•

"The Holocaust Mother" (excerpt)

Although it was not yet noon, a small line had already formed at the hostess's station in the small restaurant that only New Yorkers would call a luncheonette. Tiffany lamps dangled from the fake wood beams of the low ceilings, and the chairs around the mahogany-stained Formica tables were of a rich maroon leatherette, their color matching the coarse carpeting. It was called a luncheonette, he supposed, because paper doilies rather than tablecloths covered the tables and because counter service was available. Every stool there was already occupied by men and women who ate quickly with fierce concentration, glancing from their unread paperbacks to their watches. Muzak teased the air with a medley of songs resurrected from the fifties. "Dance, Ballerina, Dance," "Harbor Lights," "In the Sleepy Town of San Juanita . . ." Vaughn Monroe's voice carried him back to distant days when he and Ina danced to caressing tones in tiny Cambridge bars, listened to the car radio in Ray's old Dodge, their bodies pressed close in warmth and promise.

Ray took a place in line and watched the entry. Just as the last chorus of "The Miracle of the Bells" came to its mournful end, Shirley Cherne pushed through the revolving doors and walked immediately to his side. She had not doubted that he would be there before her. She did not expect to be kept waiting and seldom was. Even Jeddy, an inveterate dawdler, hurried when he had to meet his grandmother.

She wore a pale lilac linen suit with a matching blouse of fine batiste, and when she stood on tiptoe to kiss him, he smelled her perfume—the thickly sweet aroma of early spring flowers seeped from her pores and mingled with the dusty rose scent of her thick face powder. Silver waves crested across the upswept torrent of her chestnut hair, teased and lacquered into submission, each hair fearfully, obediently, in place. She worked long and diligently at teasing her hair into a semblance of thickness. It had grown back after the war but not as heavy and luxuriant as the fabled tresses of her girlhood.

"Ray-Mond, how are you?" She always pronounced his name as though it were two separate words, and he smiled because he had, long ago, decided that that indicated affection rather than affectation.

"Fine. Good. You look marvelous, Shirley."

"Saks." She patted her skirt, her fingers knowledgeably appreciating the fabric. "The blouse from Bendel's." She touched its tie. She was a manufacturer and had access to showrooms and wholesale houses, but she would buy only in the best Fifth Avenue stores.

"I like the salesgirl to wait on me," she said half defiantly, half apologetically, but Ray suspected that what she liked was the catering to her individuality, the calling of her name, the gentle obsequiousness and subtle pampering she received from the elegant saleswomen. She had, after all, spent long years of her young womanhood in ragged scraps of clothing, in threadbare uniforms that did not fit, and then in hand-me-down dresses plucked from the overcrowded closets of the benevolent. She had earned the luxury of trying on carefully selected garments in private dressing rooms with thickly carpeted floors through which soft music floated gently, persuasively.

"Hostess! A table for two, please," she called out.

There were two couples ahead of them, but the hostess, a tall blonde woman who stared sadly out at her customers through eyes weighted down with thick blue mascaraed lids, motioned them forward with her great fan of oversized maroon menus.

"These people called for a reservation," she said defiantly to those who stood ahead of them, and she winked at Shirley Cherne, whose mascara matched her own. Survivor blue, Ina called it bitterly, Ray remembered. The hostess, he decided, was probably divorced and supported an autistic child and an invalid mother. Tragedies, like opposites, attract. As they sat down and she handed them their menus, Ray saw a dollar bill slip from his mother-in-law's hand into her fringed pocket. He was annoyed but said nothing. It would, after all, do no good. Shirley Cherne was an expert on the handling of queues—years of her life had been spent standing on them.

In return, the hostess herself took their orders—a tunafish salad for him and a cottage cheese salad plate for her. There was a choice between a large salad or a small one, and she ordered the large one although she would not finish it. She enjoyed seeing food on her plate when she was through eating. In this she was very unlike her brother-in-law, Bette's father. Ray thought of him now as Shirley spread a luncheon roll with a thick cloak of butter. She would take only a single bit of it, he knew, and then lavishly butter another before the end of the meal.

When Bette's father died, Ray and Ina had helped to close his tiny Bronx apartment because Bette was so distraught. He had lived alone and bought little because he ate little, yet his refrigerator had been packed with tiny packets of leftovers, encased in torturously constructed envelopes of plastic, silver foil, brown paper. Ancient crusts, dried scraps of meat, pale and brittle, withered rinds of cheese covered with verdant mold, had flaked and crumbled in their hands. Lemon peels, faded to the color and thinness of old gold, gravies congealed into graying masses of fat trapped in tiny jars, had crouched in corners of the greasy shelves. Peshi, his wife, Bette's mother, had starved to death. So had his parents, a brother and sister, a half-remembered infant son. He took no chances now and walked always in the shadow of fear, scooping packets of sugar and crackers into his pockets when he ate his solitary meals at restaurant counters. When Ray opened a cabinet in that fetid kitchen, dozens of cellophane-wrapped clusters of Ry-Krisp and Melba Toast tumbled out, and Ina filled three paper bags with hardened clumps of restaurant sugar.

Ray had vomited in the dead man's bathroom. It was not the decay that upset him but the sour miasma of terror that hung like a mist in those three sad rooms where a man (his children's great-uncle), who had escaped death, had lived in fear of life. That same nausea teased him when Shirley Cherne overordered and then looked with satisfaction at a plate still full, as though she had won a victory, had outwitted a malevolent schemer who would see her wanting. Waste triumphed over want. He thought too of a distant cousin of Ina's, a veteran of Terezin, who spent two hours over a simple dinner, masticating each bite soberly, reverently, and he wondered if anyone had done a study of the eating patterns of survivors. If they had not, surely they would. The Holocaust was academically fashionable just now.

"So how is Ina this morning?" she asked.

"Isaacs removed the fibroma. It was a very short procedure, and it was larger than he thought it would be, but everything went well. Ina was a little more upset than I expected." He added this cautiously, hesitantly, a verbal fisherman slowly extending a lure.

Shirley Cherne turned to her salad, carved a tomato rosette into small petals that bled across the lettuce.

"Always women are upset when something affects the breast," she said harshly. She bit into her carrot and thought of the German guard with whom she had sat in the fire-rimmed darkness. The woman had wept, and Shirley (Shaindel then) had comforted her in word and wished her dead in thought. Not one cancer but a thousand should grow within that body, within all their bodies. She speared an olive and spat the pit out, unashamed of her thought, her memory. Hatred was a weapon, and it had sustained her. It was impossible to fight without hating the enemy.

"Yes, that's what Isaacs said," Ray replied.

Shirley nodded. He was a nice boy, Ina's Raymond. She had always liked him, from the very first day that Ina brought him to the house. She had known it would be all right even if they had decided so quickly. He was so soft and gentle, with a winsome helplessness in his eyes, an awkwardness in the way he moved his long, too-thin body. It came, maybe, from being orphaned so suddenly, when he was too old to be called a boy and too young to be recognized as a man. His sister, that Dorothy with the empty womb and open arms, had given him support yes, love yes, but not strength. Well, you could not give a child everything. You could say, maybe, that she had given Ina strength but not love, and Ina, maybe, would say she had given her nothing. All right. Let her say what she will. After all, so smart, computer lady. She, Shirley Cherne, knew what she knew. And Raymond, as it turned out, was a good boy and not weak. She had sensed that. He was good, competent, and only a strong man could be that gentle with his children. And he had wonderful hands. Long fingers. Yedidiah had had such hands. Yedidiah. She filled her mouth too full of cottage cheese and spoke with the snowy granules trailing from the corners of her lips.

"Maybe it's something else Ina is upset about?"

"Yes. There is something else." He hesitated, always uneasy with his wife's mother, whom he thought he loved but knew he did not understand. "Ina's pregnant. She's about five or six weeks pregnant, and I guess you realize we never planned on having another baby."

"So you didn't plan. So, an accident." Words did not frighten her. She used them harshly, accurately. "Cancer," she said aloud while others whispered: "It's very serious, dangerous." "Cancer," she said. "He has cancer." Never would she say "in financial difficulties—troubled times." "Bankrupt," she mouthed loud and clear. Not for her the euphemistic "We didn't plan another baby"—no, "an accident." A careless collision of ovum and sperm resulting in the casualty of a zygote, an embryo, a wriggling worm of life generated by an accident.

"So what do you do about such an accident?" She took a bite of coleslaw, snipped the head off her pickle, and pushed the plate away. It was still covered with vegetables and half a scoop of cheese.

"We're not sure," he said. He wanted her carrot, but then she would have less food to discard and he would deprive her of the pleasure of waste, of the temptation she tossed at gods she did not believe in.

"Not sure. For not sure you don't stay in the hospital an extra few days."

"We're undecided," he amended, weakly.

The waitress brought their coffee and gave Shirley two creams. She would open them both but use only half of each, he knew, but wondered how the waitress had known. He was right. She laced the coffee with sugar and stirred it. Often she ordered a side dish of whipped cream which she spooned onto the top of the cup, but seldom did she empty it. Once, in a restaurant Ina had protested when Shirley ordered coffee, called for whipped cream and brandy, stirred them in, and discarded the concoction after a single sip.

"Let your mother eat the way she wants," Norman Cherne had said loudly. "What do you know? American princess!"

Ina had blushed, and her father had looked sorrowfully at her. He spoke to his daughter rarely but looked at her a great deal. She looked so like his mother, whom he had last seen walking with his father down a wide Warsaw boulevard, hugging a bundle to her as though she cuddled a very young infant. Like Ina, his mother had been a tall woman who wore her long black hair caught in a knot at the nape of her neck.

"Ina wants an abortion?" Shirley asked.

Ray was startled. She had not said "You and Ina . . ." but only "Ina," as though she had some defined prescience of their situation, of their conversations, of his urging and her reticence, his growing certainty and her slowly evolving ambivalence.

"I think," he replied, "she's not sure of what she wants."

"Sure. What's sure? No one is sure of anything. Only dying. You do what you have to do."

To his surprise, she lifted her coffee cup and drained it, even spooning up the sugar encrusted at the bottom, as though suddenly hungry for sweetness, for energy, for life sustenance.

"You want the baby" she said, and it was not a question.

He nodded.

She picked up her white leather pocketbook, extracted her makeup case, and painted her mouth a shade of lilac that matched her suit, adding a layer of powder to the dusty veil that shrouded her skin. Her fingers were twisted with arthritis and weighted down with heavy rings, but they moved to these small tasks of vanity with surprising deftness. She did not wait for the waitress to bring the bill but stood. Again, he smelled the springtime sweetness of her perfume as she bent to kiss him on the cheek.

"I must hurry now. A big shipment of fabric comes this afternoon, and I have to check the bills of lading. They would steal from the blind, these suppliers. And I go first to see Ina. Thank you for the lunch. It will be all right, Ray-Mond."

Her lips brushed his cheek, and then she was on her way, walking briskly, rushing past two young girls who stood in her way. At the exit she paused to study herself in the mirror above the cigarette machine. She returned a stray tendril to her upswept crown of hair and hurried out. The waitress arrived with the check, but Ray ordered another cup of coffee and drank it very slowly.

"You do what you have to do," his mother-in-law had said, but then how did anyone know what he had to do? The simple imperatives of his life trotted through his thoughts, clearly defined. He *had* to earn a living, pay his bills, stop for red lights, make sure his children were in good health, properly cared for, and educated. But in all other things he was trapped in the dangerous prison of freedom. He did not have to urge his wife to have a child she did not want. And yet, and yet. Who was it who said, "We may not know what is right or wrong, but we always know where our duty lies"? Goddamn it, it had been Churchill, and he had not been thinking about abortions but about the future of Europe. For the first time that day Ray smiled, and he took up the check, leaving the waitress a very large tip.

Shirley Cherne took a cab across town and stared at the newly blooming foliage with the avid interest of an infrequent theatergoer absorbed by a unique stage set. She did not often see trees in great number or a wild overgrowth of vines and bushes. A neat parade of skinny maples marched up her Forest Hills street, and even the grass that thrust its green teeth tenaciously through pavement cracks was clipped away by the fastidious custodians who pruned the puny hedges and mowed balding patches of green. In Long Island City, where Cherne Knitwear occupied a narrow gray stone building, scrawny ailanthus trees struggled in sandy yards, and dusty urban sparrows perched on leafless bushes. Yet once trees and greenery had been an intrinsic part of her life, part of her personal landscape.

She had grown up in the Polish countryside, and the woodlands had been the playgrounds of her childhood. With Polish playmates she had scaled the great oak trees, slid down vines, gathered berries from bushes hidden in deep tents of soaring evergreens. When she married Nachum Czernowitz and went to live in Warsaw, they found a flat near the great municipal park so that when she awakened each morning she could see the branches of trees scraping the sky. When the war came and rumors of a ghetto began, she turned for refuge to the forest of her childhood, but her wilderness playmates were pale-eyed strangers. They had forgotten her laughter and remembered only her Jewishness, now a crime for which they, like their German masters, found her guilty. They stared resentfully at her fine city boots, her lined cloak, and turned away from her.

Still, she and Nachum wandered briefly with her sister, Peshi, and Peshi's husband. It was summer, and they found a hunter's shack with a pine-needle floor. On that harsh and fragrant bed, she and Nachum had come together in urgent passion, breathing in the odors of earth and growth, grasping at life as death pursued them hard. But of course they had to leave the forest and the tenuous shelter of that shack. Winter was coming, and the infant children, Bette and Ina, shivered constantly. Yedidiah, the toddler, blew on his fingers and hugged his small body but rarely cried. Perhaps he had known even then that tears were futile. Crying, their children had discovered, was a luxury reserved for Aryan children.

She stared out now, as Central Park rolled past, and breathed deeply, contentedly, at the sight of a small pine copse at the bottom of a gentle hill. The cab slowed, and the driver reached for a cigarette. He was a heavy, pleasant-faced man with sandy hair and blue eyes. A picture of twin girls with hair that matched his own, wearing matching white organdy communion dresses, was taped to his windshield. Shirley Cherne looked at his name on the medallion and saw with relief that he was Michael Flanagan. How long would it be, she wondered, until men who looked like Michael Flanagan did not fill her with uncertainty, fear? Even on her Forest Hills street she pressed herself close against a building when a group of boys wearing club jackets passed.

"You are a stupid woman" she told herself severely, and turned her thoughts, forcefully, back to the fabric shipments she expected that afternoon, the load of zippers she had accepted on consignment, the defective trimmings she had received that morning. The rickrack had been faded. Such *chutzpah* to send her faded goods. By the time the cab stopped in front of Mount Lebanon, she had stirred herself into an anger that threatened neither mood nor memory.

"You have very pretty daughters," she told Michael Flanagan, and gave him an extra dollar.

"Thanks." But he did not turn or smile, and she did not care. She had given him the dollar because his name had not been Mueller or Krantz.

She bought a box of candy for Ina in the hospital gift shop and knew that Ina would accept it with a thin, accusing smile. She should have gone to a store, not stopped at a convenience shop. She should have taken the time to buy a present that mattered—to think, touch, consider. Once, when Ina was away at college, she had told her mother that she was the only girl in her dormitory who did not receive packages of homebaked cakes, carefully selected clothing. The Chernes sent her money, generous checks, but Ina wanted the talismans of caring—the hand-knit sweater, the freshly baked cookies. It was not the candy Ina would object to, but the implied thoughtlessness.

"That should be all you're missing," Shirley Cherne had countered then, but she had known she was wrong, just as she knew she was wrong today. You did not bring a daughter still recovering from surgery, however minor, a box of chocolates she would not want to eat. Still, what could she do? She was what she was, just as Ina was what she was. And today they had more important things to discuss than why Ina had no mother-knitted vests. The woman next to Shirley at the gift shop cash register held an oversized blue velour elephant.

"For my new grandson," she said, smiling. "I know it's silly, but I couldn't resist it."

"Very nice," Shirley assured her. She had bought her own grandchildren's layettes in Altman's and warm comforters in Bloomingdale's, but never had she bought a newborn infant an overstuffed animal.

Ina was sitting up in bed when Shirley arrived. Her dark hair was caught back in a neat coil, and she wore a negligee of buttercup yellow. Shirley saw the bulk of the bandage through the thin fabric, and her heart turned. She did not like to think of a surgeon's scalpel cutting through Ina's pale flesh. How close to the nipple was the incision? she wondered, and remembered how Ina had hugged her small body as a child, always covering the rose-brown tips of flesh at her breasts, fearful always of nakedness. She and Bette had known, with the sly wisdom of children, that there was only nakedness in the death camp, that the deadly gas sprayed down on vulnerable unclothed bodies, and in their last moments men hugged their genitals and women concealed their milkless breasts. A small boy who worked as a *sonderkommando* had shared his knowledge with the little girls, and they had accepted it as they accepted the blue mist of smoke that hovered over the camp, the stinking of charred flesh, the incandescent fires that burned fiercely through the night amid the moans and muted crying. Children are like that, a Warsaw psychiatrist who worked in the quarry with her had told Shaindel. If they are born in a forest, they think the whole world is nothing but woods. If they grow up in a concentration camp, for them the world is nothing but flames and misery. The psychiatrist had choked to death on a rusk of bread three days before the liberation, but Shaindel had told the woman's son, who sought her out at war's end, that his mother had died of heart failure. She could not tell him how another inmate had thrust her hand into the dead woman's throat, removed the masticated hunk of food, and eaten it hungrily, huddled in a corner. Shaindel had not, could not, condemn her. She had been human enough to be shamed by her action and brave enough to struggle for survival.

"Mother you look marvelous." Ina set aside the book she had been reading.

Shirley kissed her awkwardly on the cheek, her fingers passing expertly over the fabric of the nightgown. "Batiste. Very nice material," she said.

"Ray picked it up at Bloomingdale's."

"Very nice detail work. Good smocking." Shirley held out the box of candy and saw a large red Blum's box on Ina's table.

"Mmm. Chocolate mints. Thanks, but I don't feel like any just now. Dot sent that box from Blum's."

"She had a good time on St. Thomas, your sister-in-law?"

"She was in the Bahamas, not St. Thomas," Ina said, and wondered why it was her mother did not like Dot. Everyone liked Dot. Not that Shirley had ever said anything—nor would she admit to her dislike. "Why shouldn't I like her?" she protested when Ina discussed it. "She ever did anything to me?" And of course there was no answer. Ina shrugged and lifted the box of mints.

"Miriam, would you like a mint?" she called to the young woman in the next bed.

"No thank you."

"Mother, this is Miriam Gottlieb. Miriam, this is my mother, Shirley Cherne. Miriam has a new baby. He's had some problems, but today he is doing better."

"Much better," Miriam said emphatically.

Shirley looked at her uneasily. She had heard that tone before, that urgent emphasis, that near-belligerence of voice in which dying women insisted they were fine, and mothers whose children writhed in the last stage of dysentery said over and over: "It's just diarrhea. She'll be fine. Just a little diarrhea." Later, standing over a small lifeless body, a weak voice protested: "She's just sleeping. She's not dead. She's just sleeping."

Ach, she was reading too much into things today. The girl had said her baby was much better, so let her baby be much better.

"Good," Shirley told Miriam Gottlieb. "A lot of babies are born a little weak. It's okay. It will be okay. You should have a mint."

"All right."

Ina smiled. Miriam clearly knew when someone was in command. If Shirley Cherne told her to have a mint, she had damn well better have a mint.

"That's a sensible fabric," Shirley said approvingly, looking at Miriam's striped nightgown. "That you don't have to send to a hand laundry. Now, you don't mind if I close the curtain? I have to talk to my daughter private. Business matters. You understand?"

"No. Of course not," Miriam said, and Shirley drew the curtain around Ina's bed and pulled the bedside chair close to her daughter.

"That was very rude," Ina said, her lips set in a thin line. Her breast was beginning to throb fiercely, and she felt the flesh beneath the dressing to be searing with heat. When her mother left, she would ask the nurse for something for the pain. Soon her mother would leave. She never stayed very long. Not at the apartment or the Amagansett house, not at weddings or funerals. Shirley Cherne was a busy woman who had to keep moving, who could not and would not remain still. Oddly enough, Dr. Berenson had once said that about Ina herself. Why, the analyst had asked in her noncommittal professional voice, did Ina Feldman have to keep moving?

"It wasn't rude," Shirley retorted. "It was necessary. I have things to tell you. Important things." She looked at her daughter and saw the glint of febrile pain in her eyes. "You don't feel good?"

"Not so good. But it will pass.

"Everything passes," Shirley said.

She poured a cup of water and held it to Ina's lips, supporting her head. Once, in the camp, Ina had become feverish, and Shirley had managed to obtain a cup of water from that guard who thought herself a friend. She had fed it to Ina, holding her head just as she held it now. She wondered if Ina remembered that time. No. Of course not. Ina, and Bette too, remembered little, if anything of those years. Most of the children—those who had been children then—did not. She envied them. It was a blessing to be able to forget. She and Nachum remembered everything, everything. She sighed and looked at the large garnet ring, twisted into a setting of antique gold, on her middle finger.

"I feel much better. Really. What did you want to talk about?" Ina asked.

"I had lunch with Ray-Mond." Her voice sank to a whisper. "He told me you're pregnant."

"Yes. But only a few weeks."

"And you think about an abortion."

"We've talked about it." Ina's tone was guarded. Care was necessary in any exchange with Shirley Cherne. Verbal shafts had to be swift and accurate. Her mother was a dangerous sparring partner.

They spoke very softly now. Beyond the screen Miriam Gottlieb chatted into the phone. "He's so much better. I even went to peek at him today. He has the sweetest hands."

Shirley Cherne sighed and licked her lips. Always they spoke of the hands and fingers, the new mothers. And who could blame them? There was such a miracle in the formation of those tiny hands, those soft, perfect fingers. A scrap of lipstick settled on her tongue. It tasted of lilacs, the wild purple sprays that had flourished across the verdant meadows that dotted the lost landscape of her childhood. She turned back to Ina.

"Don't talk about it. Forget from it. I know what you should do." Her voice was quiet, defiantly definite.

"What do you know? How can you know?" Ina's eyes flashed with anger, and she forgot that only a moment before her head had rested in her mother's hand. Her back was tensed, and a new pain shot through the breast. She struck her fingers together in a fist, useless and impotent.

"I know that you shouldn't have an abortion," Shirley persisted. "And how do I know? I know because I had one, and I know what it did to me."

"You had one? When? Where?"

Ina sank back against the pillow, weak, disbelieving. She knew about abortions. Her college classmates had had them in dimly lit offices on narrow streets, offering names that were not their own for records that would not be kept. Women in her consciousness-raising group had had abortions in clinics run as efficiently as supermarkets—paper gowns and paper slippers, ERA literature and copies of *Ms.* on bedside tables, gynecologists who talked as fast as they worked: "A second of pain—that's all. Here, we're through. Have you thought about an IUD—having your tubes tied—how about your old man getting a vasectomy? Off you go. There'll be some pain, but don't worry."

And occasionally young programmers or a secretary in her office had taken Monday off and returned to work pale and sad-eyed. By week's end both the pallor and sadness were gone, and a subtle hardness lurked in their eyes. But classmates, friends, and young employees were not Shirley Cherne/Shaindel Czernowitz, her mother.

Always, Ina thought of her mother in two dimensions. Shaindel was the bald woman shrunk to skeletal thinness, whose bony arms hurt the child Ina when they reached around her for a desperate hug. Shaindel stood straight among the women, broken and crippled, and her voice rang with strength and certainty when others wept and moaned. It was she who managed always to find an extra crust of bread, a wizened graying morsel of meat; it was she who knew that the soup meted out for lunch should be saved until evening when it would have jelled and thus could line the stomach so that sleep was not made impossible by hunger. Shaindel, the mama, meant life and hope to the child who played on the splintered floor of a barrack room fetid with the stink of vomit and ordure, where tired women lived in a miasma of disbelief.

Ina, the woman, remembered so little. ("Anything that comes to mind," Eleanor Berenson always urged gently.) The recalled incidents were small flashes of remembrance, isolated splinters of terror from which she could not construct a single plank. Even the dream offered no clues, no scraps of insight. But she did remember her mother's face, so strong, so sharply beautiful in its determination, the features carved starkly out of the bone of the fleshless skull. "Mama!" the small Ina had called in the night, the terrible fire-spewing night, and Shaindel's arms, her milky bones luminous through the wasted skin, would come around her child's body and rock her gently into the safety of sleep.

Shirley Cherne was the woman her mother had become in America—a transmogrified figure with newly fleshy arms and newly grown chestnut hair, who rocketed into the new American life, startling her husband with a talent for business he had not known she possessed, with ambition and determination. Shirley Cherne was the businesswoman who came home from the factory irritable and exhausted and seemed surprised to find Ina in the apartment. Sometimes Ina, growing up lonely and alone, only Mary Noble, Backstage Wife, and Stella Dallas peopling her wintry afternoons (she envied then, with all her heart, Stella's daughter, Laurel, whose mother talked to her), thought that she had dreamed up the person who had been Shaindel Czernowitz, because certainly Shirley Cherne had never come to comfort her as she lay crying softly in the darkness.

"When did you have an abortion?" Ina asked. (Who asked a mother such a question? And yet she had asked it and had to know.)

"In the camp. The second week we were there. You won't remember. I was like you—only a few weeks pregnant, and I knew that for pregnant women there was no chance. Once you showed, they killed you. The women, even the guards, told stories. Almost all pregnant women were sent to the gas chambers. On some few others, they said, they did medical experiments. Monster babies were born. Monsters. You remember maybe the Grunwalds—second cousins to your father. Chana Grunwald gave birth to such a child—a head as big as a watermelon because of some hormone injections they gave her. Chana went to London after the war, and she had two more children—normal babies—but she killed herself. They told stories. A Latvian woman they let go to her eighth month, and then they induced labor—when the baby was born, they killed it, and the mother saw. She saw and died on the table. Her heart stopped."

"But why? Why did they kill it?" Ina whispered. She felt that her heart, too, would stop. Her breast throbbed, and her mouth was dry.

"Why? They needed reason? Maybe they had a new drug to try, to see how fast it could kill a newborn. Such important experiments they had—sterilizing young women, making twins. That was an important one for them—to make twins and double the Aryan population. That's what the world needed—twice as many Nazi animals to turn all of Europe into a death camp. Ach, I can't even think about it. I can't." She reached into her bag and found a tissue to wipe her eyes. Drops of mascara dripped like blood and stained the tissue blue. Ina turned her head. Her mother almost never cried. The last time had been at Bette's father's funeral, and her weeping then had been swift and silent.

"What did you do—about the pregnancy?" Ina asked softly.

Ben Gottlieb came into the room and waved to her. She heard his voice, soft and controlled, and Miriam's brittle laugh traveled over the curtained screen. "Cute," Miriam said, and there was the rustle of paper as a gift was unwrapped, held up, admired. All visitors to hospitals should be like Ben, carrying clever talismans of the world outside, cheerful tales of health and normalcy. Ina did not want to hear what her mother had come to tell her. She wanted to see Miriam's present, listen to her gentle laughter, her new optimistic plans. Where would they hold the circumcision celebration? What food should be served?

"What could I do?" Shirley offered a question in reply—a Shirley technique. The buck does not stop here—it goes on and on. "Someone told me about a woman doctor—a prisoner. A brave woman. She changed names on medical charts—the living became the dead so that they could escape the appel, the roll call. She was everywhere, hiding the sick, stealing antibiotics. Somehow she got hold of a set of surgical instruments. How she kept them hidden in the barracks I don't know except that maybe she made a deal with the guards—helped them. They needed doctors also, believe me. From the highest social classes they didn't get concentration camp guards. Maybe she helped cure them from venereal disease, performed secret abortions. Do I know? But something she did because they let her keep those surgical tools. I went to her, and in a corner of the barracks, with the other women forming a screen in case a guard should come, she aborted that baby, scraped out my womb. She had no drugs, no chloroform. They stuffed a rag in my mouth so I couldn't scream, and two of the stronger women held me down while she worked. They put newspapers on the floor where I lay, and I watched my blood soak through the headlines, and then a small thing, a bloody bit of flesh, maybe the size of a small mouse, fell onto the paper. I thought it moved, but later they said I imagined that. I fainted then. See—who says God isn't full of mercy? And she was finished when I opened my eyes. She was a tall woman, that doctor, with green eyes the color of tears. 'I'm sorry,' she said. 'Thank you,' I told her. I never saw her again, although I heard that she survived the war and went to Israel. I hope it's true. And for what I did, God will forgive me." She did not cry now but stared toward the window where the spidery green leaves of a newly foliated tree pressed gently against the smoked glass pane.

"You did what you had to do," Ina said gently. She touched her mother's arms and moved her hand up to stroke the hair, rigid within its lacquer prison.

A small, bloodied thing, the size of a mouse, her mother had said. Was sex determined at six weeks' gestation? She could not remember. Had it been her brother or her sister, that embryo, the bloodied bit of human detritus scraped from her mother's womb that distant day? She would never know, nor would it, should it, make any difference. They called a parentless child an orphan. Was there a word, then, for a child bereft of siblings? Her mother had undergone the abortion their second week in the concentration camp—only two weeks then after Yedidiah's death in the transit camp. Twice then, in only a single month, Shaindel had been bereft. Pregnant with a child she could not bear, she had watched the silken lash of her dead son tremble on her finger. Poor Shaindel. Poor Shirley. Poor Mama. Ina's eyes burned.

She busied herself with words so that her heart would not break, because she remembered suddenly Yedidiah's laugh and how he could twist his fingers into strange contortions. He had been double-jointed, just as Jeddy was. She had forgotten that, or perhaps she had not wanted to remember it. Her mother had not wanted her to give Jeddy Yedidiah's name, but Ina had insisted on it. Her brother had been denied his life, but she would keep him alive within her own. Atonement perhaps, or guilt—what would Eleanor Berenson call it? Survivor guilt, perhaps. Certainly she would not call it love. Love was not a neurosis.

"Yes," Shirley said, "I did what I had to do. You're right. But for me it was the end. It dried me up. When they took that life from me, from my body, something ended. A snap. A dying. I was finished. Nothing. I thought of only one thing. To keep you alive. To see you strong. And I did keep you alive. I made you strong. You blame me for a lot—that I know. But this you have to give me—I made you strong."

She sat back in her chair, spent. The tie of her blouse had become undone, and the crisp linen of her suit was wilted. Her face, beneath its mask of rouge and powder, sagged. Ina saw her for the first time as an old woman, weak with age and memory.

"Mama." She had not used that word for a long time. "Mother," she said, cool and removed. She took Shirley's hand in her own and pressed it hard so that the rings cut into her skin. "Why did you tell me all this now?"

"Why? Because I don't want you to live like I do. With regret. With wondering. With sorrow. Because I don't want to happen to you what happened to me. I dried up, Ina. I was a young woman—much younger than you today. But from that day, when life was scraped from me, I became old, dry. When they took that baby, they took from me my life. That shouldn't happen to you. It wasn't for that that I kept you alive, made you strong."

"Mama. You did what you had to do. You had no choice."

"I know. But you, Ina—you have a choice. And something else I want to tell you. You know we go to *shul*, your father and I—we support the temple. Good Jews, they think we are. Your father believes in God. Still, he believes. He's a sick man. Stomach trouble. High blood pressure. But on Yom Kippur he fasts. A whole day. And sometimes he goes to *minyan* three times a day. More often with each year. It's a miracle. A man who saw his mother go in an action, whose son died in the night—he goes and thanks a

God full of mercy. *Nu*—so I go with him. I wear a hat, a nice suit. I kiss the Torah. But in God I don't believe. What I believe in is the Jewish people. Every Jewish baby born is a slap in Hitler's face. A new baby to take the place of my Yedidiah and of that bloody little mouse from my body that the women wrapped in newspaper and hid in the bottom of the garbage. They thought I didn't know, but I knew. From my body they took a life, wrapped it in a Polish newspaper, and hid it with the eggshells and potato peels. They had no choice. I had no choice. But you, Ina, you have a choice. So choose right. This I came to say to you today. Was I wrong to tell you? With you, sometimes I think that whatever I do is wrong."

But she had recovered her strength. She sat up straighter in the chair, retied the bow on her blouse, reached into her purse for her makeup bag, for the lipstick that tasted of wild lilacs, for the powder that would mask the tiny lines the trailing tears had left on her dry and withered cheeks.

Miriam Gottlieb's phone rang. A radio played too loudly in the room across the hall. Two interns and two nurses paused in their doorway. The young doctors were very tall and the women were very short. They laughed in unison, and sunlight from the wide hall window fell in dazzling golden petals across their white uniforms. Nurse Li slid into the room with a paper cup of pills for Ina. The red capsules gleamed like tiny rubies. She smiled at Shirley Cherne and crossed to Miriam's bed.

"I've just been to see your baby, Mrs. Gottlieb," she said, "and he's sleeping so sweetly."

"Doesn't he have wonderful fingers?" Miriam asked.

"Wonderful."

Ina's phone rang, and she spoke very briefly and hung up.

"That was Bette," she told her mother. "She said hello."

"She's coming to visit today?" Shirley stood up, brushing a speck of dust from her skirt. She was tired, very tired. Perhaps she would not go to the factory at all. Nachum could check on that fabric shipment. She would go home. No. She would go to Ina's apartment and see the children. She would take them for ice cream sodas to Baskin-Robbins.

"You think the children would like it if I took them for ice cream after school? And I could go with Rachel to buy the ballet dress she needs. She'll go alone, they'll sell her some junk. They take advantage of children."

"That would be wonderful," Ina said.

Shirley did not bend to kiss her. She touched instead the thin batiste sleeve of the yellow nightgown.

"This," she said "you'll have to wash by hand. All right. Why not?"

She moved aside the screen. Ben Gottlieb slept in the chair next to Miriam's bed, and the three women smiled maternally at him.

"Good-bye and good luck to you," Shirley said to Miriam, and walked from the room, her heels clicking sharply as she walked too quickly to the elevator.

When she reached the street, she saw that it had begun to rain. A light spring drizzle spattered the pavement with tiny teardrops. Two mothers, wheeling children in bright canvas strollers, walked past her. Laughing, talking, they moved slowly through the gently falling rain, and the children held up their faces and laughed as the droplets fell upon their eyes.

Ruth Knafo Setton

For many years, American Jewish male writers have been familiarizing the American reading public with the particulars of the Eastern European Jewish heritage as it has been experienced on both sides of the Atlantic ocean. The heritage and experiences of Sephardi Jews, however, have been little explored in American Jewish fiction; even more so, the lives of Sephardi Jewish women have seldom appeared in published fictional works.

Ruth Knafo Setton is one of several young American Jewish women of Sephardi extraction publishing fiction today. Setton holds a doctorate from the California State College at Sonoma and currently teaches comparative literature and creative writing at Lehigh University in Pennsylvania. She reports that her fiction draws on many aspects of her own personal experience, from childhood in a Moroccan family living in "white bread America" to her current situation as a wife and mother trying to pass on a distinctive heritage to her children. She remembers growing up in a lively, intensely verbal family and eating *burrechas* instead of bagels and lox, traveling to Montreal to visit other Sephardi relatives, singing Judeo-Spanish songs—and often feeling isolated not only from her gentile neighbors but from her Ashkenazi-Jewish friends as well. She has published many short stories in magazines and anthologies and is now at work on a novel about an American Sephardi extended family. Her story "Street of the Whores" shows that even in Israel, where Jews from around the globe should supposedly be welcome and equal, Moroccan Jews often face discrimination. Such bigotry can be experienced in a particularly intense way by women, who are struggling with two forms of discrimination at once.

•

"Street of the Whores"

I was a child again, feeling insulated from the world outside by the wall of laughter, by the globe in the window, by the music in the kitchen, by the smells and sounds of Morocco. I was 14, returning home from the library, books piled high against my chest, going to my room and opening *The Royal Road to Romance*, poring over the photo of Richard Halliburton, the traveller, turbanned and bronzed, arms akimbo, laughing with white teeth, the Taj Mahal behind him. That's me, I'd thought, that's going to be me. I'm going to go everywhere and do everything and die exhausted but satisfied that I've never said no to an experience, never refused a challenge.

Hours later, my eyes burning from reading under the weak yellow bulb, I'd come down and see my father sitting at the living room window, looking out. He'd never even notice me if I didn't speak. I'd go over to him and hug him and he'd smile faintly but keep staring outside. "What is it, Daddy?" I'd ask. "What are you doing?"

He'd turn and look at me with an odd light in his green-brown eyes, almost coldly, as if I were a stranger. I always expected him to say next: who are you? what are you to me? why are you touching me?

I felt no claim on my father. Ever. I'd retreat invisibly, shrinking in myself, but too proud to move back. I'd stand my ground, refusing to budge until the man returned from wherever he'd fled, until he acknowledged me as blood of his blood.

Finally, after an eternity of waiting, he'd return and soften slightly and say, "Bring the globe."

Together we'd sit near the window, moonlight shining in, illuminating his expressionless face, and he'd say, "You first."

I'd shut my eyes hard and spin the globe and let my finger choose a place to stop. And wait for judgment.

"Wisconsin?" he'd say, disappointed. "Ah, *ma fille*, so little sense of adventure. What are they known for, their cheese?"

"I'll try again! Let me try again. I wasn't ready."

He'd pretend to consider, then hold the globe out to me once more. "This time don't be afraid," he'd tell me. "The world is yours. You have only to choose."

I'd take a deep breath—thinking, did you choose, Daddy?—and I'd spin it violently, with everything inside me—a matter of life and death—and my finger would shoot out, independent of me. And wait.

"Japan. A good choice, *ma fille*. There we could have many adventures. A country unlike ours, a place where we could disguise ourselves and wander forever. We would have to learn their rituals, you'd paint your face white and serve me tea, I would let my hair grow perhaps and pin it up—so—with bamboo sticks pointing through it. We would live by the sea and eat seaweed and swim. The water is different there, even a different color. And it's so buoyant, you can't sink no matter how hard you throw yourself into the waves. It crashes you back against the cliffs. A fine choice." He'd smile at me.

And I'd wilt in relief. "Now your turn, Daddy."

"I am sleepy now. Next time."

"Then will you tell me again how you skated on the mountain lake of Ifrane with the Sultan? How when he fell, his two bodyguards had to fall, too?" Trying to hold him near me. Him already elusive, slipping away. The invisible barricade erected around him.

"Not now. *Bonne nuit, cherie*." He'd kiss me lightly and go up to his room where my mother waited for him, also restless in her sleep.

I'd follow quickly, afraid to stay alone downstairs in the dark. Seeing men with rolls of black hair pinned up with long sticks and women with white faces screaming in a sea of roaring waves.

He should have been buried with a globe, I thought after the funeral. Because until the end, he was seeking, seeking, and I didn't think he'd ever found it. Every land was a promise to him; and what had they promised? Death. The ultimate promise, the one that never lies. The dark wind blowing from the future, Camus had called it. And now I watched my father being buried on a windy day in Jerusalem. My mother and my brother Ben and me. The mourners. For Joseph Lek, a wandering Jew, a businessman whom no one had ever known. Daddy's legs blown off, his face exploded, his body shattered, the Israelis used to dealing with bodies that arrive in pieces, of gluing them back together as if they were a jigsaw puzzle, Daddy lovingly, professionally, reconstructed. A puzzle in little pieces, to be put together again. A hopeless, terrible puzzle in which the pieces never fit and for which I can't cry.

At the hotel we sat in our room. The fan whirring until Ben, with a curse, rose on a chair and turned it off. But he couldn't figure out how to keep the light on without the fan, so we sat on the chairs and the bed in the dark. Mom crying helplessly, ceaselessly. Startled, I saw how far back the gray roots of her hair extended. She looked dumpy, a round little old woman. "Everyone is gone now," she said. "My parents, my husband. I'm alone."

"You have us," I said, from the corner near the window, where I sat huddled in a chair.

She didn't seem to hear me. "I'd always hoped we'd get back somehow," she said. "I kept waiting for him to call or write and tell me, Bathsheba, I made a mistake. Can I come home?"

Ben sighed from the edge of the bed. "Don't, Mom," he said. "Please don't."

"He never called," she said, surprised. "I waited and waited and he never called or wrote. I gave him my life. He was the only man I'd ever known. And he left me alone. I loved him. I thought he loved me."

"He did love you," Ben said. "Sometimes it just isn't enough."

"No," she said. "I wasn't enough. Your father always wanted the green grass. Nothing was ever enough. 'It's gray here,' he told me once." Her voice broke. "'It's gray and you're gray and I'm gray when I'm with you.'"

"Mom." I went over to her, kneeled by her chair, put my head on her lap. But what could I say? Suddenly, there was absolutely nothing to say. It was all lies. For five years she'd stayed in the cocoon of her apartment and cooked twenty-course Moroccan feasts for Ben and me. It was pathetic. I looked up at her face and saw the twitch, deeper and more pronounced than ever, moving with a life of its own. Giving a jarring, odd look to her face. A mechanical doll. My name is Bathsheba. And she twitches. The gray hair in front, reddish henna-tinted brown in back. Straggly now and uncombed. Her brown eyes, always expressive, always volatile. But her face spotted, strange, white dots and brown dots, as if she were moldy, left unused for too long. Her father had sold her in marriage to the first bidder. She had given everything she had to her husband and her children. We'd left her behind and now she had nothing. Alone—now even the dream of my father returning was gone—and she didn't know what to do.

Israel. The Promised Land. Milk and honey. I hadn't allowed myself to look around yet, to see my surroundings, but now I was here alone. Tel Aviv was new, white, unlike Jerusalem where I seemed to hear screams under every cobblestone, feel hands grasping, clawing at me, from every crevice. Early this morning Mom, Ben and I had prayed at the Western Wall—in rain and wind—and had added our prayers written on scraps of paper to the notes stuffed in every opening. "May we all be free," I'd written, and backed off quickly, looking at the Orthodox men in black, separated from the women by a partition. Swaying and moaning, their voices rising above the wind, they frightened me. There was something ancient, disturbing, terribly sad and futile about being a Jew standing and praying before a wall of gray rocks. I wanted to feel inspired; instead I felt crushed by thousands of years of persecution and bloodshed.

"There's so much I still have to tell you," my mother had said afterwards at the airport, clutching my hand in hers. "Are you sure you want to stay in Israel all by yourself? What if I never see you again?"

"You will, Mom, you will," and suddenly, unbidden, the tears fell from my eyes. I cried for my mother, for my father, for Benny, for the Jews, for Israel, for the Arabs, for me. I stood and wept, Benny and my mother holding me, and I thought, it's true what my mother said: even if I see them again, it will never be the same, nothing I do or say will ever be the same.

Two weeks since my father's funeral. I'd received a letter from my boss at Bowden Press. He'd been furious at me, but was giving me a month to reconsider my resignation, during which my assistant editor would take care of my *Breathless* contemporary erotic line.

No, I thought, I'm never going back.

An old couple, the man in a clerical collar, stumbled on the rocks past me as I sat on the beach. "I can't believe it," the man said to the woman. "I still can't believe it. Prostitutes in the Holy Land. What is this world coming to?"

I looked at them in disbelief, and for the first time in days, roused myself from my stupor and walked the few steps to them. I knew I looked wild, my hair uncombed. I hadn't washed or changed out of my black sweatsuit in days. "This is a real land," I told the man, my voice rusty. I cleared my throat.

The old woman put a hand to her heart as if to ward me off. I saw the pink powder cracking on her cheeks. "Bert," she said feebly.

"Now see here," Bert said.

"Now see here," I said. "This is a country like any other country. What did you expect? That people don't live and eat and die here? It's not still in the Bible. So what if there are prostitutes here? You've got them back in Iowa, or wherever you're from. And there are thieves here and gamblers and liars, too, goddamn it. Israel doesn't just exist in your dreams." I stared at their amazed faces for a second, then walked away, my heart pounding. What had I done that for? What's it to me if Reverend Bert sees a whore? What do I care? I laughed suddenly and started running. I was still alive.

The next day I bought the *Jerusalem Post* and sat at a sidewalk cafe on Dizengoff and read the news for the first time in weeks. Months? April 12, 1975. Everything seemed new, yet unchanged. The same problems, the same shit—now Lebanon, now Syria, now Iran, now the West Bank—but here on Dizengoff—where, the manager of my building had told me, if you sit at a cafe long enough, you'll see everyone in Israel—the sun was shining and women flirted, soldiers stared, children laughed on their way home from school, tourists snapped photos. I had washed and put on a green sweater and jeans. Drinking black coffee as thick as mud, I told myself, ok, you're back, Lek. Maybe not in top form, but you're back. Now . . . to find a job, make aliyah. To learn Hebrew at an ulpan. To meet people, maybe make friends . . . I felt excited, ready to begin again.

There were no jobs in the *Post*, so I checked the bulletin board at the American Consulate: English teachers needed, no experience necessary. *Makhon leSafot Tzion*, Tzion Language Institute.

I walked lightly down the street, past the cafes and exclusive boutiques, towards the more residential area. Here it was: Tzion Language Institute. I went inside, climbed a flight of dark stairs and entered a large airy room, filled with people at students' desks, scribbling. A thin, freckled young woman gave me an application form. "English teacher?" she asked me.

"Yes."

"Fill it out and bring it back to me. Then wait your turn. You'll meet with the director and he'll let you know if you're in." The application form was ridiculously simple. Name, address, birthdate, place. Education and experience. I wondered if it would be to my advantage to mention that I had been a senior editor of female romances for the past five years. I decided it couldn't hurt.

"How long will it be?" I asked the freckled woman.

"At least two hours," she said. "Go and eat. Take your time."

I went outside and bought a falafel, then explored the area. The houses here were lovely, shady and secluded, with courtyards and inner gardens. Maybe if I found a roommate, I could afford to rent a room here. But I vetoed that instantly. I didn't want anybody—woman or man—peering into my existence, witnessing my unsteady return to life. Staring at a lush pink flower, I tore it from the branch. Almost intoxicatingly sweet, it dizzied me, reminded me of Central Park in the spring.

Back upstairs, a handful of us remained. We sat on the narrow balcony outside the classroom and talked about Israel. They were all American and all younger than I. Jim had come to play on a basketball team, but had found himself in need of money so his coach had advised him to try for a job here.

"Do you know anything about teaching English?" I asked him.

"Nah." He grinned. "I'm nineteen. I just got out of high school."

Meggie was twenty-two, a college student who'd dropped out and was drifting through the world, taking odd jobs everywhere she went.

"Do you feel free?" I asked her.

She looked at me uncomprehendingly. "I guess."

Tom and Gina had met on a kibbutz in the south and had decided to try life in the city. They were old-timers, already in Israel for a year. "It's awesome," Tom said. "I mean the mood here is really awesome. You feel like you're on the edge of an explosion any second."

I shuddered, turned away. A man, buried in pieces.

"Besides," Gina added, "now that they've got a MacDavid's here—you know like MacDonald's—there's no reason to go back, right?"

It was after four when Jim was finally called in. He came out ten minutes later, slinging his backpack. "No problem," he said, "as long as you can talk English." Tom and Gina went in next. They came out, grinning with relief. "This'll keep us going till we decide what to do," they told Meggie and me. "Good luck!"

I was next. I went down a narrow hallway to an office where a bald, stocky man sat, impatiently ruffling papers. He glanced at me for a moment, then indicated a chair. He studied my application. "Oh, you're Anne Lek."

"Yes?" I didn't understand his tone. An air of subtle disapproval.

"You're thirty-six."

"Yes." Was it my age? I knew I was older than the others, but—

"I see you received your master's degree in English from Columbia University in New York. A good school."

"Yes," I said again.

"Anne Lek." He studied me uncomfortably. "I'm sorry. We have no openings. Thank you for coming."

"Wait a minute." I felt a slow rumbling deep inside me, almost like a train roaring through my body. "I was under the impression that you had quite a few openings—"

"Miss Lek," he said, emphasizing the "miss." "Your qualifications are not what we're seeking. Good-bye."

I sat stubbornly. "My qualifications are not sufficient? But a high school graduate's are? What exactly are you looking for here? What is this all about?"

He sighed, toyed with his pencil. "Miss Lek, shall I be honest?"

"Please."

"I see here that you were born in Morocco."

"Yes?" I was in a tunnel. I still couldn't see the light. "So?"

"So I know Moroccans."

I stared at him blankly.

"Don't get the wrong idea. Some of my best friends are Moroccans. You're warm people. Fun-loving people. Religious. But not reliable. Not good workers."

"Not good workers?" I echoed his words. "What the hell are you talking about?"

"Miss Lek." He stood up. "I'm going to have to ask you to leave."

"Just a minute, Mr.—Mr.—"

"Mr. Levy."

"Mr. Levy. I left Morocco when I was four years old. I was raised in America. But what does that matter anyway? I deal with the English language as an editor every day. I'm afraid I still don't understand."

"Then let me spell it out for you, Miss Lek." He leaned over his desk, a twisted smile on his face. "I don't hire Moroccans. Is that clear enough for you? Now, *shalom*. I have work to do. And please send in the last girl."

I was so angry I wanted to take his smiling red face and smash it against the wall like a fruit. And scream at him: that's your Moroccan, here's your Moroccan for you. You son of a bitch. But I was civilized, so I walked out silently, gesturing to Meggie to go in, seeing her out of the corners of my eyes staring at me, but incapable of stopping to say a word. I went down the stairs and walked nonstop to the beach, my familiar stretch with the rocks and the dunes, and I stood at the very edge, the waves rushing in and trickling over my shoes, and I bent over and dipped my hands in the cold, salty water, splashing it on my face, over and over, until I was dripping and shivering. But I still didn't feel clean.

My day, ever since the Moroccan incident (the way I termed it in my mind), consisted of a long stroll along the beach during which I felt open, raw, as if I were drawing strength from the water, and the walk up the winding Street of the Whores. I fell in love with the name first. In Hebrew or English, it rolled on the tongue. And the women fascinated me. These were not the prime whores—those were gathered off of Allenby, also near the beach, but closer to downtown, near the port area and cafes and shady characters. I walked there sometimes, too; it reminded me of New York. The whores who sat on the rocks of this abandoned, twisting road were fewer, older, even wizened, a few leathery-skinned from the sun. But they were not sad or beaten. As they got used to me, carrying a sketchbook I'd bought on Allenby to pretend I was an artist, they'd cackle and wave at me. I wondered how Reverend Bert would react if he saw them. Women the same age as his wife pursuing man's oldest profession.

I knew I should be looking for another job. My one-month lease on the apartment would run out in a week. I couldn't live on my savings forever. I knew Mr. Levy was probably an aberration. The Civil Liberties Union in America could have had a field day with him. I knew—I knew—I knew—there was so much I should do. Life decisions, major major, looming over me. I should look seriously for a job, for friends. There were many support groups for American immigrants, even special ones for single women. My experience of Israel was so hazy, so dreamlike. Something was preventing me from sinking roots here, as if I were afraid to stay.

I love Israel, but it's not a promised land, I suddenly realized, stopping on the side of the road, near the oldest whore, the one who fascinated me most. My words to Reverend Bert boomeranging and coming back to hit me between the eyes. Of course, there are whores here, and prejudice, too. What a strain to put on a land, to call it promised. There are no promised lands, no promised endings. Oh God, Lek, I thought, pretending to stare at the rocks behind the old woman, are you finally going to open your eyes and face the void?

The woman stared back at me from under her coquettishly tilted straw hat. She never smiled like the others. She waited, straddling her rock as if she were on a horse, her bare legs falling over the sides, the coarse grass and sand of the small hill between her red toenails. Her stomach was flat under a white and red embroidered peasant blouse, her skirt flounced up around her thighs. A man in a black car, driving down towards the beach, stopped in front of her. I slowed down, too, across the street, slowly moving sideways, like a crab, back towards the car to see her mysterious, ever-shaded face exposed at last, naked to the daylight and the man and me. She was talking and laughing. She didn't move from her rock, but made him lean out his window to talk to her. Closer, closer I came, so slyly, so silently, like a spy, like a cat on soundless feet when she noticed me, so close I could touch the black car.

She took off her hat and spit. Staring at her face, I was suddenly afraid—not of the network of lines crisscrossing her brown face, but of the startling hunger in her eyes. It doesn't die, does it, grandmother? It stays and grows until it eats you alive. A low spark, nearly forgotten, bursts into life.

I forced myself to walk past her and the man watching me from his car, to push on, past the hunger in her face that I knew mirrored my own. Hunger—not for a man, nor even for money—but for oneself. Hunger that will never die, not until it's fed.

I stopped at the top of the hill and looked back down—at the women like spiders, legs and toes spread out and crawling over their rocks, at the sea sparkling and foaming—and I saw that it was desire that had led my father here to Israel, and desire—for myself—that would lead me away now, far from the Street of the Whores and back to the world, not as I knew it, but as I would re-learn it, perhaps re-create it.

Gloria Kirchheimer

For Sephardi Jews who live together in urban pockets, Americanization can take longer to transform the family unit than for those who are scattered in small towns. Gloria Kirshheimer, who grew up in a Ladino-speaking Sephardi family among a large Sephardi community in New York, has devoted much of her professional life to maintaining her ethnic heritage. In addition to recording an album of folk songs, she has published short stories in a number of literary magazines. Her vignette of life in a Sephardi family in transition, "Food of Love," first appeared in the feminist magazine *Shmate*. The mother in Kirchheimer's story is "queen of all Sephardic womanhood" only in her own environment; although "she can recite entire scenes from Racine and Corneille," she is afraid to go into the public library because she does not know how to apply for a library card. Her husband insists that even Jewish organizational activity is a form of disloyalty to him and his needs. Yet, as the protagonist and the reader discover together, this overtly dominated woman sometimes behaves with a daring, independence, sensuality, and spontaneity that her liberated daughter envies.

•

"Food of Love"

A woman drags a shopping cart up the 181st Street hill, looking furtively over her shoulder. She is sixty-five, wears a kerchief, the hem of her coat is undone in the back. Another woman appears with a cart. After a hurried conversation a parcel is transferred from the first cart to the second.

This is not a dope drop. The first woman is my mother who, after evading my father's questions with the excuse that she is going shopping, has secretly entrusted ten pounds of phyllo dough to her friend who will store it *sub rosa* in her refrigerator. My father does not like Mother to engage in extra-marital culinary activities. With the same subterfuge she might employ to meet a lover, she sneaks out to bake delicacies for the organization of which she is president. Because she has interests outside the home my retired father calls her a part-time wife. "Why don't you throw me out like a dog?" he says whenever she pleads an important committee meeting.

A tigress to her board members, my mother is too timid to go to a box office and buy theater tickets; though she has arranged gala functions for hundreds of people at the best hotels, she cannot bring herself to enter a public library for fear that she will not know how to ask for a library card.

However, within the confines of the synagogue where her organization has its office, she is—as Isabella was Queen of all the Americas—queen of all Sephardic womanhood.

She is forced to work with a vice-president who lacks authenticity. A descendant of Revolutionary War generals, the woman is made to feel like an outcast. She was elected because her name is embroidered on seat cushions and inscribed on the Declaration of Independence. Mother gives her useful work to do, stuffing envelopes. What can she know of Sephardic culture, a woman who cooks with safflower oil?

The event for which Mother is preparing is a fund-raising luncheon to be held in the synagogue community room. The entertainment will consist of a Sephardic sing-along and a short lecture with slides on Our Unique Heritage, designed to wring some money out of our brethren, particularly the Sephardim from Salonika, many of whom are regarded as moguls of the garment business. Their wives cook with olive oil and have been discouraged from aiding in the kitchen by the faction from Izmir.

This is an orthodox synagogue, though half the members travel on the Sabbath to attend services. Mother cooks with a grain of salt and, in her fantasy, with a little unconsecrated cheese, which she sprinkles onto the spinach pastries when no one is looking. Hawkeyed, the rabbi's wife watches to see that all is kosher. She comes from Rhodes where (Mother says) they speak an inferior Ladino, the now archaic Spanish we carried with us after the Expulsion.

Long before the luncheon takes place I know I will be approached to attend. Except for me, daughters always attend their mothers' functions, however dull. For years I was successful in avoiding them, but this time it will be difficult. It is Mother's show and she will receive a plaque.

Knowing she will never ask me outright, I wait. Campaigning starts early.

Invited for lunch at my apartment one Saturday two months before the event, she arrives bearing her usual food parcel. She has never come to my house and eaten my food. Perhaps some bread and coffee, but in between she is her own caterer. She wants to spare me the trouble.

"Umm, isn't this good," she says, licking her fingers. It could be sawdust for the effort it takes me to swallow.

She has brought a new dress to show me. Do I think it suitable for the luncheon?

"What luncheon?" I ask.

The luncheon. She expects two hundred people. There is already a waiting list. They have hired Aryeh the accordionist and his international band. Did I know they made a recording recently?

"A lot of people make recordings."

"You and I could make one. You have such a lovely voice. I know so many songs. Soon our music will die out if young people like you don't preserve it."

To parricide and fratricide we now add culturicide, with myself the first offender.

I crumple up her tinfoil wrappings and stuff them into the trash can which is overfull.

"Relax," Mother says, "I'll clean up, you rest." This is a woman who always insists upon carrying the fifty-pound grocery load on the grounds that I look tired.

Now she is hovering over my new electric typewriter. "Does it give you shocks?" she asks, standing back a respectful foot and a half.

"Sometimes." All those xxxx'd-out lines.

Watching her reach out to touch the keys I can't help remembering the time I demonstrated to her the instant cash apparatus found at many banks, the kind where you insert your special bank card, push a few buttons and receive cash.

We were short of money one day while shopping on Fifth Avenue. I found a bank and she watched me set the process in motion. When the computer screen said, *Hello, is there anything I can do?* she shrieked with wonder. When it asked if I wished to proceed in English or Spanish, she clutched her throat and said, *Que maravilla!* Reading over my shoulder she said that the computer was more polite than the bank tellers she dealt with. I invited her to take the money from the open cylinder, but to be quick about it at the risk of having her hand clamped in its turning maw.

"Do you know," she said when the transaction was completed, "an ignorant person might think there was a devil in there. I mean someone superstitious." Then she uttered an imprecation in Arabic to the effect that the evil eye should keep its distance from us and our loved ones.

Her campaign to get me to the luncheon is spread over several weeks. "Did I tell you that Professor Asher Halifa will be addressing us?" I had once made the error of saying that I had read an article of his in *Commentary*.

Another time: "You have a beautiful print dress. You don't wear it enough." Translation: "Wear it to the luncheon." I say nothing.

And finally: "I have a ticket reserved for you. It's a nice table, all young people."

I consult my calendar, playing for time. The date is filled. "But Mother, I'm seeing a matinee that Sunday."

"Do you have to go?"

"I don't *have* to go, I *want*—"

"No problem then. They'll exchange the ticket. You have plenty of time."

Trying to salvage some pride I offer to pay my way to the luncheon, but she won't allow it. It's for a good cause. "Relax," she says. It is her battle cry.

The day before the luncheon takes place, she calls me. Do I have a tape recorder?

"I have a cassette, but the sound is not very good."

"You know we have Aryeh and his accordion. If you feel like taping the music—"

"Mother," I say, "I will not *feel* like taping. If you want me to, just say so and I'll be glad to do it. I'll go and buy some tape—"

"No, why should you, all that bother. It's too complicated."

"It's not complicated. If you want it, I'll do it. Really, Mom."

"No, no, forget about it. It's all right."

It's not all right. I should have volunteered of course. Another black mark against this unnatural daughter.

At the luncheon I am embraced by people who knew me when I was a little girl, handsome men and beautiful women with names like Diamante, Joya, Fortunee. "Will you sing for us?" "You have such a lovely voice." As a teenager I sang here a few times, accompanying myself with primitive guitar chords. I sang, with my American accent, songs that brought tears to their eyes. It was a phase, folksinging. I haven't been in this building for years.

Mother makes a welcoming speech thanking her vice-president and conveying regrets from the distinguished professor Asher Halifa who was to have addressed us today. The main drawing card as far as I was concerned. No wonder she was afraid to tell me.

Mother's speech is concise and charming. She worries needlessly about her English. My father is watching her as though he has just fallen in love with her. They met forty years ago after a fortune teller predicted that a dark stranger from Turkey would carry her off from Alexandria. She was twenty-three then, teaching French in an Arabic school, working to support her family while her brothers were at the university. Her father, a dapper gentleman who wore spats and a boutonniere, was a gambler. My grandmother had learned to read, rare for a woman in those days in Egypt. Even now, my mother talks wistfully about taking college courses, but is afraid people will laugh at her. She has always been interested in literature and can recite entire scenes from Racine and Corneille. She used to do it often—at home, in supermarkets and especially in front of my friends. If she weren't worried about my father catching her, she would watch the advanced Italian course given at seven in the morning on television.

The rabbi makes a speech. In spite of his degrees and erudition, his public relations manner and his Sephardic wife, he is barely tolerated as a man of the somewhat worn cloth. An Ashkenazi presiding over a Sephardic congregation. *He* doesn't need to tell us how unique we are, as he invites us to go from strength to strength.

Mother is everywhere as people begin to eat. I invite her to sit, but she says she doesn't have to eat. Aryeh is playing tunes from a popular Yiddish-American musical on his accordion and Mother is incensed. She whispers something to him and he switches in mid-chord to a Greek song. Five women, all in their sixties, walk up to the stage and begin to dance. There is a soupçon of belly dance movements, but not enough to cause embarrassment. Though the Greek song is about a whore, the rabbi is beaming. One of the women puts a coin on her forehead and throws her head back, arching her whole body. The others make a circle around her. The rest of the audience is clapping in time. A man leaps onto the stage—he must be at least seventy-two—and whips out a handkerchief. The woman with the coin takes hold of a corner of the handkerchief, the man is down on one knee. The music becomes faster and faster and, at the last chord, Mother takes the microphone and announces that dessert is being served.

Now it is time for the plaque. The vice-president, in perfect Vassar English, thanks the lady who has given so much of herself. Mother is blowing her nose. I notice a run in her stocking; one shoe has been slipped off. I know she would like nothing better than to loosen her girdle.

The ovation forces Mother back up to the mike. No more speeches, she promises, and suggests we get on with the sing-along. She wants only to say how happy she is that her daughter could be here today to honor her, and they all know how much joy her daughter used to give them with her beautiful voice but "she said, 'Mother, please don't ask me to sing' and so I won't ask her—"

Pandemonium—my name shouted from every corner of the room, spoons tinkling against the demitasses. The accordion starts up, sounding like the bark of a mad dog. Mother smiles, shrugs—it is out of her hands—.

People push me out of my seat and up to the stage. "Only if you sing with me," I say, trying not to cry out. They have song sheets, but they don't need them. The accordion helps, Mother helps, I sing. I'll get them, I'll get her, they'll be eating out of the palm of my hand. People put down their cups, their baklava, lean back, sigh, sing with me in Ladino, songs about their countries, the almond tree, the sea that brings no letters, the daughters in exile, the smoldering mountains. . . . Why have I waited so long to do this? Looking at her, my mother, I understand for the first time what it is to have a "maternal language." I feel that I am singing in tongues, astonishing myself with those archaic syllables, these Moorish melodies. I could swear I smell jasmine blossoms.

"Isn't she grand?" Mother says to the audience at last. While she is making her financial report, I escape to the ladies room and wash my shaking hands with the kosher soap.

I return to hear Aryeh play a flourish and the start of a lively Arabic song. The curtain, which was drawn across the stage, now parts, revealing my mother transformed into a *houri,* a harem woman clad in gold embroidered silk pantaloons, a silk blouse and vest, pointed velvet slippers with coins jingling at their tips, a silk kerchief at her hair with a fringe of coins over her forehead, finger cymbals in her hands. I stand up. I have never seen this outfit. Where does she keep it? Why did she never show it to me? It must be at least a hundred and fifty years old. It belongs in the Metropolitan Museum or on me. She shakes her shoulders and starts to sing in Arabic and people go mad with delight. She leans into the microphone, still shaking her shoulders in rhythm. "Sing, everyone. . . . You like it?" Roars, whistles, pounding on the tables, "It's to make up for my lack of voice. We want to give you your money's worth. . . ."

A woman with a face like a gnarled pomegranate stretches out her hands to my mother, then makes her way to me and kisses me on both cheeks as though to confer upon me the Legion d'Honneur which I deserve today.

"The truth," Mother says on the phone later that night. "From you I want the truth."

"Really, you were great."

"Honest?" She giggles.

"Would I lie?"

"Not you. You always speak your mind. You are direct, like me."

I shuffle papers around on my desk while she talks. I had just been contemplating writing her an irate and formal note about her treachery to me at the microphone. Instead I ask if she was nervous. To get up on stage, all those people.

She has to confess to a little "reinforcement." Before leaving home, without my father seeing, she poured a thimblefull of scotch into an empty aspirin bottle.

I'm shocked. A nip before lunch? She should have offered me some. I catapult a paper clip across the room. She continues to question me—about the food, the seating arrangements, the color of the napkins. . . .

What is this sheet of paper on my desk with words typed on it? I did not type them. Now I remember my mother hanging around the typewriter, gingerly touching the keys.

The words on the paper are: "Amérique. America. Maman I am here."

Rebecca Goldstein

Rebecca Goldstein, who earned her Ph.D. in philosophy at Princeton University, has been a New Yorker for most of her life. She has taught philosophy at Barnard College but today is best known as a novelist. In addition to *The Mind-Body Problem*, Goldstein recently published a second novel, *The Late-Summer Passion of a Woman of Mind*, which was prominently reviewed in the *New York Times Book Review*. The winner of an American Council of Learned Societies grant for her work in progress, "The Concept of Body," she continues to write both philosophical essays and fictional works dealing with aspects of the modern Jewish experience.

The Mind-Body Problem is distinguished by its nuanced handling of the intricacies of both academe and contemporary American religious life. Its protagonist, Renee Feuer, is a "brainy and beautiful" Ph.D. candidate in philosophy at Princeton University. She has rejected the Orthodox Jewish environment of her youth, partially because she does not like the limited role of women within Orthodoxy and partially out of rebellion against her domineering mother. Yet Renee has many misgivings about this decision. First, there is much she values about Jewish tradition. She fondly remembers her deceased father, who was a cantor, a fine, gentle, affectionate man who loved Jewish music and loved his daughter. She sees that her ultra-Orthodox brother and his wife live a restricted but nonetheless affectionate and meaningful, coherent Jewish life. Second, she recoils from the ignorance and apathy of "the Jewish goyim" whom she finds at Princeton. Third, she discovers, much to her shock, that assimilation is no guarantee of feminist liberation; indeed her thoroughly assimilated Jewish husband wants her to serve as his enabler and organizer—a role she thought she had left behind when she abandoned traditional Jewish life-styles. Moreover, even women who, like her best friend Ava, regard traditional Judaism with disdain, often have trouble integrating the different pieces of their lives. Renee discovers that there are no ready-made formulas, that every thinking person is "alone" in the individual attempt to integrate Jewish values and Western humanism, science and spirituality, mind and body.

•

"Why God Gave You Brains" (excerpt)

One hour after Noam's proposal and my immediate and euphoric acceptance, I was standing out on the golf course in front of the Graduate College searching the darkened skies for three stars. Let me explain.

The minute Noam proposed to me I wanted to tell my mother. That was about the second or third thought that flashed through my triumphant head. (Can thoughts go faster than the speed of light? I wonder.) Not that my mother and I are that close. Quite the contrary. But I very much wanted to tell someone the news, someone who would consider it momentous. And my mother, who had greeted each announcement of my educational plans with "Nu, Renee, is this going to help you find a husband?" so that the consequence of all my academic honors, Phi Beta Kappa, *summa cum laude*, scholarships, fellowships, prizes, was only a deepening sense of guilty failure; my mother, who had always taught me that a woman is who she marries, that "There's more than one hole a man has to fill in a woman": my mother was such a person. Noam had proposed to me on a Saturday evening. My mother would not answer the phone until three stars were visible, indicating that the skies had truly darkened and Shabbos was over. That night in June, Shabbos wasn't over until after nine.

"*Gute voch*," she answered the phone. The Yiddish phrase means "good week."

"Hi, Mom, it's me."

"Renee! *Gevalt!* Is something wrong? What's the matter?"

"No, Mom, what makes you say that?"

"Well, here you are calling a minute after *Havdalah*, so anxious." (Havdalah is a ceremony that uses wine, a candle and sweet-smelling spices to bid farewell to the Sabbath. The word literally means division—the division of the Sabbath from the rest of the week, of the sanctified from the secular.) "Of course, maybe you didn't know it was a minute after *Havdalah*. Maybe you didn't even know that today was Shabbos?"

"Sure, Mom, I knew. I just came in from counting the stars."

"Renee darling, you're keeping Shabbos?"

"No, Mom, I just knew it would be futile to try and call you too early."

"Nu, so at least you still remember a little something. If you still remember, there's hope."

"Listen, Mom, I have something to tell you."

"I'm listening."

"I'm getting married."

A gasp. Then: "*Oy gevalt*!" Then the question: "Is he Jewish?"

Sadistically, I paused several seconds before answering her. "Yes, Mom. He's Jewish."

Total silence. I couldn't even detect any breathing.

"Mom, are you still there?"

"Yes, of course, Renee, I'm here. When isn't your mother here? I'm just a little speechless with surprise. A daughter calls me up out of the blue, I don't know *how* long it's been, and tells me she's getting married. I don't even know she's going with someone. How *should* I know? So I'm surprised."

"Aren't you happy? Isn't this what you always wanted?"

"Yes, of course I'm happy. Of course this is what I always wanted."

But she didn't sound all that happy. All that anxiety over whether and whom I would marry should, one might have thought, have made this moment one of great jubilation. A giant hosanna ought to be swelling out of the phone. I had pictured my mother—a little woman, barely five feet tall, dark and very thin, for she can't eat when she's worried, which means she averages maybe one good meal a week—bursting out into *Hallel*, the song of praise to God, in which He is called by every good name in the Hebrew vocabulary. How had I failed her this time? What maternal expectations was I once again in the process of thwarting?

And then I understood, saw it as I had never seen it before. My mother's whole life is devoted to worry. In the last few years she had been consumed in despair about two things: Would my brother's wife, Tzippy, who had been trying to have a child for two years, never succeed? And would her prodigal daughter, Renee, remain forever single (I was, after all, an overripe and bruised twenty-two), or worse, marry a *goy*? These were big, satisfying worries, requiring constant attention.

Then a few weeks ago she had learned that Tzippy was pregnant, and now I was calling to tell her that I'm marrying. A Jew yet. No wonder she sounded wounded. We children had callously deprived her life of its substance and meaning. She was holding the telephone receiver and staring down into the existential abyss.

"Of course I'm happy," she repeated weakly, "Overjoyed. Tell me, what is the young man like? What does he do? Don't tell me, he's also a philosopher." Do tell me, do tell me, her voice was begging.

"He's a mathematician."

"A mathematician? From numbers he makes a living?" Her voice gathered some strength.

"Yes, Mom. He's famous. He's one of the greatest living mathematicians. He's a genius. He was written up in *Life* magazine." This is true. When Harvard had offered Noam an appointment at age twenty, *Life* had done a story on "the youngest American professor."

"Really? A famous genius? *Life* magazine? This is really something then. This is real *yiches*." (*Yiches* is prestige.) "You should be very proud, Renee, that such a man should love you. Of course, I know you're not just any girl. Who should know if not me? This is why God gave you such good brains, so that you could make such a man like this love you. I only wish your father were alive today to hear such news."

•

"Lessons from Mrs. Einstein" (excerpt)

My sister-in-law Tzippy gave birth in December to a six-pound, twelve-ounce boy. The baby was named Reuven, after my father. Reuven Feuer.

My mother's chief worry had been Caesarean section, or, as she put it, "the knife." Tzippy is very slight, "not built for childbearing," my mother repeated throughout the five months she knew of Tzippy's pregnancy. Tzippy had been reading about pregnancy, birth, breast-feeding, toilet training, sibling rivalry—the whole megillah—ever since she felt the first kick in the fifth month and began really to trust in this third pregnancy. She had become a firm believer in the Lamaze method of childbirth, but this required a partner and my brother Avram wanted no part of it. It was *weibeszachen,* woman's business. (Not surprisingly, the Yiddish term has a pejorative connotation.) Miriam Teitelbaum, whose husband also "learned" at Lakewood and who was herself still childless, came to the rescue. Miriam and Tzippy had gone through all the grades of *Bais Yaakov* together. (*Bais Yaakov* means "house of Jacob." There is an international chain of very Orthodox *Bais Yaakov* schools for girls. The high school that had so disastrous an effect on my future religiosity was one.) They went together to the Lamaze classes, and then finally to the birth. The closeness that developed between them shone from their faces at the *bris* of little Reuven. Tzippy's delivery had been a difficult one, seventeen hours in hard labor.

"I could never have done it without Miriam. I can't begin to tell you how she helped me. I was ready to give up. I told the doctor, all right already, put me out. But Miriam and he overruled me." Tzippy was radiant.

"I knew she was near the end by then," Miriam radiated back. "She was in transition, and people always feel pessimistic then. They had warned us at class."

"Just think, if not for Miriam I would have missed seeing Reuven in those first moments of his new life. Oh, Renee, I still can't get over it. Every time I close my eyes I see it. As soon as he came out and the doctor lifted him up, he turned his head very quickly from side to side, three times: 'Nu, so what's this?' I'm going to see that my whole life."

"Tzippy didn't have any drugs at all. That's why Reuven was born so alert. When we brought him to the nursery, all the nurses commented on how alert he was. He was given a nine-point-nine Apgar out of ten. The nurse told me none of them gets a ten," Miriam bragged. "Already he's getting the best grades."

I regarded little Tzippy with awe. The years of worry over her infertility had lightly written over her sweet face. There was a certain pinched expression that hadn't been there before, and three vertical lines between the eyes. But hers was still very much the face of a child. And this child-woman had passed through the vastness of the experience of giving birth, and now looked back at me from across its great distance. For the first time I felt that she was the woman and I the girl.

Little Reuven regarded everything, including me, with immense dark eyes that spoke of infinite wisdom. He protested loudly at the indignities he was made to suffer at the hands of the mohel, but was quickly pacified by a Q-tip dunked in sweet red wine. I searched the little face closely for signs of similarity between the two Reuven Feuers, suddenly quite receptive to the superstition that lies perhaps behind the Jewish naming tradition. Let it be, I kept thinking, let this be my father returned.

Noam had come along with me to the *bris,* after some pleading on my part. He seemed very uncomfortable for the first fifteen minutes or so, standing among the *davening* men. But then he simply tuned out, became involved in his own thoughts, swaying slightly back and forth as he does when unable to pace. He looked like a natural, as I had known he would, the yarmulke perched on his head, *shuckling* in the midst of the *shuckling* men. Several people, I learned, assumed he was one of the *rebbayim* from the yeshiva, and when told he was my husband, those who knew the sad history of my profligacy rejoiced over my return to the fold. My mother was very pleased with this misinterpretation and didn't correct it. Noam remained tuned out.

Two of my mother's three sisters had made it to Lakewood from their homes in the Flatbush section of Brooklyn. The third, a xenophobic, agoraphobic hypochondriac, never travels past Ocean Avenue. They had all been born in Brooklyn. My mother was the only one whom cruel fate had tossed out of that yiddishe paradise into the Westchester wilderness, and from the way she spoke it might have been the Dakotas. She always complained bitterly that of all her sisters she, the most pious, had to live out her life in exile. The funny thing is, after my father died, leaving her free to move where she wanted, she had stayed put in the desert.

My mother was at her peak at the *bris*, *shepping naches*, presenting to the world at large, and the aunts in particular, her triumphs: her grandson and son-in-law. The expression on her face was pure bliss as she led the aunts over to be introduced to Noam, who greeted them all with his most absent stare and an occasional "hmmmm." To be able to maintain one's inner peace and psychic distance in the midst of that group requires true greatness of mind. They're all thin and under five feet tall, but they take up a lot of space.

Aunt Sophie is a bargain mavin whose life is devoted to the cause of getting shlock for less than half. Almost all her conversation revolves about this one issue, relating the ecstasies of bargaining merchants down below cost, the agonies when she suspects she could have gotten something for less. Hers is a fairly deep gray mattering zone. She feels genuine outrage for those who overpay. And yet I have a warm spot for her; she had been my unexpected ally in the war I waged to go to Barnard.

"How can you not let her accept that scholarship? Do you realize what a school like that costs? Don't you see what a bargain you're getting?" (Can I help it if I come from a family of Jewish-American stereotypes?)

My Aunt Myra was also at the *bris*, and she was really pouring it on for Noam. She's the prettiest of the sisters, managing to look, in her thinness, chic rather than scrawny. She's always smartly dressed, with her hair somewhere or other in the blondred range. Right now her thin voice was trickling out, in Noam's honor, in her version of an educated accent. Knowing that Noam wasn't Orthodox, she even made some mildly mocking noises about the *bris*:

"What did you think of our little religious ritual?" Little laugh, type consistent with accent.

"Hmmmm," Noam answered, his eyes darting about in that way that told me he hadn't heard a word.

"A littie barbaric, perhaps"—tiny laugh—"but it's supposed to be hygienic. Even the gentiles do it now." Smile, faded-blue questioning stare.

"Hmmmmm."

The aunts Sophie and Myra exchanged glances.

Aunt Myra apologized to my mother for her daughter Felicia's absence.

There was a very important sale at Bloomingdale's today, and even though Felicia "really argued with me, put up such a fight to come to the *bris*, I knew she had been waiting so long for this sale, I just couldn't let her miss it."

My aunt then turned to me and began, in sweet charity, to fill me in on every detail of Felicia's recent goings-on. My infelicitously named cousin is Myra's only child, and as a kid I had spent a good amount of time fantasizing that I was she. (That was before I learned to tame my fantasizing to the possible.) I had never seen a mother so in love with a daughter. (My mother, too, was in love, but with my brother.) Myra's husband, Harry, had a rather limited role to play. He had been required, of course, to make Felicia's existence a reality. After that I'm sure his services in *that* department were never again called upon. The meaning of the remainder of his life has lain in his fur business, which has kept his daughter in the best of everything money can buy. I still remember Felicia's canopy bed, all creamy eyelet embroidery floating on the thick apricot rug in that apricot room. Is this where my passion for the color stems from—from the green envy of those days? How I used to imagine myself in that bed. (You see that my fantasies have involved a bed from the earliest.) We always used to play the princess and her slave when I came over. Very occasionally, she'd let me be the princess.

My cousin is exactly my age, or actually ten days younger, so naturally we've been compared since infancy. (She walked before me, but I was toilet-trained first.) The sole comfort my mother took from my going to Barnard was Barnard's having rejected Felicia. I had always been the better student. One might expect this superiority to have given me the lead in the race with my cousin. Forget it. There's no way I could ever win. She, you see, is described by her mother, whose faith has never wavered, while I am represented by mine, whose attitude is at best lukewarm.

I see I can't probe the old wound, no matter how gently, without the pain bursting forth in full dazzling vigor. In a moment I shall start sobbing that my mother has never loved me, that she cared only for my brother. What a bore; so banal a solution to the mystery of my personality. And yet there it is. I've done what I can. I've transformed the woman into a parody (perhaps you've noticed) in the attempt to dilute some of her awesome strength. But though that's the picture I present to you, it's not the view I naturally occupy. I can maintain it only with great effort before the pull of subjectivity becomes too strong. In the end it is a feeble attempt, as are they all, the pathetically elaborate battlements we construct against the power absolute: the power of the parent. The effects keep on long after the exertion itself has ceased. For they're woven into the very fabric of one's soul. They are one's self. *Can nothing be done?* Must the self that one is, this poor "I" that I am and that I feel myself to be, remain permanently disfigured—encrusted with the oozing scabs of ancient bruises even as the Others are admiring the self-applied surgical dressing? Must the old pain influence every action, as a dull ache shapes a limp?

As a child I was full of schemes for winning her love. Of course my father loved me, but not in the partial way I craved. He loved everybody. He didn't favor me over Avram, as my mother favored Avram over me. He didn't love me *exclusively*. (Thus is a father-fixation forged.) For some reason (perhaps because I'm Jewish) I hooked onto the idea that I had to be smarter. I had always brought home straight A's, so I asked the teachers for extra work and carried home their praise. My fifth-grade teacher gave me a ninth-grade math book to work on. I wrote poems and stories and won prizes for them. And only watched my mother's anger grow. I really was dopey not to catch on, for she could be pretty explicit:

Some friends of my parents were visiting for Shabbos, and we were all sitting at the dining room table, having Friday night dinner. Avram, as was his way, hadn't said a word all through the meal, and I, as was my way, had been chattering throughout, wisecracking and telling stories. My mother got me into the kitchen on some pretext, where her gracious company face instantaneously transformed itself into wild rage. (These transformations were terrifying.)

"You're embarrassing me and your father with all your showing off. You're just a girl," she hissed, trying to pack all the anger into her voice without raising it, for fear the guests would overhear. "You're pretty enough. Why are you always trying to show off how smart you are? Why must you always outshine your brother? Can't you ever give him a chance?"

Avram and me. Felicia and me. Descriptions have always come in pairs, in contrapuntal duets. The good and the bad, the perfect and the problem, the *naches* and the *tsuris*.

But no matter how biased the maternal descriptions, the objective fact is that I got married before my cousin. And my husband is a genius. That's on the plus side. But on the minus side, and this must be weighted very heavily, he is *fifteen* years older than I am. Let's not total up the points until we see whom Felicia finally condescends to marry. She's still roaming the Catskills, seeking her intended (doctor) at singles weekends at Grossinger's and the Concord.

There have always been, since the birth of Felicia, states of the world to provoke Aunt Myra's indignation: girls chosen before Felicia to play Queen Esther in the Purim plays; teachers who marked her compositions in ignorance and apathy. But none of this compares to the present singles situation. These young men (especially the Jewish doctors) were spoiled rotten. None of them wanted to get married anymore because these other stupid girls were all giving it away for nothing.

"And they talk about Jewish *princesses,*" my mother had sympathetically quoted my aunt quoting my cousin, who—sorry, coz—will for me always present an ostensive definition for that hated term.

My mother always keeps me informed of the aunts' views on my life. They had all been "overjoyed" to learn I was getting married, "except your Aunt Myra, that jealous witch," my mother had chirped in ecstasy. They had been "very impressed" to learn of my husband's prominence. (My mother had found the old *Life* article at the library and sent them all xeroxed copies.) They were also "a little surprised" when their arithmetical computations revealed the age difference between Noam and myself. My mother had never commented directly on Noam's age. She frequently chooses the medium of "the aunts" to make her points. Then, if I react very badly, she can say sympathetically, "Well, you know your aunts."

The morning after the *bris* my mother called with the reactions of the aunts on meeting Noam in the flesh.

"Well, they thought he seemed a little eccentric, but of course that's a mark of his genius, as I told them. You can't expect geniuses to be normal. They were surprised at how good-looking he still is. They all said he doesn't look his age."

I thought often of my little nephew and spoke to Tzippy at least once a week. At three months Reuven began to sleep through the night, and Tzippy, after happily informing me of this, said:

"Now I can finally invite you and Noam for a Shabbos."

Noam absolutely refused. "No, Renee, I couldn't take it. I couldn't take a whole Shabbos. And I certainly couldn't take your brother for that long. I can tolerate the word 'pagan' just about twenty times in one day. That's my limit and it's surpassed in five minutes with Avram."

So I went to Lakewood by myself, after making sure that Noam had invitations for dinner Friday and Saturday.

Lakewood has two identities. It's a pretty little resort community, and it's also the Princeton of *yiddishkeit*. Life there presents Judaism at its purest: the men learning in the elite *kollel,* which is like a graduate department for Talmud; the women producing children and also teaching or running little businesses in their basements to augment the meagre stipends the *kollel* pays their husbands. Some of the families actually live quite well, supported by the wife's father. This is one of the great blessings of wealth, to be able to buy a scholar for a son-in-law and support him in the way of life one couldn't choose for oneself.

Reuven had changed tremendously in three months, as people his age tend to do, I guess. I was initially disappointed to see that he had lost the look of ineffable knowledge, but I soon became enchanted. He was delicate-featured and pale-skinned, and the hair that was coming in was the blond of my father, my brother, and me. He was a real Feuer. He seemed to me to be remarkably beautiful, although I was somewhat skeptical of my aesthetic judgement. I have heard parents of pathetically homely children marvel at their offspring's beauty and debate the pros and cons of a career in child modeling. For all I knew, such creative perception might extend to doting aunts as well.

Tzippy was completely absorbed in her maternity. She was nursing Reuven, and he was a hungry little soul (my mother worried he wasn't getting enough), feeding for about forty-five minutes every four hours. Tzippy, though much larger on top than before, was thinner every place else; especially her little face, which was more pinched than at the bris. But she was ebulliently happy:

"I have to restrain myself when he's sleeping not to wake him, I miss him."

I didn't mind the exclusiveness of her concerns. In fact, I enjoyed this glimpse into the maternal world-view. I was rather glad that Noam hadn't come after all.

Avram was also overjoyed in his role as a parent. When I watched him play with Reuven, throwing him high in the air as Tzippy begged him to be careful, making silly faces and noises, I felt for the first time in fifteen years like hugging my holy brother.

Friday night, after the Shabbos meal, Avram sat at the table swaying over a Gemara, and Tzippy and I went into the tiny bedroom so we wouldn't disturb him with our talk. There was a little night light casting a soft glow on the white walls and pink bedspreads. Reuven fell asleep at the breast, and Tzippy looked down at him.

"Ah, Reuven, you have a *tzaddik's shaym*" (a saint's name). "You should only have his *neshuma*" (his soul).

All at once I was crying, and Tzippy silently joined in. She had only known my father in the last year of his life, but a strong and special closeness had developed almost immediately between them. It was she who had shown my numbed family the way when he lay dying in the final days. We had already distanced ourselves from the man lying there, smelling of death and wearing the face of martyrdom. That wasn't my father suffering; my father had already gone. But little Tzippy had shown us who that person was, had walked into the room and straight over to him, kissing him, holding him, talking to him as she always had. How he had smiled at her with that wasted face. Were it possible to feel envy for Tzippy, I would certainly have envied her that last smile. It was four years since my father had died, and still when I spoke or thought of him my eyes often welled up. When I was with Tzippy, her eyes did the same in response.

We didn't speak for a while. The only sounds were the clock on the night table ticking, Reuven's soft breathing, and out in the living room the rhythmic squeak of Avram's chair under his swaying. Tzippy finally broke the silence:

"Oh, Renee, I almost forgot. I'm so absent-minded these days. You have an old friend here in Lakewood, a school friend. Her husband is learning here. She was so excited when she discovered you're my sister-in-law. Her name now is Fruma Friedbaum, but I can't remember her maiden name."

"Not Fruma Dershky? Thin, red hair, great giggle?"

"That's her, but she's not so thin anymore. She's expecting her fifth child, *kayn aynhoreh*." (This is a Hebrew phrase automatically uttered when any good news is spoken. It's actually an incantation to ward off the evil eye, although now it is hardly ever spoken with that intent. It's like saying "God bless you" after someone sneezes, the original purpose of which, according to Bertrand Russell, was to keep the devil from jumping in as the soul momentarily leaves the body.)

"You're kidding," I said. Again I felt my childishness, felt that I'd been left behind. And left behind by Fruma! We had been best friends in high school, and she had accompanied me, always a step in back, in that heady first flush of doubting. In our schools, as in most yeshivas, the morning classes were devoted to religious studies, taught by rabbis with beards and *rebbetsens* (rabbis' wives) with *sheitels*. In the afternoon we were taught secular subjects by moonlighting public school teachers. Fruma and I called the morning the dark ages, and the afternoon the enlightenment:

"It's like experiencing the renaissance every day of our lives."

We often cut the morning classes and hid down in the lunchroom, where I'd propound the narrowness of Judaism, the naivete of theism. We read Spinoza and Nietzsche, Freud and Bertrand Russell; and, most glorious of all, David Hume. Oh, what David Hume and his *Dialogues Concerning Natural Religion* did for my life.

Imagine the exhilaration of a chronic invalid suddenly transformed into an Olympic athlete and you glimpse my mood of those days. Judged by religious standards my want of belief was a weakness, an ailment requiring therapy. I was always being told to go and speak to this rabbi or that *rebbetsen*. And so I went, like a barren woman wandering from one fertility doctor to another. But barren I remained. They offered me reasons, which I criticized. They told me the criticisms were beside the point because the reasons were really beside the point. They're a crutch for those who need them. The good and the strong get there without them. But I couldn't get there, with or without them. Can you imagine, then, what it was like to turn from the spirit of religion to the spirit of philosophy, or, as I liked to call it in those days, the spirit of rationality? For here, reasons for beliefs are never beside the point but are the entire substance of the matter. The distinction between the mere belief and the reasoned belief is the distinction that grounds all philosophy. If truth is our end (and what else should be?) we must reason our way there.

The leap of faith is not heroic but cowardly, has all the virtues, Russell said, of theft over hard labor. (And we can take his word for it. After all, he was described, in the squabble over whether he should be allowed a professorship at City College of New York because of his book *Marriage and Morals*, as "lecherous, libidinous, lustful, venerous, erotomaniac, aphrodisiac, irreverent" and more; which is recommendation enough for me. Einstein, a habitual scribbler of doggerel verse, wrote him: *Es wiederholt sich immer wieder / In dieser Welt so fein und bieder / Der Pfaff den Pobel alarmiert / Der Genius wird exekutiert.* [It keeps repeating itself / In this world so fine and honest / The parson alerts the mob / The genius is executed.] The controversy brought Russell an invitation to Princeton, where he spent the next four years at the Institute. Anyone who is anyone in our world has done time here.)

For me, in those days, the turn from religion to philosophy was like stepping from one ethical system into another, which was the inversion of the first. My moral weakness became my moral strength, the barrenness of my belief was in truth the fertility of my rationality, and I was saved at last.

I had been in the habit since childhood of sending up urgent little prayers: God make me know the answer; make my mother love me; let me not strike out with the bases loaded. The original intent was religious, but over the years the words had simply become a formula for expressing these surges of desire. Now, in high school, the little plea became: God make me rational—even though part of what I meant by being rational was ceasing to believe in the divine presence.

My goal was Barnard, for me the beacon of reason, shining forth on the shores of the Hudson, beckoning to me like a liberation. Smart girls went to Barnard, and I wanted like hell to be one of them. The college's acceptance was not sufficient. I also had to overcome the undertow of religion, in the persons of my mother and the rabbis and *rebbetsens* she enlisted, trying to sweep me out to sea where I would drown. No high has ever quite equaled that first time I took the Seventh Avenue subway uptown and got off in the general exodus at 116th Street, *my* promised land.

And Fruma, whose name derives from the Yiddish-German *frum,* for pious, was there with me at the time of my conversion, sometimes arguing the other side but usually ending up agreeing with me. Finally we were ready to act. We walked into a McDonald's and ordered a cheeseburger each. Not just a plain *trayf* hamburger, you understand, but a *trayf* hamburger with cheese, meat and milk together. We discovered, however, that it's one thing to reach a conclusion and another to act on it. After an hour of sitting and staring shamefaced, we walked out, leaving behind two untouched cheeseburgers.

My friend and I had sporadically kept in touch our first year out of high school, when I was at Barnard and she was going to Brooklyn College at night and the *Bas Yaakov* seminary during the day. ("I have to. My parents expect it.") But we soon drifted apart. The last time I had seen her was at her wedding, when we were both eighteen. We spoke on the phone a few times after, but our increasing estrangement was both annoying and painful. So far as I was concerned, her brief experiment in thinking was over; she had returned to the proper role of the *Bas Yaakov*, the little girl who never questions or challenges, but patters through life collecting little gold stars for good behavior. She had also been, I now learned, accumulating children, one a year since her marriage, not at all unusual in her world.

My first reaction upon seeing Fruma again was shock. I would never have recognized her. She was in the advanced stages of pregnancy and was absolutely enormous, probably because this was her fifth child and she hadn't many stomach muscles left. There had been an all-round thickening of the thin body I remembered; the arms, the neck, the calves and ankles. The gorgeous red hair had been cut off and replaced by a brown *sheitel* with demure red highlights. Only the clear blue eyes were as I remembered them.

But the minute she began to talk in her fast bubbly way, I knew it was the old Fruma.

"Renee, Renee, look at you! You're exactly the same, only better. Tzippy told me you just got married. *Mazel tov!* Look at you. I can't believe it, what a beauty. But why shouldn't I believe it? You were always beautiful. So how are you, what's new?"

We exchanged summaries of our lives.

"I wish your husband was here. I'd love to meet him, he sounds so fascinating. Is he *frum*?" she asked, trying to sound casual.

"No, not at all. I'm his first brush with Orthodoxy. Not that I'm at all observant anymore," I added hastily.

"So you finally tasted the cheeseburger." Fruma grinned. I nodded and grinned back. "Was it good?"

"I don't know. I really don't. Not half so delicious as we imagined."

"None of it?"

"So you're still wondering. You look as if you had put all doubts aside long ago."

"Yeah, I do look it, don't I? I look in the mirror and I can't believe what

I see. I look just like our teachers." She grinned. "Our dark-age teachers. In fact, I do teach in the local *Bas Yaakov*. But I'm really a fake. I only look the part. I live a *frum* life, but I don't live it out of my own convictions."

"You don't believe in it?"

"I don't know if I do or I don't. The choice wasn't mine to decide what I believe in. Maybe I would have discovered that I actually do believe in it. I don't know. I went right from my parents' home to my husband's," she said very slowly. "Do you see? Tzvi would be so horrified if he heard me talking like this. I never talk like this."

"I always was your *yaytzah harah*." That's the evil inclination, dear reader, the snake in the Garden of Eden.

"Yeah." She grinned and then immediately became serious.

"Once I said something mildly skeptical to Tzvi and he told me he wondered if I was fit to be the mother of our children. You can't believe what that did to me. More than anything else I want to be a good mother to them, just as I wanted to be a good daughter."

"You know, it's funny my talking to you like this after all these years," Fruma mused. "Don't think that I'm unhappy, that I go in a blue funk all the time. I'm very happy. It's just that deep down I feel like I'm not really an adult yet, that I haven't reached maturity, because I've never decided for myself how I want to live my life. Someone just handed me the script and I started reading. I don't think I'd even know how to make up my own words, the way you have. I wouldn't know how to decide for myself, to go against everybody else. But you know," she giggled, the same little-girl giggle I remembered, "sometimes I cheat on Tzvi."

"What?" I stared at her, dumbfounded. I thought myself not easily shocked anymore, but I was having trouble assimilating Fruma's words. Was there wife-swapping going on in Lakewood? Was the *sheitel* crowd swinging? Impossible! Fruma looked at me, as if a little puzzled at the effect of her statement. Then she suddenly burst out laughing.

"Oh, Renee! Oh, is this beautiful! Too bad I can't tell Tzvi. Renee, you nut, I didn't mean *that* kind of cheating!" Her laughter was always infectious, and I was laughing, too. The great low belly was bobbing up and down so violently that I feared for the child inside. "What I *meant*—oh boy, is this going to sound ridiculous after what you thought—what I *meant* was that sometimes I don't wait the full six hours between *flayshig* and *milchik*, and once—boy, I thought I was going to shock you with this." She was laughing so hard that she had trouble speaking and the tears were streaming down her face, "Once, Renee, they were offering free samples of a *trayf* cheese spread on *trayf* crackers in the supermarket and I ate one. In fact, it was so good I ate two."

I had planned to leave Saturday night night after *Havdalah,* but I hung around talking with Tzippy and playing with Reuven until it was quite late. And when Tzippy suggested I spend another night on their lumpy little couch, I happily agreed.

Sunday morning, as I made the trip back to Princeton, I considered for the first time whether I wanted to have a baby. It wasn't a question of whether to have one at all. I'd always taken for granted that I would someday become a mother. The question was whether this was, metaphorically speaking, the day. Why not? I was a married woman. Noam was already forty. I wouldn't want my child to be embarrassed by a father whom other children mistook for a grandfather. (Would he come with me to Lamaze or, like my brother, decline any involvement in *weibeszachen*?)

I had always pictured myself with a daughter—a golden child, loving the world and herself. And now there was the possibility that she would inherit her father's genius. (I remembered, but briefly, the sorry hopes of Mother Himmel, weeping at her Formica kitchen table.) I could be the mother of a Marie Curie. How's that for compensation for not being a genius oneself? Wife *and* mother of. And if she were brilliant—not that she need be; my love would be unconditional—but if she were, I'd make sure the flames of her creativity were never smothered by self-doubt. It was an exciting thought: Daddy's mind, Mommy's body. And what, Shaw's unbidden ghost whispered in my mind's ear, what if she inherited Mommy's mind and Daddy's body? No matter! She would be loved.

Now, I'm not saying that I was really at the point of taking the step and discarding the remainder of my birth-control pills. I had discovered a new identity to fantasize about, and this was exciting. I don't know if the excitement would have been sufficient to carry me into action. It is, after all, quite a choice: whether to create a person, to take responsibility for another's existence and, to some extent, essence. "Mother" is not an identity one can just try on for size, as I have others. How do all these people do it, I've always wondered, cavalierly *do* it?

But then I have noticed that others don't seem to have quite the problem with freedom that I have, to suffer the burden of choice as I do. Most seem to have their fixed solid natures, cast in one form or another, not this liquefied matter flowing first one way and then another. Fruma wondered whether she had it in her to make up her own words. My problem is, I can think up too many words. Freedom for me is a pain in the Buridan's ass.

And now having a child has been taken out of the sphere of biological determinism and placed instead in the domain of intentional action. Another option to consider and decide upon. And this one qualifies, in the terminology that William James formulated to characterize religious choices, as a momentous decision: not to choose is to choose. I really needed this. Wouldn't I have been better off without so many options before me requiring my attention? I haven't been *bred* to make choices.

Consider my forebears. Consider my maternal great-grandmother, who was married at twelve and lived to have sixteen children and sixty grandchildren before she was carted off, at ninety-four, to Auschwitz. I'm named after her: she was Reine, which means pure. (Fruma and I used to joke about our names: "Pious and Pure, what choice did our parents give us?" But that was the idea, wasn't it?) Since I was her namesake, my grandmother used to feel it was only right for me to hear stories about her. Most of them emphasized her saintliness, but my favorite was this:

It was shortly after her marriage, one Shabbos morning when all the men were in *shul*, and she and her friends were out playing in some mud they made by peeing in the dirt lane that ran through the town. My great-grandmother was using her *sheitel* to mix the mud in. Suddenly the men were spotted returning from *shul*, my great-grandfather among them. And here was his wife with her head uncovered. So she dumped the *sheitel* (after all, what choice did she have?), mudpie and all, on her head and ran.

You know, I think I would have functioned tolerably well in such a world. My energies are considerable, quite equal to sixteen children, I think, if only they weren't being constantly dissipated in making fundamental decisions as to my essential nature. In any case, this new fantasy of mothering—of mothering a genius—was so exciting that I actually mentioned something to Noam that night at dinner.

"Noam, how would you feel about having a child?"

"A child?"

"You know, Noam, children. You've seen them around. Very young people, tend to be rather short."

"Don't attempt sarcasm, Renee, you haven't the wit. A child is out of the question. A wife is distraction enough." He stared at me coldly for several seconds. "You know, hardly any of the great mathematicians in history were married, and I've come to know why."

That was March; so Noam's hostility had already started by then, that deep numbing anger. When had it first begun? I find it hard to pinpoint, since the change was gradual. There were the walks, I remember.

Noam and I both enjoy walking. We used to love to tramp through the extensive Institute woods where so many great minds have wandered, pursuing so many great thoughts. In the good days, certainly before our marriage and after our return to Princeton as well, we had walked there together often, talking the whole time. Even in the course of our mad Viennese ambulations, when Noam was so preoccupied with his search for personal identity, the conversation had hardly ever let up. I had always loved listening to Noam, talking on a wide range of topics, always interesting and original. But gradually, over the course of that first year of marriage, the nature of the walks changed until they had become almost silent. The conversation had always been dominated by Noam, but now he seldom wanted to speak. On occasions when I'd break the silence with a comment, it would be followed by more silence, during which I'd consider the now apparent absurdity of my remark, whose existence, however brief, I regretted and he ignored. He wouldn't even acknowledge it with his usual absent-minded "hmmmm." And to think that in Rome I had been annoyed by the abundance of Noam's conversation, at least in bed.

Okay, so he was preoccupied with his thoughts. The world inside his head is more interesting than anything outside, I told myself. That's what makes Noam Noam. Perhaps he's working out something very important. Perhaps he's on the trail of something surpassing even the supernaturals. Don't distract him with your petty childish needs.

Think of the two Mrs. Einsteins, I told myself (I had just finished Ronald Clark's biography of the great man): the bad, complex Mileva and the good, simple Elsa. Mileva had been a (failed) physicist herself, bitter and brooding, whereas Elsa is described by Clark as "placid and housewifely, of no intellectual pretensions, but with a practiced mothering ability which made her the ideal organizer of genius." There! That was the description for me to assume. My instructions were clear. And just in case I didn't yet understand, Elsa, good, stolid, contented Elsa, told me again: "When the Americans come to my house they carry away details about Einstein and his life, and about me they say incidentally: he has a good wife, who is very hospitable, and offers a good table." I would have to work on myself until that is what the Americans would say of *me*.

The most persuasive statement of all came from Einstein himself: "I'm glad my wife doesn't know any science. My first wife did." Succinct and clear. Mileva's insistence on her own intellectual identity had doomed her to divorce, while Elsa had ridden out her marriage in relative peace and contentment, sharing in the glory of her husband. Elsa Einstein had not gone mooning around because her husband didn't take her mind seriously. She mothered him and understood: "You cannot analyze him, otherwise you will misjudge him," she wrote a friend. "Such a genius should be irreproachable in every respect. But no, nature doesn't behave like this. Where she gives extravagantly, she takes away extravagantly." So even Einstein, most noble of men, had had his faults.

Couldn't I be satisfied? I was the wife of a genius, for Godssakes. *I* was a malevolent Mileva with intellectual pretensions and, if not careful, would end up as Noam's first wife. Grow up grow up, grow up, I chanted to myself as we trampled through the snow. I didn't know what Noam was working on. He didn't discuss his work with me anymore. When I asked him once he said I wouldn't be able to understand it and I never asked agaln. Why didn't I simply stop tagging along on those ever more painful walks? Because I kept hoping I suppose, remembering and hoping. Noam's natural gait is much faster than mine, really very brisk, and even though I had compromised my vanity and bought some very sensible boots, I had difficulty keeping up with him for long periods. After a while he'd be twenty paces ahead of me, and I'd bleat out: "Noam." Sometimes he'd mumble "Sorry"; usually he didn't say a word, but would just pause a few seconds while I ran to catch up. Then the whole painful process would begin again. It was obvious that he had forgotten my existence, and, dependent as I am on others' assurances that I do indeed exist, this made me wretched. Still I struggled for objectivity: Can't you stop worrying about yourself? Can't you ever get beyond yourself, you petty-spirited woman? Don't blame him because he's different from other people. That's why you married him.

But there was actually very little danger of my blaming him. It was clear whose fault it was. The explanation was ready at hand, because it was the thing I had feared from the first, even before Noam had sat down with me on the dinky. If Noam wasn't interested in talking to me anymore, it was because he had discovered what an idiot I am. How could I have hoped that he would fail to do so? Had I, in my heart of hearts, even wished him to? Fear that *p* is not always incompatible with fear that not-*p*. One by one the sacred symbols of intelligence had lost their meaning for me, as I managed, with little effort, to collect them. How many of one's idols can one bear to see exposed?

I believed in genius. Genius that remained duped would try my faith. Noam's infatuation had provided the explanation for his mistaken regard for me. His besotted perception had wrapped me in an intellectual grace and loveliness. His interpretation of my remarks had been generous, often creatively so, making of them something far more brilliant than I had intended, than I ever could intend. I had enjoyed an intelligence of his own making, a little runoff from the great gushing well of his mind. He had finally located the leak.

It's hard to remember the exact timetable of the breakdown between us. I can remember lovely times that first year, when Noam spoke to me as in the old days, the golden spring days when we had first come together, excitement and intensity lighting up his vivid eyes. Sometimes he would come home from Fine Hall full of something to discuss, rushing into the kitchen where I was preparing supper. There was the famous incident I have mentioned of his getting burned when he stuck his head over the pot of soup I was stirring, in an effort to catch my gaze, just as he so often used to place his head over the steering wheel.

But now so many times the face he turned to me was frozen over in anger. That seemed to be the heart of the matter. He was furious with me. It became increasingly obvious that he harbored a very deep and constant rage that would come bursting through with great violence at unexpected moments. When I said something vague, unclear, half-baked, he'd pounce, tearing away with a ferocity that seemed no longer impersonal but vengeful. He wouldn't stop until I was completely broken. Now he's getting back at me, I'd think, for having hidden my membership in the class of dopes he despises.

The attacks paralyzed my mental processes so that I couldn't think, would blather out idiocies, contradict myself left and right; in short, produce ample evidence for his opinion that I didn't know what I was talking about. Once he said to me, it was shortly after our first anniversary: "Now I see why you're having so much trouble hacking it in philosophy."

Noam knew what such a statement would do to me, particularly coming from him. He knew the damage inflicted on my sense of self by my failure to be appreciated by the Princeton philosophers. I had poured out all to him, in the glowing days before our marriage, and he had listened sympathetically, and encouraged me:

"Don't be overwhelmed by this technical turn in philosophy. They're trying to turn philosophy into math, which can't be done. Not that I'm an expert on philosophy, but I know enough about math to know it can't be done. There's a great story about a debate between Euler and Diderot on the existence of God." (Euler, you'll remember, was on Noam's roll call of mathematical minor deities.) "Euler was supposed to take the pro side and Diderot the con. Diderot didn't know much mathematics and Euler decided to trick him. He got up and said that he could prove the existence of God mathematically, that God's being is a mathematical theorem." Noam was laughing. "Then he wrote down some equations, concluding on the last line: therefore God exists, Q.E.D. There's some uncertainty as to how the debate ended. Actually, there are two endings. One says that Diderot walked out in great embarrassment, unable to follow the so-called proof; the other, which I hope is the true one, maintains that Diderot called Euler's bluff.

"Anyway, Renee, I suspect that a lot of contemporary philosophers are playing Euler's trick, probably on themselves, too. Don't let them fool you. Call their bluff."

•

"Feminine Is Dumb" (excerpt)

One night I came very close to telling Ava about my problems, prodded by her own self-revelations. It had started off by her complimenting me:

"You know, Renee, you really look great. You're a damn good-looking woman."

I probably did look particularly good at this time. I had lost all interest in food, something I would never have imagined could happen to me. (But then I would never have thought I'd become frigid, either.) I had lost a few pounds and always look best when underweight and Camille-like. In the past I had only been able to maintain my matter in this form for short periods before my love of food brought me back to my healthy-looking self. (This love, finally acquired sometime in later childhood, is one of my mother's minor triumphs. "If only I live to see my children someday dieting.") But now it was hard to eat, for I always had the feel of cinders in my mouth.

"Look at me, on the other hand," Ava was saying. "I've really deteriorated since college."

Unfortunately, this was true. Ava was about fifteen pounds heavier than she'd been at Barnard and seemed on the whole to take no trouble with her appearance. Her thin hair, shaped like a monk's in college, now drooped unbecomingly down the sides of her too full face. She never wore a trace of makeup (as she had at Barnard) and her wardrobe was confined to jeans, which did not sit particularly well on her zaftig bottom.

"And you know this uglification is intentional, in the sense that compulsive hand-washing is intentional. There's a need behind it. I don't really want to look pretty. I don't want to look feminine. You know why? Because feminine is dumb. Or at least that's how I feel. Look around at the women in academia, the women who make their living from their brains—especially those in the so-called masculine disciplines like math and physics, to take two random examples. They all feel it too. They're telling you with the way they look and dress, the way they hold themselves and speak: feminine is dumb. You've got to stamp out all traces of girlishness if you want to be taken seriously by the others, but more importantly by yourself. I know. I can see it in myself and can't do anything about it. It was okay to be a girl when I was only a student, but not anymore. When I'm attracted to a man and start playing the part of a woman, there's a voice sneering inside me: Dumb. You dumb cunt. You just can't be a cunt with intelligence. You can have a brain and a prick, there's no incompatibility there. 'Brainy prick' sounds all right, but 'intelligent cunt' is ridiculous, a contradiction in terms. We've all swallowed it. I tell you, I think it would be an act of feminist heroism, an assertion of true liberation from the chauvinist myth, to wear eyeliner and mascara. If I ever saw a female physicist dressed to kill and wearing makeup, I'd be impressed.

"But it won't be me," she continued. "I don't care what the others will think; I care what I'll think, what I'll feel like. I can't manage to regard myself as a woman and a physicist, so one of them's got to go. And I suppose being a physicist is more important to me, so goodbye, sex. Men don't have to make the choice, but we do. For us it's either-or."

"Either mind or body," I said.

Cynthia Ozick

One of the most important and prolific figures in contemporary American Jewish literature, Cynthia Ozick was born in 1928 into a Yiddishly fluent home in the Bronx. She is a Phi Beta Kappa graduate of New York University, where she had studied Hebrew as well as English literature, and received her M.A. degree from New York University. During her student years, her interests focused on English literature, especially Henry James. However, after graduation, when Ozick was occupied in writing poetry, translating Yiddish poetry, and working as an advertising copywriter at Filene's Department Store in Boston, she became extensively involved in reading Jewish literature, history, and philosophy. Some of the authors she studied included Leo Baeck, Martin Buber, Franz Rosenzweig, and Hermann Cohen. Furthermore, during the long process of writing her first published novel, *Trust* (1966), she became more and more involved in Judaic study and thought.

Unlike the majority of American Jewish authors, Ozick does not frequently focus on the typical Eastern European Jewish immigrant/urban milieu in her novels and short stories, and yet her work is far more deeply and passionately Jewish than most. She uses not only all aspects of her own Jewish reading, thinking, and experience but also her broad knowledge of Jewish texts in her writing. As a result, her fiction has the kind of dense Jewish texture that is more typical of the Yiddish writers. For example, the short story "Puttermesser and Xanthippe," reprinted here in its entirety, is overtly about the exploitation of female employees and about urban planning—the attempt to correct and perfect New York City. However, the story plays with Jewish motifs going back to the Bible and working forward through medieval European Jewish history. A few examples of Ozick's allusions: (1) The heroine's name is Puttermesser, "butter knife" in Yiddish; (2) the mayor's name is Malachi Mavett, or Matt, which translated from the Hebrew mean, respectively, "angel of death" and "dead person"; (3) the agent of change is a golem, a powerful but mindless legendary creature that captured the imaginations of powerless, overintellectualized Jews in Diaspora Jewish communities for hundreds of years.

•

"Puttermesser and Xanthippe"

I. Puttermesser's Brief Love Life, Her Troubles, Her Titles

Puttermesser, an unmarried lawyer and civil servant of forty-six, felt attacked on all sides. The night before, her lover, Morris Rappoport, a married fund-raiser from Toronto, had walked out on her. His mysterious job included settling Soviet Jewish refugees away from the big metropolitan centers; he claimed to have fresh news of the oppressed everywhere, as well as intimate acquaintance with malcontents in numerous cities in both the Eastern and Western hemispheres. Puttermesser suspected him of instability and overdependency: a future madman. His gripe was that she read in bed too much; last night she had read aloud from Plato's *Theaetetus*:

THEODORUS: What do you mean, Socrates?

SOCRATES: The same thing as the story about the Thracian maidservant who exercised her wit at the expense of Thales, when he was looking up to study the stars and tumbled down a well. She scoffed at him for being so eager to know what was happening in the sky that he could not see what lay at his feet. Anyone who gives his life to philosophy is open to such mockery. It is true that he is unaware what his next-door neighbor is doing, hardly knows, indeed, whether the creature is a man at all; he spends all his pains on the question, what man is, and what powers and properties distinguish such nature from any other. You see what I mean, Theodorus?

Rappoport did not see. He withdrew his hand from Puttermesser's belly. "What's the big idea, Ruth?" he said.

"That's right," Puttermesser said.

"What?"

"That's just what Socrates is after: the big idea."

"You're too old for this kind of thing," Rappoport said. He had a medium-sized, rather square, reddish mustache over perfect teeth. His teeth were more demanding to Puttermesser's gaze than his eyes, which were so diffidently pigmented that they seemed whited out, like the naked eyes on a Roman bust. His nose, however, was dominant, eloquent, with large deep nostrils that appeared to meditate. "Cut it out, Ruth. You're behaving like an adolescent," Rappoport said.

"*You'll* never fall down a well," Puttermesser said. "You never look up." She felt diminished; those philosophical nostrils had misled her.

"Ruth, Ruth," Rappoport pleaded, "what did I do?"

"It's what you didn't do. You didn't figure out what powers and properties distinguish human nature from any other," Puttermesser said bitterly; as a feminist, she was careful never to speak of "man's" nature. She always said "humankind" instead of "mankind." She always wrote "he or she" instead of just "he."

Rappoport was putting on his pants. "You're too old for sex," he said meanly.

Puttermesser's reply was instantly Socratic: "Then I'm not behaving like an adolescent."

"If you know I have a plane to catch, how come you want to read in bed?"

"It's more comfortable than the kitchen table."

"Ruth, I came to make love to you!"

"All I wanted was to finish the *Theaetetus* first."

Now he had his coat on, and was crossing his scarf carefully at his throat, so as not to let in the cold. It was a winter night, but Puttermesser saw in this gesture that Rappoport, at the age of fifty-two, still obeyed his mother's doctrines, no matter that they were five decades old. "You wanted to finish!" he yelled. He grabbed the book from her lap. "It goes from page 847 to page 879, that's thirty-three pages—"

"I read fast," Puttermesser said.

In the morning she understood that Rappoport would never come back. His feelings were hurt. In the end he would have deserted her anyway—she had observed that, sooner or later, he told all his feelings to his wife. And not only to his wife. He was the sort of man who babbles.

The loss of Rappoport was not Puttermesser's only trouble. She had developed periodontal disease; her dentist reported—with a touch of pleasure in disaster—a sixty percent bone loss. Loss of bone, loss of Rappoport, loss of home! "Uncontrollable pockets," the dentist said. He gave her the name of a periodontist to consult. It was an emergency, he warned. Her gums were puffy, her teeth in peril of uprooting. It was as if, in the dread underworld below the visible gums, a volcano lay, watching for its moment of release. She spat blood into the sink.

The sink was a garish fake marble. Little blue fish-tiles swam around the walls. The toilet seat cover had a large blue mermaid painted on it. Puttermesser hated this bathroom. She hated her new "luxury" apartment, with its windowless slot of a kitchen and two tiny cramped rooms, the bathroom without a bathtub, the shower stall the size of a thimble, the toilet's flush handle made of light blue plastic. Her majestic apartment on the Grand Concourse in the Bronx, with its Alhambra spaciousness, had been ravaged by arsonists. Even before that, the old tenants had been dying off or moving away, one by one; junkies stole in, filling empty corridors with bloodstained newspapers, smashed bottles, dead matches in random rows like beetle tracks. On a summer evening Puttermesser arrived home from her office without possessions: her shoes were ash, her piano was ash, her piano teacher's penciled "Excellent," written in fine large letters at the top of "Humoresque" and right across the opening phrase of "Für Elise," had vanished among the cinders. Puttermesser's childhood, burned away. How prescient her mother had been to take all of Puttermesser's school compositions with her to Florida! Otherwise every evidence of Puttermesser's early mental growth might have gone under in that criminal conflagration.

The new apartment was crowded with plants: Puttermesser, who was once afflicted with what she called a "black thumb," and who had hitherto killed every green thing she put her hand to, determined now to be responsible for life. She dragged in great clay urns and sacks of vitamin-rich soil bought at Woolworth's and emptied dark earth into red pots. She seeded and conscientiously watered. Rappoport himself had lugged in, on a plastic-wheeled dolly, a tall stalk like a ladder of green bear's ears: he claimed it was an avocado tree he had grown from a pit in Toronto. It reminded Puttermesser of her mother's towering rubber plants on the Grand Concourse, in their ceiling-sweeping prime. Every window sill of Puttermesser's new apartment was fringed with fronds, foliage, soaring or drooping leaf-tips. The tough petals of blood-veined coleus strained the bedroom sunset. Puttermesser, astonished, discovered that if she remained attentive enough, she had the power to stimulate green bursts. All along the bosky walls vegetation burgeoned.

Yet Puttermesser's days were arid. Her office life was not peaceable;

nothing bloomed for her. She had fallen. Out of the blue, the Mayor ousted the old Commissioner—Puttermesser's boss, the chief of the Department of Receipts and Disbursements—and replaced him with a new man, seven years younger than Puttermesser. He looked like a large-eared boy; he wore his tie pulled loose, and his neck stretched forward out of his collar; it gave him the posture of a vertical turtle. His eyes, too, were unblinkingly turtlish. It was possible, Puttermesser conceded to herself, that despite his slowly reaching neck and flattish head, the new man did not really resemble a turtle at all; it was only that his name—Alvin Turtelman—suggested the bare lidless deliberation of that immobile creature of the road. Turtelman did not preen. Puttermesser saw at once, in all that meditated motionlessness, that he was more ambitious than the last Commissioner, who had been satisfied with mere prestige, and had used his office like a silken tent decorated with viziers and hookahs. But Turtelman was patient; his steady ogle took in the whole wide trail ahead. He spoke of "restructuring," of "functioning," of "goals" and "gradations," of "levels of purpose" and "versus equations." He was infinitely abstract. "None of this is personal," he liked to say, but his voice was a surprise; it was more pliable than you would expect from the stillness of his stare. He stretched out his vowels like any New Yorker. He had brought with him a score of underlings for what he called "mapping out." They began the day late and ended early, moving from cubicle to cubicle and collecting resumes. They were all bad spellers, and their memos, alive with solecisms, made Puttermesser grieve, because they were lawyers, and Puttermesser loved the law and its language. She caressed its meticulousness. She thought of law as Apollo's chariot; she had read all the letters of Justice Oliver Wendell Holmes, Jr., to Harold Laski (three volumes) and to Sir Frederick Pollock (two). In her dream once she stood before a ship captain and became the fifth wife of Justice William O. Douglas; they honey-mooned on the pampas of Argentina. It was difficult to tell whether Turtelman's bad spellers represented the Mayor himself, or only the new Commissioner; but clearly they were scouts and spies. They reported on lateness and laxness, on backlogs and postponements, on insufficiencies and excesses, on waste and error. They issued warnings and sounded alarms; they brought pressure to bear and threatened and cautioned and gave tips. They were watchful and envious. It soon became plain that they did not understand the work.

They did not understand the work because they were, it turned out, political appointees shipped over from the Department of Hygienic Maintenance; a handful were from the Fire Department. They had already had careers as oligarchs of street-sweeping, sewers and drains, gutters, the perils of sleet, ice, rainslant, gas, vermin, fumigation, disinfection, snow removal, water supply, potholes, steam cleaning, deodorization, ventilation, abstersion, elutriation; those from the Fire Department had formerly wielded the scepter over matters of arson, hydrants, pumps, hose (measured by weight, in kilograms), incendiary bombs, rubber boots, wax polish, red paint, false alarms, sappers, marshals. They had ruled over all these corporealities, but without comprehension; they asked for frequent memos; they were "administrators." This meant they were good at arrest; not only at making arrests (the fire marshals, for instance), but at bringing everything to a stand-still, like the spindle-prick in Sleeping Beauty. In their presence the work instantly held its breath and came to a halt, as if it were a horse reined in for examination. They walked round and round the work, ruminating, speculating. They could not judge it; they did not understand it.

But they knew what it was for. It was for the spoils quota. The work, impenetrable though it was to its suzerains, proliferated with jobs; jobs blossomed with salaries; salaries were money; money was spoils. The current Mayor, Malachy ("Matt") Mavett, like all the mayors before him, was a dispenser of spoils, though publicly, of course, he declared himself morally opposed to political payoffs. He had long ago distributed the plums, the high patronage slots. All the commissioners were political friends of the Mayor. Sometimes a mayor would have more friends than there were jobs, and then this or that commissioner would suddenly be called upon to devise a whole new management level: a many-pegged perch just between the heights of direct mayoral appointment and the loftier rungs of the Civil Service. When that happened, Puttermesser would all at once discover a fresh crew of intermediate bosses appointed to loiter between herself and the Commissioner. Week after week, she would have to explain the work to them: the appointed intermediate bosses of the Department of Receipts and Disbursements did not usually know what the Department of Receipts and Disbursements did. By the time they found out, they vanished; they were always on the move, like minor bedouin sheikhs, to the next oasis. And when a new commissioner arrived right after an election (or, now and then, after what was officially described as "internal reorganization"—demoralization, upheaval, bloodbath), Puttermesser would once again be standing in the sanctuary of the Commissioner's deep inner office, the one with the mottled carpeting and the private toilet, earnestly explaining his rich domain to its new overlord.

Puttermesser was now an old hand, both at the work and at the landscape of the bureaucracy. She was intimate with every folly and every fall. (Ah, but she did not expect her own fall.) She was a witness to every succession. (Ah, but she did not expect to be succeeded herself.) The bureaucracy was a faded feudal world of territory and authority and hierarchy, mainly dusty, except at those high moments of dagger and toppling. Through it all, Puttermesser was seen to be useful: this accounted for her climb. She had stuck her little finger into every cranny of every permutation of the pertinent law. Precedents sped through her brain. Her titles, movable and fictitious, traveled upward: from Assistant Corporation Counsel she became Administrative Tax Law Associate, and after that Vice Chief of Financial Affairs, and after that First Bursary Officer. All the while she felt like Alice, swallowing the potion and growing compact, nibbling the mushroom and swelling: each title was a swallow or a nibble, and not one of them signified anything but the degree of her convenience to whoever was in command. Her titles were the poetry of the bureaucracy.

The truth was that Puttermesser was now a fathomer; she had come to understand the recondite, dim, and secret journey of the City's money, the tunnels it rolled through, the transmutations, investments, multiplications, squeezings, fattenings and battenings it underwent. She knew where the money landed and where it was headed for. She knew the habits, names, and even the hot-tempered wives of three dozen bank executives on various levels. She had acquired half a dozen underlings of her own—with these she was diffident, polite; though she deemed herself a feminist, no ideology could succeed for her in aggrandizing force. Puttermesser was not aggressive. She disdained assertiveness. Her voice was like Cordelia's. At home, in bed, she went on dreaming and reading. She retained a romantic view of the British Civil Service in its heyday: the Cambridge Apostles carrying the probities of G. E. Moore to the far corners of the world, Leonard Woolf doing justice in Ceylon, the shy young Forster in India. Integrity. Uprightness. And all for the sake of imperialism, colonialism! In New York, Puttermesser had an immigrant's grandchild's dream of merit: justice, justice shalt thou pursue. Her heart beat for law, even for tax law: she saw the orderly nurturing of the democratic populace, public murals, subway windows bright as new dishes, parks with flowering borders, the bell-hung painted steeds of dizzying carousels.

Every day, inside the wide bleak corridors of the Municipal Building, Puttermesser dreamed an ideal Civil Service: devotion to polity, the citizen's sweet love of the citizenry, the light rule of reason and common sense, the City as a miniature country crowded with patriots—not fools and jingoists, but patriots true and serene; humorous affection for the idiosyncrasies of one's distinctive little homeland, each borough itself another little homeland, joy in the Bronx, elation in Queens, O happy Richmond! Children on roller skates, and over the Brooklyn Bridge the long patchwork-colored line of joggers, breathing hard above the homeland-hugging green waters.

II. Puttermesser's Fall, and the History of the Genus Golem

Turtelman sent his secretary to fetch Puttermesser. It was a new secretary, a middle-aged bony acolyte, graying and testy, whom he had brought with him from the Department of Hygienic Maintenance: she had coarse eyebrows crawling upward. "This isn't exactly a good time for me to do this," Puttermesser complained. It was as if Turtelman did not trust the telephone for such a purpose. Puttermesser knew his purpose: he wanted teaching. He was puzzled, desperate. Inside his ambitiousness he was a naked boy, fearful. His office was cradled next to the threatening computer chamber; all along the walls the computer's hard flanks glittered with specks and lights. Puttermesser could hear, behind a partition, the spin of a thousand wheels, a thin threadlike murmur, as if the software men, long-haired chaps in sneakers, had set lyres out upon the great stone window sills of the Municipal Building. Walking behind the bony acolyte, Puttermesser pitied Turtelman: the Mayor had called for information—figures, indexes, collections, projections—and poor Turtelman, fresh from his half-education in the land of abstersion and elutriation, his frontal lobes still inclined toward repair of street-sweeping machinery, hung back bewildered. He had no answers for the Mayor, and no idea where the answers might be hidden; alas, the questions themselves fell on Turtelman's ears as though in a foreign tongue.

The secretary pushed open Turtelman's door, stood aside for Puttermesser, and went furiously away.

Poor Turtelman, Puttermesser thought.

Turtelman spoke: "You're out."

"Out?" Puttermesser said. It was a bitter Tuesday morning in mid-January; at that very moment, considerably south of the Municipal Building, in Washington, D.C., they were getting ready to inaugurate the next President of the United States. High politics emblazoned the day. Bureaucracies all over the world were turning on their hinges, gates were lifting and shutting, desks emptying and filling. The tide rode upon Turtelman's spittle; it glimmered on his teeth.

"As of this afternoon," Turtelman said, "you are relieved of your duties. It's nothing personal, believe me. I don't know you. We're restructuring. It's too bad you're not a bit older. You can't retire at only forty-six." He had read her resume, then; at least that.

"I'm old enough," Puttermesser said.

"Not for collecting your pension. You people have a valuable retirement system here. I envy you. It drains the rest of us dry." The clack of his teeth showed that he was about to deliver a sting: "We ordinary folk who aren't lucky enough to be in the Civil Service can't afford you."

Puttermesser announced proudly, "I earn my way. I scored highest in the entire city on the First-Level Management Examination. I was editor-in-chief of Law Review at Yale Law School. I graduated from Barnard with honors in history, *summa cum laude*, Phi Beta Kappa—"

Turtelman broke in: "Give me two or three weeks, I'll find a little spot for you somewhere. You'll hear from me."

Thus the manner of Puttermesser's fall. Ignoble. She did not dream there was worse to come. She spilled the papers out of her drawers and carried them to a windowless cubicle down the hall from her old office. For a day or so her ex-staff averted their eyes; then they ceased to notice her; her replacement had arrived. He was Adam Marmel, late of the Bureau of Emergencies, an old classmate of Turtelman's at New York University, where both had majored in Film Arts. This interested Puttermesser: the Department of Receipts and Disbursements was now in the hands of young men who had been trained to pursue illusion, to fly with a gossamer net after fleeting shadows. They were attracted to the dark, where fraudulent emotions raged. They were, moreover, close friends, often together. The Mayor had appointed Turtelman; Turtelman had appointed Marmel; Marmel had succeeded Puttermesser, who now sat with the *Times*, deprived of light, isolated, stripped, forgotten. An outcast. On the next Friday her salary check came as usual. But no one called her out of her cubicle.

Right in the middle of business hours—she no longer had any business, she was perfectly idle—Puttermesser wrote a letter to the Mayor:

The Honorable Malachy Mavett
Mayor, City of New York
City Hall

Dear Mayor Mavett:

Your new appointee in the Department of Receipts and Disbursements, Commissioner Alvin Turtelman, has forced a fine civil servant of honorable temperament, with experience both wide and impassioned, out of her job. I am that civil servant. Without a hearing, without due process, without a hope or appeal or redress (except, Mr. Mayor, by you!), Commissioner Turtelman has destroyed a career in full flower. Employing an affectless vocabulary by means of which, in a single instant, he abruptly ousted a civil servant of high standing, Commissioner Turtelman has politicized a job long held immune to outside preferment. In a single instant, honor, dignity, and continuity have been snatched away! I have been professionally injured and personally humiliated. I have been rendered useless. As of this writing I am costing the City's taxpayers the price of my entire salary, while I sit here working a crossword puzzle; while I hold this very pen. No one looks at me. They are embarrassed and ashamed. At first a few ex-colleagues came into this little abandoned office (where I do nothing) to offer condolences, but that was only at first. It is like being at my own funeral, Mr. Mayor, only imagine it!

Mr. Mayor, I wish to submit several urgent questions to you; I will be grateful for your prompt views on these matters of political friendships, connections, and power.

1. Are you aware of this inequitable treatment of professional staff in the Bureau of Summary Sessions of the Department of Receipts and Disbursements?

2. If so, is this the nature of the Administration you are content to be represented by?

3. Is it truly your desire to erode and undermine the professional Civil Service—one of democratic government's most just, most equitable, devices?

4. Does Commissioner Alvin Turtelman's peremptory action really reflect your own sensibility, with all its fairness and exuberant humaneness?

In City, State, and World life, Mr. Mayor (I have observed this over many years), power and connections are never called power and connections. They are called principle. They are called democracy. They are called judgment. They are called doing good. They are called restructuring. They are called exigency. They are called improvement. They are called functioning. They are called the common need. They are called government. They are called running the Bureau, the Department, the City, the State, the World, looking out for the interests of the people.

Mr. Mayor, getting the spoils is called anything but getting the spoils!

Puttermesser did not know whether Malachy ("Matt") Mavett's sensibility was really fair and exuberantly humane; she had only put that in to flatter him. She had glimpsed the Mayor in the flesh only once or twice, at a meeting, from a distance. She had also seen him on Sunday morning television, at a press conference, but then he was exceptionally cautious and sober; before the cameras he was neuter, he had no sensibility at all; he was nearly translucent. His white mustache looked tangled; his white hair twirled in strings over his temples.

Puttermesser's letter struck her as gripping, impressive; copying it over on the typewriter at home that night, she felt how the Mayor would be stabbed through by such fevered eloquence. How remorseful he would be, how moved!

Still another salary check arrived. It was not for the usual amount; Puttermesser's pay had been cut. The bony acolyte appeared with a memo from Turtelman: Puttermesser was to leave her barren cubicle and go to an office with a view of the Woolworth Building, and there she was to take up the sad life of her demotion.

Turtelman had shoved her into the lowliest ranks of Taxation. It was an unlikely post for a mind superfetate with Idea; Puttermesser felt the malignancy behind this shift. Her successor had wished her out of sight. "I do not consort with failure," she heard Adam Marmel tell one of the auditors. She lived now surrounded by auditors—literal-minded men. They read best-sellers; their fingers were smudged from the morning papers, which they clutched in their car pools or on the subway from Queens. One of them, Leon Cracow, a bachelor from Forest Hills who wore bow ties and saddle shoes, was engaged in a tedious litigation: he had once read a novel and fancied himself its hero. The protagonist wore bow ties and saddle shoes. Cracow was suing for defamation. "My whole love life's maligned in there," he complained to Puttermesser. He kept the novel on his desk—it was an obscure book no one had ever heard of, published by a shadowy California press. Cracow had bought it remaindered for eighty-nine cents and ruminated over it every day. Turning the pages, he wet two of his fingers repeatedly. The novel was called *Pyke's Pique*; a tax auditor named John McCracken Pyke was its chief character. "McCracken," Cracow said, "that's practically Cracow. It sounds practically identical. Listen, in the book this guy goes to prostitutes. I don't go to prostitutes! The skunk's got me all wrong. He's destroying my good name." Sometimes Cracow asked Puttermesser for her opinion of his lawyer's last move. Puttermesser urged him on. She believed in the uses of fantasy. "A person should see himself or herself everywhere," she said. "All things manifest us."

The secret source of this motto was, in fact, her old building on the Grand Concourse. Incised in a stone arch over the broad front door, and also in Puttermesser's loyal brain, were these Roman-style tracings: LONGWOOD ARMS, NO. 26. GREENDALE HALL NO. 28. ALL THINGS MANIFEST US. The builder had thought deep thoughts, and Cracow was satisfied. "Ruth," he said, "you take the cake." As usual, he attempted to date her. "Any concert, any show, you name it," he said; "I'm a film buff." "You fit right in with Turtelman and Marmel," Puttermesser said. "Not me," Cracow retorted, "with me it's nostalgia only. My favorite movie is Deanna Durbin, Leopold Stokowski, and Adolphe Menjou in *One Hundred Men and a Girl*. Wholesome, sweet, not like they make today. Light classical. Come on, Ruth, it's at the Museum of Modern Art, in the cellar." Puttermesser turned him down. She knew she would never marry, but she was not yet reconciled to childlessness. Sometimes the thought that she would never give birth tore her heart.

She imagined daughters. It was self-love: all these daughters were Puttermesser as a child. She imagined a daughter in fourth grade, then in seventh grade, then in second-year high school. Puttermesser herself had gone to Hunter College High School and studied Latin. At Barnard she had not renounced Catullus and Vergil. *O infelix Dido*, chanted the imaginary daughter, doing her Latin homework at Puttermesser's new Danish desk in the dark corner of the little bedroom. It was a teak rectangle; Puttermesser still had not bought a lamp for it. She hated it that all her furniture was new.

No reply came from the Mayor: not even a postcard of acknowledgment from an underling. Malachy ("Matt") Mavett was ignoring Puttermesser.

Rappoport had abandoned the Sunday *Times*, purchased Saturday night at the airport; he had left it, unopened, on the Danish desk. Puttermesser swung barefoot out of bed, stepped over Plato, and reached for Rappoport's *Times*. She brooded over his furry chest hair, yellowing from red.

Now the daughter, still in high school, was memorizing Goethe's *Erlkonig:*

Dem Vater grauset's, er reitet geschwind,
Er halt in Armen des achzende Kind,
Erreicht den Hof mit Muhe und Not:
In seinem Armen das Kind war tot.

The words made Puttermesser want to sob. The child was dead. In its father's arms the child was dead. She came back to bed, carrying Rappoport's *Times*. It was as heavy as if she carried a dead child. The Magazine Section alone was of a preternatural weight. Advertising. Consumerism. Capitalism. Page after page of cars, delicately imprinted chocolates, necklaces, golden whiskey. Affluence while the poor lurked and mugged, hid in elevators, shot drugs into their veins, stuck guns into old grandmothers' tremulous and brittle spines, in covert pools of blackness released the springs of their brightflanked switchblades, in shafts, in alleys, behind walls, in ditches.

A naked girl lay in Puttermesser's bed. She looked dead—she was all white, bloodless. It was as if she had just undergone an epileptic fit: her tongue hung out of her mouth. Her eyelids were rigidly ajar; they had no lashes, and the skin was so taut and thin that the eyeballs bulged through. Her palms had fallen open; they were a clear white. Her arms were cold rods. A small white square was visible on the tongue. The girl did not resemble Puttermesser at all; she was certainly not one of the imaginary daughters. Puttermesser moved to one side of the bed, then circled back around the foot to the other side. She put on her slippers; summoning reason, she continued to move around and around the bed. There was no doubt that a real body was in it. Puttermesser reached out and touched the right shoulder—a reddish powder coated her fingers. The body seemed filmed with sand, or earth, or grit; some kind of light clay. Filth. A filthy junkie or prostitute; both. Sickness and filth. Rappoport, stalking away in the middle of the night, had been careless about closing the apartment door. God only knew where the creature had concealed herself, what had been stolen or damaged. When Puttermesser's back was turned, the filthy thing had slid into her bed. Such a civilized bed, the home of Plato and other high-minded readings. The body had a look of perpetuity about it, as if it had always been reclining there, in Puttermesser's own bed; yet it was a child's body, the limbs stretched into laxity and languor. She was a little thing, no more than fifteen: Puttermesser saw how the pubic hair was curiously sparse; but the breasts were nearly not there at all. Puttermesser went on calculating and circling: should she call the super, or else telephone for an ambulance? New York! What was the good of living in a tiny squat box, with low ceilings, on East Seventy-first Street, a grudging landlord, a doorman in an admiral's uniform, if there were infiltrators, addicts, invaders, just the same as on the fallen Grand Concourse?

Puttermesser peered down at the creature's face. Ugly. The nose and mouth were clumsily formed, as if by some coarse hand that had given them a negligent tweak. The vomerine divider was off-center, the nostrils unpleasantly far apart. The mouth was in even worse condition—also off-center, but somehow more carelessly made, with lips that failed to match, the lower one no better than a line, the upper one amazingly fat, swollen, and the narrow tongue protruding with its white patch. Puttermesser reached out a correcting hand, and then withdrew it. Once again the dust left deep red ovals on her fingertips. But it was clear that the nostrils needed pinching to bring them closer together, so Puttermesser tentatively pinched. The improvement was impressive. She blew into the left nostril to get rid of a tuft of dust; it solidified and rolled out like a clay bead. With squeamish deliberation she pushed the nose in line with the middle space where the eyebrows ought to have been. There were no eyebrows, no eyelashes, no fingernails, no toenails. The thing was defective, unfinished. The mouth above all required finishing. Forming and re-forming the savage upper lip, getting into the mood of it now, Puttermesser wished she were an artist or sculptor: she centered the mouth, thickened the lower lip with a quick turn smoothed out the hunch of the upper one—the tongue was in the way. She peeled off the white square and, pressing hard, shoved the tongue back down into the mouth.

The bit of white lay glimmering in Puttermesser's palm. It seemed to be nothing more than an ordinary slip of paper, but she thought she ought to put it aside to look it over more carefully after a while, so she left the bed and set it down on the corner of the teak desk. Then she came back and glanced up and down the body, to see whether there was anything else that called for correction. A forefinger needed lengthening, so Puttermesser tugged at it. It slid as if boneless, like taffy, cold but not sticky, and thrillingly pliable. Still, without its nail a finger can shock; Puttermesser recoiled. Though the face was now normal enough, there was more to be done. Something had flashed upward from that tongue-paper—the white patch was blank; yet it was not only blank. Puttermesser carried it in her palm to the window, for the sake of the light. But on the sill and under the sill every pot was cracked, every green plant sprawled. The roots, skeletal and hairy, had been torn from their embracing soil—or, rather, the earth had been scooped away. The plain earth, stolen. Puttermesser, holding the white scrap, wandered from window to window. There was no pot that had not been vandalized in the same way—Rappoport's big clay urn was in shards, the avocado tree broken. A few sparse grains of soil powdered the floor. Not a plant anywhere had been left unmolested—all the earth in Puttermesser's apartment was gone; taken away; robbed.

In the bedroom the girl's form continued its lethal sleep. Puttermesser lifted the tiny paper to the bright panes. Out of the whiteness of the white patch another whiteness flickered, as though a second version of absence were struggling to swim up out of the aboriginal absence. For Puttermesser, it was as if the white of her own eye could suddenly see what the purposeful retina had shunned. It was in fact not so much a seeing as the sharpness of a reading, and what Puttermesser read—she whose intellectual passions were pledged to every alphabet—was a single primeval Hebrew word, shimmering with its lightning holiness, the Name of Names, that which one dare not take in vain. Aloud she uttered it:

השם

whereupon the inert creature, as if drilled through by electricity, as if struck by some principle of instantaneous vitality, leaped straight from the bed; Puttermesser watched the fingernails grow rapidly into place, and the toenails, and the eyebrows and lashes: complete. A configuration of freckles appeared on the forehead. The hair of the head and of the mons Veneris thickened, curled, glistened dark red, the color of clay; the creature had risen to walk. She did it badly, knocking down the desk-chair and bumping into the dresser. Sick, drugged, drunk; vandal; thief of earth!

"Get your clothes on and get out," Puttermesser said. Where were the thing's clothes? She had none; she seemed less pale moment by moment; she was lurching about in her skin. She was becoming rosy. A lively color was in her cheeks and hands. The mouth, Puttermesser's own handiwork, was vivid. Puttermesser ran to her closet and pulled out a shirt, a skirt, a belt, a cardigan. From her drawers she swept up bra, pantyhose, slip. There was only the question of shoes. "Here," she said, "summer sandals, that's all I can spare. Open toes, open heels, they'll fit. Get dressed. I can give you an old coat—go ahead. Sit down on the bed. Put this stuff on. You're lucky I'm not calling the police."

The creature staggered away from the bed, toward the teak desk.

"Do what I say!"

The creature had seized a notepad and a ballpoint pen, and was scribbling with shocking speed. Her fingers, even the newly lengthened one, were rhythmically coordinated. She clenched the pen, Puttermesser saw, like an experienced writer: as if the pen itself were a lick of the tongue, or an extension of the thinking digits. It surprised Puttermesser to learn that this thief of earth was literate. In what language? And would she then again try to swallow what she wrote, leaving one untouchable word behind?

The thing ripped away the alphabet-speckled page, tottered back with the pad, and laid the free sheet on the pillow.

"What's the matter? Can't you walk?" Puttermesser asked; she thought of afflicted children she had known, struck by melancholy witherings and dodderings.

But the answer was already on the paper. Puttermesser read: "I have not yet been long up upon my fresh-made limbs. Soon my gait will come to me. Consider the newborn colt. I am like unto that. All tongues are mine, especially that of my mother. Only speech is forbidden me."

A lunatic! Cracked! Alone in the house with a maniac; a deaf-mute to boot. "Get dressed," Puttermesser again commanded.

The thing wrote: "I hear and obey the one who made me."

"What the hell *is* this," Puttermesser said flatly.

The thing wrote: "My mother," and rapidly began to jerk herself into Puttermesser's clothes, but with uneven sequences of the body—the more vitality the creature gained, the more thinglike she seemed.

Puttermesser was impatient; she longed to drive the creature out. "Put on those shoes," she ordered.

The thing wrote: "No."

"Shoes!" Puttermesser shouted. She made a signpost fist and flung it in the direction of the door. "Go out the way you came in!"

The thing wrote: "No shoes. This is a holy place. I did not enter. I was formed. Here you spoke the Name of the Giver of Life. You blew in my nostril and encouraged my soul. You circled my clay seven times. You enveloped me with your spirit. You pronounced the Name and brought me to myself. Therefore I call you mother."

Puttermesser's lungs began to roil. It was true she had circled the creature on the bed. Was it seven times around? It was true she had blown some foreign matter out of the nose. Had she blown some uncanny energy into an entrance of the dormant body? It was true she had said aloud one of the Names of the Creator.

The thing wrote again: "Mother. Mother."

"Go away!"

The thing wrote: "You made me."

"I didn't give birth to you." She would never give birth. Yet she had formed this mouth—the creature's mute mouth. She looked at the mouth: she saw what she had made.

The thing wrote: "Earth is my flesh. For the sake of my flesh you carried earth to this high place. What will you call me?"

A new turbulence fell over Puttermesser. She had always imagined a daughter named Leah. "Leah," she said.

"No," the creature wrote. "Leah is my name, but I want to be Xanthippe."

Puttermesser said, "Xanthippe was a shrew. Xanthippe was Socrates' wife."

"I want to be Xanthippe," the thing wrote. "I know everything you know. I am made of earth but also I am made out of your mind. Now watch me walk."

The thing walked, firmly, with a solid thump of a step and no stumbling. She wrote on the pad: "I am becoming stronger. You made me. I will be of use to you. Don't send me away. Call me what I prefer, Xanthippe."

"Xanthippe," Puttermesser said.

She succumbed; her throat panted. It came to her that the creature was certainly not lying: Puttermesser's fingernails were crowded with grains of earth. In some unknown hour after Rappoport's departure in the night, Puttermesser had shaped an apparition. She had awakened it to life in the conventional way. Xanthippe was a golem, and what had polymathic Puttermesser *not* read about the genus golem?

Puttermesser ordered: "All right, go look on the bookshelves. Bring me whatever you see on your own kind."

The creature churned into the living room and hurried back with two volumes, one in either hand; she held the pen ready in her mouth. She dumped the books on the bed and wrote: "I am the first female golem."

"No you're not," Puttermesser said. It was clear that the creature required correction. Puttermesser flew through the pages of one of the books. "Ibn Gabirol created a woman. This was in Spain, long ago, the eleventh century. The king gave him a dressing-down for necromancy, so he dismantled her. She was made of wood and had hinges—it was easy to take her apart."

The creature wrote: "That was not a true golem."

"Go sit down in a corner," Puttermesser said. "I want to read."

The creature obeyed. Puttermesser dived into the two volumes. She had read them many times before; she knew certain passages nearly verbatim. One, a strange old text in a curiously awkward English translation (it was printed in Austria in 1925), had the grass-green public binding of a library book; to Puttermesser's citizenly shame, she had never returned it. It had been borrowed from the Crotona Park Branch decades ago, in Puttermesser's adolescence. There were photographs in it, incandescently clear: of graves, of a statue, of the lamp-hung interior of a synagogue in Prague—the Altneuschul—, of its tall peaked contour, of the two great clocks, one below the cupola, the other above it, on the venerable Prague Jewish Community House. Across the street from the Community House there was a shop, with a sign that said V. PRESSLER in large letters; underneath, his hand in his pocket, a dapper mustached dandy in a black fedora lounged eternally. Familiar, static, piercingly distinct though these illustrations were, Puttermesser all the same felt their weary old ache: phantoms—V. PRESSLER a speck of earth; the houses air; the dandy evaporated. Among these aged streets and deranged structures Puttermesser's marveling heart had often prowled. "You have no feelings" Rappoport once told her: he meant that she had the habit of flushing with ideas as if they were passions.

And this was true. Puttermesser's intelligence, brambly with the confusion of too much history, was a private warted tract, rubbled over with primordial statuary. She was painfully anthropological. Civilizations rolled into her rib cage, stone after graven stone: cuneiform, rune, cipher. She had pruned out allegory, metaphor; Puttermesser was no mystic, enthusiast, pneumaticist, ecstatic, kabbalist. Her mind was clean; she was a rationalist. Despite the imaginary daughters—she included these among her losses—she was not at all attached to any notion of shade or specter, however corporeal it might appear, and least of all to the idea of a golem—hardly that, especially now that she had the actual thing on her hands. What transfixed her was the kind of intellect (immensely sober, pragmatic, unfanciful, rationalist like her own) to which a golem ordinarily occurred—occurred, that is, in the shock of its true flesh and absolute being. The classical case of the golem of Prague, for instance: the Great Rabbi Judah Loew, circa 1520–1609, maker of that renowned local creature, was scarcely one of those misty souls given over to untrammeled figments or romances. He was, instead, a reasonable man of biting understanding, a solid scholar a pragmatic leader—a learned quasi-mayor. What he understood was that the scurrilous politics of his city, always tinged with religious interests, had gone too far. In short, they were killing the Jews of Prague. It had become unsafe for a peddler to open his pack, or a merchant his shop; no mother and her little daughter dared turn into an alley. Real blood ran in the streets, and all on account of a rumor of blood: citizens of every class—not just the guttersnipes—were muttering that the Jews had kneaded the bodies of Christian infants into their sacral Passover wafers. Scapegoat Jews, exposed, vulnerable, friendless, unarmed! The very Jews forbidden by their dietary code to eat an ordinary farmyard egg tainted with the minutest jot of fetal blood! So the Great Rabbi Judah Loew, to defend the Jews of Prague against their depredators, undertook to fashion a golem.

Puttermesser was well acquainted with the Great Rabbi Judah Loew's method of golem-making. It was classical; it was, as such things go, ordinary. To begin with, he entered a dream of Heaven, wherein he asked the angels to advise him. The answer came in alphabetical order: *afar, esh, mayim, ruach:* earth, fire, water, wraith. With his son-in-law, Isaac ben Shimshon, and his pupil, Jacob ben Chayim Sasson, the Great Rabbi Judah

Loew sought inner purity and sanctification by means of prayer and ritual immersion; then the three of them went out to a mud-bed on the banks of the River Moldau to create a man of clay. Three went out; four returned. They worked by torchlight, reciting Psalms all the while, molding a human figure. Isaac ben Shimshon, a descendant of the priests of the Temple, walked seven times around the clay heap bulging up from the ground. Jacob ben Chayim Sasson, a Levite, walked seven times around. Then the Great Rabbi Judah Loew himself walked around once only, and placed a parchment inscribed with the Name into the clay man's mouth. The priest represented fire; the Levite water; the Great Rabbi Judah Loew designated himself spirit and wraith, or air itself. The earth-man lay inert upon earth, like upon like. Fire, water, air, all chanted together: "And he breathed into his nostrils the breath of life; and man became a living soul"—whereupon the golem heated up, turned fiery red, and rose! It rose to become the savior of the Jews of Prague. On its forehead were imprinted the three letters that are the Hebrew word for truth: *aleph, mem, tav*.

This history Puttermesser knew, in its several versions, inside out. "Three went out; four returned"—following which, how the golem punished the slaughterers, persecutors, predators! How it cleansed Prague of evil and infamy, of degeneracy and murder, of vice and perfidy! But when at last the Great Rabbi Judah Loew wished the golem to subside, he climbed a ladder (a golem grows bigger every day), reached up to the golem's forehead, and erased the letter *aleph*. Instantly the golem fell lifeless, given back to spiritless clay: lacking the aleph, the remaining letters, *mem* and *tav*, spelled *met*—dead. The golem's body was hauled up to the attic of the Altneuschul, where it still rests among ever-thickening cobwebs. "No one may touch the cobwebs," ran one of the stories, "for whoever touches them dies."

For Puttermesser, the wonder of this tale was not in any of its remarkable parts, familiar as they were, and not even in its recurrence. The golem recurred, of course. It moved from the Exile of Babylon to the Exile of Europe; it followed the Jews. In the third century Rabbi Rava created a golem, and sent it to Rabbi Zera, who seemed not to know it was a golem until he discovered that it could not speak. Then realization of the thing's true nature came to him, and he rebuked it: "You must have been made by my comrades of the Talmudic Academy; return to your dust." Rabbi Hanina and Rabbi Oshaya were less successful than Rabbi Rava; they were only able to produce a very small calf, on which they dined. An old kabbalistic volume, the Book of Creation, explains that Father Abraham himself could manufacture human organisms. The Book of Raziel contains a famous workable prescription for golem-making: the maker utilizes certain chants and recitations, imprinted medals, esoteric names, efficacious shapes and totems. Ben Sira and his father, the prophet Jeremiah, created a golem, in the logical belief that Adam himself was a golem; their golem, like Adam, had the power of speech. King Nebuchadnezzar's own idol turned into a living golem when he set on its head the diadem of the High Priest, looted out of the Temple in Jerusalem; the jeweled letters of the Tetragrammaton were fastened into the diadem's silver sockets. The prophet Daniel, pretending to kiss the king's golem, swiftly plucked out the gems that spelled the Name of God, and the idol was again lifeless. Even before that, thieves among the wicked generation that built the Tower of Babel swiped some of the contractor's materials to fashion idols, which were made to walk by having the Name shoved into their mouths; then they were taken for gods. Rabbi Aharon of Baghdad and Rabbi Hananel did not mold images; instead, they sewed parchments inscribed with the Name into the right arms of corpses, who at once revived and became members of the genus golem. The prophet Micah made a golden calf that could dance, and Bezalel, the designer of the Tabernacle, knew how to combine letters of the alphabet so as to duplicate Creation, both heaven and earth. Rabbi Elazar of Worms had a somewhat similar system for golem-making: three adepts must gather up "virginal mountain earth," pour running water over it, knead it into a man, bury it, and recite two hundred and twenty-one alphabetical combinations, observing meticulously the prescribed order of the vowels and consonants. But Abraham Abulafia could make a man out of a mere spoonful of earth by blowing it over an ordinary dish of water; undoubtedly this had some influence on Paracelsus, the sixteenth-century German alchemist, who used a retort to make a homunculus: Paracelsus's manikin, however, was not telluric, being composed of blood, sperm, and urine, from which the Jewish golem-makers recoiled. For the Jews, earth, water, and the divine afflatus were the only permissible elements—the afflatus being summoned through the holy syllables. Rabbi Ishmael, on the other hand, knew another way of withdrawing that life-conferring holiness and rendering an active golem back into dust: he would recite the powerful combinations of sacred letters backward, meanwhile circling the creature in the direction opposite to the one that had quickened it.

There was no end to the conditions of golem-making, just as there was no end to the appearance of one golem after another in the pullulating procession of golem-history; but Puttermesser's brain, crowded with all these acquisitions and rather a tidy store of others (for instance, she had the noble Dr. Gershom Scholem's bountiful essay "The Idea of the Golem" virtually by heart) was unattracted either to number or to method. What interested Puttermesser was something else: it was the plain fact that the golem-makers were neither visionaries nor magicians nor sorcerers. They were neither fantasists nor fabulists nor poets. They were, by and large, scientific realists—and, in nearly every case at hand, serious scholars and intellectuals: the plausible forerunners, in fact, of their great-grandchildren, who are physicists, biologists, or logical positivists. It was not only the Great Rabbi Judah Loew, the esteemed golem-maker of Prague, who had, in addition, a reputation as a distinguished Talmudist, reasoner, philosopher; even Rabbi Elijah, the most celebrated Jewish intellect of Eastern Europe (if Spinoza is the most celebrated on the Western side), whose brilliance outstripped the fame of every other scholar, who founded the most rigorous rabbinical academy in the history of the cold lands, who at length became known as the Vilna Gaon (the Genius of the city of Vilna, called, on his account, the Jerusalem of the North)—even the Vilna Gaon once attempted, before the age of thirteen, to make a golem! And the Vilna Gaon, with his stern refinements of exegesis and analysis, with his darting dazzlements of logical penetration, was—as everyone knows—the scourge of mystics, protester (mitnagid) against the dancing hasidim, scorner of those less limber minds to the Polish south, in superstitiously pious Galicia. If the Vilna Gaon could contemplate the making of a golem, thought Puttermesser, there was nothing irrational in it, and she would not be ashamed of what she herself had concocted.

She asked Xanthippe: "Do you eat?"

The golem wrote, "*Vivo, ergo edo.* I live, therefore I eat."

"Don't pull that on me—my Latin is as good as yours. Can you cook?"

"I can do what I must, if my mother decrees it," the golem wrote.

"All right," Puttermesser said. "In that case you can stay. You can stay until I decide to get rid of you. Now make lunch. Cook something I like, only better than I could do it."

III. The Golem Cooks, Cleans and Shops

The golem hurried off to the kitchen. Puttermesser heard the smack of the refrigerator, the clatter of silver, the faucet turned on and off; sounds of chopping in a wooden bowl; plates set out, along with an eloquent tinkle of glassware; a distant whipping, a distant sizzling; mushroom fragrances; coffee. The golem appeared at the bedroom door with a smug sniff, holding out her writing pad:

"I can have uses far beyond the mere domestic."

"If you think you're too good for kitchen work," Puttermesser retorted, "don't call yourself Xanthippe. You're so hot on aspiration, you might as well go the whole hog and pick Socrates."

The golem wrote: "I mean to be a critic, even of the highest Philosophers. Xanthippe alone had the courage to gainsay Socrates. Nay, I remain

Xanthippe. Please do not allow my Swedish mushroom souffle to sink. It is best eaten in a steaming condition."

Puttermesser muttered, "I don't like your prose style. You write like a translation from the Middle Finnish. Improve it," but she followed the golem into the little kitchen. The golem's step was now light and quick, and the kitchen too seemed transformed—a floating corner of buoyancy and quicksilver: it was as if the table were in the middle of a Parisian concourse, streaming, gleaming: it had the look of a painting both transient and eternal, a place where you sat for a minute to gossip, and also a place where the middle-aged Henry James came every day so that nothing in the large world would be lost on him. "You've set things up nicely enough," Puttermesser said; "I forgot all about these linen placemats." They were, in fact, part of her "trousseau"; her mother had given her things. It was expected, long ago, that Puttermesser would marry.

The golem's souffle was excellent; she had also prepared a dessert that was part mousse, part lemon gelatin. Puttermesser, despite her periodontic troubles, took a greedy second helping. The golem's dessert was more seductive even than fudge; and fudge for Puttermesser was notoriously paradisal.

"First-rate," Puttermesser said; the golem had been standing all the while. "Aren't you having any?"

Immediately the golem sat down and ate.

"Now I'm going for a walk," Puttermesser announced.

"Clean all this up. Make the bed. Be sure to mop under it. Look in the hamper, you'll find a heap of dirty clothes. There's a public washing machine in the basement. I'll give you quarters."

The golem turned glum.

"Well, look," Puttermesser argued, "I can use you for anything I please, right?"

The golem wrote, "The Great Rabbi Judah Loew's wife sent the golem of Prague to fetch water, and he fetched, and he fetched, until he flooded the house, the yard, the city, and finally the world."

"Don't bother me with fairy tales," Puttermesser said.

The golem wrote, "I insist I am superior to mere household use."

"No one's superior to dirty laundry," Puttermesser threw back, and went out into the great city. She intended to walk and brood; though she understood at last how it was that she had brought the golem to life, it disturbed her that she did not recall *making* her—emptying all the plant pots, for instance. Nor was Puttermesser wise to her own secret dictates in creating the golem. And now that the golem was actually in the house, what was to be done with her? Puttermesser worried about the landlord, a suspicious fellow. The landlord allowed no dogs or—so the lease read—"irregular relationships." She thought of passing Xanthippe off as an adopted daughter—occasionally she would happen on an article about single parents of teen-age foster children. It was not so unusual. But even that would bring its difficulty, because—to satisfy the doorman and the neighbors—such a child would have to be sent to school; and it was hardly reasonable, Puttermesser saw, to send the golem to an ordinary high school. They would ship her off to an institution for deaf-mutes, to learn sign language—and it would become evident soon enough, wouldn't it, that the golem was not the least bit deaf? There was really no place for her in any classroom; she probably knew too much already. The erratic tone of her writing, with its awful pastiche, suggested that she had read ten times more than any other tenth-grader of the same age. Besides, did the golem *have* an age? She had the shape of a certain age, yes; but the truth was she was only a few hours old. Her public behavior was bound to be unpredictable.

Puttermesser was walking northward. Her long introspective stride had taken her as far as Eighty-sixth Street. She left Madison and veered up Lexington. She had forgotten her gloves; her fingers were frozen. February's flying newspapers scuttled over broken bottles and yogurt cups squashed in the gutter. A bag lady slept in a blue-black doorway, wrapped in a pile of ragged coats. Dusk was coming down; all the store windows, without exception, were barred or shuttered against the late-afternoon Sunday emptiness. Burglars, addicts, marauders, the diverse criminal pestilences of uptown and downtown, would have to find other ways of entry: breaking through a roof; a blowtorch on a steel bar; a back toilet window with a loose grill. Ingenuity. Puttermesser peered around behind her for the mugger who, in all logic, should have been stalking her; no one was there. But she was ready: she had left her wallet at home on purpose; a police whistle dangled on a cord around her neck; she fondled the little knife in her pocket. New York! All the prisons in the metropolitan area were reputed to be hopelessly overcrowded.

At Ninety-second Street she swung through the revolving doors of the Y to warm up. The lobby was mostly uninhabited; a short line straggled toward the ticket office. Puttermesser read the poster: a piano concert at eight o'clock. She headed downtown. It was fully dark now. She reflected that it would be easy enough to undo, to reverse, the golem; there was really no point in keeping her on. For one thing, how would the golem be occupied all day while Puttermesser was at work? And Puttermesser was nervous: she had her demotion to think about. Stripped. Demoralized. That pest Cracow. Turtelman and Marmel. The Civil Service, founded to eradicate patronage, nepotism, favoritism, spoils, payoffs, injustice, corruption! Lost, all lost. The Mayor had no intention of answering Puttermesser's urgent letter.

Taking off her coat, Puttermesser called to the golem, "What's going on in there?" An unexpected brilliance out of the bedroom: a lamp in the form of the Statue of Liberty stood on the teak desk. "What's this?"

"I bought it," the golem wrote. "I did everything my mother instructed. I cleaned up the kitchen, made the bed"—a new blue bedspread, with pictures of baseball mitts, covered it—"mopped the whole house, did the laundry, ironed everything, hung my mother's blouses and put my mother's pantyhose into the drawer—"

Puttermesser grabbed the sheet of paper right off the golem's pad and tore it up without reading the rest of it. "What do you mean you bought it? What kind of junk is this? I don't want the Statue of Liberty! I don't want baseball mitts!"

"It was all I could find," the golem wrote on a fresh page. "All the stores around here are closed on Sunday. I had to go down to Delancey Street on the Lower East Side. I took a taxi."

"Taxi! You'll shop when I tell you to shop!" Puttermesser yelled. "Otherwise you stay home!"

"I need a wider world," the golem wrote. "Take me with you to your place of employment tomorrow."

"My foot I will," Puttermesser said. "I've had enough of you. I've been thinking"—she looked for a euphemism—"about sending you back."

"Back?" the golem wrote; her mouth had opened all the way.

"You've got a crooked tooth. Come here," Puttermesser said, "I'll fix it."

The golem wrote, "You can no longer alter my being or any part of my being. The speaking of the Name fulfills; it precludes alteration. But I am pleasant to look on, am I not? I will not again gape so that my crooked tooth can offend my mother's eye. Only use me."

"You've got rotten taste."

The golem wrote, "It was my task to choose between baseball mitts and small raccoons intermingled with blue-eyed panda bears. The baseball mitts struck me as the lesser evil."

"I never *wanted* a bedspread," Puttermesser objected. "When I said to make the bed I just meant to straighten the blankets, that's all. And my God, the Statue of Liberty!"

The golem wrote, "A three-way bulb, 150 watts. I thought it so very clever that the bulb goes right into the torch."

"Kitsch. And where'd you get the money?"

"Out of your wallet. But see how pleasantly bright," the golem wrote. "I fear the dark. The dark is where pre-existence abides. It is not possible to think of pre-existence, but one dreads its facsimile: post-existence. Do not erase, obliterate, or annihilate me. Mother, my mother. I will serve you. Use me in the wide world."

"You stole my money right out of my wallet, spent a fortune on a taxi, and brought home the cheapest sort of junk. If you pull this kind of thing in the house, don't talk to me about the wide world!"

IV. Xanthippe at Work

But the next morning the golem was in Puttermesser's office.

"Who's the kid?" Cracow asked.

"Marmel's letting me have a typist," Puttermesser said.

"Marmel? That don't make sense. After demoting you?"

"I was reassigned," Puttermesser said; but her cheeks stung.

"Them's the breaks," Cracow said. "So how come the royal treatment? You could use the typing pool like the rest of us."

"Turtelman's put me on a special project."

"Turtelman? Turtelman kicked you in the head. What special project?"

"I'm supposed to check out any employee who broods about lawsuits on City time," Puttermesser said.

"Oh come on, Ruth, can the corn. You know damn well I've been maligned. My lawyer says I have a case. I damn well have a case. What's the kid's name?"

"Leah."

"Leah." Cracow pushed his face right into the golem's. "Do they hire 'em that young? What are you, Leah, a high-school dropout?"

"She's smart enough as is," Puttermesser said.

"Whyn't you let the kid answer for herself?"

Puttermesser took Cracow by the elbow and whispered, "They cut out her throat. Malignancy of the voicebox."

"Whew," Cracow said.

"Get going," Puttermesser ordered the golem, and led her to the ladies' room. "I told you not to come! I'm in enough hot water around here, I don't need you to make trouble."

The golem plucked a paper towel from the wall, fetched Puttermesser's ballpoint pen from the pocket of Puttermesser's cardigan (the golem was still wearing it), and wrote: "I will ameliorate your woe."

"I didn't say woe, I said hot water. *Trouble*. First kitsch, now rococo. Observe reality, can't you? Look, you're going to sit in front of that typewriter and that's it. If you can type half as well as you cook, fine. I don't care *what* you type. Stay out of my way. Write letters, it doesn't matter, but stay out of my way."

The golem wrote, "I hear and obey."

All day the golem, a model of diligence, sat at the typewriter and typed. Puttermesser, passing en route from one fruitless meeting to another, saw the sheets accumulating on the floor. Was Xanthippe writing a novel? a memoir? To whom, after all, did she owe a letter? The golem looked abstracted, rapt. Puttermesser was hoping to patch together, bit by bit, her bad fortune. The gossips ran from cubicle to cubicle, collecting the news: Turtelman's niece, an actress—she had most recently played a medieval leper, with a little bell, in a television costume drama—was engaged to the Mayor's cousin. Marmel's aunt had once stayed in the same hotel in Florida with Mrs. Minnie Mavett, the Mayor's elderly widowed adoptive mother. (The Mayor had been an adopted child, and campaigned with his wife and four natural children as a "lucky orphan.") Marmel and Turtelman were said to have married twin sisters; surely this was a symbolic way of marrying each other? Or else Marmel was married to a Boston blueblood, Turtelman to a climber from Great Neck. On the other hand, only Marmel was married; Turtelman was an austere bachelor. One of the secretaries in the Administrative Assistant's office had observed that Marmel, Turtelman, and the Mayor all wore identical rings; she denied they were school rings. Turtelman's "restructuring," moreover, had begun (according to Polly in Personnel) to assume telltale forms. He was becoming bolder and bolder. He was like some crazed plantation owner at harvest time, who, instead of cutting down the standing grain, cuts down the conscientious reapers. Or he was like a raving chessmaster who throws all the winning pieces in the fire. Or he was like a general who leads a massacre against his own best troops. All these images tailed. Turtelman was destroying the Department of Receipts and Disbursements. What he looked for was not performance but loyalty. He was a mayoral appointee of rapacious nature conniving at the usual outrages of patronage; he was doing the Mayor's will. He did not love the democratic polity as much as he feared the Mayor. Ah, Walt Whitman was not in his kidneys. Plunder was.

Cracow, meanwhile reported that several times Adam Marmel had telephoned for Puttermesser. It was urgent. "That new girl's no good, Ruth. I'm all in favor of hiring the handicapped, but when it comes to answering the telephone what's definitely needed is a larynx. I had to pick up every damn time. You think Marmel wants to put you back up there in the stratosphere?"

Puttermesser said nothing. Cracow thought women ought to keep their place; he took open satisfaction in Puttermesser's flight downward. He nagged her to tell him what Turtelman's special project was. "You'd rather do special projects for the higher-ups than date a nice guy like me," he complained. "At least let's have lunch." But Puttermesser sent the golem out to a delicatessen for sandwiches; it was a kosher delicatessen—Puttermesser thought the golem would care about a thing like that. By the middle of the afternoon the golem's typed sheets were a tall stack.

At a quarter to five Turtelman's bony acolyte came puffing in. "Mr. Turtelman lent me to Mr. Marmel just to give you this. I hope you appreciate I'm not normally anyone's delivery boy. You're never at your desk. You can't be reached by phone. You're not important enough to be incommunicado, believe me. Mr. Marmel wants you to prepare a portfolio for him on these topics toot sweet."

Marmel's memo:

Dear Ms. Puttermesser:

Please be good enough to supply me with the following at your earliest convenience. A list of the City's bank depositories. Average balance in each account for the last three years. List of contact people at banks—names, titles, telephone numbers. List of contacts for Department of Receipts and Disbursements (referred to below as "we," "our," and "us") in Office of Mayor, Department of Budget, relevant City Council committees, Office of Comptroller. Copies of all evaluation reports published during past year. Current organization chart showing incumbent, title, and salary for each of our Office Heads. Why do we not have any window poles? Where have all the window poles gone? How to get toilet paper and soap regularly replaced in executive washroom? What kind of Management Information System files do we have on the assessed value of City real estate? How effective was our last Investors' Tour? Old notes disclose visit to sewage disposal plant, helicopter ride, fireboat demonstration, lunch and fashion show for the ladies—how to win goodwill this year front these heavy pockets? What hot litigation should I know about in re our Quasi-Judicial Division?

It was the old story: the floundering new official perplexed and beleaguered. Puttermesser felt a touch of malicious pleasure in Marmel's memo; she had known it would come to this—Turtelman, having thrown her out, now discovered he could not clear a space for himself without the stirring of Puttermesser's little finger. Marmel, spurred by Turtelman (too high-and-mighty to ask on his own), had set out to pick Puttermesser's brain. He was appealing to Puttermesser to diaper him. Each item in Marmel's memo would take hours and hours to answer! Except for the window poles. Puttermesser could explain about the window poles in half a second.

"Stand by," she said to the bony acolyte. And to Xanthippe: "Take a letter!"

Mr. Adam Marmel
First Bursary Officer
Bureau of Summary Sessions
Department of Receipts and Disbursements
Municipal Building

Dear Mr. Marmel:

Window poles are swiped by the hottest and sweatiest secretaries. The ones located directly above the furnace room, for instance. Though lately the ones who jog at lunchtime are just as likely to pinch poles. When they get them they hide them. Check out the second-floor ladies' room.

The fresh air of candor is always needed whenever the oxygen of honest admission has been withdrawn. Precisely WHY ["Make that all capitals," Puttermesser said, dictating] have I been relieved of my position? Precisely WHY have you stepped into my job? Let us have some fresh air!

Yours sincerely,
R. Puttermesser, Esq.

The bony acolyte snatched the sheet directly from the golem's typewriter. "There's a lot more he wants answers to. You've left out practically everything."

"Window poles are everything," Puttermesser said. "The fresh air of candor is all." She observed—it was a small shock—that the golem's style had infected her.

The bony acolyte warned, "Fresh is right. You better answer the rest of what he wants answered."

"Go home," Puttermesser told the golem. "Home!"

During dinner in the little kitchen Puttermesser was nearly as silent as the golem. Injustice rankled. She paid no attention to the golem's scribblings. The nerve! The nerve! To throw her out and then come and pick her brain! "No more Swedish souffle," she growled. "Cook something else for a change. And I'm getting tired of seeing you in my old sweater. I'll give you money, tomorrow go buy yourself some decent clothes."

"Tomorrow," the golem wrote, "I will again serve you at your place of employment."

But in the morning Puttermesser was lackadaisical; ambition had trickled away. What, after so much indignity, was there to be ambitious *for?* For the first time in a decade she came to the office late. "What's the special project, Ruth?" Cracow wanted to know right away. "The kid was burning up the typewriter yesterday. What is she anyhow, an illegal alien? She don't look like your ordinary person. Yemenite Israeli type? What is this, already she don't show up, it's only the second day on the job? The phone calls you missed! Memos piled up! That gal from Personnel back and forth two, three times! They're after you today, Ruth! The higher-ups! What's the special project, hah? And the kid leaves you high and dry!"

"She'll turn up." Puttermesser had given the golem a hundred and twenty dollars and sent her to Alexander's. "No taxis or else," Puttermesser said; but she knew the golem would head downtown to Delancey Street. The thronged Caribbean faces and tongues of the Lower East Side drew her; Xanthippe, a kind of foreigner herself, as even Cracow could see, was attracted to immigrant populations. Their tastes and adorations were hers. She returned with red and purple blouses, narrow skirts and flared pants of parrot-green and cantaloupe-orange, multicolored high-heeled plastic shoes, a sunflower-yellow plastic shoulder bag with six double sets of zippers, a pocket mirror, and a transparent plastic comb in its own peach tattersall plastic case.

"Hispanic absolutely," Cracow confirmed—Cracow the bigot—watching Xanthippe lay open boxes and bags.

But Puttermesser was occupied with a trio of memos. They appeared to originate with Marmel but were expressed through Polly, the Atropos of Personnel, she who had put aside her shears for the flurry of a thousand Forms, she who brooded like Shiva the Destroyer on a world of the lopped.

Memo One:

You are reported as having refused to respond to requests for information relating to Bureau business. You now are subject to conduct inquiry. Please obtain and fill out Form 10V, Q17 with particular reference to Paragraph L, and leave it *immediately* with Polly in Personnel.

Memo Two:

In consideration of your seniority, Commissioner Alvin Turtelman, having relieved you of Level Eleven status in the Bureau of Summary Sessions, Department of Receipts and Disbursements, due to insufficient control of bursary materials, weak administrative supervision as well as output insufficiency, has retained you at Level Four. However, your work shows continued decline. Lateness reported as of A.M. today. Fill out Below-Level-Eight Lateness Form 14TG. (Submit Form to Polly in Personnel.)

Memo Three:

As a result of a determination taken by Commissioner Alvin Turtelman in conjunction and in consultation with First Bursary Officer Adam Marmel, your Level Four appointment in the Department of Receipts and Disbursements is herewith terminated. Please submit Below-Level-Six Severance Form A97, Section 6, with particular reference to Paragraph 14b, to Polly in Personnel.

Severed! Sacked! Dismissed! Let go! Fired! And all in the space of three hours! "Output insufficiency," a lie! "Decline," a fiction! "Conduct inquiry"—like some insignificant clerk or window-pole thief! Late once in ten years and Cracow, litigious would-be lover, snitches to Polly, the Atropos, the Shiva, of Personnel! Who else but Cracow? Lies. Fabrications. Accusations. Marmel the hollow accuser. Absence of due process!

The Honorable Malachy Mavett
Mayor, City of New York
City Hall

Dear Mayor Mavett:

Where is your pride, to appoint such men? Men who accuse without foundation? An accuser who seizes the job of the accused? Suspect! Turtelman wanted me out in order to get Marmel in! I stand for Intellect and Knowledge, they stand for politics and Loyal Cunning. Hart Crane, poet of New York, his harp the Brooklyn Bridge, does that harp mean nothing to you? Is Walt Whitman dead in your kidneys? Walt Whitman who cried out "numberless crowded streets, high growths of iron, slender, strong, light, splendidly uprising toward clear skies," who embraced "a million people—manners free and superb—open voices—hospitality . . ." Oh, Mayor Mavett, it is Injustice you embrace! You have given power to men for whom Walt Whitman is dead in their kidneys! This city of masts and spires opens its breast for Walt Whitman, and you feed it with a Turtelman and a Marmel! Ruth Puttermesser is despised, demoted, thrown away at last! Destroyed. Without work. Doer of nought, maker of nothing.

This letter remained locked inside Puttermesser's head. Cracow was trying hard not to look her way. He had already read Marmel's memos manifested through Polly the Destroyer; he had surely read them. He stood behind the golem's chair, attentive to her fingers galloping over the typewriter keys—including the newly lengthened one; how glad Puttermesser was that she had fixed it! "Hey Ruth, take a gander at this stuff. What's this kid *doing*? That's some so-called special project for Turtelman."

"The special project for Turtelman," Puttermesser said coldly, "is my vanquishment. My vanishing. My send-off and diminishment. So long, Leon. May you win your case against the mediocre universality of the human imagination."

"You been canned?"

"You know that."

"Well, when Polly walks in you figure what's up. You figure who's out."

"Beware of *Schadenfreude*, Leon. You could be next."

"Not me. I don't look for trouble. You look for trouble. I knew right away this whole setup with the kid was phony. She's typing up a craziness—whatever it is, Bureau business it isn't. You let in the crazies, you get what you expect."

At that moment—as Cracow's moist smile with its brown teeth turned and turned inside Cracow's dark mouth—a clarification came upon Puttermesser: no: a clarity. She was shut of a mystery. She understood; she saw.

"Home!" Puttermesser ordered the golem. Xanthippe gathered up her clothes and shoved the typewritten sheets into one of the blouse bags.

V. Why the Golem Was Created; Puttermesser's Purpose

That night the golem cooked spaghetti. She worked barefoot. The fragrance of hot buttered tomato sauce and peppers rushed over a mound of shining porcelain strands. "What are you doing?" Puttermesser demanded; she saw the golem heaping up a second great batch. "Why are you so hungry?"

The golem looked a little larger today than she had yesterday.

Then Puttermesser remembered that it was in the nature of a golem to grow and grow. The golem's appetite was nevertheless worrisome—how long would it take for Xanthippe to grow out of over one hundred dollars' worth of clothes? Could only a Rothschild afford a golem? And what would the rate of growth be? Would the golem eventually have to be kept outdoors, so as not to crash through the ceiling? Was the golem of Prague finally reversed into lifelessness on account of its excessive size, or because the civic reforms it was created for had been accomplished?

Ah, how this idea glowed for Puttermesser! The civic reforms of Prague—the broad crannied city of Prague, Prague distinguished by numberless crowded streets, high growths of iron, masts and spires! The clock-tower of the Jewish Community House, the lofty peaked and chimneyed roof of the Altneuschul! Not to mention Kafka's Castle. All that manifold urban shimmer choked off by evil, corruption, the blood libel, the strong dampened hearts of wicked politicos. The Great Rabbi Judah Loew had undertaken to create his golem in an unenlightened year, the dream of America just unfolding, far away, in all its spacious ardor; but already the seed of New York was preparing in Europe's earth: inspiration of city-joy, love for the comely, the cleanly, the free and the new, mobs transmuted into troops of the blessed, citizens bursting into angelness, sidewalks of alabaster, buses filled with thrones. Old delicate Prague, swept and swept of sin, giving birth to the purified daylight, the lucent genius, of New York!

By now Puttermesser knew what she knew.

"Bring me my books," she ordered the golem. And read:

> A vision of Paradise must accompany the signs. The sacred formulae are insufficient without the trance of ecstasy in which are seen the brilliance of cities and their salvation through exile of heartlessness, disorder, and the desolation of sadness.

A city washed pure. New York, city (perhaps) of seraphim. Wings had passed over her eyes. Her arms around Rappoport's heavy *Times*, Puttermesser held to her breast heartlessness, disorder, the desolation of sadness, ten thousand knives, hatred painted in the subways, explosions of handguns, bombs in the cathedrals of transportation and industry, Pennsylvania Station, Grand Central, Rockefeller Center, terror in the broadcasting booths with their bustling equipment and seductive provincial voices, all the metropolitan airports assaulted, the decline of the Civil Service, maggots in high management. Rappoport's *Times*, repository of a dread freight! All the same, carrying Rappoport's *Times* back to bed, Puttermesser had seen Paradise.

New York washed, reformed, restored.

"Xanthippe!"

The golem, who had been scrubbing spaghetti sauce off the dishes in a little cascade of water-thunder under the kitchen faucet, wiped her hands on her new orange blouse, snatched up ballpoint pen and notepad, and ran to Puttermesser.

Puttermesser asked, "When you woke into life what did you feel?"

"I felt like an embryo," the golem wrote.

"What did you know?"

"I knew why I was created," the golem wrote.

"Why were you created?"

"So that my mother should become what she was intended to become," the golem wrote.

"Bring me that stack of stuff you were fooling around with in the office," Puttermesser ordered, but the golem had already scampered off to the bedroom closet to rummage among her boxes and bags of new clothes.

So Puttermesser set aside her books about the history and nature of the genus golem and settled down to contemplate all the pages the golem had typed for two days in Puttermesser's sorrowful cubicle, shared with Cracow—the cubicle of her demotion, denigration, disgrace—in the Taxation Section of the Bureau of Summary Sessions of the Department of Receipts and Disbursements of the City of New York.

What the golem had composed was a *PLAN*. Puttermesser recognized everything in it. It was as if she had encountered this *PLAN* before—its very language. It was as if, in the instant it had occurred to her to make the golem, she had read the *PLAN* in some old scroll. Ah, here was a stale and restless truth: that she did not recollect the actual fabrication of the golem, that she had helplessly, without volition, come upon Xanthippe in her bed as if the golem were some transient mirage, an aggressive imagining, or else a mere forward apparition—this had, with a wearisome persistence, been teasing at the edge of Puttermesser's medulla oblongata all along, ever since the first mulling of it on her desolate walk to the Y. It was like a pitcher that will neither fill nor pour out. But it was now as plain as solid earth itself that the golem was no apparition. Apparitions do not, in hideous public jargon, type up exhaustive practical documents concerning civic reform! Puttermesser knew what she knew—it unraveled before her in the distance, the *PLAN* approaching, approaching, until it crowded her forebrain with its importuning force: how she had set Rappoport's *Times*, record of multiple chaos and urban misfortune, down on the floor beside the bed, where the *Theaetetus* already lay. How, with a speed born of fever and agitation, she had whirled from window sill to window sill, cracking open clay plant pots as though they were eggs, and scooping up the germinative yolks of spilling earth. How she had fetched it all up in her two palms and dumped it into the bathtub. How only a half-turn of the tap stirred earth to the consistency of mud—and how there then began the blissful shudder of Puttermesser's wild hands, the molding and the shaping, the caressing and the smoothing, the kneading and the fingering, the straightening and the rounding, but quickly, quickly, with detail itself (God is in the details) unachieved, blurred, completion deferred, the authentic pleasure of the precise final form of nostril and eyelid and especially mouth left for afterward. Into the hole of the unfinished face of clay Puttermesser pressed a tag of paper, torn from the blank upper margin of Rappoport's *Times*, on which she had written in her own spittle two oracular syllables. The syllables adhered and were as legible as if inscribed in light. Then Puttermesser raised up out of the tub the imponderous damp relentless clay of a young girl—a lifeless forked creature in the semblance of a girl—and smelled the smell of mud, and put her down in her own bed to dry. The small jar to that small weight loosened crumbs of earth wherever a limb was joined to the trunk, and where the neck was joined, and where the ears had their fragile connecting stems. The crumbs sprinkled down. They crept under Puttermesser's fingernails.

And all this Puttermesser performed (aha, now it beat in hindbrain and in forebrain, she saw it, she knew it again!) because of agitation and fever: because of the wilderness inside Rappoport's *Times*. Why should the despoiled misgoverned miscreant City not shine at dawn like washed stones? Tablets of civilization, engraved with ontological notations in an ancient tongue. Puttermesser craved. Her craving was to cleanse the wilderness; her craving was to excise every black instance of injustice; her craving was to erase outrage. In the middle of her craving—out of the blue—she formulated the *PLAN*.

She was thumbing it now, it was in her hands:

PLAN
FOR THE
RESUSCITATION,
REFORMATION,
REINVIGORATION
& REDEMPTION
OF THE
CITY OF NEW YORK

"Where did you get this?" Puttermesser demanded.

"I am your amanuensis," the golem wrote. "I express you. I copy and record you. Now it is time for you to accomplish your thought."

"Everyone has funny thoughts," Puttermesser croaked; an uneasiness heated her. She was afraid of the last page.

"No reality greater than thought," the golem wrote.

"Lay off the Middle Finnish. I want to hear the truth about all this. Where'd this stuff come from? You *couldn't* copy it, I never put any of it down."

The golem wrote: "Two urges seeded you. I am one, this is the other. A thought must claim an instrument. When you conceived your urge, simultaneously you conceived me."

"Not simultaneously," Puttermesser objected; perhaps the golem could not be trusted with chronology. She breathed outside history. Puttermesser reimagined the electric moment exactly: the *PLAN* swimming like an inner cosmos into being, the mere solid golem an afterthought.

"No matter; I will serve your brain. I am your offspring, you are my mother. I am the execution of the grandeur of your principles. Grand design is my business. Leave visionary restoration to me." After which the golem put the ballpoint pen in her mouth and patiently sucked.

A fatigue seeped into Puttermesser; a tedium. It struck her that the golem was looking sly. She noticed that the seams along the armholes in the golem's orange blouse had begun to open. Growth. Enlargement. Swelling. Despite distraction Puttermesser read on. The *PLAN* though it had originated in her own mind, nevertheless smacked of Marmel's lingo, Turtelman's patois. It appeared to derive, in truth, from the Form-language of Polly the Destroyer. A starkness penetrated Puttermesser; the dead words themselves depressed her. Her wrists shook. Was it not possible to dream a dream of City without falling into the mouth of the Destroyer? Behold the conservation of residential property through the exclusion of depreciating factors. Compute twelve hundred and fifty zoning codes. Note physical aspects. Social aspects. Retail and wholesale business. Manufacturing. Shipping. Single and multiple residences. Cultural institutions. Parks, public buildings, amusements, schools, universities, community objectives, rapidity and feasibility of transportation via streets and transit lines. Health, traffic, safety public assembly conveniences. Sanitation. Prevention of slums. Transformation of slums. Eradication of poverty. Morality and obedience to law. Ordinances. Trust and pension funds. Treasury, public works, water. Public library. Police. Inspection. Councils and commissions. Welfare. Trustees. Revenue forecasting. Remote teleprocessing systems, computerized key-entry, restructuring of assessment districts, liens, senior-citizen rent-increase exemptions, delinquency centralization, corporate billings!

"My God," Puttermesser said.

"My mother has mastered and swallowed all of it," the golem wrote. "All of it is inside my mother's intelligence."

"I only meant—" Weak, Puttermesser wondered what it was she had meant. "Gardens and sunlight. Washed stones. Tablets. No; tables. Picnic tables."

Xanthippe stood nodding. The slyness powered her eyes. "My mother will become Mayor," she wrote.

The golem took the stack of typed sheets from Puttermesser's unquiet hands and held out the last page:

BY ORDER OF
RUTH PUTTERMESSER,
MAYOR
OF THE
CITY OF NEW YORK

"Drivel. Now you've gone too far. I never thought of that."

"Sleep on it," the golem wrote.

"That's your idea. You're the one who put that one in."

"Creator and created," the golem wrote, "merge," scribbling this with a shrug; the shrug made the ripped seams in her orange blouse open a little more.

The Honorable Malachy Mavett
Mayor
City Hall

Dear Mayor Mavett:

It is not respectful of a citizen's conception of the Mayor's office as "responsive" that you ignore my letter about possible spoils and other abuses. Still less is it respectful of me as a living human being and as a (former, now dismissed) Civil Servant. Shame! Shame!

Very sincerely yours,
THE HONORABLE RUTH PUTTERMESSER

This letter too remained locked inside Puttermesser's head. The signature was experimental—just to see what it looked like.

"No use, no use," the golem wrote on her notepad. "Mayor Puttermesser, by contrast, will answer all letters."

VI. Mayor Puttermesser

And so Puttermesser becomes Mayor of New York. The "and so" encloses much—but not so much as one might think. It is only a way of hastening Puttermesser's blatant destiny, of avoiding—never mind that God is in the details!—a more furrowed account of how the golem, each day imperceptibly enlarging, goes about gathering signatures for a citizens' petition. The golem is above all a realist; Puttermesser will run as an independent. There is not the minutest hope that the county leaders of either the Democratic or the Republican party will designate, as preferred candidate for Mayor of the City of New York, Ruth Puttermesser, Esq., a currently unemployed attorney put out in the street, so to speak, by Commissioner Alvin Turtelman of the Department of Receipts and Disbursements, in conjunction and in consultation with First Bursary Officer Adam Marmel. The golem is Puttermesser's campaign manager. She has burst out of all her new clothes, and has finally taken to extra-large men's denim overalls bought in the Army-Navy store on the corner of Suffolk and Delancey. The golem's complexion has coarsened a little. It is somehow redder, and the freckles on her forehead, when gazed at by an immobile eye, appear to have the configuration of a handful of letters from a generally unrecognizable alphabet:

+ 𐤌 K

Puttermesser has not failed to take note of how these letters, *aleph, mem,* and *tav,* in their primal North Semitic form, read from right to left, have extruded themselves with greater and greater clarity just below the golem's hairline. Puttermesser attributes this to pressure of the skin as the golem gains in height and thickness. She orders the golem to cut bangs. Though she is periodically alarmed at what a large girl Xanthippe is growing into, otherwise Puttermesser is pleased by her creation. Xanthippe is cheerful and efficient, an industrious worker. She continues to be a zealous cook. She remains unsure about time (occasionally she forgets that Wednesday intrudes between Tuesday and Thursday, and she has not quite puzzled out the order of all the months, though she has it splendidly fixed that November will embrace what has now become the sun of Puttermesser's firmament—Election Day); she is sometimes cocky; often intrepid; now and then surly; mainly she smiles and smiles. She can charm a signature out of anyone. At her own suggestion she wears around her neck a card that reads DEAF-MUTE, and with this card dangling on her bosom, in overalls, she scrambles up and down tenement steps as far away as Bensonhurst and Canarsie, in and out of elevators of East Side and West Side apartment buildings. She churns through offices, high schools and universities (she has visited Fordham, L.I.U., Pace, N.Y.U., Baruch College, Columbia; she has solicited the teaching staffs of Dalton, Lincoln, Brearley, John Dewey, Julia Richman, Yeshiva of Flatbush, Fieldston, Ramaz, as well as Puttermesser's own alma mater, Hunter High), supermarkets, cut-rate drugstores, subway stations, the Port Authority bus terminal. Wherever there are signers to be found, the golem appears with her ballpoint pen. The petition is completed. The golem has collected fourteen thousand five hundred and sixty-two more signatures than the law calls for.

All this must be recorded as lightly and swiftly as possible; a dry patch to be gotten through, perhaps via a doze or a skip. For Puttermesser herself it is much more wretched than a mere dry patch. She suffers. Her physiological responses are: a coldness in the temples, blurring of the eyes, increased periodontic difficulties. She is afflicted with frequent diarrhea. Her spine throbs. At night she weeps. But she keeps on. Xanthippe gives her no peace, urges her to rephrase her speeches with an ear for the lively, insists that she sport distinctive hats, glossy lipstick, even contact lenses (Puttermesser, edging into middle age, already owns reading glasses).

The golem names Puttermesser's party as follows: Independents for Socratic and Prophetic Idealism—ISPI for short. A graphic artist is hired to devise a poster. It shows an apple tree with a serpent in it. The S in ISPI is the serpent. Puttermesser has promised to transform the City of New York into Paradise. She has promised to cast out the serpent. On Election Day, Malachy ("Matt") Mavett, the incumbent, is routed. Of the three remaining candidates, two make poor showings. Puttermesser is triumphant.

Puttermesser is now the Mayor of the City of New York!

Old ardors and itches wake in her. She recites to herself: Justice, justice shalt thou pursue. Malachy ("Matt") Mavett takes his wife and family to Florida, to be near Mrs. Minnie Mavett, his adoptive mother. He is no longer a lucky orphan. He gets a job as a racetrack official. It is a political job, but he is sad all the same. His wife bears his humiliation gracelessly. His children rapidly acquire accents that do not mark them as New Yorkers. Turtelman and Marmel vanish into rumor. They are said to be with the F.B.I. in Alaska, with the C.I.A. in Indonesia. They are said to have relocated at Albany. They are said to be minor factotums in the Federal Crop Insurance Corporation, with offices in Sourgrass, Iowa. They are said to have mediocre positions in the Internal Revenue Service, where they will not be entitled to Social Security. They are said to have botched a suicide pact. No one knows what has become of Turtelman and Marmel. But Puttermesser is relieved; she herself, by means of a memo from City Hall, has dismissed them. Turtelman and Marmel are sacked! Let go! Fired!

Malachy ("Matt") Mavett, following protocol, telephones to congratulate Puttermesser on her victory. But he confesses to bafflement. Where has Puttermesser come from? An ordinary drone from the Bureau of Summary Sessions of the Department of Receipts and Disbursements! How can she, "an unknown," he asks, "a political nonentity," have won the public over so handily? Puttermesser reminds him that some months ago she wrote him a letter asking for justice, condemning patronage and spoils. "You did not reply," she accuses him in a voice hoarse from speech-making. The ex-Mayor does not remember any letter.

Though Puttermesser is disconcerted by the move to Gracie Mansion (in her dreams her mother is once again rolling up winter rugs and putting down summer rugs in the wide sun-periled apartment on the Grand Concourse), the golem immediately chooses the most lavish bedroom in the Mayor's residence for herself. It contains an antique dresser with gryphon feet and a fourposter arched by a lofty tester curtained in white velvet. Old brass bowls glint on the dresser-top. The golem fills one whole closet with fresh overalls. She wanders about studying the paintings and caressing the shining banister. She exhorts Puttermesser to rejoice that she no longer has her old suspicious landlord on East Seventy-first Street to worry about. Millions of citizens are her landlord now!

Puttermesser cannot pay attention to the golem's sprightliness. She is in a frenzy over the job of appointing commissioners and agency heads. She implores Xanthippe to keep away from City Hall—the campaign is over, she will only distract from business. The new Mayor intends to recruit noble psyches and visionary hearts. She is searching for the antithesis of Turtelman and Marmel. For instance: she yearns after Wallace Stevens—insurance executive of probity during office hours, enraptured poet at dusk. How she would like to put Walt Whitman himself in charge of the Bureau of Summary Sessions, and have Shelley take over Water Resource Development—Shelley whose principle it is that poets are the legislators of mankind! William Blake in the Fire Department. George Eliot doing Social Services. Emily Bronte over at Police, Jane Austen in Bridges and Tunnels, Virginia Woolf and Edgar Allan Poe sharing Health. Herman Melville overseeing the Office of Single Room Occupancy Housing. *"Integer vitae scelerisque purus,"* the golem writes on her notepad, showing off. "That's the ticket," Puttermesser agrees, "but what am I supposed to do, chase around town like Diogenes with a lantern looking for an honest man?" Xanthippe writes philosophically, "The politics of Paradise is no longer politics." "The politics of Paradise is no longer Paradise," Puttermesser retorts; "don't annoy me anyhow, I have to get somebody fast for Receipts and Disbursements." "You could promote Cracow," the golem writes. "I already have. I moved him over to Bronx Landfill and Pest Control. That's two levels up. He's got a good idea for winter, actually—wants to convert that garbage mountain out near the bay to a ski jump. And he's stopped asking me out. Thank God he's scared of dating the Mayor." "If you would seek commissioners of integrity and rosy cleverness," the golem writes, "fashion more of my kind." Fleetingly, Puttermesser considers this; she feels tempted. The highest echelons of City management staffed by multiple members of the genus golem! Herself the creator, down to the last molecule of ear-wax, of every commissioner, deputy, bureau chief, executive director! Every mayoral assistant, subordinate, underling, a golem! She looks over at Xanthippe. Twice already Xanthippe has quarreled with the Mansion's official cook. The cook has refused to follow the golem's recipes. "One is enough," Puttermesser says, and hurries down the subway and off to City Hall.

Despite its odious language reminiscent of Turtelman and Marmel, Puttermesser repeatedly consults the

PLAN
FOR THE
RESUSCITATION,
REFORMATION,
REINVIGORATION
& REDEMPTION
OF THE
CITY OF NEW YORK.

She blames Xanthippe for such a preposterous text: only two days spent in the Bureau of Summary Sessions, and the golem has been infected by periphrasis, pleonasm, and ambagious tautology. But behind all that there glimmers a loveliness. To Puttermesser's speeding eye, it is like the spotted sudden flank of a deer disturbing a wood. There *will* be resuscitation! There *will* be redemption!

And it begins. Mayor Puttermesser sends the golem out into the City. At first she tends to hang out among the open-air stalls of Delancey Street, but Puttermesser upbraids her for parochialism; she instructs the golem to take subways and buses—no taxis—out to all the neighborhoods in all the boroughs. It goes without saying that a robust reformist administration requires a spy. The golem returns with aching tales of what she has seen among the sordid and the hopeless; sometimes she even submits a recommendation on a page of her notepad. Puttermesser does not mind. Nothing the golem reports is new to Mayor Puttermesser. What is new is the discovery of the power of office. Wrongdoing and bitterness can be overturned: it is only a matter of using the power Puttermesser owns.

Crowds of self-seeking importuners float up the steps of City Hall; Mayor Puttermesser shoos them away. She admits visionary hearts only. She tacks signs up all around her desk: NO MORE SPOILS QUOTA. MERIT IS SWEETER THAN GOLD. WHAT YOU ARE, NOT WHOM YOU KNOW.

Lost wallets are daily being returned to their owners. Now it is really beginning—the money and credit cards are always intact. The golem ascends from the subway at Sixty-eighth and Lexington (this is the very corner where Puttermesser's alma mater, Hunter High, used to stand), looking slightly larger than the day before, but also irradiated. The subways have been struck by beauty. Lustrous tunnels unfold, mile after mile. Gangs of youths have invaded the subway yards at night and have washed the cars clean. The wheels and windows have been scrubbed by combinations of chemicals; the long seats have been fitted with velour cushions of tan and blue. Each car shines like a bullet. The tiles that line the stations are lakes of white; the passengers can cherish their own reflections in the walls. Every Thursday afternoon the youths who used to terrorize the subways put on fresh shirts and walk out into Central Park, reconnoitering after a green space; then, they dance. They have formed themselves into dancing clubs, and crown one another's heads with clover pulled up from the sweet ground. Foliage is browning, Thursday afternoons grow cold and dusky. But the youths who used to terrorize the subways are whirling in rings over darkening lawns.

The streets are altered into garden rows: along the curbs, between sidewalk and road, privet hedges shake their little leaves. The open sanitation carts are bright, like a string of scarlet chariots. They are drawn by silent horses who sniff among the new hedges. Flutes and clarinets announce the coming of the cart procession every day at noon, and children scramble to pick up every nub of cigarette or scrap of peel or paper wrapper, pressing with fistfuls toward the singing flutes and gravely marching horses, whose pairs of high nostrils flare outward like trumpets.

The great cargo trucks still spill into the intersections, carrying bolts of cloth, oranges, fowl, refrigerators, lamps, pianos, cards of buttons, lettuces, boxes of cereal, word processors, baby carriages, pillowcases with peacocks imprinted on them; some deliver uptown, others downtown; they pant and rumble freely, unimpeded; buses and taxis overtake them effortlessly. Except for fire engines and ambulances, there are no other motored vehicles. Little girls dare, between buses, to jump rope in the middle of the street. Some roads, though, have been lushly planted, so that lovers seek them out to hide in one another's breast. The tall grasses and young maples of the planted roads are haunted by pretzel sellers, hot-chestnut peddlers, hawkers of books in wheelbarrows. The children are often indoors after school, carpentering bookshelves. The libraries are lit all night, and the schools are thronged in the evenings by administrative assistants from the great companies, learning Spanish, Portuguese, Russian, Hebrew, Korean, and Japanese. There are many gardeners now, and a hundred urban gardening academies. There is unemployment among correction officers; numbers of them take gardening jobs. No one bothers to drag the steel shutters down over storefronts after closing. The Civil Service hums. Intellect and courtliness are in the ascendancy. Mayor Puttermesser has staffed the Department of Receipts and Disbursements with intelligent lawyers, both women and men, who honor due process. Turtelman and Marmel are replaced by visionary hearts. Never again will an accuser take the job of the accused, as Marmel did with Puttermesser! There is no more rapaciousness in the Bureau of Summary Sessions.

A little-known poet who specializes in terza rima is put in charge of Potter's Field. For each sad burial there, she composes a laudatory ode; even the obscure dead are not expendable or forlorn. The parks, their arbors and fields, are speckled with wide-mouthed terra-cotta urns; no one injures them. Far away in the Bronx, the grape-wreathed heads of wine gods are restored to the white stelae of the Soldiers' Monument, and the bronze angel on top of the Monument's great stone needle glistens. Nothing is broken, nothing is despoiled. No harm comes to anything or anyone. The burnt-out ruins of Brownsville and the South Bronx burst forth with spinneys of pines and thorny locusts. In their high secret pride, the slums undo themselves: stoops sparkle, new factories and stores buzz, children gaze down in gladness at shoes newly bought, still unscratched; the shoe stores give away balloons, and the balloons escape to the sky. Everywhere former louts and loiterers, muggers and thieves, addicts and cardsharps are doing the work of the world, absorbed, transformed. The biggest City agency is what used to be called Welfare; now it is the Department of Day Play, and delivers colored pencils and finger paints and tambourines to nurseries clamorous as bee-loud glades, where pianos shake the floors, and storytellers dangle toddlers in suspense from morning to late afternoon, when their parents fetch them home to supper. Everyone is at work. Lovers apply to the City Clerk for marriage licenses. The Bureau of Venereal Disease Control has closed down. The ex-pimps are learning computer skills.

Xanthippe's heels have begun to hang over the foot of her fourposter bed in Gracie Mansion. The golem is worn out. She lumbers from one end of the City to the other every day, getting ideas. Mayor Puttermesser is not disappointed that the golem's ideas are mainly unexciting. The City is at peace. It is in the nature of tranquility—it is in the nature of Paradise—to be pacific; tame; halcyon. Oh, there is more to relate of how Mayor Puttermesser, inspired by the golem, has resuscitated, reformed, reinvigorated and redeemed the City of New York! But this too must be left to dozing and skipping. It is essential to record only two reflections that especially engage Mayor Puttermesser. The first is that she notices how the City, tranquil, turns toward the conventional and the orderly. It is as if tradition, continuity, propriety blossom of themselves: old courtesies, door-holding, hat-tipping, a thousand pleases and pardons and thank-yous. Something in the grain of Paradise is on the side of the expected. Sweet custom rules. The City in its redeemed state wishes to conserve itself. It is a rational daylight place; it has shut the portals of night.

Puttermesser's second reflection is about the golem. The coming of the golem animated the salvation of the City, yes—but who, Puttermesser sometimes wonders, is the golem? Is it Xanthippe or is it Puttermesser? Puttermesser made Xanthippe; Xanthippe did not exist before Puttermesser made her: that is clear enough. But Xanthippe made Puttermesser

Mayor, and Mayor Puttermesser too did not exist before. And that is just as clear. Puttermesser sees that she is the golem's golem.

In the newborn peaceable City, Xanthippe is restless. She is growing larger. Her growth is frightening. She can no longer fit into her overalls. She begins to sew together pairs of sheets for a toga.

VII. Rappoport's Return

On a late spring afternoon about halfway through her mayoral term, and immediately after a particularly depressing visit to the periodontist (she who had abolished crime in the subways was unable to stem gum disease in the hollow of her own jaw), Puttermesser came home to Gracie Mansion to find Rappoport waiting in her private sitting room.

"Hey, you've got some pretty tough security around here. I had a hell of a time getting let in," Rappoport complained.

"Last time I saw you," Puttermesser said, "you had no trouble letting yourself out."

"How about we just consider that water under the bridge, Ruth, what do you say?"

"You walked out on me. In the middle of the night."

"You were liking Socrates better than me," Rappoport said.

"Then why are you back?"

"My God, Ruth, look who you've become! I can't pass through New York without seeing the Mayor, can I? Ruth," he said, spreading his impressive nostrils, "I've thought about you a lot since the election. We read all about you up in Toronto."

"You and Mrs. Rappoport?"

"Oh come on, let's give it another try. Not that I don't understand you have to be like Caesar's wife. Above susp—"

"I have to be Caesar," Puttermesser broke in.

"Well, even Caesar gives things another try."

"You're no Cleopatra," Puttermesser said.

There was a distant howl; it was the cook. She was fighting with the golem again. In a moment Xanthippe stood in the doorway, huge and red, weeping.

"Leave that woman alone. She'll cook what she'll cook, you can't tell her anything different," Puttermesser scolded. "She runs a strictly kosher kitchen and that's enough. Go and wash your face."

"Plump," Rappoport said, staring after Xanthippe in her toga. "Right out of Caesar's Forum."

"A growing girl. She wears what she pleases."

"Who is she?"

"I adopted her."

"I like a big girl like that." Rappoport stood up. "The town looks terrific. I came to congratulate you, Ruth."

"Is that why you came?"

"It turns out. Only I figured if you could bring a whole city back to life—"

"There are some things, Morris, that even the Mayor can't revive."

Rappoport, his briefcase under his arm, wheeled and hesitated. "It didn't make it through the move? My avocado tree that I grew from a pit in Toronto? It was doing fine in your old apartment."

"I don't have it any more."

"Aha, you wanted to dispose of me lock, stock, and barrel. You got rid of every symptom and sign. The least bit of green leaf—"

"All my plants are gone."

"No kidding. What happened?"

"I took their earth and made a golem."

Rappoport, flaunting his perfect teeth under his mustache, laughed out loud. In the middle of his laughter his head suddenly fell into the kind of leaning charm Puttermesser recalled from long ago, when they had first become lovers; it almost made her relent.

"Goodbye, Ruth. I really do congratulate you on civic improvement." Rappoport held out his hand. "It's one terrific town, I mean it. Utopia. Garden of Eden. In Toronto they run articles on you every day."

"You can stay for dinner if you like," Puttermesser offered. "Though I've got a meeting right after—municipal bonds. Myself, it's eat and get on down to City Hall."

Someone had seized Rappoport's outstretched hand and was shaking it; it was not Puttermesser. Xanthippe, practiced politician, her wide cheeks refreshed and soap-fragrant, had sped forward out of nowhere. Rappoport looked stunned; he looked interested. He slipped his fingers out of the golem's grasp and moved them upward against her chest, to catch hold of the card that twirled there: DEAF-MUTE.

"That's awfully generous of you, Ruth, adopting someone like that. You're a wonderful person. We really ought to get together again. I *will* stay for a bite, if you don't mind."

The golem did not bring her ballpoint to the table. She dealt with her soup spoon as if it were her enemy, the cook. Disgruntled, she heaped a fourth helping of mashed potatoes onto her plate. But her eye was on Rappoport, and her mouth was round with responsiveness: was it his teeth? was it his reddish mustache, turning gray? was it his wide welcoming nostrils? was it his briefcase bulging with worldly troubles?

Rappoport was talkative. His posture was straight-backed and heroic:

he told of his last clandestine trip to Moscow, and of the turmoil of the oppressed.

When Puttermesser returned at midnight from the meeting on municipal bonds, the golem was asleep in her fourposter bed, her heels thrust outward in their pink socks over the footboard, and Rappoport was snoring beside her.

Eros had entered Gracie Mansion.

VIII. Xanthippe Lovesick

Consider now Puttermesser's situation. What happens to an intensely private mind when great celebrity unexpectedly invades it? Absorbed in the golem's *PLAN* and its consequences—consequences beyond the marveling at, so gradual, plausible, concrete, and sensible are they, grounded in a Policy of civic sympathy and urban reasonableness—Puttermesser does not readily understand that she induces curiosity and applause. She has, in fact, no expectations; only desires as strong and as strange as powers. Her desires are Pristine, therefore acute; clarity is immanent. Before this inward illumination of her desires (rather, of the *PLAN*'s desires), everything else—the clash of interests that parties, races, classes, are said to give rise to—falls away into purposelessness. Another way of explaining all this is to say that Mayor Puttermesser finds virtue to be intelligible.

Still another way of explaining is to say that every morning she profoundly rejoices. There is fruitfulness everywhere. Into the chaos of the void (defeat, deception, demoralization, loss) she has cast a divinely clarifying light. Out of a dunghill she has charmed a verdant citadel. The applause that reaches her is like a sea-sound at the farthest edge of her brain; she both hears it and does not hear it. Her angelic fame—the fame of a purifying angel—is virtue's second face. Fame makes Puttermesser happy, and at the same time it brings a forceful sense of the penultimate, the tentative, the imperiled.

It is as if she is waiting for something else: for some conclusion, or resolution, or unfolding.

The golem is lovesick. She refuses to leave the Mansion. No more for her the daily voyage into the broad green City as the Mayor's ambassador and spy. She removes the DEAF-MUTE card and substitutes another: CONTEMPLATIVE. Puttermesser does not smile at this: she is not sure whether it is meant to be a joke. There is too much gloom. There are hints of conspiracy. Anyhow the golem soon takes off the new sign. In the intervals between Rappoport's appearances Xanthippe languishes. Rappoport comes often—sometimes as often as three or four times a week. Xanthippe, moping, thumps out to greet him, trailing a loose white tail of her toga;

she escorts him straight into her bedroom. She turns on the record player that Rappoport has brought her as a birthday gift. She is two years old and insatiable. God knows what age she tells her lover.

Rappoport steals out of the golem's bedroom with the dazzled inward gaze of a space traveler.

The Mayor upbraids Xanthippe: "It's enough. I don't want to see him around here. Get rid of him."

Xanthippe writes: "Jealousy!"

"I'm tired of hearing complaints from the cook. This is Gracie Mansion, it's not another kind of house."

"Jealousy! He used to be yours."

"You're stirring up a scandal."

"He brings me presents."

"If you keep this up, you'll spoil everything."

"My mother has purified the City."

"Then don't foul it."

"I am in contemplation of my future."

"Start contemplating the present! Look out the window! Fruitfulness! Civic peace! You saw it happening. You caused it."

"I can tear it all down."

"You were made to serve and you know it."

"I want a life of my own. My blood is hot."

The Mansion thickens with erotic airs. Heavy perfumes float. Has Rappoport journeyed to mysterious islands to offer the golem these lethargic scents, these attars of weighty drooping petals? The golem has discarded her sewn-together sheets and looms with gemlike eyes in darkling passageways, wrapped in silks, vast saris that skim the carpets as she goes; each leg is a pillar wound in a bolt of woven flowers.

The summer deepens. A dry dust settles on the leaves in the Bronx Botanical Gardens, and far away the painted carousels of Brooklyn cry their jollities.

The Mayor: "I notice Rappoport hasn't been around lately."

Xanthippe writes: "He left."

"Where?"

"He clouded over his destination. Vienna. Rome. Jerusalem. Winnipeg. What do I care? A man of low position. Factotum of refugee philanthropy, twelve bosses over him."

"What happened?"

"I wore him out."

"I need you right away," Puttermesser urges. "We're putting in new tiles on the subway line out toward Jamaica Avenue. With two-color portraits baked right into the glaze—Thoreau, Harriet Beecher Stowe, Emerson so far. You can decide who else."

"No."

"You haven't been anywhere in months."

"My mother speaks the truth. I thirst for the higher world. Office and rank. Illustrious men."

Puttermesser is blighted with melancholy. She fears. She foresees. In spite of fruitfulness and civic peace (rather, on their account), it is beginning to be revealed to her what her proper mayoral duty directs.

She does nothing.

In pity, she waits. Sometimes she forgets. How long did the Great Rabbi Judah Loew of Prague wait, how often did he forget? There are so many distinguished visitors. The Emperor of Japan takes the elevator to the top of the Empire State Building. Puttermesser gives an astronaut a medal on the steps of City Hall; he has looked into the bosom of Venus. The mayors of Dublin, San Juan, and Tel Aviv arrive. In the Blue Room, Puttermesser holds a news conference about interest rates. She explains into the television cameras that the City of New York, in its abundance, will extend interest-free loans to the Federal government in Washington.

Now and then Xanthippe disappears. She does not return to the Mansion at night. Frequently her fourposter stands empty.

Early one morning, the golem, her eyes too polished, her cheeks too red, her silk windings torn, the tiny letters on her forehead jutting like raw scars, thumps home.

"Four days gone without a word!" Puttermesser scolds.

Xanthippe writes impatiently: "Been down to Florida."

"Florida!"

"Been to visit ex-Mayor Malachy ('Matt') Mavett."

"What for?"

"Remember Marmel?"

"What's this about?"

"Been out West to visit him. Him and Turtelman."

"What is this?"

But Puttermesser knows.

There are curious absences, reports of exhaustion, unexplained hospitalizations. The new Commissioner of Receipts and Disbursements whispers to Puttermesser, in confidence, that he will divorce his wife. His eyeballs seem sunken, his lips drop back into a hollow face. He has lost weight overnight. He will not say what the trouble is. He resigns. The Executive Director of the Board of Education resigns. It is divulged that he suffers from catarrh and is too faint to stand. The Commissioner of the Department of Cultural Affairs has been struck stone-deaf by a horrible sound, a kind of exultant hiss; he will not say what it was. The City's managers and executives all appear to sicken together: commissioner after commissioner, department after department. Puttermesser's finest appointments—felled; depleted. There is news of an abortion in Queens. A pimp sets himself up in business on Times Square again, in spite of the cherry trees the Department of Sanitation has planted there; the Commissioner of Sanitation himself stalks under the hanging cherries, distracted, with a twisted spine and the start of a hunch. Two or three of the proud young men of the dancing clubs defect and return to mugging in the subways. The City's peace is unraveling. The commissioners blow their noses into bloody tissues, drive their little fingers into their ears, develop odd stammers, instigate backbiting among underlings.

The golem thirsts. "Stay home," the Mayor pleads. "Stay out of the City."

The golem will no longer obey. She cannot be contained. "My blood is hot," Xanthippe writes; she writes for the last time. She tosses her ballpoint pen into the East River, back behind the Mansion.

IX. The Golem Destroys Her Maker

Mayor Puttermesser's reputation is ebbing. The cost of municipal borrowing ascends. A jungle of graffiti springs up on the white flanks of marble sculptures inside museums; Attic urns are smashed. Barbarians cruise the streets. O New York! O lost New York!

Deputy commissioners and their secretaries blanch at the sound of a heavy footstep. Morning and afternoon the golem lumbers from office to office, searching for high-level managers. In her ragged sari brilliant with woven flowers, her great head garlanded, drenched in a density of musky oils, Xanthippe ravishes prestigious trustees, committee chairmen, council members, borough presidents, the Second Deputy Comptroller's three assistants, the Director of the Transit Authority, the Coordinator of Criminal Justice, the Chief of the Office of Computer Plans and Controls, the Head of Inter-governmental Relations, the Chancellor of the City University, the Rector of the Art Commission, even the President of the Stock Exchange! The City is diseased with the golem's urge. The City sweats and coughs in her terrifying embrace. The City is in the pincer of the golem's love, because Xanthippe thirsts, she thirsts, she ravishes and ravages, she ambushes management level after management level. There is no Supervising Accountant or Secretary to the Minority Leader who can escape her electric gaze.

Sex! Sex! The golem wants sex! Men in high politics! Lofty officials! Elevated bureaucrats!

Mayor Puttermesser is finished. She can never be reelected. She is a disgrace; her Administration is wrecked. Distrust. Desolation. It is all over for Mayor Puttermesser and the life of high politics. The prisons are open again. The press howls. Mayor Puttermesser is crushed. The golem has destroyed her utterly.

X. The Golem Snared

Puttermesser blamed herself. She had not forestalled this devastation. She had not prepared for it; she had not acted. She had seen what had to be done, and put it off and put it off. Dilatory. She could not say to herself that she was ignorant; hadn't she read in her books, a thousand times, that a golem will at length undo its creator? The turning against the creator is an "attribute" of a golem, comparable to its speechlessness, its incapacity for procreation, its soullessness. A golem has no soul, therefore cannot die—rather, it is returned to the elements of its making.

Xanthippe without a soul! Tears came to Puttermesser, her heart in secret shook. She was ready to disbelieve. A golem cannot procreate? Ah, but its blood is as hot as human blood. Hotter! A golem lusts tremendously, as if it would wrest the flame of further being from its own being. A golem, an earthen thing of packed mud, having laid hold of life against all logic and natural expectation, yearns hugely after the generative, the fructuous. Earth is the germ of all fertility: how then would a golem not dream itself a double? It is like a panting furnace that cries out for more and more fuel, that spews its own firebrands to ignite a successor-fire. A golem cannot procreate! But it has the will to; the despairing will; the violent will. Offspring! Progeny! The rampaging energies of Xanthippe's eruptions, the furious bolts and convulsions of her visitations—Xanthippe, like Puttermesser herself, longs for daughters! Daughters that can never be!

Shall the one be condemned by the other, who is no different?

Yet Puttermesser weeps. The golem is running over the City. She never comes home at all now. A ferry on its way from the Battery to Staten Island is terrorized; some large creature, bat or succubus, assaults the captain and causes him to succumb. Is it Xanthippe? Stories about "a madwoman on the loose, venomous against authority" ("unverifiable," writes the City Hall Bureau of the *Times*) wash daily over Mayor Puttermesser's desk. The secret chamber where sleeps the President of the Chase Manhattan Bank has had its windows brutally smashed; a bit of flowered silk clings to the jagged glass.

Xanthippe! Xanthippe! Puttermesser calls in her heart.

Every night pickets parade in front of Gracie Mansion, with torches and placards:

MAYOR PUTTERMESSER WHAT HAS HAPPENED TO THE SUBWAYS?
HIGH HOPES THE HIGH ROAD TO HELL.
SHE WHO SPARED SNUFFED.
PUTTERMESSER'S BITTER MESSES.
RUTHIE WITH SUCH A DOWN WE NEEDED YOUR UP?
FROM SMASH HIT TO SMASH.
KAPUT-TERMESSER!

Every day there are speakers on the steps of City Hall, haranguing; when the police chase them, they vanish for ten minutes and reappear. Mobs bubble, hobble, guffaw.

Puttermesser composes a letter to ex-Mayor Malachy ("Matt") Mavett:

Gracie Mansion
City of New York

Dear Matt [she permits herself this liberty]:

My campaign manager's recent Florida visit may have caused you some distress. I did not authorize it. Your defeat via the ballot box, which eliminated the wrongdoers Turtelman and Marmel from City officialdom, was satisfaction enough. Please excuse any personal indignities my campaign manager (who is now on my personal staff) may have inflicted. She expresses her nature but cannot assume responsibility for it.

Dilatory! Procrastinator! Imaginary letters! Puttermesser's tears go on falling.

Gracie Mansion
City of New York

Dear Morris:

Please come.

In friendship
Ruth

She hands this to one of the window-pole thieves to mail. In a few days it brings Rappoport, out of breath, his once-pouting briefcase hollow, caved in; Rappoport himself is hollow, his stout throat caved in, as if he had ejected his Adam's apple. His nose and chin, and the furless place between his eyebrows, have a papery cast. His beautiful teeth are nicked. His mustache looks squirrelly, gray.

"Xanthippe's left home," Puttermesser announces.

"You're the Mayor. Call the Missing Persons Bureau."

"Morris. Please."

"What do you want?"

"Bring her back."

"Me?"

"You can do it."

"How?"

"Move in."

"What? Here? In Gracie Mansion?"

"In Xanthippe's bed. Morris. Please. She likes you. You're the one who started her off."

"She got too big for her britches. In more than a manner of speaking, if you don't mind my saying so. What d'you mean, started her off?"

"You excited her."

"That's not my fault."

"You created desire. Morris, bring her back. You can do it."

"What for? I've had enough. No more. Drained. Drained, believe me, Ruth."

"Lie in her bed. Just once."

"What's in it for me? I didn't come back to this rotten town for the sake of a night's sleep in Gracie Mansion. The novelty's worn off. The bloom is no longer on the rose, you follow? Besides, you've gone downhill, Ruth, did you see those pickets out there?" He shows her his sleeve—two buttons ripped off. "They treated me like a scab, walking in here—"

"Just lie down in her bed, Morris. That's all I'm asking."

"No."

"I'll make it worth your while."

"What're you getting at? You're getting at something."

"You're a fund-raiser by profession," Puttermesser says meditatively; a strangeness rises in her. A noxious taste.

"Something like that. There's a lot of different things I do."

"That's right. Plenty of experience. You're qualified for all sorts of fine spots."

"I'm qualified for what?"

"The truth is," Puttermesser says slowly, "I'm in possession of a heap of resignations. Several of my commissioners," Puttermesser says slowly, "have fallen ill."

"I hear there's typhoid in some of those buildings along Bruckner Boulevard. What've you got, an epidemic? I heard cholera in Forest Hills."

"Rumors," Puttermesser spits out. "People love to bad-mouth. That's what makes the City go down. The banks are leaving, nobody worries about *that*. I'm talking resignations. *Openings,* Morris. You can take your pick, in fact. How about the Department of Investigation? Run the Inspectors General. Or I can appoint you judge. How about Judge of the Criminal Court? Good spot, good pay. Prestige, God knows. Look, if you like you can take over Receipts and Disbursements." Rappoport stared. "Commissioner of Receipts and Disbursements?"

"I can go higher if you want. Fancier. Board of Water Supply's a dandy. Nice remuneration, practically no show."

"Ruth, Ruth, what is this?"

Justice, justice shalt thou pursue!

It is Mayor Puttermesser's first political deal.

"Stay a night in Xanthippe's bed and any job you want is yours. The orchard's dropping into your lap, Morris, I'm serious. Plums."

"A spot in your Administration actually?"

"Why not? Choose."

"Receipts and Disbursements," Rappoport instantly replies.

Puttermesser says sourly, "You're at least as qualified as Turtelman."

"What about my wife?"

"Keep her in Toronto."

Standing in solitude in the night fragrance behind Gracie Mansion, Puttermesser catches river-gleams: the Circle Line yacht with its chandelier decks; a neon sign pulsing; the distant caps of little waves glinting in moonwake, in neonwake. White bread baking on the night shift casts its faintly animal aroma on the waters: rich fumes more savory than any blossom. It is so dark in the back garden that Puttermesser imagines she can almost descry Orion's belt buckle. One big moving star twins as it sails: the headlights of an airliner nosing out toward Europe. Plane after plane rises, as if out of the black river. Puttermesser counts them, each with its sharp beams like rays scattered from the brow of Moses, arching upward into the fathomless universe. She counts planes; she counts neon blinks; she counts the silhouettes of creeping scows; she counts all the mayors who have preceded her in the City of New York. Thomas Willett, Thomas Delavall . . . William Dervall, Nicholas De Meyer, Stephanus Van Cortlandt . . . Francis Rombouts . . . Isaac de Reimer, Thomas Noell, Philip French, William Peartree, Ebenezer Wilson . . . DeWitt Clinton . . . Gideon Lee . . . Smith Ely . . . Jimmy Walker . . . John P. O'Brien, Fiorello H. LaGuardia . . . Robert F. Wagner, John V. Lindsay, Abraham D. Beame, Edward I. Koch! She counts and waits. She is waiting for the golem to be lured homeward, to be ensnared, to lumber groaning with desire into her fourposter bed.

In the golem's fourposter, Commissioner Morris Rappoport, newly appointed chief of the Department of Receipts and Disbursements, lies in sheets saturated with a certain known pungency. He has been here before. He recoils from the familiar scented pillows.

Indoors and out, odors of what has been and what is about to be: the cook's worn eggplant au gratin, river smells, the garden beating its tiny wings of so many fresh hedge-leaves, airplane exhaust spiraling downward, the fine keen breath of the bread ovens, the golem's perfumed pillows—all these drifting smokes and combinations stir and turn and braid themselves into a rope of awesome incense, drawing Xanthippe to her bed. Incense? Fetor and charged decay! The acrid signal of dissolution! Intimations of the tellurian elements! Xanthippe, from wherever she has hurtled to in the savage City (savage once again), is pulled nearer and nearer the Mansion, where the portraits of dead mayors hang. Scepter and status, all the enchantments of influence and command, lead her to her undoing: in her bed lies the extremely important official whose job it is to call the tune that makes the City's money dance. She will burst on him her giant love. On the newly appointed Commissioner of Receipts and Disbursements the golem will spend her terrible ardor. Then she will fall back to rest, among the awful perfumes of her cleft bed.

Whereupon Mayor Puttermesser, her term of office blighted, her comely *PLAN* betrayed, will dismantle the golem, according to the rite.

XI. The Golem Undone, and the Babbling of Rappoport

The City was ungovernable; the City was out of control; it was no different now for Mayor Puttermesser than it had ever been for any mayor. In confusion and hypocrisy, Puttermesser finished out what was left of her sovereign days.

One thing was different: a certain tumulus of earth introduced by the Parks Commissioner in the mournful latter half of Mayor Puttermesser's Administration.

Across the street from City Hall lies a little park, crisscrossed by paths and patches of lawn fenced off by black iron staves. There are benches set down here and there with a scattered generosity. There is even an upward-flying fountain. Perhaps because the little park is in the shadow of City Hall and, so to speak, under its surveillance, the benches have not been seriously vandalized, and the lawns not much trampled on. Best of all, and most alluring, are the flower beds, vivid rectangles of red geraniums disposed, it must be admitted, in the design of a miniature graveyard. Civil servants peering down from high windows of the elephant-gray Municipal Building can see the crimson slash that with wild brilliance cuts across the concrete bitterness below. Some distance behind the flower beds rise those great Stonehenge slabs of the Twin Towers; eastward, the standing zither that is Brooklyn Bridge.

From the Mayor's office inside City Hall the park is not visible, and for Puttermesser this is just as well. It would not have done for her to be in sight of Xanthippe's bright barrow while engaged in City business. Under the roots of the flower beds lay fresh earth, newly put down and lightly tamped. Mayor Puttermesser herself, in the middle of the night, had telephoned the Parks Commissioner (luckily just back from Paris) and ordered the ground to be opened and a crudely formed and crumbling mound of special soil to be arranged in the cavity, as in an envelope of earth. The Parks Commissioner, urgently summoned, thought it odd, when he arrived at Gracie Mansion with his sleepy diggers, that the Mayor should be pacing in the back garden behind the Mansion under a veined half-moon; and odder yet that she should be accompanied by a babbling man with a sliding tongue, who identified himself as the newly appointed Commissioner of Receipts and Disbursements, Morris Rappoport.

"Did you bring spades? And a pickup truck?" the Mayor whispered.

"All of that, yes."

"Well, the spades won't do. At least not yet. You don't shovel up a floor. You can use the spades afterward, in the park. There's some dried mud spread out on a bedroom floor in the Mansion. I want it moved. With very great delicacy. Can you make your men understand that?"

"Dried mud?"

"I grant you it's in pieces. It's already falling apart. But it's got a certain design. Be delicate."

What the Parks Commissioner saw was a very large and shapeless, or mainly shapeless, mound of soil, insanely wrapped (so the Parks Commissioner privately judged) in a kind of velvet shroud. The Parks Commissioner had been on an official exchange program in France, and had landed at Kennedy Airport less than two hours before the Mayor telephoned. The exchange program meant that he would study the enchanting parks of Paris, while his Parisian counterpart was to consider the gloomier parks of New York. The Parks Commissioner, of course, was Puttermesser's own appointee, a botanist and city planner, an expert on the hardiness of certain shade trees, a specialist in filigreed gazebos, a lover of the urban nighttime. All the same, he was perplexed by the Mayor's caprice. The mound of dirt on the bedroom floor did not suggest to him his own good fortune and near escape. In fact, though neither would ever learn this, the Parks Commissioner and his Parisian counterpart were both under a felicitous star—the Parisian because his wife's appendectomy had kept him unexpectedly and rather too lengthily in Paris so that he never arrived in New York at all (he was an anxious man), and the Parks Commissioner because he had not been at home in his lower Fifth Avenue bed when the golem came to call. Instead, he had been out inspecting the Bois de Boulogne—consequently, the Parks Commissioner was in fine mental health, and was shocked to observe that the newly appointed Commissioner of Receipts and Disbursements was not.

Rappoport babbled. He followed after Puttermesser like a dog. He had performed exactly as she had instructed, it seemed, but then her instructions became contradictory. First he was to circle. Then he was not to circle.

Rather, he was to scrape with his penknife. There he was, all at once a satrap with a title; the title was as palpable as a mantle, and as sumptuous; overhead drooped the fourposter's white velvet canopy with its voluptuous folds and snowy crevices—how thickly warm his title, how powerful his office! Alone, enclosed in the authority of his rank, Rappoport awaited the visitation of the golem. Without a stitch, not a shred of sari remaining, her burnished gaze on fire with thirst for his grandeur, she burst in, redolent of beaches, noisy with a fiery hiss; Rappoport tore the white velvet from the tester and threw it over burning Xanthippe.

Rappoport babbled. He told all the rest: how they had contended; how he had endured her size and force and the horror of her immodesty and the awful sea of her sweat and the sirocco of her summer breath; and how he—or was it she?—had chanted out the hundred proud duties of his new jurisdiction: the protocol and potency of the City's money, where it is engendered, where it is headed, where it lands: it could be said that she was teaching him his job. And then the Mayor, speaking through the door, explaining the depth of tranquility after potency that is deeper than any sleep or drug or anesthesia, directing him to remove Xanthippe in all her deadweight mass from the fourposter down to the bare floor, and to wind her in the canopy.

Rappoport babbled: how he had lifted Xanthippe in her trance, the torpor that succeeds ravishment, down to the bare floor; how he had wound her in white velvet; how pale Puttermesser, her reading lenses glimmering into an old green book, directed him with sharpened voice to crowd his mind with impurity—with everything earthly, soiled, spoiled, wormy; finally how Puttermesser directed him to trail her as she weaved round Xanthippe on the floor, as if circling her own shadow.

Round and round Puttermesser went. In the instant of giving the golem life, the just, the comely, the cleanly, the Edenic, had, all unwittingly, consummated Puttermesser's aspiring reflections—even the radiant *PLAN* itself! Now all must be consciously reversed. She must think of violent-eyed loiterers who lurk in elevators with springblades at the ready, of spray cans gashing red marks of civilization-hate, of civic monuments with their heads knocked off, of City filth, of mugging, robbery, arson, assault, even murder. Murder! If, for life, she had dreamed Paradise, now she must feel the burning lance of hell. If, for life, she had walked seven times clockwise round a hillock of clay, now she must walk seven times counterclockwise round captive Xanthippe. If, for life, she had pronounced the Name, now she must on no account speak or imagine it or lend it any draught or flame of breath; she must erase the Name utterly.

And what of Rappoport, Rappoport the golem's lure and snare, Rappoport who had played himself out in the capture of Xanthippe? He too must walk counterclockwise, behind Puttermesser, just as the Great Rabbi Judah Loew had walked counterclockwise with his disciples when the time came for the golem of Prague to be undone. The golem of Prague, city-savior, had also run amok!—terrorizing the very citizens it had been created to succor. And all the rites the Great Rabbi Judah Loew had pondered in the making of the golem, he ultimately dissolved in the unmaking of it. All the permutations and combinations of the alphabet he had recited with profound and holy concentration in the golem's creation, he afterward declaimed backward, for the sake of the golem's discomposition. Instead of meditating on the building up, he meditated on the breaking down. Whatever he had early spiraled, he late unraveled: he smashed the magnetic links that formed the chain of being between the atoms.

Puttermesser, circling round the torpid Xanthippe in her shroud of white velvet, could not help glancing down into the golem's face. It was a child's face still. Ah, Leah, Leah! Xanthippe's lids flickered. Xanthippe's lips stirred. She looked with her terrible eyes—how they pulsed—up at Puttermesser.

"My mother."

A voice!

"O my mother," Xanthippe said, still looking upward at Puttermesser, "why are you walking around me like that?"

She spoke! Her voice ascended!—a child's voice, pitched like the pure cry of a bird.

Puttermesser did not halt. "Keep moving," she told Rappoport.

"O my mother," Xanthippe said in her bird-quick voice, "why are you walking around me like that?"

Beginning the fifth circle, Rappoport gasping behind her, Puttermesser said, "You created and you destroyed."

"No," the golem cried—the power of speech released!—"it was you who created me, it is you who will destroy me! Life! Love! Mercy! Love! Life!"

The fifth circle was completed; still the golem went on bleating in her little bird's cry. "Life! Life! More!"

"More," Puttermesser said bitterly, beginning the sixth circle. "More. You wanted more and more. It's more that brought us here. More!"

"You wanted Paradise!"

"Too much Paradise is greed. Eden disintegrates from too much Eden. Eden sinks from a surfeit of itself."

"O my mother! I made you Mayor!"

Completing the sixth circle, Puttermesser said, "You pulled the City down."

"O my mother! Do not cool my heat!"

Beginning the seventh circle, Puttermesser said, "This is the last. Now go home."

"O my mother! Do not send me to the elements!"

The seventh circle was completed; the golem's small voice piped on. Xanthippe lay stretched at Puttermesser's feet like Puttermesser's own shadow.

"Trouble," Puttermesser muttered. "Somehow this isn't working, Morris. Maybe because you're not a priest or a Levite."

Rappoport swallowed a tremulous breath. "If she gets to stand, if she decides to haul herself up—"

"Morris," Puttermesser said, "do you have a pocket knife?"

Rappoport took one out.

"O my mother, mother of my life!" the golem bleated. "Only think how for your sake I undid Turtelman, Marmel, Mavett!"

Huge sly Xanthippe, gargantuan wily Xanthippe, grown up out of the little seed of a dream of Leah!

Rappoport, obeying Puttermesser, blew aside the golem's bangs and with his small blade erased from Xanthippe's forehead what appeared to be no more than an old scar—the first on the right of three such scars—queerly in the shape of a sort of letter K.

Instantly the golem shut her lips and eyes.

The *aleph* was gone.

"Dead," Rappoport said.

"Returned," Puttermesser said. "Carry her up to the attic."

"The attic? *Here?* In Gracie Mansion? Ruth, think!"

"The Great Rabbi Judah Loew undid the golem of Prague in the attic of the Altneuschul. A venerable public structure, Morris, no less estimable than Gracie Mansion."

Rappoport laughed out loud. Then he let his tongue slide out, back and forth from right to left, along the corners of his mouth.

"Bend down, Morris."

Rappoport bent down.

"Pick up her left hand. By the wrist, that's the way."

Between Rappoport's forefinger and thumb the golem's left hand broke into four clods.

"No, it won't do. This wasn't well planned, Morris, I admit it. If we try to get her up the attic stairs—well, you can see what's happening. Never mind, I'll call the Parks Commissioner. Maybe City Hall Park—"

Then began the babbling of Rappoport.

XII. Under the Flower Beds

Garbage trucks are back on the streets. Their ferocious grinders gnash the City's spew. Traffic fumes, half a hundred cars immobile in a single intersection, demoralization in the ladies' lavatories of the Municipal Building, computers down, Albany at war with City Hall, a drop in fifth-grade reading scores—the City is choking. It cannot be governed. It cannot be controlled. There is a rumor up from Florida that ex-Mayor Malachy ("Matt") Mavett is scheming to recapture City Hall. As for current patronage, there is the egregious case of the newly appointed Commissioner of Receipts and Disbursements, said to be the Mayor's old lover; he resigns for health reasons even before taking office. His wife fetches him home to Toronto. Mayor Puttermesser undergoes periodontal surgery. When it is over, the roots of her teeth are exposed. Inside the secret hollow of her head, just below the eye sockets, on the lingual side, she is unendingly conscious of her own skeleton.

The *Soho News* is the only journal to note the Mayor's order, in the middle of a summer night, for an extra load of dirt to be shoveled under the red geraniums of City Hall Park. Parks Department diggers have planted a small wooden marker among the flower beds: DO NOT TOUCH OR PICK. With wanton contempt for civic decorum, passersby often flout the modest sign. Yet whoever touches or picks those stems of blood-colored blossoms soon sickens with flu virus, or sore throat, or stuffed nose accompanied by nausea—or, sometimes, a particularly vicious attack of bursitis.

And all the while Puttermesser calls in her heart: O lost New York! And she calls: O lost Xanthippe!

Glossary

Aggadah. (Hebrew.) Literally, narrative or legend; the nonlegal portions of rabbinic literature; often ethical, homiletical, or inspirational in nature.
Agunah. (Hebrew.) A woman whose husband has disappeared or abandoned her. According to Jewish law, she is unable to remarry until evidence of his death is established or until he returns to divorce her.
Akedat Yitzhak. (Hebrew.) The binding of Isaac by his father, Abraham, as a test of Abraham's faith in God. This story is found in Genesis and has become one of the central motifs in Jewish literature, theology, and philosophy.
Ashkenazi. (Hebrew.) Jewish person of central and northern European descent.
Baal Teshuva. (Hebrew.) A person who has "returned" to traditional Jewish observances and beliefs; colloquially might be called a "born-again Jew."
Bais Yakov. (Hebrew.) A religious day school providing intensive Orthodox Jewish education for girls. See note 38 for history.
Chollent (Yiddish.) An Eastern European Sabbath casserole dish put on to cook slowly well before sundown on Friday night; it is not tampered with until it is served for the noon meal on Saturday.
Dos pintele yid. (Yiddish.) The hidden spark of Jewishness that is traditionally thought to survive in every Jewish soul.
Dreck. (Yiddish.) Excrement.
Flaishig. (Yiddish.) Meat and meat products, traditionally kept separate from dairy products.
Frum. (Yiddish.) Religious or piously observant of Jewish rituals.
Gefilte fish. (Yiddish.) Cooked ground fish, either in a loaf, inside a fish skin, or in balls, traditionally served with horseradish on Sabbaths and holidays.
Goy, goyim. (Hebrew, Yiddish.) Literally, nation(s) of the world; usually taken to mean non-Jew(s).
Halakhah. (Hebrew.) A complex system of laws pertaining to nearly every aspect of life.
Haskalah. (Hebrew.) The Jewish Enlightenment, which began in Germany in the nineteenth century and spread later into Eastern European Jewish communities.
Havdalah. (Hebrew.) Literally, separation; a service to demarcate the holy time of the Sabbath and holidays from the workdays of the week; performed after sundown on Saturday nights with a braided candle, wine, and a spicebox.
Iggeret Hakodesh. (Hebrew.) Literally, Holy Epistle; an anonymous thirteenth-century Kabbalistic work that broke ground in applying Jewish mystical teach-

ings openly to everyday behavior, particularly to sexual relations between a husband and wife.

Kayn aynhoreh. (Yiddish.) Literally, without any evil eye; traditionally invoked to avert any bad fate or retribution for praising a person or his good fortune.

Kosher, Kashrut. (Hebrew, Yiddish.) A complex system of dietary regulations whose earliest formulation is found in a few biblical phrases, extensively developed and codified within rabbinic law. The laws of Kashrut provide for the exclusion of certain animal types from the diet, prohibit the ingestion of blood, and require the complete separation of meat and dairy products.

Mazal Tov. (Hebrew.) Literally, good luck, but colloquially used to mean "congratulations, may all go well."

Mekhitzah. (Hebrew.) Partition in Orthodox synagogues separating the women from the men. Often the women's section is off to the side, hidden behind a curtain, or in a balcony.

Midrash. (Hebrew.) Compilations of homilies, biblical exegesis, and legends that form a running commentary on specific books of the Bible.

Mikveh. (Hebrew, Yiddish.) A ritual bath that must contain a proportion of water from a natural, nonstagnant source, such as a river or stream or fresh rainwater. It is traditionally used by Jewish women for ritualistic purification each month after the cessation of their menses and after seven "white days" have passed; also used by Jewish men on a less regular basis.

Milchig. (Yiddish.) Dairy products, traditionally kept separate from meat products.

Minyan. (Hebrew, Yiddish.) Quorum of ten Jewish men necessary for certain prayers to be read.

Nahas. (Hebrew, Yiddish.) Pleasure, contentment, often derived from pride in one's children or other family members.

Neshamah. (Hebrew, Yiddish.) Soul.

Niddut. (Hebrew.) The time during a woman's menstrual cycle when she is unavailable to her husband for sexual or physical relations.

Pesach. (Hebrew.) Passover, the major, eight-day Jewish holiday in the spring that commemorates the exodus of the Israelites from Egypt. It is marked by the use of unleavened matzoh products rather than bread and by the Seder—festive meals held on the first two nights of the holiday at which the biblical story of the exodus is retold.

Pishachs. (Yiddish.) Urine.

Puttermesser. (Yiddish.) Butter knife.

Rabbi Akiva. Probably the foremost scholar, patriot, and martyr of his age, 50–135 C.E., born in the lowlands of Judea. He exercised a decisive influence in the development of Halakhah.

Rashi. Solomon ben Isaac (1040–1105 C.E.), the leading commentator on the Bible and Talmud, from Troyes, France.

Rebbetsin. (Yiddish.) Rabbi's wife.

Sephardi. (Hebrew.) Jewish person of Spanish or Portuguese descent.

Shadchen. (Yiddish.) Matchmaker.

Shaitel. (Yiddish.) Wig, often worn for modesty's sake by Orthodox Jewish women in Orthodox settings because the uncovered hair of a married Jewish woman was seen as an incitement to lust.

Shalom Bayit. (Hebrew.) Literally, the peace of the house. The serene and orderly household was perceived as the basic building block of Jewish society.

Shiksa. (Yiddish.) Unmarried gentile woman.

Shmate. (Yiddish.) Rag.

Taalith. (Hebrew.) Prayer shawl.

Taharat Hamishpakhah. (Hebrew.) Literally, the purity of the family; refers to the complex set of laws regarding marital purity in matters of sexual and physical relations.

Talmud. (Hebrew.) Literally, study; volumes transcribing the "Oral Law," the vast body of teaching, including discussions surrounding the Mishnah of Rabbi Judah ha-Nasi and later commentaries. There are, in fact, two "Talmuds," the Jerusalem Talmud and the Babylonian Talmud. Traditionally, the Jewish man devoted as much time as he was able to the study of Talmud.

Teffilin. (Hebrew.) Phylactories, small leather boxes containing a few biblical passages that a Jewish man traditionally binds with leather thongs on the arm nearest his heart and over his forehead during weekday morning prayers. They recall the biblical requirement to love God "with your heart, your soul, and all your might."

Trayf. (Hebrew, Yiddish.) Non-kosher.

Tsnies, tsniut. (Hebrew, Yiddish.) Modesty in dress and behavior.

Tzaddik. (Hebrew.) Righteous person, usually implying both moral and ritual piety.

Shul. (Yiddish.) Synagogue.

Yaytzer Harah. (Hebrew.) The evil inclination in each individual soul, which tries to lead a person astray.

Yeshiva. (Hebrew, Yiddish.) A school of higher learning for the study of classical Jewish texts, especially for the study of Talmudic literature.

Yente. (Yiddish.) Originally a proper name, probably a diminutive of the Yiddish name Genendel (genteel, refined), which is itself a Yiddishization of the Romance language word *Gentile*. However, in popular usage it has acquired a connotation of an overbearing, gossipy busybody.

Yiddish. A complex language composed primarily of Germanic and Hebraic elements but liberally sprinkled with vocabulary from the many lands in which Jews resided.

Zohar. (Hebrew.) Literally splendor; the central work in the literature of the Kabbalah, or the movement of Jewish mysticism, compiled in the thirteenth and fourteenth centuries.

Suggestions for Further Reading: A Selected Bibliography

Abel, Elizabeth, Marianne Hirsch, and Elizabeth Langland, eds. *The Voyage In: Fictions of Female Development*. Hanover, N.H.: University Press of New England, 1983.

Adler, Rachel. "The Jew Who Wasn't There," *Response* (Summer 1973): 77–82.

Adler, Ruth. "Mothers and Daughters: The Jewish Mother as Seen by American Jewish Women Writers." *Yiddish* 6 (1987): 87–92.

Asch, Sholem. *The Mother* (fiction). New York: G. P. Putnam's Sons, 1937.

Ashton, Dianne C., and Ellen Umansky, eds. *Piety, Persuasion, and Friendship: A Sourcebook of Women's Spirituality*. Boston: Beacon Press, 1991.

Baskin, Judith R. "Rabbinic Reflections on the Barren Wife," *Harvard Theological Review* 82, no. 1 (1989).

——— "Some Parallels in the Education of Medieval Jewish and Christian Women," *Jewish History* 5 (1991).

———, ed. *Jewish Women in Historical Perspective*. Detroit, Wayne State University Press, 1991.

Bayer, Linda. *The Blessing and the Curse* (fiction). Philadelphia and New York: The Jewish Publication Society, 1988.

Beck, Evelyn Torten. "The Many Faces of Eve: Women, Yiddish and I. B. Singer," *Studies in American Jewish Literature* 1 (1981): 112–23.

———. *Nice Jewish Girls: A Lesbian Anthology*. Watertown, Mass.: Persephone Press, 1982.

Brown, Cheryl, and Karen Olsen, eds. *Feminist Criticism: Essays on Theory, Poetry, and Prose*. Metuchen, N.J.: Scarecrow Press, 1987.

Brownstein, Rachel M. *Becoming a Heroine: Reading about Women in Novels*. New York: Viking Press, 1982.

Burch, C. Beth. "Johanna Kaplan's *O My America!*: The Jewish Female Claim to America." *Studies in American Jewish Literature* 9, no. 1 (Spring 1990): 36–47.

Burstein, Janet. "Jewish-American Women's Literature: The Long Quarrel with God." *Studies in American Jewish Literature* 8, no. 1 (Spring 1989): 9–25.

Cantor, Aviva. *The Jewish Woman: 1900–1980 Bibliography*. Fresh Meadows, N.Y.: Biblio Press, 1982.

Chesler, Phyllis. *Women and Madness*. Garden City, N.Y.: Doubleday, 1972.

Chodorow, Nancy. *The Reproduction of Mothering: Psychoanalysis and the Sociology of Gender*. Berkeley: University of California Press, 1978.

Christ, Carol P., and Judith Plaskow. *Womanspirit Rising: A Feminist Reader in Religion*. New York: Harper & Row, 1979.

Cohen, Arthur A. *An Admirable Woman* (fiction). Boston: David R. Godine, 1983.

Cohen, Sarah Blachor. "Hens to Roosters: Isaac Bashevis Singer's Female Species." *Studies in American Fiction* 10, no. 2 (Autumn 1982): 173–84.

Dally, Ann. *Inventing Motherhood: The Consequences of an Ideal*. New York: Schocken Books, 1983.

Daly, Mary. *Beyond God the Father*. Boston: Beacon Press, 1973.

———. *Gyn/Ecology: The Metaethics of Radical Feminism*. Boston: Beacon Press, 1978.

Davidson, Cathy N., and Esther M. Broner, eds. *The Lost Tradition: Mothers and Daughters in Literature*. New York: Frederick Ungar, 1980.

Day, Peggy L., ed. *Gender and Difference in Ancient Israel*. Minneapolis: Fortress Press, 1989.

Devault, Marjorie. "Novel Readings: The Social Organization of Interpretation." *American Journal of Sociology* 95, no. 4 (January 1990): 887–921.

Diamond, Arlyn, and Lee Edwards, eds. *The Authority of Experience: Essays in Feminist Criticism*. Amherst: University of Massachusetts Press, 1977.

Dinnerstein, Dorothy. *The Mermaid and the Minotaur: Sexual Arrangements and Human Malaise*. New York: Harper & Row, 1976.

Drucker, Sally Ann. "Yiddish, Yidgin, and Yezierska: Dialect in Jewish-American Writing." *Yiddish* 6, no. 4: 99–113.

Du Plessis, Rachel Blau. *Writing beyond the Ending: Narrative Strategies of Twentieth-Century Women Writers*. Bloomington: Indiana University Press, 1985.

Elwell, Sue Levi, and Edward R. Levenson. *Jewish Women's Study Guide*. New York: Biblio Press, 1982.

Falk, Marcia. *The Song of Songs: A New Translation and Interpretation*. San Francisco: Harper & Row, 1990.

Fiorenza, Elisabeth Schussler. *Bread Not Stone: The Challenge of Feminist Biblical Interpretation*. Boston: Beacon Press, 1985.

Flax, Jane. "The Conflict Between Nurturance and Autonomy in Mother-Daughter Relationships and within Feminism." *Feminist Studies* 4, no. 1 (February 1978): 171–89.

Flynn, Elizabeth A., and Patrocinio P. Sweikart, eds. *Gender and Reading*. Baltimore: Johns Hopkins Press, 1977.

Fried, Lewis, ed. *Handbook of Jewish-American Literature: An Analytical Guide to Themes and Sources*. New York; Westport, Conn.; London: Greenwood Press, 1988.

Friedan, Betty. *The Feminine Mystique*. New York: Norton, 1963.

Friedman, Reena Sigman. "Send Me My Husband Who Lives in New York City: Husband Desertion in the American Jewish Immigrant Community, 1900–1926." *Jewish Social Studies* 44, no. 1 (Winter 1982), pp. 1–18.

Friedman, Theodore. "The Shifting Role of Women, from the Bible to the Talmud." *Judaism* 36, no. 4 (Fall 1987): 479–87.

Fuchs, Esther. *Israeli Mythogynies: Women in Contemporary Hebrew Fiction* (Albany: State University of New York Press, 1987).

Gilbert, Sandra M., and Susan Gubar. *The Madwoman in the Attic: The Woman Writer and the Nineteenth-Century Literary Imagination*. New Haven, Conn., and London: Yale University Press, 1979.

———. *Shakespeare's Sisters: Feminist Essays on Women Poets*. Bloomington: Indiana University Press, 1979.

Gilligan, Carol. *In a Different Voice: Psychological Theory and Women's Development*. Cambridge, Mass.: Harvard University Press, 1982.

Glazer, Miryam. "Male and Female, King and Queen: The Theological Imagination of Anne Roiphe's *Lovingkindness*." *Studies in American Jewish Literature* 10 (Spring 1991): 81–92.

Goodman, Allegra. *Total Immersion: Stories* (fiction). New York: Harper & Row, 1989.

Grade, Chaim. *Rabbis and Wives* (fiction). 1982. Reprint. New York: Schocken Books, 1987.

Graetz, Naomi. "The Discredited Prophetess." *The Melton Journal* (Winter 1987).

Greenberg, Joanne. *O My America* (fiction). New York: Harper & Row, 1980.

———. *Other People's Lives* (fiction). New York: Knopf, 1975.

Grossman, Susan, and Rivka Haut, eds. *Daughters of the King: Women in the Synagogue*. Philadelphia and New York: Jewish Publication Society, 1991.

Hadda, Janet. *Passionate Women, Passive Men: Suicide in Jewish Literature*. Albany: State University of New York Press, 1988.

Handelman, Susan A. *The Slayers of Moses: The Emergence of Rabbinic Interpretation in Modern Literary Theory*. Albany: State University of New York Press, 1982.

Harap, Louis. *The Image of the Jew in American Literature: From Early Republic to Mass Immigration*. Philadelphia: The Jewish Publication Society, 1974.

Heilbrun, Carolyn G. *Writing a Woman's Life*. New York: W. W. Norton, 1988.

Hellerstein, Kathryn. "Kadya Molodowsky's Froyen-Lider: A Reading." *Association of Jewish Studies Review* (Fall 1988).

Hoch-Smith, Judith, and Anita Spring, eds. *Women in Ritual and Symbolic Roles*. New York: Plenum Press, 1978.

Kaufman, Debra Renee. "Patriarchal Women: A Case Study of Newly Orthodox Jewish Women." *Symbolic Interaction* 12, no. 2.

———. *Rachel's Daughters: Newly Orthodox Jewish Women*. New Brunswick, N.J.: Rutgers University Press, 1991.

Kauffman, Linda, ed. *Gender and Theory: Dialogues on Feminist Criticism*. Oxford: Basil Blackwell, 1989.

Kolodny, Annette. "A Map of Rereading: Or, Gender and the Interpretation of Literary Texts." *New Literary History* 11, no. 3 (1980): 451–67.

Kraemer, David, ed. *The Jewish Family: Metaphor and Memory*. New York: Oxford University Press, 1989.

Kraemer, Ross Shepard. *Gender, Cult and Cosmology: Women's Religions among Jews, Christians and Pagans in the Greco-Roman World*. New York: Oxford University Press, 1991.

———. *Maenads, Martyrs, Matrons, Monastics: A Sourcebook on Women's Religions in the Greco-Roman World*. Philadelphia: Fortress Press, 1988.

Lerman, Rhoda. *God's Ear* (fiction). New York: Henry Holt, 1989.

Lyons, Bonnie. "Grace Paley's Jewish Miniatures." *Studies in American Jewish Literature* 8, no. 1 (Spring 1989): 26–33.

———. "Sexual Love in I. B. Singer's Work." *Studies in American Jewish Literature* 1 (1981): 61–74.

Marks, Elaine, and Isabelle de Courtivron, eds. *New French Feminisms*. New York: Schocken Books, 1981.

Mazow, Julia Wolf, ed. *The Woman Who Lost Her Names* (fiction). New York: Harper, 1980.

Miller, Jean Baker. *Toward a New Psychology of Women*. Boston: Beacon Press, 1976.
Mills, Sara, Lynn Pearce, Sue Spaull, and Elaine Millard, eds. *Feminist Readings/ Feminists Reading*. Charlottesville: University Press of Virginia, 1989.
Moskowitz, Faye. *A Leak in the Heart: Tales from a Woman's Life* (fiction). Boston: Godine, 1985.
Newton, Judith, and Deborah Rosenfelt, eds. *Feminist Criticism and Social Change: Sex, Class, and Race in Literature and Culture*. New York: Methuen, 1985.
Niederman, Sharon, ed. *Shaking Eve's Tree: Stories by American Jewish Women* (fiction). Philadelphia and New York: Jewish Publication Society, 1990.
Norich, Anita. "The Family Singer and the Autobiographical Imagination." *Prooftexts* 10, no. 1 (January 1990): 91–107.
Ochs, Vanessa. *Words on Fire: One Woman's Journey into the Sacred*. San Diego, Calif.; New York; London: Harcourt Brace Jovanovich, 1990.
Olsen, Tillie. *Silences*. New York: Delacorte Press, 1978.
Ostriker, Alicia Suskin. *Stealing the Language: The Emergence of Women's Poetry in America*. Boston: Beacon Press, 1986.
———. *Writing Like a Woman*. Ann Arbor: University of Michigan Press, 1983.
Ozick, Cynthia. *Art and Ardor: Essays*. New York: Alfred A. Knopf, 1983.
Parent, Gail. *A Little Bit Married* (fiction). New York: G. P. Putnam, 1984.
———. *Sheila Levine Is Dead and Living in New York* (fiction). New York: G. P. Putnam, 1972.
Piercy, Marge. *Summer People* (fiction). New York: Fawcett Crest, 1989.
Plaskow, Judith, and Carol P. Christ. *Weaving the Visions: New Patterns in Feminist Spirituality*. New York: Harper & Row, 1989.
Pratt, Norma Fain. "Anna Margolin's Lider: A Study in Women's History, Autobiography and Poetry." *Studies in American Jewish Literature* 3 (1983): 11–25.
———. *Culture and Radical Politics: Yiddish Women Writers, 1880–1940*. Vol. 3, *Decades of Discontent*. Westport, Conn., and Boston: Greenwood Press and Northeastern University Press, 1987.
Rapoport, Nessa. *Preparing for Sabbath* (fiction). New York: Morrow, 1981.
Reich, Tova. *Mara* (fiction). New York: Farrar, Straus, Giroux, 1978.
———. *Master of the Return* (fiction). San Diego, Calif.: Harcourt Brace Jovanovich, 1988.
Reuther, Rosemary, ed. *Religion and Sexism*. New York: Simon & Schuster, 1974.
———. *Sexism and God-Talk: Toward a Feminist Theology*. Boston: Beacon Press, 1983.
———. *Womanguides: Readings toward a Feminist Theology*. Boston: Beacon Press, 1985.
Roiphe, Anne. *Generation without Memory: A Jewish Journey in Christian America*. New York: The Linden Press/Simon & Schuster, 1981.
Rosen, Norma Stahl. *Touching Evil* (fiction). New York: Harcourt, Brace, 1969.
Ruddick, Sara. "Maternal Thinking." *Feminist Studies* 6 (Summer 1980): 342–67.
Russel, Letty M., ed. *Feminist Interpretation of the Bible*. Philadelphia: Westminster Press, 1985.
Schaeffer, Susan Fromberg. *Anya* (fiction). New York: Macmillan, 1974.
Schiff, Ellen. *From Stereotype to Metaphor: The Jew in Contemporary Drama*. Albany: State University of New York Press, 1982.
Schneider, Susan Weidman. *Jewish and Female: Choices and Changes in Our Lives Today*. New York: Simon & Schuster, 1984.

Schwartz, Lynne Sharon. *Acquainted with the Night and Other Stories* (fiction). New York: Harper & Row, 1984.
Seller, Maxine S. "World of Our Mothers: The Women's Page of the *Jewish Daily Forward*." *Journal of Ethnic Studies* 18, no. 2 (Summer 1988): 85–118.
Shapiro, Ann R. "The Novels of E. M. Broner: A Study in Secular Feminism and Feminist Judaism." *Studies in American Jewish Literature* 10, no. 1 (Spring 1991): 93–102.
Sheridan, Judith Rinde. "Isaac Bashevis Singer: Sex as Cosmic Metaphor." *The Midwest Quarterly*, 30 (1982): 367–79.
Showalter, Elaine, ed. *The Female Malady: Women, Madness, and English Culture, 1830–1980*. New York: Pantheon Books, 1985.
———. *A Literature of Their Own*. Princeton, N.J.: Princeton University Press, 1977.
———. *The New Feminist Criticism: Essays on Women, Literature and Theory*. New York: Pantheon, 1986.
Silman, Roberta. *Blood Relations* (fiction). Boston: Little, Brown, 1977.
———. *Boundaries* (fiction). Boston: Little, Brown.
Sklare, Marshall. *American Jews: A Reader*. New York: Behrman House, 1983.
———. *America's Jews*. New York: Random House, 1971.
Spolsky, Ellen, ed. *The Uses of Adversity: Failure and Accommodation in Reader Response*. Lewisburg, Pa.: Bucknell University Press, 1990.
Suleiman, Susan R., ed. *The Female Body in Western Culture: Contemporary Perspectives*. Cambridge, Mass.: Harvard University Press, 1986.
Tax, Meredith. *Union Square* (fiction). New York: William Morrow, 1988.
Thorne, Barrie, and Marilyn Yalom. *Rethinking the Family: Some Feminist Questions*. New York: Longman, 1982.
Thurm, Marian. *These Things Happen* (fiction). New York: Poseidon Press, 1988.
Todd, Janet. *Women's Friendships in Literature*. New York: Columbia University Press, 1980.
Trible, Phyllis. *God and the Rhetoric of Sexuality*. Philadelphia: Fortress Press, 1978.
———. *Texts of Terror: Literary-Feminist Readings of Biblical Narratives*. Philadelphia: Fortress Press, 1984.
Vendler, Helen. "Feminism and Literature." *New York Review of Books* 37 (May 31, 1990): 19–25.
Weissler, Chava. "For Women and for Men Who Are Like Women: The Construction of Gender in Yiddish Devotional Literature." *Journal of Feminist Studies in Religion* 5, no. 2 (Fall 1989).
———. "The Traditional Piety of Ashkenazic Women." In *A History of Jewish Spirituality*, edited by Arthur Green. Crossroads, 1986.
Wenger, Beth. "Jewish Women and Voluntarism: Beyond the Myth of Enablers." *American Jewish History* 79 (Autumn 1989).
Wenkart, Henny, ed. *Sarah's Daughters Sing: A Sampler of Poems by Jewish Women*. New York: Ktav, 1990.
Yaeger, Patricia. *Honey-Mad Women: Emancipatory Strategies in Women's Fiction*. New York: Columbia University Press, 1987.
Yalom, Marilyn. *Maternity, Mortality, and the Literature of Madness*. University Park: Pennsylvania State University Press, 1985.
Yezierska, Anzia. *Bread Givers* (fiction). 1925. Reprint. New York: Persea Books, 1975.

———. *Hungry Hearts and Other Stories*. New York: Persea Books, 1985.

Zborowski, Mark, and Elizabeth Herzog. *Life Is with People: The Culture of the Shtetl*. New York: Schocken Books, 1952.

Zimmerman, Bonnie. *The Safe Sea of Women: Lesbian Fiction, 1969–1989*. Boston: Beacon Press, 1990.

Acknowledgments

Permission to reprint the following material is gratefully acknowledged:

Poem on p. vii: Rajzel Zychlinska, "Everything will remember," trans. Lucy S. Dawidowicz and Florence Victor, *A Treasury of Yiddish Poetry*, ed. Irving Howe and Eliezer Greenberg (New York, Chicago, and San Francisco: Holt, Rinehart and Winston, 1969), p. 231. Zychlinska, born in Poland in 1910, left Warsaw during World War II and lived for a time in Russia and Paris. She emigrated to New York in 1951 and has published several volumes of poetry in Yiddish.

Excerpt from *Three Cities* by Sholem Asch (1933), published by Carroll & Graf. Copyright © 1983 and reprinted by permission of Miriam Mazower for the Estate of Sholem Asch.

Excerpts from *Yekl and the Imported Bridegroom* by Abraham Cahan (1898). Courtesy of Dover Publications, Inc., 1970 rpt.

Sections of *Leah* by Seymour Epstein. Copyright © 1987 and reprinted by permission of the Jewish Publication Society.

Selection from *Four Days* by Gloria Goldreich. Copyright © 1980 and reprinted by permission of the author.

Selections from *The Mind-Body Problem* by Rebecca Goldstein. Copyright © 1983 by Rebecca Goldstein. Reprinted by permission of the Harriet Wasserman Literary Agency, Inc.

Excerpts from *Fierce Attachments* by Vivian Gornick. Copyright © 1987 by Vivian Gornick. Reprinted by permission of Farrar, Straus and Giroux, Inc.

Excerpts from *My Mother's Sabbath Days* by Chaim Grade, trans. Channa Kleinerman Goldstein and Ina Hecker Grade. Copyright © 1986 by the Estate of Chaim Grade. Reprinted by permission of Alfred A. Knopf, Inc.

"Food of Love" from *The Tribe of Dina* by Gloria L. Kirchheimer. Copyright © 1986, 1989 by Melanie Kaye/Kantrowicz and Irena Klepfisz. Reprinted by permission of Beacon Press.

Excerpts from *The Assistant* by Bernard Malamud. Copyright © 1957 and renewed 1985 by Bernard Malamud. Reprinted by permission of Farrar, Straus and Giroux, Inc.

"Tell Me A Riddle" from *Tell Me A Riddle* by Tillie Olsen. Copyright © 1956, 1957, 1960, 1961 by Tillie Olsen. Reprinted by permission of Delacorte Press/Seymour Lawrence, a division of Bantam, Doubleday, Dell Publishing Group, Inc.

Excerpt from *The Cannibal Galaxy* by Cynthia Ozick. Copyright © 1983 by Cynthia Ozick. Reprinted by permission of Alfred A. Knopf, Inc.

"Puttermesser and Xanthippe" from *Levitation: Five Fictions* by Cynthia Ozick. Copyright © 1982 by Cynthia Ozick. Reprinted by permission of Alfred A. Knopf, Inc.

"Dreamer in a Dead Language" from *Later the Same Day* by Grace Paley. Copyright © 1985 by Grace Paley. Reprinted by permission of Farrar, Straus and Giroux, Inc.

"A Marred Holiday" and "A Woman's Wrath" from *In This World and the Next* by I. L. Peretz, translated by Moshe Speigel. Copyright © 1958 by Thomas Yoseloff, Inc., and renewed 1986 by Oak Tree Publications.

Selections from *Lovingkindness* by Anne Richardson Roiphe. Copyright © 1987 by Anne Roiphe. Reprinted by permission of Summit Books, a division of Simon and Schuster, Inc.

Excerpts from *Call It Sleep* by Henry Roth. Copyright © 1934, 1962 by Henry Roth. Reprinted by permission of Roslyn Targ Literary Agency.

Excerpts from *Portnoy's Complaint* by Philip Roth. Copyright © 1969 by Philip Roth. Reprinted by permission of Random House, Inc.

Excerpts from *Goodbye Columbus* by Philip Roth. Copyright © 1959 by Philip Roth. Reprinted by permission of Houghton Mifflin Co.

"Street of the Whores" by Ruth Knafo Setton. Copyright © 1991 and reprinted by permission of the author.

"Hodel" by Sholem Aleichem, translated by Julius and Francis Butwin from *A Treasury of Yiddish Stories*, edited by Irving Howe and Eliezer Greenberg. Copyright © 1968 and reprinted by permission of The Viking Press, a division of Random House, Inc.

"Yentl the Yeshiva Boy" from *The Collected Stories* by Isaac Bashevis Singer. Copyright © 1961, 1962, 1982 by Isaac Bashevis Singer. Reprinted by permission of Farrar, Straus and Giroux, Inc.

Excerpts from *Marjorie Morningstar* by Herman Wouk. Copyright © 1955 by Herman Wouk. Reprinted by permission of Doubleday, a division of Bantam, Doubleday, Dell Publishing Group, Inc.

"The Fat of the Land" from *Hungry Hearts and Other Stories* by Anzia Yezierska. Copyright © 1985 and reprinted by permission of Louise Levitas Henriksen.

"Everything Will Remember," by Rajzel Zychlinska, translated by Lucy S. Dawdowicz and Florence Victor, from *A Treasury of Yiddish Poetry*, edited by Irving Howe and Eliezer Greenberg. Copyright © 1969 by the editors and reprinted by permission of Henry Holt and Company.

UNIVERSITY PRESS OF NEW ENGLAND publishes books under its own imprint and is the publisher for Brandeis University Press, Brown University Press, Clark University Press, University of Connecticut, Dartmouth College, Middlebury College Press, University of New Hampshire, University of Rhode Island, Tufts University, University of Vermont, and Wesleyan University Press.

Library of Congress Cataloging-in-Publication Data

Follow my footprints : changing images of women in American Jewish fiction / edited and with introductory essay and notes by Sylvia Barack Fishman.
p. cm. — (The Brandeis series in American Jewish history, culture, and life)
Includes bibliographical references.
ISBN 0–87451–544–0. — ISBN 0–87451–583–1 (pbk.)
1. Women, Jewish—United States—Fiction. 2. American Fiction—Jewish authors. 3. Jews—United States—Fiction. I. Fishman, Sylvia Barack. II. Series.
PS648.J4F65 1992
813.008′09287′089924—dc20 91–50813

♾